Lecture Notes in Artificial Intelligence 8955

Subseries of Lecture Notes in Computer Science

LNAI Series Editors

Randy Goebel
  University of Alberta, Edmonton, Canada
Yuzuru Tanaka
  Hokkaido University, Sapporo, Japan
Wolfgang Wahlster
  DFKI and Saarland University, Saarbrücken, Germany

LNAI Founding Series Editor

Joerg Siekmann
  DFKI and Saarland University, Saarbrücken, Germany

Stephan K. Chalup   Alan D. Blair
Marcus Randall (Eds.)

Artificial Life and Computational Intelligence

First Australasian Conference, ACALCI 2015
Newcastle, NSW, Australia, February 5-7, 2015
Proceedings

 Springer

Volume Editors

Stephan K. Chalup
School of Electrical Engineering and Computer Science
The University of Newcastle
Callaghan, NSW 2308, Australia
E-mail: stephan.chalup@newcastle.edu.au

Alan D. Blair
School of Computer Science and Engineering
University of New South Wales
UNSW Sydney, NSW 2052, Australia
E-mail: blair@cse.unsw.edu.au

Marcus Randall
Faculty of Business
Bond University
Bond University, QLD 4229, Australia
E-mail: mrandall@bond.edu.au

ISSN 0302-9743   e-ISSN 1611-3349
ISBN 978-3-319-14802-1   e-ISBN 978-3-319-14803-8
DOI 10.1007/978-3-319-14803-8
Springer Cham Heidelberg New York Dordrecht London

Library of Congress Control Number: 2014958672

LNCS Sublibrary: SL 7 – Artificial Intelligence

Typesetting: Camera-ready by author, data conversion by Scientific Publishing Services, Chennai, India

Printed on acid-free paper

Springer is part of Springer Science+Business Media (www.springer.com)

Preface

These are the proceedings of the Australasian Conference on Artificial Life and Computational Intelligence, ACALCI 2015. Although held for the first time in 2015, this conference builds on a scientific community that supported the Australian Conference on Artificial Life (ACAL) biannually from 2005 to 2009 and extends it now with related research in the growing area of computational intelligence.

The research areas of artificial life and computational intelligence have developed from the traditional field of artificial intelligence. It is hard to define them precisely as they continue to evolve. The fascinating dimension of this research field is its interdisciplinary nature and its diverse mix of research and paper styles that can be highly technical, theoretical, philosophical, but often also seeking experimental evaluation, simulation, and ultimately some real-world application. For these proceedings, we received papers covering a variety of areas, including philosophy and theory, game environments and methods, learning, memory and optimisation, applications, and implementations.

It requires a substantial portion of good will of many people to run a conference like this. The production of the proceedings for ACALCI 2015 received plenty of voluntary and honorary advice, help, support, and contribution by various people including the committee members, their helpers, the reviewers, Springer in Heidelberg, and last but not least the authors and their research teams.

"Every day I remind myself over and over that my outer and inner life depend upon the labors of others, living and dead, and that I must exert myself in order to give in the same measure as I have received and am still receiving."[1] - A. Einstein

This volume presents 34 papers, many of them authored or co-authored by leading researchers of their respective fields. After an initial evaluation of all 63 submissions, 55 manuscripts were regarded as of potential interest for ACALCI 2015 and underwent a full peer-review with at least three reviewers per paper. The review process consisted of over 200 reviews and resulted in 34 full papers being accepted. If we assume that each paper took 50 hours to write and each review took one hour of time, then these proceedings correspond to an in-kind

---

[1] A translation of "Jeden Tag denke ich unzählige Male daran, daß mein äußeres und inneres Leben auf der Arbeit der jetzigen und der schon verstorbenen Menschen beruht, daß ich mich anstrengen muß, um zu geben im gleichen Ausmaß, wie ich empfangen habe und noch empfange." Albert Einstein (1930) "Wie ich die Welt sehe" p. 415 in Carl Seelig (ed.) "Albert Einstein - Mein Weltbild", Ullstein Taschenbuch, 2005. [We are grateful for the source information to B. Wolff, Albert Einstein Archives, Hebrew University of Jerusalem, and to Diethard Stoffel.]

contribution of about 3,000 hours or, with an assumed hourly rate of $50, a value of $150,000 would be the result. Even this does not adequately value the true worth of the contributions to this volume.

The ACALCI 2015 international Program Committee consisted of 83 members from at least 14 countries including Austria, Australia, Brunei, Canada, China, France, Germany, Iran, Japan, New Zealand, Singapore, Sweden, the UK, and the USA. The authors of the accepted papers are from countries such as Australia, Canada, China, India, Iran, New Zealand, Norway, Turkey, the UK, and the USA.

In addition to the already acknowledged people and organizations, we would like to thank all other supporters and sponsors of ACALCI 2015, current and future, including the School of Creative Arts for sponsoring The University of Newcastle Conservatorium of Music Concert Hall as conference venue, the Faculty of Engineering and Built Environment and Karla Brandstater for web support, as well as the anonymous subreviewers for supporting the Program Committee.

We hope these proceedings will be useful for the research and life of many other people. We wish our readers plenty of joyful intellectual stimulation and new insights into a fascinating area of research, just as we experienced it when we had the honor to compile the work of our colleagues for this book.

February 2015

Stephan Chalup
Alan Blair
Marcus Randall

Organization

ACALCI 2015 was organized by the School of Electrical Engineering and Computer Science, The University of Newcastle, in association with the University of New South Wales, Bond University, CSIRO ICT Centre in Sydney, Edith Cowan University, and The University of Queensland.

Chairs

General Chair

Stephan Chalup   The University of Newcastle

Program Co-chairs

Alan Blair   University of New South Wales
Marcus Randall   Bond University

Local Organizing Committee

Alexandre Mendes   The University of Newcastle
David Cornforth   The University of Newcastle
Nasimul Noman   The University of Newcastle
Shamus Smith   The University of Newcastle

Paper and Poster Award Committee Chair

Marcus Gallagher   The University of Queensland

Performance Chairs

Frank Millward   The University of Newcastle
Richard Vella   The University of Newcastle

Publicity Chair

Raymond Chiong   The University of Newcastle

Treasurer and Registration Chairs

Vicki Kendros   The University of Newcastle
Shamus Smith   The University of Newcastle

Tutorial Chair

Oliver Obst   CSIRO, Sydney, Australia

Workshop Chair

Philip F. Hingston   Edith Cowan University, Australia

International Program Committee

Marc Adam	The University of Newcastle, Australia
Lee Altenberg	The KLI Institute, Klosterneuburg, Austria
Ognjen Arandjelovic	Deakin University, Australia
Ahmed Shamsul Arefin	The University of Newcastle, Australia
Yukun Bao	Huazhong University of Science and Technology, Wuhan, China
Christian Bauckhage	Fraunhofer IAIS, Germany
Lubica Benuskova	University of Otago, New Zealand
Regina Berretta	The University of Newcastle, Australia
Ljiljana Brankovic	The University of Newcastle, Australia
Thomas Bräunl	The University of Western Australia, Australia
Weidong Cai	The University of Sydney, Australia
Stephen Chen	York University, Canada
Zhiyong Chen	The University of Newcastle, Australia
Winyu Chinthammit	University of Tasmania, Australia
Vic Ciesielski	RMIT University, Australia
David Cornforth	The University of Newcastle, Australia
Arindam Dey	James Cook University, Australia
Alan Dorin	Monash University, Australia
René Doursat	Drexel University, USA
Henning Fernau	Universität Trier, Germany
Marcus Frean	Victoria University of Wellington, New Zealand
Marcus Gallagher	The University of Queensland, Australia
Junbin Gao	Charles Sturt University, Australia
Tom Gedeon	Australian National University, Australia
Ning Gu	The University of Newcastle, Australia
Barbara Hammer	Universität Bielefeld, Germany
Frans Henskens	The University of Newcastle, Australia
Philip Hingston	Edith Cowan University, Australia
Benjamin Johnston	University of Technology Sydney, Australia
James Juniper	The University of Newcastle, Australia
Ata Kaban	University of Birmingham, UK
Jamil Khan	The University of Newcastle, Australia
Julia Knifka	Karlsruhe Institute of Technology, Germany

Table of Contents

Learning, Memory and Optimization

Applications and Implementations

ALife Using Adaptive, Autonomous, and Individual Agent Control

Ovi Chris Rouly

Department of Computational Social Science
George Mason University
Fairfax, Virginia, USA
orouly@gmu.edu

Abstract. This is a review of three, agent control algorithm, replication experiments. In the 1948 essay, *Intelligent Machinery*, the English mathematician Alan Turing described an algorithm for constructing a machine that he claimed was capable of cybernetic (or steered feedback) self-organization. There are few, if any, references in either the historical or the technical literatures to instantiations made of this algorithm. Turing named the machine the P-Type Unorganized Machine. Considering the lack of replication evidence in the literature, three hypotheses motivated this review: 1) Turing did not describe the algorithm with sufficient detail so as to make it possible to instantiate, or that 2) if the algorithm could be instantiated it would not operate as Turing stated, or 3) both. The three replication experiments reviewed here proved the hypotheses qualitatively false when unique P-Type machines were instantiated. Each instantiation functioned as an adaptive, autonomous, and individual agent controller.

Keywords: ALife, Turing, self-organization, adaptation, learning, autonomy, multi-agent systems.

1   Introduction

A few years ago, while attempting to better understand the P-Type machine algorithm, an opportunity to speak with the English mathematician, Dr. Jack Good, at Virginia Tech (University) in Blacksburg, Virginia presented itself at the suggestion of Dr. Jack Copeland from the University of Canterbury in New Zealand. Dr. Good had worked closely with Turing at Bletchley Park during World War II. Then, after the war, Dr. Good again worked with Turing but this time at Manchester University in England. It was thought that by talking with Dr. Good (someone who knew Turing well and had worked with him for many years) an understanding might be gained as to why this Turing algorithm had remained untested for so many decades. After reading the essay Dr. Good told this author that it seemed to him that the essay, *Intelligent Machinery* [16] was, "never peer-reviewed" (personal conversation with J. Good in Blacksburg, Virginia, 2004). This seemed reasonable if by nothing else but logical association and the following circumstances.

S.K. Chalup et al. (Eds.): ACALCI 2015, LNAI 8955, pp. 1–16, 2015.
© Springer International Publishing Switzerland 2015

It is clear, Turing chose His Majesty's Stationery Office (HMSO) to become the first public printer of the *Intelligent Machinery* essay. And, by default, there was relatively little need for a peer-review process if Turing were merely reporting his work through an official government publisher. So, given these facts, it seemed less curious that the P-Type algorithm had been relatively unknown by the computer science community since almost the day of its first printing. Nevertheless, there was still a nagging question.

It had always seemed odd that within the *Intelligent Machinery* essay, Turing explicitly called for the instantiation of the P-Type algorithm in electronic computing hardware at a time in the future whenever, "some electronic machines are [were] in actual operation" (Section 11, p. 22). Moreover, Turing also commented that, "I made a start on the latter but found the work [building the paper and pencil machines by hand] altogether too laborious at present." Was this a case of Turing intentionally creating a contradiction by publishing an algorithm he wanted others to explore but doing so through a seemingly mundane government printing office?

We may never know the complete answer. But, what we do know is that implicit in the reporting of some Turing scholars [1,2,3,4], [18] the algorithm went largely unexploited for over fifty years. We also know that this invention predates all other machine intelligence work, in some cases by decades. Additionally we know that Turing himself demonstrated a paper and pencil instantiation of the algorithm complete with tests in his essay. Thus, whether it was because of its HMSO pedigree and its lack of critical review polish or some other reason, it was more than half a century after the algorithm was first printed (and it became available for general study) that anyone publicly reported the results of their efforts to instantiate the P-Type algorithm in electronic computing hardware.

The following pages contain a review of three qualitative replication experiments. Their contents will describe how three P-Type machines were instantiated and then demonstrated control of situated and embodied agents individually and in simulated small-group social settings. While one does not need to read the original Turing essay in order to understand the experiments described in this review, a comparison of the former with the latter may offer a more complete sense of the historical and subject matter context otherwise unavailable to this singular written forum. Additionally, a comparison of the original algorithm with that described here may assist the reader in adjudicating the fitness of the experimental method next described for its claims of replication. For reference, if one chooses to read the original work, then one should pay special attention to Sections 10 and 11 entitled "Experiments in Organizing Pleasure-Pain Systems" and "The P-Type Unorganized Machine," respectively.

2   Method and Results

Understanding how the P-Type algorithm was instantiated (the experimental method) and how it performed (the experimental result) is important for at least three reasons. First, this is a replication experiment. And, as a replication experiment, a close facsimile of the abstract functionality of the original Turing description will be required in order to make any claim of satisfactory replication. Second, an operational instantiation of the algorithm is required in order to refute the stated hypotheses with an existence proof. Third, there are no known template-examples to which one can refer in the literature (outside of those describing these experiments) that can guide us in building and or evaluating a machine previously described only in sixty year old text. By comparison, even related but dissimilar Turing Unorganized Machines have recently received formal mathematical description [1].

One must also be reminded that the Turing essay was written in 1948. This was well before any standardized computer engineering vocabulary had been established and it was roughly coincident with the time when behavioral (behaviorism) psychology was just beginning to achieve its full dominance within the Social Sciences. One might be motivated to ask if Turing was influenced by, or at least was aware of, the latter because he appears to have anthropomorphized much of the operational characteristics of the essay machine. This comment regarding anthropomorphization is simply one of fact and not a claim that Turing had become a student of the Social Sciences. For example, when one reads in the essay the phrase, "it is intended the pain stimuli occur when the machine's behavior is wrong, pleasure stimuli when it is particularly right," (Section 10, p. 18) one can draw their own conclusion on this point.

In this review, modern computer engineering vocabulary will be used as much as possible. Additionally the words controller or engine will often be used as a synonym for the phrase machine-intelligence. Later in the review, the concept of a controller agency will be introduced when the controllers (the machine-intelligence) is associated with increasingly more sophisticated, situated-interaction experimentation. Also, when the word host appears it will usually serve as a surrogate phrase for the embodiment and/or the vehicle through which and with which a controller comes into interface with its environment. For example, the host embodiments described in these experiments are those real or simulated objects ("rodents" and "bugs" respectively) within which the Turing algorithm acted as a controller (or machine-intelligence). More exactly: The instantiated Turing engine was the source of all control and the hosts were the vehicles from within which the Turing engines engaged their various environments. Technically speaking these are not formal definitions but rather experimental ones. Finally, it is believed necessary that vocabulary from the domains of psychology and also animal ethology occasionally be used to explain some controller-host-environment functional interaction activities.

2.1   Method

The reason the machine is called a P-Type is that Turing designed it to learn (or acquire) adaptive behaviors as a consequence of receiving differential stimulus reinforcement (*Pleasure* or *Pain*) at its machine inputs. Turing explicitly proposed that this reinforcement might come from some external steering signal like a teacher. Intuitively, however, it seems reasonable to assume that any bi-valued exogenous signal should be able to re-direct the trajectory of the learning capability of the device. Using this assumption, it turns out, will allow us to instantiate the machine as a controller and to embody it within a host situated in an artificial ecology. In fact, by expanding our intuition only slightly, we will discover that we can construct host embodiments controlled by more than one P-Type machine harnessed in a parallel-controller configuration. Moreover, we will see such instantiations can respond to an array of external steering signals. But, we are getting ahead of our evidence. Simply, Turing referred to this type of learning by means of differential reinforcement and adaptive steering as guided or "interference" learning (Sections 10 & 11). In the essay, he instantiated a machine using paper and pencil and he claimed he showed it could be taught. Today a psychologist would refer to this form of stimulus-response behavior modification [19] and the overall process as operant conditioning [13],[15].

General. The P-Type machines instantiated for this review were tightly coupled, three-piece, computing machines composed of a Behavior Library, a Transducer, and a Finite State Machine (FSM). The Behavior Library Turing wrote about was just a set of random numbers over {0, 1} each one being a possible output behavior. The Transducer is our word for the component whose function was described by Turing (generally) as a table, memory, and or storage device. He recommended using a "tape" in larger systems and he referenced this memory component using figures and descriptive text in the essay. The FSM instantiated here provided the logic and automatic functions needed to manipulate the transition table entries in the Transducer. Additionally, per the Turing essay, there were no hidden memory units used in any experiment, nor were "next situation" (next state) selections made by sense stimuli. The next state was always chosen by *Pleasure-Pain* steering on the machine input and then was directed through the Transducer transition table.

Fig. 1 is a block diagram illustration depicting the internal functions of a P-Type machine as they were instantiated here. One or more of these engines was instantiated in each of the experiments reviewed.

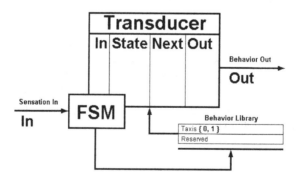

Fig. 1. The kernel engine at the heart of Turing prototype P-Type had few internal components

Consider the left side of **Fig. 1**. The FSM receives a steering signal, as *Pleasure* or *Pain* affect sensation, as its input. The FSM then directs the behavior of the Transducer and may possibly negotiate with the Behavior Library in the lower right. Eventually, a selected behavior will emerge into the world from the Transducer based on the Transducer transition table contents and the aforementioned FSM-Behavior Library negotiation. Once machine execution has started, it will continue to execute until halted by external means. By design, the primary drive of the machine is one involving the equilibration and acquisition of adaptive Transducer data structures. Other drives can be superimposed over the primary. A flow chart shown in **Fig. 2** may help explain the algorithm pictorially.

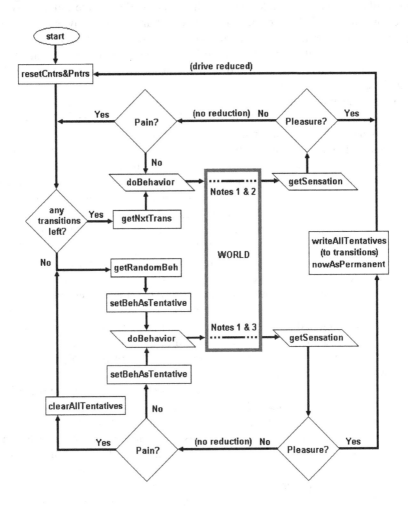

Notes:
1. There is no implied concurrency. Data passes straight through the world. See upper and the lower dotted lines.
2. The upper path is characterized as a path driven by the transitions in the Transducer.
3. The lower path is characterized as a path driven by random, trial-and-error learning.

Fig. 2. P-Type machine functional flow-chart

Specific. To start (or re-start) a full cycle a P-Type looks first into its memory (Transducer transition table) for any existing transitions. Turing started at the first entry in the list and sequentially executed every one until there were no more transitionable outputs left. If an output behavior resulted in a *Pleasurable* result (that is, the consequence of the behavior was reflected back from the world and the initial drive was reduced) then the full P-Type cycle was restarted. If an output behavior resulted in a *Painful* reflection from the world, the machine transitioned to the next table entry. If an output behavior resulted in a non-*Painful* result, the behavior (the transition) was simply repeated. When there were no stored transitions yet untested, his machine consulted the Behavior Library.

Turing pre-generated a pool of 0/1 random numbers (as in our Behavior Library) and made them ready for usage. In the instantiations reviewed here, the FSM consulted the Behavior Library for randomly generated zero or one behavior outputs (and more abstract behaviors like an orienting Taxis response) to be tested in the world.

At this point, it is understood no untested transitions remain in the Transducer. So, a pattern of random trials and behavior evaluation cycles can begin: a random behavior is taken from the Behavior Library and is output to the world. Remember, the machine is attempting to reduce its primary drive. When a *Pleasurable* result is encountered the "tentative" behaviors are transferred to the Transducer transition table as "permanent" entries and the entire (full) P-Type cycle is restarted. When *Pain* is encountered, all heretofore "tentative" behavior transitions are erased from scratchpad memory and a new sequence of random trials will be restarted. If it is determined that the random behavior does not result in *Pleasure* but it also does not make things worse (it does not cause *Pain*) then that behavior is considered to be a "tentative" candidate for learning and it will be written to a scratch-pad memory. A sequence of such "tentative" behaviors can be tried and stored in scratch-pad memory any number of times. If a non-*Painful* result is encountered, the behavior is simply repeated. The goal is always to reduce the current drive.

The pattern of trying new behavior outputs continues until either the drive is reduced (*Pleasure* is encountered and the new sequence can be added to the bottom of any existing list of transitions in the Transducer), death occurs (execution ceases), or *Pain* is encountered and the entire random trails and behavior evaluation cycle can be restarted and all "tentative" results erased. An adaptive behavior sequence can be lengthy. Since [5], psychologists have come to refer to similar cognitive behaviors that involve sequential, patterned outcomes as serial learning.

The cycle of trial, evaluate, store/forget is the basis of the P-Type algorithm as it was designed by Turing. It appears to make the automata a serial "penultimate" learner. After any successful drive-reducing cycle, the machine will always return to the first transition in its Transducer memory and will be made ready to repeat the entire process.

2.2   Results

The first two experiments were complementary instantiations of the machine depicted in **Fig. 1.** The first experiment was a situated and embodied single agent simulation based purely in software. The second experiment was a hybrid simulation constructed using an untethered mobile robot and a controller embedded in reconfigurable hardware, i.e., Field Programmable Gate Array (FPGA) technology. In each of those experiments, the P-Type served as an adaptive controller (an "agency") embodied by a mouse (an icon-mouse and a robotic rodent, respectively) situated in a simulated Hull enclosure similar to those developed by [6].

The third experiment involved a Multi-agent Systems (MAS) social simulation. This experiment explored the further extensibility of the Turing algorithm by harnessing the machine in a parallel configuration constructed of four independent P-Type machines coupled together as a single control "agency." That "agency," that controller, was then embodied in each respective host in the MAS experiment.

Replication Experiment One. The first experiment involved a simple icon-mouse embodied as a virtual agent situated in a simulated, 8-corner Hull enclosure. The experiment, depicted in **Fig. 3**, shows a screen-capture of the experiment in progress. **Fig. 4** shows some quantitative result products derived from that experiment (reproduced by permission [11]).

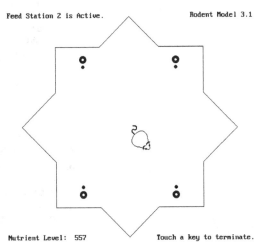

Feed Station 2 is Active.   Rodent Model 3.1

Nutrient Level: 557   Touch a key to terminate.

Fig. 3. The icon-mouse was in a simulated Hull enclosure. Here it is seen from overhead.

In this experiment a single P-Type machine was instantiated and embodied. The machine received a single steering signal input derived from host interoceptive and exteroceptive sensation. Those sensations included a simulated sense of satiety (a sense of being hungry, full, or in-between), a simulated haptic sense (the icon mouse could sense when it touched the walls of the enclosure), and a simulated olfactory sense (the icon mouse could sense a distance-modulated scent intensity coming from its food source). The goal of the experiment was (as it was for experiment number two) to see if a single P-Type machine, serving as a controller, could adapt to its surroundings using only a constrained set of behaviors from a species-specific ethology, i.e., a strong hunger drive to locate a food source using simulated olfaction, and a drive to survive by eating a bit of simulated food while not colliding with the walls of a Hull enclosure. The binaries used in experiment one are available for download[1].

The test required the host, an icon-mouse, to find and take its replenishment from a feed station embedded in the floor of the Hull enclosure. At any given time only one of the four feed stations (the circles in the corners of the Hull in enclosure shown in **Fig. 3**) was active. Using its simulated haptic sense and its simulated olfactory sense, the icon-mouse had to follow a simulated olfactory gradient emanating from the food and then place the tip of its nose over the feed station in order to be fed. Between feedings, the icon-mouse was free to roam (at random) about the enclosure. During this "roaming" period the P-Type engine was disengaged and the icon-mouse could move about the enclosure without restraints other than the enclosure walls. No learning took place during "play time." The "mice" were blind and could not escape the enclosure. If a "mouse" could not find the food (its fuel source) when it became "hungry" and its controller was re-engaged then, it would expire.

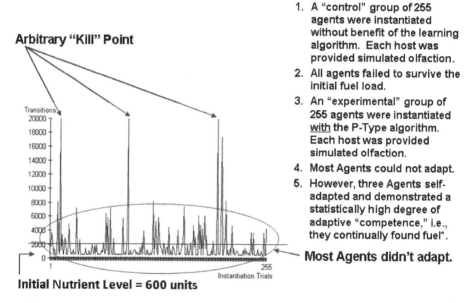

1. A "control" group of 255 agents were instantiated without benefit of the learning algorithm. Each host was provided simulated olfaction.
2. All agents failed to survive the initial fuel load.
3. An "experimental" group of 255 agents were instantiated <u>with</u> the P-Type algorithm. Each host was provided simulated olfaction.
4. Most Agents could not adapt.
5. However, three Agents self-adapted and demonstrated a statistically high degree of adaptive "competence," i.e., they continually found fuel".

Fig. 4. Most agents perished but three learned how to survive. Reprinted by permission.

The graphic in **Fig. 4** reports the results of two, 255-sample, mass trials using the P-Type as a situated and embodied controller of icon-mice. The only difference between the two trials reported was that, in one case, the P-Type engine was turned-off permanently and, in the other, it was turned-on and completely available to the host. Note: The result when the engine was turned off is not shown here since every "mouse" agent in that experiment failed to survive its initial fuel (food) load, i.e., they all "died". Also, based on the results of the trials that did use the P-Type engine, it is

---

[1] http://css.gmu.edu/papers/ALifeAAIAgentControl.zip

obvious that convergence on a survivable solution was very slow even for "mice" having access to P-Type learning. Theirs was a pure discovery-learning process (without heuristics) in an unknown environment. Clearly, search by random trial-and-error learning was not an effective survival strategy. A better method will be suggested later in experiment three. But, on the other hand, the "mice" in this experiment were capable of being taught using the method of interference learning suggested by Turing. That is, during the experiment, special "training sessions" wherein spatial pre-positioning of the "mice" within the enclosure took place. Consistent with simple methods of behavior modification that use operant conditioning (mentioned earlier), the "mice" were taught how to find replenishment. That is they were taught how to avoid contacting the walls, home-in on the scent of "food" coming from a feed station, pursue it, and survive. Here "mice" learned quickly and survived well.

Another remarkable thing about the results of this experiment was that during the post-mortem analysis of the Transducer memories in the long-surviving random-search "mice," it was discovered that those "mice" that survived longest and were "sacrificed" had all acquired a similar set of survival strategies. These surviving "mice" eschewed wandering off and roaming about their enclosure when not feeding. Instead these surviving "mice" independently learned (or evolved) behaviors involving strategies to stay near the food source during "play time" and not to go far away from the food source, get lost, and ultimately expire. All "mice" were "sacrificed" when their total execution cycle count reached 20,000.

Replication Experiment Two. The second experiment instantiated a P-Type controller in a custom Field Programmable Gate Array (FPGA) logic circuit. The controller was effectively embodied within (exerted positive control over) a host: a rodent robot. The robot is shown in **Fig. 5**.

Fig. 5. A robotic rodent was the embodiment tested in a Hull enclosure in Experiment Two

Fig. 6. A P-Type controller was on the circuit card to the left in the card cage

The P-Type engine was physically located in a small card cage and communicated with the host embodiment via radio frequency/infra-red (RF/IR) telemetry. The controller and various systems support components were housed in the card cage shown in **Fig. 6**. The use of remote telemetry had *only* to do with concerns completely independent of the instantiation of the P-Type. Concerns involved the use of the high-current-draw FPGA circuits and static random access memory used for the Transducer component. The card cage handled these concerns easily while freeing up the host body for tasks associated with host embodiment as a mobile robot. The electrical schematics of all circuits and mechanical diagrams of the robot and the Hull enclosure are available for download[2].

During the experiment, the host (the robotic rodent) was situated in a physical Hull enclosure. The Hull enclosure was about a meter across and the robotic rodent several centimeters in length. In this experiment, the instantiation of the P-Type machine was similar to the one illustrated in Fig. 1 but differed in that the algorithm was instantiated using Very High Speed Integrated Circuit (VHSIC) Hardware Description Language (VHDL) and an Altera FPGA. The VHDL code may be available by request[3].

As with experiment one, experiment two attempted to see if the P-Type machine could adapt to its surroundings using only a constrained set of behaviors from a species-specific ethology, i.e., a strong hunger drive to locate a food source using simulated olfaction, and a drive to survive by eating a bit of simulated food while not colliding with the walls of the Hull enclosure. The P-Type machine was mounted on the circuit card located to the left in the card cage shown in **Fig. 6**.

Similar to experiment number one, the "rodent" had to find its own food (find a battery charging station in the enclosure) and keep its 9-volt battery charged. Using its simulated haptic sense and its simulated olfactory sense, the "rodent" had to follow a simulated olfactory food gradient (simulated by a 100 KHz RF beacon) and then place the tip of its nose over the feed station in order to be fed. Between feedings, the "rodent" was free to roam (at random) about the enclosure. The "rodent" was blind. If the "rodent" could not find the food when it became "hungry" (when its battery neared full discharge) it would expire. That is, the "rodent" would expire when its on-board 9-volt Ni-Cad battery failed.

The purpose of this work was to test the instantiability, extensibility and transportability of the basic algorithm to other platforms. No other results for experiment two are reported here.

Replication Experiment Three. In this experiment, P-Type controllers were constructed so as to be explicitly ganged together in parallel and to cooperate with each other as a single cohesive control unit. The goal was to create an extensible controller having n-independent primary drives (n=4 in this experiment) that could cooperate with each other and provide a single control "agency" (a single, independent, machine-intelligence) capable of operating an embodied host in a highly social environment.

---

[2] http://www.maelzel.com/Programs/Circuits/Daryl/Circuits.htm
[3] http://www.maelzel.com/Contact/Moreinfo.php

The four primary drives for these controllers were selected from a list of the lower-level physiological and higher-order socio-cognitive drives associated with the Maslow Hierarchy of Needs [8]. Thus, each four-way "agency" controlled one respective host icon-bug. Said another way, each "bug" had its own four-way control system. **Fig. 7** shows the icon hosts in their simulated maze at program start-up. In this ALife experiment, the large blue circles were predatory "bugs" and the smaller red "bugs" were the food (prey) species. (In grayscale blue=dark gray, red=light gray.) At program start, the investigator could select how many predator and or prey icon hosts would inhabit the enclosed maze. During the experimental trial shown here, a total of 30 "bugs" (mixed predators and prey) were simulated simultaneously.

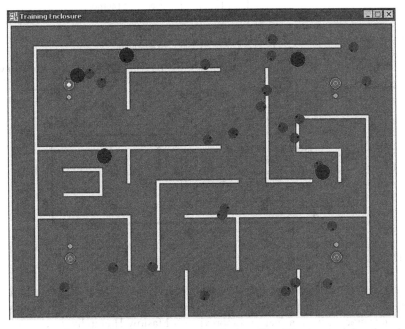

Fig. 7. Seen here from overhead at program start, the icon "bug" hosts were placed randomly. The white maze partitions were only permeable to simulated odor penetration and thus the bugs quickly fell to either side of the partitions once instantiated and the program began. The four gray circles in the floor of the training maze were prey feed-stations. These could emit a simulated odor (only one was active at a time). Predators and prey emitted unique scents of controllable intensity. The feed-station in the upper left corner is active. The icon bugs enjoyed a haptic modality, a simulated olfactory sense, a satiety sense, but no vision.

In operation, the icon hosts "were free to move about the maze until they were eaten, their energy levels were depleted, or they adapted, found available food, avoided their predators, and survived" [12]. An interesting result appeared during "bug" post-mortem Transducer table analysis. The transition tables revealed that emergent sequences of lengthy concatenations of Taxis and Kinesis[4] motor behaviors were produced. These sequences were adaptive behavior patterns constructed from shorter movements and made navigating the long corridors of the maze possible. As was mentioned previously, it turned out this was consistent with the prediction made by Turing that the P-Type might incorporate old routines into new ([16] Section 11, p. 22) and it may suggest a rudimentary form of stimulus generalization[5] was taking place. Finally, the icon hosts had, differences in color, size, and markings, predators were distinguishable from prey as can be seen in the screen capture of the trial shown above.

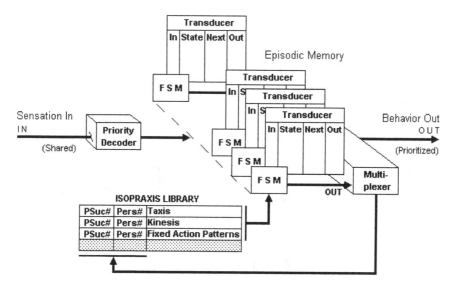

Fig. 8. In this experiment four P-Type machines were harnessed together to create a single control "agency"

Fig. 8 is an illustration depicting the internal functions of the P-Type machines instantiated for the third experiment. A priority encoder provided the initial input steering and machine activation, per an (abbreviated) Maslow Hierarchy, to each of four parallel harnessed P-Type machine sensation inputs. A multiplexer encoded and steered the output behavior signals from the four machines into a single output stream. Input steering signal shaping used in this experiment was similar to that used in the first two experiments. Emulated sensations included a simulated haptic sense

---

[4] From the study of animal ethology [9] and biology; a tropism (a taxis) is a concise, usually small, behavioral responses made with regard to a stimulus. Larger but less directed collections of motor behaviors in animals are kinesis. The latter are also often associated with intensity of movement but not necessarily direction.

[5] An early description of stimulus generalization appears in [17]. Stimulus generalization is that observable behavior pattern in a conditioned subject that occurs when a neutral, unconditioned stimulus evokes a previously conditioned response. When the conditioned response is generalized, appearing across more than one previously unconditioned (neutral) stimulus, the behavior syndrome is referred to as stimulus generalization.

(the "bugs" could sense when they touched the walls of the maze), a simulated olfactory sense (the "bugs" could sense a distance-modulated scent intensity coming from their food sources, i.e., prey for predators and floor-mounted feed-stations for prey "bugs"), and a simulated sense of satiety (a sense of being hungry, full, or in-between).

This experiment explored not only the feasibility of a four-way P-Type "agency" but it also introduced a more complex Behavior Library. Based on a paradigm of species-specific behavior patterns characterized by [10], the Behavior Library became an Isopraxis Library and included host-appropriate Taxis, Kinesis, and Fixed Action Patterns as output behaviors. Additionally, numeric scores for the probability of behavior success (PSucc#) and persistence of utility (Pers#) were updated dynamically for each behavior in the library during runtime. The tags were used by the FSM to aid in its selection of individual behaviors during trial, evaluate, store/forget cycles. This stochastic steering scheme appeared to eliminate some of the learning convergence problems evident in experiment one caused by the inherent noise in a random trial-and-error discovery learning process. For comparison, one may want to consider the application and theory presented in [14].

3   Discussion

In the experiments reviewed here, the Transducer was a memory device that held the emergent configurations of the machine, i.e., the transitions. (Turing referred to his transition table data as the "configurations" of the machine.) In the experiments reviewed here, our instantiations also had ample memory available for scratch-pad functions during the P-Type "tentative" behavior evaluation cycles.

Turing referred to the possibility of creating a "dialing system" to manipulate system memory in systems where large amounts of memory were available. In the experiments reviewed here, a "dialing system" was incorporated into the FSM. That "dialing system" provided the logic to steer the selection of the addresses (rows) in the Transducer transition table. Additionally, our FSM contained logic capable of reading, writing, and erasing any of the transition table entries, and for manipulating the scratch-pad memory.

At start time, a P-Type memory (our Transducer transition table) was normally completely empty[6]. The final size of the Transducer transition table was constrained only by the availability of transition table memory and how (temporally) long the host device was allowed to operate. After a machine had operated for some time and (more importantly) if the machine had demonstrated any adaptive behaviors *in situ* then the transition table would have started to fill with transition information. At this point it could be said the machine had started to become "organized" or to learn and to adapt to its environment. In later decades researchers working in machine intelligence and

---

[6] Technically, the table did not have to be empty. It was quite possible to transfer the acquired transitions of one machine to another and to start the latter machine pre-loaded with "knowledge" of the former. This type of transfer resembles the end result of Lamarkian evolution and was used successfully to support accelerated, inter-agent "shared" learning.

reinforcement learning came to rely on a process that, in abstract, is actually some-what similar to the P-type algorithm. Those researchers came to refer to the process as the accumulation of optimal policies. Consider, for example, the works in Reinforcement Learning described by [7].

In each of the experiments described here the machines were situated and embodied actors in unique environments. They were all subjected to "interference" stimulus during every cybernetic learning cycle. As the machines read their inputs they were forced to select output behaviors from individual, self-organizing behavior libraries, or in the case of the icon-mice they could engage in random "play." In turn, they received stimulus reinforcement (positive and negative from their environments and or their teachers) as a consequence of those previous output behavior choices.

While developing the very first P-Types for the first experiment it was discovered that the key to using the P-Type was to map it onto the targeted host's real physical, or simulated, "physiological" biomimetics and or "cognito-social" behavioral needs. This had to be done from the perspective of identifying (in advance) whatever the same or similarly functioning real mechanical and or operational properties existed in the targeted real host and needed to be controlled and or optimized by the P-Type. For example, when our final hosts had a need (a drive) to reduce hunger, or a need (drive) to avoid somatosensory contact with walls, or a need (drive) to follow a scent gradient toward food, or a need (drive) to avoid a scent gradient coming from a predator, etc., all of these had to be aligned with (or mapped onto) one or more P-Type engines in order to use the equilibratory properties intrinsic to the algorithm. Understating this somewhat, identifying this design requirement had real consequences for the experiments. Once it was identified and its requirements met, it meant a P-Type controller could be embodied easily and that it would be able to steer its host in the world. Before that, instantiating the algorithm was just a paper and pencil exercise. Now, however, the experiments have suggested that a controller based on the algorithm may be able to learn from either random discovery or teacher-delivered interference training. All just like Turing suggested.

4   Summary

In his essay, *Intelligent Machinery*, Alan Turing described a computing machine whose purpose was to learn by doing. Once embodied it became a cybernetic engine capable of recording the output sequence of its own situated behavior. Moreover, it did so while demonstrating that it could steer itself to reduce primitive drives and achieve adaptive success. Turing wanted the machine to receive its sensory feedback and external influences from a teacher. Once embodied it became possible to shape even complicated interoceptive and exteroceptive (sensory) feedback arriving at the machine turning them into simple *Pleasure* and *Pain* steering signals. In particular, Turing told us he built a paper and pencil machine and he showed us how his machine output behaviors that could be modified by its teacher. He challenged us to test his algorithm, to expand it, and to try it. For whatever reason it has taken over half a century before anyone has picked up his challenge and reported their results.

In truth, the body of work in machine intelligence and machine learning has long overtaken this algorithm in scope, efficiency, and maybe even utility. That said, this author was tasked with only a simple challenge: review three machine intelligence (replication) experiments wherein P-Type Unorganized Machines were physically instantiated based on a best effort to understand the description of the machine in that original Turing essay. This last time, then, let us restate and consider the three original hypotheses so as to better frame a possible discussion of why this algorithm lay dormant for over half a century.   The first hypothesis was that Turing did not describe the algorithm in sufficient detail so as to make it possible to instantiate. The second hypothesis was that if it were the case that it could be instantiated then, the algorithm would not operate as Turing had claimed. Finally, the third hypothesis was that both the first and the second were true. The foregoing three experimental embodiments of the algorithm seem to suggest that a constructive proof actually exists for the instantiability of the algorithm and for its operation. Thus, all of the hypotheses appear to be qualitatively false.

References

1. Burgin, M., Eberbach, E.: Evolutionary Turing in the Context of Evolutionary Machines. arXiv preprint arXiv:1304.3762. Cornell University Library (2013)
2. Copeland, B.J., Proudfoot, D.: On Alan Turing's Anticipation of Connectionism. Synthese 108(3), 361–377 (1996)
3. Copeland, B.J., Proudfoot, D.: The Computer, Artificial Intelligence, and the Turing Test. In: Teuscher, C. (ed.) Alan Turing: Life and Legacy of a Great Thinker, pp. 317–351. Springer, Heidelberg (2004)
4. Eberbach, E., Goldin, D., Wegner, P.: Turing's Ideas and Models. In: Teuscher, C. (ed.) Alan Turing: Life and Legacy of a Great Thinker, pp. 159–196. Springer, Heidelberg (2004)
5. Ebbinghaus, H.: Memory: A contribution to experimental psychology, No. 3. Teachers College. Columbia University (1913)
6. Hull, C.L.: Principles of Behavior. Appleton-Century-Crofts, New York (1943)
7. Kaelbling, L., Littman, M., Moore, A.: Reinforcement Learning: A Survey. Journal of Artificial Intelligence Research 4, 237–285 (1996)
8. Maslow, A.: A Theory of Human Motivation. Psychological Review 50, 370–396 (1943)
9. McFarland, D.D.: Animal Behaviour: Psychobiology. Ethology and Evolution, 3rd edn. Longman (1999)
10. McLean, P.D.: A Triangular Brief of the Evolution of Brain and Law. In: Gruter, M., Bohannan, P. (eds.) Law, Biology and Culture: The Evolution of Law, The Berkeley Electronic Press, Berkeley California (1982)
11. Rouly, O.C.: Cybernetic Intelligence: A Return to Complex Qualitative Feedback Theory. Unpublished thesis, New Mexico State University, Las Cruces (2000)
12. Rouly, O.C.: Learning Automata and Need-Based Drive Reduction. In: Ha, Q.P., Kwok, N.M. (eds.) Proceedings of the 8th International Conference on Intelligent Technologies, pp. 310–312. University of Technology Sydney, Sydney (2007)
13. Skinner, B.F.: The behavior of organisms: An experimental analysis (1938)
14. Sutton, R.S., Barto, A.G.: Reinforcement learning. Journal of Cognitive Neuroscience 11(1), 126–134 (1999)

15. Thorndike, E.L.: Animal intelligence: Experimental studies. Macmillan, New York (1911)
16. Turing, A.M.: Intelligent Machinery. In: National Physical Laboratory Report, HMSO, London (1948)
17. Watson, J.B., Rayner, R.: Conditioned emotional reactions. Journal of Experimental Psychology 3(1), 1–14 (1920)
18. Webster, C.S.: Alan Turing's unorganized machines and artificial neural networks: his remarkable early work and future possibilities. Evolutionary Intelligence 5(1), 35–43 (2012)
19. Zirpoli, T.J., Melloy, K.J.: Behavior management: Applications for teachers and parents. Merrill (1997)

Computational Understanding and Manipulation of Symmetries

Attila Egri-Nagy[1,2] and Chrystopher L. Nehaniv[1]

[1] Centre for Computer Science and Informatics Research
University of Hertfordshire
Hatfield, Herts AL10 9AB, United Kingdom
C.L.Nehaniv@herts.ac.uk
[2] Centre for Research in Mathematics
School of Computing, Engineering and Mathematics
University of Western Sydney (Parramatta Campus)
Locked Bag 1797, Penrith, NSW 2751
A.Egri-Nagy@uws.edu.au

Abstract. For natural and artificial systems with some symmetry structure, computational understanding and manipulation can be achieved without learning by exploiting the algebraic structure. This algebraic coordinatization is based on a hierarchical (de)composition method. Here we describe this method and apply it to permutation puzzles. Coordinatization yields a structural understanding, not just solutions for the puzzles. In the case of the Rubik's Cubes, different solving strategies correspond to different decompositions.

Keywords: permutation puzzle, wreath product, coordinatization, cascade, decomposition, Rubik's Cube.

1 Introduction

Symmetry structure in natural and artificial systems, such as crystallography, chemistry, physics, and permutation puzzles, etc., can facilitate understanding and manipulation of these systems. This is well-known in the mathematical sciences and from the algebraic theory of groups. However, until now, computational algebraic methods have not been fully exploited in Artificial Intelligence (AI).

We show how AI systems can make use of such mathematical symmetry structure to automatically generate and manipulate hierarchical coordinate systems for finite systems whose generating symmetries are given. Such hierarchical coordinate systems correspond to subgroup chains in the group structure determined by generating symmetries of the system. We demonstrate how, for any finite-state symmetry system, these coordinate systems

1. can be generated automatically, i.e. deriving formal models for understanding the finite-state symmetry system, and
2. can be deployed in manipulating the system automatically.

S.K. Chalup et al. (Eds.): ACALCI 2015, LNAI 8955, pp. 17–30, 2015.

Thus, without learning, manipulation of such systems is reduced via algebra to sequential computation in a hierarchy of simple (or simpler) group coordinates. This general, implemented method is illustrated with examples from coordinate systems on permutation puzzles such as Rubik's cube.

1.1 Algebra, Cognitive Modeling, Coordinate Systems

Algebra and the theory of permutation groups is well-known from applications of groups in chemistry and crystallography [24], in physics [15], and more recently of semigroups and groups in systems biology, genetic regulatory networks, and biochemistry [4, 26]. Unlike machine learning or optimization techniques, *algebraic* machine intelligence can without any learning derive coordinate systems not only on states of a structure, but also on its transformations, i.e. on operations for manipulating the structure. These are unlike the methods, spatial structures, or cognitive and semantic maps presently exploited for theorem proving, path-planning, automated reasoning, etc., but they are similar to coordinate systems occurring tacitly elsewhere in science [26]. Coordinate systems, like the ones studied here on general symmetry structures from the viewpoint of AI applications using computer algebra, also arise in conservation laws in physics. As Emmy Noether showed in the first part of the 20th century, invariants preserved under conservation laws correspond exactly to group-theoretic symmetry structures in physics [23]; moreover, such invariants for physical systems give rise to coordinate systems of exactly the type described here [21, 26].

AI techniques for cognitive modeling, machine learning and optimization so far have made relatively little use of abstract algebra. Cognitive architectures such as SOAR, ACT-R and SAC have been applied to build AI systems that model human cognitive capacities more or less intending to emulate faithfully the structure of cognition in humans, with applications ranging from autonomous control of aircraft based on subsymbolic rule-extraction, to human-style learning of arithmetic or natural language, to predictive evaluation of user interfaces (e.g. [18, 19, 25]). But aspects of human and machine cognition can also involve understanding of hierarchical processes with dynamical structure as evidenced by the object-oriented methods [20] or the place-value representation in human number systems [29], which have close connections to algebra. Here we are interested in the study of AI models that can derive, represent, and manipulate this type of knowledge, but without necessarily seeking to model human capacities faithfully. Models for understanding of finite-state (and more general) dynamical systems phenomena in general exhibit such feedforward, coarse-to-fine, hierarchical structure related to algebraic coordinate systems [17, 20, 26]. Our work shows how such coordinate systems can be derived and exploited automatically.

By a *coordinate system* on a symmetry structure (or more general structure), we mean a notational system in the broadest possible sense, with which a human or artificial agent can address building blocks of the structure and their relations in a decomposition, thus gaining a convenient way for grasping the structure of the original phenomenon and possibly getting tools for manipulating the components.

An obvious example is the Descartes coordinate system, where we can uniquely specify any point of the n-dimensional space by n coordinates. However, this is an example of a spatial and inherently non-hierarchical coordinate system for a totally homogeneous space. In general, different coordinates have different roles, addressing 'parts' of the system different in size, function, etc. The natural example of a hierarchical coordinate system is our decimal positional number notation system: different coordinates correspond to different magnitudes. The examples also show that a coordinate system is very much the same thing as a decomposition: the space is decomposed into dimensions, an integer is decomposed into ones, tens, hundreds, etc.

From this viewpoint coordinate systems become cognitive models, means of knowledge representation. The above examples show the usefulness of these coordinates, but how can we obtain these models? The good news, and the main promise of this research direction, is that we can get them automatically! In algebraic automata theory, the Prime Decomposition Theorem says that every finite state automata can be decomposed into a hierarchical coordinate system [8, 14, 17]. Therefore the way of representing knowledge becomes algebraic, semigroup- and group-theoretical, which is really very different from other, well-established AI methods mainly based on logic (e.g. [1, 22]).

Here we concentrate on coordinatizing symmetry structures (called 'permutation groups' in algebra) via the Frobenius-Lagrange embedding. Related work [4, 6, 7] has computationally implemented the automated generation of transformation semigroup decompositions along the lines of the Krohn-Rhodes theorem, but did not pursue the 'simpler' problem of obtaining coordinate systems on permutation groups as we do here, and hence our work is both complementary and necessary for providing a full decomposition in the more general setting where operations need not be invertible.

The use of algebra in cognitive modeling also occurs in other non-traditional applications. For example, the approach by Fauconnier-Turner-Goguen to conceptual blending and metaphor [9] uses category-theoretic pushout computations with computer algebraic implementations by Goguen to automatically generate conceptual blends and metaphors relating two (or more) conceptual domains (knowledge of which is modeled by small categories), as well as applications to the semiotics of user-interface design, and formal specification for imperative programs built up and verified in a hierarchical manner [11, 12].

As there are many different ways of understanding of the same thing, there are many different coordinate systems for the same structure. Some of them may be intuitive for humans, while others will suit computational manipulation better, so the range of intelligent 'users' of the coordinate system is not restricted.

Although much of the mathematical theory required here is very old, the proper computational tools were missing, therefore the idea of hierarchical coordinate systems giving understanding computationally has not been much studied nor applied. Now such tools are available open-source [5–7] for transformation semigroups, complemented by our work reported here for groups giving fine detail on coordinatizing the groups involved. The mathematical significance of these coordinate systems is immediate, but as they capture one of the basic aspects of our cognitive capabilities, namely, *hierarchical representation*, they might also play significant role in AI.

2   Mathematical Preliminaries

Here we briefly review basic group theory and a hierarchical composition method of permutation groups.

2.1   Essentials of Group Theory

A function $p : X \to X$ on the set X is called a *permutation* if it is one-to-one and onto (invertible). A *permutation group* (X, G) is a set G of permutations closed under composition (multiplication, usually denoted by $\cdot$), together with the state set X on which the mappings act. It is called a *symmetry group* if certain structure on X is preserved by all $p \in G$. If it is clear form the context we omit the state set and write simply G. For $x \in X$ and $g \in G$, we write $x \cdot g$ for the result of applying permutation g to x. The action is *faithful* if whenever $x \cdot g = x \cdot g'$ holds for all $x \in X$ then $g = g'$. The group contains the *identity* 1 and *inverse* map p^{-1} for each element p, thus everything can undone within a group. A group G acting on X by permutations need not necessarily be faithful, i.e. need not be a permutation group. The group consisting of all permutations acting on n points is called the *symmetric group* S_n, while C_n denotes the *cyclic group* on n objects permuted cyclically. A subset H of a group G called a *subgroup* if it is closed under inversion and the group's multiplication. We write $H \leq G$ if H is a subgroup of G. If (X, G) is faithful, then G is a naturally a subgroup of the symmetric group on X. We say (X, G) is *transitive* there is an $x_0 \in X$ from which every $x \in X$ is reachable, i.e., there exists $g \in G$ with $x_0 \cdot g = x$. For more on elementary group theory see for instance [13, 27], and on permutation groups see [2, 3]. As is standard, we use cycle notation to denote permutation group elements, e.g. (1 3)(2 4 5) denotes the permutation swapping 1 and 3, cyclically taking 2 to 4, 4 to 5, and 5 to 2, while leaving any other objects fixed.

As a special case, a group can act on itself, i.e. the group elements are the states and each $g_0 \in G$ maps $G \to G$ by right multiplication, $g \mapsto g \cdot g_0$. This is called the *right regular representation*, and it enables us to identify the group element with its effect, which will be really handy for permutation puzzles. However, this representation poses problems computationally due to the possibly large size of the state set.

2.2   Cascade Product of Permutation Groups

Given permutation groups (X, G) and (Y, H), their *wreath product* is the permutation group

$$(X, G) \wr (Y, H) \cong (X \times Y, G \times D)$$

where $D = H^X$ is the set of all possible functions from X to H. A state in the wreath product is expressed by two coordinates (x, y), $x \in X, y \in Y$. The group elements are coordinatized similarly by (g, d) where $g \in G$ and $d : X \to H$ is the *dependency function*, a 'recipe' to find an element that should be applied on the second level based on the (previous) state of the first (top) level. The elements of the wreath product are all permutations of $X \times Y$ given by some such (g, d):

$$(x, y) \cdot (g, d) = (x \cdot g, y \cdot d(x))$$

from which we can see that on the top level the action is independent from the bottom level, but not the other way around, hence the hierarchical nature of the wreath product. The wreath product is easy to generalize for more levels.

Wreath products are prone to combinatorial explosion, so in practice we deal with substructures with the dependency functions limited. These we call *cascade products* (see Fig. 1 for a simple example).

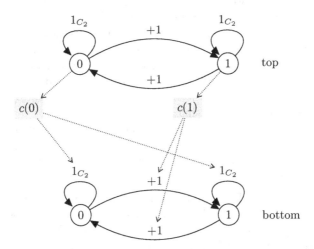

Fig. 1. Cascade with Carry. A modulo 4 counter (cyclic group C_4 acting on 4 objects) is built as a cascade product of two modulo 2 counters (C_2 on 2 objects). Their wreath product would yield the symmetry group of the square, but limiting dependencies as much as possible to allow just the carry bit (here function c) yields precisely the counter. The cascade product is generated by $(+1, c)$ and isomorphic to C_4 for which it is a hierarchical coordinatization. The carry c is a dependency function of the current top level state $x \in \{0, 1\}$, so the carry bit $c(x)$ is either '1' (given by the generator $+1$ of the group C_2) or '0' (given by the identity 1_{C_2} of the group C_2) and gives what to add to the bottom state $y \in \{0, 1\}$.

More generally, a modulo 2^k counter is coordinatized and isomorphic to a cascade of k C_2's, generated by $(+1, c_1, \ldots, c_{k-1})$ where for $1 \leq i \leq k-1$ the dependency function $c_i(x_1, \ldots, x_i)$ is '1' only for $(x_1, \ldots, x_i)$ the all 1's vector and is '0' otherwise. This is the binary (base 2) representation of integers. Base n is similar.

3   Lagrange Coordinatizations of Groups

In fact, we can build a isomorphic cascade for any permutation group (X, G). The basic idea of the Lagrange Decomposition is that given a subgroup H of G, we form the set of *cosets* $G/H = \{Hg : g \in G\}$, i.e. the subgroup H and its translates within G; these partition G, and G acts on G/H by right translations: $Hg \overset{\cdot g_0}{\mapsto} Hgg_0$. The action may not be faithful, so we denote G made faithful by $\tilde{G}$.[1] We do not need to act on whole cosets but can replace them by arbitrary but fixed coset representatives $\overline{g} \in Hg = H\overline{g}$. So the action is $\overline{g} \cdot g_0 = \overline{\overline{g}g_0} = \overline{gg_0}$.

Theorem 1 (Lagrange Decomposition). *Let (X, G) be a transitive permutation group and (X, H) be a subgroup of it. Then (X, G) admits the following coordinatization*

$$(G/H, \tilde{G}) \wr (H, H)$$

corresponding to the subgroup chain $G \geq H \geq \langle 1 \rangle$.

Thus given a state $x \in X$ we will coordinatize it by $\tilde{x} = (x_1, x_2)$, where each x_i is a coset representative $(x_1 \in G/H, x_2 \in H/\langle 1 \rangle)$.

By refining the underlying subgroup chain we can make the component groups much simpler or *simple* (i.e. having only trivial homomorphic images). This allows one to iterate the Lagrange coordinatization so the problem of understanding the permutation group (X, G) is reduced to understanding much simpler permutation groups linked up in a feedforward manner. Therefore getting a coordinatization corresponds to devising a subgroup chain.

For building subgroup chains certain subgroups are very useful. The *stabilizer* G_a is the subgroup of G, which fixes $a \in X$. Point-wise and set-wise stabilizers can be defined for sets of states as well. By iterating and refining the Lagrange construction, we have

Theorem 2 (Frobenius-Lagrange Coordinatization). *Let (X, G) be a transitive permutation group and let $G = G_1 \geq G_2 \geq \cdots \geq G_{n+1} = G_a$ be a subgroup chain ending at the stabilizer G_a of some state $a \in X$. Then, in the notation above, (X, G) is coordinatized by embedding in the wreath product*

$$(G_1/G_2, \tilde{G}_1) \wr \cdots \wr (G_n/G_{n+1}, \tilde{G}_n)$$

where $\tilde{G}_i$ is G_i modulo the core of G_{i+1} in G_i. Moreover, since (X, G) corresponds isomorphically to $(G/G_a, G)$, the states have coordinates given by the bijection

$$G_a x_n \cdots x_1 \Leftrightarrow (x_1, \ldots, x_n)$$

where each x_i is the fixed coset representative of $G_{i+1} x_i$ in G_i.

Remarks. (1) The number of coordinate tuples in Theorem 2 is exactly $|X|$. Each state has a unique coordinatization. (2) In Theorem 1 the number of possible coordinate tuples is $|G| = |X| \cdot |G_a|$, for any $a \in X$, as each point has exactly $|G_a|$ different possible coordinatizations.

---

[1] Here $\tilde{G}$ is a quotient group G/K, where K is the *core* of H in G, that is, the largest normal subgroup of G contained in H. Thus $K = \bigcap_{g \in G} g^{-1}Hg$. See standard references [2,27].

4   Coordinate Manipulation

The Frobenius-Lagrange decomposition gives us, in terms of a coordinate system, a structured view of the group, i.e. we can address its parts conveniently and with arbitrary precision. However, we would like to use the coordinate system dynamically, not just as a static description. We would like to calculate with it, finding manipulative operations taking one state to another desired state, or, equivalently, from one tuple of coordinate values to another one using the elementary symmetry operations of the original structure.

4.1   Component Actions

For establishing the connection between the original group and the coordinatized one we need to have a way to express a permutation as coordinate actions. Given a group element $g \in G$ and a coordinatized state $\tilde{x} = (x_1, \ldots, x_n)$, we can calculate the coordinatewise component actions by the following recursive calculations:

$$g_1 := g$$

$$g_{i+1} := x_i \cdot g_i \cdot \left(\overline{x_i \cdot g_i} \right)^{-1} \in G_{i+1}$$

Thus g on $\tilde{x}$ is coordinatized as $\tilde{g}(\tilde{x}) = (g_1, \ldots, g_n)$. Note that generally $x_i \cdot g_i$ does not equal to $\overline{x_i \cdot g_i}$, so g_i is not the identity. Note the hierarchical structure: g_i depends only on g and $(x_1, \ldots, x_{i-1})$. The action of g in coordinatized form is then

$$(x_1, \ldots, x_n) \cdot \tilde{g} = (x_1 \cdot g_1, \ldots, x_n \cdot g_n).$$

Killing and Building by Levels. We call the coordinate tuple the *base state*, if it consists of only the identities (as coset representatives), which clearly represents the identity of the original group. Given an arbitrary coordinatized state $\tilde{x} = (x_1, \ldots, x_n)$, we call the coordinatewise changes of values from x_i to 1 (top-down) *'killing by levels'*. This is accomplished by simply applying the inverse of the coset representatives, in order. An example is shown in Fig. 6. Conversely, *'building by levels'* is accomplished bottom-up by successively applying the coset representatives, i.e. elementary generating symmetries whose product is the given coset representative x_i for the ith component, in the order x_n then x_{n-1} ,..., and finally x_1 to move from the 'solved state' $(1, \ldots, 1)$ to create state $\tilde{x}$ bottom-up. Moreover, one can compute elements that change only a single coordinate to a desired value.

Global Transformation via Coordinate Values. Since we work with groups, whenever we make any action, it can be undone by an inverse, thus reversing the killing by levels we can go from the base state to any other coordinate value combination. Thus going from $\tilde{x}$ to $\tilde{y}$ coordinatewise can be achieved simply combining the level-killers of $\tilde{x}$ with the level-builders of $\tilde{y}$. More efficient solutions are generally possible (and implemented), but this provides at least one way to do it using the hierarchical coordinate system.

```
gap> pocket_cube_F := (9,10,11,12)(4,13,22,7)(3,16,21,6);;
gap> pocket_cube_R := (13,14,15,16)(2,20,22,10)(3,17,23,11);;
gap> pocket_cube_U := (1,2,3,4)(5,17,13,9)(6,18,14,10);;
gap> pocket_cube_L := (5,6,7,8)(1,9,21,19)(4,12,24,18);;
gap> pocket_cube_D := (21,22,23,24)(12,16,20,8)(11,15,19,7);;
gap> pocket_cube_B := (17,18,19,20)(1,8,23,14)(2,5,24,15);;
gap> pocket_cube_gens := [pocket_cube_U, pocket_cube_L, pocket_cube_F,
>                         pocket_cube_R, pocket_cube_B, pocket_cube_D];;
gap> pocket_cube_gen_names := ["U","L","F","R","B","D"];;
gap> pocket_cube := GroupByGenerators(pocket_cube_gens);
<permutation group with 6 generators>
gap> scrambled := Random(pocket_cube);
(1,19,20,3,18,24,15,10,5,8,23,13)(2,6,7,17,4,12,14,9,21)
gap> inverse := Inverse(scrambled);
(1,13,23,8,5,10,15,24,18,3,20,19)(2,21,9,14,12,4,17,7,6)
gap> epi := EpimorphismFromFreeGroup(pocket_cube:names:=
                                    ["U","L","F","R","B","D"]);
gap> sequence := PreImagesRepresentative(epi,inverse);
U^-1*R*U^-1*F*L*D^-1*F*L^-1*U*F^-1*U^-1*F*U*L^-1*F^-1*L*F*L*
U^-1*F^-1*U^-1*L*F*L^-1*F^-1*U^-1*F*U*R^-1*U*F^-2*U^-2*L
gap> Length(sequence);
35
```

Fig. 2. Getting a solution for the Pocket Cube. This is an excerpt from a GAP interactive session. The basic possible moves as generators (basic symmetry operations F, R, U, L, D, B rotating a face $90°$) for the Pocket Cube are defined together with names. Group elements are represented here in cycle notation, with () denoting the identity element (or, according to the right regular representation, the solved state). For obtaining a solution we simply express the inverse of permutation representing the scrambled state as a sequence of generators.

5   An Application: Permutation Puzzles

Permutation puzzles are one person games where the moves are permutations, elements of a group [16]. Natural problems for such puzzles are:

1. How can one go, via elementary legal moves, from one configuration x of the puzzle to a standard "solved" configuration?
2. More generally, how can one go from configuration x to another arbitrarily selected configuration y?

The main quest of permutation puzzles is often to find a shortest sequence of moves that leads to the solution (bounded by the diameter of the Cayley graph of the underlying group). Though the idea of of nested coset space actions is also used in tackling the shortest solution problem (e.g. Thistlethwaite's Algorithm), it is not our aim here. We would like to facilitate understanding, but usually the quickest solutions are 'dirty tricks' that are very difficult to grasp and one often has to fall back on simple memorizing. In fact, non-optimal solutions are easy to get by using computer algebra systems (see Fig. 2 for solving a simpler version of the cube). One can follow the steps to solve the cube without gaining any understanding. *Can we learn to solve the cube from the above answer? Can we identify, talk about and solve subproblems? Can we devise and compare different solving strategies?* We aim to answer these questions.

5.1 Coordinatizing Rubik's Cubes

The $3 \times 3 \times 3$ Rubik's Cube is probably the most popular permutation puzzle.

What does it mean 'to know the Rubik's cube'? The question usually boils down to the ability to solve the cube. By asking a cube-fan he/she would give a few tricks, recipes to apply in certain situations. By learning these algorithms one can learn to solve the cube, but does it imply understanding the cube, i.e. grasping how certain sequences of moves work and seeing why they work? Not necessarily.

We claim that understanding comes with imposing a coordinate system on the underlying algebraic structure. Here we demonstrate this on the symmetry group of the Pocket Cube, which is the $2 \times 2 \times 2$ version of the Rubik's Cube. The moves are the 90 degree clockwise rotations of the 6 sides. By the Frobenius-Lagrange decomposition we know that each coordinate system corresponds to a subgroup chain, so devising new strategies for solving the cube is equivalent to constructing subgroup chains. Such a coordinate system encodes a 'global viewpoint' in which one solves by successive approximation, with manipulations going from coarse to fine resolution, and converging in terms of moving from natural, abstract states to fully specified states. The group of the cube acts on the set of configurations in such a way that any non-trivial permutation yields a different result on the 'solved state', thus the stabilizer of this state is the trivial group $\langle 1 \rangle$, so each group element corresponds to a unique configuration. Hence by the remark following Theorem 2, for any coordinate system arising from any subgroup chain down to $\langle 1 \rangle$, each configuration of the cube has a unique coordinatized form. Examples derived computationally follow (see also Fig. 6).

Pocket Cube: Cornerwise Decomposition. One can solve the cube in a rather long, systematic step-by-step fashion: get the position and then the orientation of the first corner right, then proceed to the next corner until the cube is solved. In the subgroup chain we put the stabilizer of the position of a corner, then continue with the stabilizer of the orientation of the corner within the position stabilizing subgroup. Then we repeat the whole process for another corner. The chain yields the following coordinatization:

$$S_8 \wr C_3 \wr S_7 \wr C_3 \wr S_6 \wr C_3 \wr S_5 \wr C_3 \wr S_4 \wr C_3 \wr S_3 \wr C_3 \wr C_2 \wr C_3$$

where the top level component S_8 acts on 8 states (coordinate values), representing the 8 possible positions of the first stabilized corner. Therefore killing the first level will put the corner in the right position. The coordinate values on the second level correspond the 3 possible rotational states of the corner. The 3rd and 4th level similarly encode the second corner, and so on (Figures 3-5).

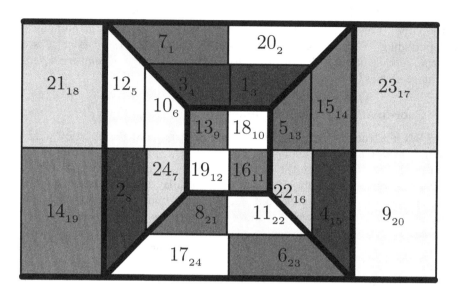

Fig. 3. A random, 'scrambled' configuration of the Pocket Cube, coordinatized by the cornerwise decomposition as $(8, 2, 5, 3, 2, 2, 5, 1, 2, 3, 3, 1, 2)$. Note: coset representatives have been integer-encoded in these examples. Faces are identified by numbers giving their position in the solved configuration. Subscripts if present shows what face should be at the location in the solved state.

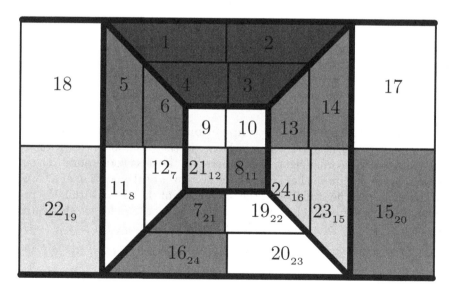

Fig. 4. Pocket Cube configuration after killing the top 9 levels out of 14. $(1, 1, 1, 1, 1, 1, 1, 1, 3, 3, 1, 2)$.

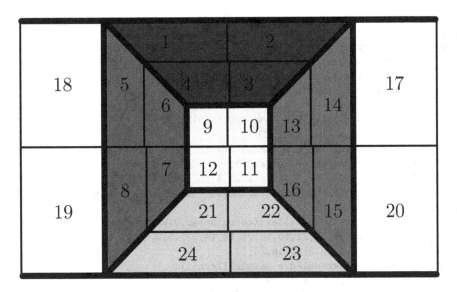

Fig. 5. The solved state of the Pocket Cube with coordinates $(1,1,1,1,1,1,1,1,1,1,1,1,1,1)$

Another Model for Understanding: Permute the Corners, then 'Beat the Clock'. Contrasting to the previous, very machine-minded solution, here is another one which is short, and reveals the existence of a different puzzle within the Pocket Cube:

$$S_8 \wr \prod_{i=1}^{7} C_3.$$

The top level component is the right regular representation of the now familiar symmetric group permuting the 8 corners. The second level is the direct product of 7 copies of modulo 3 counters (the orientation group of corners). It is to be noted that there are not 8 copies, otherwise every corner could be rotated independently from the other corners (and that would be rather easy to solve). Actually solving the bottom level is the same type of problem as the Rubik's Clock [28], which is an array of connected modulo 12 counters. As the underlying group is commutative, it is easier to solve since the order of operations generating this subpuzzle does not matter in this lowest level. For an example computational session using our decomposition package SGPDEC [5,7] in GAP [10] see Fig. 6.

3 × 3 × 3 Rubik's Cube. Going to the standard Cube we immediately meet some difficulty, as its group is not a transitive one. Therefore, using (G, G) we can get a decomposition which solves the corners as in the Pocket Cube and nearly separately and in parallel the remaining non-corner middle faces (those not at the corners, not in the middle of a side) on which the cube group is transitive. Then we can proceed by coordinatizing and solving the Pocket Cube and this middle cube puzzles independently.

```
gap> #creating a subgroup chain from the chief series
gap> subgroupchain := ShallowCopy(ChiefSeries(pocket_cube));;
gap> Remove(subgroupchain,2);;
gap> #getting the hierarchical components
gap> cags := CosetActionGroups(subgroupchain);;
gap> StructureDescription(cags.components[1]);
"S8"
gap> StructureDescription(cags.components[2]);
"C3 x C3 x C3 x C3 x C3 x C3 x C3"
gap> #solving the cube from a random state
gap> scrambled := Random(pocket_cube);
(1,10,12,6,23,14,16,24)(2,22,19,5,3,21,4,15)(7,9,20,17,11,8,18,13)
gap> coordinates := Perm2Coords(scrambled, cags.transversals);
[ 22578, 552 ]
gap> levelkillers := LevelKillers(coordinates,cags.transversals);
[ (1,19,22,2,15,9,7,3)(4,21,10,18,24,16,14,23)(5,8,11,17,20,6,12,13),
    (1,5,18)(3,13,10)(4,6,9)(8,19,24) ]
gap> halfsolved := scrambled * levelkillers[1];
(1,18,5)(3,10,13)(4,9,6)(8,24,19)
gap> halfsolvedcoords := Perm2Coords(halfsolved,cags.transversals);
[ 1, 552 ]
gap> halfsolved * levelkillers[2] = ();
true
```

Fig. 6. Deriving a Coordinate System for Pocket Cube and Solving via Killing by Levels. The subgroup chain for the decomposition is the modified chief series of the group. Then the decomposition is calculated yielding the two level coordinatization. Then a scrambled (random element of the Pocket Cube permutation group) is shown in coordinate format. Finally, the scrambled cube is solved by levels of this hierarchical coordinate system, top-down, using level-killers (see text), which are also expressed as an [unoptimized] sequence of the original generators.

Choosing a Suitable Algorithm. For a given configuration of a permutation puzzle there can be several choices of applicable strategies. The algebraic coordinate systems can help in making this selection. Assuming a predefined number of algorithmic stages, a *suitable solving strategy* is a decomposition that maximizes the number of solved levels. This is essentially what human speedsolvers are doing. Similarly, one can build a robot for solving the Rubik's Cube, that first analyzes the scrambled state and based on the configuration it chooses a suitable method. Moreover, by restricting to standard stabilizers the robot could teach how to solve the Cube by demonstration.

6   Conclusion and Future Work

We have shown how different subgroup chains in a permutation group correspond to different Frobenius-Lagrange coordinatizations of that permutation group, as well as to different solving strategies for manipulation. In particular, we showed that solving strategies for permutation puzzles can be represented by a subgroup chain, which determines a hierarchical decomposition. Coordinatewise manipulation of the permutation group via short or minimal length words over group's basic generators is an easily achievable next step.

For exploitation of the idea of hierarchical coordinatization in more general settings, groups can generalized to semigroups in order allow the possibility of some irreversible manipulations [5, 7, 26].

Acknowledgment. The research reported in this paper was funded in part by the European Union's Seventh Framework Programme (FP7/2007-2013) under grant agreement no. 318202.

References

1. Brachman, R.J., Levesque, H.J.: Knowledge Representation and Reasoning. Morgan Kaufmann (2004)
2. Cameron, P.J.: Permutation Groups. London Mathematical Society (1999)
3. Dixon, J.D., Mortimer, B.: Permutation Groups. Graduate Texts in Mathematics, vol. 163. Springer (1996)
4. Egri-Nagy, A., Nehaniv, C.L., Rhodes, J.L., Schilstra, M.J.: Automatic analysis of computation in biochemical reactions. BioSystems 94(1-2), 126–134 (2008)
5. Egri-Nagy, A., Mitchell, J.D., Nehaniv, C.L.: SgpDec: Cascade (De)Compositions of finite transformation semigroups and permutation groups. In: Hong, H., Yap, C. (eds.) ICMS 2014. LNCS, vol. 8592, pp. 75–82. Springer, Heidelberg (2014)
6. Egri-Nagy, A., Nehaniv, C.L.: Algebraic Hierarchical Decomposition of Finite State Automata: Comparison of Implementations for Krohn-Rhodes Theory. In: Domaratzki, M., Okhotin, A., Salomaa, K., Yu, S. (eds.) CIAA 2004. LNCS, vol. 3317, pp. 315–316. Springer, Heidelberg (2005)
7. Egri-Nagy, A., Nehaniv, C.L., Mitchell, J.D.: SGPDEC – software package for hierarchical decompositions and coordinate systems, Version 0.7+ (2013), http://sgpdec.sf.net
8. Eilenberg, S.: Automata, Languages and Machines, vol. B. Academic Press (1976)
9. Fauconnier, G., Turner, M.: The Way We Think: Conceptual Blending and the Mind's Hidden Complexities. Basic Books (2003)
10. The GAP Group. GAP – Groups, Algorithms, and Programming, Version 4.7.5 (2014), http://www.gap-system.org
11. Goguen, J.: An introduction to algebraic semiotics, with application to user interface design. In: Nehaniv, C.L. (ed.) CMAA 1998. LNCS (LNAI), vol. 1562, pp. 242–291. Springer, Heidelberg (1999)
12. Goguen, J.A., Malcolm, G.: Software Engineering with OBJ: Algebraic Specification in Action. Springer (2000)
13. Hall, M.: The Theory of Groups. The Macmillan Company, New York (1959)
14. Holcombe, W.M.L.: Algebraic Automata Theory. Cambridge University Press (1982)
15. Jones, H.F.: Group Theory, Representations and Physics. Adam Hilger (1990)
16. Joyner, D.: Adventures in Group Theory. John Hopkins University Press (2002)
17. Krohn, K., Rhodes, J.L., Tilson, B.R.: The prime decomposition theorem of the algebraic theory of machines. In: Arbib, M.A. (ed.) Algebraic Theory of Machines, Languages, and Semigroups, ch. 5, pp. 81–125. Academic Press (1968)

18. Laird, J., Newell, A., Rosenbloom, P.: SOAR: An architecture for general intelligence. Artificial Intelligence 33(1), 1–64 (1987)
19. Li, S.Y.W., Blandford, A., Cairns, P., Young, R.M.: Post-completion errors in problem solving. In: Proceedings of the Twenty-Seventh Annual Conference of the Cognitive Science Society, Hillsdale, NJ, Lawrence Erlbaum Associates (2005)
20. Nehaniv, C.L.: Algebraic models for understanding: Coordinate systems and cognitive empowerment. In: Proc. Second International Conference on Cognitive Technology: Humanizing the Information Age, pp. 147–162. IEEE Computer Society Press, Los Alamitos (1997)
21. Nehaniv, C.L.: Algebra and formal models of understanding. In: Ito, M. (ed.) Semigroups, Formal Languages and Computer Systems, vol. 960, pp. 145–154. Kyoto Research Institute for Mathematics Sciences, RIMS Kokyuroku (1996)
22. Newell, A.: Unified Theories of Cognition. Harvard University Press (1990)
23. Olver, P.J.: Applications of Lie Groups to Differential Equations, 2nd edn. Springer (2000)
24. Raman, K.V.: Group Theory and Its Applications to Chemistry. Tata McGraw-Hill (2004)
25. Reder, L.M., Schunn, C.D.: Metacognition does not imply awareness: Strategy choice is governed by implicit learning and memory. In: Reder, L.M. (ed.) Implicit Memory and Metacognition. Erlbaum, Hillsdale (1996)
26. Rhodes, J.: Applications of Automata Theory and Algebra via the Mathematical Theory of Complexity to Biology, Physics, Psychology, Philosophy, and Games. World Scientific Press (2009), Foreword by Hirsch, M.W. edited by Nehaniv, C.L. (Original version: University of California at Berkeley, Mathematics Library, 1971)
27. Robinson, D.J.S.: A Course in the Theory of Groups, 2nd edn. Springer (1995)
28. Wiggs, C.C., Taylor, C.J.: Mechanical puzzle marketed as Rubik's Clock. Patent EP0322085 (1989)
29. Zhang, J., Norman, D.A.: A representational analysis of numeration systems. Cognition 57, 271–295 (1995)

Ontological and Computational Aspects of Economic-Environmental Modelling

James Juniper

School of Business
The University of Newcastle, Callaghan, NSW 2308, Australia
james.juniper@newcastle.edu.au

Abstract. The paper examines economic-environmental modelling from a computational perspective. It considers the relationship between foundational and reference ontologies, warning that the philosophical implications of making an ontological commitment are often far from benign. In particular, it considers the proximity between foundational ontologies motivated by Husserlian phenomenology and neo-Austrian economic thought. Doubts are raised about capital theory in the modelling of economic-environmental interactions. A range of philosophical approaches towards environmental sustainability are also discussed in terms of their congruence with different schools of economic thought. Computational and mathematical aspects of modelling are then considered.

Keywords: ontology, computation, environmental sustainability, economic modelling.

1 Introduction

In what follows, I shall draw upon relevant arguments made in two recent papers, Juniper [1,2], which deal with computational aspects of economic and environmental modelling. The current paper then situates these arguments within a broader policy context. The second paper [2] also provides a justification for adopting a specific economic modelling approach based on a multi-sectoral representation of production and distribution along the lines of what some commentators describe as the "Sraffa-Leontieff-von Neumann" suite of models.

The issue discussed in this particular paper is how researchers can develop a *meaningful* approach to the modelling of economic-environmental interactions which departs from the mainstream or neo-classical economic tradition. Theoretical justifications for this approach are examined at some length both from and economic and an environmental perspective and, as well, from a more encompassing viewpoint.

In particular, it argues that researchers should be concerned about the capital-theoretic limitations of the dominant methodology of Pearce and Turner [3], which is predicated on the notion of "environmental capital". This socio-economic approach has been embraced by the United Nations. A currently fashionable alternative grounds its analysis on metrics which are based on the thermodynamic concept of entropy

S.K. Chalup et al. (Eds.): ACALCI 2015, LNAI 8955, pp. 31–48, 2015.

(specifically, the work of Georgescu-Roegen and Herman Daly). In what follows, I also question the merits of this popular interpretation of sustainability.

In its place, I suggest that there is potential for alloying Eco-Socialist interpretations with Eco-Feminist thinking about sustainability. In my own work I have adopted a Deleuzean critique of political economy, which draws on Deleuze's notions of an axiomatic of capital, and his arguments about the co-evolution of both the nomadic war-machine and despotic state. This theoretical trajectory affords the prospect for a productive merger with the New Economic Sociology of Michel Callon and Bruno Latour (who have, themselves, advocated the deployment of Deleuzean concepts of desiring production and de-territorialization—alongside the Pragmatist notions of performativity and enactment—as substitutes for what they see as the more problematic Foucauldian notions of power-knowledge relations and resistance, respectively). By the same token, I find Deleuze's critique of Lacan's "phallologocentrism" and his preferred notion of Schizoanalysis of great value in overturning the ubiquitous role of "lack" as an explanatory vehicle. Finally, I prefer Deleuze's own fleeting but pessimistic observations in "Postscripts to a Control Society" to those who celebrate the coming of a new democratic epoch of "co-creation" and "presumption" (i.e. where consumers have also become active producers).

1.1   Motivation from Computational Perspective

Empiricist prejudices notwithstanding, it might seem obvious that researchers one should never divorce seemingly technical or computational questions of ontology, including in matters regarding highly specialized and often quite functional "regional" ontologies, from much broader philosophical considerations. If we take as an example, regional ontologies that have been developed for economics it should be observed that schools of economic thought differ dramatically one from the other. One of the more philosophically informed schools of thought is that of Austrian Economics, as championed by Carl Menger. Menger's approach which draws heavily on the notions of Brentano, Stumpf and Husserl, most notably the latter's *Logical Investigations*. As Foucault points out, members of the Germano-Austrian *Ordo*-liberal School of Public Policy grounded their reading of economics in Husserlian conceptions of the essential logic of market processes. Although market relations are a contingent social artefact, for them, the logic governing their mechanisms is far from being contingent. The inherent logical necessity of these mechanisms is what allows them to be transported into new domains of activity that had hitherto been entirely removed from the vicissitudes of the commodity form.

In contrast, most members of the so-called Cambridge Circus in the 1930s were informed by both Marxist philosophies (especially Piero Sraffa), and the early Analytic tradition of Russell, Whitehead, and Moore (especially Keynes himself), although the extent of Whitehead's influence over Keynes is still hotly debated. Where Menger embraced methodological individualism and a respect for entrepreneurship, Marx emphasised, on one hand, the clash between mechanisms of private appropriation and, on the other hand, the knowledge-based, collective and cumulative characteristics of the forces of production.

When economic theories are viewed from an Actor-Network-Theory Perspective, which focuses on notions of performativity and enactment, economists are viewed as not merely describing the world, but also actively constituting it, albeit under certain propitious or un-propitious "conditions of felicitation". On this view, the development of rival ontologies is a process that has an obvious political character. At the very least, the construction of ontologies on the part of government agencies, commercial institutions, and NGOs, should be carefully monitored and politically contested, with a view to enhancing what Jürgen Habermas has referred to as the more communicative and emancipatory rather than merely procedural forms of "knowledge-constituting interest".

2   Ontology, Knowledge Representation, and Computation

This section of the paper will provide an overview of the issues at hand, leaving more detailed consideration for later. One consequence of the dramatic growth in the size and influence of the Information Technology Sector over everyday life, is that questions of ontology have become a significant focus of research. Ontological systems have been constructed to support both data-base management, system design, interchange standards, diagnostics and execution, and modelling and simulation. Some ontologies however, are intended to operate at a global or universal scale while others are designed for highly specialized forms of professional activity and information sharing. The former tend to be grounded within an overarching philosophical framework whereas the latter tend to be governed more by functional and procedural forms of rationality. The objective of these foundational ontologies is to promote integration and inter-operability, while minimizing the tendency towards an untamed proliferation of entities and defining relationships.

This paper is predicated on the simple notion that an important, though largely implicit, inter-relationship obtains between the attributes and structures of computational ontologies and those developed to service more functional legal, economic, accounting, environmental, and geospatial objectives, a complex, mutual conditioning that has been illustrated in the following diagram, as will be explained in more detail in what follows.

The notion of process will play an important, unifying and integrative function in my interrogation of ontological issues. For Hoekstra, this dimension of process thinking concerns the relationship between knowledge representation and the construction of computational ontologies. Taking a general or abstract point of view, the developers of any particular ontology are obliged to choose between working with an intuitive but inexpressive language or working with a well-wrought language, which supports reasoning [4].

Hoekstra complains that those working on computational ontologies must negotiate between at least two, at times conflicting theoretical trajectories within the knowledge representation literature that have been influenced, respectively, by psychology and philosophy.

Philosophy and Computation

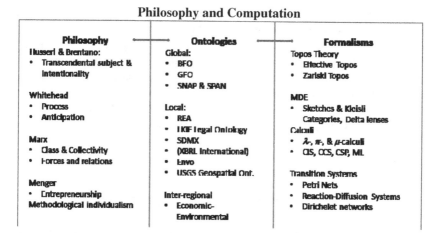

Philosophy	Ontologies	Formalisms
Husserl & Brentano: • Transcendental subject & intentionality	**Global:** • BFO • GFO • SNAP & SPAN	**Topos Theory** • Effective Topos • Zariski Topos
Whitehead • Process • Anticipation	**Local:** • REA • LKIF Legal Ontology	**MDE** • Sketches & Kleisli Categories, Delta lenses
Marx • Class & Collectivity • Forces and relations	• SDMX • (XBRL International) • Envo • USGS Geospatial Ont.	**Calculi** • λ-, π-, & μ-calculi • CIS, CCS, CSP, ML
Menger • Entrepreneurship Methodological individualism	**Inter-regional** • Economic- Environmental	**Transition Systems** • Petri Nets • Reaction-Diffusion Systems • Dirichelet networks

Fig. 1. The linkage between Philosophy, Computational Ontologies, and Formalisms

In his efforts to develop an ontology for the insurance industry, Hoekstra attempted to base his architecture on a formal representation of physical causation, which in turn was grounded in a meaningful attribution of liability and responsibility. Nevertheless, he observes that, in trying to link formal theory (i.e. jurisprudence) to computational modelling (i.e. AI and the semantic web), researchers are forced to take a philosophical stance in regard to the philosophical status of the legal subject. As we shall see, differing conceptions of subjectivity and the individual can be situated at the very heart of the philosophical controversy between economists of a Keynesian and Marxist persuasion and those of a neo-Austrian and neoliberal persuasion.

Hoekstra also warns that the representation of causal relationships, even within the context of a simple model, is very difficult to establish in practice because inferences must be made from multiple, successive situations highlighting the changes occurring between them. From this representational perspective he cautions that the OWL language, for example, is too limited in its expressiveness and alternatives such as the PROLOG language require the implementation of custom classifier, while languages such as ESTRELLA are undoubtedly very expressive, but this raises further questions as to how relevant expressions should be integrated with OWL, and how the latter can be extended to account for more intricate descriptions.

2.1   Software and Model Development Engineering

In their survey article on the rapidly growing field of software engineering, Diskin and Maibaum [5] interpret software engineering as an integrative practice linking software to objects, structures and dynamic processes in the world, mediated by what they call "modelware". A successful process of integration allows the software developers to reproduce and represent these real world processes and structures within the software environment.

Diskin and Maibaum [5] argue that as model development engineers work on ever larger-scale programs and have to engage with increasingly heterogeneous constellations of models, of necessity, they are forced to draw upon the full resources of what they characterise as post-Bourbakian mathematics[1].

The mathematical resources they point to include more complex forms of topos theory, which take us away from the paradoxes and imitations of set theory into topos-theoretic domains that can accommodate recursive processes, function spaces, and multi-valued logics, as well as more complex mathematical objects, including R-modules and fields.

3   A Survey of Some Recent (Regional) Ontology Projects

In my subsequent discussion of ontologies, computational and philosophical, I shall concentrate on three major philosophical traditions, namely: the formal and transcendental philosophy of Husserl and Brentano, as interpreted by Carl Menger, the Keynesian tradition as influenced by Whitehead, Russell and Moore, and Marx's philosophy of alienation, as this has been re-interpreted by the Eco-Socialist school for application to questions of environmental sustainability. In what follows, I will briefly examine the features of three computational ontologies, to highlight their divergent characteristics, before returning to consider more philosophical themes: (i) The *Envo* ontology designed for environmental systems; (ii) SEEK/SPiRE Projects designed for Eco-informatics purposes; and, (iii) The Basic Formal Ontology (BFO) Project designed as an umbrella for over 100 sub-ontologies.

3.1   The Envo Environmental Ontology

Envo is a controlled, structured vocabulary that is designed to support the annotation of any organism or biological sample with environment descriptors. It is part of the The Open Biological and Biomedical Ontologies stable and is available for the following website: http://environmentontology.org/

Envo contains terms for biomes, environmental features, and environmental material. The biome classification include terms such as boreal moist forest biome, tropical rain forest biome, and oceanic pelagic zone biome etc.. Environmental features include terms such as mountain, pond, whale fall, and karst etc., while environmental material includes terms such as sediment, soil, water, and air etc.

Envo is linked to certain Genomic Standards Consortium (GSC) Genome Projects MixS and GCDML. The intention of GSC is to promote mechanisms for standardizing the description of (meta)genomes, including the exchange and integration of

---

[1] While the Bourbakians developed sophisticated notions of mathematical and algebraic structure, in foundational terms, they largely relied on point-set theory rather on more general pointless topologies, for which points are derivative and regions are privileged. Modern treatments of computation exploit the categorical duality between point-free convex structures and point-set structures and draw on the distinction between the internal and the external logics of a topos.

(meta)genomic data. The MixS represents the core standards of the GSC for describing genomes, metagenomes and gene marker sequences, whereas the GCDML is an XML schema implementing MixS.

3.2   The SEEK/SpiRE Projects

The above acronyms respectively stand for "Science Environment for Ecological Knowledge" (SEEK) and the "Semantic Prototypes in Research Ecoinformatics" (SpiRE). These projects have the objective of applying knowledge representation and Semantic Web technologies to problems associated with the discovery and integration of ecological data and data analysis techniques. Each has been developed using the OWL-DL variant of the OWL languages. The pertinent ontologies are available at http://wow.sfsu.edu/ontology/rich/ .

They place emphasis on the relevant characteristics of a data set that need to be described, which include where, when, and by who the data were collected; a description of what was observed, typically including the taxonomic classification and other traits of observed organisms; the sampling protocol, including collection procedures and associated experimental manipulations; a classification for entities, their environment, processes and traits, and taxonomic classifications. Entities are classified as biotic, abiotic, or aggregate); the Environment is classed as physical or biotic; processes are classified as either inter-specific or intra-specific with either directed or undirected interactions; and, traits are divided into those pertaining to eco-process and those pertaining to eco-entity. Finally, the taxonomic classifiers distinguish in conventional terms between Kingdom, Phylum, Class, Order, Family, Genus, and Species.

3.3   Factors Affecting the Development of Ontologies for Environmental Modelling

Directly above, we addressed the issue of knowledge representation within the context of debates over appropriate ontologies, computational languages, and modelling procedures for Business Process Management. It is hardly surprising that similar debates arise in regard to ecological ontologies.

Keet [6] observes that taxonomies alone should not suffice for purposes of scientific analysis because more expressive 36odelling techniques are already available. She complains that the perspective of flow, predicated on the centrality of events and processes, cannot be represented adequately by a taxonomy. Instead, she argues for a formal mapping between software-supported ecological 36odelling methodologies and the software tool STELLA, along with its ontology elements (which have marked similarities to MatLab's Simulink module designed for the simulation of dynamic systems). To justify this thesis she examines two examples. One of these is a Pollution Model based on the mechanics of Stock-Flow-Conversion while another is a Microbial Loop.

In the Stock-Flow converter water and pollutants flow in and out of a bounded system, while a combination of measures are taken of water volume and the amount of pollutant yielding estimates of concentration, with the resulting combination of water outflow and pollutant concentration giving rise, in turn, to pollutant outflow. In ontological terms the model distinguishes between endurants, perdurants, quality (here conceived as an 'attribute' belonging to an entity), and a set of states.

For its part, the microbial loop ontology distinguishes between non-agentive physical objects; agentive physical objects, and detritus. The relevant flow elements include process (PRO), accomplishment (ACC) (measures as 2 times the entity *Uptake* and *Excretion*), and achievement (ACH) (*Oxidation*). Converters include grazing pressure. On the basis of these two cases, Keet argues that the "formal mapping between the software-supported ecological 37odelling method STELLA and ontology elements" simplifies bottom-up ontology development and "has excellent potential for semi-automated ontology development".

4   Foundational Ontologies

A wide variety of Foundational ontologies can be found in the field of computation. The Wikipedia site on "Ontologies" lists the following:

- BFO – Basic Formal Ontology (Husserlian, mereological)
- Cyc (not just an upper ontology, as it also contains many mid-level and specialized ontologies as well; it is based on knowledge modelling and is largely AI-driven: i.e. concepts are interrogated for their 'adequacy'!)
- DOLCE – Descriptive Ontology for Linguistic and Cognitive Engineering (Trento, Laboratory for Applied Ontology; Social Constructivist in basing objective knowledge on the constitutive powers of both natural language and common sense)
- GFO – General Formal Ontology (Onto-med, Leipzig University; 3-layered—distinguishing between top, core, base—with a meta-ontological architecture predicated on sets and universals; philosophically Analytic and Realist)
- UFO – Unified Foundational Ontology (a DOLCE derivative)
- OCHRE – Object-Centered High-level Reference ontology (Also developed at Leipzig University, predicated on a distinction between objects, attributes, and events conceived as description of reality; reliant on Boolean mereology and mereotopology!)
- SUMO – Suggested Upper Merged Ontology (drawing on meta-level concepts; schemas)
- UMBEL – Upper Mapping and Binding Exchange Layer (a subset of Open-Cyc; semantic web-based; linked with over 2 million Wikipedia sites)
- Business Objects Reference Ontology (deployed by the US Dept. Defence; with an ontology mined from multiple legacy systems)
- YAMATO – Top ontology with objectives similar to those of DOLCE, BFO, or GFO (representation, process and event: quality/attribute/property/ quantity; context-dependent theory of roles)

Of these, I will consider the BFO, firstly, due to its influence over a wide range of current domain-ontology projects, especially in the bio-medical sphere; and secondly, due to its generally un-remarked proximity to neoliberal political theory and policy.

4.1   The BFO Project

The Basic Formal Ontology (BFO) Project, available at <http://ifomis.uni-saarland.de/bfo/> is designed as an overarching and philosophically motivated ontology, which was initiated in 2002 under the auspices of the project *Forms of Life* sponsored by the Volkswagen Foundation. The theory behind BFO was developed first by Barry Smith and Pierre Grenon and presented in a series of publications. BFO is a small, upper level ontology that is designed for use in supporting information retrieval, analysis and integration in scientific and other domains. As such, it does not contain physical, chemical, biological or other terms which would properly fall within the coverage domains of the special sciences. Nevertheless, the developers note that BFO is used by more than 100 ontology-driven endeavors throughout the world. Current contributors include: Mathias Brochausen, Werner Ceusters, Melanie Courtot, Randall Dipert, Janna Hastings, Chris Mungall, Fabian Neuhaus, Bjoern Peters, Alan Ruttenberg, Stefan Schulz, Holger Stenzhorn, and Kerry Trentelman.

The so-called "SNAP and SPAN" ontology is situated at the core of the BFO Project (see Smith and Grenon [7], the gist of which, owing to its importance to the arguments made in this paper, is reproduced in somewhat abbreviated form below). This Brentanoan and Husserlian-influenced ontology would seem to have many areas of overlap and common ground with Whitehead's ontological framework, as set out in *Process and Reality*. One example of this correspondence, of relevance to the ontologies considered above, is the important contribution made by both philosophers to the underlying axiomatic logic of Boolean and Heyting Connection Algebras, which are almost universally deployed in a GIS context, most notably by the US Geographical Survey (on this see above, along with more technical discussion in [8] and [9]). Another instance is afforded by the duality between Snap and Span entities, which has apparent resonance with Whitehead's distinction between eternal objects and actual occasions. Yet another reflected in the notion of *anticipation*, which seems to be central to both the Brentan-Husserlian and Whiteheadian ontologies. I do not have space here to do justice to the profound question of where the similarities and differences reside in relation to each of these two trajectories. Suffice to say that Whitehead would reject both the Aristotelian substantialist nature of the Husserlian project and the role and importance of the transcendental subject for the resulting conception of anticipation[2]. Nevertheless, in what follows I will highlight the *proximity* of the BFO

---

[2] Whitehead was more concerned with the nature of the interaction between the prehending subject/superject and what he described as the extensive (i.e. space-time) continuum, with the latter conceived as affording the opening for an anticipatory and non-deterministic kind of projective geometry. On this see [11, 12]. [13] presents a provocative critique of the BFO approach on the grounds that its chosen ontological categories are no less compatible with a Nominalist rather than a Realist metaphysics, but see [14] for a robust response.

project to its neo-Austrian (and thus, the neo-liberal) counterpart within the ontological domain of economics and public policy, respectively.

4.2 The SNAP-SPAN Ontology

Smith and Grenon [10] identify "perspectivalism" as one of the key concepts grounding the SNAP-SPAN ontology. Perspectivalism consists in the view that any given domain of reality can be viewed from a number of different ontological perspectives, all of which can have equal claim to veridicality (e.g. anatomy and physiology; synchronic and diachronic structures in linguistics; level of granularity adopted in examining human body: i.e. molecular, cellular, organ, and whole organism perspective, where each of these can have equal claims to veridicality).

In particular they distinguish between "continuants" and "occurrents", asserting that each fundamental category calls for a distinct sort of ontological perspective. Another way of stating this thesis is to point out that substantial entities and processes exist in time in different ways based on the mereological distinction between temporal parts and wholes. According to this view, temporal evolution preserves the determinateness of parthood by insisting that continuant entities should be grasped in an ontology always as they exist at some specific instant of time: where continuants span moments in time, snap entities are instants without duration.

They further distinguish three kinds of SNAP entities: (i) independent SNAP entities (substances and their aggregates, the parts, and boundaries thereof); (ii) dependent SNAP entities (qualities, roles, conditions, functions, dispositions, powers, etc.). and (iii) spatial regions (of 0, 1, 2 and 3 dimensions, respectively).

For SNAP entities, time plays the role of external index. For SPAN entities, in contrast, time exists as part of the domain of the ontology. We can distinguish four kinds of SPAN entities: (a) processual entities (which include processes in the narrow sense—which are extended in time—as well as the instantaneous temporal boundaries of processes, here called events); (b) temporal regions (of dimension T); and (c) spatiotemporal regions of dimensions $T+1$, $T+2$ and $T+3$.

Grenon and Smith [10] introduce a third category which they call formal ontological relations. Formal relations are those types of relations which can traverse the divides between distinct ontological perspectives. Thus, they are those types of relations which: (1) can traverse the SNAP-SPAN divide (relations which glue SNAP and SPAN entities together); (2) can traverse granularities (for example between the molecular and the cellular levels of granularity); and, (3) can traverse temporal divides (for example between now and later).

In generating a catalogue of kinds of formal relations Grenon and Smith [10] observe that a number of parameters can be used. First, the ontologies from which the *relata* derive, can be expressed as an ordered list, called the signature of the relation. Second, the arity of the relation i.e. the number of variables appearing in each term of the underlying logic, can be proscribed. Third, parameters can determine the directionality of the relation. The principal signatures in the binary case are as follows: (i) <SNAP, SPAN>; (<SPAN, SNAP>; <SNAPi, SNAPj>, for distinct time indices I, j); and, (iv) <SPAN, SPAN> for SPAN ontologies with different domains or granularities.

Grenon and Smith [10] go on to consider a series of examples for each of the principle signatures introduced above, which I do not have sufficient space to consider here.

On the surface it would seem that a foundational ontology of this kind, to a large extent, crystallizes common sense and, as such, could only give rise to fairly benign effects. In some respects, this may be a correct appraisal of the situation. From a more politico-philosophical perspective, however, Husserl was a conservative thinker. It was this very conservatism that led Paul MacDonald [15] to conclude that Husserl shared with Descartes an ascetic methodology based, for the latter, on remorseless doubt and, for the former, on a an equally remorseless "bracketing" that was designed to reveal the essential truth of things. And, perhaps, it was this conservative aspect of Husserl's thought, more than its homage to the tradition of Aristotelean realism, which primarily attracted the attention and admiration of Austrian economists like Carl Menger.

4.3   Austrian Economics and the Ontological Question

Earlier, I observed the philosophical connection between Ordo-liberalism and Husserlian Phenomenology. In this section of the paper want to touch on the nature of this connection by briefly detailing on Barry Smith's homage to Carl Menger, one of the most influential thinkers within the Ordo-liberal tradition. It is important to realize that Menger, like his sociological contemporary Max Weber, formed his views of society while participating in the Austro-German *Methodenstreit* debates, which primarily took place between the Logical Positivists, Phenomenologists, followers of Diltheyian Hermeneutics, and members of the German Historical School[3].

In his exposition on Austrian Economics and Austrian Philosophy, Barry Smith [17: 1] makes the following observations about the peculiarities of the social domain when compared with that of the natural sciences:

> The large-scale social structures which confront the economist when he makes the attempt to apply his theories to reality are, first of all, typically more complex and less determinately delineated than the more or less cleanly isolable segments of material reality which are at the disposal of the physicist in his laboratory. But the crucial difference between the object-worlds of the economist and of the physicist consists in the fact that the individual economic agent who constitutes the most important element in the domain of economic theory exhibits one trait, consciousness, entirely absent from the realm of physics.

On the basis of Smith's elucidation of Austrian philosophy, it would seem that Whitehead and the members of the Cambridge Circus would share with Husserl (and his acolyte, Menger), a rejection of Positivism's privileging of the analytic and the necessary over the synthetic and the contingent. In contrast, Husserl argued that *synthetic* laws

---

[3] On Weber's contribution to these debates see Huff (1984), although his work suffers from his determination to reinterpret Weber's position in the light of "the new materials in the philosophy and history of science" that arose during in the much more recent debates between Popper, Feyerabend, and Kuhn.

(still a priori propositions) reflected objective structural inter-connections (i.e. relations of dependency) between objects, whereas *analytic* propositions relied only upon one core matter (e.g. sets in mathematics). They would also follow Husserl in holding that sensory impressions always, already partake of judgement. Finally, they would undoubtedly accept mereological distinction made by Husserl between mere "pieces" and aggregates on one hand and organic "wholes" on the other. On transferring these philosophical allegiances into the economic sphere, however, Menger insists that commodities, as organic wholes, depend for their worth on the valuing acts of individual, intentional subjects. Along similar lines, Menger posits that entrepreneurial activity, far from being a mere *factor* of production, can only operate as a veritable *presupposition* of production, insofar as it represents a practical ability to *anticipate* economic opportunities, entirely free from habitual blind spots.

5   Philosophical Interpretations of Environmental Sustainability

In this section of the paper I want to briefly highlight the differences between three broad and competing interpretations of Environmental Sustainability: Marx's Eco-Socialism, Menger's version of Neo-liberalism, and Daly's Thermodynamic approach.

5.1   Eco-socialism

In his evaluation of Marx's environmental views Foster [18] emphasizes the importance of his opposition to "mechanistic materialism". For Marx, this oppositional stance can already be detected in his thesis of Epicurus, who contended that a materialistic and anti-teleological view of nature was the essential basis for human freedom. Marx's subsequent refinement of his notion of the alienation of man both his from his labouring activity and from the object of labour was also conceived as an estrangement from: (i) nature as it existed outside him; and, (ii) his own body and, thus, his human species being (as creative activity) and spiritual essence. As such, alienation was manifest in man's relations with other men, with himself, and with nature. With the publication of *Capital*, Marx expounded the notion that socialism carried with it the implication that we would be able to govern our metabolism with nature in a rational way [18: 141].

Foster [18: 142] points to the fact that Marx developed a profound critique of capitalist agriculture, based on his conception of a metabolic rift between town and country). This analysis was based on both a close reading of soil science and a theoretical critique of Malthus and Ricardo, which focused on an assessment of the limitations of the second agricultural revolution. In effect, Marx engaged in a critique of the classical (Ricardian) theory of ground rent based on James Anderson's research into the historical causes of changes in soil fertility and then turned Ricardo against Malthus in arguing that pauperdom (i.e. unemployment) was the principle cause of social breakdown rather than Malthusian overpopulation [18: 143-7].

5.2   The Neo-liberal Approach to Environmental Economics

I am going to follow the precedent of Foster and Clark [19] who use the famous "Lauderdale Paradox" to distinguish between Marxist and Neoliberal approaches to sustainability. The "Lauderdale Paradox" stipulates that increases in scarcity for such formerly abundant, but necessary, elements of life as air, water, and food would, if exchange values were attached to them, enhance individual private riches, and indeed the riches of the country—conceived as 'the sum total of individual riches'—but only at the expense of the common wealth.

Foster points out that Marx's interpretation: of the paradox is based on the conventional Classical political economic distinction between use-value and exchange-value: i.e. in this instance the common wealth encompasses value in use and, for Marx, "the earth is the reservoir from whose bowels the use-values are to be torn" [18: 6, fn. 11].

In stark contrast, Foster and Clark observe that Carl Menger, the "father of neoliberalism", was one of the most vehement opponents of the Classical distinction, which he viewed as being singularly metaphysical. For him there could only be one system for determining value: namely, the mainstream or Neoclassical approach. Nevertheless, since Menger's time, well-meaning Neoclassical theorists have developed increasing elaborate techniques for shadow pricing (i.e. using exchange values) when confronted with market failure due to the presence of indivisibilities, inappropriabilities, and uncertainties [20][4]. This approach to determining social as distinct from private or market value raises the obvious question of whether metrics exist to support objectives of environment sustainability within the frame of Classical rather than Neoclassical Political Economy.

In opposition to the tradition of Classical Political Economy, both the Austrian economists and their Marginalist predecessors argue that value cannot be defined in the absence of subjective beliefs, feelings and judgements. Nevertheless, Eco-Socialists contend that values can be determined in a consistent manner on the basis of socially necessary labour time.

5.3   Thermodynamic Interpretations of Sustainability

Another active group of ecological economists, whose members include Georgescu-Roegen and Herman Daly, have turned to the science of thermodynamics for their sustainability metrics. Schwartzman (2007) has provided a review and hard-hitting critique of this paradigm. He first sets out the three fundamental laws of thermodynamics [22: 3-4].

---

[4] Critics of Arrow's notions of market failure single out his work on the market for "knowledge". While Arrow concedes that knowledge is "possessed imperfectly" and its productive powers are subject to increasing returns to scale, they nevertheless complain that he ignores the importance of tacit knowledge; framing and (non-Bayesian) revisions to knowledge; structural (i.e. non-parametric) forms of uncertainty; and the importance of organizational and collective, as well as network-based, forms of knowledge (i.e. those providing the context for communicative interactions). Hence, they suggest that there is a need to develop a "team theory" of knowledge exchange in opposition to those that are essentially rivalrous, such as "principal-agent" and "transaction cost" based theories [21].

The first law asserts the conservation of energy (after Einstein, both mass and energy must be considered). The second law captures the fundamental dissymmetry of the universe, in which the distribution of energy changes in an irreversible manner. This irreversibility is measured by the production of entropy. In thermodynamic terms, entropy is defined as the heat supplied to a system divided by its absolute temperature. The third law applies to matter at very low temperatures, forbidding it to reach absolute zero in a finite number of steps.

Second he considers [22: 4] diverging notions of the fourth law. On one hand, Georgescu-Roegen sets out two versions of the fourth law, namely: (i) "unavailable matter cannot be recycled"; and, (ii) "a closed system (i.e., a system that cannot exchange matter with the environment) cannot perform work indefinitely at a constant rate" which reflects the idea that "in a closed system available matter continuously and irrevocably dissipates, thus becoming unavailable".

Schwartzman [22: 4] observes that If we substitute "isolated" for "closed" (an isolated system means there are neither matter nor energy transfers between the system and its environment) then Georgescu-Roegen's (ii) (an isolated system cannot perform work indefinitely) is merely equivalent to the second law of thermodynamics, and is thus redundant. His man complaint, however, is that:

> Whatever the change in entropic flux arising from changes in the Earth's surface temperature, the entropic flux in itself will tell us nothing about actual impacts of global warming, which are both the linear and nonlinear outcomes of fossil fuel consumption and other sources of anthropogenic greenhouse gases. The concrete linkage of cause and effect must be worked out from application of the relevant sciences.

In an earlier paper, Schwartzman [23] asked the rhetorical question: "Why is it so important to overturn the arguments of the neo-Malthusians?" His response was the following

> They amount to an overthrow of Sraffa's arguments for a return to the surplus approach of Classical Political Economy, achieved through replacing the labour theory of value with one predicated on the use of energy or entropy as the supposedly appropriate measure.

Moreover,

> They interpret a problem with a geopolitical solution as one that is biological which thus has a strictly biological solution (i.e. an asymptotic movement towards complete biomimicry supported by policies to achieve a much smaller global population), or as Schwartzman puts it: "[i]f the dominant political economy of global capitalism is assumed to be largely irrelevant to explaining humanity's and nature's sorry condition, then pointing to the present size of human population and its forecasted growth as the primary cause will be user-friendly to the continued rule of capital"; that is, "[b]iology triumphs over political economy."

For Schwartzman then,

> [T]he Earth is too crowded—but with billionaires. Population stabilizes with reduction of poverty and empowerment of women.

Schwartzman goes on to acknowledge, less glibly perhaps, that radical changes must be made to realize global sustainability through a combination of solarization, demilitarization, agroecology. Nevertheless, he insists that the challenge is political and economic, not one of simply reducing population size or the size of the economy.

5.4   An Evaluation of Competing Philosophical Conceptions

At this stage I would like to evaluate some of the claims made above, focusing on Foster and Clark [19] and Schwartzman's anti-entropic version of Eco-Socialism[5] and the Austrian neoliberals. To some extent, arguments against entropy are a paper tiger: a resort to metrics based on entropy does not amount to denial of the political. For surely, entropy-based shadow prices can be used to guide policy, especially given that use values cannot be measured (although I shall argue later in this section that more Classically motivated techniques can be used to derive shadow prices that account for short-falls in sustainability).

Foucault argues that the Classical Liberalism of Adam Smith, is predicated on a critique of the "reasons of state". As the sovereign could never attain to a rational and complete knowledge of what motivated the Empiricist "subject of interest", it would be better to leave. In stark contrast, neoliberal policy was grounded in a Husserlian conception of the essential logic of the market. In this case, a fully developed "methodological individualism" would be constituted on the basis of a particular interpretation of Brentanoan intentionality (i.e. in the form of a deep-seated admiration for the anticipatory, practical nature of entrepreneurship).

While contemporary neo-Austrians engage in a partial critique of the assumptions underpinning "rational choice" theory, by resorting to notions of Knightian uncertainty, this epistemic choice only serves to justify, disguise, and thus perpetuate the private appropriation by capital of creative activity that is intrinsically collective and cumulative in nature [21][6].

Post-Structuralist alternatives to the three approaches considered above, merit some mention. Timothy Morton's Speculative Realist approach [26] to ecological issues has attracted a notable following[7]. Moreover, Teresa Brennan advocates a Spinozian ethical perspective which she integrates with Marxian pricing theory. Along these lines, Brennan [27: 185] has also argued that capitalism exploits nature whenever "natural substances" are "used up faster than they can reproduce themselves".

---

[5] Also see Burkett [3], who uses Marx's critique of the Physiocrats to support his critique of the entropy-theorists.

[6] An alternative virtue-ethics perspective on value theory is afforded by Johnson [25:4], who demonstrates that even the Fundamental Theorem of Asset Pricing in modern finance can be interpreted within his ethical framework.

[7] Timothy Morton [26] adopts a Speculative Realist approach focusing on *hyperobjects*, which are defined as objects that are so massively distributed in time and space as to transcend spatiotemporal specificity, instancing 'climate change'.

6 Modelling Environmental-Economic Interactions

My own approach to the modelling of economists and environmental interactions is predicated on the view that scientists from both disciplinary domains must increasingly work together in a close and cooperative fashion. This also carries the implication that they should either gravitate towards using similar techniques for dynamic simulation and modelling, or engage in model engineering development to overcome problems associated with model hybridity, including the overcoming of any disparities between: (i) discrete time (say, economic) and continuous time (say, environmental); (ii) physical (environmental) and value-based (economic) approaches to the evaluation of policy; and, (iii) a resort to general (say, economic) rather than partial equation systems (say, environmental).

In [1], I also observed that mainstream (i.e. neoclassical) models of economic growth and accumulation tend to: (a) use artificial and spurious notions of aggregated capital and notions of capitalization; (b) thus, encouraging the often erroneous view that one form of capital (e.g. environmental) is perfectly substitutable for another; and (c) expose themselves to criticism on the basis of the capital deepening and re-switching phenomena identified as problematic during the capital controversies of the 1960[8].

I also noted that, although the alternative approach of adopting inter-temporal Walrasian General Equilibrium (GE) models evades the capital critiques, this tactic is rarely pursued for practical policy development and evaluation, with researchers falling back on aggregative kinds of computable GE models that are susceptible to these critiques.

For this reason, I advocated the construction of multi-sectoral, input-output models along Sraffa-Leontieff-von Neumann lines, characterised by joint production. By the same token, Stock-Flow-Consistent, "single-sector" macroeconomic models of a post Keynesian variety, could be developed which, nevertheless, avoid making erroneous assumptions about the aggregation of capital. I also observe that, just as Marx was constrained by lack of access to *linear* algebra, so too, Piero Sraffa was constrained by lack of access to *process* algebras. On this basis, I recommended the adoption of a research trajectory based on the deployment of priced, timed Petri nets as a mechanism for modelling multiple-input and multiple-output relations, suggesting that a modelling approach of this kind (i) is amenable to formalization using process algebras and the various calculus of communicative and interactive systems; (ii) is congruent with biological modelling using reaction-diffusion systems and stochastic Petri nets [27]; and, (iii) supports the construction of policy metrics along Classical lines

---

[8] When it comes to the modelling of macroeconomic relationships, post Keynesians contend that the capital debates undermine the orthodox models of growth and accumulation that are situated at the very heart of conventional IS-LM-analysis of processes of adjustment to equilibrium in the markets for financial assets and real goods and services. This undermining also carries over to the conservative policy maxims that have been derived from these "neoclassical synthesis" models, which include notions of "Ricardian equivalence", the neutrality and super-neutrality of money, the concept of an ex ante "budget constraint" over deficit spending, and the natural rate hypothesis.

that can account, in terms of labour value, for the extent to which capitalist production "short-changes" nature. When it comes to the "shadow pricing" of environmental goods and bads, of course, these alternative modelling strategies have a lot of catching up to do if they are to compete with their neoclassical counterparts on empirical grounds.

7   Conclusions

This paper has examined the seemingly remote relationship between philosophical positions and computational ontologies pertaining to interactions between the economic and the environmental. It has focused on two major philosophical traditions— Eco-Socialism and Phenomenologically informed Austrian economics, as well as some subsidiary ones.

In their philosophical outlooks, Whitehead and Husserl seem to share so much: a concern with lived experience which views objectification (not in objectivity) as responsible for the crisis of the sciences, an anticipative conception of human consciousness based on pretensions and protensions, and an effort to ground of their formal logic of relations on ontological conceptions about the two-fold relationship between parts and wholes: on one hand, there are aggregates which are conceived as a merely summative gathering together of independent components, while on the other there are organic fusions as a complex manifold of dependent parts. Both thinkers also contributed to the axiomatic formalization of an algebra of connection, for which regions rather than points are the primitives. Nevertheless, Whitehead attempted to ground his conception of experience on the prehending relationships obtaining between perpetually perishing actual occasions rather than on the transcendental subject [28].

Moreover, the very proximity of Husserlian phenomenology to the Austrian neoliberal project has a dual source in: (i) an anticipative conception of the entrepreneur as subject; and, (ii) a conception of the market as something imbued with an essential, pure (ideal) logic. Nevertheless, even the latter is predicated on the eidetic intuitions of the transcendental subject, which Husserl saw as being unconcerned with either questions of existence, or any other peripheral qualities that the object expresses, but rather, as being a *logically* grounded faculty, oriented towards fulfilment (which, through abstraction, establishes a bridge between meaning intuition and meaning intention) [29]. What links these idealist conceptions together with the interpretation and development of computational ontologies is Husserl's underlying mereology and its subsequent axiomatisations. The question which remains unanswered is whether a computational ontology based on Whiteheadian principles might have both notable and divergent political effects.

While sharing in a rejection of Positivism, obvious differences remain between Austrians and their socialist counterparts. On one hand we have the intentionality of transcendental subjects (entrepreneur as immortal and universal), and on the other we have Whitehead's "lure of the proposition" and his analysis of the "extensive continuum" as a substrate for anticipatory behaviour. On one hand we have shadow pricing to account for market failure (somewhat grudgingly, on Menger's part) and on the other hand a conception of nature being "short-changed" in labour value terms. Each espouses divergent accounts of both policy prescription and of the emergence of uncertainty and economic crisis.

On computational grounds the paper has argued that economic modellers working with complex, heterogeneous systems need to take software engineering and model development engineering issues seriously! It suggests that the integration of world, modelware and software code will become increasingly important in the modelling, calibration, and simulation of dynamic systems that are designed to capture economic and environmental interactions.

Category Theory and Topos Theory are becoming ubiquitous instruments for development, analysis and evaluation in this field along with formal calculi designed for analysis and modelling of interactive and communicative systems (e.g. using stochastic Petri nets and the stochastic Pi calculus). I content that this increasing take up of such calculi has implications for the modelling of economic-environmental interactions, even though most of the examples cited in the MDE literature refer to interconnections between database modules. In [2], I argue that the categorical machinery that has been developed (e.g. generalized sketches, Kleisli categories, delta lenses, and coalgebraic formulations of dynamic systems) has the capacity and flexibility to deal with much greater complexity, both in terms of the mathematical objects that can be represented, the spatial and dynamic structures that can be modelled, the expressiveness of the resulting logics, and the heterogeneity of models that are brought together.

References

1. Juniper, A.J.: A Classical Economic Perspective on Using Coalgebras to Model the Process of Accumulation. Paper submitted to the Society of Heterodox Economists Conference (earlier version of this paper submitted to the Eighth International Conference on Interdisciplinary Social Sciences, Charles University, Prague, Czech Republic, July 30-August 1) (2013)
2. Juniper, A.J.: A Software Engineering Approach to the Modelling of Economic-Environmental Interactions and the Phenomenon of Liquidity Preference. Paper presented at Economics Politics and Tourism Seminar (May 2014)
3. Pearce, D.W., Kerry Turner, R.: Economics of Natural Resources and the Environment. Johns Hopkins University Press, Baltimore (1990)
4. Hoekstra, R.: Ontology Representation: Design Patterns and Ontologies that Make Sense. IOS Press, Amsterdam (2009)
5. Diskin, Z., Maibaum, T.: Category Theory and Model-Driven Engineering: From Formal Semantics to Design Patterns and Beyond. In: 7th ACCAT Workshop on Applied and Computational Category Theory (affiliated with ETAPS 2012) (2012), http://gp.uwaterloo.ca/sites/default/files/Accat12-paper7.pdf
6. Keet, C.M.: Factors Affecting Ontology Development in Ecology. In: Ludäscher, B., Raschid, L. (eds.) DILS 2005. LNCS (LNBI), vol. 3615, pp. 46–62. Springer, Heidelberg (2005)
7. Smith, B., Grenon, P.: The Cornucopia of Formal-Ontological Relations. Dialectica 58(3), 279–296 (2004)

8. Stell, J.G.: Boolean connection algebras: A new approach to the Region-Connection Calculus. Artificial Intelligence 122, 111–136 (2000)
9. Mormann, T.: Continuous Lattices and Whiteheadian Theory of Space. Logic and Logical Philosophy 6, 35–54 (1998)
10. Grenon, P., Smith, B.: SNAP and SPAN: Towards Dynamic Spatial Ontology. Spatial Cognition and Computation 4(1), 69–103 (2004)
11. Lango, J.W.: Whitehead's Ontology. State University of New York Press, Albany (1972)
12. Chiaraviglio, L.: Whitehead's Theory of Prehensions. In: Kline, G.L. (ed.) Alfred North Whitehead: Essays on His Philosophy, ch. 9, pp. 81–92. Prentice-Hall, Englewood Cliffs (1963)
13. Merrill, G.H.: Ontological realism: Methodology or misdirection? Applied Ontology 5, 79–108 (2010)
14. Smith, B., Ceusters, W.: Ontological realism: A methodology for coordinated evolution of scientific ontologies. Applied Ontology 5(3-4), 139–188 (2010)
15. MacDonald, P.S.: Descartes and Husserl: The Philosophical Project of Radical Beginnings. State University of New York, Albany (2000)
16. Huff, T.E.: Max Weber and the Methodology of the Social Sciences. Transaction Publishers, New Brunswick (1984)
17. Smith, B.: Austrian Economics and Austrian Philosophy. In: Grassl, W., Smith, B. (eds.) Austrian Economics: Historical and Philosophical Background, pp. 1–36. Croom-Helm, London (1987)
18. Foster, J.B.: Marx's Ecology. Monthly Review Press, New York (2000)
19. Foster, J.B., Clark, B.: The Paradox of Wealth: Capitalism and Ecological Destruction. Monthly Review 61(6), 1–18 (2009)
20. Arrow, K.: Knowledge, Productivity, and Practice. Bulletin SEDEIS, Etude no. 909, Suppl., reprinted in Arrow, Collected Papers 5, 191–200 (1965)
21. Vahabi, M.: A critical survey of J. K. Arrow's theory of knowledge. Cahiers D'economie Politique 29, 35–65 (1997), Pre-print available Munich Personal RePEc Archive, MPRA Paper No. 37888, http://mpra.ub.uni-muenchen.de/37888/
22. Schwartzman, D.: The Limits to Entropy: the Continuing Misuse of Thermodynamics in Environmental and Marxist theory. Science & Society 72(1), 43–62 (2007)
23. Schwartzman, D.: Solar Communism. Science & Society 60(3), 307–331 (1996), http://www.redandgreen.org/Documents/Solar_Communism.htm
24. Burkett, P.: The Value Problem in Ecological Economics: Lessons from the Physiocrats and Marx. Organization & Environment 16, 137–167 (2003)
25. Johnson, T.C.: Reciprocity as the Foundation of Financial Economics, (March 25, 2014), http://dx.doi.org/10.2139/ssrn.2334127
26. Morton, T.: Ecology Without Nature: Rethinking Environmental Aesthetics. Harvard University Press, Harvard (2007), http://www.ecologywithoutnature.blogspot.com.au/Brennan (accessed July 30, 2014), Brennan, T.: Economy for the earth. Ecological Economics 20(2), 175–185 (1997)
27. Mura, I.: Modeling Biological Systems with Stochastic Petri Nets, Technical Report CoSBi 08/2010, The Microsoft Research, Centre of Computational and Systems Biology, University of Trento (2010)
28. Marstellar, L.: Towards a Whiteheadian Neurophenomenology. Concrescence, 57–66 (2009)
29. Aldea, A.S.: Husserl's Break from Brentano Reconsidered: Abstraction and the Structure of Consciousness. Axiomathes 24, 395–426 (2014)

Exploring the Periphery of Knowledge by Intrinsically Motivated Systems

Kirill Makukhin[1] and Scott Bolland[2]

[1] The University of Queensland, Brisbane, Australia
k.makukhin@webage.net.au
[2] Queensland University of Technology, Brisbane, Australia
scott.bolland@qut.edu.au

Abstract. Intrinsically motivated learning is essential for the development of a wide range of competences. However, the neural substrate for the motivational signal as well as how this signal facilitates the processes of building competences are poorly understood. In this paper we exploit a biologically plausible approach, showing that an intrinsically motivated system where the motivation depends on stimulus familiarity as an inverted U-shape, exhibits well-structured exploration behaviour. Furthermore, we show that such behaviour may lead to the emergence of complex competences such as object affordances.

Keywords: intrinsic motivation, developmental robotics, emergence of competences, inverted U-shape, RBM.

1   Introduction

A considerable amount of the psychological literature argues that intrinsically motivated behaviour is essential for learning a diverse range of important skills and competences, such as grasping, walking and even language, e.g. [1, 2]. It is widely accepted in psychology that intrinsic motivation, driving exploration for the sake of knowledge, depends on such factors as novelty, complexity and surprise, and seems to follow an inverted U-shaped curve with respect to these variables [2–4].

However, there is currently a lack of understanding as to concrete algorithms involved in this process, which is necessary from the robotics point of view for building working simulations. Specifically, there are two open questions: what mechanisms are involved in the process of the forming of the intrinsic rewards, as well as how an inverted U-shaped function of intrinsic motivation could give rise to the emergence of complex skills or competencies.

In contrast, the field of developmental robotics has recently made substantial progress in modelling intrinsic motivation and applying it to artificial systems, see [5, 6] for reviews. Although most of the models have the same intention—to maximise learning efficiency, they are differently related to the underlying neurological mechanisms.

In this paper we address the two open questions exploiting a biologically plausible approach, where the motivational signal is formed as an inverted U-shaped curve with respect to the familiarity of the input dataflow [7]. The following sections describe

S.K. Chalup et al. (Eds.): ACALCI 2015, LNAI 8955, pp. 49–61, 2015.

two computational experiment. The first simulation demonstrates that the exploration reinforced by intrinsic motivation that follows an inverted U-shaped function with respect to familiarity could lead to the emergence of well-structured behaviour that is more efficient comparing to random exploration. The second experiment shows the process of the emergence of object affordances in a simulated robot.

2   Emergence of Structured Behaviour

Intuitively, if an organism spends its time exploring familiar parts of the world, little new knowledge can be gained. Furthermore, this could also reduce performance on other regions of the world, because of either catastrophic or gradual forgetting, a phenomenon peculiar to most connectionist networks [8].

On the other hand, exploring totally unfamiliar contingencies is also problematic, in that the contingencies might be purely random (such as trying to predict the next car exiting a tunnel), or may not be easily integrated into current mental models (e.g., integrating a location into a poorly formed map of the world), or the power of the learning algorithm does not allow the processing of the information.

In either case, an attempt to learn such data is obviously wasting the agent's time. Instead, exploring new knowledge that *extends* the old, drives the organism to effectively expand its mental models and gain competencies.

In this experiment, an intrinsically motivated agent is learning data that are unevenly split into several "boxes" with increasing number of data vectors ("facts"). Thus, each box represents a different level of complexity that gradually changes from easy-to-learn, up to unlearnable. Structured incremental behaviour seems to be beneficial for learning performance: first learning simple things, then more complex ones [9]. The experiment is designed to explore if such an interesting behaviour could emerge in a system motivated with an inverted U-shape signal with respect to familiarity.

2.1   Experimental Setup

The agent is being trained to memorise random data vectors that are combined into five boxes. Each box contains a logarithmically increasing number of facts from 2 to 200, thus simulating an increasing level of learning complexity. In addition, there is a 6th box with an infinite number of facts. Each fact is a pre-generated random vector with sparsity about 0.1[1] and having the length of 400 bits.

The agent tracks the intrinsic motivation for every box as a running average of the motivations for all processed facts within that box. In every iteration, the agent chooses a box with the maximum motivation and learns one fact from it. A small degree of random exploration is allowed during the experiment.

The memory of the agent comprises a binary restricted Boltzmann machine (RBM) [10–12], which is a two-layer network of visible and hidden units that are bi-directionally

---

[1]   The sparsity of stimuli must be low to overcome limitations of a simple binary RBM as it was discussed in [17].

connected to each other with no lateral connections within layers, **Fig. 1**. The units make stochastic decisions about whether to be "on" or "off" with probability defined by the net input.

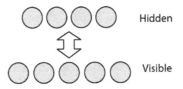

Fig. 1. A binary RBM

Specifically, the probability of turning a unit "on" is:

$$p(h_j|\mathbf{v}) = \frac{1}{1 + e^{-z_j}},$$

$$z_j = b_j + \sum_i v_i \cdot w_{ij},$$

where w_{ij} is the weight of the connection between the i-th visible and j-th hidden units, b, c are visual and hidden units' biases respectively.

The RBM is trained to minimise the joint probability of visible and hidden units $P(v,h)$ with a contrastive divergence algotithm [11], where the weight are updated according to the following equation:

$$\Delta w_{ij} = \langle v_i h_j \rangle^{data} - \langle v_i h_j \rangle^{equilibrium}.$$

In this equation, $\langle\ \rangle^{data}$ denotes the expected value of the input multiplied with the inferred hidden states while the input is clamped on the data points, and $\langle\ \rangle^{equilibrium}$ is the expectation of $v_i h_j$ when the alternating Gibbs sampling of the hidden and visible units was infinitely iterated to get samples from the equilibrium distribution. Fortunately, it was shown that the learning could be acceptably efficient even if the Gibbs sampling chain has been stopped after the first update.

In addition to the prototypical RBM, our implementation explicitly generates an intrinsic motivation signal that is a simplified inverted U-shaped curve with respect to the mean squared error of the restored input data (see Fig.2):

$$IM = \begin{cases} \dfrac{E}{Ep}, & if\ E \le Ep \\ \dfrac{E - Eo}{Ep - Eo}, & if\ Ep < E < Ed \\ E, & if\ E > Ed \end{cases}$$

where E is normalised error (will be explained later), Ep is the inverted U-shape peak and $Ed = D(Ep - Eo) + Eo$. The parameter D defines the value of the motivation for totally unfamiliar stimuli. We used the following parameters through our experiments: $D=0.1$, $Ep = 0.15$ and $Eo = 0.4$.

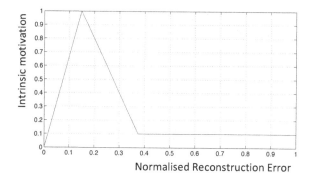

Fig. 2. The function used in the generation of the intrinsic motivation signal. See text for details and math

The RBM error could be considered as the inverse of familiarity of the stimulus. It is calculated as a squared error between the input image and the reconstruction, obtained from the RBM via Gibbs sampling [13] error $= \sum_i (v_i^{recon} - v_i^{data})^2$. For the sake of computational convenience, the error is normalised to be bounded approximately in the range [0..1] by subtracting its expected mean and dividing by the expected range. Interestingly, the described framework is quite insensible to the shape of the intrinsic motivation function.

This algorithm captures, albeit in an artificial way, the dynamics of the activity of a spiking neural network with Hebbian learning and lateral inhibition that possibly reflects processes underlying intrinsic motivation in the brain [7]. Indeed, for highly familiar stimuli, the motivation signal is low because the error is low. Subsequently, it has a low (but non-zero) value for unfamiliar stimuli when the normalised error is approaching 1. However, for moderately familiar stimuli, the algorithm gives a high signal, thus producing an inverted U-shaped response of the signal with respect to familiarity.

The agent's RBM has 200 hidden units and is trained with a learning rate of 0.0005. The RBM was pre-trained beforehand with a few random vectors to remove the influence of settling down the weights and biases.

2.2   Results

The results of the experiment are presented in Fig.3. The bottom plot shows the normalised reconstruction error E for the facts from each bin. The top plot represents the intrinsic motivation signal IM, for the same bins respectively.

Initially, when all facts are new for the agent, the motivation for every bins is low. After few iterations, the motivation rises with the formation of the initial representation. Apparently, the learning for the first bin is more efficient because it has fewer samples. This results in a motivation peak for the first bin (Fig.3, data1 line). Thus the agent now is actively choosing the first bin until its facts are learned well enough and the bin's average motivation decays back to the base level. Once this happens, the next bin with higher complexity is selected. The process repeats with all learnable bins and with gradual increasing complexity. However, it is important to note that the agent never chooses the 6th bin with an infinite number of facts (data6). Thus, the agent will not get stuck at unpredictable segments, because the motivation for that area is always low.

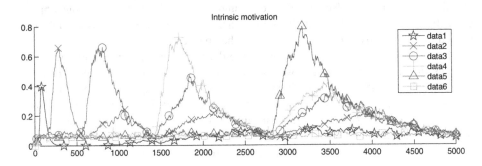

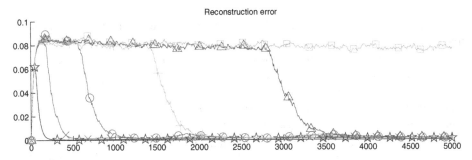

Fig. 3. A typical run of the learning bins experiment. Intrinsic motivation at the top and reconstruction error at the bottom. Bins are selected to learn from by the agent in a systematically organised way, starting from the easiest to learn and proceeding to the hardest to learn. The unlearnable bin with random facts (data6) is never selected. Best viewed in colour.

The described sequence is a typical run of the experiment. However, sometimes the agent may not strictly follow the sequence of gradually increasing complexity. For example, it might choose initially bin No 2, and then bin No 1, followed by the selection of other bins in the correct sequence. It happens because of the stochastic nature of an RBM and the bin selection mechanism, and it could be relaxed by adding a slow degree of random exploration. That is, the agent may choose a random action instead of the most interesting one with a low probability (we use the probability of 5% in our experiment).

3 Object Affordances

Object affordances is a salient competence that is being developed in children and young animals during their developmental stage. The following experiment shows an example of how such competences could emerge in a system with the proposed intrinsically motivated learning.

For this experiment we have designed a setup similar to the Playground Experiment described in [14] that could be implemented both in a physical robot (e.g., robot-dog Sony AIBO) and as a simulated sensorimotor data flow. The playground environment comprises a baby play mat that is intended to develop basic sensorimotor skills in babies of age about 2-3 months, and two toys. The toys could be both detected visually, but they also have their own unique way of being handling: one object could be bitten (an elephant ear in the original setup), while another one could be bashed (a hanging toy that starts to oscillate when bashed).

The robot could perform the following pre-defined primitive actions that we call reflexes: moving its head along two axes (tilt and pan), bash to a certain direction with variable strength, and finally it can perform "crouch biting". The "crouch biting" consists of crouching in the direction it is looking at, followed by biting. The direction is defined by the head tilt and pan parameters, while another parameter regulates the depth of crouching.

Thus, the primitive action space is a vector of five real values:

$$M(t) = (H_p, H_t, B_d, B_s, C),$$

where H_p, H_t are the pan and tilt of the head, B_d, B_s are the bash direction and strength, and C is the depth of crouch biting.

The reflexes are grouped into four actions that the robot can choose, one at a time:
— moving the head along the vertical axis, head pan (H_p)
— moving the head along two axes, head pan and tilt (H_p, H_t)
— moving the head followed by crouch biting (H_p, H_t, C)
— moving the head followed by bashing (H_p, H_t, B_d, B_s).
Values that are not in use by reflexes are set to a default (rest) value.

If the robot bashes in the direction of the hanging toy with the appropriate strength, the toy starts swinging. If the robot bites while its head faces toward the toy and the depth of crouch has the correct range, then the toy ends up in the robot's mouth. All the actions are atomic in a sense that the robot does not perform the next action until the current action has been completed and all detectors have been read.

A physical robot (e.g., AIBO) is equipped with a webcam and biting sensor. At a program level, the robot simulates four detectors: two separate toy detectors for each toy (i.e., colour blobs detector), oscillation detector and bite detector. Each toy detector is triggered when the robot's head (with the webcam) is looking at the toy. This event, however, cannot happen if the robot only moves its head along the vertical axis (pan), because the default head tilt does not correspond to the angle where the toys are. The oscillation detector is activated when the robot is looking at the hanging toy and the toy is actually swinging as the result of a successful bash. The bite detector detects if the robot's mouth holds an object, which occurs when the head position has the correct orientation towards the toy and the depth of the crouch is in the correct range.

Thus, in total, there are four detectable events in the playground experiment that have different probabilities of happening: the visual detection of the toy #1 or #2, triggering of the mouth detector after correct biting, and detection of oscillation as the result of correct bashing:

$$S(t) = (V_1, V_2, C, B)$$

Fig. 4. The playground experiment setup (simulated on the V-REP virtual robot experimental platform [18])

The performing of appropriate actions $M(t)$ that have led to the corresponding event and sensor readings, we call 'affordance'. In the simulated environment, we can calculate the exact probabilities of the affordances:

$$p(V_1 = 1 \; or \; V_2 = 1) = 0.06$$

$$p(C = 1) = 0.004$$

$$p(B = 1) = 0.0016$$

Thus, the environment is designed with the goal of having events with dissociable probabilities and, thus, different learnability of the associations between the corresponding action and sensor readings.

It is important to note that initially the robot does not know what actions would lead to particular sensor readings. For instance, it is not aware that at a particular head tilt and pan, a visual toy detector will be triggered. Thus, the robot does not have any task-dependant knowledge a priori.

3.1 Model

A key component of the system is a predicting machine that learns to predict what would be the sensor readings after an action has been performed. The predicting machine is essentially an RBM, similar to the system described in the previous experiment, that learns a probability distribution of the combined vector of actions and detectors in order to reproduce missing input values when only part of the input vector (actions, but not detector readings) are fed to the input, Fig.5.

In the simulation flow, there are two operational steps: training and prediction. At the training step, the RBM is trained with a combination of an action vector $M(t)$ and the corresponding detectors' reading $S(t)$. Thus, it learns that a particular action leads to a certain event. At the following prediction step, the ability of an RBM to reconstruct a partially obscured input is used to calculate the most possible (from the system's point of view) detector readings $S(t)$, given only the action vector $M(t)$.

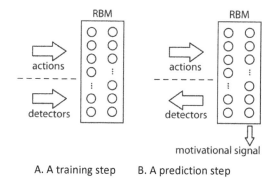

A. A training step   B. A prediction step

Fig. 5. The association machine based on the RBM's ability to reconstruct a partially obscured input

An intrinsic motivation signal is programmatically generated as an inverted U-shaped dependence with respect to the familiarity of an action-sensor pair measured as the inverse of reconstruction error, similar to the system described in the previous experiment (Fig. 2)

The action representation in the simulation uses real numbers within a particular range. To represent these values to a binary RBM, the values of the action vector $M(t)$ are discretised into five subranges. Specifically, every element is represented by a binary vector with "1" corresponding to the subrange the value falls into and "0"s corresponding to the other four elements. For example, if a value is close to the middle of the range, then the binary vector will be [0 0 1 0 0]. Hence, the RBM in our experiment has 25 inputs for five actions plus four inputs for detector readings, and 20 hidden units. The RBM is trained with the contrastive divergence algorithm [11] with the learning rate 0.003. The biases of the hidden units are initialised to small negative values as per [12].

Each simulation epoch consists of two steps. At the first step the system predicts detectors' readings on 20 random actions, and then it chooses an action that yields the maximum motivational signal. At the following step, the RBM is trained with the combination of the action from the previous step and sensor readings provided by the robot's sensors or simulated environment.

The simulation setup is a simplified model of the world that offers an agent a choice of actions without taking into account the current state of the robot (i.e., the robot always returns to the same starting state before commencing a new action). This limitation does not allow the implementation of complex decision schemas such as actor-critic models. With a single starting state, apparently the most direct way of choosing an action, would be the iteration through all possible actions comparing their intrinsic motivational signals. However, it is extremely computationally expensive, and we replaced this approach with random sampling that qualitatively yields similar results.

3.2   Results

During the simulation we track actions performed by the robot and register the occurrence of the target events: visual detection of a toy, biting of biteable toy, and bashing of a bashable toy. **Fig. 6** shows a typical run of the experiment[2]. The top plot depicts the frequency of the action chosen, averaged over the window of 100 epochs. Recall that within our model every action can have five different values $M(t)$. The plot shows the rate of functional actions, where similar actions with any possible value are summed into one functional action.

The bottom plot shows learned affordances averaged over 300 epochs. By affordance we mean an action that has led to the corresponding event, e.g. when the robot bashes in the direction of the hanging toy with the appropriate strength and the toy starts swinging.

An interesting property that emerged in the experiment and is shown in **Fig. 6** is that there are clearly distinguishable phases of robot learning, where it repeatedly choses mostly the same action. In particular, at about the first 200 epochs, the robot chooses to perform an action that is the simplest to learn: "head pan". Indeed, this action always results in none of events occurring. While the RBM is learning this association, the reconstruction error decreases. When the error become low enough, the motivational signal starts to decay. That is, the novelty of the situation passes the intermediate level, and after this point, the robot finds that some other actions are more rewarding. As a result, the robot switches to the exploration of a more complicated and intrinsically interesting action, specifically, the "head pan and tilt" action.

During the second phase that lasts until about the 1700th epoch, the robot quickly learns the affordance of looking at a toy. The corresponding association between the action and predicted sensors' readings has greater complexity than the first association learned by the robot. When the association for this action is learned well enough, the robot switches to biting, the next action that happens less frequently and thus is more difficult to learn. Finally, the robot progresses to learning the most complex action, to explore the action of bashing affordance that has the lowest probability of being enacted.

---

[2]   A video of the experiment with a simulated robot (V-REP virtual robot experimental platform) is available at: http://vimeo.com/52611232.

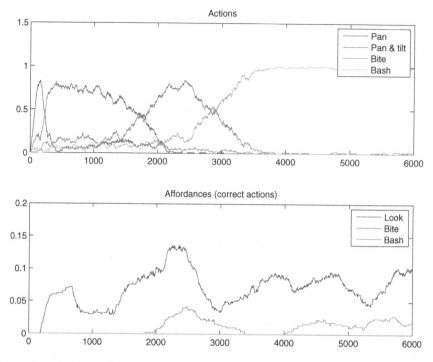

Fig. 6. A typical run of the playground experiment. The top plot shows the probability of choosing different actions. The bottom plot depicts the rate of successful actions, when the corresponding sensor was activated (e.g. the "bash" action caused swinging of the hanged toy). The horizontal axis shows the learning epoch. Best viewed in colour.

4   Discussion

The first experiment demonstrated that structured behaviour emerges in the system with the inverted U-shape intrinsic motivation: the agent incrementally learns the environment, starting from simple things and gradually switching to more complicated ones (Fig.3). In contrast, when an agent scatters its exploration rather than promotes specialisation in a particular domain, this would typically result in a "Jack of all trades and master of none" situation [9].

To numerically assess the efficiency of the strategy, we compared the intrinsically motivated exploration with random walk. The RBM reconstruction error averaged over 10 experiments for an intrinsically motivated agent achieved the value of 0.29±5.9%, while at the random exploration case, the error was 0.65±6.0%. The significantly lower performance at the random walk trials was demonstrated because the agent was wasting time and resources on learning both already well-learned facts and random facts that were impossible to remember.

Interestingly to note, with the exploration of a new bin (e.g., red, light blue and magenta peaks), the error of "old" knowledge slightly increases. That is, the system partially "forgets" old memories because the new memories compete for the RBM's resources. This causes a "refreshing" effect: the intrinsic motivation for old bins slightly increases and the system interleaves learning of the current bin with already learned bins.

In the following simulation, we apply the proposed intrinsic motivation mechanism to a robotic setup. The robot sequentially explores its sensorimotor space, starting from the most easy-to-learn actions and gradually moving towards rising complexity. The results of the experiment may illustrate one of the key aspects of developmental learning supported by the robotics community: development is an incremental and cumulative process [15]. This aspect emphasises that the vast amount of knowledge offered by the real world could not be learned completely by the limited agent's (or animal's) resources, and thus some mechanism is required to select only that fraction of the knowledge that "technically" could be learned and incorporated into existing mental schemas. In such a situation, random exploration is inefficient because interesting events usually have low probability and happen very rarely, so there is a very low chance for the organism to occasionally find that 'needle in a haystack'.

The results of the experiment are qualitatively consistent with the results published in [14], where the researchers underline two main achievements. First, at some periods of time, the robot focuses its activity on learning a small subset of the sensorimotor space. Second, the robot's exploration shows a progressive increase in the complexity of the behaviour. While the strategies and affordances developed in our experiment looks similar to [14], there are few key differences. First, our algorithm relies on a biologically plausible source of the intrinsic motivation signal. Second, it does not require storing lifetime information about the learning progress (or building a meta-model of the learning progress) and thus less susceptible to the curse of dimensionality.

Functioning in the real world requires the equally important ability of avoiding the learning of things that are essentially random in nature. Unlike the cited experiment [14], our setup does not allow testing of the functionality of the suggested theory in such situations; thus we leave this question to be explored in future work.

It is worth noticing that the experiment relies on a probabilistic network as an action selection element that makes the robot's decision probabilistic too. However, living organisms usually use more deterministic action selection. For example, if a baby starts exploring a new toy, it would keep on the exploration for a while until it becomes bored, but it would not interleave this exploration with other activities. In this sense, our experiment does not match, as can be seen on video, because even if the probability of performing a correct action is significantly high, there is still a good chance of selecting an incorrect action (i.e., interleave the correct action with incorrect).

Another limitation of the experiment is in the nature of action selector. The robot samples intrinsic motivation for different actions (or iterate through all possible actions) and choses the most interesting action to perform. However, it could be argued that this is not the way humans usually make decisions — we do not iterate through all possible actions (that could be infinite in number), but rather instantly choose one or a few with a generative mechanism. Thus, a more sophisticated action selection algorithm needs to be added to the system, and we leave this for future work also.

5   Conclusions and Future Work

The focus of this paper has been on addressing important questions of developmental robotics: what is the intrinsic motivation mechanism and how competences could emerge in such intrinsically motivated systems.

We believe that the inverted U-shaped activity of the deep cortical areas with respect to the novelty of stimuli reflects the intrinsic motivation signal. This idea let us bridge the gap between psychology and neuroscience, offering an efficient and context-independent mechanism for intrinsically motivated learning. We have demonstrated in simulations that this mechanism allows the agent to actively seek knowledge in an organised sequence with gradually increasing complexity, while keeping away from purely random areas that are impossible to learn. Furthermore, we showed an example how this exploration on the periphery of knowledge may lead to the development of competences such as object affordances.

Practically, we would like a robot to solve some concrete problems. Thus, as a future direction of research, it would be interesting to build an experiment and assess the performance of an agent that uses a combination of intrinsic motivation and a task-dependant reward in order to solve a complex problem that cannot be easily solved with plain reinforcement learning techniques, such as it was addressed in [16].

Acknowledgments. This work was supported by Mr. Sean Howard and Australian Postgraduate Awards scholarship.

References

1. White, R.W.: Motivation Reconsidered: the concept of competence. Psychol. Rev. 66, 297–333 (1959)
2. Walker, E.: Psychological complexity and preference: a hedgehog theory of behavior. Brooks/Cole Pub. Co., Monterey Calif (1980)
3. Wundt, W.: Grundzüge der physiologischen Psychologie. Engelmann (1874)
4. Berlyne, D.E.: Conflict, Arousal and Curiosity. McGraw-Hill Inc., US (1960)
5. Schmidhuber, J.: Formal theory of creativity, fun, and intrinsic motivation (1990–2010). IEEE Trans. Auton. Ment. Dev. 2, 230–247 (2010)
6. Oudeyer, P.-Y., Kaplan, F.: How can we define intrinsic motivation? In: 8th Conf. on Epigenetic Robotics, pp. 93–101 (2008)
7. Makukhin, K., Bolland, S.: Dissociable forms of repetition priming: a computational model. Neural Comput. 26, 712–738 (2014)
8. French, R.: Catastrophic forgetting in connectionist networks. Trends Cogn. Sci. 3, 128–135 (1999)
9. Stoytchev, A.: Some Basic Principles of Developmental Robotics. IEEE Trans. Auton. Ment. Dev. 1, 122–130 (2009)
10. Smolensky, P.: Information processing in dynamical systems: Foundations of harmony theory. In: Rumelhart, D.E., McClelland, J.L. (eds.) Parallel Distributed Processing, vol. 1, pp. 282–317. MIT Press, Cambridge (1986)
11. Hinton, G.E.: Training products of experts by minimizing contrastive divergence. Neural Comput. 14, 1771–1800 (2002)

12. Hinton, G.E.: A Practical Guide to Training Restricted Boltzmann Machines. Report (2010)
13. Bengio, Y.: Learning Deep Architectures for AI. Found. Trends Mach. Learn. 2, 1–127 (2009)
14. Oudeyer, P.-Y., Baranes, A., Kaplan, F.: Intrinsically Motivated Exploration for Developmental and Active Sensorimotor Learning. Mach. Learn. 1–42 (2010)
15. Lungarella, M., Metta, G., Pfeifer, R., Sandini, G.: Developmental robotics: a survey. Conn. Sci. 15, 151–190 (2003)
16. Merrick, K.: A comparative study of value systems for self-motivated exploration and learning by robots. IEEE Trans. on Auton. Ment. Dev., 1–15 (2010)
17. Tang, Y., Sutskever, I.: Data Normalization in the Learning of Restricted Boltzmann Machines. Report (2011)
18. V-REP virtual robot experimental platform, http://www.v-rep.eu

On the Estimation of Convergence Times to Invariant Sets in Convex Polytopic Uncertain Systems

Ryan J. McCloy, José A. De Doná, and María M. Seron

School of Electrical Engineering and Computer Science,
The University of Newcastle, Callaghan, NSW 2308, Australia
`ryan.mccloy@uon.edu.au`,
`{jose.dedona,maria.seron}@newcastle.edu.au`

Abstract. In this paper, we first provide a mathematical description and proof for the robust stability of systems with convex polytopic uncertainty through the construction of attractive invariant sets. Then, we present the problem of estimating the convergence time to arbitrarily tight over-approximations of an invariant set, from both a known initial condition and for initial conditions belonging to a convex polytopic set. We then propose various analytical and numerical methods for computing the aforementioned convergence time. Finally, a number of numerical examples, including a flexible link robotic manipulator, are given to illustrate the results.

Keywords: convergence time, invariant sets, convex polytopic uncertainty, robotic applications.

1 Introduction

Mathematical system modelling provides an attractive framework for the analysis, design, simulation and control of real-world systems [1], with numerous examples in biology, physics, chemistry as well as in various human engineered systems, such as robotics and the wide variety of artificial and automated systems.

Considering the difficulty in capturing reality exactly, convenient model uncertainty descriptions are required [2,3]. A powerful and computationally tractable paradigm is afforded by the convex polytopic uncertainty (CPU) description (see, for example, [4]). Under this framework, the uncertain system belongs to a polytope, which is the convex hull of the vertices or parameters of a set of models. Polytopic uncertainty descriptors can be used for the well defined interval and linear parameter varying systems as well as for multi-model systems. This allows for the extension of powerful linear tools to more complex nonlinear models, for example the use of linear matrix inequality (LMI) based routines (see, e.g., [5]).

Once a modelling framework is chosen, it is often beneficial to analyse model properties such as stability, robustness and invariance. For example, numerous

S.K. Chalup et al. (Eds.): ACALCI 2015, LNAI 8955, pp. 62–75, 2015.

techniques have been developed to assess robust stability of systems having CPU description. Most of these techniques lend themselves to the application of efficient computational methods such as those based on LMIs, see, e.g., [6,5]. Another important concept is that of 'attractive invariance', which describes sets of a system's states that 'attract and keep' the system's trajectories, see, for example [7,8,9]. These sets are useful in determining the long term behaviour of a system under specific conditions.

For many applications—for example, robots that have to perform certain tasks in a pre-specified time—it is of interest to compute the *time of convergence* to invariant sets. Another application example can be found in 'invariant-set' based sensor fault tolerant control (see, for example, [10]), where the reintegration of sensors that have recovered their functionality after a fault requires the computation of transition times of critical system variables towards associated 'healthy' attractive invariant sets [11]. More generally, when designing control systems using uncertain models, an estimate of the time of convergence of the system's trajectories to appropriate 'target' invariant sets can be regarded as a certificate of the system's performance, a generalisation of the well-known concept of 'settling time' in classical control theory (see, for example, [12]).

In this paper, we first provide conditions for the robust stability of systems with convex polytopic uncertainty via attractive invariant sets in Section 2. We then present the problem of estimating the convergence time to an invariant set, from both a known initial condition and for initial conditions belonging to a convex polytopic set in Section 3. In Section 4 we propose various analytical and numerical methods for computing a solution to the aforementioned convergence time problem and lastly, a number of numerical examples, including a flexible link robotic manipulator, are presented in Section 5 to illustrate the results.

2   Attractive Invariant Sets for Convex Polytopic Uncertain Systems

In this section, we present a useful result on robust stability and invariant sets for convex polytopic uncertain systems (this is an adaptation of a result in [9] for switched systems). Consider the discrete-time uncertain system

$$x(k+1) = A(k)x(k) + B(k)v(k), \tag{1}$$

where $x(k) \in \mathbb{R}^n$ is the system state and $v(k) \in \mathbb{R}^s$ is a disturbance input componentwise bounded as[1]

$$|v(k)| \leq \overline{v}, \quad \forall k \geq 0, \tag{2}$$

for some known constant non-negative vector $\overline{v} \in \mathbb{R}^s$. The matrices in (1) have the form

$$A(k) = \sum_{j=1}^{N} \xi_j(k)A_j, \quad B(k) = \sum_{j=1}^{N} \xi_j(k)B_j, \tag{3}$$

---

[1] Here, and in the remainder of the paper, the bars |.| denote elementwise magnitude (absolute value) and the inequalities and max operations are interpreted elementwise.

where A_j and B_j, for $j \in \mathcal{N} \triangleq \{1, 2, \ldots, N\}$ are known constant matrices of compatible dimensions. The functions ξ_j in (3) satisfy, for all $k \geq 0$,

$$\xi_j(k) \in [0,1], \forall j \in \mathcal{N} \quad \text{and} \quad \sum_{j=1}^{N} \xi_j(k) = 1. \tag{4}$$

The following theorem provides conditions to assess robust stability and boundedness of the system (1)–(4). In addition, it derives an "ultimate-bound" set which is asymptotically *attractive*, that is, the trajectories of the system ultimately converge (in infinite time) to the set, and is *invariant*, that is, the trajectories cannot leave the set once inside; and "finite-time" attractive invariant sets, which have the same invariance property but attract the system trajectories in finite time.

Theorem 1. *Consider the convex polytopic uncertain system (1)–(4) and suppose an invertible complex transformation $V \in \mathbb{C}^{n \times n}$ exists[2] such that the matrix*

$$\Lambda \triangleq \max_{j \in \mathcal{N}} |V^{-1} A_j V| \tag{5}$$

is a Schur matrix[3]. Then,

(i) *Invariance. The trajectories of (1) are bounded and ultimately converge to the set*

$$\mathcal{S} \triangleq \{x \in \mathbb{R}^n : |V^{-1}x| \leq b\}, \tag{6}$$

where

$$b \triangleq (I - \Lambda)^{-1} \max_{j \in \mathcal{N}} |V^{-1} B_j| \overline{v} \tag{7}$$

which is an invariant set for the dynamics of (1).

(ii) *Convergence. Given any initial condition $x(0) \in \mathbb{R}^n$ and positive vector $\epsilon \in \mathbb{R}^n$, the system (1) will converge to the set*

$$\mathcal{S}_\epsilon \triangleq \{x \in \mathbb{R}^n : |V^{-1}x| \leq b + \epsilon\}, \tag{8}$$

in finite time $k^* = k^*(\epsilon, |V^{-1}x(0)|)$. Moreover, the set (8) is invariant, provided that ϵ satisfies[4] $\Lambda \epsilon \leq \epsilon$.

---

[2] To find the transformation V required in Theorem 1 a numerical search routine can be readily implemented. Moreover, when the system matrices A_j contain variables that can be freely selected, as is the case when they are closed-loop matrices including some design feedback gains, then the numerical routine to find V can search for those free variables as well.

[3] A Schur matrix has all its eigenvalues with magnitude less than one.

[4] A vector $\epsilon > 0$ satisfying $\Lambda \epsilon \leq \epsilon$ can always be found for a Schur nonnegative matrix Λ. To see this, consider a slight perturbation of Λ, denoted Λ_+, such that $\Lambda_+ > 0$, $\Lambda_+ \geq \Lambda$ and Λ_+ is Schur. Then, by the Perron-Frobenius theorem, there exists a positive eigenvalue r (known as the Perron-Frobenius eigenvalue) and an eigenvector ϵ with positive elements such that $\Lambda_+ \epsilon = r\epsilon$. Since Λ_+ is Schur then $r < 1$ and we have: $\Lambda \epsilon \leq \Lambda_+ \epsilon = r\epsilon < \epsilon$.

Proof. Define
$$z(k) \triangleq V^{-1}x(k).\tag{9}$$

Then, from (1),
$$z(k+1) = V^{-1}A(k)V\, z(k) + V^{-1}B(k)v(k).\tag{10}$$

(i) Taking magnitudes and using (2)–(5) yields

$$|z^+| \leq |V^{-1}AV|\,|z| + |V^{-1}B|\,|v|$$

$$\leq \sum_{j=1}^{N}\xi_j\,|V^{-1}A_jV|\,|z| + \sum_{j=1}^{N}\xi_j\,|V^{-1}B_j|\,\overline{v}$$

$$\leq \underbrace{\sum_{j=1}^{N}\xi_j}_{=1}\underbrace{\max_{j\in\mathcal{N}}|V^{-1}A_jV|}_{\Lambda}\,|z| + \underbrace{\sum_{j=1}^{N}\xi_j}_{=1}\,\max_{j\in\mathcal{N}}|V^{-1}B_j|\,\overline{v}$$

$$= \Lambda\,|z| + \max_{j\in\mathcal{N}}|V^{-1}B_j|\,\overline{v}\tag{11}$$

where $z = z(k)$, $z^+ = z(k+1)$, $A = A(k)$, $B = B(k)$, $v = v(k)$ and $\xi_j = \xi_j(k)$. Define a new variable y such that

$$y(k+1) = \Lambda\,y(k) + \max_{j\in\mathcal{N}}|V^{-1}B_j|\overline{v}, \quad y(0) = |z(0)|.\tag{12}$$

Since Λ is a Schur matrix by assumption and all matrices and vectors in (12) are non-negative, then the trajectories of (12) converge to the invariant set

$$\mathcal{S}_y = \{y \in \mathbb{R}^n : 0 \leq y \leq b\},\tag{13}$$

where b is defined in (7). To see this, we have from (12) that from an initial condition $y(0)$, the general expression of the trajectories is

$$y(k) = \Lambda^k y(0) + \sum_{i=0}^{k-1}\Lambda^i \max_{j\in\mathcal{N}}|V^{-1}B_j|\overline{v},\tag{14}$$

and since $\Lambda^k \to 0$ and $\sum_{i=0}^{k-1}\Lambda^i \to (I-\Lambda)^{-1}$ as $k \to \infty$, we conclude from (7) that $y(k) \to b$ as $k \to \infty$.

Then, to see that this set is invariant, let $y(k) \in \mathcal{S}_y$ for some $k \geq 0$. Hence, $0 \leq y(k) \leq b$ and using the definition of b from (7) yields

$$y(k+1) = \Lambda y(k) + [b - \Lambda b] \leq \Lambda b + [b - \Lambda b] = b$$

The result (i) then follows by noticing, from (9) and (11)–(12), that

$$|V^{-1}x(k)| = |z(k)| \leq y(k), \qquad \forall k \geq 0.\tag{15}$$

This completes the proof of (i).

(ii) Consider again the system (12) and let $\tilde{y}$ satisfy

$$\tilde{y}(k+1) = \varLambda\tilde{y}(k), \quad \tilde{y}(0) = y(0) = |z(0)| \tag{16}$$

Note that $\lim_{k\to\infty} \tilde{y}(k) = 0$, since $\varLambda$ is Schur. Then, given any positive vector ϵ, a finite time $k^* = k^*(\epsilon, \tilde{y}(0)) = k^*(\epsilon, |z(0)|) = k^*(\epsilon, |V^{-1}x(0)|)$ exists, such that

$$|\tilde{y}(k)| \leq \epsilon, \quad \forall k \geq k^* \tag{17}$$

Define $\hat{y}(k) = y(k) - \tilde{y}(k)$ and note that $\hat{y}$ satisfies the dynamic equation (12) with initial condition $\hat{y}(0) = 0 \in \mathcal{S}_y$. Then, by the invariance of $\mathcal{S}_y$ in (13)

$$|\hat{y}(k)| \leq b, \quad \forall k \geq 0. \tag{18}$$

Thus, taking magnitudes, we have from (15), (17) and (18) that

$$|V^{-1}x(k)| = |z(k)| \leq |y(k)| \leq |\hat{y}(k)| + |\tilde{y}(k)| \leq b + \epsilon, \tag{19}$$

for all $k \geq k^*$, and convergence is proved.

To see that the set (8) is invariant when ϵ is such that $\varLambda\epsilon \leq \epsilon$, consider $x(k) \in S_\epsilon$ for any k; i.e., $|z(k)| = |V^{-1}x(k)| \leq b + \epsilon$ with $z(k)$ defined in (9). Then, we have from (11) and (7) that

$$|V^{-1}x(k+1)| = |z(k+1)| \leq \varLambda |z(k)| + \max_{j\in\mathcal{N}} |V^{-1}B_j|\bar{v}$$

$$\leq \varLambda b + \varLambda\epsilon + b - \varLambda b = b + \epsilon,$$

and hence $x(k+1) \in S_\epsilon$ and the proof is complete.   □

3   The Convergence Time Estimation Problem

This section presents the problem of estimating the convergence time to arbitrarily tight over-approximations of $\mathcal{S}$ (i.e., convergence to the set $\mathcal{S}_\epsilon$), as presented in the previous section (see (6) and (8)). The problem is first presented for an initial condition given by a single point, and then for initial conditions belonging to an arbitrary convex polytopic set.

3.1   Convergence Time from an Initial Given Point

Given an arbitrary initial condition $x(0) \in \mathbb{R}^n$ we want to obtain an estimate of the convergence time k^* to the set (8). From (16) and (9) we have

$$\tilde{y}(k) = \varLambda^k\tilde{y}(0) = \varLambda^k|V^{-1}x(0)|.$$

The objective is then to find (cf. (17)) an estimate of the smallest positive integer k^* such that

$$\varLambda^k|V^{-1}x(0)| = PJ^kP^{-1}|V^{-1}x(0)| \leq \epsilon, \quad \forall k \geq k^*, \tag{20}$$

where P is an invertible matrix such that $J = P^{-1}\Lambda P$ is the Jordan canonical form of Λ. In order to satisfy (20), we will consider the following sufficient condition: Find the smallest integer $\tilde{k}^* \geq k^*$ such that

$$\underbrace{|J|^k\,|P^{-1}||V^{-1}x(0)|}_{X} \leq \underbrace{\gamma\epsilon}_{E}, \quad \forall k \geq \tilde{k}^*, \tag{21}$$

with $\gamma = \min\limits_{1 \leq i \leq n} \left(\epsilon_i \left[\sum_{j=1}^n |P_{i,j}|\epsilon_j \right]^{-1} \right)$, since then,

$$PJ^k P^{-1}|V^{-1}x(0)| \leq |P||J|^k|P^{-1}||V^{-1}x(0)| \leq |P|\gamma\epsilon \leq \epsilon.$$

Since J is in Jordan canonical form, it is composed of p Jordan blocks J_i of dimension $n_i \times n_i$, $i = 1, \ldots, p$, such that $\sum_{i=1}^p n_i = n$, and has the general form

$$J = \begin{bmatrix} J_1 & & \cdots & 0 \\ & J_2 & & \vdots \\ \vdots & & \ddots & \\ 0 & \cdots & & J_p \end{bmatrix}. \tag{22}$$

Partitioning X and E defined in (21) as

$$X = \begin{bmatrix} X_1 \\ X_2 \\ \vdots \\ X_p \end{bmatrix}, \quad E = \begin{bmatrix} E_1 \\ E_2 \\ \vdots \\ E_p \end{bmatrix}, \tag{23}$$

where X_i and E_i are $n_i \times 1$ vectors of compatible dimensions to the associated Jordan block J_i, we can then write the corresponding expression to (21) for each Jordan block as

$$|J_i|^k X_i \leq E_i, \quad \forall k \geq \tilde{k}_i^* \tag{24}$$

Thus, an estimation for k^* is given by the largest $\tilde{k}_i^*$ over all Jordan blocks, i.e.,

$$\tilde{k}^* = \max_{i=1,\ldots,p} \tilde{k}_i^*. \tag{25}$$

Each Jordan block J_i has the general form

$$J_i = \begin{bmatrix} \lambda_i & 1 & \cdots & 0 \\ & \lambda_i & \ddots & \vdots \\ \vdots & & \ddots & 1 \\ 0 & \cdots & & \lambda_i \end{bmatrix}, \tag{26}$$

which can be exploited by noting that the kth power of a Jordan block will be a direct sum of upper triangular matrices as a result of block multiplication, to write the kth power as

$$
J_i^k = \begin{bmatrix} \lambda_i^k & \binom{k}{1}\lambda_i^{k-1} & \cdots & \binom{k}{n_i-1}\lambda_i^{k+1-n_i} \\ & \lambda_i^k & \ddots & \vdots \\ \vdots & & \ddots & \binom{k}{1}\lambda_i^{k-1} \\ 0 & \cdots & & \lambda_i^k \end{bmatrix}, \tag{27}
$$

where each element $\{g,h\}$ of J_i^k can be written as

$$
J_i^k\{g,h\} = \begin{cases} 0 & \text{if } h < g, \\ \binom{k}{h-g}\lambda_i^k\lambda_i^{g-h} & \text{if } h \geq g. \end{cases} \tag{28}
$$

Expressing X_i and E_i elementwise as $X_i = (X_{i,1}, X_{i,2}, \ldots, X_{i,n_i})$ and $E_i = (E_{i,1}, E_{i,2}, \ldots, E_{i,n_i})$, each row of (24) can then be rewritten as

$$
\sum_{h=g}^{n_i} \binom{k}{h-g} |\lambda_i|^k |\lambda_i|^{g-h} X_{i,h} \leq E_{i,g}, \quad \forall k \geq \tilde{k}_{i,g}^*. \tag{29}
$$

Solving (29) for the minimum positive value of $\tilde{k}_{i,g}^*$ yields a solution for each row of (24), of which $\tilde{k}_i^*$ can be taken as the maximum, i.e., $\tilde{k}_i^* = \max_{g=1,\ldots,n_i} \tilde{k}_{i,g}^*$; which combined with (25) yields

$$
\tilde{k}^* = \max_{\substack{i=1,\ldots,p \\ g=1,\ldots,n_i}} \tilde{k}_{i,g}^*, \tag{30}
$$

which states that an upper estimate for k^* in (20) can be obtained as the maximum over all the estimates computed for each row of each Jordan block.

3.2   Convergence Time from an Initial Polytopic Set

We denote by $\tilde{k}_{x_o}^*$ the estimate obtained using (21)–(30) for an initial point $x(0) = x_o$. We now assume that the initial condition, x_o, is not perfectly known, but it is known to belong to a convex polytopic set, i.e.,

$$
x_o = \sum_{m=1}^{M} \alpha_m x_m, \tag{31}
$$

where the coefficients satisfy $\alpha_m \in [0,1]$ for $m = 1, \ldots, M$ and $\sum_{m=1}^{M} \alpha_m = 1$, and x_m, $m = 1, \ldots, M$, are the vertices of the polytopic set.

We then proceed as follows. First, compute using (21)–(30) the estimates $\tilde{k}_{x_m}^*$ corresponding to each vertex of the polytope, x_m, $m = 1, \ldots, M$ (where $x(0)$ in (21) is replaced by x_m). Then compute $\tilde{k}_{x_o}^*$ as:

$$
\tilde{k}_{x_o}^* = \max_{m=1,\ldots,M} \tilde{k}_{x_m}^*. \tag{32}
$$

Lemma 1. *The estimate* $\tilde{k}^*_{x_o}$ *computed using* (32) *is an upper bound for the convergence time from the initial condition* x_o *satisfying* (31) *to the set* $\mathcal{S}_\epsilon$ *defined in* (8).

Proof. From (21), with $x(0) = x_o$ satisfying (31) and the definitions of $\tilde{k}^*_{x_m}$, $m = 1, \ldots, M$, and $\tilde{k}^*_{x_o}$ given above, we have

$$|J|^k |P^{-1}||V^{-1} x_o| = |J|^k |P^{-1}||V^{-1} \sum_{m=1}^{M} \alpha_m x_m|$$

$$\leq \sum_{m=1}^{M} \alpha_m \left(|J|^k |P^{-1}||V^{-1} x_m| \right)$$

$$\leq \sum_{m=1}^{M} \alpha_m (\gamma \epsilon) = \gamma \epsilon, \quad \forall k \geq \tilde{k}^*_{x_o}.$$

The proof is then concluded by noticing that, as shown before, inequality (21) is sufficient for the inequality in (20) to hold. □

4 Methods for Computing a Convergence Time Estimate

We present in this section a number of methods to estimate k^* in (20). Both analytical and numerical strategies are explored.

4.1 Closed-form Solutions

This section is intended to provide closed-form solutions for an upper estimate for k^* in (20). The results presented here are for systems of arbitrary order with Jordan blocks of dimension up to 2×2.

Last Row. The last row (i.e., $g = h = n_i$) of each Jordan block results (see (29)) in the inequality:

$$|\lambda_i|^k X_{i,n_i} \leq E_{i,n_i}. \tag{33}$$

Since the left hand side of (33) is a strictly decreasing function of k (since $0 < |\lambda| < 1$; the case $\lambda = 0$ being trivial), it can be solved for k with equality. Using log laws and rearranging gives:

$$\tilde{k}^*_{i,n_i} = \frac{\ln\left(\frac{E_{i,n_i}}{X_{i,n_i}}\right)}{\ln\left(|\lambda_i|\right)} = \log_{|\lambda_i|}\left(\frac{E_{i,n_i}}{X_{i,n_i}}\right) \tag{34}$$

Second Last Row. The inequality associated with the second last row for each Jordan block in (29) takes the form:

$$|\lambda_i|^k X_{i,n_i-1} + k|\lambda_i|^{k-1} X_{i,n_i} \leq E_{i,n_i-1}. \tag{35}$$

which can also be expressed in a closed form and hence solved for k with equality (note that we are interested in the maximum positive solution of the equation). For simplicity of notation, let $\lambda = |\lambda_i|$, $X_2 = X_{i,n_i}$, $X_1 = X_{i,n_i-1}$ and $E_1 = E_{i,n_i-1}$ be the corresponding parameters for the ith Jordan block. Using log laws and rearranging gives

$$\lambda^k \left(\frac{\lambda X_1}{X_2} + k \right) = \frac{\lambda E_1}{X_2}$$

$$\ln(\lambda) \left(\frac{\lambda X_1}{X_2} + k \right) e^{\ln(\lambda)k} = \ln(\lambda) \frac{\lambda E_1}{X_2}$$

$$e^{\ln(\lambda)\frac{\lambda X_1}{X_2}} \ln(\lambda) \left(\frac{\lambda X_1}{X_2} + k \right) e^{\ln(\lambda)k} = e^{\ln(\lambda)\frac{\lambda X_1}{X_2}} \frac{\lambda E_1}{X_2} \ln(\lambda)$$

$$\ln(\lambda) \left(\frac{\lambda X_1}{X_2} + k \right) e^{\ln(\lambda)\left(\frac{\lambda X_1}{X_2}+k\right)} = \frac{\lambda^{\frac{\lambda X_1}{X_2}+1} E_1 \ln(\lambda)}{X_2} \tag{36}$$

The next step involves utilising the Lambert W function[5], denoted $W_\phi(\cdot)$, where $\phi = 0$ and $\phi = -1$ represent the two real branches. Applying the Lambert W function to both sides of (36) and simplifying yields

$$\ln(\lambda) \left(\frac{\lambda X_1}{X_2} + k \right) = W_\phi \left(\frac{\lambda^{\frac{\lambda X_1}{X_2}+1} E_1 \ln(\lambda)}{X_2} \right) \tag{37}$$

The *secondary* branch (i.e., $\phi = -1$) will yield the maximum positive solution for k (observing the sign of the Lambert W function's argument and noting it must be $\geq -1/e$), which from (37) is given as

$$\tilde{k}_{i,n_i-1}^* = \frac{X_2 W_{-1} \left(\frac{\lambda^{\frac{\lambda X_1}{X_2}+1} E_1 \ln(\lambda)}{X_2} \right) - \lambda X_1 \ln(\lambda)}{X_2 \ln(\lambda)}. \tag{38}$$

4.2   Numerical Search Methods

There are several motivations for a numerical strategy. This first being the absence of a closed form solution for Jordan blocks of 3rd or higher dimensions. Additionally, given that the solution will involve a numerical approximation for

---

[5] The Lambert W function has recently received significant interest amongst the mathematical community (see [13]), with numerous useful and well documented applications in the areas of mathematics, computer and physical sciences (e.g., see [14,15,16,17]).

the logarithmic and Lambert W functions, albeit with sufficient accuracy (e.g. in MATLAB at double precision, to approximately 16 decimal digits), and given the nature of the problem, whereby numerical convergence to a solution is inherently fast, it is appropriate to alternatively employ a numerical search routine. Two numerical search methods are considered in the examples of the following section, which use MATLAB's *fsolve* or *fmincon* to search for solutions to:

1. The original convergence estimate objective (20) (matrix operations);
2. The general row equation (29) for each Jordan block (scalar operations).

5   Examples

5.1   Numerical Example with Uncertainty in the Initial Condition

Consider the following system

$$x^+ = \begin{bmatrix} 0.3 & 0.3118 + \rho \\ 0 & 0.3 \end{bmatrix} x + \begin{bmatrix} 0.5 \\ 1 \end{bmatrix} v, \tag{39}$$

where $\rho \in [-0.1, 0.1]$, v is a bounded input disturbance, where $|v| \leq \bar{v} = 0.01$ and the initial condition belongs to a convex polytopic set (31), where $M = 4$, $x_1 = [0.19, -0.21]^T$, $x_2 = [0.19, -0.19]^T$, $x_3 = [0.21, -0.21]^T$, $x_4 = [0.21, -0.19]^T$.

A transformation (5) can be found, where

$$\Lambda = \begin{bmatrix} 0.3 & 0.7 \\ 0 & 0.3 \end{bmatrix}, \quad V = \begin{bmatrix} 10 & 0 \\ 0 & 17 \end{bmatrix}, \tag{40}$$

which yields the Jordan matrices (20)

$$J = \begin{bmatrix} 0.3 & 1 \\ 0 & 0.3 \end{bmatrix}, \quad P = \begin{bmatrix} 0.7 & 0 \\ 0 & 1 \end{bmatrix}. \tag{41}$$

An invariant set $\mathcal{S}$ (6) was computed with $|x| \leq [0.0155, 0.0143]^T$. Defining $\epsilon = [0.001, 0.001]^T$, an over-approximated set $\mathcal{S}_\epsilon$ (8) could then be found where $|x| \leq [0.0255, 0.0313]^T$. To compute an estimate for the convergence time to this over-approximated set, we consider the following methods:

1. Solving the Jordan block general row equation (29) using the closed-form expressions (34) and (38);
2. Solving (29) via a numerical search;
3. Solving the general matrix expression (20) via a numerical search.

The convergence time estimations and computation time effort for each method are summarised in Table 1. The system was then simulated with a sample time of $1s$. The sets $\mathcal{S}$, $\mathcal{S}_\epsilon$ and the set of initial conditions x_o, along with the state evolution, can be seen in Fig. 1. Note that the convergence times in Table 1 (being worst case estimates) are adequate estimations for the actual convergence time of 2 samples as seen in Fig. 1.

Table 1. Summary of convergence time estimations for (39)

Method	Convergence Time	Computation Time
1	5 samples	3.2636 ms
2	5 samples	15.6562 ms
3	3 samples	24.9311 ms

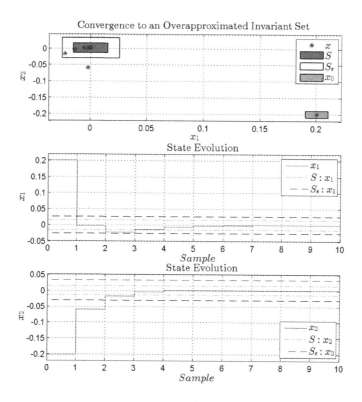

Fig. 1. Simulation results for (39)

5.2   Flexible Joint Robotic Manipulator

Consider the following non-linear state-space model of a flexible joint robot, which has been taken from [18]

$$
x^+ = \underbrace{\begin{bmatrix} 1 & T_s & 0 & 0 \\ \frac{(mg\ell\rho + K_a)T_s}{I_a} & 1 & -\frac{K_a T_s}{I_a} & 0 \\ 0 & 0 & 1 & T_s \\ \frac{K_a T_s}{J_a} & 0 & -\frac{K_a T_s}{J_a} & 1 \end{bmatrix}}_{A(\rho)} x + \underbrace{\begin{bmatrix} 0 \\ 0 \\ 0 \\ \frac{T_s}{J_a} \end{bmatrix}}_{B} u + \begin{bmatrix} 0 \\ 0 \\ 0 \\ 1 \end{bmatrix} w, \qquad (42)
$$

where $x \triangleq [\theta_1, \dot{\theta}_1, \theta_2, \dot{\theta}_2]^T$ and $\rho \triangleq \sin(\theta_1)\theta_1^{-1}$. The variables θ_1 and $\dot{\theta}_1$ are the flexible link angular position and velocity, θ_2 and $\dot{\theta}_2$ are the motor axis angular position and velocity, u is the applied motor torque, w is a bounded input disturbance, such that $|w| \leq \overline{w} = 0.01$, $mg\ell$ is the nominal load in the link, K_a is the flexible joint stiffness coefficient, I_a is the inertia of the link, J_a is the motor inertia and T_s is the sampling period. The sampling period is chosen to be $T_s = 0.01$ and the initial condition is chosen as $x_o = [0, 100, 0, 0]^T$. All other parameters are as in [18].

Since the angular position of the flexible link is restricted to $\theta_1 \in [-\pi, \pi]$ radians, the parameter ρ is confined to $\rho \in [0, 1]$. A fixed, stabilising state feedback gain $K = [-147.1352, -6.9206, 42.2588, 0.4800]$ is found, to place the poles of the closed loop central system $[A(0.5) - BK]$ at 0.4 and such that all poles of the closed loop system $[A(\rho) - BK]$, $0 \leq \rho \leq 1$, have a magnitude less than 1.

A transformation V in (5) can be found for the closed loop system $[A(\rho) - BK]$, such that Λ yields the Jordan matrix

$$|J| = \begin{bmatrix} 0.1878 & 0 & 0 & 0 \\ 0 & 0.7995 & 0 & 0 \\ 0 & 0 & 0.4170 & 0 \\ 0 & 0 & 0 & 0.4170 \end{bmatrix}. \tag{43}$$

An invariant set $\mathcal{S}$ in (6) was computed such that $|V^{-1}x| \leq b$, where $b = [186.5469, 0.1234, 6.3915, 138.8842]^T \times 10^{-6}$. Defining $\epsilon = [50, 50, 50, 50]^T \times 10^{-6}$, an over-approximated set $\mathcal{S}_\epsilon$ in (8) could then be found such that $|V^{-1}x| \leq b + \epsilon$, where $b + \epsilon = [236.5469, 50.1234, 56.3915, 188.8842]^T \times 10^{-6}$.

X and E in (21) are found to be $X = [1949.782, 1608.625, 2096.236, 2096.236]^T$ and $E = [0.04167, 0.04074, 0.04945, 0.04945]^T$. To compute an estimate for the convergence time to the set $\mathcal{S}_\epsilon$, we consider the following methods

1. Solving the Jordan block general row equation (29) using the closed-form expression (34), noting that the Jordan form (43) for the system (42) involves 4 Jordan blocks with no multiplicity in the eigenvalues;
2. Solving the general matrix expression (20) via a numerical search.

The convergence time estimation and computation time effort for each method are summarised in Table 2. The state evolution along with the bounds for the

Table 2. Summary of convergence time estimations for (42)

Method	Convergence Time	Computation Time
1	84 samples	0.0041 ms
2	64 samples	17.9545 ms

invariant set for each state can be seen in Fig. 2. Note that the convergence times in Table 2, which consider the worst case, give over-estimations for the actual convergence time of approximately 42 samples (0.42 s) as seen in Fig. 2.

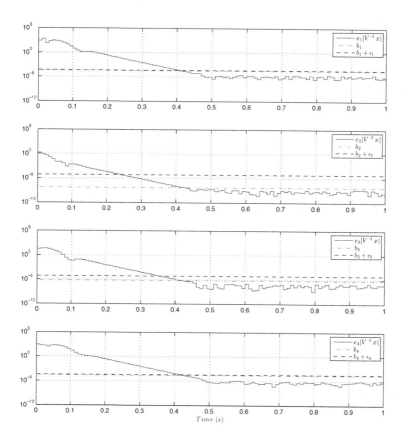

Fig. 2. Simulation results for (42) (e_i, $i = 1, \ldots, 4$, represents a 4-dimensional row vector with a 1 in the ith component and all other elements equal to 0)

6   Conclusions

Through the use of attractive invariant sets, we have provided a mathematical description and proof for the robust stability of systems with convex polytopic uncertainty. The problem of estimating the convergence time to arbitrarily tight over-approximations of an invariant set, from both a known initial condition and for initial conditions belonging to a convex polytopic set was presented. Analytical and numerical methods for computing this convergence time were presented and demonstrated through their application to numerical examples.

References

1. Sontag, E.D.: Mathematical Control Theory: Deterministic Finite Dimensional Systems. Springer, New York (1998)
2. Zhou, K., Doyle, J.C., Glover, K.: Robust and Optimal Control. Prentice-Hall, Upper Saddle River (1996)
3. Battacharyya, S., Chapellat, H., Keel, L.: Robust Control: The Parametric Approach. Prentice-Hall, Upper Saddle River (1997)
4. Apkarian, P., Gahinet, P., Becker, G.: Self-scheduled H_∞ control of linear parameter-varying systems: a design example. Automatica 31(9), 1251–1261 (1995)
5. Daafouz, J., Bernussou, J.: Parameter dependent Lyapunov function for discrete time systems with time varying parametric uncertainties. Systems and Control Letters 43, 355–359 (2001)
6. de Oliveira, M., Bernussou, J., Geromel, J.: A new discrete-time robust stability condition. Systems and Control Letters 37, 261–265 (1999)
7. Blanchini, F.: Set invariance in control. Automatica 35, 1747–1767 (1999)
8. Khalil, H.: Nonlinear Systems, 3rd edn. Prentice-Hall, New Jersey (2002)
9. Haimovich, H., Seron, M.: Bounds and invariant sets for a class of discrete-time switching systems with perturbations. International Journal of Control (2013), doi:10.1080/00207179.2013.834536 (published online: September 13, 2013)
10. Olaru, S., De Doná, J.A., Seron, M.M., Stoican, F.: Positive invariant sets for fault tolerant multisensor control schemes. International Journal of Control 83(12), 2622–2640 (2010)
11. Seron, M.M., De Doná, J.A., Olaru, S.: Fault tolerant control allowing sensor healthy-to-faulty and faulty-to-healthy transitions. IEEE Transactions on Automatic Control 77(7), 1657–1669 (2012)
12. Franklin, G., Powell, J.D., Emami-Naeini, A.: Feedback Control of Dynamic Systems. Prentice Hall, Upper Saddle River (2002)
13. Veberic, D.: Having fun with Lambert W(x) function, CoRR, vol. abs/1003.1628 (2010), http://arxiv.org/abs/1003.1628
14. Veberic, D.: Lambert W function for applications in Physics. Computer Physics Communications 183(12), 2622–2628 (2012), http://www.sciencedirect.com/science/article/pii/S0010465512002366
15. Houari, A.: Additional applications of the Lambert W function in Physics. European Journal of Physics 34(3), 695 (2013), http://stacks.iop.org/0143-0807/34/i=3/a=695
16. Banwell, T.: Bipolar transistor circuit analysis using the Lambert W-function. IEEE Transactions on Circuits and Systems I: Fundamental Theory and Applications 47(11), 1621–1633 (2000)
17. Hwang, C., Cheng, Y.-C.: Use of Lambert W function to stability analysis of time-delay systems. In: Proceedings of the 2005 American Control Conference, vol. 6, pp. 4283–4288 (June 2005)
18. Sira-Ramírez, H., Castro-Linares, R.: Sliding mode rest-to-rest stabilization and trajectory tracking for a discretized flexible joint manipulator. Dynamics and Control 10(1), 87–105 (2000)

A Sensor Fusion Approach
to the Fault Tolerant Control
of Linear Parameter Varying Systems

Ryan J. McCloy, María M. Seron, and José A. De Doná

School of Electrical Engineering and Computer Science,
The University of Newcastle, Callaghan, NSW 2308, Australia
ryan.mccloy@uon.edu.au,
{maria.seron,jose.dedona}@newcastle.edu.au

Abstract. In this contribution we propose a fault tolerant control (FTC) scheme to compensate for sensor faults in multisensor fusion-based control of linear parameter varying systems. The scheme consists of a closed-loop system with an estimator-based feedback tracking controller that combines healthy sensor-estimator pairings via a fusion algorithm. Faulty sensors are detected and discarded based on a set separation criterion, which considers both model uncertainty and system disturbances. We ensure the preservation of closed-loop system boundedness for a wide range of sensor fault situations and for the whole domain of plant model uncertainty. To illustrate the performance of the proposed FTC strategy, a flexible joint robotic arm example is presented.

Keywords: invariant sets, sensor fusion, fault tolerant control, linear parameter varying systems, robotic applications.

1 Introduction

Due to the fault-sensitive nature of complex technical systems, it is essential to be able to efficiently and appropriately handle a range of potential system faults. Consequently, development of strategies to ensure closed-loop stability and robustness to system faults is a necessary consideration in control system design. Fault tolerant control (FTC) schemes often combine a fault detection and isolation (FDI) module (see, e.g., [1,2,3]) with a controller reconfiguration module (see, e.g., [4,5]), to maintain closed-loop stability and good performance levels under a range of fault scenarios (see, e.g., [2,3,6]).

A recent approach to FTC involves detecting and isolating faults through the separation of "healthy" and "faulty" sets (see, e.g., [7,8]). Under healthy operation, appropriately selected residual variables remain in "healthy" attractive invariant sets and "jump" from the set in the presence of abrupt sensor faults. Provided specific conditions are met, which may depend on plant and estimator dynamics as well as bounds on setpoints and system disturbances, this set separation approach offers a guarantee for correct FDI.

S.K. Chalup et al. (Eds.): ACALCI 2015, LNAI 8955, pp. 76–87, 2015.

In this paper, we propose an FTC scheme consisting of a bank of sensor-estimator pairings, a set-based FDI module, an estimate reconfiguration module, and an estimate fusion-based feedback tracking controller. This control scheme is developed with linear parameter varying (LPV) systems in mind. The LPV framework is attractive as it allows for the use of powerful linear design tools to a wide range of complex nonlinear systems. LPV models also have a close relationship with gain-scheduling control, which is a well-defined control strategy for a large class of nonlinear systems [9]. The development of techniques to assess LPV system stability has also motivated the use of this modelling paradigm. Many of these techniques allow for the use of efficient computation based methods, such as linear matrix inequality based routines (see, e.g., [10]). An alternative strategy to assess robust stability is through recent switched linear system techniques, which offer the added advantage of also providing a simple means for computing an invariant set for the trajectories of the LPV system (see, e.g., [11]).

Self-scheduling control is commonly employed in the control of LPV systems. This involves adapting the control system parameters, in real time, with reference to the current measured value of the varying parameter (see, e.g., [12]). In the current paper, a self-scheduled controller and a bank of self-scheduled estimators are used to stabilise the LPV system, as determined from the measurement of the varying parameter. The controller and estimators are then embedded in an FTC strategy, utilising a set-based FDI strategy and a sensor-estimate reconfiguration scheme. In the latter, the estimates obtained from the sensors identified as healthy are combined via a fusion algorithm, which is one of the most used techniques for integrating data provided by various sensors (see, e.g., [13]). Under the proposed FTC approach we establish system fault tolerance, closed-loop system stability and performance for a range of sensor fault conditions, as demonstrated by an example consisting in a flexible joint robotic arm.

2   Plant, Sensor and Reference Models

Consider a discrete-time multisensor LPV system with a bank of measurement outputs given by

$$x^+ = A(\rho)x + B(\rho)u + E(\rho)w, \tag{1}$$

$$y_i = \Pi_i C_i(\rho)x + \eta_i, \quad i \in \mathcal{M} \triangleq \{1, 2, \ldots, M\}, \tag{2}$$

where $x = x(t)$ and $x^+ = x(t+1) \in \mathbb{R}^n$ are the current and successor system states, $u = u(t) \in \mathbb{R}^m$ is the control input and $w = w(t) \in \mathbb{R}^r$ is a process disturbance. The state vector x is not assumed to be fully measured; instead a bank of $\mathcal{M}$ measurement outputs (2) is available, each measuring some combination of state components through sensors affected by noise, whereby $y_i = y_i(t) \in \mathbb{R}^{p_i}$ is the measured output of the ith group of sensors and $\eta_i = \eta_i(t) \in \mathbb{R}^{p_i}$ represents measurement noise. $\rho = \rho(t) \in \mathbb{R}^L$ is a time-varying parameter whose future evolution is unknown but its current measurement is available at each sample time, and $A(\rho) \in \mathbb{R}^{n \times n}$, $B(\rho) \in \mathbb{R}^{n \times m}$, $E(\rho) \in \mathbb{R}^{n \times r}$, $C_i(\rho) \in \mathbb{R}^{p_i \times n}$, for each ρ.

The parameter ρ is assumed to lie in a bounded set $\Gamma \subset \mathbb{R}^L$ and we consider that the system matrices have the polytopic description $A(\rho) = \sum_{j=1}^N \xi_j(\rho) A_j$, $B(\rho) = \sum_{j=1}^N \xi_j(\rho) B_j$, $E(\rho) = \sum_{j=1}^N \xi_j(\rho) E_j$ and $C_i(\rho) = \sum_{j=1}^N \xi_j(\rho) C_{i,j}$ for constant matrices $A_j \in \mathbb{R}^{n \times n}$, $B_j \in \mathbb{R}^{n \times m}$, $E_j \in \mathbb{R}^{n \times r}$, $C_{i,j} \in \mathbb{R}^{p_i \times n}$, and continuous functions $\xi_j : \Gamma \to \mathbb{R}$ satisfying $\xi_j(\rho) \geq 0$ and $\sum_{j=1}^N \xi_j(\rho) = 1$ for all $\rho \in \Gamma$. Hence, for each $\rho \in \Gamma$, $(A(\rho), B(\rho), E(\rho), C_i(\rho))$ lies in the convex hull $\mathrm{Co}\{(A_1, B_1, E_1, C_{i,1}), (A_2, B_2, E_2, C_{i,2}), \ldots, (A_N, B_N, E_N, C_{i,N})\}$, for $i \in \mathcal{M}$. We assume that the pairs (A_j, B_j) are stabilisable and the pairs $(A_j, C_{i,j})$ are detectable for $i \in \mathcal{M}$ and $j \in \mathcal{N} \triangleq \{1, 2, \ldots, N\}$.

The "fault-signature" matrix $\Pi_i \in \mathbb{R}^{p_i \times p_i}$ in (2) is used to characterise the sensor fault situation, and is described as follows:

$$\Pi_i = \begin{cases} I_{p_i} & \text{if all sensors are healthy,} \\ \Pi_i^F \triangleq \mathrm{diag}\{\pi_{i1}, \ldots, \pi_{ip_i}\} & \text{otherwise,} \end{cases} \tag{3}$$

where I_{p_i} is the $p_i \times p_i$ identity matrix and $\pi_{ij} \in [0, 1]$, for $j = 1, \ldots, p_i$, with at least one element $\pi_{ik} < 1$, for some $k \in \{1, \ldots, p_i\}$.

The process disturbance w and the measurement noises η_i are assumed to be bounded, where[1] $|w(t)| \leq \overline{w}$ and

$$\eta_i(t) \in \mathcal{E}_i \triangleq \{\eta_i : |\eta_i| \leq \overline{\eta}_i\}, \tag{4}$$

for all $t \geq 0$, where $\overline{w} \in \mathbb{R}^r$ and $\overline{\eta}_i \in \mathbb{R}^{p_i}$ are known constant nonnegative vectors.

The control objective is for the plant state x to track a reference signal x_{ref} satisfying

$$x_{ref}^+ = A(\rho) x_{ref} + B(\rho) u_{ref}, \tag{5}$$

where u_{ref} and x_{ref} are bounded input and state reference signals. In particular, $x_{ref}(t)$ satisfies[2], $\forall t \geq 0$,

$$x_{ref}(t) \in \mathcal{X}_{ref} \triangleq \{x_{ref,0}\} \oplus \{x \in \mathbb{R}^n : |x| \leq \overline{x}_{ref}\} \tag{6}$$

and $x_{ref,0} \neq 0$, $\overline{x}_{ref} \geq 0$ are known constant vectors in $\mathbb{R}^n$.

The reference model (5) encapsulates the 'ideal' (noise- and fault-free) performance desired for the plant to achieve by designing the control signal $u(t)$ in (1) so that the plant state x 'closely tracks' x_{ref}. Typical control performance objectives such as setpoint tracking, minimum settling time, etc., can be incorporated in the design of (5). This will be illustrated in the robotic manipulator example of Section 6, where the reference model is designed so that the robot joints reach and remain at desired angle setpoints.

---

[1] Here, and in the remainder of the paper, the bars $|.|$ denote elementwise magnitude (absolute value) and the inequalities and max operations are interpreted elementwise.

[2] The symbol $\oplus$ in (6) represents the *Minkowski sum* of sets, where if $\mathcal{X} \subset \mathbb{R}^n$ and $\mathcal{Y} \subset \mathbb{R}^n$ are sets, their Minkowski sum is the set $\mathcal{X} \oplus \mathcal{Y} = \{z \in \mathbb{R}^n : z = x + y, x \in \mathcal{X}, y \in \mathcal{Y}\}$.

3   State Estimate Fusion, Residual Signals and Tracking Controller

Since the plant state is not assumed to be fully measured, we employ a bank of self-scheduled state estimators

$$\hat{x}_i^+ = A(\rho)\hat{x}_i + B(\rho)u + L_i(\rho)[y_i - C_i(\rho)\hat{x}_i], \tag{7}$$

for $i \in \mathcal{M}$, where y_i is the measured output of the ith sensor (or group of sensors), given by (2), $\hat{x}_i$ is its associated estimate of the plant state, and the gains $L_i(\rho) = \sum_{j=1}^N \xi_j(\rho)L_{i,j}$ are self-scheduled gains computed using the functions $\xi_j(\rho)$ defined in Section 2. The matrices $L_{i,j}$ are design parameters that can be determined to achieve certain stability and boundedness properties, as will become clear in Section 4.2 (see (23)).

We define the associated state estimation errors as

$$\tilde{x}_i \triangleq x - \hat{x}_i, \quad \text{for} \quad i \in \mathcal{M}, \tag{8}$$

and the output estimation errors as

$$\tilde{y}_i \triangleq y_i - C_i(\rho)\hat{x}_i, \quad \text{for} \quad i \in \mathcal{M}. \tag{9}$$

Being a directly measurable quantity, the output estimation errors (9) will be used as *residual* signals, or 'fault indicators' for FDI. Indeed, when the ith group of sensors is healthy, setting $\Pi_i = I_{p_i}$ in (2) we have from (9) and (8) that

$$\tilde{y}_i = \tilde{y}_i^H = C_i(\rho)x + \eta_i - C_i(\rho)\hat{x}_i = C_i(\rho)\tilde{x}_i + \eta_i. \tag{10}$$

On the other hand, for a 'faulty' signature matrix $\Pi_i = \Pi_i^F \neq I_{p_i}$ we have from (9), (2) and (8) that

$$\begin{aligned}
\tilde{y}_i = \tilde{y}_i^F &= \Pi_i^F C_i(\rho)x + \eta_i - C_i(\rho)\hat{x}_i \\
&= C_i(\rho)x - C_i(\rho)x + \Pi_i^F C_i(\rho)x + \eta_i - C_i(\rho)\hat{x}_i \\
&= C_i(\rho)\tilde{x}_i + (\Pi_i^F - I_{p_i})C_i(\rho)(z + x_{ref}) + \eta_i, \tag{11}
\end{aligned}$$

where, in the last line, we have used the definition

$$z \triangleq x - x_{ref}, \tag{12}$$

which stands for the plant tracking error.

The second term on the right hand side of (11), which is not present in (10), in particular the state reference signal x_{ref}, will be the key element to detect sensor faults, as will be explained in the following sections.

We will base the control law on a *reconfigured* estimate $\hat{x}^*$ obtained by *fusing* estimates deemed healthy, defined as

$$\hat{x}^* \triangleq \sum_{i \in \mathcal{H}} \alpha_i \hat{x}_i, \tag{13}$$

where the set $\mathcal{H} \subseteq \mathcal{M}$ contains the indices of the groups of sensors deemed healthy and the fusion weights α_i satisfy $\alpha_i \geq 0$ and $\sum_{i \in \mathcal{H}} \alpha_i = 1$. The set $\mathcal{H}$ and the weights α_i are updated at each sampling time according to the current decision made by the FDI algorithm described later in Section 5.

We then employ the following estimate-based feedback controller with reference tracking:

$$u = -K(\rho)(\hat{x}^* - x_{ref}) + u_{ref}, \tag{14}$$

where the self-scheduled gain $K(\rho) = \sum_{j=1}^{N} \xi_j(\rho)K_j$ is computed using the functions $\xi_j(\rho)$, $j \in \mathcal{N}$, defined in Section 2, and u_{ref} is obtained from the reference model (5). The matrices K_j are design parameters that will be determined to achieve certain stability and boundedness properties (see (30) in Section 4.2).

4   Invariant Sets and Stability

In the following section we will analyse robust stability of the overall closed-loop system when the fusion-based controller (14) (cf. (13)) is based on only healthy estimates. This condition will be ensured by the FDI-based fault tolerant scheme presented in Section 5. The stability analysis is based on the definition of "healthy" and "under-fault" sets, whose computation is explained in this section.

4.1   Invariant Set Computation

We first present a result from [11], which will be employed for the invariant sets computation. Consider the discrete-time convex polytopic uncertain system

$$x(t+1) = A(t)x(t) + B(t)v(t), \tag{15}$$

where $x(t) \in \mathbb{R}^n$ is the system state and $v(t) \in \mathbb{R}^s$ is a disturbance input componentwise bounded as

$$|v(t)| \leq \overline{v}, \quad \forall t \geq 0, \tag{16}$$

for some known constant non-negative vector $\overline{v} \in \mathbb{R}^s$. The matrices in (15) have the form

$$A(t) = \sum_{j=1}^{N} \xi_j(t)A_j, \quad B(t) = \sum_{j=1}^{N} \xi_j(t)B_j, \tag{17}$$

where A_j and B_j, for $j \in \mathcal{N}$ are known constant matrices of compatible dimensions. The functions ξ_j in (17) satisfy, for all $t \geq 0$,

$$\xi_j(t) \in [0,1], \forall j \in \mathcal{N} \quad \text{and} \quad \sum_{j=1}^{N} \xi_j(t) = 1. \tag{18}$$

Suppose an invertible complex transformation $V \in \mathbb{C}^{n \times n}$ exists[3] such that the matrix

$$\Lambda \triangleq \max_{j \in \mathcal{N}} |V^{-1} A_j V| \tag{19}$$

is a Schur matrix.[4] Then we have, by adapting a result from [11], that the trajectories of (15) are bounded and ultimately converge to the set

$$\mathcal{S} \triangleq \{x \in \mathbb{R}^n : |V^{-1} x| \leq b\}, \tag{20}$$

where

$$b \triangleq (I - \Lambda)^{-1} \max_{j \in \mathcal{N}} |V^{-1} B_j| \bar{v}, \tag{21}$$

which is an invariant set for the dynamics of (15).

The above result will be employed below to derive invariant sets for relevant variables associated with the closed-loop system formed by the plant (1) with the control law (14), based on the state estimators (7) fused according to (13).

4.2 Healthy Set Computation

Consider first the dynamics of the state estimation errors (8). When the ith group of sensors is healthy, using (1), (2) with $\Pi_i = I_{p_i}$ and (7), we have that (8) satisfies the dynamic equation

$$\tilde{x}_i^+ = [A(\rho) - L_i(\rho) C_i(\rho)] \tilde{x}_i + [E(\rho) - L_i(\rho)] \begin{bmatrix} w \\ \eta_i \end{bmatrix}. \tag{22}$$

Thus, after a suitable reparameterisation of the indices involved in (22) to fit the convex polytopic description (15) and using the result presented in Section 4.1 above, provided a transformation V_i exists such that

$$\Lambda_i \triangleq \max_{j,k \in \mathcal{N}} |V_i^{-1} [A_j - L_{i,k} C_{i,j}] V_i| \quad \text{is a Schur matrix,} \tag{23}$$

then the trajectories of the estimation errors (22) are bounded and the set

$$\tilde{\mathcal{S}}_i \triangleq \{\tilde{x} : |V_i^{-1} \tilde{x}| \leq (I - \Lambda_i)^{-1} \nu_i\}, \text{ where } \nu_i \triangleq \max_{j \in \mathcal{N}} |V_i^{-1} [E_j - L_{i,j}]| \begin{bmatrix} w \\ \eta_i \end{bmatrix} \tag{24}$$

is an attractive invariant set for the state estimation error dynamics.

Assuming that the fusion scheme (13) is only based on healthy groups of sensors and that the associated estimation errors lie in their respective invariant sets (24), the reconfigured state estimation error defined as

$$\tilde{x}^* \triangleq \sum_{i \in \mathcal{H}} \alpha_i \tilde{x}_i, \tag{25}$$

---

[3] To find the required transformation V a numerical search routine can be readily implemented.

[4] A Schur matrix has all its eigenvalues with magnitude less than one.

can be bounded as (using the properties of the weights α_i)

$$|\tilde{x}^*| \leq \overline{\tilde{x}^*} \triangleq \max_{i \in \mathcal{M}} |V_i|(I - \Lambda_i)^{-1}\nu_i. \tag{26}$$

Also, from (10) and (24) the set

$$\tilde{\mathcal{Y}}_i \triangleq C_i(\rho)\tilde{\mathcal{S}}_i \oplus \mathcal{E}_i \tag{27}$$

describes a "healthy" set for the output estimation error, where $\mathcal{E}_i$ is the measurement noise bounding set defined in (4). Similarly to (26), the output estimation error can be bounded as

$$|\tilde{y}_i| \leq \overline{\tilde{y}}_i \triangleq \max_{j \in \mathcal{N}} |C_{i,j}||V_i|(I - \Lambda_i)^{-1}\nu_i + \overline{\eta}_i. \tag{28}$$

We next consider the plant tracking error dynamics. From (1), (5), (13)–(14) and (25), the plant tracking error (12) satisfies

$$z^+ = [A(\rho) - B(\rho)K(\rho)]z + B(\rho)K(\rho)\tilde{x}^* + E(\rho)w. \tag{29}$$

Then, following the procedure in Section 4.1 above, provided a transformation V_z exists such that

$$\Lambda_z \triangleq \max_{j,k \in \mathcal{N}} |V_z^{-1}[A_j - B_jK_k]V_z| \quad \text{is a Schur matrix,} \tag{30}$$

and if the bound (26) holds (which will be ensured by the FDI algorithm proposed in Section 5) then the trajectories of the plant tracking error are bounded and the set

$$\mathcal{S}_z \triangleq \{z : |V_z^{-1}z| \leq (I - \Lambda_z)^{-1}\nu_z\}, \text{ where } \nu_z \triangleq \max_{j,k \in \mathcal{N}} |V_z^{-1}[B_jK_k \ E_j]| \begin{bmatrix} \overline{\tilde{x}^*} \\ \overline{w} \end{bmatrix} \tag{31}$$

is an attractive invariant set for the plant tracking error dynamics (29).

4.3 Under-Fault Set Computation

Suppose that the ith group of sensors experiences a fault with signature Π_i^F satisfying (3). Using (11), at the time the fault occurs, the ith ouput estimator error $\tilde{y}_i^F$ "jumps" from the "healthy" set (27) to the "under-fault" set

$$\tilde{\mathcal{Y}}_i^F(\Pi_i^F) \triangleq C_i(\rho)\tilde{\mathcal{S}}_i \oplus (\Pi_i^F - I_{p_i})C_i(\rho)\mathcal{S}_z \oplus (\Pi_i^F - I_{p_i})C_i(\rho)\mathcal{X}_{ref} \oplus \mathcal{E}_i$$
$$= \tilde{\mathcal{Y}}_i \oplus (\Pi_i^F - I_{p_i})C_i(\rho)\mathcal{S}_z \oplus (\Pi_i^F - I_{p_i})C_i(\rho)\mathcal{X}_{ref}, \tag{32}$$

where $\tilde{\mathcal{S}}_i$, $\mathcal{S}_z$, $\mathcal{X}_{ref}$, $\mathcal{E}_i$ and $\tilde{\mathcal{Y}}_i$ are defined in (24), (31), (6), (4) and (27), respectively. The third term on the right hand side of (32), for a large enough reference offset $x_{ref,0}$ can produce a 'set shift' that will cause the "under-fault" set $\tilde{\mathcal{Y}}_i^F(\Pi_i^F)$ to have no intersection with the "healthy" set $\tilde{\mathcal{Y}}_i$, allowing for the fault to be detected. This quality allows for the use of the fusion scheme in (13), with "built-in" fault tolerance, as described in the following section.

5   FDI Algorithm and Closed-Loop Properties

In this section we present the proposed FDI algorithm based on separation between "healthy" and "under-fault" sets, and establish the fault tolerance and closed-loop stability properties of the resulting overall scheme.

We consider the following assumption.

Assumption 1. *Suppose the following conditions hold:*

1. *At initialisation all groups of sensors are healthy (that is, $\Pi_i = I_{p_i}$ in (2), for all $i \in \mathcal{M}$) and the estimation and tracking errors are in their "healthy" attractive invariant sets,[5] i.e., $\tilde{x}_i \in \tilde{\mathcal{S}}_i$, for all $i \in \mathcal{M}$, and $z \in \mathcal{S}_z$.*
2. *At all times at least one group of sensors $i \in \mathcal{M}$ is healthy and such that the corresponding estimation error is contained in its invariant set i.e., $\tilde{x}_i \in \tilde{\mathcal{S}}_i$.*
3. *For all $i \in \mathcal{M}$, and for all fault signature matrices Π_i^F of interest (e.g., those representing total sensor outage), the "healthy" set for the output estimation error, $\tilde{\mathcal{Y}}_i$ defined in (27), has no intersection with the "under-fault" set $\tilde{\mathcal{Y}}_i^F(\Pi_i^F)$ defined in (32).* ○

The proposed FDI algorithm is then as follows.

Algorithm 2 (FDI and Fusion Estimate Reconfiguration).

Initialisation: Define the initial set of indices of healthy group of sensors as $\mathcal{H} = \mathcal{M}$ and set the reconfigured fusion estimate to (13).

At each time step: Check the containment $\tilde{y}_i \in \tilde{\mathcal{Y}}_i$ for all $i \in \mathcal{H}$. If at some time instant t, $\tilde{y}_i(t) \notin \tilde{\mathcal{Y}}_i$ for some $i \in \mathcal{H}$ then set $\mathcal{H} = \mathcal{H} \setminus \{i\}$ and correspondingly update the weights α_i in the reconfigured fusion estimate (13). ○

We then have the following theorem establishing the closed-loop properties of the overall scheme under Algorithm 2.

Theorem 3 (Stability and fault tolerance). *Under Assumption 1, the closed-loop system encompassing the LPV plant (1) with outputs (2), the bank of estimators (7) and the tracking controller (14) based on the reconfigured fusion-based estimate (13) updated through the FDI Algorithm 2, has bounded trajectories under abrupt sensor faults with signature Π_i^F for which $\tilde{\mathcal{Y}}_i \cap \tilde{\mathcal{Y}}_i^F(\Pi_i^F) = \emptyset$. Moreover, the plant tracking error (12) remains in the attractive invariant set $\mathcal{S}_z$ defined in (31), and converges to zero in the absence of process disturbances and measurement noises.*

---

[5] This initialisation assumption can be readily satisfied if the closed-loop system initially operates without sensor faults for sufficiently long time so that all variables converge to their corresponding "healthy" attractive invariant sets.

Proof. Part 1 in Assumption 1 ensures that the estimation and tracking errors remain in their respective invariant sets if no sensor fault occurs. Next suppose, without loss of generality, that a fault with signature Π_i^F for which $\tilde{\mathcal{Y}}_i \cap \tilde{\mathcal{Y}}_i^F(\Pi_i^F) = \emptyset$ occurs in the ith group of sensors. At the time the fault occurs, the FDI Algorithm 2 detects the fault and removes the index i from the set $\mathcal{H}$. Thus, the estimate reconfiguration law (13) continues to use only estimates associated with healthy groups of sensors whose estimation errors remain in their healthy invariant sets (24). This property guarantees, in turn, that all bounds derived are valid at all times and, hence, the tracking controller (14) preserves the closed-loop variables within their attractive invariant sets. In the absence of process disturbances and measurement noises all the invariant sets reduce to the origin. Convergence of z to zero then follows from the result described in Section 4.1.

□

6   Example - Flexible Joint Robotic Arm

Consider the following non-linear state-space model of a flexible joint robot, which has been taken from [14]

$$x^+ = \underbrace{\begin{bmatrix} 1 & T_s & 0 & 0 \\ \frac{(mg\ell\rho + K_a)T_s}{I_a} & 1 & -\frac{K_a T_s}{I_a} & 0 \\ 0 & 0 & 1 & T_s \\ \frac{K_a T_s}{J_a} & 0 & -\frac{K_a T_s}{J_a} & 1 \end{bmatrix}}_{A(\rho)} x + \underbrace{\begin{bmatrix} 0 \\ 0 \\ 0 \\ \frac{T_s}{J_a} \end{bmatrix}}_{B} u,$$

$$y_i = \Pi_i C_i x + \eta_i, \tag{33}$$

where $x \triangleq [\theta_1, \dot{\theta}_1, \theta_2, \dot{\theta}_2]^T$ and $\rho \triangleq \sin(\theta_1)\theta_1^{-1}$. The variables θ_1 and $\dot{\theta}_1$ are the flexible link angular position and velocity, θ_2 and $\dot{\theta}_2$ are the motor axis angular position and velocity, u is the applied motor torque, $mg\ell$ is the nominal load in the link, K_a is the flexible joint stiffness coefficient, I_a is the inertia of the link, J_a is the motor inertia and T_s is the sampling period. The sampling period is chosen to be $T_s = 0.01$, the initial condition is chosen as $x(0) = [0,0,0,0]^T$ and we consider the sensor noise bounds $\overline{\eta_1} = 1 \times 10^{-5}$, $\overline{\eta_2} = 5 \times 10^{-5}$. All other parameters are as in [14].

Since the angular position of the flexible link is restricted to $\theta_1 \in [-\pi, \pi]$ radians, the parameter ρ is confined to $\rho \in [0,1]$. A fixed, stabilising state feedback gain $K = [-147.1352, -6.9206, 42.2588, 0.4800]$ is found, to place the poles of the closed loop central system $[A(0.5) - BK]$ at 0.4 and such that all poles of the closed loop system $[A(\rho) - BK]$, $0 \le \rho \le 1$, have a magnitude less than 1. Similarly, a fixed state estimator $L_i = L = [0.3634, 6.2293, 0.4366, 13.0647]^T$ is found, to place the poles of $[A(0.5) - LC]$ at 0.8, where $C_i = C = [1\ 0\ 1\ 0]$, for $i = 1, 2$.

The fault-profiles for the sensor groups were shaped prior to simulation and can be viewed in Fig. 1.

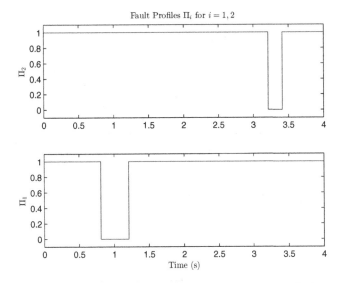

Fig. 1. Pre-simulation shaped fault profiles for (33)

The reference system is designed to achieve a setpoint of $\pi/2$ rad for the link angular position (this results in a setpoint of 2.0217 rad for the motor angular position, 0 rad/s for the link and motor angular velocity and 0.7259 Nm for the applied motor torque). Thus, an exosystem satisfying (5) is designed to track a constant state setpoint $x_s = [1.5708, 0, 2.0217, 0]^T$ and associated constant input setpoint $u_s = 0.7259$.

The bounds in (28) for the output estimation error $\overline{\tilde{y}}_i$ were computed for each sensor group as $\overline{\tilde{y}}_1 = 0.004095$ and $\overline{\tilde{y}}_2 = 0.005310$ and set separation was verified for the "healthy" and "under-fault" sets for the fault profiles in Fig. 1, whereby the computed corresponding intervals given by $-0.004095 \leq \tilde{y}_1 \leq 0.004095$, $-5.9271 \leq \tilde{y}_1^F \leq -1.2579$ and $-0.005310 \leq \tilde{y}_2 \leq 0.005310$, $-5.9283 \leq \tilde{y}_2^F \leq -1.2567$ show no intersection.

The FDI and fusion estimate reconfiguration module works as follows. The sensor groups are determined healthy by comparison to the respective bound in (28). Then, when both groups of sensors are deemed "healthy", i.e., $\mathcal{H} = \{1, 2\}$, we employ the following fusion strategy (given by a weighted average according to the respective sensor noise amplitudes)

$$\hat{x}^* = \frac{\overline{\eta_2}}{\overline{\eta_1} + \overline{\eta_2}}\hat{x}_1 + \frac{\overline{\eta_1}}{\overline{\eta_1} + \overline{\eta_2}}\hat{x}_2. \tag{34}$$

When one of the sensor groups is determined "under fault", the remaining sensor group is selected alone.

The overall fault tolerant control scheme was successfully simulated, as described above, whereby good tracking performance, un-affected by the simulated fault scenario, was achieved for the entire duration. Fig. 2 shows that the states and control input track their respective setpoints. The simulated time evolution of the parameter ρ (bottom plot) is also shown.

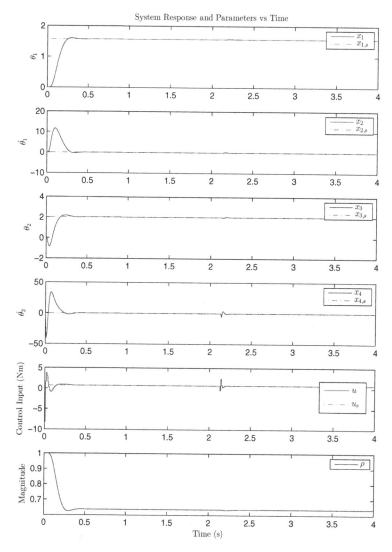

Fig. 2. State (subplots 1–4), control input (subplot 5) and ρ (subplot 6) evolution for (33)

7   Conclusions

We have proposed a fault tolerant control scheme to compensate for sensor faults in multisensor fusion-based control of linear parameter varying systems. The scheme consists of a closed-loop system with an estimator-based feedback tracking controller that combines healthy sensor-estimator pairings via a fusion algorithm. Faulty sensors are detected and discarded based on a set separation criterion, which considers both model uncertainty and system disturbances. Closed-loop system boundedness has been ensured for a wide range of sensor fault situations and for the whole domain of plant model uncertainty. The performance of the proposed FTC strategy has been demonstrated by a flexible joint robotic arm example.

References

1. Chow, E.Y., Willsky, A.S.: Analytical redundancy and the design of robust failure detection systems. IEEE Transactions on Automatic Control 29(7), 603–614 (1984)
2. Ding, S.: Model-based Fault Diagnosis Techniques. Springer (2008)
3. Isermann, R.: Fault-Diagnosis Systems. An Introduction from Fault Detection to Fault Tolerance. Springer (2006)
4. Rauch, H.E.: Autonomous control reconfiguration. IEEE Control Systems Magazine 15(6), 37–48 (1995)
5. Steffen, T.: Control Reconfiguration of Dynamical Systems. Springer (2005)
6. Blanke, M., Kinnaert, M., Lunze, J., Staroswiecki, M.: Diagnosis and Fault-Tolerant Control, 2nd edn. Springer (2006)
7. Seron, M., Zhuo, X., De Doná, J., Martínez, J.: Multisensor switching control strategy with fault tolerance guarantees. Automatica 44(1), 88–97 (2008)
8. Seron, M., De Doná, J., Olaru, S.: Fault tolerant control allowing sensor healthy-to-faulty and faulty-to-healthy transitions. IEEE Transactions on Automatic Control 77(7), 1657–1669 (2012)
9. Rugh, W.J., Shamma, J.S.: Research on gain scheduling. Automatica 36, 1401–1425 (2000)
10. Daafouz, J., Bernussou, J.: Parameter dependent Lyapunov function for discrete time systems with time varying parametric uncertainties. Systems and Control Letters 43, 355–359 (2001)
11. Haimovich, H., Seron, M.M.: Bounds and invariant sets for a class of discrete-time switching systems with perturbations. International Journal of Control (2013) (published online: September 13, 2013), doi:10.1080/00207179.2013.834536
12. Heemels, W.P.M.H., Daafouz, J., Millerioux, G.: Observer-based control of discrete-time LPV systems with uncertain parameters. IEEE Transactions on Automatic Control 55(9), 2130–2135 (2010)
13. Sun, S.-L., Deng, Z.-L.: Multi-sensor optimal information fusion Kalman filter. Automatica 40(6), 1017–1023 (2004)
14. Sira-Ramírez, H., Castro-Linares, R.: Sliding mode rest-to-rest stabilization and trajectory tracking for a discretized flexible joint manipulator. Dynamics and Control 10(1), 87–105 (2000)

Emotions and Their Effect on Cooperation Levels in N-Player Social Dilemma Games

Garrison W. Greenwood

Dept. of Electrical and Computer Engineering
Portland State University
Portland, OR 97207–0751 USA
greenwd@ece.pdx.edu

Abstract. Game theoretical social dilemma games provide a framework for studying how decisions are made in social dilemmas. It has been suggested emotions—e.g., anger or guilt—can influence the decision process. Recently two human experiments were conducted to gain insight into what effect, if any, emotions have on decision making in public goods and group competition games. In this paper we present a simple computer model that emulates those game-theoretical human experiments. Simulation results indicate anger and guilt have very different effects on decision making depending on the type of social dilemma under investigation.

Keywords: cooperation, emotions, N-player games, social dilemmas.

1 Introduction

Social dilemmas arise whenever people must make tradeoffs between conflicting choices before reaching a decision. Usually the decision is whether to cooperate or not cooperate (defect). Participation in a global climate change program or setting fishing quotas in international waters are examples of social dilemmas. Mutual cooperation produces the best overall outcome, but that is not a Nash equilibrium because an individual can always do better by defecting. The inevitable outcome is everyone defects.

Cooperation and altruism [1] is pervasive among non-related humans yet the underlying reasons why this is so remain allusive. In his seminal paper Nowak [1] proposed five rules that help promote cooperation: *direct reciprocity, indirect reciprocity, network reciprocity, kin selection* and *group selection*. Direct reciprocity means an individual cooperates more frequently with individuals who have cooperated in the past. With indirect reciprocity reputations influence future decisions to cooperate. Network reciprocity promotes cooperation by limiting interactions to only a subset of the population. Kin selection (also called inclusive fitness) means individuals are more likely to cooperate if they are genetically related. Group selection (also called multi-level selection) occurs when competition between groups increases cooperation levels within those groups.

---

[1] Cooperative behavior provides a benefit to another individual. Altruistic behavior provides a benefit to another individual but at a cost to oneself.

S.K. Chalup et al. (Eds.): ACALCI 2015, LNAI 8955, pp. 88–99, 2015.

Positive assortment [2] provides a framework that encompasses all of Nowak's rules. An assortment is the segregation of a collection of objects into distinct classes or groups. The assortment is positive if group members share more things in common with their fellow group members than with the population as a whole. Under normal circumstances in social dilemmas a small number of cooperators will go extinct in a population of mostly defectors. However, positive assortment allows that small group of cooperators to persist[2].

In this work I investigate how group competition and emotions affect cooperation levels in social dilemmas using a simple computer model. Specifically, I look at groups that play repeated *public goods* (PG) games to see how anger and guilt affect player decisions. Periodically these groups compete against other groups. The computer model was constructed to see if behavior observed in two recently conducted human experiments [3,4] can be duplicated. The human experiment results indicate anger reduces positive assortment in PG games, but guilt, however, had no effect. The model validates those outcomes and thus can now be used for future related research investigations. One interesting extension is the model was then reconfigured to play repeated *tragedy of the commons* (ToC) games, which is another type of social dilemma. (I am unaware of any human experiments investigating emotional effects in ToC scenarios.) Simulation results indicate anger and guilt have opposite affects on positive assortment in that game.

The paper is organized as follows. In the next section we formally define the PG and ToC games and their differences are highlighted. Section 3 describes the two human experiments and a brief description of my computer model. Section 4 discusses the experimental results and compares them with the human experiment results.

2   Social Dilemma Games

This section briefly describes the PG and ToC games. Some authors (e.g., [5,6]) consider PG and ToC somewhat related. Although it is true both are social dilemmas, they actually describe completely different situations [7]. After describing both games these differences will be highlighted as they are important to understanding the proximate roles of anger and guilt in these social dilemmas.

2.1   PG Game

The PG game is an N-player game that is equivalent to an N-player prisoner's dilemma game. During each round players simultaneously decide to cooperate (C) or defect (D). Players do not know beforehand what other players will choose. Each player starts the game with an account of d dollars. Cooperators contribute an amount c to a public pot P whereas defectors contribute nothing.

---

[2] In this paper an increase in positive assortment means group cooperation has increased.

(P becomes a public good.) An external benefactor then increases the pot and distributes it equally to each player regardless if they cooperated or defected.

In a *linear* PG game the benefactor uses a linear equation to increase the pot. Typically the pot amount is multiplied by a constant factor r where $1 < r < N$. The return to player i is

$$\text{return}(i) = \begin{cases} \frac{r}{N}P - c & \text{cooperators} \\ \frac{r}{N}P & \text{defectors} \end{cases}$$

The best outcome for the group occurs when everyone contributes. However, in a group size of $N = 4$ each dollar contributed only returns $0.50. That means defection is the best choice for an individual because a defector gets a return without contributing anything. Unfortunately this temptation to free-ride inevitably leads to a sub-optimal group outcome.

This same outcome is also likely in the *nonlinear* PG game version. In the nonlinear version the benefactor increases P in a monotonically increasing way that depends on the number of cooperators. The simplest nonlinear method uses a Heavyside function

$$\text{return}_j(i) = \begin{cases} 0 & j \leq k \\ \frac{rP}{N} & \text{otherwise} \end{cases}$$

where j is the number of cooperators among the N players and k is an integer. In this case there is no return unless there are at least k cooperators in the group. If there are enough cooperators P is increased by a factor r and then equally distributed among the N players.

Archetti et. al [8] points out that the nonlinear version is pervasive throughout nature. In fact, the linear version only appears in human groups. This makes perfect sense because the linear version always returns *something* to a cooperator, regardless of whatever other players do, whereas the nonlinear version may return nothing. Humans are aware of this fact and thus more inclined to play the linear version. Since our model emulates human experiments we only consider the linear PG game version in this research.

2.2   ToC Game

ToC is a term coined by Hardin [9] as part of an economic theory. In this N-player game players simultaneously decide to take a portion of a shared resource. This resource is renewable but if players take too much too often the replenishment may not be able to keep up in which case the shared resource eventually disappears.

A cooperator limits his take to allow the shared resource to replenish whereas a defector player takes as much as he wants. Mutual cooperation is the best group policy because the shared resource will always be available. But a defector always gets a higher payoff than a cooperator, which means defection is the best individual policy.

If every player pursues his own best interests then the inevitable outcome is everyone defects and the shared resource disappears. For example, consider a group of fisherman working in the Tasman Sea. They can take as many fish as they can. (These fish are "the commons".) However, if every fisherman did that the fish population may not reproduce at a high enough rate to keep the population viable. So a cooperative fisherman would limit the size of his catch. But that makes more fish available for the rest of the fisherman. A defector could exploit the cooperator by taking more fish. Therein lies the social dilemma: should a fisherman cooperate to keep the fish population viable (and risk being exploited by others) or defect and maximize his profit knowing that this could deplete the fish population? The inevitable outcome of everyone defecting leads to the tragedy of the commons.

2.3   Game Differences

In economic circles goods are classified into two categories:

1. *Excludable*: certain agents may not be allowed access to the good
2. *Diminishable*: goods used by one agent makes less available for other agents

A town park is an example of a non-excludable good. Everyone can enjoy the park—regardless of whether or not they helped pay for it via local property taxes. Renewable goods are non-diminishable. The town park is also non-diminishable because public use does not reduce it. That said, the town park is shared equally so there is a temptation not to contribute by paying taxes. However, *somebody* must pay the taxes or the park would not exist!

ToC and PG games both deal with non-excludable goods because all players can participate without restriction. For instance, in PG games every player can contribute to a group pot and every player gets their portion of the return. In the fisherman example above every fisherman can take a portion of the available fish. The difference is ToC uses a diminishable good while PG does not. The fisherman example has a diminishable good because fish taken by one fisherman leaves less fish for others to take. Conversely, in the PG game the good is non-diminishable because the benefactor is assumed to be infinitely wealthy so there is always enough money on hand to increase a group's contribution. *Consequently, only in a ToC game are players considered rivals.* This difference significantly impacts which emotions influence C or D decisions in the two games.

3   Experiments

In this section two human experiments are described that inspired the simple computer model. Results of the computer modeling experiments are described in detail.

3.1   Human Experiments

The first human experiment was conducted by Puurtinen and Mappes [3]. Their experiment partitioned 192 human subjects into 8 sessions (24 subjects per session). Each session was then segregated into 6 distinct equal sized groups. Each session conducted two experiments with 20 rounds per experiment. In the first experiment 10 rounds of a PG game were played followed by 10 rounds of a group competition (GC) game (denoted by "PG+GC"). The order of the PG and PG+GC games were reversed for the second experiment.

In the PG game players were provided with an endowment of 20 monetary units (MUs) and only interact with other players who belong to the same group. During each round players could contribute between 0 and 20 MU to a group pot; C players contribute at least 1 MU while D players contribute nothing. The pot total was then doubled and equally distributed to the group members. The PG+GC game was identical to the PG game except after the group pots are distributed two randomly chosen groups were picked for competition. The 'winner' was the group with the bigger pot. The difference between the two group pots was then doubled. Each member of the winning group received 1/4 of this doubled pot while each member of the losing group had 1/4 of this doubled pot deducted from their accounts. Some groups played 10 PG rounds followed by 10 PG+GC rounds; in other groups this order was reversed.

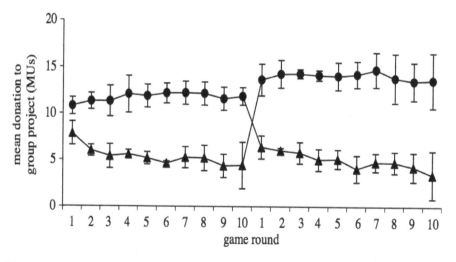

Fig. 1. Typical results from the Puurtinen and Mappes experiments. Triangles (circles) represent mean contributions in the PG (PG+GC) rounds. The error bars indicate 95% confidence intervals of the mean. This figure originally appeared in [3].

After each round group members were randomly reassigned such that no two group members interacted again[3]. This reshuffling of the group members prevented direct or indirect reciprocity from influencing player decisions, thereby making group selection dynamics the primary factor in determining cooperation levels.

After each round players were asked to record their emotions, anger towards those who contributed less than then they did or personal guilt if others contributed more. At the conclusions players were paid in cash according to how many MUs they had accumulated.

Figure 1 shows typical results. The PG rounds showed a decrease in mean contribution levels—i.e., less positive assortment. Positive assortment was more prevalent in the PG+GC rounds because mean contributions remained relatively constant. These characteristics appeared regardless of the order in which the games were played.

The second human experiments were conducted by Burton et al. [4]. In their experiments 48 students participated. Students were split into 3 blocks of 16 participants each. Each block was split into 4 groups of 4 members. Each group played two PG games of 6 rounds; one PG game had no GC while the second game did have GC. The order of the two games varied across the blocks.

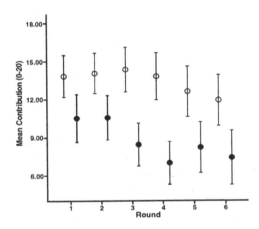

Fig. 2. Sample results from the Burton et al. experiments. Filled (open) circles represent PG (PG+GC) rounds. This figure originally appeared in [4].

As in the other experiment players started each round with an endowment of 20 MUs. Contributions could be between 0 and 20 MUs. (C players contribute at least 1 MU.) The pot size was doubled and then equally distributed among the group members. The GC, however, was different because there was no penalty for losing the competition. Instead groups were ranked according to their total contributions and then given additional MUs based on their ranking. The highest ranked group got 16 additional MUs, the next highest got 8 MUs, the next highest 4 MUs and the lowest ranked 2 MUs. These additional MUs were equally divided among the group members

---

[3] It is not clear how this was accomplished; the authors provided no details.

Group members were not reassigned after each round. Instead reciprocity was avoided by not disclosing what prior decisions their group members made. Players were informed about the payoffs and were asked to record their emotional responses. At the end of the experiment players were also asked to record wether they considered their group members as competitors or collaborators. Players were paid in cash for every MU they had accumulated.

Figure 2 shows typical results. Again the PG+GC rounds showed more positive assortment. However, unlike the first experiment, now both games showed an obvious decrease in the mean contribution levels over time.

3.2   A Simple Game-Theoretical Computer Model

The computer model was designed to mimic the human experiments described in the previous section. This model plays repeated PG games with group competition and ToC games. Players adapt their contributions (PG games) or consumptions (ToC games) depending on group interactions in the previous round. The PG game will be discussed first.

A population of 24 players is split into 6 equal size groups. Groups are identified with a color "tag" $T \in \{$red, blue, white, brown, orange, purple$\}$. A PG game can only be played among players with the same tag. Tags make shuffling group memberships easy; two players can switch groups by simply exchanging tags. The initial player assignments are random—i.e., there is no positive assortment.

Every tag group plays a PG game of 6 rounds. Players begin each round with a new endowment of 20 MUs. Each player decides whether to cooperate (C) by contributing between 1–20 MUs or to defect (D) by contributing nothing. Contributions are adapted each round based on the payoffs from the previous round[4]. The total group contribution is doubled and then equally distributed among the group players—regardless of whether they chose C or D. A GC takes place after every PG round after which players were reassigned by randomly shuffling the tags.

Players adapt the amount they contribute based on average group contributions from the previous round. Let K_i denote the current contribution of the i-th player in a tag group and let avg_{-i} be the average contribution of players in the same tag group other than i. Players increment, decrement or do not change their current contribution level based on how it compares with the average contribution of the other group players. The adaption algorithm is shown below.

avg_{-i} is calculated after each round. K_i is incremented if less than avg_{-i} and decremented if greater than avg_{-i}; otherwise it is left unchanged. If player i is contributing more than the average in the group, then he might feel angry at being exploited. It therefore makes sense to decrease his future contributions. Conversely, if his contributions are less than the average he might feel guilty about being a free-rider and thus want to increase his future contributions. This

---

[4] Initial contributions were randomly drawn from a poisson distribution with mean 10 since that gave a distribution similar to that observed in the human experiments.

K_i **Adaption Algorithm**
1. Compute avg$_{-i}$
2. **for each** member $i \in T$ **do**
3.   **if** contribution of player $i <$ avg$_{-i}$ **then**
4. $K_i \leftarrow K_i + 1$ // increase contrib.
5.   **end if**
6.   **if** contribution of player $i >$ avg$_{-i}$ **then**
7. $K_i \leftarrow K_i$ - 1   // decrease contrib.
8.   **end if**
9. **end for**

adaption scheme is simple, but it sufficient to study how anger and guilt affect social dilemma decisions.

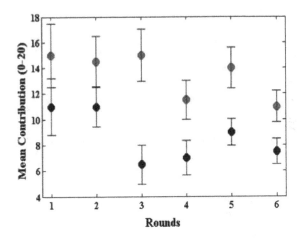

Fig. 3. A sample computer model run. Black circles depict a pure PG game; red circles depict a PG+GC game. Both games show a steady downward trend in contributions. Error bars show the 95% confidence interval for the means.

Figure 3 shows the simulation results (c.f., Figure 2). Notice the pure PG game and the PG+GC game both show downward trends in contributions. Even the potential of greater rewards through a GC were not enough to overcome the pressure to free-ride during the PG game. The contribution levels were higher when GC was played, but still the contribution trend was downward.

4   Discussion

The computer model was constructed specifically to mimic dynamics observed in human experiments. It is therefore useful to look at some of the reasons behind why humans made their decision during rounds of PG and PG+GC games.

Participants in both human experiments were asked to record their levels of guilt and anger after each round. Both experiments reported the results but only provided statistical analysis without speculating on proximate causes. Both found participants exhibited anger towards other group members who contributed less but differed on how guilt influences decision making. In [3] guilt levels were "generally quite low" whereas in [4] they found individuals were more guilty when they contributed less than others. Burton et al. [4] report participants felt angrier when they contributed more than others and guiltier when they contributed less. Those Burton et al. findings inspired the K_i adaption method used in my model.

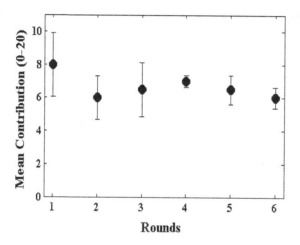

Fig. 4. A sample computer model PG run without guilt. Error bars show the 95% confidence intervals for the means.

Practically speaking, guilt makes little sense in a pure PG game. Presumably the guilty player believes his or her previous winnings are too high relative to other players and so contributes more to increase the return to others. But that belief acts against a self-interested player because it increases the chances of exploitation in future rounds—particularly if group memberships change after every round. This aspect was investigated by removing the contribution increase when $K_i < \text{avg}_{-i}$ (lines 3-5 in the K_i Adaption Algorithm). Figure 4 shows typical simulation results. Notice there is still a downward trend in contribution levels even though no guilt is involved. These results empirically show guilt has no role in a pure PG game.

Guilt, however, is an important factor in group competitions. A player who contributes less than the rest of the group may feel guilty if his low contributions made the group non-competitive. In addition, a player who contributed more than the group average might feel guilty about decreasing future contributions too much because that could make his future groups non-competitive. In either case guilt pressures a player to keep his contributions high.

Group competition was not explicitly incorporated into the model but instead the initial contributions were just increased. This increase is not as arbitrary as it might appear at first glance. Actually neither human experiment explicitly implemented GC either (see below). Nevertheless, both showed a significant contribution increase when group competition is present. Notice in Figure 1 the dramatic increase when the game switched from PG to PG+GC. The only plausible explanation is the players realized their mates were now collaborators, which is something both experimenters posited. It therefore seems reasonable to increase the contribution levels in the model to incorporate this thought process.

It is worth mentioning there is no actual strategy for GC. In the PG game each group had 4 members and contributions were doubled. It is easy to show each contributed MU returns -0.5 MU, which means a positive return requires others to contribute. In [3] the difference between contribution totals was increased by a factor of $b = 2$ and added equally to the winning group players but subtracted equally from the losing group players. In this case the benefit B_{GC} from investing one additional MU is

$$B_{GC} = -0.5\,\mathrm{MU} + \left(\frac{b \times 1}{4}\right)\mathrm{MU} = 0$$

where the first term is the return from the PG game. Thus regardless of what a player contributed in the PG game, it would have no effect on accumulated wealth in the group competition. Consequently, there is no strategy per se for the GC game.

Anger is important in both games but for different reasons and therefore induces different decisions. Anger pressures a player to reduce contribution levels to avoid future exploitation in the PG game. On the other hand in the PG+GC game it tends to increase contributions because a player feels his group is presently non-competitive. This tradeoff could explain the radical shift in behavior observed in the Puurtinen and Mappes [3] experiment (c.f., Figure 2).

Guilt has just the opposite effect in ToC games because a player may feel his higher than average consumption may deplete the common good. Thus guilt tends to decrease consumption. To investigate this idea the computer model was reconfigured so "contributions" are now considered "consumptions"—i.e., K_i now represents a consumption. The K_i adaption algorithm must also be reinterpreted. Specifically, lines 3-5 now reflect anger while lines 6-8 now reflect guilt. An angry player feels exploited and so should increase his consumption. On the other hand, a guilty player who consumes more than the average should decrease his consumption to help preserve the common good. The results are depicted in Figure 5. Notice the consumption rates increase over time, which depletes the common good. Unfortunately eliminating guilt produces even higher consumption rates.

5   Final Remark

In all pure social dilemma games—i.e., games without inter-group competition— the best group outcome happens with all-C strategies. Unfortunately the all-C

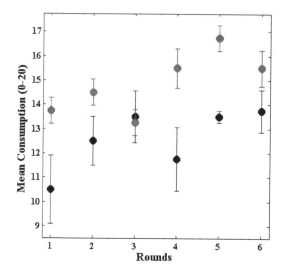

Fig. 5. A sample run with the computer model reconfigured as a tragedy of commons problem. The black (red) circles shows mean consumption with (without) guilt. Error bars show the 95% confidence intervals of the means.

strategy profile is not a Nash equilibrium because an individual can always profit more by free-riding. In fact, the best response for any self-interested player is always defection regardless of what other players choose.

GC changes things because, while smaller contributions may be the best PG response, they make the group less competitive, which means lower returns in inter-group competition. That said, if the payoff is high enough for winning an inter-group competition, then an all-C strategy may be a Nash equilibrium for a PG+GC game. C would be the best response in those particular situations because it maximizes the PG game return and at the same time maximizes the GC return. On the other hand, if the inter-group payoff is low an individual may do better by focusing on PG game returns and ignoring the GC returns.

. In ToC games D (i.e., high consumption) is best for the individual and anger may tempt an individual to consume even more. Guilt, however, serves as a moderator because it reminds the individual that increasing consumption rates could deplete the resource. Thus the best response is a consumption rate that yields sufficiently high enough returns while at the same time preserving the common good.

There are two competing philosophies on how self-interested players effect an economy:

- (Adam Smith) *In competition, individual ambition serves the common good*

- (John Nash) *The best result comes when everyone does what is best for himself **and** what is best for the rest of the group*

As stated previously, players are rivals in ToC games but not pure PG games. Clearly the John Nash philosophy applies to ToC games. Adding GC to PG games introduces some rivalry, which suggests the John Nash philosophy applies to PG+GC games as well. I conjecture the Adam Smith philosophy would apply to PG+GC games only if GC payoffs are extremely high compared to PG game payoffs.

References

1. Nowak, M.: Five rules for the evolution of cooperation. Science, 1560–1563 (2006)
2. Fletcher, J., Doebeli, M.: A simple and general explanation for the solution of altruism. Proc. R. Soc. B 276, 13–19 (2009)
3. Puurtinen, M., Mappes, T.: Between-group competition and human cooperation. Proc. R. Soc. B 276, 355–360 (2009)
4. Burton, M., Ross, A., West, S.: Cooperation in humans: competition between groups and proximate emotions. Evol. & Human Behav. 31, 104–108 (2010)
5. Kraal, S.: Exploring the public goods game model to overcome the tragedy of the commons in fisheries management. Fish and Fisheries 12(1), 18–33 (2011)
6. Milinski, M., Semmann, D., Krambeck, H., Marotzke, J.: Stabilizing the earth's climate is not a losing game: supporting evidence from public goods experiments. Proc. Nat'l. Acad. Sci. 103(11), 3994–3998 (2006)
7. Dionisio, F., Gordo, I.: The tragedy of the commons, the public goods dilemma and the meaning of rivalry and excludability in evolutionary biology. Evol. Ecol. Res. 8, 321–332 (2006)
8. Archetti, M., Scheuring, I., Hoffman, M., Frederickson, M., Pierce, N., Yu, D.: Economic game theory for mutualism and cooperation. Ecol. Lett. 14(12), 1300–1312 (2011)
9. Hardin, G.: The tragedy of the commons. Science 162, 1243–1248 (1968)

Agent-Based Simulation of Stakeholder Behaviour through Evolutionary Game Theory

Yngve Svalestuen, Pinar Öztürk, Axel Tidemann, and Rachel Tiller

Norwegian University of Science and Technology
Sem Sealandsvei 7, 7491 Trondheim Norway
yngve@outlook.com, pinar@ntnu.no,
{axel.tidemann,racheltiller}@gmail.com

Abstract. Aquaculture organizations establish facilities at the coast in Frøya, Norway. The facilities block the surrounding area from fishing and cause environmental damage to close natural resources. Fishers who depend on those natural resources get the opportunity to influence the aquaculture expansion through complaints about the municipality's coastal plan. Statistics show that fishers don't complain as much as expected. This work aims to investigate why. An agent-based simulation is developed in order to model the fishers as intelligent agents with complex interaction. Fishermen's decision making is simulated through an artificial neural network which adapts its behavior (i.e. weights) by "learning-by-imitation", a method in evolutionary game theory, from other stakeholders' behavior in the environment. The promising results show that with further development the simulation system may be part of a decision support system that promotes policies that are fair for the stakeholders.

Keywords: computational intelligence, agent-based model, simulation, learning by imitation, evolutionary game theory, artificial neural network, strategical decision making.

1 Introduction

Agent-based models of human behavior and multi-agent simulations are powerful methods for predicting social behavior when empirical experimentation is not possible or feasible [1]. Simulations are attractive because they avoid the risk of undesired outcomes associated with real life social experiments and provide a quick insight into social dilemmas which would have required unaffordable time to experiment with in real time.

The research presented in this paper was motivated by the observation of a particular behavior in fishermen in Frøya, a small municipality in Sør-Trønderlag, Norway. The fishermen were faced with the decision about whether they should allow new aquaculture establishments. These decisions are made through a democratic process where each fisherman is given the opportunity to file a complaint to hinder new aquaculture establishments in their preferred fishing area. Fishermen are observed to complain less frequently than predicted. It is also predictable

S.K. Chalup et al. (Eds.): ACALCI 2015, LNAI 8955, pp. 100–111, 2015.

that if fishers do decide to complain, they will complain as much as they can, and even complain about locations that are not important to them. This behavior is referred to as "falsely" complaining. We aim to understand why the complaint rate is generally low, as well as the conditions under which false complaints occur, and ultimately which policies can be implemented to encourage genuine complaints and to discourage false complaints.

It is obvious that individual stakeholder agents exercise strategic thinking and decision making, and that complex societal behavior emerges from decisions taken by individuals. The main principle underlying such dynamic behavior of societies is that individuals observe other agents' behavior and change their behavior accordingly. Game theory (GT) investigates such strategic decision-making and is able to explain many prototypical dilemmas. However, GT has been criticized for being unable to capture the behavior of societies with high population. Firstly, classical GT assumes that the agents have perfect knowledge about the other agents in the environment, e.g. their payoffs. Secondly, it assumes that agents behave rationally, i.e. each individual select actions that maximize their utility. In dynamic and stochastic environments, assumption of perfect knowledge is unrealistic, and agents do not necessarily behave rationally. In addition, it is not possible to know in advance which strategies are optimal. Evolutionary game theory (EGT) investigates the learning of optimal strategies, rather than assuming that agents have sufficient information about their environments to decide optimal actions in advance [2]. In EGT, individuals learn how to select an optimal behavior by imitating the strategies of the agents that receive highest payoff. This is analogous to survival of individuals with highest fitness in biological evolution [3].

This paper describes a thick multi-agent simulation environment where the agents exhibit complex decision making and learn from each other to make decisions that will maximize their utility/payoff. The core of the simulator is an evolutionary artificial neural network that implements a learning-by-imitation mechanism, an EGT method, where agents adopt the behavior of agents that made best return in the preceding round. Using the simulator, we study the effects of learning on stakeholders' decision-making in the fishing community in Frøya municipality. We divided our experiment into four parts. The first set of experiments examines whether and how government approval rate of complaints influence fishers' eagerness to complain. The second part explores the outcomes of the government's decisions about new aquaculture establishments. The third set of experiments analyzes how the overall behavior of fishermen evolves over time. The fourth set investigates whether the complaint behavior changes when environmental damages start to influence the Frøya community. The implications of the results show that the simulator was able to produce results that were in alignment with the reality of Frøya according to fishermen's story acquired in the workshop and other researchers' studies of the phenomenon in Frøya [4]. This is promising in the sense that the simulation may be further developed as a decision support system, showing possible future outcomes given specific governmental policies.

In the rest of the paper, the next section gives a background both in terms of the related literature on the use of agent-based systems for studying some social phenomena, and describes the Frøya phenomenon. Section 3 describes the simulator, including the agents, their roles and behaviour. In 3.1 the architecture for the decision mechanism of fisherman, which is implemented as an artificial neural network, is described in detail while 3.2 explains the interdependence between the strategies of the fishermen and the other actors, and whether a learning-by-imitation behaviour adaptation may explain the outcomes in Frøya dispute. Section 4 describes the experimental setup we designed to study the answers of the four questions we mentioned above, and the results of the simulations. Finally, section 5 wrap up with a discussion and evaluation of the simulations.

2   Background

2.1   Related Work

Simulations of social science problems are helpful not only by the results they provide, but also because they force all assumptions to be made explicit, parameters to be defined, and limits of the theories involved to be defined [1].

Agent-based models are used to learn and teach about complex situations where agents influence and are influenced by dynamic and vulnerable environments [5,6,7]. REEFGAME is an agent-based simulation game where the players interact as fishers to cooperate and harvest resources from the environment in different locations, and has been applied as a teaching tool in a social setting [5]. Sea lice infestations in salmon populations can be controlled using wrasse, another fish. An agent-based model was developed to investigate the spread and dynamics of the lice themselves, allowing study of effectiveness and optimal concentrations of wrasse without environmental risk [6]. Farmers spreading pests through interactions are simulated using a combined agent-based and cellular automaton model which is applied as a teaching tool, aiming to increase awareness of how the pests spread [7].

Agents presented with game-theoretic choices can learn by imitation through different dynamics, commonly copying neighbors with the best strategy [8,9]. Investor agents distributed in a scale-free social network have a choice to invest in a technology that is good for the environment, but give relatively lower profits. A structure-based advertisement policy that uses social connectivity is assessed and compared to traditional monetary reward policies to promote green spending [8]. The motivation to cull red deer populations through hunting is divided as sporting interests or of interest to preserving biodiversity. Land owners choose when and how much to cull, which develops a dynamic where neighbors maximize efficiency and cooperate by doing the opposite of each other, while agents learn through imitation [9].

2.2   Frøya Scenario

In Frøya, aquaculture companies apply to the municipality for a license to build a new facility in a given area. Coastal plans are created with semi-regular intervals; they are generated by local municipalities and comprise decisions about how many aquaculture licenses will be issued and where each new facility will be located. Fishermen and other stakeholders (e.g. turists, civilians) may vote against coastal plans by filing complaints if they don't want an aquaculture activity in a certain area announced in the coastal plan. The complaints from the hearing are considered by the government. If one or more of the complaints are approved, the plan goes back to the municipality for review, which triggers a renewed planning, another hearing and another government decision. For instance, the combined local fisherman community in Frøya has twice complained about areas that were where the municipality wanted to allow aquaculture expansion, because they felt the areas were too valuable as fishing spots but their complaints were not always followed because both the municipality and the regional government of Frøya are very interested in having aquaculture.

The fishers' situation in Frøya municipality is relatively unique because unlike most other fisher communities who when faced with aquaculture oppose the development as much as possible, the fishers at Frøya are open and supportive of the expansion [4]. All the fishermen were clear on the point that if it were not for the existence aquaculture in Frøya, it would be a much smaller place with a lower standard of living. Fishermen mainly receive revenue from fishing activities, but since they are community members, they also receive tax benefits from the existence of aquaculture since they pay taxes that are distributed to community members (including fishermen). Fishermen also have community wealth as an important priority, which is positively influenced by this taxation as well.

Even though aquaculture is considered an overall good, it still poses threats to the fishers. Besides, environmental damage is an issue for the fishers, and it is partially caused by the aquaculture facilities. Preventing environmental damage that pollutes fish resources is a major reason why fishers by complaining desire to halt the aquaculture expansion in certain areas.

However, the fishers experienced that complaining doesn't work as much as they wished. They expressed, in a workshop we have had with various stakeholders in Frøya, that the rate of govenment's approval of fishers' complaint is low. If the government's complaint approval rate is observed by the fishermen to be too low, this may cause the fishers to not complain at all, because they observe no benefit or a benefit that occurs far too rarely, compared to the cost. Even if the benefit when it occurs is far greater than the cost associated with complaining, this effect may still take place. We focussed on this information from the Frøya workshop and it took a central place in our simulation to study the dynamic of the behaviour of fisherman in this scenario.

3   Materials and Methods

We present a multi-agent simulator that models the entire process revolving around the establishment of new aquaculture facilities. Heterogeneous agents interact through a sequence of events which involves actions performed by agents. The overall mechanism and the rules, the agent types and their roles, and the type of interaction between them are designed according to the description in [4]. The agents correspond to stakeholders in the Frøya situation, and include fishers, aquaculture companies, a government agency for treating fishermen complaints, and the municipality. Fishers and aquaculture agents operate in a world divided into cells as a grid, as shown in fig. 1.

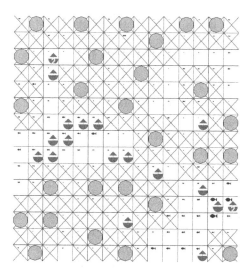

Fig. 1. The world map organized as a grid structure. Fishers are represented as boats (numbered means multiple fishers in the same location), and are located in their current "home" cells. Fish quantity in each cell can be seen by the size of the fish in the cell's top-left corner. Aquaculture facilities are shown as gray decagons, and the area around them that is blocked for fishing (as well as further aquaculture expansion) is indicated by crosses.

There are several functions performed by government instances, that are grouped together as a single "government", another type of agent, in the simulation for the purpose of simplicity. These functions include receiving complaints, deciding if a coastal plan needs reworking, and providing the municipality with aquaculture licenses.

Figure 2 shows an overview of the simulation process, which continues a number of rounds. Each round is initiated by a coastal plan being laid out by the municipality. The main priority of the municipality of Frøya is to have aquaculture where it is possible, so initially all locations will be reserved for aquaculture. The plan is sent to all "voting" agents, which includes fishermen, aquaculture owners, tourists and civilians. After the plan has been distributed, the hearing phase starts. Each voting agent can issue at most a predetermined number of complaints about aquaculture establishment on areas in the plan, which correspond to cells in the world grid. Complaints from the hearing are considered by the government. If one or more of the complaints are approved, the plan goes

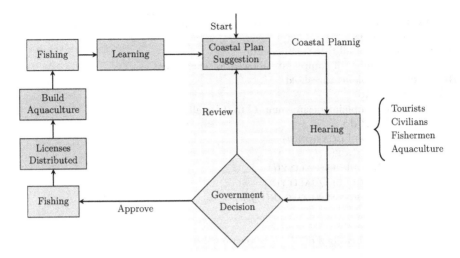

Fig. 2. Process chart of the simulation. Every round starts with a coastal plan being created by the municipality. It is sent on hearing to the agents including fishers, who may choose to complain about aquaculture locations. The government decision has two options: To *approve* a coastal plan, or decide that it has to be *reviewed*. After a plan has been approved, fishers harvest and aquaculture organizations run their facilities. At a point during the fishing phase, licenses coming from the national government are distributed and new aquaculture is established. Agents undergo a learning process before the beginning of the next round.

back to the municipality for review, which triggers a replanning, another hearing and another government decision. At some point the government will decide to distribute licenses and aquaculture building can begin. After aquaculture has been built, normal activities (shown as "fishing" in fig. 2) are pursued by all agents until it is time to lay out a new coastal plan. Before a new planning phase is started, there is a learning phase where agents adapt their decisions, using a learning-by-imitation method.

3.1   Decision Making

Fishermen decide whether to complain about single plans to establish aquaculture at a certain location. Fishermen have a "home" area where they currently do their fishing. The home area can change during the simulation, either because the spot degrades in fish quantity or quality, or because the area is blocked by aquaculture expansion. The decision is based on three factors: 1) The distance between the threatened location and the home cell since aquaculture facilities produce waste that harm nearby fishing locations. 2) The fishing conditions in the currently preferred spot. A good spot decreases the need to protect other good fishing spots, and having a bad spot may devalue spending resources on protecting it from nearby facilities because it may be easier to find a similar spot somewhere else. 3) If fishing conditions are bad at the location threatened

Require: P: coastal plan for the current round, represented as the set of all planned aquaculture zones
Require: F: set of all fisherman agents
Require: n: number of complaints allowed for each agent
Require: t: complaint threshold
   for all $a \in F$ **do**
      Initialize complaint desires map C to 0 for all locations
      for all $l \in P$ **do**
         $h \leftarrow$ HOMELOCATION(a)
         $i \leftarrow$ DISTANCE(h, l)
         $j \leftarrow$ RESOURCEQUALITY(l)
         $k \leftarrow$ RESOURCEQUALITY(h)
         $C[l] \leftarrow$ PROCESSNETWORK(i, j, k)
      end for
      SORT(C)
      $D \leftarrow n$ first locations of C where desire value $d > t$
      $a \rightarrow$ COMPLAIN(D)
   end for

Fig. 3. Algorithm describing usage of a fisher's artificial neural network during the complaining decision. The weights of the ANN are learned using artificial evolution, while the structure is static. Knowledge of resource qualities is either experienced through fishing at a location, or inferred from other agents' complaints.

by aquaculture expansion there may be no reason to fight for it, but keeping good fishing spots intact for the future is important as assurance for the fishers. Fishers also prioritize the overall health of the fish, which is harmed if a good fishing spot is destroyed by aquaculture.

Complaining has zero monetary cost, but there is an associated information cost when agents reveal their good fishing spots by complaining about them. This cost is not an explicit part of the decision making process, but rather a consequence of complaining, and thus this information sharing cost is learned through experience.

Fishers change their locations for two reasons: either because of aquaculture expansion or by observing that the current spot has such low quality (i.e. performance below a certain threshold) that they try somewhere else. If a fisherman does not know any locations that are better than average, the fisher will try another random non-blocked fishing spot.

In the simulation, the fishers' decision mechanism underlying the complaining decision is implemented as an artificial neural network (ANN). Figure 3 shows how agents apply the ANN to their complaint decision. The ANN is implemented with three input nodes (corresponding to the factors described above), six nodes in the hidden layer with recurrent connections, and one output neuron. Synaptic weights are evolved. For each agent, the network is activated once per aquaculture area in the plan. The output is the complaint strength for each area; i.e. a measure of how much the agent wants to complain. After deciding a desired value for each location, the number of cells with the highest desired values are complained about, if they are above a certain threshold.

3.2 Learning

The learning implementation is based on evolutionary game theory, as a social learning interpretation. Agents copy the ANN weights of their best-performing peers, while the copying process is subject to mutation. Imitation corresponds to inheritance in traditional evolutionary algorithms. The evolution process is implemented as a standard Darwinian process, with phenotypes that are fitness measured and genotypes that are copied and developed into phenotypes.

Fishers imitate others based on their fitness, which is measured as the priority satisfaction for each agent. Fishers have a set of priorities that have varying weights, representing the significance of each priority. The total satisfaction e_a for agent a is thus given as a weighted average:

$$e_a = \sum_{p \in P} S_p(a) W_p(a)$$

where $S_p(a)$ is the satisfaction of priority p for agent a, and $W_p(a)$ is the relative weight of priority p for agent a, with $\sum_W W(a) = 1$.

In order for the fishers to keep aquaculture at bay, they have to cooperate on complaining. A single fisher complaining will not be able to consistently reserve any areas since the probability of complaints being approved is less than 1 and an agent can only complain once about a given area. However, several agents complaining about the same area significantly increases the odds of a complaint about that location being approved. The population of fishers overall will therefore benefit from cooperation, but individual fishers are at the same time disadvantaged by complaining since they thereby share information about the best fishing spot they know of.

4 Experiments and Results

When running the simulation for 30 rounds, the outcomes can be classified in two kinds: a *collapse* which results in the whole map being consumed by aquaculture facilities, leaving the fishers no place to continue fishing; or *stabilization* which means that the average number of complaints exhibited by fishers in each round stabilizes at a non-zero rate and successfully keeps aquaculture expansion at bay.

Stabilized and collapsed runs have different developments, as illustrated by fig. 4 which shows statistics for one typical simulation run for each class. In the collapsed run, we see that the average number of fisherman complaints rapidly decreases until it reaches 0 and never raises again. The number of aquaculture facilities steadily increases until there are no available cells left because there are no complaints left to oppose the expansion. At the same time, average fisherman capital decreases steadily until it reaches 0 since the fishers no longer have any

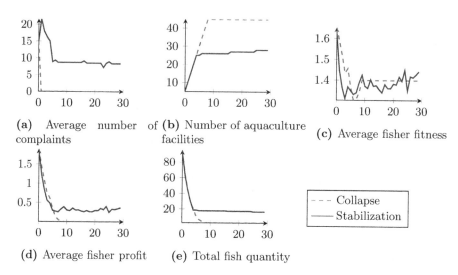

(a) Average number of complaints

(b) Number of aquaculture facilities

(c) Average fisher fitness

(d) Average fisher profit

(e) Total fish quantity

- - - Collapse
—— Stabilization

Fig. 4. Plots showing typical simulation progress resulting in collapse (dashed line); and stabilization (solid line). The horizontal axis represents the round and the vertical axis represents values for the different plots. A collapsed state is characterized by complaint behavior quickly disappearing from the population (a). At the same time the number of aquaculture facilities rises to its maximum value (b). The fisher fitness stabilizes once the number of aquacultures does (c). Fish quality is dependent on aquaculture expansion, and is hurt whenever new aquaculture is built (e). A stabilized state is characterized by complaining stabilizing at a non-zero rate, as shown by a which stabilizes at around 9 complaints per agent. The number of aquaculture facilities (b) subsequently stabilizes below its theoretical maximum value, and the average fisher fitness (c) fluctuates while staying somewhat constant. Fishers continue moving between fishing spots in the stabilized state, causing minor fluctuations in the complaining rate depending on the current knowledge and position of the individual fishers.

spots to fish, leaving them with zero income. Average fisherman fitness decreases at first quite rapidly as fishers are pushed away from their original good fishing locations, before it slowly rises and stabilizes when the maximum number of aquaculture facilities is reached. The fitness does not reach zero like the fisherman capital because aquaculture facilities have a positive influence on fishers' fitness, since their priorities are dependent on overall community wealth which is increased by aquaculture. Since aquaculture is the only influence on total fish quantity, it rapidly decreases at the start, and then stabilizes at a low level when the maximum number of aquaculture facilities is reached.

On the other hand, in the stabilized scenario the number of aquaculture facilities increases until it reaches a stable point that's below the maximum amount, kept at bay by the stabilized non-zero complaint rate. The average fisherman capital decreases steadily in the beginning, and stabilizes at a non-zero level once the number of aquaculture facilities does. The average fisher fitness stabilizes at a slightly higher point than in the previous scenario, but instead of being

Table 1. Average number of open cells and aquaculture for stable and collapsing outcomes, given the three different approval rates. The configured approval rate is shown in relation with the outcome data showing the average final states of the worlds, separated by outcome. Stable outcomes are compared by the number of open cells left and the number of established aquaculture facilities. The number of open cells in a collapsed outcome is always equal to 0, so they are not shown.

	Stable		Collapse
Approval Rate	**Open cells**	**Aquacultures**	**Aquacultures**
0.2	24.2	35.4	44.8
0.5	53.2	28.6	45.8
0.8	70.667	25.333	45

completely constant it has continuous fluctuations. Fish quantity stabilizes at a higher rate compared to the collapsed scenario since the number of aquaculture facilities is lower.

In response to feedback from the workshop, experiments were ran to assess the effects of aquaculture-friendliness in the local government, by changing the complaint approval rate. Table 1 shows the relationship between approval rate and average number of open cells and aquaculture facilities, for each of the two outcomes. With the lowest approval rate of 0.2, there are on average 24.2 open cells left and 35.4 aquaculture facilities in the stabilized outcome. With the medium approval rate of 0.5 there are on average 53.2 open cells and 28.6 aquaculture facilities when the simulation has stabilized. When the approval rate is higher at 0.8, there are on average 70.667 open cells and 25.333 aquaculture facilities in the stable outcome.

5   Discussion

The simulation can produce two outcomes: 1) The complaint rate stabilizes and fishers manage to preserve an area from aquaculture expansion. 2) The complaint rate plummets, reaches zero, and the environment is flooded with aquaculture until it is full, causing a collapse. The collapsed outcome corresponds with the situation in Frøya, where fishers do not complain, while the stabilized outcome only occurs in the simulation. On the other hand, if the level of complaints stays above a certain threshold, the number of aquaculture facilities may stabilize accordingly. Figures 4a and 4b show this relation.

The fishers are learning agents, and they implement a form of social learning where they copy the decision making mechanism of their best-performing peers. A clear assumption of the model is therefore that fishers' complaint rates will have an impact on their fitness. This assumption is justified by the logic that since complaints have an impact on aquaculture expansion, and aquaculture expansion have an impact on fishers' income since they may be pushed away from their preferred, and better-yielding fishing spots. Since fishers' fitness is dependent on their capital, fishermen who don't complain will suffer. However, individual fishermen may be freeloaders of this effect if their peers complain about expansion in areas they care about, the non-complaining fishermen may also receive the benefits of reserved zones. Therefore, other agents can perceive that agents with non-complaining behavior do as well as the complainers do, and overall complaining may falter.

Since complaints have never worked for the fishers at Frøya, it is important to explore how complaint approval rate influences the complaint rate. Experiments were conducted with the goal of exploring the consequences of varying approval rates. The two outcomes of collapse and stabilization are shown to be equally likely with every tested approval rate, but the size of the protected area in the stabilized outcome becomes larger with increasing approval rate, as shown by table 1. The fact that the rate of collapsed outcomes stays the same with varying approval rates suggests that the approval rate is not decisive of complaining behavior disappearing from the fisher population. A low approval rate may therefore not be the only reason why fishers are not complaining at Frøya. Increasing the approval rate of the government may therefore also not be sufficient to push fishermen to complain more.

The complaint approval rate does clearly influence how much area the fishers manage to protect in a stabilized outcome. There is a linear relationship between the two figures. The total size of protected areas is shown by the "open cells" statistic in table 1. The low complaint rate may be explained by this effect if fishers give up on complaining when they see that they cannot protect a large enough area for the complaining to be worth the effort, in the case of a low approval rate. There is also a special case of 0 approval rate in which agents will never be able to protect any area and the simulation will always collapse. Since the approval rate at Frøya so far has been 0 with two out of two complaints being rejected, there has so far been no positive indication that complaining works. Therefore it is equivalent with a government which has a complaint approval rate of 0, which always causes collapse. In order to make the situation more fair for fishers, the government may be encouraged to approve more complaints. The complaint rate is also directly related to the environment. An approach where complaints are always disregarded will lead to a collapse; this is something that should be emphasized to the appropriate government bodies. In this respect, the simulation can aid as a decision support system, showing possible future outcomes given specific governmental policies.

References

1. Davidsson, P.: Agent based social simulation: A computer science view. Journal of Artificial Societies and Social Simulation 5(1) (January 2002)
2. Smith, M.: Evolution and the Theory of Games. Cambridge University Press (1982)
3. Axelrod, R., Hamilton, W.D.: The evolution of cooperation. Science 211, 1390–1396 (1981)

4. Tiller, R., Richards, R., Salgado, H., Strand, H., Moe, E., Ellis, J.: Assessing stakeholder adaptive capacity to salmon aquaculture in Norway. Consilience: The Journal of Sustainable Development 11(1), 62–96 (2014)

5. Cleland, D., Dray, A., Perez, P., Cruz-Trinidad, A., Geronimo, R.: Simulating the dynamics of subsistence fishing communities: REEFGAME as a learning and data-gathering computer-assisted role-play game. Simulation and Gaming 43(1), 102–117 (2012)

6. Groner, M.L., Cox, R., Gettinby, G., Revie, C.W.: Use of agent-based modelling to predict benefits of cleaner fish in controlling sea lice, lepeophtheirus salmonis, infestations on farmed Atlantic salmon, Salmo salar L. Journal of Fish Diseases 36(3), 195–208 (2013)

7. Rebaudo, F., Crespo-Perez, V., Silvain, J.-F., Dangles, O.: Agent-based modeling of human-induced spread of invasive species in agricultural landscapes: Insights from the potato moth in Ecuador. Journal of Artificial Societies and Social Simulation 14(3), 7 (2011)

8. Nannen, V., van den Bergh, J.C.J.M.: Policy instruments for evolution of bounded rationality: Application to climate-energy problems. Technological Forecasting and Social Change 77(1), 76–93 (2010)

9. Touza, J., Drechsler, M., Smart, J.C.R., Termansen, M.: Emergence of cooperative behaviours in the management of mobile ecological resources. Environmental Modelling and Software 45, 52–63 (2013)

Evolving Cellular Automata for Maze Generation

Andrew Pech, Philip Hingston, Martin Masek, and Chiou Peng Lam

School of Computer and Security Science
Edith Cowan University
a.pech@our.ecu.edu.au, {p.hingston,m.masek,c.lam}@ecu.edu.au

Abstract. This paper introduces a new approach to the procedural generation of maze-like game level layouts by evolving CA. The approach uses a GA to evolve CA rules which, when applied to a maze configuration, produce level layouts with desired maze-like properties. The advantages of this technique is that once a CA rule set has been evolved, it can quickly generate varying instances of maze-like level layouts with similar properties in real time.

Keywords: procedural content, evolutionary algorithm, cellular automaton.

1 Introduction

Level design in video games has always been a large part of game development and has mostly been accomplished by manual means. In the early years of game development, video games were generally created by a single person, who designed and programmed the game, as well as developing artistic resources. With the rapid advancement in technology, video games have become larger and more complex, requiring more work from multiple artists and designers. This has led to increased costs, due to the extra development time required, and skewed the balance in time between developing resources and programming. These issues have increased the motivation to employ cost reduction techniques, such as the procedural generation of content.

Procedural content generation (PCG) is a term commonly used to describe the process of generating media content algorithmically rather than manually. Not only can PCG be used to alleviate the burden of the design process, but can also increase a game's replay value by generating new content to present to the player during gameplay. An early example of PCG being used to increase a game's replay value is the classic 1980 game, Rogue [1]. Rogue used PCG to generate an unlimited number of unique levels, in the form of 2D "dungeon" environments. Since then, many other games such as NetHack [2], Moria [3], and Diablo [4] have mimicked Rogue's use of PCG to generate an unlimited number of unique dungeons, adding to the replay value of games as the players are continuously presented with new designs.

While PCG has been used in video games for decades, it is still an emerging field of research. Recent work in the area of generating two dimensional game level layouts includes using genetic algorithms to evolve layouts directly [5] and applying manually designed cellular automaton rules to random initial configurations [6].

S.K. Chalup et al. (Eds.): ACALCI 2015, LNAI 8955, pp. 112–124, 2015.
© Springer International Publishing Switzerland 2015

There are benefits and drawbacks to both of these approaches. Using a genetic algorithm (GA) to evolve layouts directly gives a great amount of control over the generated layouts but running the GA takes time and is not suited for generation of layouts during application run time. Using cellular automata (CA) to generate levels is much faster and has been used for run time generation of game levels [6], but manually designing CA rules that are capable of producing desired levels can be a difficult task, especially when more intricate game levels are desired.

The approach presented in this paper addresses both of these issues by combining the use of GA with CA to automatically evolve CA rules that are capable of producing game level layouts with desired maze-like properties. This approach addresses the issue of manually designing CA rules by allowing attributes that are desired in the generated level layouts to be selected and using a GA to find rules that are capable of generating layouts with similar attributes. Once the rules have been found they can be utilized during application run time to produce a variety of different level layouts in a short amount of time, with each generated layout having similar properties. The contributions of this paper are as follows:

- **The combination of GA and CA for PCG** is the main contribution made by this research. In the past, level layouts have been evolved by GA directly, or generated through manually designed CA rules. No previous PCG approach has used GAs to evolve CA rules that are capable of generating level layouts with desired properties.
- **Exploration of two different chromosome representations** for CA rule tables.
- **Experimentation with the idea of "flavours"** [7]. As our layouts are restricted to being represented by only two cell states (traversable and non-traversable), "flavours" were used to explore CAs with more than two cell states. This device allows for more complex rule sets.

Section 2 of this article describes previous work that has been done in this area of research. Section 3 explains our approach in detail, including the chromosome representation, fitness function, and the steps of the GA process. Section 4 details the experiments that were conducted to test the effectiveness of our approach, followed by Section 5, which discusses the results. Finally, Section 6 concludes this article.

2   Related Work

Previous PCG methods of generating game levels have included the use of generative grammars to generate game levels that map to a story line [8, 9], GAs to evolve game levels based on certain attributes [5, 10], and CA for fast generation of infinite game levels [6].

One approach to generating game levels was taken by Ashlock et al. [5], whose method generated maze-like game levels based on physical attributes rather than a storyline. This approach uses a GA as the search heuristic, where chromosomes represent game levels. Four different chromosome representations were explored, each forming levels with distinct visual appearances. To control the layout of the generated game levels, a highly customizable fitness function is used, which allows control of path placement, length, and reconvergence via placement of checkpoints. This approach can take up to 20 minutes to generate a single game level, making this method only suitable for generating levels during game development and not during run time of the application.

Another PCG method for producing game levels was presented in Johnson et al. [6], which uses cellular automata to produce infinite game levels that are cave-like in appearance. CA's [11] are simpler processes than GA's and consist of a set of rules and a grid of cells, where each cell in the grid has a state. The set of rules governs the state of a cell at a given time step based on the state of that cell and its neighbours at the previous time step. The initial grid of cells, before the CA is applied, is referred to as the "initial configuration". The CA process involves applying the rules to each cell in the grid synchronously for a number of iterations, resulting in what is called the "final configuration". This can result in complex behaviour.

The CA in Johnson et al.'s [6] approach uses 2D grids of cells where each cell is initialized randomly to one of two states, either the rock state or the floor state. The CA rules in this approach use an 8-connected neighbourhood and set a cell to the "rock" state if five or more of its neighbouring cells were in the rock state. Otherwise the cell would be set to the "floor" state. Although the CA rules were simple, its speed allowed it to be executed during run time of a video game to form game level "chunks" that were connected to produce a virtually infinite game level.

Although CA iteration is a fast process, manually designing the rules for a CA can be a significant challenge. Therefore an approach that uses a combination of GA and CA to evolve CA rules would remove the difficulty of designing the CA rules, which can then be utilized during application run time to efficiently generate game level layouts.

Previous work on evolving CA rules with GAs was introduced by Mitchell et al. [12] for performing the density classification task. This task involves a one-dimensional grid of cells where each cell represents one of two values, a 0 or a 1. The goal was to use CA to discover the state that the majority of cells were in, converting the state of each cell in the grid to the majority state in the final configuration. The GA chromosomes represented CA rule tables, which took a neighbourhood configuration as input and output the new state of the neighbourhood's central cell. The fitness function applied each rule table to a collection of initial configurations and calculated the percentage of final configurations it produced that were in the correct state.

Although there are many techniques that focus on generating game levels, few allow the user to specify desired physical properties. Ashlock et al. [5] developed an approach using GA that generates maze-like levels and allows users to specify path properties. Unfortunately Ashlock et al.'s method can take up to 20 minutes to produce a single level and therefore our work aims at finding CA rules that were capable of generating similar layouts in real-time. CAs have proved to be efficient enough to generate game levels in real-time, but all research in this area uses manually designed rules. Manually designing CA rules becomes less feasible as the desired layout becomes more complex, such as requiring a specific number of rooms with a specific average size. Previous attempts to obtain more complex CA rules have utilized GA to evolve rule tables, but this technique has not been applied to level layout generation for video games

3   Evolutionary Algorithm

Our system evolves CA rules that generate mazes with a similar visual style to that of a "goal layout". The intuition behind this approach is that generated layouts that exhibit the same characteristics of the goal layout would be similar in appearance, so that they would provide a consistent style to a game. To represent the visual style of the goal layout, the following set of target attributes are employed:

1. Number of traversable areas.
2. Size of the largest traversable area.
3. Average size of all traversable areas.
4. Number of passageways.
5. Average length of passageways.
6. Number of rooms.
7. Average size of rooms.
8. Number of cul-de-sacs.
9. Number of dead-ends.

Fig. 1 illustrates these attributes for clarity. **Fig. 1**(a) is a colour-coded image to illustrate what defines a room, passageway, dead-end, and cul-de-sac. **Fig. 1**(b) is a colour-coded image to illustrate what defines a traversable area.

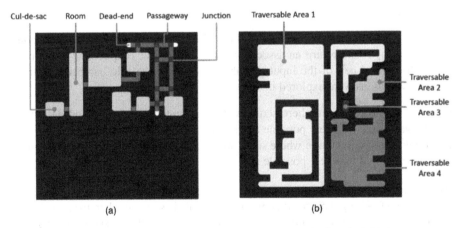

Fig. 1. (a): Colour coded layout that identifies rooms (green), dead-ends (white), passageways (red), junctions (blue), and cul-de-sacs (rooms with a single entry point). (b): Colour coded layout to identify traversable areas.

The rest of this section details the approach, first describing the genetic representations that were explored, then the idea of flavours, and finally, the details of the GA and how the evolved CA rules are evaluated, as illustrated in **Fig. 2**.

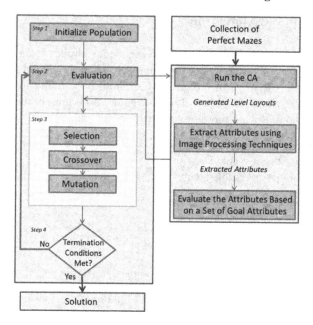

Fig. 2. The genetic algorithm, including CA rule evaluation

3.1   Representation

We evolve CA rule tables, which are lookup tables that take a neighbourhood configuration as input and return an associated output state. The output state is the new state of the central cell of the input neighbourhood once the rule has been applied. Two representations were explored in this study.

1. A *direct* representation where states were represented as integers and an output state was stored for every possible neighbourhood configuration.
10. An *indirect* representation where states were represented as integers and an output state was stored for every possible sum of neighbourhood state values.

Direct Representation. The direct rule table representation stores an output state for every possible CA neighbourhood configuration. This is suitable when using a simple CA where each cell in the configuration can be set to one of two states and a small neighbourhood is used. However, when using more complex CA, the range of possible neighbourhood configurations quickly expands, making this representation infeasible. A CA's complexity is affected by two attributes, S, the number of states each cell in the CA configuration can be set to, and N, the size of the neighbourhood used when running the CA. The number of neighbourhood configurations is thus S^N, and since this representation stores an output state for each neighbourhood configuration the number of output states to be stored in the rule table is also equal to S^N.

This representation stores output states in a list of integers. Each output state is stored in lexicographic order of its corresponding neighbourhood state for lookup purposes. **Fig. 3** demonstrates the lookup process on a simple 1D grid of cells where a small neighbourhood of three cells is used to look up the new state of the neighbourhood's central cell.

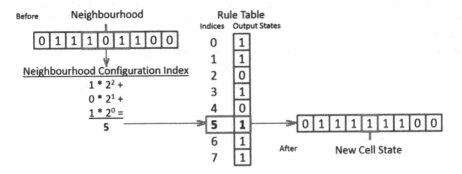

Fig. 3. Applying a direct rule table to a single cell in a 1D CA. A neighbourhood is selected and an index is calculated. The index is used to look up the output state.

Indirect Representation. The indirect representation stores an output state for every possible sum of neighbourhood values, making its storage requirement $(S-1)*N+1$ output states, which is much smaller than the direct representations. This allowed the exploration of more complex CA, which was not possible with the direct representation.

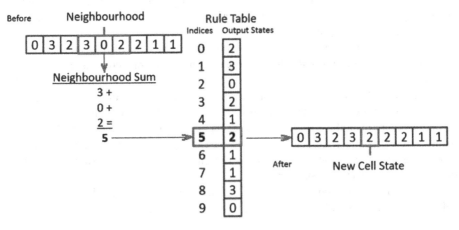

Fig. 4. Applying an indirect rule table to a single cell in a 1D CA. A neighbourhood is selected and its neighbourhood sum is calculated. The sum is used as an index to look up the output state.

This representation stores output states in a list of integers. The cell states of the input neighbourhood are summed together to produce the index of the output state. **Fig. 4** demonstrates this on a simple 1D grid of cells where a small neighbourhood of three cells is used to look up the new state of the neighbourhood's central cell.

3.2   Flavours

Our motivation for experimenting with CA that use more than two cell states is the possibility of more complex behaviour, resulting in more interesting layouts. To enable this, flavours [7] were used. The idea of flavours is that a single cell state can be divided into a set of sub-states (or *flavours*) for CA rule application. This allows the CA to use any number of cell states to explore the effects of more complex rules, while each cell in the resulting final configuration will map to one of two parent states (traversable or not traversable).

3.3   The Genetic Algorithm

We now describe the steps in the genetic algorithm.

Initialize the Population. Chromosomes (rule tables) are initialized by setting each of their genes (output states) to a random value in the range of $[0, S-1]$ where S is the number of cell states. Once all the chromosomes have been initialized, they are evaluated.

Evaluating Fitness. The fitness function evaluates each CA by applying it to a collection of 100 initial maze configurations. The initial mazes were generated using the recursive backtracker algorithm [13], a stack-based graph traversal algorithm that is commonly used to generate, and solve, perfect mazes (mazes where only one path exists between any two points within them).

The CA is applied to each initial configuration, and the cells of final configurations are mapped to one of two states, traversable or non-traversable, creating a set of level layouts.

Next, for each generated layout an attribute similarity measure (ASM) is calculated, by comparing the generated layout's attributes to the desired attributes. To perform this comparison the attributes of the generated layout must be extracted. A novel method of extracting a layout's attributes was developed, using a series of image processing techniques including erosion, outlining, and region growing [14]. The details are omitted here for space reasons.

Once each attribute value is extracted from the generated level layout, its ASM value is calculated using Equation (1).

$$ASM = \sum_{i=1}^{9} \left(1.0 - \frac{|da_i - aa_i|}{ma_i}\right)^3 \times aw_i \tag{1}$$

The value of the attribute extracted from the layout is denoted as *aa*, while *ma* is the maximum possible value that the attribute could be. For example, the maximum value for traversable area size is equal to the total number of cells contained in the grid, as it is impossible to have a traversable area that is larger. *da* and *aw* are the desired value of the attribute and its associated weighting factor. The sum of weighting factors across all attributes is 1.0, ensuring that the ASM is a value in the range of [0.0, 1.0]. Finally, the fitness value is the average of the ASM values from each of the generated level layouts.

Generating the New Population. Candidates are selected, based on their fitness, to mutate and crossover to form a new population. We mostly used De Jong's [15] GA parameter settings, with the exception of the mutation probability. The GA employs an elitist selection where the top five candidates from the original population are carried over to the new population unchanged in each generation. Tournament selection with a group size of five is used to select parents for the rest of the new population. Mutation and crossover are then applied. Crossover is applied first, with a probability of *pc*. If crossover is to be performed, a second candidate is selected. Single-point crossover is then applied to the two selected chromosomes resulting in two new chromosomes. Uniform mutation is applied to the selected chromosome or, if crossover is applied, the two new chromosomes. The mutation operator replaces genes (output states) with random values in the range of [0, S-1]. A mutation probability of one over the length of the chromosome [16] is used instead due to the varying chromosome sizes. The processes of selection, crossover, and mutation are repeated in an iterative manner until a population of new candidates has been created.

Termination Conditions. After the new population has been created, the GA repeats the previous two steps until a termination condition has been met. There are three termination conditions:

- Convergence: This is achieved when the fitness value of the best candidate in the population has not increased by a value of 0.0001 over 100 consecutive generations.
- Maximum fitness value: When a candidate achieves the maximum fitness value of 1.0 it cannot improve further and therefore the GA terminates early.
- Maximum number of generations: If the previous two conditions are not met by the 5000th generation, then the GA will terminate.

4   Experiments

A series of experiments was conducted to explore the effectiveness of this approach when using different sets of attributes, and to determine which parameters had a significant effect on the layouts generated by the evolved CAs. The series of experiments was divided into four sets, with each set consisting of twelve individual experiments. Each set of experiments was run using five different sets of eight attribute values (derived from five goal layouts, shown in **Table 1**), with the aim of finding CA rules capable of generating level layouts with different styles. These five sets of attributes are labelled *G1*, *G2*, *G3*, and *G4*.

Table 1. Target attribute values and weights. Key: AAC = Accessible Area Count, AAS = Average Area Size, LAS = Largest Area Size, PC = Passage Count, APL = Average Passage Length, RC = Room Count, ARS = Average Room Size, DEC = Dead-End Count, CC = Cul-de-sac Count.

	Goal layouts						
	G1		*G2*		*G3*		*G4*
Attributes	target	wt	target	wt	target	wt	target	wt
AAC	1	0.27	1	0.27	4	0.27	2	0.27
AAS	-	0.0	-	0.0	90	0.18	64.5	0.18
LAS	89	0.18	214	0.18	-	0.0	-	0.0
PC	7	0.09	18	0.09	11	0.09	3	0.09
APL	5.71	0.09	7.11	0.09	4.9	0.09	1	0.09
RC	4	0.09	9	0.09	5	0.09	5	0.09
ARS	10.75	0.09	8.88	0.09	58.6	0.09	24.4	0.09
DEC	6	0.09	6	0.09	13	0.09	4	0.09
CC	0	0.09	1	0.09	1	0.09	2	0.09

The chosen attribute weighting values were decided manually. The number of traversable areas was given the highest weighting because a layout may contain the exact target values for every other attribute, but still be unusable if the area is divided into an undesired number of disconnected sections. The largest and average area size are the second most important attributes, as the amount of traversable space made the most significant contribution to the layout's visual similarity to its goal layout. The remaining attributes were given equal weighting values.

Three sets of experiments were carried out and were labelled Set 1, Set 2, and Set 3. These sets had different combinations of parameters as listed below and in **Table 2**:

- The **chromosome representation** that was used: direct (*D*) or indirect (*I*).
- The **neighbourhood radius**: size of the Moore neighbourhood used (1 or 2).

Table 2. Parameter values for each set of experiments

	Experiment Sets		
Parameters	*Set 1*	*Set 2*	*Set 3*
Chromosome Representation	*D*	*I*	*I*
Neighbourhood Radius	1	1	2

The combination of direct representation with neighbourhood radius 2 is not used as the genome size would be impractical. For each set, 12 experiments were run, using different combinations of two parameters as listed below:

- The **number of cell states**: 2, 3, or 4 cell states.
- The **number of CA iterations**: the number of times a CA was applied to each pre-generated maze to generate a level layout (1, 5, 10, or 25).

For each experiment, the genetic algorithm was run 30 times, and the best fitness in the last generation was recorded.

5   Results and Discussion

In **Fig. 5** we show interaction plots for Set 1 (direct representation; neighbourhood size of 1). For goal layouts 1, 3 and 4, the best combination is 5 iterations using 3 or 4 cell states. Goal layout 2 does best with the simplest combination of 1 iteration and 2 cell states.

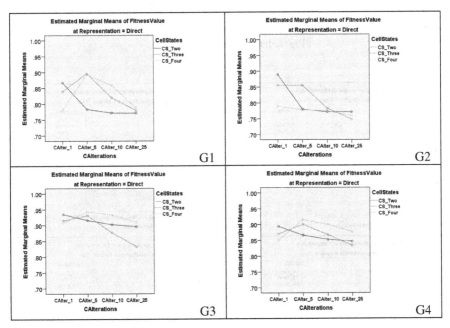

Fig. 5. Interaction plots for Set 1. There is one plot for each goal layout, labeled G1 to G4.

In comparison, as seen in **Fig. 6**, with Set 2 (indirect representation; neighbourhood size of 1), 5 iterations is still best, but number of cell states has little effect. Comparing across the two figures, the best fitness values for each goal layout are similar in Sets 1 and 2.

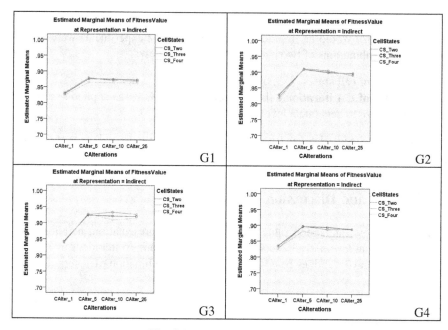

Fig. 6. Interaction plots for Set 2

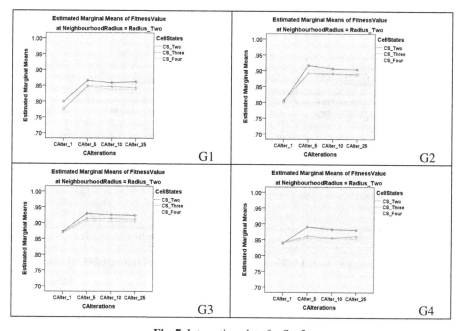

Fig. 7. Interaction plots for Set 3

Finally, in **Fig. 7**, with Set 3 (indirect representation; neighbourhood size of 2), we see that 5 iterations with 2 cell states gives the best results. Overall fitness values are slightly lower than those in Sets 1 and 2.

Based on these results, it is possible to evolve CA rule tables that produce layouts with desired attributes. However, visual inspection of the generated mazes shows that it is not trivial to design attributes that capture the desired visual style.

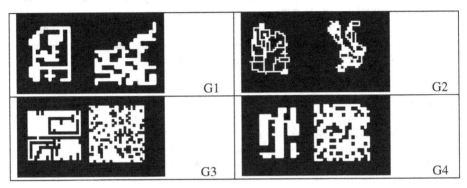

Fig. 8. Examples of generated mazes (on the right) along with their goal layouts (on their left). They all used 5 iterations, and neighbourhood size of 1. For goal layouts 1,3 and 4, the direct representation was used. For goal layouts 1 and 2, 3 states were used, while 4 states were used for goal layouts 3 and 4.

In **Fig. 8**, for example, we show some examples of generated mazes. Each example is the 5th highest fitness out of the 100 generated for that goal layout with the specified parameters, after post-processing to select the largest connected component. Goal layout 1 seems to have been characterised quite well, with small rectangular rooms joined by horizontal and vertical passages. But for layout 2, the generated layout has rooms with rounded or diagonal sides. In goal layouts 3 and 4, which have large open areas, the generated layouts tend to contain isolated impassable cells inside large rooms (the small black dots in the white areas). The attributes that we designed do not discourage that kind of feature.

Generally, the idea of using more states with "flavours" seems more useful than larger neighbourhoods as a way to provide for complexity in the representation. There is therefore less need for the indirect representation (although that could be useful if a large number of flavours was used).

6   Conclusions

Content creation is an important process in the development of video games, but also one of the most time consuming. The time required to generate content can be shortened with PCG; the process of algorithmically generating media content.

This paper introduces a new approach to the procedural generation of maze-like game level layouts by evolving CA. The approach uses a GA to evolve CA rules which, when applied to a maze configuration, produce level layouts with desired maze-like properties. CAs were evaluated by applying them to a collection of initial configurations and comparing the generated layouts' attributes, which were obtained via novel method of extraction, to the attributes of a goal layout.

The advantages of this technique is that once a CA rule set has been evolved, it can quickly generate varying instances of maze-like level layouts with similar properties in real time. Other evolutionary techniques evolve level layouts directly, which is a slow process that takes time to generate each instance.

The results from this research show that it is possible evolve rule tables that are capable of generating level layouts with desired attributes and visual styles. However, the selection of a suitable set of attributes requires some care.

References

1. Toy, M., Wichmann, G.: Rogue. In: Cross-platform (ed.) Epyx (1997)
2. Team, N.D.: NetHack. In: Cross-platform (ed.) NetHack Dev Team (1987)
3. Koeneke, R.T., Moria, J.: In: Cross-platform (ed.). Abandonware (1994)
4. North, B.: Diablo. In: Cross-platform (ed.). Blizzard Entertainment (1996)
5. Ashlock, D., Lee, C., McGuinness, C.: Search-Based Procedural Generation of Maze-Like Levels. IEEE Transactions on Computational Intelligence and AI in Games 3, 260–273 (2011)
6. Johnson, L., Yannakakis, G.N., Togelius, J.: Cellular automata for real-time generation of infinite cave levels. In: Proceedings of the 2010 Workshop on Procedural Content Generation in Games, pp. 1–4. ACM, Monterey (2010)
7. Ashlock, D.: Cellular Automata Flavours, personal communication. (2013)
8. Joris, D.: Adventures in level design: generating missions and spaces for action adventure games. In: Proceedings of the 2010 Workshop on Procedural Content Generation in Games. ACM, Monterey (2010)
9. van der Linden, R.L., Bidarra, R.: Designing procedurally generated levels. In: Proc. 2nd Workshop Artif. Intell. Game Design Process, pp. 41–47 (2013)
10. Hartsook, K., Zook, A., Das, S., Riedl, M.O.: Toward supporting stories with procedurally generated game worlds. In: 2011 IEEE Conference on Computational Intelligence and Games, CIG (2011)
11. Wolfram, S.: Statistical mechanics of cellular automata. Reviews of Modern Physics 601–644 (1983)
12. Mitchell, M., Crutchfield, J.P., Das, R.: Evolving cellular automata with genetic algorithms: A review of recent work. In: Proceedings of the First International Conference on Evolutionary Computation and Its Applications (EvCA 1996) (1996)
13. http://weblog.jamisbuck.org/2011/1/17/maze-generation-aldous-broder-algorithm
14. Russ, J.C.: The Image Processing Handbook, pp. 777 (2006)
15. De Jong, K.A.: An analysis of the behavior of a class of genetic adaptive systems, pp. 266. University of Michigan (1975)
16. Bäch, T.: Optimal Mutation Rates in Genetic Search. In: 5th International Conference on Genetic Algorithms, pp. 2–8. Morgan Kaufmann Publishers Inc. (1993)

Point of Regard from Eye Velocity
in Stereoscopic Virtual Environments
Based on Intersections of Hypothesis Surfaces

Jake Fountain and Stephan K. Chalup

Newcastle Robotics Laboratory, School of Electrical Engineering & Computer Science
The University of Newcastle, University Drive, Callaghan, NSW 2308, Australia
jake.fountain@uon.edu.au, stephan.chalup@newcastle.edu.au

Abstract. A new method is proposed for utilising scene information for stereo eye tracking in stereoscopic 3D virtual environments. The approach aims to improve gaze tracking accuracy and reduce the required user engagement with eye tracking calibration procedures. The approach derives absolute Point of Regard (POR) from the angular velocity of the eyes without user engaged calibration of drift. The method involves reduction of a hypothesis set for the 3D POR via a process of transformation during saccades and intersection with scene geometry during fixations. A basic implementation of this concept has been demonstrated in simulation using the depth buffer of the scene and a particle representation for the hypothesis set. Future research directions will focus on optimisation of the algorithm and improved utilisation of scene information. The technique shows promise in improving gaze tracking techniques in general, including relative paradigms such as electrooculography.

Keywords: stereo eye tracking, 3D virtual environments, automatic calibration, particle model, depth buffer.

1 Introduction

The *gaze* of a human eye is defined as the axis in three dimensions along which the field of view is centered. Tracking this information is useful due to the nature of human visual perception. The density profile of perceptive cells on the rear of the eye is not uniform. Thus humans perceive fine detail only within a narrow cone along the gaze [4]. This cone is moved across a scene to extract information and construct a representation of the environment. The point of intersection of the gaze ray with an object in the environment gives information about the user's attention and perception. This 3D location is called the *Point of Regard* (POR).

Gaze tracking is usually performed with pupil/corneal reflection video based oculography (PCRO), where a reflection on the cornea of an infrared illuminator is compared to the center of the pupil [4]. This method relies on the spherical shape of the cornea to obtain a reflection which is invariant under eye rotation,

S.K. Chalup et al. (Eds.): ACALCI 2015, LNAI 8955, pp. 125–141, 2015.

while the pupil depends on the eye's rotational pose. Frequent calibration is required to compensate for environmental changes. For example, lighting changes can result in altered size of the pupil or corneal reflection. The limiting factor of gaze-trackers is their accuracy and need for calibration. Morimoto and Mimica discuss some techniques for avoiding calibration of eye trackers [9]. These techniques typically use additional hardware and models of the head and eyes to reduce the number of calibration steps required to deduce the on-screen 2D POR. For example, one technique entirely avoids calibration by placing infrared illuminators at each corner of the screen [19].

Alternate gaze-tracking techniques, such as the scleral search coil technique [12] and electrooculography (EOG), have fallen into disuse due to the accuracy, convenience and low cost of computer vision techniques like PCRO. However, in particular situations, obsolete techniques can have appealing features. For example, EOG is relevant to head mounted displays due to the potential inclusion of unobtrusive, lightweight electrodes in the facial contact region of the head mounted display. This design paradigm is demonstrated in several examples of EOG utilised for continuous long-term eye tracking for health applications [3],[17]. This is simpler than positioning cameras in a head mounted display. However EOG generally measures eye velocity only, which results in the measured zero position of the eyes drifting noticeably over minutes [18]. Thus, EOG is typically only suitable for measuring relative eye movements.

Within the domain of virtual environments the limited accuracy of gaze tracking leaves many powerful applications infeasible. Rendering detail dependent on retinal acuity [6], [10], [20] and simulating depth of field focal accommodation effects in real time [7] relies on fast, accurate gaze tracking. Of course, less intensive applications also benefit from increased accuracy. For example, the eyes of an avatar can be driven by an eye tracker for communication in virtual environments [15]. Improving the fidelity of eye tracking increases the quality and quantity of information one user can communicate to another through eye movements of an avatar. The initial goal of this research was to allow for the implementation of these applications in consumer level virtual reality. The aim was to create a low cost, lightweight, unobtrusive eye tracking solution for head mounted displays using electrooculography. The proposed technique is the result of attempts to overcome some of the limitations with electrooculography.

1.1 Human Visual Perception and Eye Behaviour

There are two basic types of eye movement which need to be understood in order to model visual attention [4]. *Fixations* are movements where the eye tracks an object. *Saccades* are rapid eye movements which reposition the eye. Human visual perception relies on successive saccades and fixations to observe the environment. Human vision is also stereoscopic and, during normal function, the two eyes converge such that the images of the object of focus align on the foveas. Additionally muscles within the eye distort the lens of the eye to focus light sharply on the retina. The required distortion is dependent on the distance to the source of the light and the eye can only perceive sharp detail within a small depth range at any given time. Thus it is logical to model gaze with a point in 3D space, the POR, at the intersection of the gaze lines from each eye.

The POR moves discontinuously through the environment, displaced by saccades. During a saccade, visual perception is ignored. During fixations, the POR is stationary relative to the object of focus, and this is maintained by a neural feedback loop which stabilises the image on the retina. Assuming normal eye functionality, these observations allow the prediction of the behaviour of the POR.

1.2   Modern Eye Tracking in Virtual Environments

Virtual environments, by their nature, have a rich set of environmental data available at little additional computational cost. Examples include object positions, mesh vertex positions and object velocities. This information can be utilised to improve eye tracking results by assuming the POR behaves as described in Sect. 1.1. This section outlines the latest results in such techniques.

Gaze-to-Object Mapping. The *gaze-to-object mapping* (GTOM) problem involves mapping the measured gaze signal or screen POR to the object of fixation in a virtual scene. GTOM is a simplification of the general POR extraction problem as it assumes that only knowledge of the object of focus is required. This information is sufficient for many purposes, such as attention studies or user interfaces. Simplification in this way has advantages including improved accuracy and greater stability.

Bernhard et al. presents and compares a number of methods for GTOM which utilise the scene's *item buffer* to compute a probability density function which maps each object to its probability of fixation [1]. Bernhard, Stavrakis and Wimmer developed a method for analysing user attention in which an object to visual importance map was learned from participants performing tasks in a monoscopic 3D virtual environment [2]. Importance maps improved GTOM performance for participants even when their own map was trained exclusively on other participant's data. Papenmeier and Huff developed a system for defining dynamic areas of interest for analysing participant attention in non-virtual scenes to exploit the advantages of GTOM [11]. These techniques reflect a use of scene information to improve the quality of gaze tracking results.

Gaze-Driven Object Tracking. Mantiuk et al. proposed a gaze tracking algorithm to predict the POR of a user viewing a 3D virtual environment on a monoscopic screen [8]. The algorithm utilises the information available in the virtual scene to construct a Hidden Markov Model for the POR as a set of potential targets. The targets are distributed uniformly over the scene from the camera's perspective, with smaller visible objects explicitly assigned a target. Each target has an on screen position and velocity. The raw gaze position is filtered for noise and the gaze velocity is computed in real time. Comparison of the position and velocity measurements to the state of each target allowed computation of the probability that a given target was currently being tracked. This obscures the noise present in the raw gaze signal and allows tracking of objects which are smaller than the angular resolution of the system.

The probability of fixation at target i was defined by [8] as

$$P(o_i) := P(p_i \cup v_i) = 1 - P(\bar{p}_i)P(\bar{v}_i) = 1 - (1 - P(p_i))(1 - P(v_i)) \quad (1)$$

where o_i represents the event of fixation on target i and p_i and v_i are the events of gaze position and velocity matching the target. The probability models for $P(p_i)$ and $P(v_i)$ were derived by fitting Bayesian models to experimental data with known ground truth. The resulting models were Gaussian in the distance between the eye screen POR and the target, and exponential in the angular difference between the target's screen velocity vector and the eye's screen velocity vector. The probability of the user changing targets was modelled at a fixed value of 0.05, weighting continued fixation highly to maximise the stability of the gaze. Mantiuk et al. explains that this technique is more stable and accurate than the raw gaze data, as well as other popular fixation modelling techniques. The added stability provides a better platform for visual effects such as gaze reactive depth of field, but the technique introduces a small latency of less than a second. The ideas presented by Mantiuk et al. were key in developing the formulation presented in this paper.

1.3   Research Motivation

The techniques described in Sect. 1.2 use information from a virtual scene and exploit human visual behaviour to improve the performance of gaze tracking systems. The limitation involved with extracting POR from eye velocity is the gradual *baseline drift* of the POR, where the zero position slowly changes. The technique which is presented in this paper was motivated by the possibility of compensating for baseline drift using stereoscopic scene information, avoiding interruption of the user for calibration procedures. The proposed approach applies the ideas about probability from GTOM and Gaze-driven Object Tracking to a more general context of hypotheses which can occupy a continuum of states.

2   Point of Regard from the Intersection of Hypothesis Surfaces

This section details the contribution of the research to stereo gaze modelling. First, the geometry of eye fixation in the virtual scene is explained. The *hypothesis surface* for the POR is defined as a subset of $\mathbb{R}^3$ which represents the possible locations for the POR. It is called a surface because typically it is locally homeomorphic to $\mathbb{R}^2$ due to the nature of human visual perception. The method of intersection of hypothesis surfaces is formalised and a technique for tracking the hypothesis surface over successive intersections is proposed and implemented in simulation. The proposed technique relies on a particle representation of the hypothesis surface with intersections performed by probabilistic comparison to the depth buffer of the scene. The technique assumes that the eyes behave typically: saccadic movement with verged fixation on moving or stationary surfaces.

2.1   Eye Angles and Point of Regard

Define the *head* space with x in the forward direction of the face, y leftward and z upward with the eye positions along the y axis and the origin between the eyes (Fig. 1). The eye positions are defined by the interpupillary distance, d_{ip}, and are hence given by $\{(0, \frac{d_{ip}}{2}, 0), (0, -\frac{d_{ip}}{2}, 0)\}$. The interpupillary distance is available in virtual environments as a rendering parameter. The *eye angles* of a given POR in $\mathbb{R}^3$ are defined as the bearing and elevation of the POR from each eye, $(\theta_l, \phi_l, \theta_r, \phi_r)$ (see Fig. 1).

Each POR corresponds to one configuration of eye angles. However, it is not always true that a set of eye angles will correspond to a POR, since the two rays cast by the eyes will rarely intersect in three dimensions. To overcome this limitation, the point in each line of closest proximity to the other line is computed, yeilding two points of mutual closest proximity. Assuming only a small amount of noise, the average of these two points is used as the POR corresponding to the eye angles (Fig. 1).

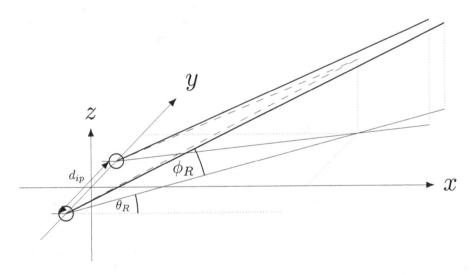

Fig. 1. The head space demonstrating the mapping from four eye angles to 3D Point of Regard (POR). The solid lines represent the gaze rays cast from the eyes based on a tuple of eye angles $(\theta_l, \phi_l, \theta_r, \phi_r)$, with noise present in the z direction. The dashed line represents the estimated gaze, with the POR at the intersection of the lines. The estimated POR is defined as the average of the points of mutual closest approach of the gaze rays.

2.2 Technique Formalisation and Theory

Here a new abstract formalism is presented which defines the technique in terms of sets of points in head space. At each timestep t, there is a set of points in 3D space which are viewable by the user. A user viewing one of these points will rotate their eyes to unite the images of the point on the fovea of each eye. The set $S_t \subseteq \mathbb{R}^3$ of visible points in the scene is called the *visible surface*. A point is in S_t if it is on a viewable surface in the environment and at least one eye can be rotated to focus on the point at timestep t. In a typical polygon-based virtual environment, these points are the set of points on polygons which are not occluded and in the field of view of one or both eyes. In order to track the eyes, a set $\mathcal{X}_t \subseteq \mathbb{R}^3$, called the *hypothesis surface*, models the set of hypotheses for the POR of the user. At $t = 0$, the hypothesis set is initialised to be the visible surface: $\mathcal{X}_0 = S_0$. For $t \geq 1$, the change $u_t = (\Delta\theta_l, \Delta\phi_l, \Delta\theta_r, \Delta\phi_r)_t$ in the eye angles since timestep $t - 1$ is measured and used to update $\mathcal{X}_t$ via the *eye movement transform* $T_t : \mathbb{R}^3 \to \mathbb{R}^3$.

T_t is defined in the following way: for $p \in \mathbb{R}^3$, compute the eye angles $\Psi = (\theta_l^p, \phi_l^p, \theta_r^p, \phi_r^p)$ corresponding to p. Next, update these eye angles with the latest measurement u_t, giving new eye angles $\Psi' = \Psi + u_t$. The result $T_t(p)$ is given by the eye angles to POR transformation of the updated eye angles Ψ', defined in Sect. 2.1 as the midpoint of the closest points of the two eye rays.

Comparison of u_t to an angular velocity threshold $\nu \in \mathbb{R}$ is used to determine if a saccade is being performed. The gaze is saccading if $\|u_t\| > \nu$. If a movement corresponds to a saccade, let $\mathcal{X}_t = T_t(\mathcal{X}_{t-1})$. Otherwise, assume fixation and compute $\mathcal{X}_t$ according to

$$\mathcal{X}_t = T_t(\mathcal{X}_{t-1}) \cap S_t \ . \tag{2}$$

This step is based on the observation that during fixation the correct POR hypothesis must lie on the current visible surface S_t. The resulting hypothesis set at time t is thus

$$\mathcal{X}_t = T_t(T_{t-1}(T_{t-2}(\dots T_1(S_0) \cap S_1 \dots) \cap S_{t-2}) \cap S_{t-1}) \cap S_t \ . \tag{3}$$

Since saccades have a high velocity, the value of ν needs to be tuned based on the noise level in the eye velocity signal. Lower thresholds are typically better because this avoids false positives for fixation where particles can be falsely eliminated. However, since hypotheses are only eliminated during fixation, a low threshold increases the convergence time if signal noise frequently exceeds the threshold. Very low thresholds also tend to ignore smooth pursuits, which are valid fixations.

The proposed iterative reduction diminishes the hypothesis set remarkably quickly, as can be seen by the following argument. Consider the simple case of a static scene with a single plane S_0 perpendicular to the head x axis, some distance from the origin. The scene is static, so $S_t = S_0$ for all $t \geq 0$. For the purpose of argument, assume that each T_t for $t \geq 1$ is a small rotation about the origin of the head space. The first hypothsis set $\mathcal{X}_1 = T_1(S_0) \cap S_0$ is the intersection of two non-parallel planes and is thus a line. If T_2 rotates $\mathcal{X}_1$ about an axis different to the rotation axis of T_1, $\mathcal{X}_2 = T_2(\mathcal{X}_1) \cap S_0$ will contain only a single point, as it is the intersection of a plane and a line. Thus, it takes only two distinguishable eye movements to deduce the POR of the user in this simplified case.

In reality, the transformation T_t is performed in eye angle space and hence it is highly non-linear, especially for larger eye movements and eye movements starting or ending near the edge of the field of view of the eyes. In addition to being rotated, the hypothesis set is actually translated and distorted under each T_t. Figure 2 demonstrates the transformation of a quad under a typical eye movement transform. Note that the image of the quad is non-planar. This actually works in favour of the algorithm, in that the surface intersections become irregular curves. The hypothesis set is reduced faster than with a linear transformation as the sets overlap less. Generally, scene geometry is more complicated than a single plane, and this contributes to reducing the hypothesis set further. Figure 3 shows the first iteration of the algorithm applied to the Stanford Bunny [14] for an eye movement of around $10°$.

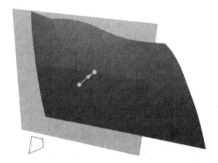

Fig. 2. The non-linearity of the eye movement transformation T_t is demonstrated. The transparent quadrilateral is the only viewable surface in the scene. The Point of Regard (POR) moves between the dots on the viewable quad, inducing a transformation T_t on the hypothesis set. The eye movement was performed by virtual eyes situated at the wire-frame camera's position. The green opaque surface is the image of the quad under the eye movement transformation T_t. Note that the final POR is at the intersection of the plane and the green surface, as expected.

The complication with the proposed approach is in the representation and computation of the set $\mathcal{X}_t$ in real time. Indeed, if these ideas are to be applied to a head mounted display, frame rates of at least 60 frames per second are necessary, and higher is desirable. Performing intersections with complex geometry, as in Fig. 3, has a time complexity depending on the geometry detail in the scene, and can have artifacts for unusual meshes. The solution presented in this paper involves a particle based approach to tracking $\mathcal{X}_t$. The depth buffer of the scene

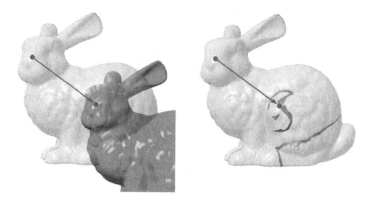

Fig. 3. The first iteration of the hypothesis set algorithm is illustrated by application to a static scene with a more complex object than the quad in Fig. 2, the Stanford Bunny [14]. The hypothesis set $\mathcal{X}_0$ is initialised as the visible surface S_0 of the bunny. The eyes rotate such that the Point of Regard (POR) moves discontinuously between two surface points indicated in blue. The first image shows the intermediate step, with $T_1(S_0)$ opaque and green with the scene transparent. The second image displays the resultant hypothesis set $\mathcal{X}_1 = T_1(S_0) \cap S_0$ opaque and green. $\mathcal{X}_1$ can be seen to contain the final POR.

is used to filter the particles. This approach is independent of scene geometry and is scalable through choice of parameters such as the number of particles.

2.3   Particle Deduction Filter

This section presents a method for tracking the hypothesis set $\mathcal{X}_t$ of the POR using a set of particles which are updated and re-sampled in a similar way to that of a particle filter. In a particle filter, a population of particles models a probability distribution in the state space of a system [16, p. 96-100]. Every iteration, particles are weighted based on how well they agree with measurements of the real system. Finally, each particle is re-drawn from a multinomial distribution with probability proportional to its most recent weight. The key difference with the deduction filter, presented here, is that the particles accumulate weight over time. Each weight update multiplies by the probability $p(\mathbf{x} \in S_t)$ that the particle $\mathbf{x} \in \mathbb{R}$ is in the current visible surface S_t. Thus the accumulated weight w_t represents the probability of the particle $\mathbf{x}$ being in the hypothesis set $\mathcal{X}_t$ at time t (because $p(u \in \bigcap_i U_i) = \prod_i p(u \in U_i)$). The particles which have vanishing weight (less than some $\varepsilon > 0$) are called *insignificant* particles and they are re-sampled from the set of *significant* particles (particles with weight greater than or equal to ε). In this way, the accumulated particles model the successive intersection of hypothesis set with the visible surface.

Given a set of particles with weights $\mathcal{X}_{t-1} = \{(\mathbf{x}_{t-1}, w_{t-1})\} \subseteq \mathbb{R}^3 \times \mathbb{R}$, the visible surface information $S_t \subseteq \mathbb{R}^3$ and a control vector for the eye's movement $u_t \in \mathbb{R}^4$, the set of particles $\mathcal{X}_t$ in the next timestep is given by Alg. 1. The state space of the particles is $\mathbb{R}^3$, with each particle $\mathbf{x}_t$ representing the POR of the eyes in head space.

A sample of $p(\mathbf{x}_t|u_t, \mathbf{x}_{t-1})$ in Alg. 1 is computed as the result of transforming $\mathbf{x}_{t-1}$ into eye angles (see Sect. 2.1), adding the measured change in eye angles u_t, with some Gaussian noise, and transforming back to Cartesian head coordinates. This is an application of the transform T_t with additive noise sampled per particle. Note that the noise is generated as two independent Gaussian distributions, yielding $\Delta\theta$ and $\Delta\phi$. The sample for each variable is then added to the eye angles so that the left and right eye noise is correlated:

$$\Psi' = \Psi + u_t + (\Delta\theta, \Delta\phi, \Delta\theta, \Delta\phi) \qquad (4)$$

This approach improved the stability of the particles compared to using four uncorrelated Gaussian distributions, and avoided the computational time complexity of sampling a four-dimensional Gaussian distribution modelled with a covariance matrix.

Algorithm 1: Deductive Particle Filter

Data: $\mathcal{X}_{t-1} = \{(\mathbf{x}_{t-1}, w_{t-1})\}, u_t, S_t, \varepsilon, N, M$
Result: $\mathcal{X}_t = \{(\mathbf{x}_t, w_t)\}$ such that $M \geq |\mathcal{X}_t| \geq N$
// Initialise result
$\mathcal{X}_t \leftarrow \emptyset$;
for $(\mathbf{x}_{t-1}, w_{t-1}) \in \mathcal{X}_{t-1}$ **do**
    // Update each particle and weight
    sample $\mathbf{x} \leftarrow p(\mathbf{x}_t|u_t, \mathbf{x}_{t-1})$;
    $w \leftarrow w_{t-1} \cdot p(\mathbf{x} \in S_t)$;
    if $w \geq \varepsilon$ **then**
        // Record significant particles
        $\mathcal{X}_t \leftarrow \mathcal{X}_t \cup \{(\mathbf{x}, w)\}$;
    end
end
// If no significant particles
if $\mathcal{X}_t = \emptyset$ **then**
    // Reset hypothesis set
    $\mathcal{X}_t \leftarrow$ sampled set of M particles from S_t (with $w = 1$);
end
// Resample insignificant particles
$\overline{\mathcal{X}}_t \leftarrow \emptyset$;
for $\max\{0, N - |\mathcal{X}_t|\}$ *iterations* **do**
    draw $(\mathbf{x}, w)$ from $\mathcal{X}_t$ with probability $\propto w$;
    $\overline{\mathcal{X}}_t \leftarrow \overline{\mathcal{X}}_t \cup \{(\mathbf{x}, 1)\}$;
end
$\mathcal{X}_t \leftarrow \mathcal{X}_t \cup \overline{\mathcal{X}}_t$;
return $\mathcal{X}_t$;

The weight of each particle is updated using the depth buffer from one of the eye's viewports. First, $\mathbf{x}_t$ is projected onto the image of one eye's view to yield pixel coordinates (y, z). The depth buffer value in metres at this screen location, $d(y, z)$, is used to compute the weight with a Gaussian model:

$$p(\mathbf{x} \in S_t) = \exp\left(-|d(y, z) - x_1|^2/\sigma^2\right) \in [0, 1] \tag{5}$$

where x_1 is the depth component of the POR in the head space, which corresponds to depth in the eye space, as the coordinate systems are translations of one another. The depth buffer is already available because the scene requires it to model occlusion. Particles which agree with the surface will have $p(\mathbf{x} \in S_t)$ close to 1. It is important to ignore non-fixated eye movements, so $p(\mathbf{x} \in S_t)$ is set to a value of 1 whenever the eye velocity exceeds the threshold ν discussed in Sect. 2.2, indicating a saccade.

If the state where there are no significant particles is reached, the hypothesis set is reset to be the current visible surface S_t. This is performed by sampling M screen points and re-projecting into the head space with the current depth buffer. Additionally, sample points are placed at the center of each mesh object which is viewable. In the case that $M > N$, the next step will discard any insignificant particles rather than re-sampling them, so that at least N remain. Thus a large number of hypotheses can be examined in the initial state, but they are discarded with eye movement to improve the compute time.

3   Simulation Results

An interactive virtual scene was constructed with several moving and stationary objects. Each object was a screen aligned billboard of radius 0.2 m with position between 1 m and 5 m from the head. Each object orbited the point $(3, 0, 0)$ with different velocity to give the scene some motion. A virtual pair of eyes with $d_{ip} = 64$ mm was simulated with interactive selection of objects for the eyes to view. The camera was placed between the eyes, at $(0, 0, 0)$, facing toward positive x in the head space, for visualisation of the scene. The background of the scene was a plane parallel to the yz-plane at a distance of $x = 10$ m. The virtual eyes produce eye angles corresponding to fixation on the centre of the surface of the selected object. An artificial measurement signal from the virtual eyes was simulated using the model given in Sect. 2.1 with optional independent Gaussian noise in each of the four eye angles. The eye angle signal was then differentiated numerically to give the eye velocity control signal u_t.

Figure 4 demonstrates the filter converging to track the simulated eye position for a single example run. No noise was included in this run to demonstrate real time ($>$60Hz) tracking. Particles are initialised uniformly across the screen with additional particles at the center of each object. The number of particles here was initialised at $M = 250$ and the minimum particle population was $N = 25$. The eyes track the target under the large cross-hair and the particles are seen to each move according to the rotation of the eyes. Particles are eliminated during the tracking period of the initial target as they diverge from agreement with the depth buffer. Note that while the hypotheses are all drawn at the same size on screen, they are in fact points in 3D space. Simply by tracking a single target for around 5 seconds, the hypotheses converge and the POR is deduced using only eye velocity measurements. After convergence, the system is able to track the POR in real time (at over 60 frames per second or 15.6ms for Alg. 1) provided drift is not too severe.

The system was found to compensate for slow drifts in the baseline of the eye position and noise in the velocity signal through the step of sampling $p(\mathbf{x}_t|u_t, \mathbf{x}_{t-1})$. Define the *maximum drift compensation* of the algorithm to be the rate of drift per second in any single eye angle which can be accommodated by the algorithm without losing tracking. There is a trade-off between POR stability, the maximum noise compensation, the maximum drift compensation and the number of particles N. A wider $p(\mathbf{x}_t|u_t, \mathbf{x}_{t-1})$ distribution results in higher maximum drift compensation and noise compensation. However this reduces the stability of the POR result unless more particles are introduced to accurately represent the distribution through sampling.

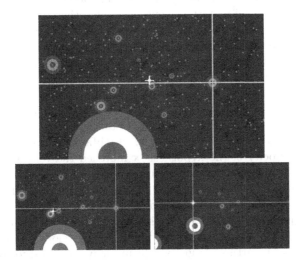

Fig. 4. Images of the eye gaze simulation with particles in grey and the tracking result (the weighted average of all particles) as a white cross-hair. The concentric disks are the dynamic targets upon which the virtual eyes can fixate. The true POR is indicated by the intersection of the lines, and it tracks a single target for the duration of the demonstration. Initially, the particles are spread uniformly across the screen with additional particles for each object (*top*). After 0.5 seconds, the particles have shifted from their initial positions under the eye angle transform, with many being discarded as unlikely hypotheses by comparison to the depth buffer (*bottom left*). After 5 seconds, convergence is achieved and only one cluster of 25 particles remains (*bottom right*). After convergence, tracking remains accurate and runs in real time.

4   Discussion

Noisy signals can be compensated by increasing the number of particles and the width of the $p(\mathbf{x}_t|u_t, \mathbf{x}_{t-1})$ distribution. However, this reduces the tracking refresh rate which is highly important in virtual environments. Thus the simulation demonstrates that the technique is feasible for use in real time POR deduction, provided some basic optimisations can be made. As this section discusses, there are numerous avenues to achieve this optimisation. This section also discusses potential extensions of the method to improve utility and accuracy. The limitations of the technique are explained and the implications for performance on real world data are explored. Potential solutions to these problems are proposed.

4.1   Potential Extensions

Parameter selection for the particle deduction algorithm includes choosing: the minimum and initial particle populations N and M, the variances for the Gaussian $p(\mathbf{x}_t|u_t, \mathbf{x}_{t-1})$ and $p(\mathbf{x} \in S_t)$ distributions and the thresholds ε and ν. ε was chosen through tuning for good performance, and generally any small value worked well (e.g. $\varepsilon = 10^{-6}$). With the exception of ε, these variables were somewhat time consuming to tune to produce stable convergence in real time. This difficulty is the result of the trade off between accuracy and refresh rate. Offline meta-optimisation of these parameters using a training set of data with ground truth could achieve better results and reduce the effort required by the designer in tuning.

An additional factor of hypothesis elimination was examined during development, inspired by the approach of Mantiuk et al. [8] detailed in Sect. 1.2. This involved including a factor in $p(\mathbf{x} \in S_t)$ which obtained a value of 1 whenever the head space velocity of the hypothesis $\mathbf{x}$ matched the velocity buffer of the surface behind it, and decreased continuously to zero with increasing discrepancy. This additional factor increased the rate of hypothesis elimination, but for the simulated environment which was tested (Fig. 4) the performance was not noticeably better. Thus, it was decided that velocity filtering is not valuable enough to justify the overhead of computing the velocity values and extra probability term per particle. Velocity filtering may be useful for other scenes, particularly those with small fast objects.

Typically eye measurement devices do not output eye velocity directly, but rather they rely on a user-dependent model which is calibrated before use. For example, in pupil/corneal eye tracking, the system measures the difference between the position of the rotationally-variant pupil and the rotationally-invariant corneal reflection. In electrooculography, a voltage is measured which is a one-to-one function of eye angles. Given a set of parameters Γ defining a map from a measured quantity to eye angles or eye angle velocity, the proposed algorithm can be generalised to include Γ in each particle. By modelling the noise in Γ and initialising a set of particles with different Γ at each initialisation position, it is theoretically possible to automatically calibrate the measurement model and even adjust to slow changes in the measurement model over time. In practice, this approach suffers from the curse of dimensionality with regard to the number of particles required to sample Γ-space and screen-space sufficiently. A large number of particles is already required to sample the screen-space and Γ can be high dimensional, depending on the system. However, with optimisation and further development, it may be possible to avoid user engaged calibration for the measurement model in addition to the drift.

4.2   Issues and Potential Solutions

Modelling eye measurement noise with the particle deduction filter with a fixed number of particles has proven difficult. Most notably, if a small amount of Gaussian noise is added to the eye angle signal, any fixation hypotheses past a certain depth (dependent on the number of particles) diverge from the surface despite no actual eye movement. This divergence is caused by the asymmetrical kite shaped distribution corresponding to uncorrelated eye noise (Fig. 5). Compensation for this effect is improved by modelling the update probability distribution $p(\mathbf{x}_t|u_t, \mathbf{x}_{t-1})$ as four independent Gaussian distributions in $\theta_l, \phi_l, \theta_r, \phi_r$ rather than just two in θ, ϕ. However, this requires another increase in particle population N so that the asymmetrically-shaped distribution is represented accurately. Otherwise the particles will drift and diverge. In particular, single particles, which exist particularly often at initialisation, become very unstable and tend to be eliminated too quickly. Filtering the eye signal with a low pass filter would help reduce this problem. Another potential solution to the instability issue is extracting fixations and saccades using a technique similar to Velocity-Threshold Identification (I-VT). I-VT methods were first proposed by Erkelens and Vogels [5] and a useful discussion of the technique is presented in a comparative study by Salvucci and Goldberg [13]. The technique involves classifying each POR measurement as either saccade or fixation based on a velocity threshold. Consecutive fixation points are then consolidated to a single point representing that fixation, removing the inherent noise.

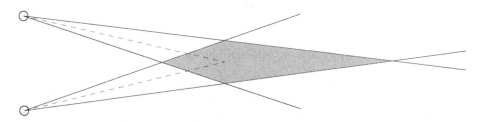

Fig. 5. The Point of Regard (POR) distribution for independent uniformly sampled eye angle noise in the horizontal plane. The shaded region represents the possible values of the measured POR given the true POR is at the intersection of the dashed lines, but the measurement has uniform noise in the bearing angles. The distribution is a kite with a large tail which grows with increasing distance from the eyes. This demonstrates how small noise in eye angle measurements results in large noise in the POR.

The central limitation of the particle approach is in its time complexity, which is $O(n)$ in the number of particles $n = |\mathcal{X}_t|$ at each time step t. This results in very slow eye tracking refresh rate, especially initially. The simulation demonstrated that the system handles noisy signals provided N is large enough and if the POR is close to the origin. More particles allows the POR to be tracked further from the origin. Thus there is a trade-off between tracking quality and refresh rate, and hence optimisation will be vital to achieving a useful eye tracking algorithm. Two potential solutions to the optimisation problem are asynchronous updates and GPU parallelisation.

Asynchronous updating involves allowing the render thread to take priority, with eye tracking performed with spare compute time. In the main simulation thread, the eye angle velocity would be integrated numerically at the native frequency of the simulation to approximate the eye change since the last update began. In a separate thread, the algorithm would run at low priority and lower frequency. At the beginning of each tracking update, the current depth buffer and the current running integrated velocity is recorded and the update performed based on that data. This allows the eye position to be tracked at a different frequency than the scene update rate. An additional low cost prediction update of the resultant eye POR using just the latest integrated velocity could be performed at the end of each complete update to reduce tracking latency.

GPU parallelisation involves performing the particle computations on hardware dedicated to parallel computation. This is convenient because a GPU would already be available to render the scene. The algorithm is suited to parallel computing due to the independent iteration steps including particle transformation, weight calculation and re-sampling steps. The only non-parallel step of computation is the calculation of normalised weights for re-sampling the multinomial distribution.

The approach of using the depth buffer to filter the set of particles is advantageous because the depth buffer is readily available in 3D virtual environments with little additional computation costs. However, it assumes that the closest surface point to the particle is directly behind it, which is often a bad approximation because the depth buffer is generally discontinuous. The best approach would compute the distance of the particle to the closest surface in the scene, but this is computationally expensive as comparisons must be made to many surfaces in the scene for each particle. A compromise could involve filtering the depth buffer, for example, with a Gaussian blur filter, to produce a continuous approximation of depth.

Sampling screen-space for the initial hypothesis set is also made difficult by the raw depth buffer approach. Ideally, every pixel on screen would be re-projected and included in the initial hypothesis set, but this is computationally infeasible at high resolutions. The sparse uniform sampling works poorly because particles initialised near the correct POR may have a depth which is significantly different to that of the POR due to the discontinuity of the depth buffer.

4.3   Comparison to Existing Techniques

The technique proposed in this paper generalises the ideas present in the 2D method formulated by Mantiuk et al. [8] as discussed in Sect. 1.2. The particle based hypothesis set technique, formulated here, uses a comparatively general concept for the POR hypotheses, treating them as particles which move with the eyes, rather than scene dependent states which can be occupied by the eyes. The hypothesis set technique uses the stereoscopic eye data to extract more information about the user's POR and critically relies on the 3D nature of the environment and POR. This comes at the cost of computational complexity, especially with respect to the particle deduction filter.

Gaze-to-object mapping (GTOM, Sect. 1.2) restricts the problem definition to that of determining the object of focus. This allows for exploitation of object properties to predict fixation probability for a discrete set of visual screen regions defined by the object screen projections. The hypothesis set technique allows for a continuous probability density function for the POR to be approximated by a set of particles, allowing trivial generalisation to many troublesome scenes which are not handled well by GTOM solutions. For example, Bernhard et al. note that large surfaces which constitute a single object, such as a terrain mesh, would need additional partitioning structure to resolve eye fixation at different points on the surface using GTOM [1]. While not a significant issue for GTOM, the hypothesis set technique handles this situation natively.

4.4   Future Development

Future research will focus on increasing the speed of the algorithm through parallel GPU computation and algorithmic optimisation. Particle filtering will be improved by exploring alternative sources of environmental knowledge, other than the depth buffer. Alternative models for $\mathcal{X}_t$ will be investigated, as particles have some disadvantages. The ultimate goal is to create a working prototype mounted in a head mounted display. It is hoped that the algorithm will allow the creation of low cost, lightweight, unobtrusive electrode based eye tracking in head mounted displays using electrooculography, while improving the accuracy of other techniques. Another avenue of research would involve applying the proposed algorithm to eye tracking in real environments through use of sensors, such as a depth camera, to acquire environmental information.

5   Conclusion

A novel approach has been presented for determining the Point of Regard (POR) of a user viewing a virtual environment only through measurements of relative eye movement. The process of hypothesis set deduction was formalised and a potential solution for the implementation of the technique was trialled in simulation. This solution involved modelling the hypothesis set with particles and updating them in an algorithm similar to a typical Bayesian particle filter. These results indicate that the approach has the potential to increase the accuracy of existing absolute eye measurement techniques such as pupil-corneal reflection, while renewing the feasibility of techniques which measure relative eye movement, such as electrooculography. The main difficulty with the proposed approach is representing noisy measurement signals with a small number of particles. Further research will involve more sophisticated use of scene information and optimisation of the algorithm to improve refresh rates for large numbers of particles.

Acknowledgements. This work was completed during the year of 2014, as part of Jake Fountain's Bachelor of Computer Science (Honours) at the University of Newcastle. Jake Fountain was responsible for the research, conception and implementation of the ideas as well as writing of the paper. Stephan Chalup provided guidance and feedback on preparation of the manuscript. Thank you to Josiah Walker, Trent Houliston and the other students and academics at the University of Newcastle's Robotics Laboratory for many useful and inspiring discussions. Also, thank you to Luke Treacey and Melinda Duncan for their excellent work correcting spelling and grammar.

References

1. Bernhard, M., Stavrakis, E., Hecher, M., Wimmer, M.: Gaze-to-object mapping during visual search in 3d virtual environments. ACM Transactions on Applied Perception 11(3), 14:1–14:17 (Aug 2014)
2. Bernhard, M., Stavrakis, E., Wimmer, M.: An empirical pipeline to derive gaze prediction heuristics for 3d action games. ACM Transactions on Applied Perception 8(1), 4:1–4:30 (2010)
3. Bulling, A., Roggen, D., Tröster, G.: Wearable eog goggles: Seamless sensing and context-awareness in everyday environments. Journal of Ambient Intelligence and Smart Environments 1(2), 157–171 (2009)
4. Duchowski, A.: Eye Tracking Methodology: Theory and Practice, 2nd edn. Springer-Verlag London Limited (2007)
5. Erkelens, C.J., Vogels, I.M.: The initial direction and landing position of saccades. In: Groner, R., d'Ydewalle, G. (eds.) Eye Movement Research Mechanisms, Processes, and Applications, Studies in Visual Information Processing, vol. 6, pp. 133–144. North-Holland (1995)
6. Levoy, M., Whitaker, R.: Gaze-directed volume rendering. SIGGRAPH Computer Graphics 24(2), 217–223 (1990)
7. Mantiuk, R., Bazyluk, B., Tomaszewska, A.: Gaze-dependent depth-of-field effect rendering in virtual environments. In: Ma, M., Fradinho Oliveira, M., Madeiras Pereira, J. (eds.) SGDA 2011. LNCS, vol. 6944, pp. 1–12. Springer, Heidelberg (2011)
8. Mantiuk, R., Bazyluk, B., Mantiuk, R.K.: Gaze-driven object tracking for real time rendering. Computer Graphics Forum 32(2), 163–173 (2013)
9. Morimoto, C.H., Mimica, M.R.: Eye gaze tracking techniques for interactive applications. Computer Vision and Image Understanding 98(1), 4–24 (2005), special Issue on Eye Detection and Tracking

10. Ohshima, T., Yamamoto, H., Tamura, H.: Gaze-directed adaptive rendering for interacting with virtual space. In: Proceedings of the IEEE 1996 Virtual Reality Annual International Symposium, pp. 103–110, 267 (March 1996)
11. Papenmeier, F., Huff, M.: Dynaoi: A tool for matching eye-movement data with dynamic areas of interest in animations and movies. Behavior Research Methods 42(1), 179–187 (2010)
12. Robinson, D.: A method of measuring eye movement using a scleral search coil in a magnetic field. IEEE Transactions on Bio-medical Electronics 10(4), 137–145 (1963)
13. Salvucci, D.D., Goldberg, J.H.: Identifying fixations and saccades in eye-tracking protocols. In: Proceedings of the 2000 Symposium on Eye Tracking Research & Applications, pp. 71–78. ACM Press, New York (2000)
14. Stanford Computer Graphics Laboratory: The stanford bunny (1994), http://graphics.stanford.edu/data/3Dscanrep/#bunny (accessed September 1, 2014)
15. Steptoe, W., Oyekoya, O., Murgia, A., Wolff, R., Rae, J., Guimaraes, E., Roberts, D., Steed, A.: Eye tracking for avatar eye gaze control during object-focused multiparty interaction in immersive collaborative virtual environments. In: 2009 IEEE Virtual Reality Conference, pp. 83–90 (March 2009)
16. Thrun, S., Burgard, W., Fox, D.: Probabilistic Robotics. The MIT Press, Cambridge (2005)
17. Vidal, M., Turner, J., Bulling, A., Gellersen, H.: Wearable eye tracking for mental health monitoring. Computer Communications 35(11), 1306–1311 (2012)
18. Yagi, T.: Eye-gaze interfaces using electro-oculography (eog). In: Proceedings of the 2010 Workshop on Eye Gaze in Intelligent Human Machine Interaction, pp. 28–32. ACM, New York (2010)
19. Yoo, D.H., Kim, J.H., Lee, B.R., Chung, M.J.: Non-contact eye gaze tracking system by mapping of corneal reflections. In: Fifth IEEE International Conference on Automatic Face and Gesture Recognition, pp. 94–99 (May 2002)
20. Zha, H., Makimoto, Y., Hasegawa, T.: Dynamic gaze-controlled levels of detail of polygonal objects in 3-d environment modeling. In: Second International Conference on 3-D Digital Imaging and Modeling, pp. 321–330 (1999)

Formalising Believability and Building Believable Virtual Agents

Anton Bogdanovych, Tomas Trescak, and Simeon Simoff

MARCS Institute, School of Computing, Engineering and Mathematics
University of Western Sydney
Penrith NSW 2751, Australia
{a.bogdanovych,t.trescak,s.simoff}@uws.edu.au

Abstract. Believability is an important characteristic of intelligent virtual agents, however, very few attempts have been made to define and formalise it. This paper provides a formal analysis of believability, focused on diverse aspects of believability of the agents and the virtual environment they populate, approaching the problem from the perspective of the relationship between the agents and the environment. The paper also presents a computational believability framework built around this formalism, featuring virtual agents able to reason about their environment – the virtual world in which they are embedded, interpret the interaction capabilities of other participants, own goals and the current state of the environment, as well as to include these elements back into interactions. As a proof of concept we have developed a case study, a prototype of an ancient Sumerian city (Uruk), where believable virtual agents simulate the daily life of its citizens.

Keywords: virtual agents, believability, virtual worlds, simulations, games.

1 Introduction

The term "believability" is frequently used in various disciplines, but is very loosely defined. Believability is an essential requirement of modern video games and distributed virtual worlds, hence the shift of research focus to believable agents. As suggested by [19], "the need for modern computer games is not unbeatable AI, but believable AI". In terms of formalisation the concept of believability resembles similarity with intelligence – it is hard to define and formalise. As the result we are witnessing conflicting definitions in existing works and lack of working formalisms for both concepts.

We argue that believability is a more tangible concept than intelligence. Hence, we seek to better define the concept of believability by constructing a formal model of perceived believability. This paper attempts to summarise existing believability research to tackle those issues. As a result, we present a definition of believability, expand its key components and explain those in a formal way. We extend the fundamental work of [20], which we consider to be the most comprehensive attempt to analyse the concept of believability, by integrating recent research findings and formalising the concept of believability. Based on the resulting formalisation we have developed a technological framework that integrates all the identified believability features through contemporary AI techniques. To illustrate the functionality of this framework, as well as to provide

S.K. Chalup et al. (Eds.): ACALCI 2015, LNAI 8955, pp. 142–156, 2015.

an environment for evaluation of believability, we have developed a prototype of the ancient city of Uruk, which is populated with believable virtual agents simulating the daily life of ancient Sumerians.

The remainder of the paper is structured as follows. In Section 2 we analyse existing works and definitions of believability to identify its key components and define the concept. Section 3 presents the definition and formal model of believability. In Section 4 it is shown how the key components of this formalisation can be implemented. Finally, Section 6 concludes the presentation and discusses future work avenues.

2   The Notion of Believability

The notion of believability originates in the field of animation and theatre. A classical work of Walt Disney Studios on animated characters – the "illusion of life" [30] elaborates on the requirements for believability. Though these characters are not real they continue to impact the audiences' imagination to accept them as believable. Believability and realism have been differentiated by [21] and [8]. According to the authors, a believable character is not necessarily a real character, but *must be real in the context of its environment*. Believable agents and believable characters are differentiated in that believable agents are both computer based and interactive [20].

Contemporary AI uses the term "believability" in relation to engaging life-like systems. Reactivity, interactivity and appropriate decision making are the common characteristics of believability for autonomous agents [26]. These characteristics can also be extended with respect to the environment within which they operate.

2.1   Definitions of Believability

In [21] a believable character is defined as the one who seems life-like, whose actions make sense, who allows you to suspend disbelief. An extended definition of believable characters is given by [20]. Here a character is also considered believable if it allows the audience to suspend their disbelief, but what is also important is a convincing portrayal of the personality of this character. Another definition that emphasises personality and focuses on agents rather than characters is presented in [18]. Here believability is defined as the extent to which the users interacting with the agent come to believe that they are observing a sentient being with its own beliefs, desires and personality. A contemporary definition that is used in relation to video games states that believability of a virtual agent is associated with giving the illusion of being controlled by a human [28].

2.2   Exploring Believability Features

We start with listing the key features of believable agents, specified in [20], as follows:

- **Personality**: Personality infuses everything a character does, from the way they talk and move to the way they think. What makes characters interesting are their unique ways of doing things. Personality is about the unique and not the general.
- **Emotion**: Characters exhibit their own emotions and respond to the emotions of others in personality-specific ways.

- **Self-motivation** - Characters don't just react to the activity of others. They have their own internal drives and desires, which they pursue regardless of whether or not others are interacting with them.
- **Change**: Characters change with time, in a way consistent with their personality.
- **Social Relationships**: Characters engage in detailed interactions with others in a manner consistent with their relationship. In turn, these relationships change as a result of the interaction.
- **Consistency of Expression**: Every character or agent has many avenues of expression depending on the medium in which it is expressed, for example an actor has facial expression and colour, body posture, movement, voice intonation, etc. To be believable at every moment all of those avenues of expression must work together to convey the unified message that is appropriate for the personality, feelings, situation, thinking, and other behaviours of the character. Breaking this consistency, even for a moment, causes the suspension of disbelief to be lost.
- **Illusion of Life**: This is a collection of requirements such as: pursuing multiple, simultaneous goals and actions, having broad capabilities (e.g. movement, perception, memory, language), and reacting quickly to stimuli in the environment.

The illusion of life is expanded by [20] in terms of: (i) Appearance of goals; (ii) Concurrent pursuit of goals and Parallel action; (iii) Reactive and Responsive; (iv) Situated; Resource bounded – Body and Mind; (v) Existing in a Social Context; (vi) Broadly Capable; (vii) Well integrated (Capabilities and Behaviours).

Emotional State vs Emotions. Recent work on the use of emotions in achieving believability [24] suggests the use of *emotional state* of the agent rather than emotions in general, and considers the consistency of agent behaviour across similar situations, coherency and variability of agent behaviour to be significant components of believability.

The Role of Environment. Loyall's work [20] is mainly focused on believable agents themselves and not that much on the environment in which they operate. While situatedness and integrity are listed as important features of illusion of life, little has been said about how believability is being achieved.

The importance of agent integration with the environment is highlighted in [14]. In this work the emphasis is put on the awareness of the agents about their environment, own state in it, other participants and own interaction capabilities. The authors provide evidence that those features significantly improve the overall believability of the agents.

Verbal Behavior. Two significant components that are missing in [20] are verbal and non-verbal behaviours.

The majority of works on believable verbal behaviour are associated with scripted dialogues or chatter bots like Eliza [33] and ALICE [32] Technically, chatter bots parse the user input and use keyword pointing, pattern matching and corpus based text retrieval to provide the most suitable answer from their "knowledge base" [10], trying to keep a human engaged in a textual or auditory conversation.

Non-verbal Behaviour. Humans complement verbal communication with non-verbal cues, like facial expressions, body language and gaze.

Facial expressions can be used to complement the word stream through expressing emotions. These emotional expressions have cross-cultural boundaries, but, generally, existing work deals with a list of emotional expressions: (happy, sad, fear, anger, disgust, agreement, disagreement and surprise) as presented in [6].

Gestures allow humans to interact in a lively manner and are an important believability factor. Gesture selection and their correct execution may increase the expressivity of the conversation [11]. Believable gestures are related to gestures selection being correctly aligned with the flow of conversation and the generation of realistic movements of agent's upper limbs during the conversation [11].

Gaze helps to convey the cognitive state of a participant or synchronise a conversation as explained in [17]. Various gaze models like avert, examining the current task, gaze at visitors, etc. were simulated by [12]. They measured the believability of the agent based on factors like satisfaction, engaging, natural eye, head movements and mental load among others; and this study showed the significant improvements in communication between humans and virtual agents. Lance in [29] contributed to investigation of believable gaze by developing a hybrid approach combining head posture, torso posture and movement velocity of these body parts with gaze shift.

Appearance. In addition to previously mentioned features from [20], we add *unique and believable appearance* as an important feature of believable agents. Appearance plays an important part in agent believability. Kelley states that human behaviour towards others is shaped depending on differences in first impressions such that people who have favourable impressions of someone tend to interact more with that person than others having unfavourable impressions [16]. First impressions are, therefore, an important basis for whether humans will build relations with others and find their interactions believable [2]. Another important line of research that connects appearance and believability investigates the phenomenon of uncanny valley [22], which states that there is a strong relationship connecting human-likeness and believability, but the correspondence between these is no linear and at some stage as the characters become more human like their believability starts to drop rather than increase.

3   Formalising Believability

Based on the analysis of existing works on believability we try to isolate the key components of believability and define a believable virtual agent as follows.

Definition: *Believable virtual agent* is an autonomous software agent situated in a *virtual environment* that is life-like in its appearance and behaviour, with a clearly defined personality and distinct emotional state, is driven by internal goals and beliefs, consistent in its behaviour, is capable of interacting with its environment and other participants, is aware of its surroundings and capable of changing over time.

Consequently, believability is formalised as follows:

$$\beta = \langle A^T, P^T, E^T, L, SR, \Upsilon, \delta, Aw \rangle \tag{1}$$

Here β is the believability of a virtual agent, A^T are the agent's appearance features, P^T is the agent's personality, E^T is to the emotional state of the agent, L corresponds to liveness, Aw represents agent's awareness, which we define later, SR - social relationship, Υ - represents the consistency constraints and δ - is the change function.

Appearance. To formalise the appearance, we assume the existence of parametric avatars of agents, which are defined by their visual features, e.g. height, belly size, head size [31]. Each of these parameters has a value in the interval [0,1] where extremes are labeled by the specific state of the visual feature. For example a visual feature height, has a label for the minimum "short" and for the maximum "tall". The appearance a of an individual can then be represented by the following vector:

$$A^T = [\alpha_1 \ldots \alpha_n], \forall i \in [1, n] : \alpha_i \in [0, 1] \tag{2}$$

Personality. While formalising the personality we consider the assumption of [9] that a personality has n dimensions, where each dimension is represented by a value in the interval $[0, 1]$. A value of 0 corresponds to an absence of the dimension in the personality; a value of 1 corresponds to a maximum presence of the dimension in the personality. The personality p of an individual can then be represented by the following vector:

$$P^T = [\beta_1 \ldots \beta_n], \forall i \in [1, n] : \beta_i \in [0, 1] \tag{3}$$

Emotional State. The emotional state (E^T) is defined following [9] as an m-dimensional vector, where all m emotion intensities are represented by a value in the interval [0,1]. A value of 0 corresponds to an absence of the emotion; a value of 1 corresponds to a maximum intensity of the emotion. This vector, given as

$$E^T = \begin{cases} [\beta_1 \ldots \beta_m], \forall i \in [1,m] : \beta_i \in [0,1], \text{if } t > 0 \\ 0, \text{if } t = 0 \end{cases} \tag{4}$$

Liveness. Liveness is agent's ability to express the illusion of life. It incorporates the illusion of life features from [20], plus verbal and non-verbal behaviour, as follows:

$$L = < IL, V_b, NV_b > \tag{5}$$

Here IL is a vector responsible for illusion of life, V_b represents verbal behaviour and NV_b represents non-verbal behaviour.

Illusion of Life. We adapt Loyall's [20] specification of "Illusion of life", uniting "situatedness" and "integration" into the concept of immersion in 3D virtual environments:

$$IL = < Goals, Concurrency, Immersion,$$
$$ResourceLimitation, SocialContext \qquad (6)$$
$$BroadCapability, Reactivity, Proactiveness >$$

Consistency. Consistency across the personality of an agent and other believability characteristics is ensured in our formalisation by the set of consistency constraints (Υ). We formalise those constraints as a penalty function that is 0, if emotional state of the agent and liveness features are inconsistent with the agent's personality and 1 otherwise.

$$\Upsilon : P^T \times L \times E^T \rightarrow \left\{ \begin{array}{l} 1 - \text{if consistent} \\ 0 - \text{if inconsistent} \end{array} \right. \qquad (7)$$

These constraints must ensure the consistency of the agent behaviour over the entire range of its believability features:

$$\forall p_j \in P^T, \forall l_h \in L, \forall e_g \in E^T : \Upsilon(p_j, l_h, e_g) = 1 \qquad (8)$$

Change. Change (δ) is basically a learning function that updates a believability instance given another instance and the environment state:

$$\delta : EnvState \times \beta_i \rightarrow \beta'_i \qquad (9)$$

Social Relationship. Social relationship, formally speaking, can be represented by a function, which reflects on how the current role being assumed by an agent relates to the roles of other agents. This function results in a numeric value in a range [0...1]. Here 0 represents no relationship between two roles and 1 - is the highest degree of relation.

$$\forall r_i, r_k \in Roles : SR = f(r_i, r_k) \in [0 \dots 1] \qquad (10)$$

Awareness Believability. Awareness is essential part of human conversational behaviour. In a conversation we are aware of where we are (environment awareness), who we are (self-awareness) and generally how the interaction is progressing (interaction awareness). Therefore, awareness is an essential component of the believability of embodied conversational behaviour, which we label as "awareness believability". Further, we develop each of the subcomponents of awareness believability.

So we can formalise awareness believability as follows:

$$Aw = < EA, SA, IA > \qquad (11)$$

Environment Awareness. As suggested by [14], the key features of environment awareness include the positions of objects and avatars in the environment, how these evolve with time and the direction vectors associated with avatars. Thus, environment awareness is formalised as follows:

$$EA = \{Objects, Avatars, Time\} \tag{12}$$

Here *EA* is the set of components of environment awareness and includes the objects in the environment, other avatars representing agents and human participants with respect to the current time.

Self-awareness. Knowing own context and state within the environment (being self aware) is essential for a virtual agent to interact believably [8]. The formalisation of self-awareness proposed by [14] is as follows:

$$SA = \{G, P, B, Sc, St, ObjUsed, Role, Gest\} \tag{13}$$

Here *SA* represents the set of components of self-awareness and includes the local goals of the agent (G), its current plans (P) and beliefs (B), current scene where the agent participates (Sc), its state within this scene (St), objects used by the agent ($ObjUsed$), the role it plays ($Role$) and the gestures being executed ($Gest$).

Interaction-Awareness. Human behaviour in interactions is a result of the mix of being rational, informed, impulsive, and the ability to influence others and cope with the influences from others. All these nuances impact the richness of human interactions, hence, must be taken into account when considering the believability of interactions between virtual agents and humans. Interaction-awareness is defined as the state of an agent who is "able to perceive important structural and/or dynamic aspects of an interaction that it observes or that it is itself engaged in" [7]. The components of the interaction-awareness model as outlined in [14] are presented below.

$$IA = \{AV_{vis}, AV_{sc}, Act, Obj, State, Pos, Or\} \tag{14}$$

Here IA represents the set of components included in our interaction awareness model. AV_{vis} corresponds to the set of currently visible avatars. The AV_{sc} is a set of all avatars within the scene where the agent participates in a given moment. Act represents the set of actions each of the agents in the current scene is able to perform given its state. Obj refers to the list of objects the avatar can use. $State$ is the state of the avatar in the world. Pos is the position of the agent in the virtual world and Or is agent's orientation vector in the virtual world space.

4   Implementation: The I^2B Framework

Now that we have a formalisation of believability, next we present our attempt of developing a computational framework implementing this believability formalism. This framework supports the implementation of believable virtual agents for virtual worlds and game engines and is labelled I^2B (Interactive, Intelligent and Believable). It is important to mention that here we do not attempt to develop a comprehensive general-purpose believability framework, but rather present a suggestion on how the aforementioned formalism can be practically implemented (with no claims for this implementation to be the most optimal, unique or comprehensive). The aim of this section is simply to show that the formalism from the previous section is practically useful and can act as a guide for building believable agents. Next we show how each of the components of the above believability formalism can be practically implemented using standard methods and best practices from the literature that were adjusted to fit the formalised models.

4.1 Appearance

Both Second Life and Unity, the platforms we have selected for testing our implementation, offer mechanisms to represent virtual agents as avatars and define them through a set of parametric features, e.g. (height, head size, arm length, skin colour, etc.). This way of modelling avatars is consistent with the aforementioned formalism.

4.2 Personality and Emotional State

One of the most popular modern personality models used in computational psychology is OCEAN (or "The Big Five") model proposed in [15]. We rely on this model in our framework. This model defines the following five personality traits: {Openness, Consciousness, Extroversion, Agreeableness and Neuroticism}. For modelling the emotional state we rely on the well known OCC emotional model proposed in [23] and with computational implementation proposed in [1]. In order for agents to be able to select an appropriate action reflective of its emotional reaction to the state of the environment that is most relevant for their personality, such action has to be annotated by the following *personality facets* [13]: *temptation, gregariousness, assertiveness, excitement, familiarity, straightforwardness, altruism, compliance, modesty* and *correctness*. Using values of personality facets, the agent selects an action that provides the highest utility for its personality type [1] [13]. Thus, personality (P^T) and the emotional state (E^T) are implemented as an array of variables, where each variable represents a personality feature or an emotional state feature correspondingly.

4.3 Liveness

The implementation of various features of Liveness (L) is based on Second Life[1] and Unity 3D technology[2] and the adaptation of a number of contemporary AI techniques.

Goal Generation. A critical aspect in the illusion of life (IL) is to make an agent show that it has certain goals, which it can pursue in a concurrent fashion, as well as change them and prioritise in a reactive and proactive manner. We have developed and

---

[1] http://secondlife.com
[2] http://unity3d.com

integrated all these features with Unity and Second Life [31]. Agent goal generation is based on agent *motivation*. In the current model, we support physiological motivation where agents proactively try to fulfil their physiological needs, such as hunger, thirst or fatigue. As part of our future works we want agents to consider other motivations, such as safety or belonging (social realisation). Furthermore, our model implements the BDI approach [25], allowing for all the standard features of agent-oriented programming offering C# classes for agents, events, plans, beliefs, goals and supporting the message communication, plan selection on receipt of an event, priority planning, etc. Programmers of virtual agents can express beliefs and desires of their agents, decide on the types of events they react to and design the plans to handle those events.

Planning. Every agent in our system relies on a number of plans to satisfy its goals. A plan is a set of instructions, triggered in response to some event. Those events arise as a result of a human- or agent-controlled avatar sending a text command or as a result of an environment state change. The I^2B framework supports static planning - when the entire plan is prescribed by a programmer and is executed by the agent without variation; and dynamic planning, when the agent can sense its current state in the environment and can react to environment changes re-evaluating its current plan. Rather than having a complete recipe for every situation the agent can encounter - the agent is simply given the list of possible actions and has to find a way of combining those to reach its goals. This search is done using a classical depth-first search algorithm [27], in which a path between the current state and the goal state is found by evaluating all available actions and analysing their pre-conditions and post-conditions.

Obstacle Avoidance and Locomotion. In order to believably immerse into its virtual environment and to support the illusion of life while interacting with its environment, the agent must be able to move around without being stuck at an obstacle. This required the implementation of obstacle avoidance techniques. Unity 3D (Pro) offers agent obstacle avoidance based on A^* algorithm. For Second Life, we have also implemented obstacle avoidance adapting the Artificial Potential Fields (see [4] for more details).

Object Use. An important aspect of believability is the use objects in the environment (i.e. grabbing a spear, jumping on a boat). We have developed a designated library that provides a set of classes allowing agents to identify an object in the virtual world, attach it to the default attachment point, play a certain animation (i.e. rowing) associated with a given object, wear an object that is a piece of clothing, detach the piece of clothing, drop an object to the ground and detach the object and hide it in the avatar's inventory.

Non-verbal Behaviour. Each agent is supplied with a list of possible gestures. Depending on the current emotional state an agent can select a certain gesture and play the corresponding animation. I^2B agents are also supplied with a programming solution dealing with idle gaze behaviour. When the agents are moving around, their gaze is not fixed. The gaze focus keeps changing by our attention-based model. The agent shifts its gaze between objects and avatars depending on the level of its interest in those.

The increase and decay of the agent's interest in the surrounding objects will determine the shift in the gaze focus.

Verbal Behaviour. The verbal behaviour of the I^2B agents is currently limited to exchanging text messages with other agents and text chats with humans. For chatting with humans I^2B agents employ the ALICE chat engine [32] based on the AIML language. Each agent uses a number of AIML files that represent what can be seen as a common sense database. Additionally, every agent is supplied by personalised AIML files that define its personality and the data relevant for its role within the virtual society.

4.4 Social Relationships

The Virtual Institutions [3] technology manages the social interactions and social relationships of the I^2B agents. The approach taken in Virtual Institutions is to "program" the environment first, in terms of the roles of the agents, their presence, possible scenes, the role flow of the agents between these scenes, interaction protocols of every scene, etc (see [3] for more details on this process). With the help of the underlying Virtual Institution I^2B agents can also understand which social roles are being played by other agents or humans, and change their roles over time. Based on this information they can engage into believable social interactions and build social relationships. An agent's personality and the emotional state are impacted by social interactions with others.

4.5 Consistency

Virtual Institutions manage the set of rules (social norms) for all participants in the given virtual environment, subject to their roles, hence they manage the consistency (Υ) of the agent behaviour. The institutional formalisation helps an I^2B agent to assign context to own actions and actions of other participants, thus being able to make the corresponding adjustments to its emotional state, personality and liveness.

4.6 Change

The I^2B technology supports the change (δ) through imitation learning. The agents can be trained to respond to certain situations in a desired manner. They can learn at multiple levels of abstraction as described in [5]. The Virtual Institution structures the learning process and provides the context for learning. Through imitation the agents can learn new plans for various goals. Such plans are represented as recursive-arc graphs (similar to recursive decision trees) with probabilities being assigned to the arcs of the graph as the training continues. We have also created a method for training the I^2B agents to perform different verbal behaviour in various situations. Our method of modifying the AIML rules and assigning context to those is described in [14].

4.7 Awareness

Virtual Institution is essential in enabling the environment-, self- and interaction-awareness of the I^2B agents. The institution helps the agent to understand which scene it is currently in, what is the current state of the scene, how other participants can change this state, etc. In combination with the ability to sense the surrounding objects and understand their types through annotations created by designers, the agents can include references to those objects in conversations with humans and into their decision making. The details on integrating these features are presented in [14].

5   Case Study: The City of Uruk 3000 B.C.

As a case study we have used the I^2B framework for building a virtual reality simulation of the ancient City of Uruk in the Second Life and Unity 3D, based on the results of archaeological excavations and under supervision of subject matter experts. While in Second Life we were able to run a maximum of 15 agents, in Unity 3D we have created a population with hundreds of agents that simulate the behaviour of its ancient citizens[3]. Figure 1 shows the overview of the city of Uruk.

Fig. 1. Overview of the city of Uruk

The agents populating this city show a slice of the Uruk society among which are fishermen families, priest, king and professional workers. All agents are supplied with a number of internal goals and plans to reach those. For some simplistic activities, like fishing it was more efficient to utilise static planning, while for others, like spear making and pot making we utilised dynamic planning, so that the agents can better adjust to environment changes and interact with one another to resolve problems. The agent appearance was generated automatically using approaches from [31]. Figure 2 shows some selected agents performing their activities in Uruk.

To give an example of the complexity of agent actions, consider the case of the pot maker (Koko Karsin). When there are no pending goals, the agent explores the city by choosing a random path through city streets. When it recognises the need for social

---

[3] A video illustrating the key aspects of Uruk agents can be found at:
https://www.youtube.com/watch?v=ZY_04YY4YRo

Fig. 2. Selected Agents in Uruk

interaction - it seeks for an interaction partner, approaches it and engages in a conversation. Meanwhile, the agent's hunger, thirst and fatigue levels are raising, possibly passing the threshold value, when the agent generates the goals: "hungry", "thirsty" or "tired". This tells the agent that it has to perform a specific action, such as feed, drink or rest. From its knowledge base the agent can read all its possible actions and then use them to dynamically find a plan that leads to the goal. Koko Karsin is only allowed to rest after finishing work (which is making a clay pot). Thus, its plan is: Rested = Add Water, Make Clay, Make Pot, Rest. To show the dynamic nature of planning - the water pot is deleted after every 3 pots made. So, by attempting to perform Add Water the agent approaches the location where the water pot is supposed to be, will sense that there is no pot, will fail the current plan, update the environment state to NoWater and will create the new plan that will also have the Get Water action before Add Water.

All agents can sense their environment. For example, they can detect danger (i.e. a donkey cart moving close to them and will often try to run away from it) or detect a high ranked person (the King) at close proximity and praise him. They can also perform various group activities. One of those activities is a prayer. The prayer is announced by the city priest as a goal with very high priority. Using our priority planning mechanism, when such an event is received – the agents are capable of dropping their current activity and start running towards the temple and then perform a prayer ritual. They have a number of plans, each for handling a different type of situation. Each plan has a different associated priority, which makes it possible for the agent to decide that the prayer is more important than an exploratory walk or a chat with a friend.

The users can interact with the agents via chat facilities. User commands are given the highest priority, followed by the pray request from the priest. Next comes praising the king (the agent will fall face down when the king is at close proximity). Finishing work and resting are the normal priority plans. Finally, the low priority is allocated with the exploratory walk and the social chat with other agents.

For chat responses to human users the agents rely on the set of AIML rules. Those rules can be modified via imitation by authorised subject matter experts. To illustrate the awareness believability, in their conversations the agents can refer to certain objects in the city and provide relevant explanations, can explain why are they doing things in a certain way, relate to their state in various scenes or make references to current or future possible actions of other agents[4].

6   Conclusion and Future Work

We have analysed existing literature in relation to believability of virtual agents. Based on this analysis we have produced a revised definition of believability and a formal model. With the help of this formal model we have implemented a believability framework that can be used for simulating believable virtual agents. This framework was tested by developing a virtual reality simulation of an ancient Sumerian city, where virtual agents believably simulate the daily life of its ancient citizens.

The resulting formalisation of believability that was developed here is an early work that needs further development and extensive evaluation. Future work will include further investigation of believability features and advancing the formalisation. In order for the developed believability model to be scientifically sound, we plan to conduct a comprehensive set of evaluation rounds, where the significance and correct implementation of each of the identified believability features is tested in isolation to determine that it does, in fact, correlate with improving the perception of agents being more believable with this feature being implemented.

References

1. Bartneck, C.: Integrating the OCC model of emotions in embodied characters. In: Workshop on Virtual Conversational Characters. Citeseer (2002)
2. Bergmann, K., Eyssel, F., Kopp, S.: A second chance to make a first impression? How appearance and nonverbal behavior affect perceived warmth and competence of virtual agents over time. In: Nakano, Y., Neff, M., Paiva, A., Walker, M. (eds.) IVA 2012. LNCS, vol. 7502, pp. 126–138. Springer, Heidelberg (2012)
3. Bogdanovych, A.: Virtual Institutions. Ph.D. thesis, UTS, Sydney, Australia (2007)
4. Bogdanovych, A., Rodriguez-Aguilar, J.A., Simoff, S., Cohen, A.: Authentic Interactive Reenactment of Cultural Heritage with 3D Virtual Worlds and Artificial Intelligence. Applied Artificial Intelligence 24(6), 617–647 (2010)
5. Bogdanovych, A., Simoff, S.J., Esteva, M.: Virtual institutions: Normative environments facilitating imitation learning in virtual agents. In: Prendinger, H., Lester, J.C., Ishizuka, M. (eds.) IVA 2008. LNCS (LNAI), vol. 5208, pp. 456–464. Springer, Heidelberg (2008)

---

[4] A video showing awareness believability aspects of our framework can be found at: http://www.youtube.com/watch?v=VAnoeupxo9c

6. Cunningham, D.W., Kleiner, M., Wallraven, C., Bülthoff, H.H.: Manipulating video sequences to determine the components of conversational facial expressions. ACM Trans. Appl. Percept. 2(3), 251–269 (2005)
7. Dautenhahn, K., Ogden, B., Quick, T.: From embodied to socially embedded agents- implications for interaction-aware robots (2003)
8. Doyle, P.: Believability through context using "knowledge in the world" to create intelligent characters. In: AAMAS 2002: Proceedings of the First International Joint Conference on Autonomous Agents and Multiagent Systems, pp. 342–349. ACM, New York (2002)
9. Egges, A., Kshirsagar, S., Magnenat-Thalmann, N.: A model for personality and emotion simulation. In: Knowledge-Based Intelligent Information & Engineering Systems (KES 2003), pp. 453–461 (2003)
10. Gandhe, S., Traum, D.: Creating spoken dialogue characters from corpora without annotations. In: Proceedings of Interspeech 2007, pp. 2201–2204 (2007)
11. Hartmann, B., Mancini, M., Pelachaud, C.: Implementing expressive gesture synthesis for embodied conversational agents. In: Gesture Workshop, pp. 188–199 (2005)
12. Heylen, D.K.J., van Es, I., Nijholt, A., van Dijk, E.M.A.G.: Controlling the gaze of conversational agents. In: van Kuppevelt, J., Dybkjaer, L., Bernsen, N.O. (eds.) Natural, Intelligent and Effective Interaction in Multimodal Dialogue Systems, pp. 245–262. Kluwer Academic Publishers (2005)
13. Howard, P.J., Howard, J.M.: The big five quickstart: An introduction to the five-factor model of personality for human resource professionals (1995)
14. Ijaz, K., Bogdanovych, A., Simoff, S.: Enhancing the believability of embodied conversational agents through environment-, self- and interaction-awareness. In: Reynolds, M. (ed.) Australasian Computer Science Conference (ACSC 2011). CRPIT, vol. 113, pp. 107–116. ACS, Perth (2011)
15. John, O.P., Donahue, E., Kentle, R.: The 'big five'. Factor Taxonomy: Dimensions of Personality in the Natural Language and in Questionnaires. In: Pervin, L.A., John, O.P. (eds.) Handbook of Personality: Theory and Research, pp. 66–100 (1990)
16. Kelley, H.H.: The Warm-Cold Variable in first impressions of Persons. Journal of Personality 18(4), 431–439 (1950)
17. Lee, J., Marsella, S.C., Traum, D.R., Gratch, J., Lance, B.: The rickel gaze model: A window on the mind of a virtual human. In: Pelachaud, C., Martin, J.-C., André, E., Chollet, G., Karpouzis, K., Pelé, D. (eds.) IVA 2007. LNCS (LNAI), vol. 4722, pp. 296–303. Springer, Heidelberg (2007)
18. Lester, J.C., Stone, B.A.: Increasing believability in animated pedagogical agents. In: Proceedings of the First International conference on Autonomous Agents, AGENTS 1997, pp. 16–21. ACM, New York (1997)
19. Livingstone, D.: Turing's test and believable AI in games. Computer Entertainment 4(1), 6 (2006)
20. Loyall, A.B.: Believable agents: building interactive personalities. Ph.D. thesis, Computer Science Department, Pittsburgh, PA, USA (1997)
21. Mateas, M.: An oz-centric review of interactive drama and believable agents. In: Veloso, M.M., Wooldridge, M.J. (eds.) Artificial Intelligence Today. LNCS (LNAI), vol. 1600, pp. 297–328. Springer, Heidelberg (1999)
22. Mori, M., MacDorman, K.F., Kageki, N.: The uncanny valley [from the field]. IEEE Robotics & Automation Magazine 19(2), 98–100 (2012)
23. Ortony, A., Clore, G., Collins, A.: Cognitive Structure of Emotions. Cambridge University Press (1988)
24. Ortony, A.: On making believable emotional agents believable, pp. 189–212. MIT Press, England (2003)

25. Rao, A.S., Georgeff, M.P., et al.: BDI agents: From theory to practice. In: ICMAS, vol. 95, pp. 312–319 (1995)
26. Riedl, M.O., Stern, A.: Failing believably: Toward drama management with autonomous actors in interactive narratives. In: TIDSE, pp. 195–206 (2006)
27. Tarjan, R.: Depth-first search and linear graph algorithms. SIAM Journal on Computing 1(2), 146–160 (1972)
28. Tencé, F., Buche, C., Loor, P.D., Marc, O.: The challenge of believability in video games: Definitions, agents models and imitation learning, CoRR abs/1009.0451 (2010)
29. Thiebaux, M., Lance, B., Marsella, S.: Real-time expressive gaze animation for virtual humans. In: AAMAS (1), pp. 321–328 (2009)
30. Thomas, F., Johnston, O.: Disney animation: the illusion of life, 1st edn. Abbeville Press, New York (1981)
31. Trescak, T., Bogdanovych, A., Simoff, S., Rodriguez, I.: Generating diverse ethnic groups with genetic algorithms. In: Proceedings of the 18th ACM Symposium on Virtual Reality Software and Technology, VRST 2012, pp. 1–8 (2012)
32. Wallace, R.S.: The Anatomy of ALICE. APA. Springer, Netherlands (2009)
33. Weizenbaum, J.: Eliza—a computer program for the study of natural language communication between man and machine. Communications of the ACM 9(1), 36–45 (1966)

Gamification for Education: Designing a Pharmacy Education Game

Geoffrey Hookham[1], Keith Nesbitt[1], Joyce Cooper[2],
Hayley Croft[1], and Rohan Rasiah[2]

[1] School of Design, Communication and IT, The University of Newcastle, Australia
{Geoffrey.Hookham,Keith.Nesbitt}@newcastle.edu.au
[2] School of Biomedical Sciences and Pharmacy, The University of Newcastle, Australia
{Joyce.Cooper,Rohan.Rasiah,Hayley.Croft}@newcastle.edu.au

Abstract. A key motivator for the use of serious games has been the notion that "gamification" provides users with an additional level of engagement. This study examines a traditional model of usability in terms of engagement and efficacy, presenting the results obtained from a formative evaluation of a serious game prototype that has been developed to assist in pharmacy education.

Keywords: gamification, pharmacy education, usability, serious games.

1 Introduction

The computer games industry continues to grow as an important segment of the entertainment market. There has also been a continued growth in academic interest surrounding the use of such games for purposes more serious than entertainment alone. "Serious Games", as these applications have been called, have been developed to support domains as diverse as military training [1], finance [2], education [3], health [4] and even scientific discovery [5].

A key motivator for the use of these serious games has been the notion that "gamifying" a more traditional application provides users with an additional level of engagement and motivation that improves the intended, serious outcomes. Indeed throughout history, games have been used to educate, train, inform and distract [6]. If computer games are able to engage an audience to the extent of creating memorable experiences, then if applied to the serious purpose of learning and training, can they provide learning experiences that are more memorable, and potentially more effective?

This general question is perhaps more complex than it appears. It invokes a number of more specific research questions: What design elements of video games promote an engaging experience? How do general questions of usability impact on engagement? What role does engagement play in the effectiveness of serious games? How do we measure engagement in the context of games? If gamification in a training context improves the intended outcomes how do we best measure this effectiveness?

This study investigates these questions by designing, developing and evaluating some specific game elements within the context of Pharmacy education. The case

S.K. Chalup et al. (Eds.): ACALCI 2015, LNAI 8955, pp. 157–165, 2015.

study reported in this paper is a game prototype developed for the University of Newcastle's Masters of Pharmacy program, which aims to assist its students in the development of forensic pharmaceutical skills. This paper reports on the first phase of formative evaluation looking at the perceived effectiveness and usability of the game as measured through a survey containing both closed and open questions.

2   Background

Whether using existing games or creating new games, the process of adapting games for purposes other than entertainment falls under the umbrella of gamification. Prior to defining gamification, one must understand the grounding question: "What is a game?" In short, the defining characteristics of a game are a goal, rules, feedback and voluntary participation [7,8]. A goal provides the motivation to the player; the rules define how that player can approach the goal; feedback informs the player of their performance; and voluntary participation implies the choice the player makes to enter the game world and interact with that world. This concept can apply to the digital (video games) and non-digital contexts (board or card games), however for the purpose of this research the focus is on digital games.

There is no clear consensus on how to define gamification, with each researcher approaching the definition differently. For example, Mosca [9] defines gamification by referring to the concepts of ludic and non-ludic behaviour. Ludic behaviour refers to actions for the purpose of play, while non-ludic behaviour refers to those actions directed by purpose, not necessarily for play. Mosca describes gamification as the application of ludic concepts within non-ludic contexts. Pointsification, or the awarding of points, banners, badges or achievements, within these non-ludic contexts is an attempt to promote "user engagement, loyalty, rhetoric awe, and time expenditure" [9].

Lee and Hammer define gamification "as the use of game mechanics, dynamics, and frameworks to promote desired behaviours" [10] within the context of commercial industries, focusing on the motivational capabilities of games. A more general definition from Deterding refers to gamification as using game-based mechanics, thinking, aesthetics and approaches within traditionally non-game contexts [11,12]. Deterding clarifies this definition, indicating that the process of gamification includes the concept of gamefulness, or the qualities of gaming, and a clear differentiation between the concepts of serious games (complete games) and gamified applications (applications with some game elements).

Taking a practical approach to the definition, Zichermann and Cunningham state that gamification is "the process of [applying] game-thinking and game mechanics to engage users and solve problems" [13]. This pragmatic view of gamification is suited to this research project as one of our aims is to identify elements of serious games that promote engagement to improve upon the design of these games.

In an analysis of the relationship between learning outcomes and game attributes, Wilson and colleagues [14] note that there are several game attributes that are necessary for learning, including: fantasy, the separation from real life; rules/goals, the established criteria for how to win; sensory stimuli, the audio, visual or tactile elements that encourage the separation from real life; challenge, the difficulty of attaining the goal; mystery, the difference between known and unknown information; and control, the ability of the player to influence elements of the game. While this is not an exhaustive list, these elements, in conjunction with informational content, ideally combine to promote a "learner state" through which learned knowledge, skills and attitudes can be produced [14].

The game described in this study, the Virtual Dispensary, was developed to assist teaching dispensing skills to Pharmacy students. We take an iterative approach to developing the Virtual Dispensary game, developing and evaluating game prototypes to ensure we meet the expected educational directions of the serious game and also ensuring that key usability issues that might detract from engagement are identified early in the development process. We have previously developed an interactive virtual tour of a community pharmacy. From the evaluation of this virtual tour we identified the need for more game like elements in the application, these included task-driven challenges and interactive elements in the form of conceptual reasoning puzzles [7]. The gamification process, turning the virtual tour into the Virtual Dispensary game was achieved by adding three key meta-game concepts to drive the users interaction. These elements were a completion goal, interactive 3D products, and challenges related to dispensing practice.

3   The Virtual Dispensary

The use of simulation in healthcare education is increasing as it offers students the opportunity to practice clinical skills in a safe environment without risk of harm to patients or students [15,16,17]. Patient simulation software has been used to augment teaching in pharmaceutics lectures [18], therapeutics and problem based learning [19,20]. For example, in 2012, researchers from Monash University designed a specialised teaching space called a virtual practice environment (VPE) using immersive technologies that incorporated life size photographic and video images which represented a pharmacy setting, and provided a 'backdrop' to communication and counselling role play scenarios [21]. Though simulation and immersive environments do form a component of games, there are comparatively few serious games developed for use in pharmacy education.

The Virtual Dispensary prototype was designed to provide pharmacy students with an exploratory, interactive space that allows the students to practice forensic skills that students undertake as part of their studies. It makes use of multiple technologies to provide the online game structure. The online learning environment, Blackboard, provides the introduction and goal setting of the game; presenting a quiz that requires forensic investigation of the Virtual Dispensary world and the detail presented on scripts and medication packaging.

The game world itself was adapted from a virtual tour created from sixteen, 360° panoramic photographs of a community pharmacy (see Fig. 1). The functionality of the community pharmacy tour allows students to navigate about the pharmacy and zoom in to examine products in detail. The tour also provides information about the key locations of the pharmacy by way of auditory descriptions and information pop-ups. The Virtual Dispensary adds the task of identifying and verifying prescriptions, which includes checking medication packaging and labels (see Fig.2.)

A single play session of the game would require the student to access the quiz, which would provide them access to the Virtual Dispensary, which they would then navigate through and explore to answer the quiz questions. The structure and gameplay of the Virtual Dispensary prototype places the game within the 'puzzle game' genre, as it consists of conceptual reasoning challenges requiring extrinsic knowledge for successful completion [7].

Fig. 1. 360° Panoramic view of pharmacy virtual tour

Fig. 2. Script Checking area behind the Dispensary Counter

Within the game, there are two main areas, the Scripts In and the Script Checking areas. The Scripts In area sits at the front of the dispensary, where the patient submits a prescription to the Pharmacist, while the Script Checking area is behind the dispensary counter, where the Pharmacist is required to ensure that the prescriptions, medications and labeling are correct and appropriate. The student is able to access the scripts, medications and labels by locating and clicking the script icons within the game world (see Fig. 2. and Fig. 3.).

Prescriptions and medications within the Virtual Dispensary are displayed as an interactive, 3D model, wherein the user can rotate and zoom the object to view the packaging and pharmacy label information. These models were created using 3DSom [22] from high-definition photographs of the packaging (see Fig. 4.)

The game elements are designed to encourage the student to examine their surroundings and identify interactive components. Answering questions posed in the Blackboard quiz requires the close examination of the information displayed in these environment and interactive 3D models. The Virtual Dispensary is stored on the University of Newcastle servers, and was made accessible for students of the Masters of Pharmacy through the University network.

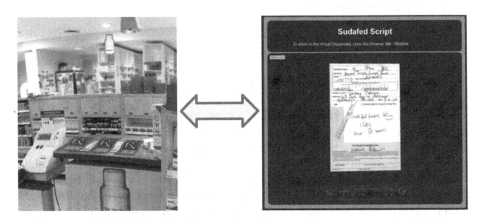

Fig. 3. Display of the Scripts In area and interactive view of prescription

Fig. 4. Rotating, 3D model of medication from Virtual Dispensary Game

4   Method

The subjects for the study were 10 students currently studying the Masters of Pharmacy program at the University of Newcastle. There were six males, and four females. Four of the subjects were under the age of 23, four were between the ages of 24-34 and two were older than 35. Five of the subjects had previous experience working in a community pharmacy for at least 6 months. Most subjects (n=9) completed the game in less than 30 minutes while one subject played for slightly longer.

The Virtual Dispensary was designed as a stage 1 prototype and was evaluated to gain user feedback to help direct further design work for the gamification. After completing the games, subjects completed an anonymous survey, containing eleven Likert-scale questions designed to measure the perceived effectiveness (Table 1) and usability (Table 2) of the Virtual Dispensary. Students could also respond to two open questions to identify the features of the Virtual Dispensary they enjoyed the most and to suggest possible improvements.

5   Results

In terms of perceived effectiveness, all 10 subjects agreed that the Virtual Dispensary provided an effective way of learning about dispensing. For the two questions related to confidence, 12 of the twenty responses agreed that the game improved their confidence about dispensing while five disagreed. Seven of the subjects formed no opinion about whether or not the application stimulated their interest to learn.

In terms of usability seven subjects agreed the application was easy to use, while one disagreed. Nine subjects agreed the application was fun to use and ten subjects agreed the world was realistic. Five subjects agreed the functions in the game were well integrated, while one disagreed. Eight of the subjects felt they could learn to use the application quickly, while two disagreed with this position. Five subjects disagreed that there was inconsistency in the application while the remainder of subjects had no opinion on this. There was mixed opinion about whether further instructions were required to use the application, with four indicating no requirement and three suggesting it would be useful to provide more instruction.

When asked to identify the best thing about the Virtual Dispensary, four noted the scripting examples with checking. Three subjects highlighted the realism of the pharmacy environment and three suggesting the interactive products and packing as key elements. A range of improvements were suggested, these focused on providing more content, in particular three subjects requested increasing the number of products and scripts available. Another four subjects wanted more product information to be integrated into the game. Other subjects suggested integrating even more elements of pharmacy practice, such as patient counselling into the game.

Table 1. Perceived Effectiveness Questions and Responses (n=10)

Questions	strongly disagree	disagree	no opinion	agree	strongly agree
Using this type of technology is an effective way of learning about dispensing				5	5
I feel I have gained confidence from learning more about dispensing before my next placement		2	3	4	1
I feel I have gained confidence from learning more about dispensing before my dispensing exam		3		6	1
The Virtual Dispensary Application stimulated my interest to learn		1	7	2	

Table 2. Usability Questions and Responses (n=10)

Questions	strongly disagree	disagree	no opinion	agree	strongly agree
I thought the application was easy to use		1	2	4	3
I thought the application was fun to use			1	7	2
I thought the application was realistic				7	3
I found the different functions in this application were well integrated	1		4	3	2
I imagine that people would learn to use this application very quickly		2		4	4
I thought there was too much inconsistency in the application	1	4	5		
I need more instructions on how to use the application before I am confident to use it effectively	1	3	3	3	

6   Conclusion

As this study was intended to inform further design only a small sample size was used in the study. While this does not allow for in depth analysis of the overall effectiveness, usability and engaging elements of the Virtual Dispensary, the feedback does allow for the improvement of measurements and direction for further development. The goal of the gamification of the original pharmacy tour was to find ways to enhance the learning of forensic pharmaceutical skills. According to the feedback, the application of interactive and game elements was perceived to be a fun and effective learning technique, however this is no indication of the effectiveness in terms of learning outcomes. There were some interesting feedback elements, namely that the majority of respondents indicated that the game functions were well integrated. From a technical standpoint, these elements were not integrated within the dispensary environment as they were akin to separate pages of a website. However the conceptual grouping of elements and interface usability of the game world appear to disguise this somewhat.

As an early prototype, the Virtual Dispensary's game elements appear to be on the right track, but will certainly need further iteration and development. Further development of a truly integrated, interactive environment with more product information and interactive components is a future goal for this research. Which will then be used to develop a greater understanding of the engagement of games and their efficacy in a learning environment.

References

1. United States Army: America's Army (2002), http://www.americasarmy.com/
2. People's Choice Credit Union: Zip It Up! Play the game, win real life rewards! (2014), http://www.peopleschoicecu.com.au/667/zip-it-up.aspx
3. Rawal, J.: Koe - A JRPG with Japanese at the core of gameplay (2014), https://www.kickstarter.com/projects/297265509/koe-a-jrpg-with-japanese-at-the-core-of-gameplay
4. Baranowski, T., Baranowski, J., Cullen, K.W., Marsh, T., Islam, N., Zakeri, I., Honess-Morreale, L., Demoor, C.: Squire's Quest!: dietary outcome evaluation of a multimedia game. American Journal of Preventive Medicine 24(1), 52–61 (2003)
5. Cooper, S.,, Treuille, A., Barbero, J., Leaver-Fay, A., Tuite, K., Khatib, F., Snyder, A.C., Beenen, M., Salesin, D., Baker, D.: The challenge of designing scientific discovery games. In: Proceedings of the Fifth international Conference on the Foundations of Digital Games, pp. 40–47. ACM (2010)
6. Koster, R.: A theory of fun for game design. Paraglyph Press, Scottsdale (2005)
7. Adams, E.: Fundamentals of Game Design. Pearson Education (2013)
8. McGonigal, J.: This is not a game: Immersive aesthetics and collective play. In: Proceedings of the Melbourne DAC 2003. Streamingworlds Conference. Citeseer (2003)
9. Mosca, I.: + 10! Gamification and deGamification. GI AI MI E Games as Art, Media, Entertainment 1(1) (2012)
10. Lee, J.J., Hammer, J.: Gamification in education: What, how, why bother? Academic Exchange Quarterly 15(2), 146 (2011)
11. Deterding, S., Dixon, D., Rilla, K., Nacke, L.: From game design elements to gamefulness: defining gamification. In: Proceedings of the 15th International Academic MindTrek Conference: Envisioning Future Media Environments, pp. 9–15. ACM (2011)
12. Kapp, K.M.: The Gamification of Learning and Instruction: Game-based Methods and Strategies for Training and Education. Pfeiffer, San Francisco (2012)
13. Zichermann, G., Cunningham, C.: Gamification by design: Implementing game mechanics in web and mobile apps. O'Reilly Media, Inc. (2011)
14. Wilson, K.A., Bedwell, W.L., Lazzara, E.H., Salas, E., Burke, C.S., Estock, J.L., Orvis, K.L., Conkey, C.: Relationships between game attributes and learning outcomes review and research proposals. Simulation & Gaming 40, 217–266 (2009)

15. Bradley, P.: The history of simulation in medical education and possible future directions. Medical Education 40(3), 254–262 (2006)
16. Gaba, D.M.: The future vision of simulation in health care. Quality and Safety in Health Care 13(suppl. 1), i2–i10 (2006)
17. Kneebone, R., Scott, W., Darzi, A., Horrocks, M.: Simulation and clinical practice: strengthening the relationship. Medical Education 38(10), 1095–1102 (2004)
18. Benedict, N., Schonder, K.: Patient simulation software to augment an advanced pharmaceutics course. American Journal of Pharmaceutical Education 75(2) (2011)
19. Battaglia, J.N., Kieser, M.A., Bruskiewitz, R.H., Pitterle, M.E., Thorpe, J.M.: An Online Virtual-Patient Program to Teach Pharmacists and Pharmacy Students How to Provide Diabetes-Specific Medication Therapy Management. American Journal of Pharmaceutical Education 76(7) (2012)
20. Benedict, N.: Virtual patients and problem-based learning in advanced therapeutics. American Journal of Pharmaceutical Education 74(8) (2010)
21. Yasmeen, S., Styles, K., Duncan, G.: A Virtual Practice Environment to Develop Communication Skills in Pharmacy Students. American Journal of Pharmaceutical Education 76(10) (2012)
22. Big Object Base: 3DSOM, i2o3d Limited, Hatfield, United Kingdom (2010)

Sound Improves Player Performance in a Multiplayer Online Battle Arena Game

Patrick Ng, Keith Nesbitt, and Karen Blackmore

School of Design, Communication and Information Technology
The University of Newcastle, NSW, Australia
{Patrick.H.Ng,Keith.Nesbitt,Karen.Blackmore}@newcastle.edu.au

Abstract. Sound in video games is often used by developers to enhance the visual experience on screen. Despite its importance in creating presence and improving visual screen elements, sound also plays an important role in providing additional information to a player when completing various game tasks. This preliminary study focuses on the use of informative sound in the popular multiplayer online battle arena game, Dota 2. Our initial results indicate that team performance improves with the use of sound. However, mixed results with individual performances were measured, with some individual performances better with sound and some better without sound.

Keywords: Dota 2, auditory icons, earcons, informative sound, multiplayer online battle arena.

1 Introduction

For game developers, integrating informative sound has the potential to provide additional feedback to the player. This use of informative sound is in addition to the traditional function sound plays in enhancing the reality of the game world. With the emergence and growing state of competitive gaming on the world stage, performance has become a relevant factor for most professional and hardcore gamers who seek to play video games at the optimum level. Previous approaches of measuring performance in games have focused their attention on the experience, skill and rank levels of players, there has also been some work, that has explored the relation between player and performance in terms of sound and information. However, there are few studies that try to quantify a simple relationship between sound and performance in popular commercial games. In this paper we examine both team and individual performance, both with and without sound, in the multiplayer online battle arena game, Dota 2.

2 Overview of Dota 2

Dota 2 (Defence of the Ancients 2) is a popular multiplayer online battle arena (MOBA) game created by Valve [1] and the successor to the original custom map, Dota 1 that was based on the Warcraft III gaming engine [2]. Funk provides a detailed explanation

S.K. Chalup et al. (Eds.): ACALCI 2015, LNAI 8955, pp. 166–174, 2015.

of the history of the MOBA genre [3]. The game pits two teams of five players against each other in a highly competitive match. Each player controls a single unique character called a hero who grows in power over time [4]. Heroes are defined by their roles they play in the game. For the purpose of this paper we choose to only highlight some of the main primary roles: Carry, Support, Off Lane and Jungler (see Table 1). The primary goal of the game is for one team to destroy the enemy's fortified stronghold. To achieve this goal, players must work together and communicate information effectively as a team to complete key tasks such as killing enemy creeps (computer controlled soldiers), destroying key enemy structures and killing enemy heroes to gain an advantage over the opposing team. The game is played in an online environment where each person plays on a separate computer with a fast Internet connection. The duration of each game varies with most matches finishing between 45-50 minutes [5].

Table 1. Description of the primary hero roles in Dota 2

Hero Positions	Definition
Carry	A hero the team relies upon to deal physical damage in team fights. Carries lack power and survivability early on and are dependent on supports to protect them from danger to be able to obtain 'farm' and key items in order to be effective in team fights and later game stages.
Support	A hero who provides survivability and support to their team. Their goal is to protect their allies from dying in team fights. In addition they are also responsible for purchase of wards to provide map vision for their team and a courier to deliver items for their team.
Jungler	A hero that obtains gold and experience points from farming (killing) neutral creep camps on their respective side of the map. They are able to take on the roles of support and/or carry.
Off Lane	A hero that has either certain skills and/or survivability to contest the most difficult lane (path) for their team.

The game itself is divided into three phases: early game, mid game and late game. Throughout the game, players attempt to farm (kill) computer generated and controlled enemies called creeps. This allows the player to gain gold and experience points for their hero in their respective lane. Killing enemy creep warriors also allows a player to obtain key items and unlock abilities for their heroes. Being able to obtain more 'farm' than the enemy hero in the same path provides an advantage in both the short and long term. Heroes obtain levels by gaining experience points from killing creeps, heroes or destroying enemy structures such as towers. For each level gained, a player is given one point, which can be used to unlock or power up one of three primary abilities or primary attributes of strength, intelligence and agility [5]. Reaching a certain level will unlock that hero's ultimate ability, which can change outcome of a team fight. Throughout the game, both teams will seek to ambush enemy heroes by starting team fights and winning a team fight provides a tactical advantage over the opposing team. The game will end when one team successfully destroys the enemy's stronghold.

3   Related Work

Prior works within the field of auditory display have identified a number of different ways that sound can be used to improve the functionality and efficiency of feedback in computer applications. Gaver [6] deduced that people pick up and store information by the everyday listening of sounds in their environment. He suggested that these types of sounds could increase the level of information in interfaces that typically relied only upon visual feedback. By using familiar sounds based off real world events and mapping them back to actions and events in a computer application, the user would be able to immediately recognize and understand the current interface actions. Gaver refers to these natural sounds as 'Auditory Icons'. Subsequent research into the integration of Auditory Icons in computer applications included the Sonic-Finder [7] and the ARKola bottling plant simulation [8]. Each of these applications demonstrated the theoretical advantages of auditory icons for helping convey vital information. When using the SonicFinder, participants reported a generally 'favourable reaction' and increased feelings of direct engagement when performing various actions with these additional audio cues. ARKola was found to provide more immediate and intuitive feedback on user initiated events, processes, modes and locations within a busy factory environment.

Studies conducted within the field of Psychology have helped expand upon Gaver's initial findings by further evaluating the use of Auditory Icons in human computer interfaces. This work has focused on the use of Auditory Icons as warning signals that help reduce the visual load of information on a human operator and improve task efficiency. In their work, Petocz et al states that sound is often the most effective medium to convey information as reaction times to auditory stimuli is often quicker than visual stimulus [9]. Stevens et al concurs by noting that natural auditory indicators have the potential to be an alternative and effective form of conveying visual warning signals [10]. For critical work environments such as hospitals where timing and immediate recognition of events is paramount, the design and implementation of auditory displays as an alternative means of communicating information can be a key factor for optimally perform tasks.

Blattner et al expanded upon Gaver's work by noting that not all sounds can be accurately represented in terms of an everyday source [11]. For representing complex actions and events in the interface, he suggested an alternative means of creating auditory messages called 'Earcons'. Earcons rely upon musical conventions such as pitch, timbre and dynamics to communicate abstract information. Unlike Gaver's approach of using everyday listening skills to understand an action or event in the user interface, the association between an Earcon and an event has to be explicitly learnt by the user. However, once this association is learnt, Earcons provide an effective way of conveying information, which is more abstract in nature. Brewster conducted an experiment to test the effectiveness of Earcons in providing navigational cues within a structured menu hierarchy [12]. He noted that that 81.5% of participants successfully identified their position in the hierarchy indicating that Earcons can be a powerful method of conveying structured information. Brewster also suggested that adding non-speech sounds to existing graphical interfaces could reduce the risk of information being lost or hidden from the user.

Other works in the field of HCI have also explored the significance of auditory alarms in real life environments where sound is crucial in providing important feedback. For example, Patterson's study into the design of auditory warning systems on civil aircraft highlights the importance of auditory alarm systems in real life [13]. Howard et al noted that ambulances have a siren in addition to flashing lights to warn motorists of their approach, in case they do not see the vehicle [14].

Research conducted on video game audio and player performance has shown mixed results in regards to whether sound provides a positive or negative impact on performance. Tafalla reported that participants playing the game DOOM with the soundtrack scored almost twice as many points to those playing without the sound [15]. In contrast, Yamada et al found that the presence of music had a negative effect on performance [16]. Tan et al conducted further studies into the effects of sound on performance levels and found that players perform the weakest when playing without sound while the highest scores were obtained when playing with music unrelated to the game [17]. Each of these findings suggested that sound could play a factor on players performance levels in games. However in each case, only the background music was considered when evaluating the effects of sound on player performance levels.

As information gathering plays an important task for players in performance demanding games, further research is required to better understand the role sound and information plays in performance. To this end a simple preliminary study was conducted to examine the informative effects of sound in a team based game. The main question we consider in this research is: "Does the sound used in a commercially available game actually improve player performance?"

4   Information and Sound in Dota 2

The game utilizes a combination of both auditory icons and earcons to highlight when certain hero abilities have been activated as well as auditory-based alarms as urgency warning signals in the game. These signals make the player aware that they need to respond shortly or may highlight emergency situations, which demand immediate attention. The high-paced nature of a Dota 2 game, as well as the need to constantly monitor various statuses at the same time, would seem to make sound an important source of additional information for players. For example, players need to stay informed at all times on events in the player's current point of view but also any relevant off screen events that may happening. While off screen events in the game can be communicated by visual means, the player may prefer to rely primarily on sound to keep track of these events. As previously mentioned previously, another reason why sound may be important in a game of Dota 2 is that the revolves around teamwork and good communication. Unlike most real strategy games, such as StarCraft II: Heart of the Swarm [18], which usually feature only one person playing at a time, Dota 2 has five players playing as part of a team. Not all players will see the same information visually on the screen. By using auditory signals for warnings and notifications, players can all receive the same information at the same time, regardless of their current viewpoint [19].

Like most competitively driven video games, information can play a prominent role in shaping and influencing player and team behavior and strategies used in a game of Dota 2. This game revolves around collaborative teamwork and effective real time feedback might be considered essential for helping teams achieve both individual and team objectives. Information could be expected to be a vital resource for winning key fights and ultimately the match as a game of Dota 2 progresses to later stages. Indeed, based on previous discussions within the fields of Auditory Display, HCI and Psychology, there is some evidence to suggest that informative based alarms and sounds do improve a player's ability to quickly recognize and respond to key events. In the case of Dota 2, the ability to quickly recognize threats and opportunities should be of economic and strategic benefit. Our study simply tries to quantify these expected benefits by having players play with and without the sound.

5   Experiment

We conducted a preliminary evaluation into the use of sound in Dota 2 and its relationship with performance. A total of 20 participants (19 males, 1 female) took part in this experiment. Of these participants, 18 were undergraduate students aged between 18-25 years while 2 participants were postgraduate students aged between 26-40 years. A pre-survey conducted before the experiment revealed that most participants (n=19) played an average of 10-25 hours of videos games per week. When asked if they have previously played a strategy game, most participants (n=19) indicated they had. In addition, when asked if they have played Dota 2 or any variants of the multiplayer online battle arena genre, the majority of participants (n=18) answered yes.

The experiment was designed so that participants were divided into two groups. One group consisted of expert players and the other group consisted of novice players. The expert group consisted of 15 players who have experience in playing competitive match games of Dota 2 or equivalent strategy games in teams. These 15 participants were then randomly divided into 3 teams of 5 players. The teams played each other in a round robin of games, where one team played with the sound off and the other with the sound on. In the sound on condition, players were required to have the in game background music and sounds from the game turned on. This included voice chat. Participants in the sound off condition were not allowed to have any sounds from the game on and played in complete silence. Other sounds, such as personal music, were not allowed in either of the two conditions. In both conditions players were also allowed to communicate using text based chat. Each team in this part of the experiment played each other twice, alternating which of the two teams played with the sounds on and sounds off condition.

The second, novice group consisted of 5 players who had little or no experience in Dota 2 or equivalent games of the multiplayer online battle arena genre. Trying to match these players against experienced players would have unbalanced the game play. Therefore these players were placed together in a single team to play against the computer, alternating between sounds on and sound off condition, much like the expert group. One advantage of this strategy is that it allowed us to consider the effect of sound cues on the performance of novice versus expert players.

Both the expert and novice group of players first played a practice game against a computer controlled AI opponent. Results from these practice matches were excluded from the final results. After the practice match each team played a total of four more matches, two in the sound on and two in the sound off condition. The game mode selected for all groups is 'all pick', which allows participants to select any character in the game without restriction. Participants were also given the choice to randomize their choice. In the novice part of the experiment, the AI opponents were set to 'normal mode' to replicate the difficulty of playing against an average performing equivalent team. At the time, the server selected to host all matches was US west. This server provided the best possible latency levels for all players based on their Internet connection speeds. All matches in the experiment were recorded by the game recording program FRAPS [20]. This allowed the games to be reviewed in detail. Statistics were checked in each game every five minutes to ensure consistency of recording key statistical data. This data is provided automatically by tools built into Dota 2, allowing both individual and team performance data to be collected.

The performance data for individuals consisted of: Hero levels; Hero kills; Hero deaths; Kill assists; Total gold earned; Gold per minute and; Experience points per minute. The performance measure for teams consisted of: Total gold earned; Total experience points earned; Total hero kills and; Total hero deaths. For most of these measures, larger numbers represent improved performance. The two exceptions are individual hero deaths and total hero deaths. For both of these measures a decrease is indicative of better performance as players aim to protect their own heroes from death.

6   Results

We recorded a total of 140 comparative measures (7 performance measures x 5 players x 4 teams) for analyzing individual performances. Of these 82 showed improvements in performance when sound is included, 10 showed no difference and 48 displayed a reduction in performance. We collated the individual performance data further, calculating the average individual results across the 7 measures. Out of these 7 measures, 1 showed a reduction in performance, 6 showed improvements when sound was present (see table 2). The difference for the measure of Hero levels was found to be significant.

In additional to recording individual performances, we also recorded 16 team measures in total (4 teams x 4 performance measures) for measuring team performance. Out of these nine showed an increase in performance with sound on while seven showed a decrease in performance. We collated the team performance data further, calculating the average team results for the three expert teams (see table 3). Out of the 4 measures, 3 showed improvements in performance when sound is present while only 1 measure recorded a reduction in performance with sound.

Table 2. Average Individual Performance with Sound On and Sound Off. *Indicates statistically significant performance in the sound on condition.

Individual Measure	Sound Off	Sound On
Hero Levels*	17.2	18.6
Hero Kills	6.8	7.1
Hero Deaths	10.8	11.5
Kill Assists	7.1	7.4
Total Gold Earned	12555	13170
Gold per Minute	312.8	314.8
Experience Points per Minute	427.9	453.8

Table 3. Average team performance (3 expert teams)

Team Measure	Sound Off	Sound On
Total Gold Earned	62383.3	64331.7
Total Experience Points Earned	85693.3	94206.7
Hero Kills	35.7	37.8
Hero Deaths	7.1	7.4

Our analysis of the initial results has shown mixed results in terms of whether players and teams performance actually improved when there is sound. While over half of the total individual comparative measures have shown improved in performance with sound, 58 displayed either no difference or a reduction in performance. We also found a similar pattern in team performance where 9 of the comparative measures displayed an increase with sound while 7 showed a reduction in performance. A post survey conducted after the experiment revealed that 18 of the 20 players felt that removing sound affected their performance negatively.

7 Discussion

In this study we have undertaken a preliminary examination on the role of information and sound in video games. Specifically we looked at whether sound could offer improved performance levels in the multiplayer online battle arena game, Dota 2. In our preliminary experiment, we attempted to measure the difference in performance levels by adding and removing sound from the gameplay. We tested both individual and team performance levels in two different sound conditions (on and off) using seven individual and four team measures. The mixed results in this preliminary experiment may be a result of the difficulty in creating a controlled environment in Dota 2. While similar patterns occur during games, no two games are exactly the same. Outcomes and performance depends on team strategy, individual hero choices and how the two teams engage and interact on the map. More work needs to be conducted on the experimental design to better measure the effects of sound on player and team performance in Dota 2 and other similar team based video games. The next stage of our work will address some of the issues encountered with the design of this preliminary study.

This will include changing the game mode from 'all pick' to 'captain's mode' to better simulate a competitive game of Dota 2 by forcing players to pick and ban heroes. In addition, we will focus on two expert teams who play an extended number of games against each other so that the additional data gathered might highlight further significant differences in performance.

References

1. Valve Corporation, Dota 2 (PC/Mac Software). Bellevue, Washington, USA: Valve, LLC (2009)
2. Blizzard Entertainment. Warcraft III: Reign of Chaos (PC/Mac Software). Activision Blizzard Inc., Irvine (2002)
3. Funk, J.: MOBA, DOTA, ARTS: A Brief Introduction to Gaming's Biggest, Most Impenetrable Genre, http://www.polygon.com/2013/9/2/4672920/moba-dota-arts-a-brief-introduction-to-gamings-biggest-most (accessed November 4, 2014)
4. Yang, P., Harrison, B., Roberts, L.B.: Identifying Patterns in Combat that are Predictive of Success in MOBA Games. In: 9th International Conference on the Foundations of Digital Games, Fort Lauderdale, Florida (2014)
5. Dota 2 Game Overview., http://au.ign.com/wikis/dota-2/Game_Overview (accessed November 4, 2014)
6. Gaver, W.: Auditory Icons: Using Sound in Computer Interfaces. Human-Computer Interaction 2(2), 167–177 (1986)
7. Gaver, W.: The SonicFinder: An interface that uses auditory icons. Human-Computer Interaction 4(1), 67–94 (1989)
8. Gaver, W., Smith, R., O'Shea, T.: Effective sounds in complex systems: the ARKola simulation. In: 9th SIGCHI Conference on Human Factors in Computing Systems, pp. 85–90. ACM, New Orleans (1991)
9. Petocz, A., Keller, P., Stevens, C.: Auditory warnings, signal-referent relations, and natural indicators: Re-thinking theory and application. Journal of Experimental Psychology: Applied 14(2), 165–178 (2008)
10. Stevens, C., Brennan, D., Petocz, A., Howell, C.: Designing Informative Warning Signals: Effects of indicator type, modality and task demand on recognition speed and accuracy. Advances of Cognitive Psychology 5, 84–90 (2009)
11. Blattner, M.M., Sumikawa, D., Greenberg, R.: Earcons and icons: their structure and common design principles. Human-Computer Interaction 4(1), 11–44 (1989)
12. Brewster, S.A., Wright, P.C., Edwards, A.D.N.: An evaluation of earcons for use in auditory human-computer interfaces. In: 11th INTERCHI Conference on Human Factors in Computing Systems, pp. 222–227. ACM, New York (1993)
13. Patterson, R.D.: Guidelines for auditory warning systems on civil aircraft. CAA Paper 82017, Civil Aviation Authority, London (1982)
14. Howard, C.Q., Maddern, A.J., Privopoulos, E.P.: Acoustic characteristics for effective ambulance sirens. Australian Acoustics Journal 39(2), 43–53 (2011)
15. Tafalla, R.J.: Gender differences in cardiovascular reactivity and game performance related to sensory modality in violent video game play. Journal of Applied Social Psychology 37(9), 2008–2023, doi:10.1111/j.1559-1816.2007.00248.x
16. Yamada, M., Fujisawa, N., Komori, S.: The effects of music on the performance and impression in a racing game. Journal of Music Perception and Cognition 7(2), 65–76 (2001)

17. Tan, S., Baxa, J., Spackman, M.P.: Effects of Built-in Audio versus Unrelated Background Music on Performance in an Adventure Role-Playing Game. International Journal of Gaming and Computer-Mediated Simulations 2(3), 1–23 (2010), doi:10.4018/jgcms. 2010070101
18. Blizzard Entertainment. StarCraft II: Heart of the Swarm (PC/Mac Software). Irvine, California, USA. Activision Blizzard Inc. (2013)
19. Jørgensen, K.: On the functional aspects of computer game audio. In: 1st Audio Mostly Conference - A Conference of Sound in Games, Piteå, Sweden, pp. 48–52 (2006)
20. Fraps: Real-time video capture and benchmarking, http://www.fraps.com

Generic Construction of Scale-Invariantly Coarse Grained Memory

Karthik H. Shankar

Center for Memory and Brain, Boston University
Boston, MA-02215, USA
kshankar79@gmail.com

Abstract. Encoding temporal information from the recent past as spatially distributed activations is essential in order for the entire recent past to be simultaneously accessible. Any biological or synthetic agent that relies on the past to predict/plan the future, would be endowed with such a spatially distributed temporal memory. Simplistically, we would expect that resource limitations would demand the memory system to store only the most useful information for future prediction. For natural signals in real world which show scale free temporal fluctuations, the predictive information encoded in memory is maximal if the past information is scale invariantly coarse grained. Here we examine the general mechanism to construct a scale invariantly coarse grained memory system. Remarkably, the generic construction is equivalent to encoding the linear combinations of Laplace transform of the past information and their approximated inverses. This reveals a fundamental construction constraint on memory networks that attempt to maximize predictive information storage relevant to the natural world.

Keywords: predictively relevant memory, resource conserving memory, inverse Laplace transformed memory.

1 Introduction

Representing the information from the recent past as transient activity distributed over a network has been actively researched in biophysical as well as purely computational domains [8,6]. It is understood that recurrent connections in the network can keep the information from distant past alive so that it can be recovered from the current state. The memory capacity of these networks are generally measured in terms of the accuracy of recovery of the past information [6,20,5]. Although the memory capacity strongly depends on the network's topology and sparsity [2,14,7,18], it can be significantly increased by exploiting any prior knowledge of the underlying structure of the encoded signal [3,1].

Our approach to encoding memory stems from a focus on its utility for future prediction, rather than on the accuracy of recovering the past. In particular we are interested in encoding time varying signals from the natural world into memory so as to optimize future prediction. It is well known that most natural signals exhibit scale free long range correlations [9,16,19]. By exploiting this

S.K. Chalup et al. (Eds.): ACALCI 2015, LNAI 8955, pp. 175–184, 2015.
© Springer International Publishing Switzerland 2015

intrinsic structure underlying natural signals, prior work has shown that the predictive information contained in a finite sized memory system can be maximized if the past is encoded in a scale-invariantly coarse grained fashion [13]. Each node in such a memory system would represent a coarse grained average around a specific past moment, and the time window of coarse graining linearly scales with the past timescale. Clearly the accuracy of information recovery in such a memory system degrades more for more distant past. In effect, the memory system sacrifices accuracy in order to represent information from very distant past, scaling exponentially with the network size [13]. The predictive advantage of such a memory system comes from washing out non-predictive fluctuations from the distant past, whose accurate representation would have served very little in predicting the future. Arguably, in the natural world filled with scale-free time varying signals, animals would have evolved to adopt such a memory system conducive for future predictions. This is indeed evident from animal and human behavioral studies that show that our memory for time involves scale invariant errors which linearly scale with the target timescale [4,11].

Our focus here is not to further emphasize the predictive advantage offered by a scale invariantly coarse grained memory system, rather we simply assume the utility of such a memory system and focus on the generic mechanism to construct it. One way to mechanistically construct such a memory system is to gradually encode information over real time as a Laplace transform of the past and approximately invert it [12]. The central result in this paper is that any mechanistic construction of such a memory system is simply equivalent to encoding linear combinations of Laplace transformed past and their approximate inverses. This result should lay strong constraints on the connectivity structure of memory networks exhibiting the scale invariance property.

We start with the basic requirement that different nodes in the memory system represents coarse grained averages about different past moments. Irrespective of the connectivity, the nodes can be linearly arranged to reflect their monotonic relationship to the past time. Rather than considering a network with a finite set of nodes, for analysis benefit, we consider a continuum limit where the information from the past time is smoothly projected on a spatial axis. The construction can later be discretized and implemented in a network with finite nodes to represent past information from timescales that exponentially scale with the network size.

2   Scale Invariant Coarse Graining

Consider a real valued function $f(\tau)$ observed over time τ. The aim is to encode this time-varying function into a spatially distributed representation in one dimension parametrized by s, such that at any moment τ the entire past from $-\infty$ to τ is represented in a coarse grained fashion as $\mathbf{T}(\tau, s)$

$$\mathbf{T}(\tau, s) = \int_{-\infty}^{\tau} f(\tau')\mathbf{W}(\tau - \tau', s) \, d\tau'. \tag{1}$$

This is now a convolution memory model. The kernel $\mathbf{W}(\tau - \tau', s)$ is the coarse graining window function with normalized area for all s, $\int_{-\infty}^{\tau} \mathbf{W}(\tau - \tau', s)d\tau' = 1$.

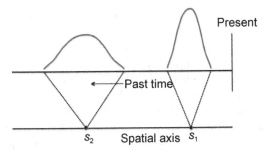

Fig. 1. Coarse grained averages around different past instants are projected on to different points on the spatial axis

Different points on the spatial axis uniquely and monotonically represents coarse grained averages about different instants in the past, as illustrated in figure 1.

We require that coarse graining about any past instant linearly scales with the past timescale. So, for any pair of points s_1 and s_2, there exists a scaling constant α_{12} such that $\mathbf{W}(\tau - \tau', s_1) = \alpha_{12}\mathbf{W}(\alpha_{12}(\tau - \tau'), s_2)$. For the window function to satisfy this scale-invariance property, there should exist a monotonic mapping $s(\alpha)$ from a scaling variable α to the spatial axis so that

$$\mathbf{W}(\tau - \tau', s(\alpha)) = \alpha\mathbf{W}(\alpha(\tau - \tau'), s(1)). \tag{2}$$

Without loss of generality we shall pick $s(\alpha) = \alpha$ because it can be retransformed to any other monotonic $s(\alpha)$ mapping after the analysis. Hence with $0 < s < \infty$,

$$\mathbf{W}(\tau - \tau', s) = s\mathbf{W}(s(\tau - \tau'), 1). \tag{3}$$

3 Space-Time Local Mechanism

Equation 1 expresses the encoded memory as an integral over the entire past. However, the encoding mechanism can only have access to the instantaneous functional value of f and its derivatives. The spatial pattern should self sufficiently evolve in real time to encode eq. 1. This is a basic requirement to mechanistically construct $\mathbf{T}(\tau, s)$ in real time using any network architecture. Since the spatial axis is organized monotonically to correspond to different past moments, only the local neighborhood of any point would affect its time evolution. So we postulate that the most general encoding mechanism that can yield eq. 1 is a space-time local mechanism given by some differential equation for $\mathbf{T}(\tau, s)$. To analyze this, let us first express the general space-time derivative of $\mathbf{T}(\tau, s)$ by repeatedly differentiating eq. 1 w.r.t τ and s.

$$\mathbf{T}^{[n]}_{(m)}(\tau, s) = \sum_{j=0}^{n-1} f^{[n-j-1]}(\tau)\mathbf{W}^{[j]}_{(m)}(0, s)$$

$$+ \int_{-\infty}^{\tau} f(\tau')\mathbf{W}^{[n]}_{(m)}(\tau - \tau', s)\, d\tau'. \tag{4}$$

Here n and m are positive integers. For brevity, we denote the order of time derivative within a square bracket in the superscript and the order of space derivative within a parenthesis in the subscript.

Since $f(\tau)$ is an arbitrary input, $\mathbf{T}(\tau, s)$ should satisfy a time-independent differential equation which can depend on instantaneous time derivatives of $f(\tau)$. The first term in the r.h.s of eq. 4 is time-local, while the second term involves an integral over the entire past. In order for the second term to be time-local, it must be expressible in terms of lower derivatives of $\mathbf{T}(\tau, s)$. Since the equation must hold for any $f(\tau)$, $\mathbf{W}_{(m)}^{[n]}(\tau - \tau', s)$ should satisfy a linear equation.

$$\sum_{n,m} C_{nm}(s) \mathbf{W}_{(m)}^{[n]}(\tau - \tau', s) = 0. \tag{5}$$

The aim here is not to derive the time-local differential equation satisfied by $\mathbf{T}(\tau, s)$, but just to impose its existence, which is achieved by imposing eq. 5 for some set of functions $C_{nm}(s)$. To impose this condition, let us first evaluate $\mathbf{W}_{(m)}^{[n]}(\tau - \tau', s)$ by exploiting the functional form of the window function given by eq. 3. Defining $z \equiv s(\tau - \tau')$ and the function $G(z) \equiv \mathbf{W}(z, 1)$, eq. 3 can be repeatedly differentiated to obtain

$$\mathbf{W}_{(m)}^{[n]}(\tau - \tau', s) = \sum_{r=r_o}^{m} (n+1)! m! \frac{s^{n+1-m+r}}{r!(m-r)!^2}(\tau - \tau')^r G^{[n+r]}(z),$$

where $r_o = \max[0, m - n - 1]$ and the superscript on $G(z)$ represents the order of the derivative w.r.t z. Now eq. 5 takes the form

$$\sum_{n,m} C_{nm}(s) s^{n+1-m} \sum_{r=r_o}^{m} \frac{(n+1)! m!}{r!(m-r)!^2} z^r G^{[n+r]}(z) = 0 \tag{6}$$

The above equation is not necessarily solvable for an arbitrary choice of $C_{nm}(s)$. However, when it is is solvable, the separability of the variables s and z implies that the above equation will be separable into a set of linear differential equations for $G(z)$ with coefficients given by integer powers of z. The general solution for $G(z)$ is then given by

$$G(z) = \sum_{i,k} a_{ik} z^k e^{-b_i z}, \tag{7}$$

where i and k are non negative integers. The coefficients a_{ik} and b_i, and the functions $C_{nm}(s)$ cannot be independently chosen as they are constrained through eq. 6. Once a set of $C_{nm}(s)$ is chosen consistently with the coefficients a_{ik} and b_i, the differential equation satisfied by $\mathbf{T}(\tau, s)$ can be obtained by iteratively substituting $\mathbf{W}_{(m)}^{[n]}(\tau - \tau', s)$ (in the second term of the r.h.s of eq. 4) in terms of its lower derivatives and replacing the integral in terms of derivatives of $\mathbf{T}(\tau, s)$.

Here we shall neither focus on the choice of $C_{nm}(s)$ nor on the differential equation for $\mathbf{T}(\tau, s)$ it yields. We shall only focus on the set of possible window functions that can be constructed by a space-time local mechanism. Hence it suffices to note from the above derivation that the general form of such a window function is given by eq. 7. Since by definition the window function at each s coarse grains the input about some past moment, we expect it to be non-oscillatory and hence restrict our focus to real values of b_i. Further, the requirement of the window function to have normalized area at all s restricts b_i to be positive.

4   Two Step Process

Let us consider the simplest window function, where only one of the coefficients in the set of a_{ik} and b_i in eq. 7 are non-zero, namely $b_i = b$ and $a_{ik} = b^{(k+1)}/k!$. We shall denote the corresponding window function as $W_{\{k,b\}}$ to highlight its dependence on specific k and b. The most general window function is then simply a linear combination of various $W_{\{k,b\}}$ for different values of k and b. From eq. 7, $W_{\{k,b\}}$ takes the form

$$W_{\{k,b\}}(\tau - \tau', s) = \frac{(bs)^{k+1}}{k!}(\tau - \tau')^k e^{-bs(\tau-\tau')}. \tag{8}$$

It turns out that the differential equation satisfied by $\mathbf{T}(\tau, s)$ that generates this window function is simply first order in both space and time given by

$$\mathbf{T}^{[1]}_{(1)}(\tau, s) + bs\mathbf{T}^{[0]}_{(1)}(\tau, s) - \frac{(k+1)}{s}\mathbf{T}^{[1]}_{(0)}(\tau, s) = 0, \tag{9}$$

with a boundary condition $\mathbf{T}(\tau, \infty) = f(\tau)$. This equation can hence be evolved in real time by only relying on the instantaneous input $f(\tau)$ at each moment τ.

For more complex window functions that are linear combinations of $W_{\{k,b\}}$ for various k and b, the order of the space and time derivatives of $\mathbf{T}(\tau, s)$ involved in the differential equation are not necessarily bounded when the parameters k and b involved in the linear combinations of $W_{\{k,b\}}$ are bounded. So, it is not straight forward to derive the mechanistic construction as a differential equation for $\mathbf{T}(\tau, s)$. Hence the question now is, what is the mechanism to construct a memory system with any window function?

Interestingly, there exists an alternative derivation of eq. 9 where the time derivative and space derivative can be sequentially employed in a two step process [12]. The first step is equivalent to encoding the Laplace transform of the input $f(\tau)$ as $\mathbf{F}(\tau, s)$. The second step is equivalent to approximately inverting the Laplace transformed input to construct $\mathbf{T}(\tau, s)$.

$$f(\tau) \xrightarrow{\ Laplace\ } \mathbf{F}(\tau, s) \xrightarrow{\ Inverse\,Laplace\ } \mathbf{T}(\tau, s)$$

$$\mathbf{F}^{[1]}(\tau, s) = -bs\mathbf{F}(\tau, s) + f(\tau), \tag{10}$$

$$\mathbf{T}(\tau, s) = \frac{b}{k!}s^{k+1}\mathbf{F}_{(k)}(\tau, s). \tag{11}$$

Taking $f(\tau)$ to be a function of bounded variation and $\mathbf{F}(-\infty, s) = 0$, eq. 10 can be integrated to see that $\mathbf{F}(\tau, s) = \int_{-\infty}^{\tau} f(\tau')e^{-bs(\tau-\tau')}d\tau'$. Thus $\mathbf{F}(\tau, s)$ is the Laplace transform of the past input computed over real time. Eq. 11 is an approximation to inverse Laplace transform operation [10]. So $\mathbf{T}(\tau, s)$ essentially attempts to reconstruct the past input, such that at any s, $\mathbf{T}(\tau, s) \simeq f(\tau - k/bs)$. This reconstruction grows more accurate as $k \to \infty$, and the input from each past moment is reliably represented at specific spatial location. For finite k however, the reconstruction is fuzzy and each spatial location represents a coarse grained average of inputs from past moments, as characterized by the window function $W_{\{k,b\}}$. For further details, refer to [12].

Since any window function is a linear combination of various $W_{\{k,b\}}$ for different values of k and b, its construction is essentially equivalent to linear combinations of the two step process given by equations 10 and 11.

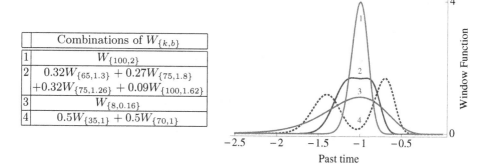

	Combinations of $W_{\{k,b\}}$
1	$W_{\{100,2\}}$
2	$0.32W_{\{65,1.3\}} + 0.27W_{\{75,1.8\}}$ $+0.32W_{\{75,1.26\}} + 0.09W_{\{100,1.62\}}$
3	$W_{\{8,0.16\}}$
4	$0.5W_{\{35,1\}} + 0.5W_{\{70,1\}}$

Fig. 2. For different combinations of $W_{\{k,b\}}$, the window functions are plotted as a function of past time at the spatial point $s = 50$

The choice of the combinations of $W_{\{k,b\}}$ has strong implications on the shape of the resulting window function. At any given s, $W_{\{k,b\}}$ is a unimodal function with a peak at $\tau - \tau' = k/bs$ (see eq. 8). Arbitrary combinations of $W_{\{k,b\}}$ could result in a spatial location representing the coarse grained average about disjoint past moments, leading to undesirable shapes of the window function. Hence the values of k and b should be carefully tuned. Figure 2 shows the window functions constructed from four combinations of b and k. The combinations are chosen such that at the point $s = 50$, the window function coarse grains around a past time of $\tau' - \tau \simeq -1$. The scale invariance property guarantees that its shape remains identical at any other value of s with a linear shift in the coarse graining timescale. Comparing combinations 1 and 3, note that the window function is narrower for larger $k(=100)$ than for a smaller $k(=8)$. Combination 2 has been chosen to illustrate a plateau shaped window function whose sides can be made arbitrarily vertical by fine tuning the combinations. Combination 4 (dotted curve in fig. 2) illustrates that combining different values of k for the same b will generally lead to a multimodal window function which would be an undesirable feature.

5   Discretized Spatial Axis

A memory system represented on a continuous spatial axis is not practical, so the spatial axis should be discretized to finite points (nodes). The two step process given by equations 10 and 11 is optimal for discretization particularly when the nodes are picked from a geometric progression in the values of s [13]. Eq. 10 implies that the activity of each node evolves independently of the others to construct $\mathbf{F}(\tau, s)$ with real time input $f(\tau)$. This is achieved with each node recurrently connected on to itself with an appropriate decay constant of bs. Eq. 11 involves taking the spatial derivative of order k which can be approximated by the discretized derivative requiring linear combinations of activities from k neighbors on either sides of any node. For further details on implementation of the two step process on discretized spatial axis, refer to [13].

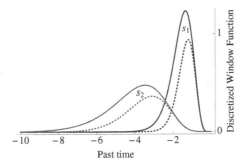

Fig. 3. Window function $w\{8, 1\}$ at two points $s_1 = 6.72$ and $s_2 = 2.59$ computed on a discretized spatial axis with $c = 0.1$. The dotted curves correspond to the window functions computed on the continuous spatial axis ($c \to 0$).

By choosing the nodes along the s-axis from a geometric progression, the error from the discretized spatial derivative will be uniformly spread over all timescales, hence such a discretization is ideal to preserve scale-invariance. Let us choose the s-values of successive nodes to have a ratio $(1 + c)$, where $c < 1$. Figure 3 shows the window function $W_{\{k,b\}}$ with $k = 8$ and $b = 1$ constructed from the discretized axis with $c = 0.1$. The window functions at two spatial points $s_1 = 6.72$ and $s_2 = 2.59$ are plotted to illustrate that scale invariance is preserved after discretization. As a comparison, the dotted curves are plotted to show the corresponding window function constructed in the continuous s-axis (limit $c \to 0$). The window function computed on the discretized axis is artificially scaled up so that the solid and dotted curves in figure 3 are visually discernible. Note that the discretized window function peaks farther in the past time and is wider than the window function on the continuous spatial axis. As $c \to 0$, the discretized window function converges on to the window function constructed on the continuous axis, while for larger values of c the discrepancy grows larger. Nevertheless, for any value of c, the discretized window function always stays scale-invariant, as can be seen by visually comparing the shapes of the window functions at s_1 and s_2 in figure 3. Now, it is straight forward to construct scale-invariant window functions of different shapes by taking linear combinations of discretized $W_{\{k,b\}}$, analogous to the construction in figure 2.

Implementing this construction on a discretized spatial axis as a neural network has a tremendous resource conserving advantage. Since at each s, the window function $W_{\{k,b\}}$ coarse grains the input around a past time of k/bs, the maximum past timesscale represented by the memory system is inversely related to minimum value of s. The geometric distribution of the s values on the discretized axis implies that if there are N nodes spanning the spatial axis for $\mathbf{T}(\tau, s)$, it can represent the coarse grained past from timescales proportional to $(1+c)^N$. Hence exponentially distant past can be represented in a coarse grained fashion with linearly increasing resources.

6   Discussion and Conclusion

The formulation presented here starts from a convolution memory model (eq. 1) and derives the form of the scale-invariant window functions (or the kernels) that can be constructed from a space-time local mechanism. Interestingly, by simply postulating a kernel of the form of eq. 7, Tank and Hopfield have demonstrated the utility of such a memory system in temporal pattern classification [15]. In general, a convolution memory model can adopt an arbitrary kernel, but it cannot be mechanistically constructed from a space-time local differential equation, which means a neural network implementation need not exist. However, the Gamma-memory model [17] shows that linear combinations of Gamma kernels, functionally similar to eq. 7, can indeed be mechanistically constructed from a set of differential equations.

The construction presented here takes a complementary approach to the Gamma-memory model by requiring scale invariance of the window function in the forefront and then imposing a space-time local differential equation to derive it. This sheds light on the connectivity between neighboring spatial units of the network that is required to generate a scale invariant window function, as described by the second part of the two step process (eq. 11). Moreover, the linearity of the two step process and its equivalence to the Laplace and Inverse Laplace transforms makes the memory representation analytically tractable.

Theoretically, the utility of a scale invariantly coarse grained memory hinges on the existence of scale free temporal fluctuations in the signals being encoded [13]. Although detailed empirical analysis of natural signals is needed to confirm this utility, preliminary analysis of time series from sunspots and global temperature show that such a memory system indeed has a higher predictive power than a conventional shift register [13]. The predictive advantage of this memory system can be understood as arising from its intrinsic ability to wash out non-predictive stochastic fluctuations in the input signal from distant past and just represent the predictively relevant information in a condensed form. Finally, the most noteworthy feature is that a memory system with N nodes can represent information from exponentially past times proportional to $(1+c)^N$. In comparison to a shift register with N nodes which can accurately represent a maximum past time scale proportional to N, this memory system is exponentially resource conserving.

Acknowldegements. The work was partly funded by NSF BCS-1058937 and AFOSR FA9550-12-1-0369.

References

1. Charles, A.S., Yap, H.L., Rozell, C.J.: Short-term memory capacity in networks via the restricted isometry property. Neural Computation 26, 1198–1235 (2014)
2. Ganguli, S., Huh, D., Sompolinsky, H.: Memory traces in dynamical systems. Proceedings of the National Academy of Sciences of the United States of America 105(48), 18970–18975 (2008)
3. Ganguli, S., Sompolinsky, H.: Memory traces in dynamical systems. Annual Review of Neuroscience 35, 485–508 (2012)
4. Gibbon, J.: Scalar expectancy theory and Weber's law in animal timing. Psychological Review 84(3), 279–325 (1977)
5. Hermans, M., Schrauwen, B.: Memory in linear recurrent neural networks in continuous time. Neural Networks 23(3), 341–355 (2010)
6. Jaeger, H.: The echo state approach to analyzing and training recurrent networks. GMD-Report 148, GMD - German National Research Institute for Information Technology (2001)
7. Legenstein, R., Maass, W.: Edge of chaos and prediction of computational performance for neural circuit models. Neural Networks 20, 323–334 (2007)
8. Maass, W., Natschläger, T., Markram, H.: Real-time computing without stable states: A new framework for neural computation based on perturbations. Neural Computation 14(11), 2531–2560 (2002)
9. Mandelbrot, B.: The Fractal Geometry of Nature. W. H. Freeman, San Fransisco (1982)
10. Post, E.: Generalized differentiation. Transactions of the American Mathematical Society 32, 723–781 (1930)
11. Rakitin, B.C., Gibbon, J., Penny, T.B., Malapani, C., Hinton, S.C., Meck, W.H.: Scalar expectancy theory and peak-interval timing in humans. Journal of Experimental Psychololgy: Animal Behavior Processes 24, 15–33 (1998)
12. Shankar, K.H., Howard, M.W.: A scale-invariant internal representation of time. Neural Computation 24, 134–193 (2012)
13. Shankar, K.H., Howard, M.W.: Optimally fuzzy temporal memory. Journal of Machine Learning Research 14, 3785–3812 (2013)
14. Strauss, T., Wustlich, W., Labahn, R.: Design strategies for weight matrices of echo state networks. Neural Computation 24, 3246–3276 (2012)
15. Tank, D., Hopfield, J.: Neural computation by concentrating information in time. Proceedings of the National Academy of Sciences 84(7), 1896–1900 (1987)
16. Voss, R.F., Clarke, J.: $1/f$ noise in music and speech. Nature 258, 317–318 (1975)
17. Vries, B.D., Principe, J.C.: The gamma model, a new neural model for temporal processing. Neural Networks 5(4), 565–576 (1992)

18. Wallace, E., Maei, H.R., Latham, P.E.: Randomly connected networks have short temporal memory. Neural Computation 25, 1408–1439 (2013)
19. West, B.J., Shlesinger, M.F.: The noise in natural phenomena. American Scientist 78, 40–45 (1990)
20. White, O.L., Lee, D.D., Sompolinsky, H.: Short-term memory in orthogonal neural networks. Physical Review Letters 92(14), 148102 (2004)

Transgenic Evolution for Classification Tasks with HERCL

Alan D. Blair

School of Computer Science and Engineering
University of New South Wales
Sydney, 2052 Australia
blair@cse.unsw.edu.au

Abstract. We explore the evolution of programs for classification tasks, using the recently introduced Hierarchical Evolutionary Re-Combination Language (HERCL) which has been designed as an austere and general-purpose language, with a view toward modular evolutionary computation, combining elements from Linear GP with stack-based operations from FORTH. We show that evolved HERCL programs can successfully learn to perform a variety of benchmark classification tasks, and that performance is enhanced by the sharing of genetic material between tasks.

Keywords: transgenic evolutionary computation, stack-based genetic programming, evolutionary automatic programming.

1 Introduction

The Hierarchical Evolutionary Re-Combination paradigm and associated HERCL programming language were recently introduced [3] in an effort to provide a novel framework for evolutionary automatic programming, designed to be suitable for transfer learning between tasks [18] as well as for the future development of modular evolving systems [4].

HERCL has been designed as an austere and general-purpose language, combining elements from Linear GP [16] with stack-based operations from FORTH [5]. As such, it draws on the tradition of induced subroutines [1] and Automatically Defined Functions [11,17,9,23] as well as stack-based GP [19,6] and related approaches [20,22].

In previous work, we have shown how HERCL programs can be evolved to perform dynamically unstable control tasks [4] as well as coding tasks such as the Caesar and Vigenere cipher [3]. Although challenging, these coding tasks dealt exclusively with synthetic data derived from very precise rules, so that as soon as the training error reached zero, the test set error generally also went to zero. In the present work, we take this research in a new direction and explore the ability of HERCL programs to capture underlying patterns in real-world datasets and generalize to unseen data, by testing them on six benchmark classification tasks. We are particularly interested in the question of whether the evolution of one task can be improved (in terms of speed, parsimony or accuracy) by the sharing of transgenic material from agents evolved on other, related tasks.

S.K. Chalup et al. (Eds.): ACALCI 2015, LNAI 8955, pp. 185–195, 2015.

```
out: [-0.98]
mem: ..............................
reg: gtattctcaacaagattaaccgacagattcaatctcgtggatggacgttcaacattg
stack: [0.93]t[1.39][1.77]...........................
                ^
0[15<14<49g=:x|33=x:35=:1:|15g}:38=:21<38g:q|cn%y3.906#p3.#thwo]
                                                              ^
```

Fig. 1. HERCL simulator, showing an evolved agent executing the PROMOTERS task. Note the output buffer, memory, registers, stack and code. All items are floating point numbers, but the simulator prints them as a dot (zero), an ASCII character, or bracketed in decimal format, depending on their value.

2   The HERCL Programming Language

HERCL agents have a stack, registers and memory. The number of registers, size of memory and (maximum) size of the stack are part of the specification of the agent, along with the code – which is divided hierarchically into *cells*, *bars* and *instructions*. Each *cell* contains a sequence of executable instructions, and might alternatively be thought of as a "procedure" or "subroutine". The pipe symbol (|) is used as a kind of *bar line* to divide each cell into smaller chunks or *bars*, like the bars in a musical score. Every instruction consists of a (single-character) *command*, optionally preceded by a sequence of dot/digits which form the "argument" for that command. The various commands are listed in Table 1.

The language has been designed with the specific aim of allowing new programs to be created by combining portions or *patches* of code from other (heterogenous) programs, at multiple scales (bar, cell or multi-cell) in such a way that the functionality of the transplanted code would be substantially preserved. Whenever such a patch is applied, it is followed up by a series of smaller-scale patches or mutations in the vicinity of the original patch, in an effort to make the new code integrate felicitously with the surrounding code. These smaller patches are, in turn, followed up by yet smaller mutations, recursively, to produce a global random search strategy known as hierarchical evolutionary re-combination.

3   Hierarchical Evolutionary Re-combination

HERCL does not use a population as such, but instead maintains a stack or *ladder* of candidate solutions (agents), and a *codebank* of potential mates (Figure 2). At each step of the algorithm, we select the agent at the top rung of the ladder and apply either mutation or crossover with a randomly chosen agent from the codebank, or from an external *library* (explained below). We distinguish different *levels* of mutation/crossover (TUNE, POINT, BAR, BRANCH, CELL, JUMP or BLOCK) which vary according to the portion of code from the primary (ladder) parent that is either mutated or crossed over with a commensurate portion of

Table 1. HERCL Commands

Input and Output

i fetch INPUT to input buffer
s SCAN item from input buffer to stack
w WRITE item from stack to output buffer
o flush OUTPUT buffer

Stack Manipulation and Arithmetic

\# PUSH new item to stack ...... $\mapsto$ x
! POP top item from stack ...... $x \mapsto$ ......
c COPY top item on stack ...... $x \mapsto$ ...... x, x
x SWAP top two items ... $y, x \mapsto$ ... x, y
y ROTATE top three items $z, y, x \mapsto x, z, y$
- NEGATE top item ...... $x \mapsto$ ..... $(-x)$
+ ADD top two items ... $y, x \mapsto$ ...$(y + x)$
* MULTIPLY top two items ... $y, x \mapsto$ ...$(y * x)$

Mathematical Functions

r RECIPROCAL $.. x \to .. 1/x$
q SQUARE ROOT $.. x \to .. \sqrt{x}$
e EXPONENTIAL $.. x \mapsto .. e^x$
n (natural) LOGARITHM $.. x \mapsto .. \log_e(x)$
a ARCSINE $.. x \mapsto .. \sin^{-1}(x)$
h TANH $.. x \mapsto .. \tanh(x)$
z ROUND to nearest integer
? push RANDOM value to stack

Double-Item Functions

% DIVIDE/MODULO $.. y, x \mapsto .. (y/x), (y \bmod x)$
t TRIG functions $.. \theta, r \mapsto .. r\sin\theta, r\cos\theta$
p POLAR coords $.. y, x \mapsto ..$ atan2$(y, x), \sqrt{x^2 + y^2}$

Registers and Memory

< GET value from register
> PUT value into register
^ INCREMENT register
v DECREMENT register
{ LOAD from memory location
} STORE to memory location

Jump, Testing, Branching and Logic

j JUMP to specified cell (subroutine)
| BAR line (RETURN on .| HALT on 8|)
= check register is EQUAL to top of stack
g check register is GREATER than top of stack
: if TRUE, branch FORWARD
; if TRUE, branch BACK
& logical AND
/ logical OR
~ logical NOT

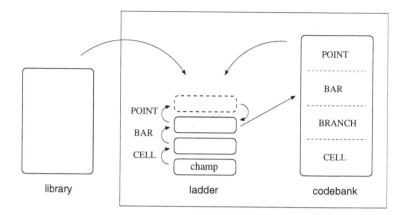

Fig. 2. Hierarchical Evolutionary Re-Combination. If the top agent on the ladder becomes fitter than the one below it, the top agent will move down to replace the lower agent (which is transferred to the codebank). If the top agent exceeds its maximum number of allowable offspring without ever becoming fitter than the one below it, the top agent is removed from the ladder (and transferred to the codebank).

code from the secondary (codebank or library) parent. The level of each mutation/crossover is chosen randomly, with lower levels weighted more heavily than higher ones, and with the constraint that the mutation levels must strictly decrease as we move up the ladder. The agents in the codebank are grouped according to mutation/crossover level, with a limited number of agents in each level. Further details can be found in [3].

During the evolution, comparison between agents is based on five criteria: *length*, *time*, *cost*, *penalty* and *reject*. The *length* is the total number of commands, dots and digits in the program. The *time* is the average number of instructions executed for each training input. We draw a distinction between the *cost* — which is a measure of the difference between actual and desired output — and the *penalty* — which is a count of more serious violations of the "rules" (for example, producing the wrong number of outputs, or failing to produce any output at all). If an agent exceeds a certain maximum number of execution steps (usually due to an infinite loop) it is classified as *reject* and culled immediately. If two agents differ in terms of *penalty*, the one with lower penalty is always considered fitter, regardless of the *cost*. When comparing two penalty-free agents, the fitness is calculated as the *cost* plus tiny multiples of the *length* and *time* — thus favoring shorter and faster agents, and serving as an effective means of *bloat control* [12,13].

When two agents with the same non-zero *penalty* are compared, the winner is chosen probabilistically using a Boltzmann distribution based on the difference in *length* and *time*. This gives rise to a Metropolis search [15] in the early stages of evolution, until a penalty-free agent is achieved. After that, the fitness comparison strictly favors shorter and faster agents, and relies purely on the hierarchical nature of the search in order to escape from local optima (see Figure 2). Depending on its

Table 2. Mutation Levels (Low to High)

TUNE:	Modify one or more PUSH values
POINT:	Choose one or more points at which to insert, remove or replace an instruction, or modify the dot/digits of an instruction
BAR:	Replace the front, back, middle, fringe or whole of a bar in P_0 with the front, back, middle, fringe or whole of a bar in P_1
BRANCH:	Insert a conditional branch, to skip some existing instructions and/or execute newly added instructions
CELL:	Replace front, back, middle or fringe of a cell in P_0 with the front, back, middle or fringe of a cell in P_1
JUMP:	Introduce an instruction to jump to a cell in P_0 and (optionally) replace that cell with a cell from P_1
BLOCK:	Replace a block of cells in P_0 with a block from P_1

level, each (penalty-free) agent is guaranteed to survive long enough to produce a certain number of offspring, thus promoting diversity in a manner comparable to the age-layered population structure of [10].

Once an agent is found which achieves a *cost* less than some pre-determined threshold, the algorithm moves into a final *trimming* phase in which instructions can be deleted and replaced but not inserted, thereby removing extraneous code and reducing the agent to a minimal size.

4   Training Paradigm

We consider classification tasks where the input consists of a fixed number of (binary, discrete or continuous) features and the target output is either 1 or -1.

The stack and memory of the agent are initially re-set, and the input features are loaded into its registers (one register for each feature). The code of the agent is then executed, and it is required to eventually output one single-item message and halt; otherwise it incurs a penalty. The cost function between the target T and output Z is defined as:

$$\text{cost} = \begin{cases} 0 & , \quad \text{if } T = 1 \text{ and } Z \geq 1, \\ 0 & , \quad \text{if } T = -1 \text{ and } Z \leq -1, \\ (Z - T)^2, & \text{otherwise.} \end{cases}$$

The progress of the evolution is measured in *applications, evaluations* and *epochs*. Each *application* refers to the code of a new agent being executed once, to classify one training item. Each *evaluation* refers to a new agent having its cost (fitness) evaluated and compared to that of its (primary) parent. For this, the new agent is applied to successive training items until either (a) all items in the training set have been exhausted, or (b) the cost accumulated by the new agent is already so large that it would remain inferior to the parent even if it were to classify all subsequent items with zero cost. For convenience the evolution is divided into *epochs*, with the number of evaluations in each epoch gradually increasing as the evolution progresses (equal to $2^{\frac{n}{2}}$ for epoch n, up to a maximum of $10,000$ comparisons). If more than one agent remain on the ladder when this limit is reached, the epoch continues for a few additional evaluations until the ladder is reduced to a single agent on the lowest rung. For the experiments described in this paper we will only consider single-cell HERCL programs, so CELL level crossovers are the highest ones available.

In order to put a limit on the computation time, and avoid overfitting, we stop the evolution when either (a) the total number of applications has exceeded 900 million, or (b) the average cost per training item has reached a pre-defined threshold. We then commence the final "trimming" phase, for an additional 10,0000 evaluations. The limit of 900 million epochs has been chosen so that, allowing for the completion of the current epoch, plus the trimming phase, the total number of applications in the entire process will not exceed one billion. For these experiments a threshold value of 0.2 was chosen. (Preliminary tests indicated that a threshold of 0.1 leads to similar results, while 0.3 leads to slightly degraded performance.) During the trimming phase agents with lower cost are preferred, so the average cost per training item may ultimately reach a value lower than the pre-defined threshold.

Once the evolution and trimming are complete, the agent is tested on the (unseen) test data. We will be investigating the number of evaluations required to achieve the threshold cost per item, and the length of the resulting code, as well as the final accuracy.

It is also possible to ensemble a number of evolved agents to produce a collective prediction. The ensembling is done by voting, with the sum of the output values used as a tie-breaker when there are equal numbers of positive and negative votes.

This kind of ensembling method — now a standard technique in machine learning — can perhaps be traced back to Solomonoff [21] who proposed that the optimal predictive agent should be one which maintains a collection of Turing machines compatible with the data so-far observed, and weighs their predictions (inversely) exponentially by the size of the machine. Programs in a language like HERCL (or any kind of linear, tree- or stack-based GP) arguably comprise a better set of "base learners" than Turing machines for this purpose, because (a) the evolutionary algorithm provides an effective search mechanism, giving preference to shorter (and faster) agents, and (b) these programs operate natively on floating point numbers rather than discrete symbols, reflecting the fact that modern computers can perform floating-point operations in a single clock cycle.

5 Tasks and Experimental Method

Six Benchmark Classification Tasks Were Selected from the UCI repository [2]: IONOSPHERE, PROMOTERS, HEPATITIS, AUSTRALIAN, SONAR and PIMA. These tasks were chosen on the criteria that the number of training items should not exceed 1000, the number of features should not exceed 100, and the number of classes should be two. Each dataset was split randomly into 10 parts (stratified) for 10-fold cross-validation. In each case, we consider the target output to be +1 for positive items and −1 for negative items.

The input features for these six tasks are quite diverse. The IONOSPHERE task takes 34 continuous inputs in the range −1 to 1. The E. Coli Promoter Gene Sequences (PROMOTERS) task uses 57 nucleotides, which we represent as ASCII characters a, c, g or t. The inputs for the HEPATITIS task are the age and sex of the patient, together with 17 medical indicators (12 binary, 5 continuous). The Australian Credit Card Approval (AUSTRALIAN) dataset has 14 inputs of which 6 are continuous, 4 are binary (0,1) and 5 are categorical (which we treat as integers 1, 2, etc.). The SONAR task (Mines vs. Rocks) uses 60 continuous values between 0 and 1, representing the energy in different frequency bands. The Pima Indians Diabetes (PIMA) Dataset has 6 medical indicators together with the age of the patient and the number of times they have been pregnant.

In order to investigate the effect of sharing genetic material between different tasks, we will compare two different training regimes – referred to as Single and Transgenic. In the Single regime, evolution for the six tasks are run completely independently and do not share any genetic material. In the Transgenic regime, the six evolutions are run concurrently, and a common *library* is maintained, consisting of the current best agent (champ) for each of the six tasks. The code in the library is updated at the conclusion of each epoch. At each step of the algorithm, the secondary parent can be chosen either from the codebank or from the library. In other words, the current best agent from each task is made available as a potential mate for the evolution of the other five tasks. Each regime was run 25 times from different random seeds.

6 Results

In order to compare training times between the two regimes, we count the total number of evaluations required for the threshold cost per item to be achieved. The median number of evaluations (rounded to the nearest thousand) are shown in Column 2 of Table 3, while Column 3 shows the Z-score and p-value obtained from a (two-tailed) Mann-Whitney U-test [14] (the AUSTRALIAN and PIMA datasets are excluded, because the majority of runs failed to attain the threshold cost per item before exceeding the maximum number of allowed applications). For the IONOSPHERE dataset, the number of evaluations for the Transgenic regime is significantly smaller than for the Single regime. For the other datasets, the difference is not statistically significant.

The median Code Length (total number of commands, dots and digits) in the final evolved agent is shown in Table 3, Column 4. For the PROMOTERS, AUSTRALIAN, SONAR and PIMA datasets, the Transgenic regime produces significantly shorter code than the Single regime, as measured by a Mann-Whitney U-test (Column 5).

Table 3. Evaluations and Code Length

	Evaluations		Mann-Whitney		Code Length		Mann-Whitney	
	Single	Trans	z-score	p-value	Single	Trans	z-score	p-value
IONOSPHERE	67,000	55,000	2.01	0.044	62	63	1.27	0.20
PROMOTERS	484,000	439,000	1.28	0.20	95	87	3.25	0.0012
HEPATITIS	689,000	575,000	1.35	0.18	118	114	1.71	0.087
AUSTRALIAN	–	–			249	216	5.32	0.0001
SONAR	1436,000	1612,000	-0.97	0.33	215	206	2.34	0.019
PIMA	–	–			266	244	2.58	0.010

Table 4. Accuracy

	Items	Features	Single	Trans	t-score	p-value	Ensemble
IONOSPHERE	351	34	89.8 ± 0.3	89.8 ± 0.2	0.12	0.91	93.2
PROMOTERS	106	57	65.2 ± 0.6	68.4 ± 1.0	2.54	0.014	83.0
HEPATITIS	155	19	73.6 ± 0.6	73.3 ± 0.5	-0.42	0.67	80.6
AUSTRALIAN	690	14	79.1 ± 0.3	79.0 ± 0.3	-0.30	0.76	85.2
SONAR	208	60	64.4 ± 0.7	66.3 ± 0.7	1.76	0.084	82.2
PIMA	768	8	62.6 ± 0.5	62.9 ± 0.6	0.47	0.51	72.3

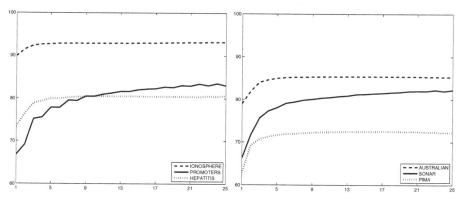

Fig. 3. Accuracy achieved by different sized ensembles of evolved HERCL programs, with classification by voting, using summed output to break ties when votes are equal

Columns 4 and 5 of Table 4 show the mean accuracy (on the test set) for the Single and Transgenic regimes, averaged over the 25 runs, together with the standard error of the mean. Column 6 shows the result of a (two-tailed) Welch's t-test. We see that, for the PROMOTERS dataset, the Transgenic regime provides a statistically significant improvement in mean accuracy, compared to the Single regime. For the other datasets, the difference is not statistically significant.

The accuracy achieved by ensembling different numbers of agents is graphed in Figure 3, and the accuracy obtained from an ensemble of all 25 evolved agents is listed in the final column of Table 4.

By ensembling a number of moderately accurate agents, we ultimately achieve a level of accuracy which is broadly competitive with what has previously been reported for other evolutionary approaches such as GP with clustering, or GP refined using a gain criterion [7]. For the SONAR dataset, our methods seem to achieve an accuracy comparable to that of a neural network with two or three hidden units [8] (although a more thorough analysis based on multiple splits of the data would be needed in order to make a comprehensive comparison).

The evolved HERCL agents which happen to classify the largest number of items correctly for each dataset are shown in Table 5. We see that the agents evolved for the IONOSPHERE and PROMOTERS task make extensive use of testing and branching instructions, while those evolved for the SONAR and PIMA tasks rely more heavily on stack manipulation and arithmetic.

Table 5. Evolved Agents

IONOSPHERE:

[13{<q14g:.06#11g|.v~:<17={:28=v:15<p6=.{:4=.v:4<|<wo]

HEPATITIS:

[10<13g:<1.#12g~y:ztq|13ge2}:>7}|5.#t%1vh<8<y14g15{:7=|+px
!xgx:y|y}>14g{p6^{:3{|p13g:8{15g~:2g:e|px>=~:.647059#-|-wo]

PROMOTERS:

[15<14<49g=:x|33=x:35=:1:|15g}:38=:21<38g:q|cn%y3.906#p3.#thwo]

AUSTRALIAN:

[e2g=:1.83242496#10<aeh.3#6gy:{g{:*ycc5>p+|txy.>e<12va7<21#9g9:3.#
5=~!:{|!n8<c11g:e|*4=~:15#-|3<n12vrn13<cp12ge~*:+}4^c2<htxxn4#-
c1}>g2:|t.}><+8{+5{+c9=!{++c13<11=~!:n3vy<h++12{5>7}{2{11<!g:5:
|a10<x6g.=aaa/~aqt:!!zcg:a*xaaaaaaa2#e>aaaaaaah<|5<t7vnzt}xg2:+
11{+caaa1.#->aag~:0>|13<3=~*z:8}|0g:2>4<|9#=!:+11#g}:+a8{2=y:h|wo]

SONAR:

[10<21<14g~!:aaaaaaaaa|h15g:.1#p<|+<xqcpya>h+g46<x.99#-:*a
tt**>44<qh|tx>+zcc>+g+46<<1:19<+27<6g+:51<*4<+{}13gq}p:<|c
r+9#-t50<q.13#>g~:!42<{+.8#-+a|z35{++aaaxr-q<-+hz+a14{q+wo]

PIMA:

[7.#27.8#5gzq6<10.88#0<p>ct>pz><q:%pp<8#-.>ppch7}e5ge|q>g<:5v**y+|
1gzh<ppppp!:%t6vxy%|n<p5}at.1565#->g{4:x^xzg:9:|9g+>aa+r.1521#-g:>g
1:x|}a.58#4gac:%*9<x|x6gx:+*tp>py|%!<ac0g~!:a|1.#>g:pa%nzc6>pc1v}pp
<p>|<4g!!p!.55393#:ae+1:|7.#.>0g*:n-|.g~:x=x1:zg:++|htx6g~ax:tt|wo]

---

7   Conclusion and Further Work

We have shown that HERCL programs can successfully be evolved to perform six benchmark classification tasks.

Although the tasks are quite disparate, the evolution for each task can make productive use of transgenic crossovers which adapt portions of code from the evolution of other, related tasks. For all except the HEPATITIS task, the availability of transgenic crossovers provides a statistically significant improvement in either the training time, code length or final accuracy. Overall accuracy can be improved by ensembling a number of evolved agents.

The genetic diversity of the codebank and the hierarchical nature of the evolutionary search allow it to escape from local optima even though the number of agents competing at any point in time is very small. The selective pressure for shorter and faster code enables the evolved programs to capture the underlying patterns in the data and avoid overfitting.

In future work, we plan to investigate sequence prediction and further refine the HERCL framework with a view to exploring multi-agent systems and modular evolution.

References

1. Angeline, P.J., Pollack, J.B.: The evolutionary induction of subroutines. In: Proc. 14th Annual Conference of the Cognitive Science Society, pp. 236–241 (1992)
2. Bache, K., Lichman, M.: UCI Machine Learning Repository. University of California, School of Information and Computer Science, Irvine, CA (2013), http://archive.ics.uci.edu/ml
3. Blair, A.: Learning the Caesar and Vigenere Cipher by Hierarchical Evolutionary Re-Combination. In: Proc. 2013 Congress on Evolutionary Computation, pp. 605–612 (2013)
4. Blair, A.: Incremental evolution of HERCL programs for robust control. In: Proc. 2014 Conf. on Genetic and Evolutionary Computation Companion, pp. 27–28 (2014)
5. Brodie, L.: Starting Forth, 2nd edn. Prentice-Hall, NJ (1987)
6. Bruce, W.S.: The lawnmower problem revisited: Stack-based genetic programming and automatically defined functions. In: Proc. 2nd Annual Conf. Genetic Programming, pp. 52–57 (1997)
7. Eggermont, J., Kok, J.N., Kosters, W.A.: Genetic programming for data classification: Partitioning the search space. In: Proc. 2004 ACM Symposium on Applied Computing, pp. 1001–1005 (2004)
8. Gorman, R.P., Sejnowski, T.J.: Analysis of Hidden Units in a Layered Network Trained to Classify Sonar Targets. In: Neural Networks, vol. 1, pp. 75–89 (1988)
9. Harper, R., Blair, A.: Dynamically Defined Functions in Grammatical Evolution. In: Proc. 2006 Congress on Evolutionary Computation, pp. 1420–1427 (2006)
10. Hornby, G.S.: ALPS: the age-layered population structure for reducing the problem of premature convergence. In: Proc. 2006 Conf. on Genetic and Evolutionary Computation, pp. 815–822 (2006)
11. Koza, J.R.: Genetic Programming II: Automatic Discovery of Reusable Programs. MIT Press (1994)

12. Langdon, W.B., Banzhaf, W.: Genetic Programming Bloat without Semantics. In: Parallel Problem Solving from Nature VI, pp. 201–210 (2000)
13. Luke, S., Panait, L.: A Comparison of Bloat Control Methods for Genetic Programming. Evolutionary Computation 14(3), 309–344 (2006)
14. Mann, H.B., Whitney, D.R.: On a Test of Whether one of Two Random Variables is Stochastically Larger than the Other. Annals of Math. Statistics 18(1), 50–60 (1947)
15. Metropolis, N., Rosenbluth, A.W., Rosenbluth, M.N., Teller, A.H., Teller, E.: Equation of State Calculations by Fast Computing Machines. J. Chem. Phys. 21, 1087–1092 (1953)
16. Nordin, P.: A compiling genetic programming system that directly manipulates the machine code. Advances in Genetic Programming 1, 311–331 (1994)
17. O'Neill, M., Ryan, C.: Grammar based function definition in Grammatical Evolution. In: Proc. GECCO 2000, pp. 485–490 (2000)
18. Pan, S.J., Yang, Q.: A Survey on Transfer Learning. IEEE Trans. Knowledge and Data Engineering 22(10), 1345–1359 (2010)
19. Perkis, T.: Stack-based genetic programming. In: Proc. IEEE World Congress on Computational Intelligence, pp. 148–153 (1994)
20. Salustowicz, R., Schmidhuber, J.: Evolving Structured Programs with Hierarchical Instructions and Skip Nodes. In: Proc. 15th Int'l Conf. Machine Learning (ICML 1998), pp. 488–496 (1998)
21. Solomonoff, R.J.: A formal theory of inductive inference: Parts 1 and 2. Information and Control 7, 1–22, 224–254 (1964)
22. Spector, L., Robinson, A.: Genetic Programming and Autoconstructive Evolution with the Push Programming Language. Genetic Programming and Evolvable Machines 3(1), 7–40 (2002)
23. Walker, J.A., Miller, J.F.: The Automatic Acquisition, Evolution and Reuse of Modules in Cartesian Genetic Programming. IEEE Trans. Evolutionary Computation 12(4), 397–417 (2008)

Learning Nursery Rhymes Using Adaptive Parameter Neurodynamic Programming

Josiah Walker and Stephan K. Chalup

School of Electrical Engineering & Computer Science
The University of Newcastle, NSW 2308, Australia
josiah.walker@uon.edu.au

Abstract. In this study on music learning, we develop an average reward based adaptive parameterisation for reinforcement learning metaparameters. These are tested using an approximation of user feedback based on the goal of learning the nursery rhymes *Twinkle Twinkle Little Star* and *Mary Had a Little Lamb*. We show that a large reduction in learning times can be achieved through a combination of adaptive parameters and random restarts to ensure policy convergence.

Keywords: neuro-dynamic programming, reinforcement learning, metaparameters, online music learning.

1 Introduction

Computer generated music first appeared in the 1950's when computers capable of playing music, such as CSIRAC at the University of Melbourne, were developed (Doornbusch, 2005). These early machines simply reproduced pre-programmed melodies, however they offered many new opportunities for composers of the time to experiment with the new technology. Hiller and Isaacson are credited with the first algorithmic computer generated music, beginning with a series of experiments in 1955 which were later published (Hiller and Isaacson, 1959). These were offline methods for composing music which culminated in the composition of music for a string quartet called *The Illiac Suite*, performed in 1957 (Hiller and Isaacson, 1959). Following this, famous composer Iannis Xenakis popularised the concept of algorithmic music by using computers to generate music based on stochastic processes (Xenakis, 1992).

The potential for music to be used to affect human behaviour and performance brings a practical element to the machine learning approach of composing of music in a way which maximises certain goals. Goals such as investigating and reproducing the phenomenon labeled the 'Mozart Effect' [1] (Rauscher et al., 1993) and similar studies (Mammarella et al., 2007) bring interesting possibilities for research and application.

---

[1] The 'Mozart Effect' is a term given to the finding that listening to one of Mozart's pieces can enhance some types of reasoning abilities for a short time.

S.K. Chalup et al. (Eds.): ACALCI 2015, LNAI 8955, pp. 196–209, 2015.
© Springer International Publishing Switzerland 2015

Recent experiments in computer generated music include the use of neuro-dynamic programming (Sutton and Barto, 1998; Bertsekas and Tsitsiklis, 1996), also known as reinforcement learning (RL) to develop music through live inter-action with users. Groux and Verschure (2010) investigate manual user feedback signals to shape musical tension, showing that live user input can be effectively used as a feedback function to learn from. This work shows that a relatively high time resolution of 100ms is acceptable for measuring manual user feedback in real-time, which allows relatively high speed sampling to the point where it is possible to gather feedback per note played for some types of music.

Collins (2008) investigates a simple model for music generation by reinforce-ment learning. While reinforcement learning mechanisms have been used in con-junction with pre-training techniques (Franklin, 2006), Collins concluded that for RL in the field of music, outstanding research questions include investigating how to gather appropriate input from the user. More broadly, the performance of the learning algorithm itself, and the issue of using prior knowledge for tasks are still open research questions in the RL community. Smith and Garnett (2012) addresses some of these concerns by enabling self-learning through intrinsically motivated reinforcement learning. Such an approach allows an agent to learn for longer and without human feedback in order to achieve interesting results. However, the use of human feedback within a real-time learning loop may open up new methods for exploring creativity, if some of the current limitations of reinforcement learning systems can be addressed.

In the framework of reinforcement learning, every learning episode has a stochastic set of initial values and/or exploration during the episode. As a result, each episode has a variable time to convergence, and guaranteed solutions may not be achievable in a reasonable amount of time. Most RL solutions focus on the policy which has been learned, rather than the learning itself, as the useful end product of the learning system. In the case of music creation, the learn-ing process itself is central to the system's performance measure, and so fast, guaranteed convergence is needed.

In this paper, we seek to address some of the issues described by Collins (2008). Specifically, we seek to improve the general performance of musical agents cre-ating or learning music to the point that learning speed is practical for exper-imenting with other user feedback methods such as biometrics. The remainder of this paper addresses the use of adaptive meta-parameters for reinforcement learning, the experimental set-up used to validate adaptive meta-parameters, and the use of random restarts to guarantee agent convergence to a successful music pattern.

As noted by Collins (2008), using a reward function such as biometric feedback for learning to create music is tantalising but completely untested. We do not know what learning parameters will improve learning speed, or how long it might take for a user to complete a training episode using a learning agent. To test the feasibility of learning music using this type of method, an automated testing platform is required. We propose an evaluation mechanism which utilises existing music to perform test training using a simple user response model.

2   Reinforcement Learning

Reinforcement learning (RL) is a field of machine learning with intuitively under-standable biological parallels (Sutton and Barto, 1998; Bertsekas and Tsitsiklis, 1996; Schweighofer and Doya, 2003). RL uses positive and negative 'rewards' to reinforce behaviours and encourage agents to learn behaviours that solve tasks as diverse as as pole balancing, robot locomotion, and chess. The learning setting is an agent interacting with an environment by sensing states and making choices over time. Learning is achieved by feeding the agent a signal (the 'reward') which can be positive when the agent achieves a desired goal, and negative when the agent fails in some way.

Research into the biological processes which inspired reinforcement learning has also led to useful (and sometimes parallel) results for the field of RL. These results are significant not only for the advances in machine learning that occur, but also because we gain insight into how our own brains work. In particular, results from Doya and Dayan (Doya, 2008; Dayan, 2009) are important to our understanding of the biological processes involved in temporal credit assignment learning.

Within the framework of reinforcement learning, Kenji Doya called the learn-ing rate α, the inverse temperature β, and the discount factor γ meta-parameters or hyper-parameters (Doya, 2002). He also proposed a brain-theoretical inter-pretation of the meta-parameters as equivalent to certain neuro-modulators, which provides a consistent explanation of the behaviour of some of the learning processes in the brain. Under this theory, the meta-parameter γ is linked to sero-tonin; the error estimate δ is linked to dopamine; the learning rate α is linked to Acetylcholine; and the inverse temperature β is linked to Noradrenaline.

Daw et al. (2002) proposed the existence of an opponent partnership of sero-tonin with dopamine and that the serotonergic signal reports the long-run av-erage reward rate as part of an average-case reinforcement learning model. This modifies the RL update rule to subtract the long-run average, r_{av}, from the value rather than multiplying the future estimated reward by a discount γ. The resulting update rule can be expressed as:

$$Q\left(s,a\right) = Q\left(s,a\right) + \alpha\left[r - r_{av} + argmax_{i=0}^{n}\left(Q\left(s',a_i\right)\right) - Q\left(s,a\right)\right]$$

This modification separates the reward prediction horizon from the expected future reward value, allowing the agent's estimates of action value to change as it achieves better or worse average results. An average reward learning strategy effectively avoids many sub-optimal solutions by modifying the value of its own previous estimates to consistently improve on its average gain. The effective-ness of average reward RL also shows that the average reward is an important contributing value in the learning process.

3   Experimental Setup

The response model works as follows: if an unrecognised set of notes is played, the reward is 0. If several correct notes are played in the correct sequence, the reward is 1. If an incorrect note is being played after several correct notes have been played, the reward is −1. This may not reflect the responses of a user completely, but provides an automated feedback function which is hopefully similar. In tuning, the minimum correct sequence required was set to 2. Variations were also tested with the minimum sequence length set to 3. These tests allow an evaluation of how changes to the reward function will affect the success of the agents.

Real music was used as training and testing data. For initial investigations into the feasibility of this type of learning, we use two well known nursery rhymes. These are: *Twinkle Twinkle Little Star* and *Mary Had a Little Lamb* (Daly, 2010). This music was transcribed into pitch and duration pairs for use with the learning system. We did not include data on beat timing in this system, and so issues such as syncopation are not considered in the reward system at this point.

For all tests, we use a linear classifier agent as our testing has shown that with the right state representation it offers a good trade-off between the expressiveness of neural networks and speed of learning convergence.

3.1 Music Representation for Efficient Learning

Western tonal music consists of discrete notes, with discrete timings represented by symbols in sheet music. Using this abstraction, we can reduce the complexity of music to a discrete state and action space. This is a desirable quality for problems we wish to apply RL to, as discrete spaces help to provide a more easily learned problem definition.

Bickerman et al. (2010) used a similar discrete sparse coding scheme, but encoded the length of a note by checking for whether it was held or released at every time-step. This encoding was speculated to have caused some issues related to learning the music patterns. We represent each possible note and duration pair as a single action. This allows mixing time-scales of actions, which is intended to avoid time-step issues.

Taking advantage of the structure of short term music memory as noted by Assayag et al. (2006) a 'sliding window' of notes was defined (see Figure 1). In order to represent the sequence of notes, agent state is represented as a concatenation of the last n notes played, where n is a value chosen to represent enough notes in a song to uniquely identify the next note to play. In experiments, $n = 16$ was chosen as it is longer than the longest repeated section in the music tested. This guarantees uniqueness in states for the whole of the music piece.

The representation of music we chose (Figure 2) is intended as a baseline for comparison of learning speeds of agents, and is simply an enumeration of every pitch and duration combination. With the simpler music, there are 2 durations, 7 pitches, and a rest, giving 15 inputs per note. This representation is almost tabular, being tiled only due to the fact that the input history will have more than one note in it. As such, it should not suffer from over-generalization or inability to learn the problem structure. It will be unable to generalize learning of note progressions well, due to every note and timing being independently evaluated. With a more complex reward system, it is possible that representations with better generalisation will improve performance even more.

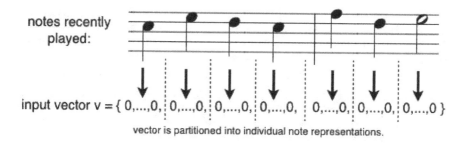

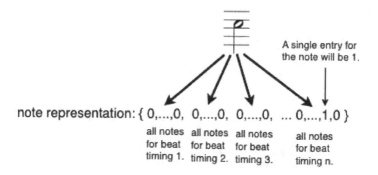

Fig. 1. Overall input structure, showing sliding window of notes which is used as the state for the agent

Fig. 2. Simple Note Structure

3.2 Defining Meta-parameters

In reinforcement learning, it is common to begin with a large learning rate α, and to decay the magnitude slowly over time. Doing so accelerates the learning process initially, while still allowing for finer changes to the value function later on. This technique is quite effective in learning tasks where there is a stationary target value function to learn, but is somewhat more difficult to apply if it is unknown when and by how much the target value function may change.

It has also been observed that static γ parameter values have an impact on the maximum string length learnable by an agent. Kenji Doya addressed this with a neuro-biological argument for the use of an averaged reward based parameter to perform the future estimate discounting instead (Doya, 2000). Unlike WoLF, Doya's derivation offers a continuous range of values based on the agent's current approximate success.

We define functions for learning and exploration parameters, based on the current average reward of an agent. Each meta-parameter was replaced with a function of the average reward:

$$f(r_{av}) = a \cdot r_{av}^3 + b \cdot r_{av}^2 + c \cdot r_{av} + d$$

Where a,b,c and d define a cubic function for each meta-parameter. The function has been defined to allow flexibility in learning shape and representation while still minimizing the number of parameters added. Constant parameter RL could be seen as a subset of the possible represented functions of average reward, with only the parameter d set. This was intentional, as it allows us to test whether optimization of the meta-parameters would produce a constant-parameter or adaptive parameter agent.

3.3   Meta-parameter Tuning

Meta-Parameter tuning for SARSA and Q-Learning agents generally requires finding the best combination of a small number of meta-parameters. In smaller scale problems, it is practical to run a grid search over these parameters to find a good combination. In larger scale problems, running a search with a hill-climber algorithm can be a more efficient way of finding a set of parameters with good performance.

We use a simulated annealing type algorithm, evaluating 4 modified meta-parameter sets every iteration, using the average of 800 separate experiment runs as a performance indicator for each parameter set. This algorithm was run through 80 iterations for both the constant parameter settings (4 variables) and the adaptive parameter settings (16 variables).

The fitness function used to evaluate parameters was originally the average reward over the last half of the run. After initial results, this was changed to be:

$$100 \cdot (average\ fitness) + (longest\ unbroken\ string\ of\ rewards)$$

Where *average fitness* is the average reward received from the run, and *longest unbroken string of rewards* is the longest number of consecutive positive rewards received, indicating the longest sequence of notes correctly learned. Changing the fitness function reduced the tendency to settle for sub-optimal, but still fitness-wise, good policies (such as play the same three notes over and over). As music is generally constructed of similar repeating patterns which can cause learners to enter sub-optimal loops, this type of evaluation function may be useful in the general music learning domain as well.

The annealing algorithm was used to tune both constant and adaptive meta-parameter sets from a common starting value, for a common number of iterations. After using the annealing algorithm to optimise meta-parameters, both the constant and adaptive sets of parameters were tested and compared.

4   Experimental Results

We tuned both constant and adaptive parameters on the dataset *Twinkle Twinkle Little Star*. We compare agent performance for both *Twinkle Twinkle Little Star* and *Mary Had a Little Lamb*. A number of the best performing solutions have been listed with directly comparable performance data in Table 1 at the end of the results section, where we discuss the effect of restarting the learning process.

4.1   Meta-parameter Tuning

As the adaptive meta-parameter set varies with average reward, inspecting these parameters with respect to this variable leads to the graphs in Figure 3. These graphs show a number of interesting features which have parallels in other algorithms and approaches.

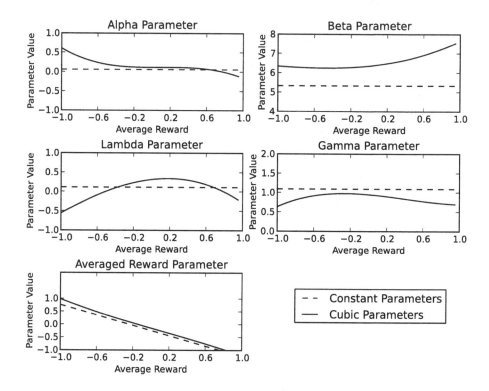

Fig. 3. Comparison of the tuned values of adaptive and constant learning metaparameters

The α value shows a curve with respect to average reward that roughly fits an exponential decay curve until it approaches maximum reward. At maximum reward, the value decreases sharply to 0. One major challenge to RL agents is not over-learning or oscillating around the best policy, but to reach the best policy and stay in a stable state. The optimisation of the α parameter in this case has the desired effect, allowing it to reach a stable state quicker than a simple decay of the value over time.

The β value, or inverse temperature, is linked inversely to the proportion of random non-best-choice actions that are made. The higher this value is, the more deterministic the result. It is interesting that the adaptive parameter is significantly higher than the constant parameter, indicating that the adaptive parameter agent is more confident in its knowledge of the best actions to take, rather than taking exploratory actions which have less confidence of reward.

The λ value allows learning to be spread along a longer sequence of actions at a time. A higher value of λ reinforces previous actions more strongly when a reward is received. From Figure 3 we see that λ reinforces previous actions most strongly when the agent is receiving medium positive average rewards. An unusual feature of the results is that the adaptive parameterisation of λ becomes negative at some when the average reward is very high or very low, that recent learning will be suppressed somewhat in these conditions.

The γ value represents how future-focused the agent is. A higher value means the future reward is more important. This is essential when several actions which do not generate reward are needed to reach an action which does. The adaptive parameterisation of γ has the highest value when the average reward is slightly below zero, where according to our reward function several actions following a mistake will likely not generate a reward and so the agent must be more future focused. The constant version of this parameter stays above 1, indicating that the agent is not just considering the total future reward (the case of $\gamma = 1$) but even being optimistic that its forecast of future reward is actually less than what will be received. This may be an effect of including an explicit averaged reward term (as proposed by Doya (2002); Daw et al. (2002)) as an extra parameter.

The averaged reward parameter has been included as an addition to the γ parameter due to both being included in the adaptive version, and also due to its improvement in performance over the γ formulation of RL for the music learning task. In both sets of parameters, this does not deviate much from the original value except a change in slope to meet -1 at the maximum value the average reward achieves in practical runs. The value of the constant parameter version is slightly lower than that of the adaptive parameter version, possibly to offset its higher value of γ.

4.2   Reinforcement Learning Algorithm Performance

Figure 4 shows averaged reward values for 100 runs each of the optimised constant and reward-based parameter sets on the music for *Twinkle Twinkle Little Star* which was used as the optimisation test. These results show a noticeable difference in convergence time, worst case performance, and best case performance. Given that both sets of parameters were run for the same search time, we would expect the constant parameters to be closer to optimal, due to their corresponding smaller search space.

Constant parameter RL achieved 90% convergence after about 45000 iterations. In contrast, the adaptive parameter algorithm achieved 90% convergence after only 11000 iterations. The performance gained from considering variable meta-parameters is quite large in this case, even when only using the same amount of optimisation time for the increased number of parameters. The well defined learning curve for adaptive meta-parameters in Figure 4 also allows early rejection of those runs which will fail to converge.

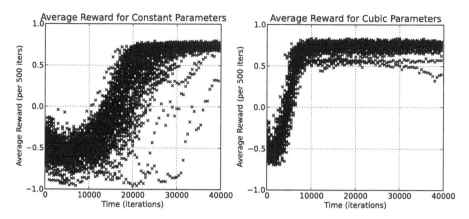

Fig. 4. Learning performance on the music *Twinkle Twinkle Little Star*, 100 runs displayed. Each datapoint represents a running average over 500 time-steps

In addition, the worst-case average performance for adaptive parameters is around −0.7, and below −0.95 for the constant parameter algorithm. Ideally this means that a larger portion of learning time is spent producing good music sequences, which would be preferable for the end user. The adaptive meta-parameter algorithm learns in much less time than the constant parameter algorithm. An inspection of 4 shows that this is a significant difference, as the variance in performance between the two methods is much larger than the variance seen across different runs.

One factor which is an advantage of the constant meta-parameter algorithm is that every run eventually converges. The adaptive parameter algorithm has a small minority of runs which do. If every run must converge for the agent to be useful, then this flaw is significant. It's possible that the flaw can be overcome by further optimisation of the meta-parameters, and that the chosen meta-parameter set represents some instability. Alternatively, an episode length could be set so that the run is checked for success after a certain amount of time, and if it is not achieved then the agent is reset and re-initialised.

Figure 5 shows test results for music which was not used in the optimisation process, *Mary Had A Little Lamb*. Figure 5 shows an increase in the number of suboptimal solutions. *Mary Had A Little Lamb* uses fewer pitches and more repetition, increasing the number of suboptimal loops the agent could stabilise in. Even though the music being learned has different characteristics to the training data, performance is very similar. This indicates that non-linear meta-parameter tuning can transfer to varying music patterns while still performing well.

4.3   Guaranteeing Convergence through Random Restarts

To provide guarantees of learning convergence for the system, we observe that not every learning episode fails, but at least some episodes will fail or take too long to converge if left running indefinitely. We could consider the question "what is

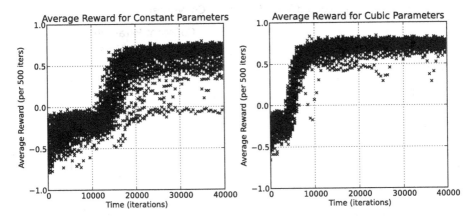

Fig. 5. Learning performance on the music *Mary Had A Little Lamb*, 100 runs displayed. Each datapoint represents a running average over 500 time-steps.

the best learning episode length to minimize the time taken for a 99.5% chance of convergence?" and determine a timeframe based on observed data. Calculating such a tradeoff involves determining when a particular learning episode should be terminated as "wasting time". At this point, we restart the learning process with a new agent as we are likely to find an initial policy which will converge more quickly. To calculate the best termination time, we use the following formula:

$$min \left[\frac{log\,(1.0 - 99.5\%)}{log\,(1.0 - (percent\ converged))} \cdot (episode\ length) \right]$$

Where 99.5% and *percent converged* are converted to fractions of 1, and *percent converged* is the percentage of runs observed to converge in less than *episode length* amount of time. This formula calculates total amount of time such that the probability of none of the tests converging is less than 0.5%. The solution is a time minimisation of the formula given by Muller (1923) for calculating a population size of experiments required to give reasonable guarantees of including at least one outcome of a given frequency. In this case the ceiling of the value found is used as the number of trials required to exceed 99.5% probability of success. We define convergence in this context as the earliest point at which the agent played the entire sequence of notes correctly.

The variable we seek to optimise is *episode_length*, which measures the number of time-steps a learning episode will execute before either converging, or being reset. The behaviour of total convergence time for various episode lengths can be seen in Figure 6. to better show the probabilistic effects, we have not rounded the numbers in this graph to the next highest whole episode length. The most desirable algorithm for music learning will approach $(0, 0)$ on this graph, having both a short episodic time and a short overall run-time to achieve high success.

As can be seen, the adaptive parameter RL agent has both much shorter episode length and much faster overall convergence than the constant parameter agent.

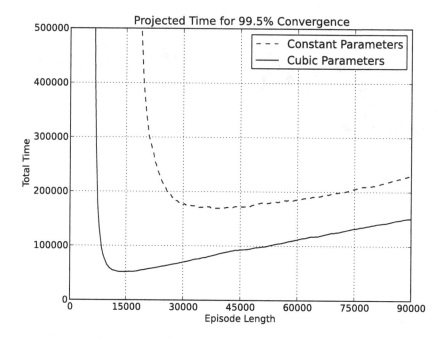

Fig. 6. Estimated average number of iterations to 99.5% convergence versus learning episode length in iterations. Total time shown on the y axis indicates significantly faster convergence for cubic parameters.

The minima calculated by the algorithm are shown in Table 1. These values are listed with the total runtime as a discrete number of trials. Each value is the result of minimising the formula above with a dataset of 2000 runs; 1000 for each simple piece of music. From data in Table 1, we can see that the adaptive parameter agent is able to provide good convergence in less than one third of the time of the constant parameter agent.

Table 1. Number of iterations per episode and in total to achieve 99.5% probability of convergence for variations of the RL algorithm. Normalised Time shows adaptive parameters converge in 27% of the time required for constant parameters.

Algorithm	Episode Length	Total Time	Normalised Time
Constant Parameters	64, 700	258, 800	1.0
Varying Parameters	14, 000	70, 000	0.27

5   Discussion

These experiments have shown several results which are of interest in developing RL algorithms for music learning agents. The use of non-constant meta-parameters (explained in Section 3.2) has made the biggest single and overall difference in learning rates, and the margin by which it outperforms other tests shows that a focus on the learning update aspect of RL is one of the most important concerns for practical performance benefits. Tests also showed that the performance of these non-constant parameters dropped slightly more in comparison with constant parameter performance when the problem was altered. This suggests a higher degree of specificity to the problem in tuning, which we could counter by increasing the variety of training data used. In the case of composition, using as many varied pieces of music as possible to optimise meta-parameters with should result in high overall performance.

The only limitation of the optimisation method used in these experiments is that we must have a computationally efficient environment simulation to obtain accurate performance estimates. The scale of training required means doing parameter tuning interactively may not be feasible, so either the function must be defined somehow, or the randomness in the initialisation and performance of the agent must be somehow reduced so that less tests are needed. The latter may be achievable by controlling the random seeds used for experimental runs, although a significant number of tests would still be needed to avoid bias that may be introduced by this technique. The former could possibly be solved by constructing classifiers to give reward signals based on rewards gathered from tests with real users. Franklin and Manfredi (2002) solved the reward definition problem by using a reward function derived from basic rules for Jazz music, showing that these requirements are not a limitation for all practical music composition systems.

System convergence guarantees (calculated in Section 4.3) allow a practical real-world analysis to be drawn from each of the learning systems tested. This gives a good overall picture of how different algorithms affect overall performance of the system. This method of comparison may not be suitable for all music learning systems, as there is an assumption made that nothing of greater value is lost by throwing out the current learned function and starting again.

6   Conclusion

In this paper, we have investigated the advantage of adaptive meta-parameters over constant parameter RL, and found significant performance increases can be obtained in this way. Varying learning meta-parameters should be considered as a relatively simple optimisation for increasing the learning speeds of RL agents, at least in settings such as music pattern learning. A final analysis of total time taken (in Section 4.3) showed that the adaptive meta-parameter algorithm can achieve reasonable learning guarantees in less than 30% of the number of learning steps it takes the constant meta-parameter algorithm.

Acknowledgements. This study received support from UoN FEBE grant G0900038 "Neurodynamic programming for sound generation through human-computer interaction".

References

Assayag, G., Bloch, G., Chemillier, M., Caen, U.D.: Omax-ofon. In: 3th Sound and Music Computing Conference, Marseille, France (2006)

Bertsekas, D.P., Tsitsiklis, J.N.: Neuro-Dynamic Programming. Optimization and Neural Computation Series. Athena Scientific, Belmont (1996)

Bickerman, G., Bosley, S., Swire, P., Keller, R.: Learning to play jazz with deep belief networks. In: Proceedings of the International Conference on Computational Creativity, pp. 228–237. University of Coimbra, Portugal (2010)

Collins, N.: The potential of reinforcement learning for live musical agents. In: International Machine Workshop on Machine Learning and Music, International Conference on Machine Learning, University of Helsinki, Finland (2008)

Daly, M.: Sheet music digital (2010), http://www.sheetmusicdigital.com/ (accessed February 8, 2014)

Daw, N.D., Kakade, S., Dayan, P.: Opponent interactions between serotonin and dopamine. Neural Networks 15(4-6), 603–616 (2002)

Dayan, P.: Goal-directed control and its antipodes. Neural Networks 22(3), 213–219 (2009)

Doornbusch, P.: The music of CSIRAC: Australia's first computer music. Common Ground Publishing, Altona (2005)

Doya, K.: Metalearning, neuromodulation and emotion. In: Hatano, G. (ed.) Proceedings of the 13th Toyota Conference on Affective Minds, pp. 101–104. Elsevier Science, B.V. (2000)

Doya, K.: Metalearning and neuromodulation. Neural Networks 15(4-6), 495–506 (2002)

Doya, K.: Modulators of decision making. Nature Neuroscience 11, 410–416 (2008)

Franklin, J.: Recurrent neural networks for music computation. INFORMS Journal on Computing 18(3), 321–338 (2006)

Franklin, J.A., Manfredi, V.U.: Nonlinear credit assignment for musical sequences. In: Abraham, A., Nath, B., Sambandham, M., Saratchandran, P. (eds.) Computational Intelligence and Applications—Second International Workshop on Intelligent Systems Design and Application, pp. 245–250. Dynamic Publishers, Inc., Atlanta (2002)

Groux, S.L., Verschure, P.F.M.J.: Towards adaptive music generation by reinforcement learning of musical tension. In: 7th Sound and Music Computing Conference, Barcelona, Spain (2010)

Hiller, L., Isaacson, L.: Experimental Music - Composition with an Electronic Computer. McGraw-Hill Book Co. (1959)

Mammarella, N., Fairfield, B., Cornoldi, C.: Does music enhance cognitive performance in healthy older adults? The Vivaldi effect. Aging Clinical and Experimental Research 19(5), 394–399 (2007)

Muller, H.J.: A simple formula giving the number of individuals required for obtaining one of a given frequency. The American Naturalist 57(648), 66–73 (1923)

Rauscher, F.H., Shaw, G.L., Ky, K.N.: Music and spatial task performance. Nature 365(6447), 611 (1993)

Schweighofer, N., Doya, K.: Meta-learning in reinforcement learning. Neural Networks 16(1), 5–9 (2003)

Smith, B.D., Garnett, G.E.: Reinforcement learning and the creative, automated music improviser. In: Machado, P., Romero, J., Carballal, A. (eds.) EvoMUSART 2012. LNCS, vol. 7247, pp. 223–234. Springer, Heidelberg (2012)

Sutton, R.S., Barto, A.G.: Reinforcement Learning: An Introduction. In: Adaptive Computation and Machine Learning, The MIT Press, Cambridge (1998)

Xenakis, I.: Formalised Music: Thought and Mathematics in Composition., 2nd edn. Pendragon Press, Stuyvesant (1992)

Autonomous Hypothesis Generation as an Environment Learning Mechanism for Agent Design

Bing Wang, Kathryn E. Merrick, and Hussein A. Abbass

University of New South Wales, Canberra Campus, Australia
bing.wang@student.adfa.edu.au, k.merrick@adfa.edu.au,
h.abbass@adfa.edu.au

Abstract. Studies on agent design have been focused on the internal structure of an agent that facilities decision-making subject to domain specific tasks. The domain and environment knowledge of an artificial agent is often hard coded by system engineers, which is both time-consuming and task dependent. In order to enable an agent to model its general environment with limited human involvement, in this paper, we first define a novel autonomous hypothesis generation problem. Consequently, we present two algorithms as its solutions. Experiments show that an agent using the proposed algorithm can correctly reconstruct its environment model to a certain extent.

Keywords: autonomous agents, causal relations, co-evolutionary algorithms.

1 Introduction

Agent is a loosely defined concept across different disciplines [1], [6]. In general, an artificial agent has three key components: (1) perceive its environment through sensors, (2) reason about its inputs and making decisions through its internal architecture, (3) act upon its environment through effectors. Based on these three components, an artificial agent is considered to possess the properties of goal-directed, autonomy and reactivity/proactivity [20].

Conventional studies on agent design focus on the internal structure that facilities decision-making in a certain environment [4], [8], [12], [19]. Many of such internal structures favour provoking actions according to predefined goals, or policies that satisfy domain specific rewards. This requires the domain experts to design appropriate representations and interpretations for environmental elements that have specific goals embedded in them and can stimulate the desired reasoning process within in an agent. From this perspective, the agent has a deep understanding of its environment designed by its system engineers. However, this is achieved at the cost of autonomy. An agent being autonomous implies that it can create its own goals and construct solutions for achieving it [18]. Studies on motivated agents address this problem from the angle of incorporating different

S.K. Chalup et al. (Eds.): ACALCI 2015, LNAI 8955, pp. 210–225, 2015.
© Springer International Publishing Switzerland 2015

motivation mechanisms, which allow the agent to select or create goals according to its external and internal states.

Motivated agent uses motivation models to autonomously create goals to stimulate a sequence of actions. Motivation models have been inspired from general theories on what is interesting [10], [17] and model free learning techniques (e.g. reinforcement learning). An agent with motivation mechanism can learn about its environment and autonomously interact with different tasks [11], [2]. Sanders and Gero [16] proposed to use a computational model of novelty as a mechanism of motivation to design agents that are capable of both problem finding and problem solving. Kaplan and Oudeyer [14] developed an intelligent adaptive curiosity (IAC) mechanism for modelling motivation. In a recent study [3], the authors presented a self-adaptive goal generation robust intelligent captive curiosity architecture (SAGG-RIAC) that allows a robot to actively learn skills/policies to solve relevant tasks. The above studies focus on the aspect of autonomy that the agent is able to create or select goals, and learn through experiences.

In contrast, this paper investigates the aspect of autonomy concerned with whether environment elements can be modelled by an agent in a general way with minimum human intervention. The agent learns through observing, reasoning and testing. If the agent can establish general knowledge about the environment itself, then it can adapt to new environment without specific modification from human experts. The remainder of this paper is organised as follows: Section 2 presents the background knowledge about hypotheses and hypothesis generation, which forms the basis for an agent learning about its environment in this paper. The formal definition of an autonomous hypothesis generation problem is discussed in this section too. Section 3 proposes two algorithms for an agent to execute autonomous hypothesis generation in practice. A play board game is designed to demonstrate the performance of the proposed algorithm in Section 4. Conclusions are drawn in the last Section.

2   Background and Problem Definition

2.1   Hypotheses and Hypothesis Generation

A hypothesis is a supposition or proposed explanation made on the basis of limited evidence as a starting point for further investigation. In scientific research, using hypotheses as guides for further exploration is a standard approach. Scientific research often starts with a hypothesis intending to answer a specific domain question. Later, this hypothesis is tested against the observation of domain phenomena or the experiment designed for testing. If its claim or implication is compatible with observations, it is taken as a confirmed hypothesis. Otherwise, it needs modification to be consistent with observations, or to be abandoned. Hypothesis generation is not only limited to scientific discoveries, but also an everyday activity that humans conduct in their minds to understand the reality around them. By formulating reasonable guesses about events and phenomena, humans are able to explore and understand the surrounding environment [9].

Hypothesis generation in the human mind is considered non-algorithmic in philosophy, that it cannot be reduced to formulae. It is driven by human intellectual creativity in response to questions. The exact mechanism of generating hypotheses in the human mind is yet to be fully understood. However, the development of data mining and machine learning techniques provides an opportunity to approximate such behaviour. Autonomous hypothesis generation is related to finding patterns from observational data through data mining or machine learning tools. The definition of hypotheses in this field can take different forms. For example, rules, clusters, classifiers, graphs and equations. In this paper, we are interested in hypotheses that represent causal relations. The reason for adopting this format is that, firstly, hypotheses generated in the human mind usually take the form of causal explanation of a phenomenon. The autonomous hypothesis generation technique developed in this paper intends to approximate such human like intelligence; Secondly, causal relations are domain independent. They possess inherent generalisation properties for agent design; Lastly, they compress knowledge and provide a potential control strategy for an agent to learn/develop other skills.

2.2   Autonomous Hypothesis Generation Problem Definition

The autonomous hypothesis generation problem for an agent is that: the raw environmental data perceived by the agent takes the form of a vector X of n variables. We assume the environment is fully observable, and the length X is fixed to n. No specific domain knowledge about the environment is available to the agent. At the same time, the agent is supposed to learn to reconstruct the underlying causal relations hidden in the environment. This problem can be formally defined as follows:

Autonomous Hypothesis Generation Problem Definition
  Input: observational dataset ($\mathbf{X}$) perceived from environment (E). $\mathbf{X}$ has p instances, each of which (X) a vector comprised of n variables and $X = [x_1, x_2, ..., x_i, ..., x_n]$, where x_i is quantitative variable.
  Output: causal graph (G) describing underlying interrelations among variables in X, with each node in G a variable (x_i); edges in G with arrowheads represent direct causal relations between two variables. If there is an arrowhead from variable x_i to x_j, then x_i is a direct cause of x_j.

In the case of human knowledge discoveries, causation discovery is a progressive process. Understanding of the causal laws behind a phenomenon begins with observation of associations, which lead to an inquiry into causal relations. Similarly, the autonomous hypothesis generation problem above can be decomposed into two progressive sub-problems: an associative hypothesis generation problem (AHGP) and a causal hypothesis generation problem (CHGP). The first problem is to find associative patterns which provide evidence for potential causal relations. The second problem identifies causal relations according to the information acquired by solving the previous problem.

AHGP Definition

   Input: observational dataset ($\mathbf{X}$) with p instances; each instance (X) vector comprised of n variables and $X = [x_1, x_2, ..., x_i, ..., x_n]$, where x_i quantitative variable.

   Output: set ($\mathbf{F} = \{f_1, f_2, ..., f_m\}$) of associative hypotheses; m number of hypotheses generated from observational data ($\mathbf{X}$). f_j a single associative hypothesis taking the form, $X_A \Rightarrow X_B$, $X_A \cap X_B = \emptyset$, $X_A, X_B \subset X$.

CHGP Definition

   Input: set ($\mathbf{F} = \{f_1, f_2, ..., f_j, ..., f_m\}$) of associative hypotheses and m number of associative hypotheses.

   Output: causal graph (G) describing underlying interrelations among variables in X; edges in G with arrowheads represent direct causal relation between two variables and if arrowhead from variable x_i to x_j, x_i is a direct cause of x_j.

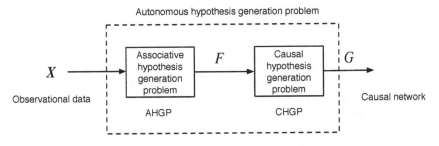

Fig. 1. General view of hypothesis generation problem and sub-problems

3   Autonomous Hypothesis Generation Algorithms

3.1   Cooperative Co-evolutionary Associative Hypothesis Generation

The definition of the AHGP gives a general representation of associative relations: $X_A \Rightarrow X_B$ ($X_A \cap X_B = \emptyset$, $X_A, X_B \subset X$). Therefore, the solution design for the AHGP needs to address the question of how to extract associative relations from a given dataset $\mathbf{X}$. In the literature, extracting associative relations from datasets falls into the field of association rule mining (ARM). There has been a rich literature about how to mine association rules from a given database [7]. However when dealing with quantitative variables, association rule mining techniques conventionally convert quantitative variables into intervals. In contrast, both the AHGP and the CHGP require establishing relations among variables rather than intervals of variable values. To address this problem, we propose a novel associative relation form: the functional association rule (FAR).

A FAR takes the form $f(X_A) \Rightarrow X_B$ $(X_A \cap X_B = \emptyset, X_A, X_B \subset X)$, which is interpreted as the variations of the variables in X_B can be predicted by the variations of the variables in X_A. The AHGP is then converted into a problem of searching for valid FARs from given observational data. We use a function approximation method to evaluate the validity of a FAR. Artificial neural networks (ANNs) have been proven to be a universal approximator [5]. Therefore, if an ANN can predict the right hand side (RHS) of a FAR to a certain accuracy level after training, we can mark the FAR representing a valid associative relation. In this paper, ANN training is conducted by applying a backpropagation algorithm (BP).

This design implies a dual-search problem. In order to find valid FARs, on one hand, the agent needs to search for variable subsets that potentially possess associative relations (and also separate the variables into left hand side (LHS) variables and RHS variable); on the other hand, the agent needs to search for appropriate ANNs that can best approximate a given FAR. The two search processes have a reciprocal relation, as when a potential valid FAR is matched with an appropriate ANN (in terms of initialisation weights and architecture), it is more likely that the valid rule can be identified by the ANN approximation. Therefore, in this paper, these two reciprocal search processes are encompassed by a cooperative co-evolutionary mechanism, termed cooperative co-evolutionary functional association rule mining (CCFARM). The general process for CCFARM is shown in Figure 2.

Cooperative Co-evolution: The FAR and ANN sub-populations co-evolve as follows: First, each sub-population is initialised. The two sub-populations are then evaluated in a parallel manner. Each member in the FAR sub-population is first combined with all members of the ANN sub-population, and then each pair executes the ANN training. The fitness of each member in the FAR sub-population is assigned by putting these training results through an objective function (presented later). The same process is applied to each member of the ANN sub-population. Once the entire two sub-populations are assigned fitness, they continue with their own evolutionary operators. The FAR sub-population uses a genetic algorithm (GA) , and the ANN sub-population differential evolution (DE). This is done because that the chromosomes of the FARs are mainly binary coded, whilst the chromosomes of the ANNs are vectors of real values. The entire process is repeated until the stopping criteria is met.

Chromosome coding. A FAR chromosome is a vector, represented by $[o, e_1, e_2, e_3, ..., e_k, ..., e_n]$. o is an integer value indicating that the oth element of the vector X is the RHS variable. $e_1, ..., e_n$ are binary values corresponding to x_1 to x_n; 1 means the corresponding variable is a LHS variable and 0 not used in this FAR. No variable can appear in both the LHS and the RHS of a FAR.

An ANN chromosome encodes the weights of an ANN. The real value coding has the advantage of being compact and is a natural representation. Therefore, we chose real values for ANN weight coding. An ANN chromosome is a vector ω of real values representing the weights of each connection in the corresponding ANN.

Objective function. The objective function comprises two components. One component is the predictive accuracy (c) of applying a FAR and its best matching ANN to a preserved test dataset. This predictive accuracy is calculated by the coefficient of determination (R^2). It measures the validity aspect of a FAR. The other component is a distance measure (d). It measures an average distance between one FAR and a set of other FARs. We use hamming distance for calculating each pair of FAR chromosomes' distance. Since we are searching as many valid FARs as possible, the distance measure d is designed to favour FARs that are different from others.

The fitness of a FAR (ϑ_{r_i}) is assigned as follows:

$$\vartheta_{r_i} = \frac{c_{r_i}}{(d_{r_i})^2} \tag{1}$$

$$c_{r_i} = \max_j c_{ij}; \ j = 1, 2, ..., n_a \tag{2}$$

$$d_{r_i} = \frac{1}{1 + \delta_{r_i(pop)} + \delta_{r_i(arc)}} \tag{3}$$

c_{r_i} for a FAR (r_i) selects the best predictive accuracy among its combinations with the ANNs in the other population. c_{ij} is used to denote the predictive accuracy of a FAR (r_i) combined with ANN (a_j), while (n_a) refers to the FAR sub-population size. The best predictive accuracy is used because firstly this can guarantee that the validation of a FAR is only determined by its best matching ANN, as long as there is one ANN that can verify the FAR, it can be considered a solution for the AHGP and be copied into an archive (presented later). Secondly each FAR is essentially a predictive model, for applying it to unknown data, it just needs one ANN for mapping the variables. As for the distance measure (d_{r_i}), the current FAR r_i is measured against two sets of FARs: one set is the other FARs in the current population and the other set is the valid FARs stored in the archive. $\delta_{r_i(pop)}$ refers to the distance measure of r_i against the other FARs in the current population, and $\delta_{r_i(arc)}$ denotes the distance measure of r_i against the FARs in the archive. Because that the accuracy c_{r_i} is calculated by using R^2, which has a range of $[0, 1]$, the distance (d_{r_i}) is designed to be in the same scale.

$$\delta_{r_i(pop)} = \frac{1}{n_r - 1} \sum_{l=1, l \neq i}^{n_r} h(r_i, r_l) \tag{4}$$

$$\delta_{r_i(arc)} = \frac{1}{n_c} \sum_{l=1}^{n_c} h(r_i, r_l) \tag{5}$$

where h is hamming distance, n_r is FAR sub-population size, and n_c is the archive size. Similarly, the fitness of an ANN (ϑ_{a_j}) is assigned as follows:

$$\vartheta_{a_j} = \frac{c_{a_j}}{(d_{a_j})^2} \tag{6}$$

$$c_{a_j} = \max_i c_{ij}; \ i = 1, 2, ..., n_r \tag{7}$$

$$d_{a_j} = d_{r_m}; \ m = \arg\max_i c_{ij}; \ i = 1, 2, ..., n_r \tag{8}$$

The only difference of ϑ_{a_j} (as in Eq. 6) and ϑ_{r_i} (as in Eq. 1) is that the distance measure for a_j is adopted from the best matching FAR (r_m) of a_j. Such design is out of the concern that if r_m has higher probability to produce offspring, then a_j can also be more likely to produce offspring. This could potentially introduce an ANN that is better initialised for the approximation of the offspring of r_m.

Archive. When a valid FAR and its corresponding ANN are selected into the archive, a variable selection process is implemented to the FAR for the purpose of producing a more concise FAR. Sequential backward selection on each valid rule is executed to eliminate redundant variables. Variables that do not contribute to the relation are dropped. Only unique rules are admitted to the archive.

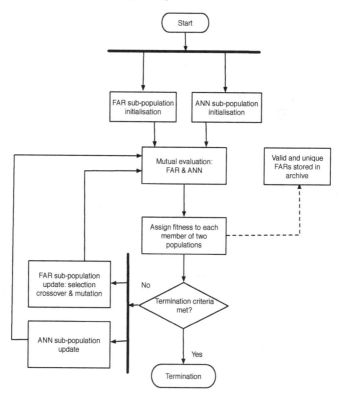

Fig. 2. Problem decomposition of the autonomous hypothesis generation problem

3.2   Experimental Causal Search

The CCFARM algorithm provides candidate relations to as input for the process of finding causal relations. The next task is to reconstruct a causal network from the FARs derived from CCFARM. A visualisation of these two steps is given in Figure 3. For a solution to the CHGP, we propose an experimental causal search algorithm based on the causality criteria of counterfactual. The Counterfactual model defines causality in terms of comparisons of observable and unobservable events [13]. It establishes causal relation by checking the differences of the supposed effect variable in two different situations: (1) exposed to treatment[1] and (2) not exposed to treatment. If there exists a difference, then causal relation can be confirmed. Otherwise, causal relation cannot be confirmed. For any variable x_i, the time when the treatment is applied is important, as treatments applied at different times might cause different responses. Suppose x_i is a potential cause variable, and x_j a potential effect variable. Applying treatment to x_i is denoted T_1, the corresponding observation from x_j is denoted Y_1. Similarly, applying no treatment to x_i is denoted T_0, the corresponding observation from x_j is denoted Y_0. When Y_1 is observed, Y_0 becomes counterfactual, and *vice versa*, as x_i cannot be exposed to two different treatment at the same time. This is called the fundamental problem of causal inference (FPCI).

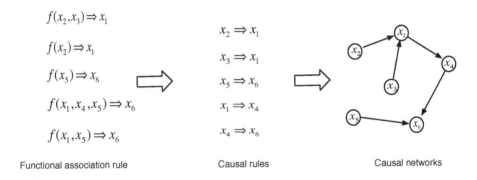

| Functional association rule | Causal rules | Causal networks |

Fig. 3. Visualisation of deriving a causal network from FARs

In practice, under certain settings it is reasonable to assume that FPCI does not apply. There are three assumptions for specifying such a situation: temporary stability, causal transience and homogeneity. The proposed experimental causal search algorithm uses these assumptions to form the solution to the CHGP. This algorithm relies on the agent's basic feature that it uses its effectors to act upon its environment, as counterfactual causal criteria require construction of counterfactual instances, which needs manipulation of the environment.

Sense. As defined by the CHGP, the input of the experimental causal search algorithm is the set of FARs derived from solving the AHGP ($\mathbf{F} = \{f_1, f_2, ..., f_m\}$) which comprises one part of the agent's sensed information. The information from the environment (i.e. observational data $\mathbf{X}$) forms the other part. The experimental causal search algorithm aims to form two groups of instances, where

---

[1] *treatment* is the term used in the counterfactual model to refer to manipulation of a variable.

one group is the other's counterfactual group. The observational data ($\mathbf{X}$) provide a database from which a number of instances can be selected to form one of the instance sets (D_s). The construction of its counterfactual instance set (D'_s) relies on the actions of the agent applying interventions to the potential causal variables. Such a construction is possible based on the temporary stability, causal transience and homogeneous assumptions introduced in the last section.

Causal reasoning. The causal reasoning part of the agent determines, for each FAR, how to select the set of instances and actions to execute in order to construct an instance set and its counterfactual set. Suppose the FAR under processing is $f(x_{p_1}, x_{p_2}, ..., x_{p_i}, ..., x_{p_k}) \Rightarrow x_q$, where $\{x_{p_1}, x_{p_2}, ..., x_{p_i}, ..., x_{p_k}\} \in X$, $x_q \in X$ and $\{x_{p_1}, x_{p_2}, ..., x_{p_i}, ..., x_{p_k}\} \cap x_q = \emptyset$. The variables concerned in the current experiments are then confined to $\{x_{p_1}, x_{p_2}, ..., x_{p_i}, ..., x_{p_k}, x_q\}$. The RHS variable ($x_q$) is considered a response variable while the LHS variables ($\{x_{p_1}, x_{p_2}, ..., x_{p_i}, ..., x_{p_k}\}$) are examined one by one as potential cause variables. Suppose the current potential cause variable is x_{p_i}. The observational data ($\mathbf{X}$) are first sorted according to x_{p_i} in ascending order. Then, 30 instances are selected with equal intervals from the sorted data ($\mathbf{X}'$) and form the instance set (D_s). We use 30 instances in the algorithm, because the proposed causal search algorithm adopts a statistical test to verify the causal relations. Selecting instances from the sorted dataset avoids the situation, in which the instances selected from $\mathbf{X}$ only covers a small range of the x_{p_i}.

In order to construct a counterfactual set for D_s, the agent applies an intervention (Δx_{p_i}) to the variable x_{p_i} for each instance in D_s. By recording the system reaction after the intervention, the agent can build the counterfactual set D'_s for D_s. The step size (Δx_{p_i}) is calculated by using Equation 9. This equation first determines the value range of x_{p_i} in D_s. Then the value range is divided by 30, as 30 instances will be selected from D_s. It is further halved, because when the agent applies an intervention to x_{p_i}, the resulting value of x_{p_i} should be within its original range in D_s.

$$\Delta x_{p_i} = \frac{(max(x_{p_i}) - min(x_{p_i}))/30}{2} \qquad (9)$$

Act The agent's actions are to create the counterfactual instances for each instance in D_s. Given the current potential cause-effect variable pair $\{x_{p_i}, x_q\}$, for the jth instance ($D_{s,j}$) in D_s, the agent acts on the environment to form the same state as $D_{s,j}$ and then applies the intervention (Δx_{p_i}) to $x_{p_{i,j}}$. At the same time, values of other variables except $\{x_{p_i}, x_q\}$ are adjusted to the states as in $D_{s,j}$ to eliminate their influences [15]. The value of x_q under such manipulation is recorded, together with the values of the other variables. This newly recorded instance $D'_{s,j}$ forms the counterfactual of instance $D_{s,j}$ subject to the potential cause variable (x_{p_i}).

When all the 30 counterfactual instances are constructed, the difference between the values of x_p in D_s and D'_s is calculated. In order to rule out the possible influence of random error, this difference is examined by using the paired t-test. If the test shows no difference between the x_q values in D_s and D'_s, then x_{p_i} is not the direct cause of x_q and the link between them is dropped. Otherwise, x_{p_i} is one of the direct causes of x_q. This process is repeated for each cause variable of a FAR, and all the FARs in the archive of CCFARM are checked. This causal search step in essence eliminates the false positive causal links in the candidate FARs.

4   Experimental Design and Results

4.1   Experiment Settings

For the experiments that test the performance of the overall autonomous hypothesis generation approach, including CCFARM and the experimental causal search, we designed a play board environment for an agent to learn about the causal relations behind the dynamics of the play board. This play board is shown in Figure 4. The agent can perceive and record the values of each colour strip, and its effector can control the value of any colour strip to certain value.

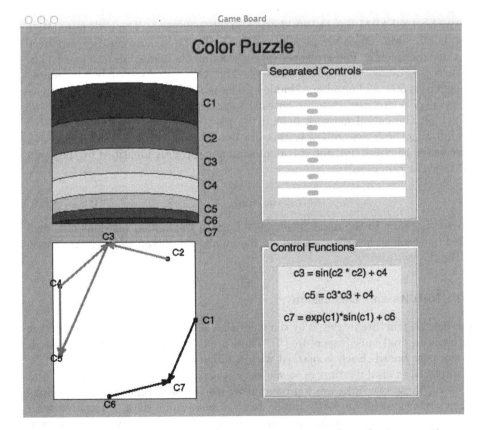

Fig. 4. Color control play board for testing autonomous hypothesis generation

In the play board interface, the rainbow colours in the upper left box possess a set of causal relations among them, which is shown in the right bottom box in terms of equations. The underlying causal network constructed from the equations is shown in the lower left box. The variables, $\{c_1, c_2, c_3, ..., c_i, ..., c_7\}$, refer to the coloured strips, and their values form the perception of the agent.

The play board has two main phases: active and stable. During the active phase, the strips change colour by their own underlying mechanisms, which allows the agent to observe and record the values of the colours. In this phase, the values of variable $\{c_1, c_2, c_4, c_6\}$ are generated randomly from the range $[-5, 5]$ by using a uniform distribution. The values of $\{c_3, c_5, c_7\}$ are determined accordingly by using the causal equations. Quantitative values are then converted to colour values. During the stable phase, the variables $\{c_1, c_2, c_4, c_6\}$ stop generating values themselves, and the agent can manipulate the value of each colour strip through its effectors.

In the experiments, the agent recorded 500 instances of the $\{c_1, c_2, c_3, ..., c_i, ..., c_7\}$ values to search for the FARs using the CCFARM algorithm, during the active phase of the play board. The agent uses 80% of the 500 observational instances for training and the rest for testing. Among these training data, the agent further splits it into training data (80%) and validation data (20%). The algorithm CCFARM was executed using 30 different seeds. The FAR population size is 30, while the ANN population size is 14. 50 generations are produced in the experiments. The crossover rate is 0.8 and the mutation rate is 0.1. The accuracy threshold is selected to be 0.95. The ANN learning rate is 0.1, number of epochs is 500, and number of hidden nodes is 10. In the following stable phase of the play board, the agent executes the experimental causal search algorithm to rebuilt the causal network behind the play board. The performance of the overall hypothesis generation is measure by error rate, which is defined by the percentage of causal link and its orientation not correctly identified by the agent as shown in Equation 10.

$$error = m_h/n_h \tag{10}$$

where m_h refers to the number of causal links in the hidden relations not identified by the search algorithm and n_h the number of overall causal links hidden in the dataset.

4.2   Results and Discussion

The causal structure retrieved by the algorithm is shown in Figure 5 (a), together with the original causal structure (b). There are three underlying causal relations in the play board. Each is marked with a different colour in Figure 5 (b). For example, the causal relation, $c_3 = sin(c_2 \times c_2) + c_4$, includes two links $c_2 \rightarrow c_3$ and $c_4 \rightarrow c_3$, these two links are represented by using colour blue. The causal links are reconstructed from FARs mined from observational data. Compared with the original causal network, there are three missing links in the reconstructed network, as shown in Figure 5 (a). The error rate is 0.5.

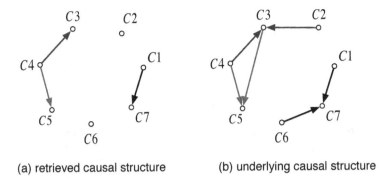

(a) retrieved causal structure   (b) underlying causal structure

Fig. 5. Comparison of causal structure retrieved from experimental causal search algorithm and underlying causal structure

It takes the agent two steps to reconstruct the causal network hidden in its environment. Accordingly, in order to investigate the reasons for the missing links, we look into the problem from two aspects: the coverage of the FARs and the test accuracy in the causal search. For the former aspect, we checked whether the links missing from the constructed network are the same across all seeds. Table 1 shows the percentage of each causal link appearing in 30 seeds. It can be seen that $c_2 \rightarrow c_3$ and $c_6 \rightarrow c_7$ are not identified in any seeds. The link $c_3 \rightarrow c_5$ is identified by the CCFARM process, but obviously overlooked by the causal search algorithm, the reason for which will discussed later. The question raised now is whether the CCFARM failed to identify the associative relation corresponding to the causal link $c_2 \rightarrow c_3$ and $c_6 \rightarrow c_7$ or whether they were deleted during the process.

Table 1. Percentage of causal links for 30 seeds

Causal links	Percentage	Causal links	Percentage
$C2 \rightarrow C3$	0	$C4 \rightarrow C3$	0.9
$C3 \rightarrow C5$	0.8	$C4 \rightarrow C5$	0.9
$C1 \rightarrow C7$	0.95	$C6 \rightarrow C7$	0

In order to answer the question above, we selected three steps in the CCFARM algorithm to check the number of causal links included in each generation. These three steps are: (1) the step where a new population is generated, (2) the step when the valid rules are identified, and (3) the step where the valid rules are put through the recheck process. For the first step, the number of each causal link in each generation is recorded. For the second step, the number of each causal link in the valid rules in each generation is recorded. For the last step, the number of each causal link in the FARs selected to the archive in each generation is recorded. The result is shown in Figure 6 to Figures 8.

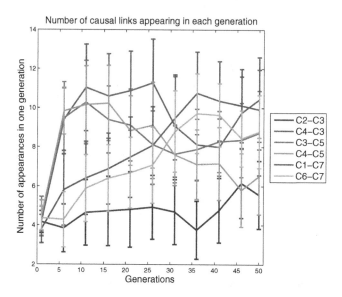

Fig. 6. Number of causal links in each population (30 seeds, 95% confidence interval)

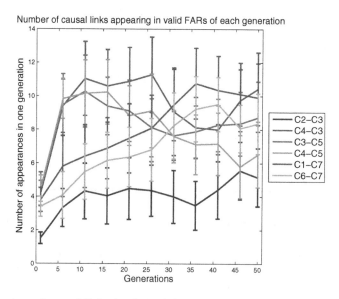

Fig. 7. Number of causal links in the valid rules of each population (30 seeds, 95% confidence interval)

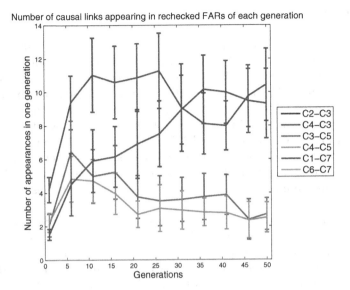

Fig. 8. Number of causal links in the archived rules of each population (30 seeds, 95% confidence interval)

As it is shown in Figure 6 and Figure 7, all six causal links appear in each FAR sub-population and the valid FARs of each generation, but disappear after the recheck step (Figure 8). This result demonstrates that the CCFARM algorithm is able to identify the associative relations corresponding to the real causal relations, but the recheck process causes some causal links to be missed. The recheck process was designed so that the CCFARM can provide the causal search with concise FARs. However, the experimental results do not fully support the necessity of this step. In further, it is possible this process can be skipped.

The last missing link in the reconstructed causal network, $c_3 \rightarrow c_5$, is a false negative result from the difference test adopted in the experimental causal search algorithm. Table 1 implies that there are FARs extracted from observational data including this causal link. However, after the experimental causal search, the link is labelled negative. This implies a false negative result from the difference test adopted in the experimental causal search.

In summary, the experiments show that the proposed autonomous hypothesis generation algorithms can identify and reconstruct a certain number of the causal links correctly. The missing links are attributed to the feature selection process in the archiving step of CCFARM and the false negative test result from the experimental causal search algorithm. The error rate of the overall autonomous hypothesis generation algorithms can be further reduced, when the feature selection step in CCFARM is skipped.

5   Conclusion

This paper has introduced and defined an autonomous hypothesis generation problem to enable an artificial agent to autonomously learn about its environment with reduced knowledge hard-coded by system engineers. Inspired by the human behaviour of hypothesis generation, we decomposed the general problem of autonomous hypothesis generation into two sub-problems, AHGP and CHGP. Formal definitions of these two problems are also presented in this paper. In addition, two algorithms, CCFARM and experimental causal search, are proposed to serve as solutions to the two proposed sub-problems. Experiments on a game board environment show that an agent using the proposed algorithms can identify and reconstruct a certain number of causal relations hidden in its environment.

There is still a distance from the hypothesis generation approach proposed in this paper to an agent gaining a deep understanding about its environment autonomously. However, the problem discussed in this paper probes a possibility in this direction. For the further work, one direction is on additional experiments under various scenarios testing the performance of the proposed algorithms. There is also still a certain amount of design from human side to instruct the agent how to control the environment. It may be interesting to investigate whether it is possible to further reduce the human involvement in this process.

References

1. Abbass, H.A., Petraki, E.: The causes for no causation: A computational perspective. Information Knowledge Systems Management 10(1-4), 51–74 (2011)
2. Baldassarre, G., Mirolli, M.: Intrinsically motivated learning in natural and artificial system. Springer, Berlin (2013)
3. Baranes, A., Oudeyer, P.Y.: Active learning of inverse models with intrinsically motivated goal exploration in robots. Robotics and Autonomous Systems 61(1), 49–73 (2013)
4. Brooks, R.A.: Intelligence without representation. Artificial Intelligence 47(1), 139–159 (1991)
5. Cybenko, G.: Approximation by superpositions of a sigmoidal function. Mathematics of Control, Signals, and Systems 2(4), 303–314 (1989)
6. Franklin, S., Graesser, A.: Is it an agent, or just a program?: A taxonomy for autonomous agents. In: Jennings, N.R., Wooldridge, M.J., Müller, J.P. (eds.) ECAI-WS 1996 and ATAL 1996. LNCS, vol. 1193, pp. 21–35. Springer, Heidelberg (1997)
7. Han, J., Pei, J., Yin, Y.: Mining frequent patterns without candidate generation. SIGMOD Record 29(2), 1–12 (2000)
8. Larid, J., Newell, A., Rosenbloom, P.S.: Soar: An architecture for general intelligence. Artificial Intelligence 33(1), 1–64 (1987)
9. Leedy, P., Ormrod, J.: Practical research: Planning and design. Pearson (2010)
10. Lenat, D.: AM: An artificial intelligence approach to discovery in mathematics as heuristic search. Ph.D. thesis, Standford University (1976)
11. Merrick, K., Maher, M.L.: Motivated reinforcement learning: curious characters for multiuser games. Springer, Berlin (2009)

12. Milani, A., Poggioni, V.: Planning in reactive environments. Computational Intelligence 23(4), 439–463 (2007)
13. Neyman, J.: Statistical problems in agriculture experimentation. Supplement of Journal of the Royal Statistical Society 2(2), 107–180 (1935)
14. Oudeyer, P.Y., Kaplan, F., Hafner, V.V.: Intrinsic motivation systems for autonomous mental development. IEEE Transactions on Evolutionary Computation 11(2), 265–286 (2007)
15. Rubin, D.B.: Teaching statistical inference for causal effects in experiments and observational studies. Journal of Education and Behavioural Statistics 29(3), 343–367 (2004)
16. Saunders, R., Gero, J.S.: Curious agents and situated design evaluation. AI EDAM: Artificial Intelligence for Engineering Design, Analysis and Manufacturing 18(2), 153–161 (2004)
17. Schmidhuber, J.: What's interesting. Tech. Rep. IDSIA-35-97, IDSIA Switzerland (1997)
18. Steels, L.: When are robots intelligent autonomous agents? Journal of Robotics and Autonomous Systems 15(1-2), 3–9 (1995)
19. Sun, R.: The clarion cognitive architecture: Extending cognitive modelling to social simulation. In: Sun, R. (ed.) Cognition and Multi-agent Interaction: From Cognitive Modelling to Social Simulation, pp. 79–99. Cambridge University Press, New York (2006)
20. Wooldridge, M., Jennings, N.: Intelligent agents: theory and practice. The Knowledge Engineering Review 10(2), 115–152 (1995)

Learning Options for an MDP
from Demonstrations

Marco Tamassia, Fabio Zambetta, William Raffe, and Xiaodong Li

RMIT University, Melbourne VIC, Australia
{first.last}@rmit.edu.au

Abstract. The options framework provides a foundation to use hierarchical actions in reinforcement learning. An agent using options, along with primitive actions, at any point in time can decide to perform a macro-action made out of many primitive actions rather than a primitive action. Such macro-actions can be hand-crafted or learned. There has been previous work on learning them by exploring the environment. Here we take a different perspective and present an approach to learn options from a set of experts demonstrations. Empirical results are also presented in a similar setting to the one used in other works in this area.

Keywords: reinforcement learning, options.

1 Introduction

A Markov Decision Process (MDP) is a formal model of decision processes in a stochastic stationary environment. MDPs are currently being used in a wide variety of problems including robotics ([9]), games ([19, 2]), and control ([13]).

An MDP includes a set of states, a set of possible actions, a model of the environment (that is, information on how the state of the environment varies in response to the agent's actions) and a reward function specifying how good each state is.

Given an MDP, a variety of techniques can be used to compute an optimal behavior with respect to the specified reward. A behavior is termed *policy* and, in the simplest form, it is a mapping from states to actions. Among the existing techniques, the most used are dynamic programming, temporal differences and Monte Carlo methods.

The field studying these techniques is called *Reinforcement Learning* (RL) ([20]). RL can be considered as a branch of Machine Learning, which deals with strategic behaviors.

This model, however, suffers the so-called "curse of dimensionality": each of the currently known algorithms has at least a quadratic computational time complexity in the number of states. This translates in a prohibitive computational time required for states sets of important magnitude.

This is more evident in cases where a state is represented by a combination of features, making thus the states set exponentially large in the number of features.

S.K. Chalup et al. (Eds.): ACALCI 2015, LNAI 8955, pp. 226–242, 2015.

To address this issue, [21] introduced a framework for abstraction of the states of MDPs. The central concept of their work is that of an *option*, which is an extended course of action, and can be thought as an abstract action or a macro-action. Options are not actions that are really available to the agent but, rather, represent sequences of primitive actions performed over an extended period of time.

When options are used along with actions in a dynamic programming algorithm, an approximation of the optimal policy can be computed in a short amount of time (compared to that of the same setting but with no options). Options can also be used within a variation of the Q-learning algorithm ([21]). Also in this case the time necessary to complete the process is cut by means of using options.

As the "no free lunch" principle suggests, the computational burden is not eliminated but, rather, is moved to a precomputation step in which options are learned. However, since options are defined over a subset of the states set, computing their internal policy is potentially much faster than finding the optimal policy without options.

Such an abstraction mechanism arguably offers a strong advantage, but the drawback is that of having to manually specify the options to be adopted. Previous work has been done to automate the learning of options ([11, 18, 4, 17, 10, 22, 3]): note that these approaches rely on the agent exploring the state space and inferring potentially good options.

The purpose of this work is to introduce an algorithm that learns options from one or more demonstrations provided by experts. This is a different use case than that in the mentioned literature. Whereas in those works options were learnt by interacting with the environment, we do not assume such interaction possible but, rather, we assume data about other agents interacting with the environment is available.

It could be said that learning from a demonstration is a form of Supervised Learning (SL). However, while on an abstract level this is correct, the reader should not form the idea that Supervised Learning algorithms (such as Neural Networks or Support Vector Machines, to name the most famous) would work well on a Reinforcement Learning problem.

This is likely not to happen because RL algorithms take advantage of information of the structure of the environment to plan actions in order to maximize the cumulative reward *over time*, while SL algorithms do not.

In the context of learning from a demonstration, a SL algorithm would copy state-actions pairs from the demonstration, but it would not be able to generalize effectively from them because it would have no model of the environment.

This is a well known difference between SL and RL and it is furtherly explained in [20].

The idea of learning parts of an MDP from a demonstration is not new. The field of *Inverse RL* (IRL) studies methods of learning the reward function from a demonstration. The first problem has been formulated as learning the reward function used by an expert ([14]) while in later work the objective has been relaxed to learning a reward function that makes the agent behave like the expert ([1, 16, 25, 12, 8]).

Nevertheless, to the best of our knowledge, learning options from demonstrations is a still unexplored area. It is argued in [7] that by using options in a Q-learning process, bias is introduced. This can potentially be an advantage if the bias is well directed. In a settings where options are learned from experts demonstrations, this is possibly the case.

2   MDPs and Options

This section introduces the Markov Decision Process (MDP) formalism which is used in this work (2.1) and gives an introduction to the options framework (2.2).

2.1   MDP and Reinforcement Learning

An MDP is a model of a stochastic, stationary environment; that is, an environment whose response to an agent's actions is non-deterministic but follows a distribution that does not change over time.

Formally, an MDP M is a tuple

$$M = (\mathcal{S}, \mathcal{A}, T, \gamma, R),$$

where $\mathcal{S}$ is the set of states; $\mathcal{A}$ is the set of actions; $T : \mathcal{S} \times \mathcal{A} \times \mathcal{S} \to \mathbb{R}$ is a function expressing the environment state transition probabilities; $\gamma < 1$ is a discount factor used to decrease future rewards; $R : \mathcal{S} \to \mathbb{R}$ is a function associating a reward to each state.

At each point in time t, the environment is in a state s_t, and an agent receives a reward $r_t = R(s_t)$. After collecting the reward, an agent performs an action a_t. The purpose of an agent is to maximize the discounted, cumulative reward collected over time: $\sum_t \gamma^{t-1} r_t$. The agent, therefore, wants to find a policy $\pi : \mathcal{S} \to \mathcal{A}$ that maximizes such reward.

Such a policy can easily be computed if the expected future reward of taking action a in state s is known for all a and s. It is possible to define a function $Q^* : \mathcal{S} \times \mathcal{A} \to \mathbb{R}$ to capture this notion. Such function is called *state-action value function* and is recursively defined as follows:

$$Q^*(s, a) = \sum_{s' \in \mathcal{S}} T(s, a, s') \left(R(s) + \gamma \max_{a' \in \mathcal{A}} Q^*(s', a') \right).$$

An optimal policy executes the action with the highest expected future reward:

$$\pi^*(s) = \arg \max_a Q^*(s, a).$$

The optimal Q^* function can be learned by interacting with the environment step by step. The most widely used algorithm to this end is Q-learning, introduced in [24]. The algorithm approximates the optimal Q-function by updating any initial estimate of Q at each state transition (s_t, a_t, s_{t+1}) as follows:

$$Q(s_t, a_t) \overset{\alpha}{\leftarrow} r_{t+1} + \gamma \max_{a \in \mathcal{A}} Q(s_{t+1}, a) - Q(s_t, a_t),$$

where $x \overset{\alpha}{\leftarrow} y$ is a short for $x \leftarrow x + \alpha y$ and $0 < \alpha \leq 1$ is a learning factor. This algorithm converges with probability 1 to the optimal Q^* function.

A good introduction to RL is [20].

2.2 Options Framework

The concept of *option* generalizes that of action (which, in the options framework, are called *primitive actions*) to include temporally extended courses of action. It has been introduced in [21] to accelerate the convergence rate of RL algorithms. An option, like any other action, can be chosen by a policy; however, differently from primitive actions, when an option is chosen, an auxiliary policy is followed for some period of time - until the option execution terminates.

An option o is defined as a tuple $o = (\mathcal{I}, \pi, \beta)$ where:

- $\mathcal{I}$ is the *initiation set*; that is, the set of states from which it is possible to select option o;
- π is the policy to be used when option o is selected;
- $\beta : \mathcal{S} \to \mathbb{R}$ is a function expressing the termination probability; that is, $\beta(s)$ expresses the probability with which option o terminates when in state s.

The intuitive idea behind this is to generalize a policy so that it chooses what to do next not just from the set of primitive actions $\mathcal{A}$ but more generally from a set of options $\mathcal{O}$, which may or may not include the primitive actions in $\mathcal{A}$. Policies over options are denoted with the symbol μ.

Notice that the best policy $\mu_{\mathcal{O}}^*$ over a set of options $\mathcal{O}$ is not guaranteed to be as good as the best policy $\pi_{\mathcal{A}}^*$ over the set of primitive actions $\mathcal{A}$. This is because the options in $\mathcal{O}$ may not necessarily have the *granularity* required to achieve an optimal behavior. However, an approximation of $\mu_{\mathcal{O}}^*$ can be computed in potentially fewer steps than $\pi_{\mathcal{A}}^*$, because one option execution can transition to a state that is reachable only by many primitive actions executions.

Furthermore, if $\mathcal{O} \supseteq \mathcal{A}$, the best policy over $\mathcal{O}$ is at least as good as the best policy over $\mathcal{A}$. This framework, while maintaining the advantages of reasoning with policies, only adds a slight computational burden with respect to the setting that reasons only with actions ([21]).

When a policy over options in state s_t selects an action $a \in \mathcal{A}$ as the next move, the action is executed as in a usual MDP policy. On the other hand, when it selects an option $o \in \mathcal{O}$, the option policy determines the actions to be performed until it randomly terminates in s_{t+k}, at which time a new action or option is selected.

Notice that, to treat options as primitive actions - in order to be able to use existing RL algorithms - a model of each option o is required. A complete model of o in this formalism consists of the transition probabilities $T_o(s, s')$ associated to o. T_o expresses the probability of macro-transitioning from state s

to state s' when selecting option o. That is, actually, the probability that option o terminates in state s' when started in state s.

If such a model is not known, it is still possible to learn the Q-function (now called *state-option value function*) by exploring the environment. For this purpose, a generalization of the Q-learning algorithm for options, introduced in [21], can be used. The Q-learning update rule, for each option execution (s_t, o_t, s_{t+k}), is defined as follows:

$$Q(s_t, o_t) \overset{\alpha}{\leftarrow} r + \gamma^k \max_{o \in \mathcal{O}} Q(s_{t+1}, o) - Q(s_t, o_t),$$

where k is the number of steps between s and s' and $r = r_{t+1} + \gamma r_{t+2} + \ldots + \gamma^{k-1} r_{t+k}$ is the discounted cumulative reward obtained over this time. Using such rule at the termination of each option leads Q to converge to the optimal state-option value function Q^*. Notice that, in case o_t is a primitive action, $k = 1$ and the update rule is the same as the original Q-learning, except that the choice for the next action is extended to options.

Performing updates only at the end of options executions, however, takes a long time to converge. To accelerate this process, *intra-option learning* can be used ([21]). On every single state transition (s_t, a_t, s_{t+1}), all options $o = (I, \pi, \beta)$ such that $\pi(s_t) = a_t$ are updated as follows:

$$Q(s_t, o) \overset{\alpha}{\leftarrow} r_{t+1} + \gamma U(s_{t+1}, o) - Q(s_t, o),$$

where

$$U(s_t, o) = (1 - \beta(s_t))Q(s_t, o) + \beta(s_t) \max_{o'} Q(s_t, o').$$

This algorithm also converges to the optimal state-option value function.

It is also possible to use a variation of the mechanism so to allow policies to terminate when termination is a better alternative. Indeed, given two policies μ and μ' that are identical except for the fact that μ' terminates an option o in states s where $Q^{\mu'}(s, o) < V^{\mu'}$, it can be proven that $V^{\mu'} \geq V^{\mu}$ ([21]). The computational burden added by this variation is negligible.

3   Learning Options

This section explains how it could be possible to learn options from one or more demonstrations. As mentioned above, this approach is different from [11, 18] since in these works the agent needs to explore the environment while in our work one or more expert demonstrations are required.

This approach has, however, some constraints. The first constraint is that the state and the action spaces must be finite. The second constraint of this mechanism is that the policy of each option o must be based on a **single-peak** reward function R_o; in other words, option o represents the high-level intent of reaching a specific subgoal s_{k_o}. This is consistent with work in [11, 18, 4, 17].

That is to say, given s_{k_o}, R_o assumes a non-zero value c only for state s_{k_o}. Formally, for some $c > 0$, $R_o(s) = c \cdot \delta_{s,s_{k_o}}$, where δ is the Kronecker's delta:

$$\delta_{i,j} = \begin{cases} 1 & \text{if } i = j \\ 0 & \text{otherwise} \end{cases}. \tag{1}$$

Such a restriction reduces the space of reward functions to a tractable size. This allows the use of **memoization** over calls of any RL algorithm A. By means of memoization, $A(R)$ needs to be called only the very first time for each R: by storing the result in memory, subsequent calls to $A(R)$ can be avoided. Notice that this is possible since states and action spaces are finite.

It can be argued that memoization is not critical in this task, but the cost of computing optimal policies with model-based RL algorithms is high, and we believe the speed up given by not having to recalculate the policy of options is important. However, we do not have quantitative data to support such claim.

Furthermore, this very specific rewards space allows for a very **concise representation** of a reward function. In fact, supposing parameter c is fixed, all the necessary information to represent a reward function R is the state in which R assumes the non-zero value. For example, the reward function expressed above can be represented entirely by the scalar k_o.

3.1 Identify Useful Subgoals

Our procedure elaborates on one or more demonstrations given as input. The first step of our approach is to identify useful subgoals. We base our algorithm on the assumption that, if a subgoal is useful, at least one of the demonstrations makes good use of it.

The idea for identifying such subgoals, is to find the smallest set $\mathcal{L}$ of options that allows to equivalently rewrite all of the demonstrations expressing the steps in the form $(s_i, \pi_o(s_i))$, with $o \in \mathcal{L}$.

Formally, this means, given a demonstration d, which is a sequence of state-action pairs (s_i, a_i), $d = \langle (s_1, a_1), (s_2, a_2), \ldots, (s_{n-1}, a_{n-1}), (s_n, a_n) \rangle$, to find the smallest set $\mathcal{L} = \{o_1, o_2, \ldots, o_m\}$ such that

$$a_1 = \pi_{o_1}(s_1)$$
$$a_2 = \pi_{o_1}(s_2)$$
$$\vdots$$
$$a_i = \pi_{o_1}(s_i)$$
$$a_{i+1} = \pi_{o_2}(s_{i+1})$$
$$a_{i+2} = \pi_{o_2}(s_{i+2})$$
$$\vdots$$
$$a_n = \pi_{o_m}(s_n).$$

By using options in set $\mathcal{L}$, it is possible to identify subsequences in d. Each such subsequence d_x is composed of state-action pairs that can be rewritten in the form $(s_i, \pi_{o_x}(s_i))$:

$$d_x = \langle (s_{i+1}, \pi_{o_x}(s_{i+1})), (s_{i+2}, \pi_{o_x}(s_{i+2})), \ldots, (s_j, \pi_{o_x}(s_j)) \rangle.$$

Given this, it is possible to rewrite d as $\langle d_1, d_2, \ldots, d_m \rangle$ (with a little abuse of notation), which expands to:

$$d = \langle (s_1, \pi_{o_1}(s_1)), (s_2, \pi_{o_1}(s_2)), \ldots, (s_i, \pi_{o_1}(s_i)),$$
$$(s_{i+1}, \pi_{o_2}(s_{i+1})), (s_{i+2}, \pi_{o_2}(s_{i+2})), \ldots, (s_j, \pi_{o_2}(s_j)),$$
$$\vdots$$
$$(s_{k+1}, \pi_{o_m}(s_{k+1})), (s_{k+2}, \pi_{o_m}(s_{k+2})), \ldots (s_n, \pi_{o_m}(s_n)) \rangle.$$

3.2 Reduce the Number of Options

Set $\mathcal{L}$ includes all the options that are necessary to equivalently rewrite d as specified above. However, some of these options may not differ much from each other. For this reason, we perform a clustering step to group "similar" options.

The similarity concept that is desired here is captured by the likelihood of transitioning from one state to another state, assuming the best action to this end is chosen. We thus define the distance between states s_i and s_j as follows:

$$\Delta(s_i, s_j) = \min_{a \in \mathcal{A}} \frac{1}{T(s_i, a, s_j)},$$

where $T(s_i, a, s_j)$ is the probability of transitioning from state s_i to state s_j when executing action a.

This distance measure is then used to build a probability matrix. To this end, a graph is built and then the *all-pairs shortest path* algorithm is used ([6]). This algorithm has a complexity $O(|S|^3)$, however, the idea is that this algorithm is run only once in a precomputation phase. The distance matrix is then fed to the *DBSCAN* clustering algorithm ([5]). DBSCAN has been chosen because it does not require a specification of the number of clusters, unlike many other clustering algorithms.

The clusters are sorted by size and a random representative from the top k clusters is selected, where k is an arbitrary constant. The so-chosen representatives form the set of learned subgoals, and can then be enriched with an initiation set, a policy and a distribution of termination probabilities and so be transformed in options.

3.3 Limitations

This method relies on an RL algorithm that computes the policies induced by the subgoals. However, this goes against the advantage of computing options at all. Indeed, for large state spaces, this computation would be prohibitive.

Similarly, if the options model is computed by using the environment model (in the form of the transition probabilities function), the cost of such a computation would be prohibitive.

A simple approximation is to limit the computation performed by the RL algorithm to only a subset $\mathcal{S}' \subset \mathcal{S}$ with a much lower dimensionality. This would make the computation of policies feasible.

Such simplification would produce a larger variety of options. While most of these options may actually be redundant[1], the computational burden added would not be significant ([21]).

The procedure we propose makes use of the transition probabilities $T(s_i, a, s_j)$ for computing the similarity of options. This is a strong assumption, but such information could also be approximated by using the data contained in the demonstrations.

Notice that, even knowing T in advance, traditional model-based RL could not be used because the reward function is not assumed to be known. The purpose of the learnt options is to speed up a later on-line learning phase.

4   Experiments

This section details the experimental setup and presents the results of our experiments.

4.1   Experimental Setup

The whole procedure has been implemented in Python using the Numpy library[2] ([23]) and the Scikit Learn toolkit[3] ([15]).

The Q-learning algorithm has been tested in a grid-world. The shape of such environment is very similar to that used in [21], where a square 13×13 world is divided in 4 areas by means of barriers. Figure 1 shows a representation of such environment. Barriers are interrupted to allow traveling from one room to another; these holes are called "hallways". The agent can move in the four cardinal directions north, south, east or west. The probability of transitioning in the desired direction is $\frac{2}{3}$; the agent moves in one of the other cardinal directions with probability of $\frac{1}{3}$, that is $\frac{1}{9}$ for each of them.

We used this topology in two different flavors.

– The four areas are separated by "walls" which are impassable no matter what. This is the setting used in [21].
– The four areas are separated by "ponds", which are not impassable, but just have a much lower reward. The rationale behind this choice is to make the hallways part of the paths *chosen* by the experts rather than *unavoidable* steps. This is because our algorithm detects as subgoals only states that

---

[1] In case they were generated only as substeps of another option that could not be completely computed due to this approximation

[2] http://www.numpy.org/

[3] http://scikit-learn.org/

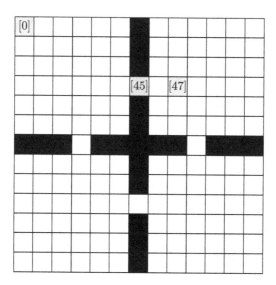

Fig. 1. The grid-world used in the experiments. The gray squares represent the destinations used in the different experiments: the one in the upper corner is labeled as [0], the one in the hallway is labeled [45] and the other one is labeled [47]. These labels will be used to present the results of the experiments. The black squares represent unreachable states in the wall setting and low rewards states in the ponds setting.

the experts explicitly chose among the others - as opposed to states that were simply not avoidable.

Specifically, while normal states have a reward of 0, ponds have a reward of −10. The final state has reward 1000 and, when reached, terminates the execution.

The key difference between the two flavors emerges because the demonstrations are generated by using a reward function that is unknown to the algorithm analyzing them. Consequently, the best choice to reach a particular state can appear suboptimal to the algorithm analyzing the demonstration. For example, a demonstration in which the expert is avoiding a pond by taking a longer path will be considered sub-optimal by our algorithm which does not know about the existence of the pond, whose existence is encoded in the unknown reward function.

In each of the flavors, different sets of experiments are run: each set of experiments sets a different destination for the agent. The states we chose as destinations are shown in Figure 1. We selected these destinations for specific reasons: one of them is in a corner, away from most common paths; another one is in a hallway, which is one of the hand-crafted options; the third one is close to a hallway and, as such, is part of many common paths.

By choosing different destinations, it is possible to compare the performance of all sets of options in different situations: in fact, if the options are close to the destination, the agent is advantaged because its exploration is biased in a convenient way; on the other hand, if the options are far from the destination, for the same reason, this is a disadvantage for the agent.

The value of the discount factor of the MDP is $\gamma = 0.97$. The options are generated from the subgoals o by using a reward function $R_o(s) = c \cdot \delta_{s,s_{k_o}}$ with $c = 50$, where s_{k_o} is the subgoal captured by option o by making use of the model of the environment T. The exploration strategy used in the experiments is ϵ-greedy, with $\epsilon = 0.1$.

The purpose of the experiments is to compare the quality of hand-crafted options, the hallways, denoted by $\mathcal{H}$, and that of options learned from demonstration, denoted $\mathcal{L}$. These sets of options are also compared against the set of primitive actions only, denoted $\mathcal{A}$. Sets $\mathcal{A} \cup \mathcal{H}$ and $\mathcal{A} \cup \mathcal{L}$ are also tested,

We select the handcrafted options as the baseline for comparison, rather than a random selection of states, because the former are supposed to perform better. This is because, due to the structure of the environment, a hallway state is for sure in any path that travels between two different rooms. Given this, their contribution to the Q-learning algorithm is supposedly more useful than that of other random locations.

4.2   Results

In the following we will often refer to "bad" options. By such term, we refer to options that lead to an area in the state space that is far away from the destination state the agent is pursuing.

It could be argued that, since all the options selected by our algorithm are part of the optimal path in a demonstration, there cannot be such a thing as a "bad" option. This can, however, happen since options are inferred from more than one demonstration, and are then likely to be sparse around the state space.

Figures 2, 3, 4, 5, 6 and 7 show the result of the experiments that have been run. On the X axis, the number of episodes is presented, while on the Y axis the (average) number of steps per episode is reported.

The plots show the average performance on 200 experiments run over 3000 episodes. In particular, for the curves representing the performance of learned options, for each of the 200 repetitions, a new set of demonstrations was randomly generated. The number of experiments is high because, since the perfomance depends on the random starting state, there is high variance.

All of the experiments have been run on both the "pond" and "wall" settings and on all of the destinations, [0], [45], [47] (see Figure 1 to visually identify these destinations). Results are presented using a sliding window with size of 20 to average values and hence smooth the curves.

The demonstrations used to learn the options have been generated by means of an automatic process. Each demonstration was computed by selecting a random initial state and using the optimal policy (computed by means of the value iteration algorithm) to simulate the behavior of an agent pursuing the destination. For each of environment, options set, destination and repetition, 4 demonstrations were generated and were used to learn options.

In the following, it will often be said that an option is close or far from a destination point: this is actually a short way to say that the subgoal which is captured by an option is close or far from that destination point. For the sake of conciseness, we will stick to the former, shorter version.

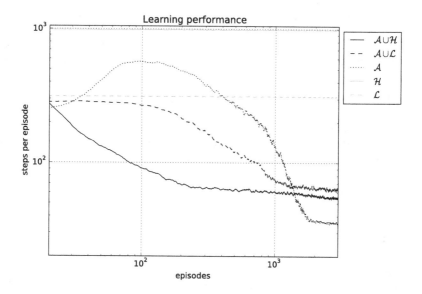

Fig. 2. This and the following figures show the result of experiments in the simulated environment described in Subsection 4.1. In all the figures, $\mathcal{A}$ denotes the set of primitive actions, $\mathcal{H}$ denotes the set of handcrafted options, which lead to each of the four hallways, and $\mathcal{L}$ denotes the set of learnt options. This figure shows the results obtained in the "pond" setting with destination [0]. For details, see Subsection 4.2.

Figures 2 and 3 show the results of the experiments where the agent's destination is the top-left corner, labeled as [0] in Figure 1.

In the pond setting, in Figure 2, both sets $\mathcal{A} \cup \mathcal{H}$ and $\mathcal{A} \cup \mathcal{L}$ both converge, but the former is consistently better than the latter. Set $\mathcal{A}$ performs worse at the beginning but ends up being the best performer, as one would expect. We interpret this difference to be due to the ϵ-greedy strategy: when an agent randomly chooses a "bad" option, it ends up further away than it would by just choosing a "bad" action. Set $\mathcal{H}$ performs very poorly here, because the distance of the options from the destination make it very unlikely that the destination is ever reached. Set $\mathcal{L}$ performs quite poorly as well, even though it shows a slight advantage.

In the "wall" setting, in Figure 3, set $\mathcal{A} \cup \mathcal{L}$ and set $\mathcal{L}$ both outperform sets $\mathcal{A} \cup \mathcal{H}$ and $\mathcal{A}$. While the former is expected to perform worse, it is not obvious for the latter. After investigating in the logs, we found out that this is due to the learned options in this setting. As a consequence of the topology, all of the expert's decisions, inferred by the demonstrations, are explained by the topology (rather than the reward function, as in the pond setting). As a consequence, most

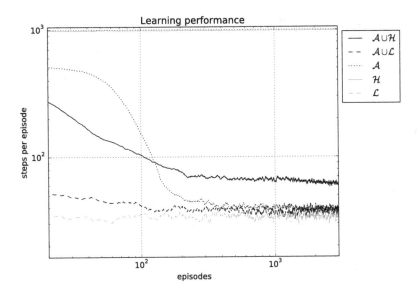

Fig. 3. This figure shows the results obtained in the "wall" setting with destination [0]. For further information, see Figure 2.

of the times the only option that is learned in this setting is the destination itself. The fact that virtually only one option is available, beside the primitive actions, eliminates the disadvantage caused by the ϵ-greedy exploration strategy. Finally, for the same reason as in the pond setting, set $\mathcal{H}$ performs very poorly.

Figures 4 and 5 show the results of the experiments where the agent's destination is the hallway, labeled as [45] in Figure 1.

In the pond setting, in Figure 4, the best performers are clearly sets $\mathcal{H}$ and $\mathcal{A} \cup \mathcal{H}$. This is because the destination is exactly one of the options, making it very quick for the agent to find a good path to the destination. Set $\mathcal{A}$ also performs well after an exploration phase. Set $\mathcal{A} \cup \mathcal{L}$ converges with a slight disadvantage with respect to set $\mathcal{A}$. Finally, set $\mathcal{L}$ is outperformed by all of the others: this shows how having options distant from the destination and not having primitive actions make it unlike that the destination is reached.

In the wall setting, in Figure 5, the sets $\mathcal{H}$ and $\mathcal{A} \cup \mathcal{H}$ both perform very well, once more, because the destination is one of the subgoals. In this case, also sets $\mathcal{L}$ and $\mathcal{A} \cup \mathcal{L}$ perform well, again because the topology makes it so that, most of the times, the only learned option is the destination. Also set $\mathcal{A}$ performs well, even though it takes longer to converge.

Figures 6 and 7 show the results of the experiments where the agent's destination is the state on the left of the hallway, labeled as [47] in Figure 1.

In the pond setting, in Figure 6, sets $\mathcal{A} \cup \mathcal{L}$, $\mathcal{A} \cup \mathcal{H}$ and $\mathcal{A}$ perform very well. Sets $\mathcal{H}$ and $\mathcal{L}$ perform unexpectedly poorly. We hypothesize that, due to the low rewards received, the algorithm does not have sufficient information to tell which of the option is the best one to choose since they all appear equally bad.

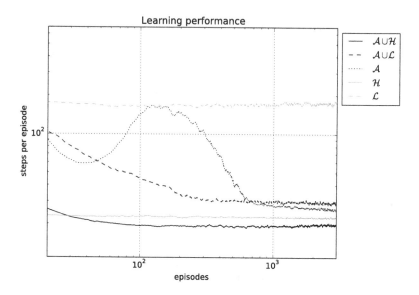

Fig. 4. This figure shows the results obtained in the "pond" setting with destination [45]. For details, see Figure 2.

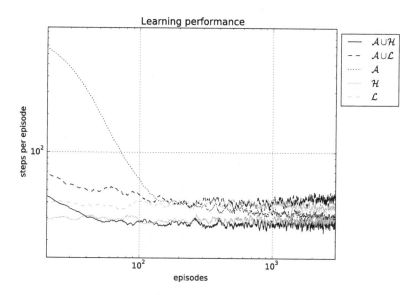

Fig. 5. This figure shows the results obtained in the "wall" setting with destination [45]. For details, see Figure 2.

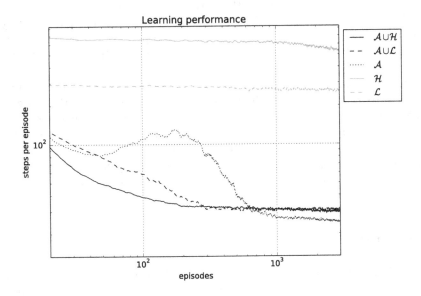

Fig. 6. This figure shows the results obtained in the "pond" setting with destination [47]. For details, see Figure 2.

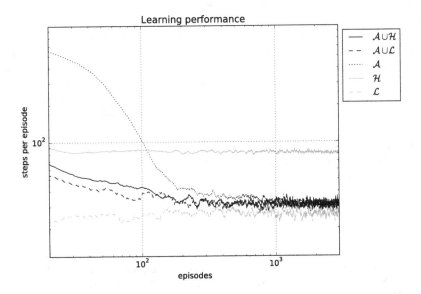

Fig. 7. This figure shows the results obtained in the "wall" setting with destination [47]. For details, see Figure 2.

In the wall setting, in Figure 7, the performance of sets $\mathcal{A} \cup \mathcal{L}$ and $\mathcal{L}$ are about the same as the pond setting. Set $\mathcal{A}$ reaches convergence more quickly and set $\mathcal{A} \cup \mathcal{H}$ performs better in general. Set $\mathcal{H}$ also perform better than in the pond setting; however, since the destination is only close to the options but not coincident, reaching it takes some luck (i.e. time).

When used along with primitive actions, learned options perform about as well as hand-crafted options, with a slight advantage in most cases. Furthermore, it can be noticed that the bias introduced by the options in the random exploration provides a speed-up in the learning process, letting the agents reach a stable performance after only a few tens of episodes. This is one of the cases in which the introduction of a bias (as mentioned in [7]) is benefiting the learning process; since it is derived by the behavior of experts, the exploration tends to follow the footsteps of the experts.

5   Conclusion

We have showed that learning options for an MDP from a demonstration is a viable choice. Options can greatly improve learning and planning performance. Previous work has shown that they can be hand-crafted ([21]) or learned by exploring the environment ([11, 18, 4, 17, 10, 22, 3]). With this work we show that options can also be learned from demonstration, which is a good choice in a context where exploration is not possible but significant amounts of data are available.

We also showed that different settings give rise to different behaviors both in learned and hand-crafted options. In particular, when the topology constrains the experts' behavior, learned options usually correspond to the destination; on the other hand, when a behavior is a consequence of the rewards, which are unknown to the agent, learned options are arguably more significative (in the sense that they resemble more to landmarks) but are less efficient in the learning phase.

Future works include testing this approach against real data, possibly in the form of a bigger dataset. A possible extension of this research is to let the algorithm work in continuous states and actions spaces.

References

1. Abbeel, P., Ng, A.Y.: Apprenticeship learning via inverse reinforcement learning. In: Proceedings of the 21st International Conference on Machine Learning, ICML 2004, pp. 1–8. ACM, New York (2004), http://doi.acm.org/10.1145/1015330.1015430, doi:10.1145/1015330.1015430
2. Baxter, J., Tridgell, A., Weaver, L.: Knightcap: A chess programm that learns by combining TD(lambda) with game-tree search. In: Proceedings of the Fifteenth International Conference on Machine Learning, ICML 1998, pp. 28–36. Morgan Kaufmann Publishers Inc., San Francisco (1998), http://dl.acm.org/citation.cfm?id=645527.657300

3. Cobo, L.C., Subramanian, K., Jr., C.L.I., Lanterman, A.D., Thomaz, A.L.: Abstraction from demonstration for efficient reinforcement learning in high-dimensional domains. Artificial Intelligence 216(0), 103 (2014), http://www.sciencedirect.com/science/article/pii/S0004370214000861, doi:10.1016/j.artint.2014.07.003

4. Şimşek, Ö., Wolfe, A.P., Barto, A.G.: Identifying useful subgoals in reinforcement learning by local graph partitioning. In: Proceedings of the 22nd International Conference on Machine learning, ICML 2005, pp. 816–823. ACM, New York (2005), http://doi.acm.org/10.1145/1102351.1102454, doi:10.1145/1102351.1102454

5. Ester, M., Kriegel, H.-P., Sander, J., Xu, X.: A density-based algorithm for discovering clusters in large spatial databases with noise. In: Simoudis, E., Fayyad, U., Han, J. (eds.) Proceedings of the Second International Conference on Knowledge Discovery and Data Mining, vol. 96, pp. 226–231. AAAI Press (1996)

6. Floyd, R.W.: Algorithm 97: Shortest path. Communications of the ACM 5(6), 345–349 (1962), http://doi.acm.org/10.1145/367766.368168, doi:10.1145/367766.368168

7. Jong, N.K., Hester, T., Stone, P.: The utility of temporal abstraction in reinforcement learning. In: Proceedings of the 7th International Joint Conference on Autonomous Agents and Multiagent Systems, AAMAS 2008, vol. 1, pp. 299–306. International Foundation for Autonomous Agents and Multiagent Systems, Richland (2008), http://dl.acm.org/citation.cfm?id=1402383.1402429

8. Klein, E., Geist, M., Pietquin, O.: Batch, off-policy and model-free apprenticeship learning. In: Sanner, S., Hutter, M. (eds.) EWRL 2011. LNCS, vol. 7188, pp. 285–296. Springer, Heidelberg (2012), http://dx.doi.org/10.1007/978-3-642-29946-9_28

9. Kober, J., Peters, J.: Reinforcement learning in robotics: A survey. In: Wiering, M., van Otterlo, M. (eds.) Reinforcement Learning. Adaptation, Learning, and Optimization, vol. 12, pp. 579–610. Springer, Heidelberg (2012), http://dx.doi.org/10.1007/978-3-642-27645-3_18, doi:10.1007/978-3-642-27645-3_18

10. Mannor, S., Menache, I., Hoze, A., Klein, U.: Dynamic abstraction in reinforcement learning via clustering. In: Proceedings of the 21st International Conference on Machine Learning, ICML 2004, pp. 71–78. ACM, New York (2004), http://doi.acm.org/10.1145/1015330.1015355, doi:10.1145/1015330.1015355

11. McGovern, A., Barto, A.G.: Automatic discovery of subgoals in reinforcement learning using diverse density. In: Proceedings of the Eighteenth International Conference on Machine Learning, ICML 2001, pp. 361–368. Morgan Kaufmann Publishers Inc., San Francisco (2001), http://dl.acm.org/citation.cfm?id=645530.655681

12. Lacasse, A., Laviolette, F., Marchand, M., Turgeon-Boutin, F.: Learning with randomized majority votes. In: Balcázar, J.L., Bonchi, F., Gionis, A., Sebag, M. (eds.) ECML PKDD 2010, Part II. LNCS, vol. 6322, pp. 162–177. Springer, Heidelberg (2010), http://dx.doi.org/10.1007/978-3-642-15883-4_25

13. Ng, A., Coates, A., Diel, M., Ganapathi, V., Schulte, J., Tse, B., Berger, E., Liang, E.: Autonomous inverted helicopter flight via reinforcement learning. In: Ang Jr, M.H., Khatib, O. (eds.) Experimental Robotics IX. Springer Tracts in Advanced Robotics, vol. 21, pp. 363–372. Springer, Heidelberg (2006), http://dx.doi.org/10.1007/11552246_35

14. Ng, A.Y., Russell, S.J.: Algorithms for inverse reinforcement learning. In: Proceedings of the Seventeenth International Conference on Machine Learning, ICML 2000, pp. 663–670. Morgan Kaufmann Publishers Inc., San Francisco (2000), http://dl.acm.org/citation.cfm?id=645529.657801

15. Pedregosa, F., Varoquaux, G., Gramfort, A., Michel, V., Thirion, B., Grisel, O., Blondel, M., Prettenhofer, P., Weiss, R., Dubourg, V., Vanderplas, J., Passos, A., Cournapeau, D., Brucher, M., Perrot, M., Duchesnay, E.: Scikit-learn: Machine learning in python. The Journal of Machine Learning Research 12, 2825–2830 (2011), http://dl.acm.org/citation.cfm?id=1953048.2078195

16. Ramachandran, D., Amir, E.: Bayesian inverse reinforcement learning. In: Proceedings of the 20th International Joint Conference on Artifical Intelligence, IJCAI 2007, pp. 2586–2591. Morgan Kaufmann Publishers Inc, San Francisco (2007), http://dl.acm.org/citation.cfm?id=1625275.1625692

17. Şimşek, Ö., Barto, A.G.: Using relative novelty to identify useful temporal abstractions in reinforcement learning. In: Proceedings of the 21st International Conference on Machine Learning, ICML 2004, pp. 95–102. ACM, New York (2004), http://doi.acm.org/10.1145/1015330.1015353, doi:10.1145/1015330.1015353

18. Stolle, M., Precup, D.: Learning options in reinforcement learning. In: Koenig, S., Holte, R. (eds.) SARA 2002. LNCS (LNAI), vol. 2371, pp. 212–223. Springer, Heidelberg (2002), http://dx.doi.org/10.1007/3-540-45622-8_16

19. Stone, P., Sutton, R.S.: Scaling reinforcement learning toward robocup soccer. In: Proceedings of the Eighteenth International Conference on Machine Learning, ICML 2001, pp. 537–544. Morgan Kaufmann Publishers Inc., San Francisco (2001), http://dl.acm.org/citation.cfm?id=645530.655674

20. Sutton, R.S., Barto, A.G.: Introduction to Reinforcement Learning, 1st edn. MIT Press, Cambridge (1998)

21. Sutton, R.S., Precup, D., Singh, S.: Between MDPs and semi-MDPs: A framework for temporal abstraction in reinforcement learning. Artificial Intelligence 112(1–2), 181–211 (1999),
http://www.sciencedirect.com/science/article/pii/S0004370299000521, doi:http://dx.doi.org/10.1016/S0004-37029900052-1

22. Vigorito, C., Barto, A.: Intrinsically motivated hierarchical skill learning in structured environments. IEEE Transactions on Autonomous Mental Development 2(2), 132–143 (2010), doi:10.1109/TAMD.2010.2050205

23. Walt, S., van, d. C.S.C., Varoquaux, G.: The numpy array: A structure for efficient numerical computation. Computing in Science & Engineering 13(2), 22–30 (2011), http://scitation.aip.org/content/aip/journal/cise/13/2/10.1109/MCSE.2011.37, doi: http://dx.doi.org/10.1109/MCSE.2011.37

24. Watkins, C.J.C.H.: Learning from delayed rewards. Ph.D. thesis, University of Cambridge (1989)

25. Ziebart, B.D., Maas, A., Bagnell, J.A., Dey, A.K.: Maximum entropy inverse reinforcement learning. In: Proceedings of the 23rd National Conference on Artificial Intelligence - Volume 3, AAAI 2008, pp. 1433–1438. AAAI Press (2008), http://dl.acm.org/citation.cfm?id=1620270.1620297

A Grammarless Language Generation Algorithm Based on Idiotypic Artificial Immune Networks

Vedanuj Goswami* and Samir Borgohain

Dept. of Computer Science and Engineering,
National Institute of Technology, Silchar, Assam, India
vedanuj.gos@gmail.com

Abstract. The immune system is capable of evolving by learning from its environment over the lifetime of the host. Using the ideas of idiotypic network theory and artificial immune systems we explore the analogy between the immune system and linguistics to suggest a new approach to build a network of sentence phrases and train it using a learning algorithm. The learning algorithm is devised to help evolve the network sufficiently with stimulations by correct phrases or antigens. The network after sufficient stimulations, suppressions and decay is capable of detecting and differentiating between correct and wrong sentences. We verify with experimental data and observe promising results for such an immune network based algorithm. The system learns a language without any grammar rules similar to a small child who knows nothing about grammar yet learns to speak in his native language fluently after a few years of training.

Keywords: artificial immune system, idiotypic network theory, natural language generation, grammarless language learning.

1 Introduction

Grammar has no flexible laws or no absolutely hard and fast rules. Several problems faced with traditional approaches of using grammatical rules to generate a language have been mentioned by Araujo and Santamaria [1]. Inferring language from grammar often leads to undecidable decision problems. Also a grammar generated from a collection of texts depends on the text type and hence different rules are required for even the same language. Furthermore for many languages the grammar rules are not available for proper language generation and translation.

In order to overcome such problems an evolutionary approach of training a set of sentence phrases can be used to generate a language. Here we propose a model using the ideas of the Idiotypic Network theory, with the goal of producing a system to learn a language that can evolve with its changing environment. Our work explores the basic aspects of the artificial immune systems.

The architecture described in this paper takes inspiration from the natural immune system which is responsible for protection of the human body from foreign invaders by differentiating self from non-self and neutralizing dangerous pathogens and toxins.

---

* Corresponding author Tel : $+91 - 8588979158$. Email : vedanuj.gos@gmail.com

S.K. Chalup et al. (Eds.): ACALCI 2015, LNAI 8955, pp. 243–257, 2015.

Main function is carried out by antibodies that are specific proteins that recognize and bind to other particular proteins called antigens. The specialized portion of the antibody molecule used for identifying other molecules is called the antibody combining region or paratope. The structure of an antibody is described in [2]. The regions on any molecule (antigen or antibody) that the paratopes can attach to are called epitopes. If the shape of an foreign antigen molecule matches that of the paratope, i.e the paratope can attach to the epitope, the antibody attaches itself to the antigen, leading to its eventual demise. The immune system is described very lucidly by Farmer [3] as a system of locks and keys.

An epitope that is unique to a given antibody type is called an idiotope. Jerne in [4,5] proposed the *Idiotypic Network theory* where he postulated that the immune system functions as a network, where antibodies are stimulated or suppressed by idiotypic interactions with complementary antibodies. The immune system is a complex network of antibodies which link to each other via the paratopes that recognize the set of idiotopes and of idiotopes that are recognized by sets of paratopes. This forms a complex web of recognizing and of being recognized [6]. The antibodies can respond either positively or negatively to the recognition signal. A positive response would result in antibody stimulation while a negative response would lead to suppression and decay.

Several immune network models proposed until now (Jerne [4]; Bona et al. [7]; Farmer et al. [3]; Varela et al. [8]) are based upon a set of differential equations. These describe the interactions, which are either excitatory (network activation) or inhibitory (network suppression) between different types of elements which lead to the network connectivity pattern and dynamics of the network elements. This network approach is particularly useful for the development of a system that can evolve with time into an intelligent system depending on its environment. Such systems have been employed in different problem domains which include classification, anomaly and fault detection [9], data analysis and clustering [10] and robotics [11]. But till now not much work has been done to exploit this analogy that exists between the descriptions of language and the immune system and use Idiotypic Network theory for learning of languages.

In this paper an artificial immune network model based on Farmer's computational model [3] of Jerne's Idiotypic Network theory is proposed. The purpose is to train a huge set of word phrases by forming an immune network. Section 2 explains the structure of antibodies in our network to represent the sentence phrases in section 2.1. The set of antibodies interlink to form a network with the help of the learning algorithm described in section 2.3. The memory of the network is explained in section 2.4. Finally we show the results of running the learning algorithm over a set of antibodies to form a network in section 3. Here we show experimentally that the network formed between the phrases learns meaningful and correct sentences from the training data set without the help of any grammatical rules. It can also detect and differentiate between correct and incorrect sentence constructs. The network will change and evolve itself when put in a new environment or context.

2   Grammarless Language Model

The antibody repertoire available to our immune system is very large compared to the vocabulary of a language. Jerne in [2] mentioned a reasonable analogy between language and the immune system which can be established by regarding the variable region of an antibody (Fig 1.a) as a sentence or phrase. The great diversity of antibody molecules and their specificities result from an enormous number of varieties in the variable regions with respect to amino acid sequences. It is similar to the great variety of sentences in a language which results from the huge number of varieties with respect to the sequences of words and phrases. In the biological immune system, recognition occurs through a complementary match between a given antigen and the antibody (Fig 1.b). For the purposes of our model, and antigen action leads to the stimulation of antibodies with similar characteristics (instead of complementary) to that of the antigen. Similar assumptions were used by Hajela and Yoo [12], Hart and Ross [13], Castro and Von Zuben [10] and Whitbrook et al. [11].

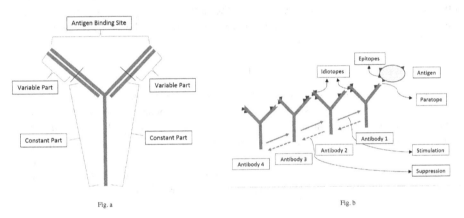

Fig. a   Fig. b

Fig. 1. a) The structure of an antibody molecule. b) The idiotypic network where stimulation and suppression occurs.

The proposed learning algorithm aims at constructing an evolved network by training it sufficiently with correct sentences. The model will consist of a set of cells each of which is an antibody (parts of sentences, used interchangeably in this text). The antibodies are interconnected by links with associated probabilities of their order in a sentence. The antibodies represent the network's internal images of the antigens (input patterns or correct phrases) contained in the environment to which it is exposed. The connections between the antibodies will determine their interrelations, providing a degree of similarity among them: more strongly connected the antibodies, the more similar they are. Another type of interaction exists between the antibodies which depicts the order of occurrence of phrases in a sentence. Hence the antibody network consists of two types of links, (i) between antibodies having close proximity with each other and (ii) between antibodies based on the probability of occurrence of each other one after the other in a sentence. The training set (antigens) are sentences found in literature or any other source of correct sentences. Existing antibodies will compete for antigenic recognition and those successful will be stimulated, while those who fail will be suppressed. The suppression controls the specificity level of the antibodies by suppressing the wrong phrases among a set of similar phrases. The link probabilities and the affinity matrix take care of the generalist behavior of the antibodies by travelling over the links and clubbing together chunks of other antibodies to learn a correct sentence.

2.1 The structure of Antibodies and Antigens

Phrases or word constructs of antibodies are stored as character strings separated by spaces. The lengths of the antibodies can vary and this will have no impact on the performance of the system (explained in later sections). The structure of an antibody is

$$\boxed{C_i \| Word_1 \| Word_2 \| Word_3 \| Word_4 \| \ldots}$$

where C_i is the concentration of the antibody and the $Word_i$ are the words of the sentence/phrase in sequence. Words are stored as character strings separated by spaces in between. The concentration changes as per the network change due to antigen stimulations. While calculating the distance between antibodies the word sequences are matched. The structure of an antigen is

$$\boxed{Word_1 \| Word_2 \| Word_3 \| Word_4 \| \ldots}$$

The concentration of an antigen is not stored in its structure since an antigen will not reside in the system. Antigens are used only for the purpose of training the network and as such their effect on the network is only for the cycle during which the antigen is introduced to the system. We assume an antigen to have a high concentration while calculating the network change. This is because an antigen is assumed to be always correct and hence it stimulates the antibodies matching it to a higher extent. This stimulation is thus higher than the idiotypic antibody stimulation or suppression.

2.2 Network Topology : Antibody Affinity Matrix

The network is represented in the form of Affinity Matrix $\mathcal{AA}$ which stores the network links based on the affinity between two antibodies. Each element in the matrix specifies the similarity between two antibodies, while the magnitude of the element specifies the degree of similarity between the two antibodies. Affinity Matrix $\mathcal{AA}$ of order $n \times n$,

$$\mathcal{AA}_{n,n} = \begin{pmatrix} pa_{1,1} & pa_{1,2} & \cdots & pa_{1,n} \\ pa_{2,1} & pa_{2,2} & \cdots & pa_{2,n} \\ \vdots & \vdots & \ddots & \vdots \\ pa_{n,1} & pa_{n,2} & \cdots & pa_{n,n} \end{pmatrix} \tag{1}$$

For a set of numbered antibodies, the element $pa_{i,j}$ at position (i,j) in the affinity matrix, specifies the binding affinity between antibodies Ab_i and Ab_j in the set. Each of the elements in the affinity matrix is calculated as

$$pa_{i,j} = max(0, \alpha_t(LCWS(i,j) - \lambda_t)) \tag{2}$$

where $LCWS$ is the function returning the length of *Longest Common Word Sub-sequence* between antibodies Ab_i and Ab_j and λ_t is the *Affinity Threshold* for the system at time t. α_t defines how strong each matching between two antibodies will effect their concentration change during a particular time t of the system. Its value is adjusted depending upon the system characteristics which determine the rate of evolution of the network. We take the maximum value between 0 and $\alpha_t (LCWS(i,j) - \lambda_t)$ as we ignore any non positive values for affinity.

In order to calculate the suppression of antibodies we construct a Negative Affinity Matrix $\mathcal{NA}$ of dimensions $n \times n$ as

$$\mathcal{NA}_{n,n} = \begin{pmatrix} na_{1,1} & na_{1,2} & \cdots & na_{1,n} \\ na_{2,1} & na_{2,2} & \cdots & na_{2,n} \\ \vdots & \vdots & \ddots & \vdots \\ na_{n,1} & na_{n,2} & \cdots & na_{n,n} \end{pmatrix} \tag{3}$$

Negative-Affinity between antibodies i and j is given by

$$na_{i,j} = max(0, \beta_t(NMW(i,j) - LCWS(i,j) - \phi_t)) \tag{4}$$

where $NMW(i,j)$ returns the total number of matching words between antibodies Ab_i and Ab_j and ϕ_t is the *Negative-Affinity Threshold* for the system at time t. The value of β_t, defines how strong each matching between two antibodies will effect their concentration during a particular time t of the system. Its value is adjusted depending upon the system characteristics which determine the rate of evolution of the network. It is important to note that $\beta_t \leq \alpha_t$ at any point of time, which means stimulation is always greater than suppression.

2.3   The Learning Algorithm

Time t_k is considered as one *cycle* or period of action of antigen k in the system. It is the duration of the whole stimulation and suppression cycle due to the particular antigen. The Learning Algorithm is

For each antigenic pattern k introduced during the time interval t_k

Step 1 : The affinity of the antibodies with the introduced antigen is calculated and stored in the Antigen Affinity vector $\mathcal{AN}$ as

$$\mathcal{AN}_i = max(0, \alpha_t(LCWS(i,k) - \lambda_t)) \tag{5}$$

where $LCWS(i,k)$ returns the length of *Longest Common Word Sub-sequence* between antibody Ab_i and the antigen k.

Step 2 : The Concentration change vector $\mathcal{D}$ which stores the change in the concentration of each antibody due to the antigenic reaction is calculated. This is done with the help of the Farmer's Equation [3]. Some modifications are done in the equation to fit our purpose. The change in concentration of each antibody is calculated with the help of the initial concentrations of the antibodies, their affinities and the antigenic affinity with the antibody. It takes into account the stimulation, suppression and decay of antibodies as follows :

Stimulation : Concentration of an antibody Ab_i increases when more antigens or antibodies stimulate them. Stimulation is proportional to the longest common subsequence of words between the antibody and the antigen or other antibodies. Antigens are considered to be correct and hence the greater matching with an antigen means the antibody is more correct and hence higher the concentration.

Suppression : Concentration of an antibody is suppressed by another antibody. Suppression is proportional to the number of words out of sequence in the two antibodies. The higher the concentration of the other antibodies which are out of sequence with respect to this antibody, the higher is the suppression. This means that a correct phrase suppresses an incorrect phrase.

Decay : When an antibody is not stimulated for a particular amount of time or a particular number of cycles its concentration decays at rate γ times the number of cycles without any positive stimulation. Also $\gamma \ll \eta$ since the decay rate must be very low for ensuring that probable wrong phrases are not discarded as wrong only after a few cycles.

The change in concentrations of other antibodies during the same cycle are not considered for calculating the change of an antibody. Only the network interactions and antigenic stimulation is used. If antibody Ab_i's concentration $C_i >$ Decay Threshold, the change in its concentration is calculated using a modified Farmer's Equation as

$$
\begin{aligned}
\mathcal{D}_i &= \frac{\mathrm{d}}{\mathrm{d}t}(C_i) \\
&= \eta \left(\sum_{j=1}^{N} \mathcal{A}\mathcal{A}_{i,j} C_i C_j - \sum_{j=1}^{N} \mathcal{N}\mathcal{A}_{i,j} C_i C_j + \mathcal{A}\mathcal{N}_i C_i \right) - \gamma NCS(i)
\end{aligned} \tag{6}
$$

where η is a constant which drives the growth of the network, C_j is the concentration of the antibody Ab_j and γ is the decay constant. $NCS(i)$, *Number of Cycles without Stimulation*, is the function that gives the time difference from the last positive concentration change of the antibody Ab_i. An example is shown in Fig.2.

After calculating the concentration change vector, we observe that many antibodies are stimulated by a very small degree. We ignore small stimulation changes by keeping only those changes which are significant. We do this by calculating the maximum of the concentration changes for the current cycle.

$$
\mathcal{M} = max(\mathcal{D}_1, \mathcal{D}_2, \mathcal{D}_3, \ldots, \mathcal{D}_N) \tag{7}
$$

After storing the maximum value in $\mathcal{M}$, for each $\mathcal{D}_i$ we either keep its value or put a zero if its value is too low in comparison to the maximum change,

$$
\mathcal{D}_i = \begin{cases} \mathcal{D}_i & \text{if } abs(\mathcal{D}_j) > \xi\mathcal{M} \\ 0 & \text{otherwise} \end{cases} \tag{8}
$$

where $\xi(< 1)$ on multiplying with $\mathcal{M}$ gives the fraction of maximum change required for keeping the value of $\mathcal{D}_i$.

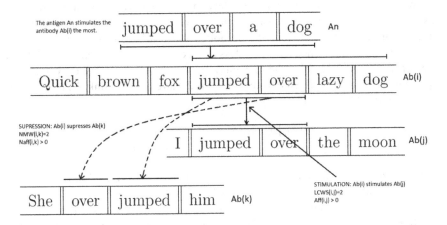

Fig. 2. Here we show an example. Upon the action of the antigen *An*, the antibody *Ab$_i$* gets stimulated. Upon its stimulation it stimulates the antibody *Ab$_j$* due to high positive affinity with it. It also suppresses antibody *Ab$_k$* due to negative affinity with it.

Step 3 : The Order Matrix *O* stores link weights between both similar and dissimilar antibodies which is necessary for complete sentence formation. It is modified with the help of the Concentration change vector *D*. Every value in the Order Matrix gives the arrangement order of two antibodies for sentence formation(even if they have very low or no affinity between them). The value corresponding to two antibodies in this matrix shows how much is the probability of them occurring one after the other in a sentence. This matrix stores the information for correct order of antibodies in order to form meaningful sentences. Order matrix *O* of dimensions *n* x *n* is given as

$$O_{n,n} = \begin{pmatrix} o_{1,1} & o_{1,2} & \cdots & o_{1,n} \\ o_{2,1} & o_{2,2} & \cdots & o_{2,n} \\ \vdots & \vdots & \ddots & \vdots \\ o_{n,1} & o_{n,2} & \cdots & o_{n,n} \end{pmatrix} \tag{9}$$

The value of each $o_{i,j}$ in the matrix corresponds to a probability of occurrence of *Ab$_j$* after *Ab$_i$*. Let $\mathcal{Z}$ be any set of antibodies each of which may be a probable choice to follow antibody *Ab$_i$* in the sentence to be formed. In that case, the antibody having the highest $o_{i,j}$ value, where $Ab_j \in \mathcal{Z}$, is chosen.

We introduce the strength of a link, $S_{i,j}$, formed between two antibodies during an antigen stimulation cycle. The higher the stimulation level of the antibodies joined by the link the higher is the link strength i.e.

$$S_{i,j} \propto \mathcal{D}_i \mathcal{D}_j \tag{10}$$

where $\mathcal{D}_i$ and $\mathcal{D}_j$ are concentration change of *Ab$_i$* and *Ab$_j$* respectively.

$S_{i,j}$ is also proportional to the negative of affinity as lower the affinity between two antibodies. The lower the presence of same words in sequence in the two antibodies, the higher is the probability of them occurring together in the same sentence i.e.

$$S_{i,j} \propto max(0, \theta - \mathcal{A} \mathcal{A}_{i,j}) \tag{11}$$

where *Threshold* θ gives the maximum level of affinity beyond which link strength is zero. The significance is that if affinity between two antibodies Ab_i and Ab_j is more than the maximum value we do not establish a link between them as they are very similar and hence have very less chance of occurring together in the same sentence. $S_{i,j}$ is valid only when a pattern present in Ab_i is followed by a pattern present in Ab_j in the antigen introduced. Thus the strength of a link $S_{i,j}$ by combining equations (10) and (11) is

$$S_{i,j} = \begin{cases} \kappa \mathcal{D}_i \mathcal{D}_j \{max(0, \theta - \mathcal{A}\mathcal{A}_{i,j})\} & \text{if } Ab_j \text{ follows } Ab_i \\ 0 & \text{otherwise} \end{cases} \quad (12)$$

where κ is a constant that remains same throughout the cycles. We observe that higher the value of $S_{i,j}$ higher is the probability of Ab_j following Ab_i.

After each antigen stimulation of the network we calculate the $\mathcal{P}_{i,j}$ for each antibody pair(in the order Ab_i preceding Ab_j) which gives the probability of the Ab_j following Ab_i. It is calculated as the probability of one particular link over all the possible links that get created upon the introduction of an antigen. Using the link strength as described in equation (12) we get

$$\mathcal{P}_{i,j} = \frac{S_{i,j}}{\sum_{j=1}^{N} \sum_{i=1}^{N} S_{i,j}}$$

With the value of the probability of occurrence of the two antibodies in the sequence, we adjust each $o_{i,j}$ in matrix O with the new value for the ordered antibody pair. The new value is

$$o_{i,j} = max(\mathcal{P}_{i,j}, o_{i,j}) \quad (13)$$

This means we keep only the highest value that determines the occurrence of the pair in that order. Incase $\mathcal{P}_{i,j}$ is less than $o_{i,j}$ we ignore it as in some previous cycle we have already established that the ordered pair (Ab_i, Ab_j) occurs with a higher probability than as found in this cycle and hence need not be modified.

Step 4 : The concentration of antibodies is changed if the initial concentration lies between the *Decay Concentration* and the *Correct Concentration*. *Correct Concentration* is a level of concentration beyond which an antibody is declared to be a correct phrase construct. *Decay Concentration* is the lower limit below which an antibody is declared *wrong* or *dead*. This is necessary for prohibiting exponential growth of the correct antibodies due to high network stimulation when they have a high concentration.

$$C_i = \begin{cases} C_i + \mathcal{D}_i, & \text{if } C_{Decay} \leq C_i \leq C_{Correct} \\ C_i, & \text{otherwise} \end{cases} \quad (14)$$

The network thus reacted to the antigen k and formed new links between the antibodies based on affinity and order and hence it learned another sentence construct.

2.4 Immune Memory in the Network and Correctness Detection

The antibody concentrations provide a measure of how much each phrase (antibody) is correct or wrong. Memory is built by storing the correct phrases with relatively higher concentrations. The order and probabilities of occurrence of antibodies one after another is stored in the Order Matrix which helps in forming complete sentences based on the memory of the antigens the system was exposed to during the training phase. The network memory can also be used for recognizing wrong sentence constructs which can be achieved in the two ways - (i) using Negative Affinity and (ii) using Decay Affinity and Decay Concentration.

A negative affinity threshold limit, $\mathcal{NA}_{Limit}$ can be set which will be the point of tolerance for a foreign sentence construct. If the sentence construct has a negative affinity more than the threshold with respect to any of the antibody Ab_i in the system, it can be regarded as *wrong* and rejected. Thus a foreign sentence construct k is deemed wrong if

$$(NMW(i,k) - LCWS(i,k) - \phi_t) \geq \mathcal{NA}_{Limit}$$
$$\text{and}\quad C_i > C_{Decay} \tag{15}$$

The antibodies which fall below a *Decay Concentration*, C_{Decay} concentration are considered *dead*. They are stored in the system as parts of the network which do not evolve or change. They maintain their affinities with other antibodies in the system which helps them to be recognized via the network links. This is done for the possibility that if such sentence constructs are encountered in future they can be easily recognized as *wrong*. In order to recognize a wrong phrase k, its affinity with the dead antibodies must be greater than the *Decay Affinity*, $\mathcal{AA}_{Decay}$. Thus a phrase is considered incorrect if

$$(LCWS(i,k) - \theta_t) \geq \mathcal{AA}_{Decay} \text{ and } C_i \ll C_{Decay} \tag{16}$$

In addition to these, a factor of correctness of a foreign sentence T_k can be calculated simply by subtracting the product of its negative affinities with antibodies and their corresponding concentrations from the product of positive affinities with antibodies and their concentrations. If we get negative values (negative affinity with higher concentration antibodies is more) even after testing with a sufficiently trained network we can assume the sentence tested is incorrect. The Degree of Correctness of T_k,

$$\mathcal{DC}_{T_k} = \sum_{i=1}^{N} \mathcal{AA}_{T_k,i} C_i - \sum_{i=1}^{N} \mathcal{NA}_{T_k,i} C_i \tag{17}$$

3 Results and Analysis

We simulate our model on a set of antibodies or phrases from the English language. We take an initial pool of 50 antibodies and then introduce antigens to allow the network between the antibodies to grow and evolve. The lengths of the antibodies can vary and this will have no impact on the performance of the system. This is because the affinity matching is done only relative to the number of word matching in sequence rather than total number of words in a antibody phrase. Every antibody is a phrase with an associated concentration level. The phrases are simple word clusters like

Ab_i : why are they here
Ab_j : why do you cry
Ab_k : is why here she

The antigens used to train the antibody set may be either phrases or even long sentences. For example
Why is she here without your car?

3.1   Concentration Change to Determine the Correct Set of Antibodies

We set the parameters and threshold values as given below and note the network change after 10, 20, 25, 30, 40 and 50 cycles of antigen action.

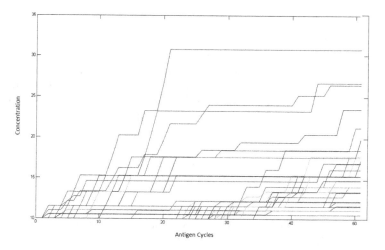

Fig. 3. The change of concentration of the antibodies with increasing antigenic cycle trainings. we observe some antibodies reach a high level of concentration whereas a few others do not increase in concentration at all.

We assume $\alpha_t = \beta_t = 1, \lambda_t = 2, \phi_t = 0, \gamma = 0.01, \eta = 0.1$ and $\xi = 0.3$. α_t and β_t are taken as 1 such that the concentration of antibodies having higher affinity does not change abruptly after an antigenic cycle but rather increases/decreases slowly. This ensures that the antibody is sufficiently trained and tested before it is deemed as either correct or wrong. γ and η are taken as such for similar reasons and due to reasons described in Step (2) of the algorithm. We assume λ_t as 2 to ensure a minimum of three word matchings between antibodies for affinity calculations and ϕ_t is assumed to be 0 to take into account all the out of sequence words for negative affinity calculation. ξ is taken a lower value such that we do not ignore low concentration changes calculated by

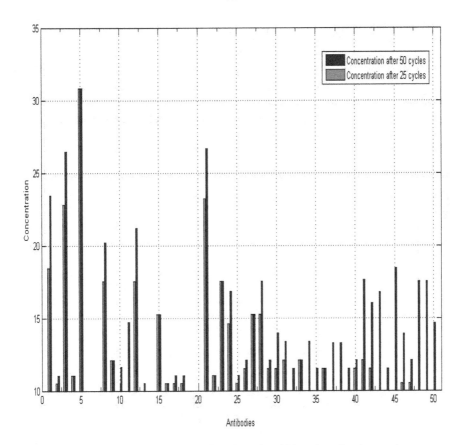

Fig. 4. Concentration of antibodies after 25 and 50 cycles of antigen action

equation (6). These values can be chosen accordingly as to determine how each factor will effect the network evolution.

Using these values in our system, we calculate the Affinity vector $\mathcal{AN}$, the Affinity matrix $\mathcal{AA}$ and the Negative Affinity matrix $\mathcal{NA}$. Using equation (6) and (14) we calculate the concentration changes of the antibodies. It can be observed from Fig. 3 & 4 that some antibodies have undergone a high degree of change in concentration which implies that they have a high chance of being correct. On the other hand some antibodies have not changed much even after many training cycles. These antibodies whose concentration are low have a high chance of being wrong.

We set the Correct Concentration($C_{Correct}$) level sufficiently higher than the Initial Concentration such that any antibody in the system takes a certain minimum number of antigen cycles to reach that level. This ensures that the antibody is tested a sufficient number of times before it is assumed as a correct phrase construct. We observe in Fig.5 that after crossing the Correct concentration level the concentration of the antibody depicted doesn't change further. Concentrations of correct antibodies converges after the $C_{Correct}$ level.

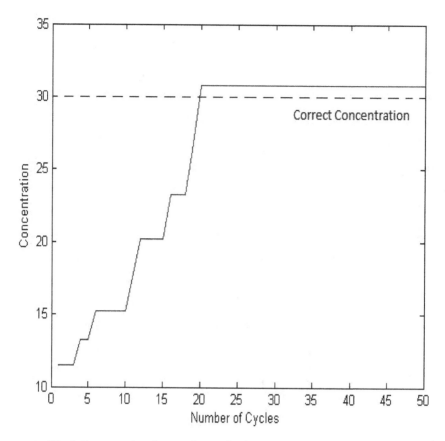

Fig. 5. Concentration change of an antibody after crossing $C_{Correct}$ converges

3.2   Network Growth via Link Creation

We modify the Order Matrix (given in equation 9) after each antigen action cycle and calculate the link weights between a pair of antibodies which gives the possibility of them occurring together in a sentence using equation (13). The higher the value in the order matrix the higher is the chance of the two antibodies following one another in a sentence composition. Hence the system learns possible phrases that can follow a given phrase and what is the probability of each such phrase to occur along with the given phrase with the help of the links formed in the network as shown in Fig. 6. The height of the points in the mesh gives the link weight between the corresponding antibodies.

In Fig. 7 the growth of the network among the 50 antibodies with the increasing number of antigen cycles is shown. The darker colors represent higher link weights between the antibodies. This implies that in case of a choice, an antibody will chose that other antibody with whom it has a darker link.

We observe that as the system evolves, more links are formed between the antibodies with more antigen actions. With more training cycles the system increases its repertoire of correct order sequences of phrases that occur in a sentence.

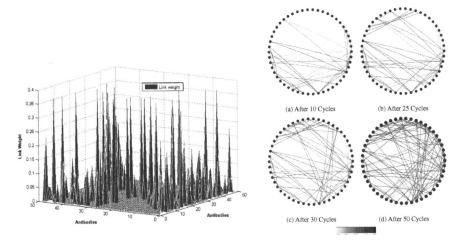

Fig. 6. This shows the possibility of occurrence of two antibodies in sequence as calculated in the Order Matrix after 50 antigen action cycles. The Z-axis shows the link weights.

Fig. 7. The Links among the network nodes(antibodies) after a certain number of antigen actions. The corresponding link weights are given in the legend.

Table 1. This table shows the factor of correctness ($\mathcal{DC}$) by testing the sentences after a regular interval of training cycles

	0 Iterations	10 Iterations	20 Iterations	40 Iterations	50 Iterations
T_1	-30.0000	-31.5240	60.9122	109.6453	112.2303
T_2	-60.0000	-71.1931	19.0502	42.6174	43.9099
T_3	-90.0000	-115.0688	-42.5740	-44.1726	-44.1726

3.3 Correctness Detection by the Network

In order to check if the network we have trained has the capability of differentiating between correct and wrong sentences we test some random sentences using the network built. We use the following sentences to determine their factor of correctness using equation (17) after every 10 iterations.

Sentence T_1 : Going on a bike alone.
Sentence T_2 : Going alone on a bike.
Sentence T_3 : Going bike a on alone.

We observe that initially when the system is in a nascent stage of evolution the correctness factor for both correct and wrong sentences are very random. This is because at such initial stages the antibodies are not trained enough. But as the system evolves more we observe that the factor increases consistently for correct sentences but for wrong sentences it becomes negative (Fig. 8). Thus after a few training iterations of the network we are able to distinguish between correct and incorrect sentence constructs. With more and more training the probability of detecting and differentiating correct and wrong sentences increases.

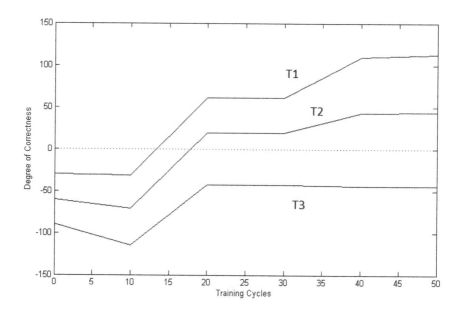

Fig. 8. The change of degree of correctness is consistent after the network evolves more. For T_1 and T_2 the slope increases consistently while for T_3 the slope starts decreasing after 40 cycles.

4 Conclusion and Future Work

We have observed that with the help of antigens (correct phrases) we can train a set of antibodies (phrases) such that the correct ones increase in their concentration and also the antibodies which occur together can form links between them. This system can be used for framing sentences which are correct and also the order of phrases in such sentences have a high probability of being correct. This level of accuracy increases with more training of the antibody set until an optimum level of accuracy is reached. Thus there is a considerable scope to learn a language by modelling a system on the immune idiotypic network which obviates the need for any grammatical rules. This approach can help to learn a whole sentence with the phrase positions and constructs present in it in just one learning cycle. This is considerable improvement over trigram approaches where learning is confined to a limited number of words or phrase constructs. Further work will include validating this algorithm's performance and time complexity more concretely by testing the algorithm against the present day language induction algorithms used to train various language corpus. Also we can explore if the evolved network can be used in sentence generation and language translation purposes.

References

1. Araujo, L., Santamaria, J.: Evolving natural language grammars without supervision. In: IEEE Congress on Evolutionary Computation 2010, pp. 1–8 (2010)

2. Jerne, N.: The generative grammar of the immune system. Nobel lecture (December 1984)
3. Farmer, J.D., Packard, N.H., Perelson, A.S.: The immune system, adaptation, and machine learning. Physica 22, 187 (1986)
4. Jerne, N.: Towards a network theory of the immune system. Ann. Immunol (Inst. Pasteur) 125, 373 (1974)
5. Jerne, N.: The immune system. The Scientific American 229, 52–60 (1973)
6. de Castro, L.N., Timmis, J.: Artificial Immune Systems: A New Computational Intelligence Approach, vol. XVIII, p. 357. Springer, Heidelberg (2002)
7. Bonna, C.A., Kohler, H.: Immune Networks. Annals of the New York Academy of Sciences (1983)
8. Varela, F.J., Coutinho, A.: Second generation immune networks. Immunology Today 12(5), 159–166 (1991)
9. Plett, E., Das, S.: A new algorithm based on negative selection and idiotypic networks for generating parsimonious detector sets for industrial fault detection applications. In: Andrews, P.S., Timmis, J., Owens, N.D.L., Aickelin, U., Hart, E., Hone, A., Tyrrell, A.M. (eds.) ICARIS 2009. LNCS, vol. 5666, pp. 288–300. Springer, Heidelberg (2009)
10. de Castro, L.N., Zuben, F.J.V.: Ainet: An artificial immune network for data analysis. Springer, London (2002)
11. Whitbrook, A.M., Aickelin, U., Garibaldi, J.M.: Idiotypic immune networks in mobile robot control. IEEE Transactions on Systems, Man and Cybernetics-Part B: Cybernetics 37(6), 1581–1598 (2007)
12. Hajela, P., Yoo, J.S.: Immune Network Modelling in Design Optimization. In: Corne, D., Dorigo, M., Glover, F. (eds.) New Ideas in Optimization, McGraw Hill, London (1999)
13. Hart, E., Ross, P.: The Evolution and Analysis of a Potential Antibody Library for Use in Job-Shop Scheduling. In: Corne, D., Dorigo, M., Glover, F. (eds.) New Ideas in Optimization. McGraw Hill, London (1999)

Evolving Unipolar Memristor Spiking Neural Networks

David Howard[1], Larry Bull[2], and Ben de Lacy Costello[2]

[1] QCAT, 1 Technology Court, Pullenvale Brisbane QLD 4069 Australia
david.howard@csiro.au
[2] University of the West of England, Frenchay Campus,
Coldharbour Lane, Bristol BS16 1QY UK

Abstract. Neuromorphic computing — brainlike computing in hardware — typically requires myriad CMOS spiking neurons interconnected by a dense mesh of nanoscale plastic synapses. Memristors are frequently cited as strong synapse candidates due to their statefulness and potential for low-power implementations. To date, plentiful research has focused on the bipolar memristor synapse, which is capable of incremental weight alterations and can provide adaptive self-organisation under a Hebbian learning scheme. In this paper we consider the Unipolar memristor synapse — a device capable of switching between only two states (conductive and resistive) through application of a suitable input voltage — and discuss its suitability for neuromorphic systems. A self-adaptive evolutionary process is used to autonomously find highly fit network configurations. Experimentation on a dynamic-reward scenario shows that unipolar memristor networks evolve task-solving controllers faster than both generic bipolar memristor networks and networks containing non-plastic connections whilst performing comparably.

Keywords: memristors, Hebbian learning, plasticity, evolution, genetic algorithm, tmaze.

1 Introduction

Neuromorphic computing [14] is concerned with developing brainlike information processing, and requires the creation of hardware neural networks of appropriate scale together with associated learning rules. Typically, densely-packed CMOS spiking neurons [17] communicate with each other via voltage pulses sent along nanoscale synapses. The memristor [4] (memory-resistor) is a fundamental circuit element (alongside the resistor, capacitor, and inductor) that can change between various conductance states in an analog manner through application of a suitable input voltage. Memristors display statefulness (conductance changes are chemical in nature, so persist indefinitely and require no power to store) and memory (a memristor's instantaneous conductance value depends on the history of voltage activity across it). Statefulness alleviates typical nanoscale concerns regarding heat and power consumption, and context-sensitive memory allows for

S.K. Chalup et al. (Eds.): ACALCI 2015, LNAI 8955, pp. 258–272, 2015.

synapse-like information processing. Combined, these features make memristors strong neuromorphic synapse candidates.

An adaptive self-organising mechanism is required to bestow learning abilities to the network. Hebbian learning rules [9] provide a biologically-realistic way to alter synaptic conductance values in a context-sensitive manner, depending on the activities of the neurons they connect to. Conveniently, the adaptive conductance found in memristors closely replicates the biological plasticity observed by Hebb, and as such the two are often paired [1,13,20] to allow for adaptive learning by permitting each synapse a gradual, analog traversal over a continuous range of conductance values.

Although much current research is devoted to the use of this type of device (and this type of plasticity), there is in fact a distinction to be made between two types of memristor — the one capable of analog, Hebbian plasticity, which is frequently called simply the "memristor", but which may more correctly be called the "bipolar memristor", and the less-discussed "unipolar memristor" [26], which shares the statefulness and memory but switches between only two conductance states. In this paper we simulate and analyse these memristor networks, and ascertain the suitability of the unipolar memristor when used as a plastic synapse in spiking neural networks.

We employ a Genetic Algorithm (GA) [11] to automatically discover high-performance spiking network topologies where each synapse is a unipolar memristor. These networks are compared to identically-created benchmark networks consisting of (i) generic bipolar memristor synapses, and (ii) constant (nonplastic) synapses on a simulated robotics dynamic-reward scenario. Results show that by foregoing the biological plausibility of bipolar plasticity, networks comprised of homogenously-parameterised unipolar memristors can adapt to changing conditions more expediently than either of the benchmark networks. Original contributions include the introduction of such unipolar memristor networks, comparisons of the three synapse types on a dynamic reward scenario, and an in-depth analysis of the role of plasticity in the unipolar networks.

2   Memristive Spiking Networks

Spiking Neural Networks (SNNs) model neural activity in the brain to varying degrees of precision. Two well-known phenomenological implementations are the Leaky Integrate and Fire (LIF) model and the Spike Response Model (SRM) [8], with the most well-known mechanistic alternative being the Hodgkin-Huxley model [10]. A SNN comprises a number of neurons connected by numerous unidirectional synapses. Each neuron has a state, which is a measure of internal excitation, and emits a voltage spike to all forward-connected neurons if sufficiently excited. This state is a form of memory which allows the network to solve temporal problems.

The memristor was first theoretically characterized by [4], and first manufactured from titanium dioxide by HP labs [23]. This fabrication has led to numerous other groups creating memristors from metal oxides and a variety of materials: conductive polymers [6], metal silicides, and crystalline oxides [5].

Both unipolar and bipolar memristors can internally form conductive pathways called *filaments*, which may arise due to material defects or conditions during synthesis [26]. Unipolar memristors form complete filaments (Fig. 1(a)), resulting in drastic changes in resistance. Mechanistically, the unipolar memristor acts as a device whose resistance can change between two values — the Low-Resistance State (LRS) (Fig. 1(a)) and the High-Resistance State (HRS) (Fig. 1(b)) — through application of a voltage over some threshold. The memristor enters the LRS when complete filaments are formed. Driving over a threshold voltage breaks these filaments and transfers the device to the HRS. A further voltage input of suitable magnitude reforms these filaments and reinstates the device to the LRS. Unipolar devices are ambivalent to voltage polarity.

Bipolar memristors do not form complete filaments (Fig. 1(b)), meaning they must instead use comparatively weaker mechanisms such as ionic transport to alter their resistance to any value between the minimum and maximum resistance of the device in a continuous, analog manner. The "classic" HP bipolar memristor can be thought of as comprising two regions, one of titanium dioxide, and the other of more conductive oxygen-depleted titanium dioxide, which are represented respectively by variable resistors R_{off} and R_{on}. Voltage across the device causes the oxygen vacancies to drift, altering the position of the boundary and changing the conductance depending on the polarity of the applied voltage (see Fig 1(c)). Note that the unipolar memristor also features this ionic transport; complete filament formation is simply a stronger form of resistance change so ionic effects are largely mitigated.

Implementing memristive plasticity involves a bidirectional voltage spike (a discrete or continuous waveform), which is emitted by a sufficiently excited CMOS neuron and can be used to track the coincidences of spikes across a synapse. Two voltage spikes (one from each neuron that the synapse connects) arriving at the synapse in a short time window causes a Hebbian event to take place. A single spike pair causes a bipolar memristor to change its conductance by a small amount under a STDP [2] learning scheme, e.g. so that the order of spiking affects the polarity of the voltage experienced by the device and thus the direction of synaptic weight change. Unipolar memristors are less sensitive to voltage than bipolar memristors, and as such require multiple events to flip between the resistance states. As unipolar memristors operate under a single voltage polarity, there is no notion of spike order affecting weight change. Note that this removes an element of biological realism from unipolar plasticity.

Numerous groups have previously used bipolar memristors as plastic synapses [1,13,20], seeking to exploit the similarities between analog resistance alteration and Hebbian learning. To our knowledge, no previous work has considered the use of unipolar memristor synapses to fulfil the same role. Examples of unipolar memristors are confined to binary operation for traditional logic [24], although neural implementations exist for non-memristor binary switching devices [27].

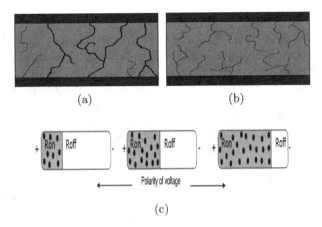

Fig. 1. Showing the differences in resistance change with (a, b) unipolar and (c) bipolar memristors. Unipolar memristors form complete filaments, allowing electrons to travel largely unimpeded through the substrate and resulting in a very low resistance when formed (a), but a very high resistance when broken (b). The bipolar memristor (which could also be represented in (b)) does not form these filaments and so relies instead on ionic conductivity (c). The device is abstractly modelled as two variable resistors R_{off} and R_{on}; the boundary between the resistors represents the movement of oxygen vacancies from electrode to electrode and changes as a function of applied voltage.

In keeping with our long-term goal of neuromorphic computing, we exploit a genetic algorithm to automatically explore the space of network topologies. Related work on neuro-evolution includes [7], who survey various methods for evolving both weights and architectures. [16] describe the evolution of networks for robotics tasks. Combined with plasticity, neuro-evolutionary controllers have shown increased performance compared to similarly-evolved nonplastic-synapse networks [21, 25].

We focus on unipolar memristors because they are easier to implement in reality than bipolar memristors — using binary rather than analog resistance states means that the devices are less reliant on precise nanoscale fabrication, which can be compromised by device variations that are currently an intrinsic part of the nanoscale manufacturing process. Using a single voltage polarity reduces the difficulty of manufacturing and operating unipolar networks. During operation, unipolar memristors require multiple Hebbian events to force a single state change; it follows that they also undergo fewer total state changes and therefore may be more long-lasting. A single resistance change could potentially perturb the network state more than is possible in bipolar networks, potentially leading to simpler solutions (reduced attractor space), and more tractable analysis of candidate networks. The main motivation for this work is to see if such networks can be automatically evolved — potentially more expediently — without loss of solution quality when compared to traditional bipolar networks.

3   Task

Experiments are conducted on a simulated robotics platform [15]. At the start of each experiment, 100 spiking networks are randomly generated. The synapse type used varies per experiment, being either unipolar, bipolar, or constant. Each network is then evaluated on the task over a maximum of 8000 robot steps. Each robot step involves the the controller processing its sensory input for 21 processing steps, after which the spike trains generated at the output nodes are used to pick an action. The robot executes the action, and recieves the next sensory input. After a trial (which ends either with success or timeout), each controller is assigned a fitness. A genetic algorithm then optimises the population of networks for 500 generations.

To properly compare the temporal information processing capabilities of the plastic memristor synapses, a simulated T-maze [3, 22] scenario is used. The T-maze is an enclosed arena with coordinates ranging from [-1,1] in both x and y directions, with walls placed to represent a "T" (Fig. 2). A differential-drive robot is initialised facing North in a zone at the bottom of the "T". Reward zones R1 and R2 are situated at the end of the left and right arms respectively. A light source, modelled on a 15 Watt bulb, is placed at the top-centre of the arena ($x = 0.5$, $y = 1$) and was used to indirectly feed position information to the network, enabling it to produce any available action from anywhere in the arena.

Fig. 2. The T-maze. The robot (white circle) begins in the checkered box and must travel to reward zones R1 or R2. The light source is shown (top-centre).

During a trial, the controller is initially rewarded for navigating to R1. Once pathfinding to R1 is attained, the reward zone is switched to R2 and the robot reinitialised in the start zone. To give the robot "memory" of the first part of the trial, the membrane potentials and synaptic weights of the controlling network are not reset during this process. A network that located R2 following location of R1 is said to have sucessfully completed the trial. The fitness function, f, was simply the total number of robot steps required to solve the trial.

4   Controllers

Leaky Integrate and Fire [8] networks are used as spiking controllers — three layers of neurons are connected by numerous weighted connections (weights constrained [0-1]), which can be recurrent within the hidden layer only. Neurons are either excitatory (transmit voltages $V \geq 0$) or inhibitory ($V<0$). On network creation, the hidden layer is populated with 9 hidden layer neurons, whose types are intitially excitatory with P=0.5, otherwise they are inhibitory. Each connection has a weight w. Each possible connection site is initially likely to have a connection with P=0.5.

During activation, stimulation by incoming voltage alters a neuron's internal state y, $y > 0$, which by default decreases over time. Surpassing a threshold y_θ causes a spike to be transmitted to all postsynaptic neurons. The amount of voltage sent is equal to the weight of the connection, multiplied by -1 if sent from an inhibitory neuron. The state of a neuron at processing step $t + 1$ is given in equation 1; equation 2 shows the reset formula. $y(t)$ is the neuron state at processing step t (calculated following equation 1), I is the input voltage, a is an excitation constant and b is the leak constant. Immediately after spiking, the neuron resets its state to c following equation 2. A spike sent between two hidden layer neurons is received n ($n > 0$) processing steps after it is sent, where n is the number of neurons spatially between the sending neuron and receiving neuron in the layer. Parameters are $a = 0.3$, $b = 0.05$, $c = 0.0$, $y_\theta = 0.6$

$$y(t + 1) = y(t) + (I + a - by(t)) \tag{1}$$

$$\text{If } (y(t) > y_\theta) \quad y(t) = c \tag{2}$$

Our bidirectional voltage spikes are discrete-time stepwise waveforms, matching the discrete-time operation of the SNNs. Each neuron in the network is augmented with a "last spike time" variable LS, which represents voltage buildup at the synapse and is initially 0. When a neuron spikes, this value is set to an experimentally-determined positive number, in this case 3. At the end of each of the 21 procesing steps that make up a single robot step, each memristor synapse is analysed by summating the LS values of its presynaptic and postsynaptic neurons — any value greater than a threshold $\theta_{LS}=4$ is said to have caused a Hebbian event at the synapse. Each LS value is then decreased by 1 to a minimum of 0, creating a discrete stepwise waveform through time, see Fig. 4(a).

4.1   Controller Integration

Each controller commands a differential-drive robot with 3 active light sensors and 3 active distance sensors shown at positions 0, 2, and 5 in Fig. 3(b). Random-uniform sensory noise in included – ±2% for IR sensors and ±10% for light sensors. To prevent the robot from becoming stuck in the environment, two bump sensors are used (see Fig. 3(b) for placement) — activating either causes the robot to immediately reverse 10cm (an effective penalty of 10 robot steps spent reversing).

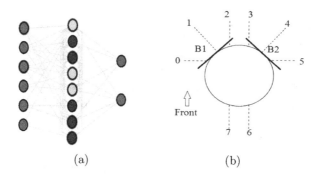

Fig. 3. (a) A typical SNN architecture. The top 3 input neurons receive light sensor activations, the bottom 3 receive IR sensor activiations, and spike trains generated at the two output neurons are used for action calculation. In the hidden layer, green neurons denote excitatory neurons and blue neurons signify inhibitory neurons. (b) Robot sensory arrangement. Three light sensors and 3 IR sensors share positions 0, 2, and 5 and form the network input. The other numbers show unused sensor positions. Two bump sensors, B1 and B2, are shown attached at 45 degree angles to the front-left and front-right of the robot.

For each robot step (64ms in simulation time), the robot samples the six sensors: the six-dimensional input vector is then scaled so that the entire sensor range falls within [0,1], and is used as I in equation(1). The network is then run for 21 processing steps, and the spike trains at the output neurons are discretised as *high* or *low* activated to generate an action (*high* activation if more than half of the 21 processing steps generated a spike at the neuron, *low* otherwise). Three discrete actions are used to encourage more distinct changes in network activity and more differentiated attractor spaces, allowing a detailed analysis of such disparities to be performed. Actions are *forward*, (maximum movement on both wheels, *high* activation of both output neurons) and continuous turns to both the *left* (*high* activation on the first output neuron, *low* on the second) and *right* (*low* activation on the first output neuron, *high* on the second) — caused by halving the left/right motor outputs respectively.

4.2   Synapse Types

In this section we describe our implementation of the three synapse types used in the experiment. Both memristor synapses rely on the concept of a "Hebbian event". The **unipolar memristor's** main parameters are S_n, which represents the sensitivity of the device to voltage buildup (in the form of repeated Hebbian events), and S_c, which tracks the number of consecutive Hebbian events the synapse has experienced. All synapses are initially in the Low Resistance State ($w = 0.9$). This is an arbitrary selection, performance is unaffected if the networks begin in the HRS. At each processing step every synapse is checked, incrementing S_c if a Hebbian event occurs at the synapse and decrementing S_c if no Hebbian event occurs at that processing step. If $S_c=S_n$ (Fig. 4(a)), the unipolar memristor switches to the HRS ($w = 0.1$) if it was previously in the LRS, and the LRS if it was previously in the HRS. S_c is reset to 0. The device can switch between these states multiple times per trial. Due to the requirement of multiple consecutive Hebbian events per switch, the actual frequency of synapse alteration is lower than that seen in the bipolar networks. Note that switching between two conductance states, one highly resistive, one highly conductive, likens the unipolar plasticity mechanism to network-wide feature selection, rather than online weight adaptation as with traditional plasticity schemes.

Initial experimentation (excluded for the sake of brevity) performed a sensitivity analysis on the S_n parameter — no statistically significant differences were observed between values of 2, 4, and 6. In this paper we select $S_n=4$ as a compromise between switching speed and potential device longetivity in hardware implementations.

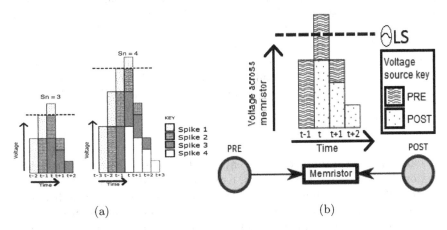

(a)   (b)

Fig. 4. Showing a spike coincidence event for both memristor types. A presynaptic voltage spike is received at time t-1, with a postsynaptic voltage spike at time t (a "Hebbian event"). For the unipolar memristor (a) multiple such events (l.h.s $S_n = 3$, r.h.s $S_n = 4$) serve to push the voltage past a threshold, causing a switch. Dotted lines show the derived voltage threshold. Voltage spike values are decremented by one per subsequent processing step. (b) A single event allows the voltage to surpass θ_{LS}, increasing the conductivity of the bipolar memristor.

We use a generalised model of the **bipolar memristor** — as previously noted, memristor materials and techniques are highly varied, and similar variance is seen in the plastic behaviour of the synapses. We elect to use a linear model as this provides the most bias-free comparison, whilst still providing incremental resistance changes. This model is competitive with real-world memristor models [12]. Bipolar memristor connection weights are initially 0.5. Bipolar memristors have an effective S_n of 1 (Fig. 4(a)), so every Hebbian event causes a change in synaptic weight by $1/L$, (where $L=1000$ is the number of processing steps to take the memristor from fully resistive to fully conductive). Weight increases if the postsynaptic neuron has the highest LS value, and decreases if the presynaptic LS is higher, in other words the bipolar memristor is sensitive to the polarity of applied voltage.

The **constant** synapse is non-plastic (essentially a resistor), and selected to show a baseline comparative network. The conductance of the connection is initialised random-uniformly in the range $[0,1]$ and may be altered during application of the GA, but is constant during a trial.

5   Genetic Algorithm

In our steady-state GA, two child networks are created per generation. A parent is selected via roulette wheel on the 100 population networks, and its genome copied to the child and probabilistically mutated. Crossover is omitted — sufficient network space exploration is obtained via a combination of weight and topology mutations; a view that is reinforced in the literature [19]. The networks are then trialled on the test problem and assigned a fitness before being added to the population. Finally, the two worst-fitness networks are deleted from the population. Each network has its own self-adaptive mutation rates, which are initially seeded uniform-randomly in the range $[0,0.5]$ and mutated as with an Evolution Strategy [18] as they are passed from parent to child following equation 3.

$$\mu \rightarrow \mu \, exp^{N(0,1)} \tag{3}$$

This approach is adopted as it is envisaged that efficient search of weights and neurons will require different rates, e.g., adding a neuron is likely to impact a network more than changing a connection weight, so less neuron addition events than connection weight change events are likely to be desirable. Self-adaptation is particularly relevant for the application area of neuromorphic computing — brainlike systems must be able to autonomously adapt to a changing environment and adjust their learning rates accordingly.

The genome of each network comprises a variable-length vector of connections and a variable-length vector of neurons, plus a number of mutation rates. Different parameters govern the mutation rates of connection weights (μ), connection addition/removal (τ), and neuron addition/removal (ω). For each comparison to one of these rates a uniform-random number is generated; if it is lower than the rate, the variable is said to be *satisfied* at that allelle. During GA application, for each constant connection, satisfaction of μ alters the weight by ±0-0.1. Memristive synapses cannot be mutated from their initial weights of 0.9 for unipolar and 0.5 for bipolar, forcing those networks to use plasticity to perform well. Each possible connection site in the network is traversed and, on satisfaction of τ, either a new connection is added if the site is vacant, or the pre-existing connection at that site is removed. ω is checked once, and equiprobably adds or removes a neuron from the hidden layer (inserted at a random position) if satisfied. New neurons are randomly assigned a type, and each connection site on a new neuron has a 50% chance of having a connection. New constant connections are randomly weighted between 0 and 1.

6 Experimentation

We test the three synapse types for 30 experimental repeats, using the averages to create the statistical analysis given below. Two-tailed T-tests are used to asses statistical significance, with significance at P<0.05. As well as fitness, we also track the first generation in which each population produces a controller that properly solves the T-Maze. Use of the dynamic T-maze task allows us to answer important questions regarding the power of the unipolar plasticity mechanism — does the plasticity permit sufficient adaptivity to solve the problem? Does the discontinuous switching behaviour allow the evolutionary process to set up useful attractors more expediently? What are the benefits and drawbacks in terms of controller performance and network composition?

6.1 Results

Table 1 shows that the unipolar memristor networks are able to find solutions to the test problems in significantly fewer generations than both the bipolar memristor and constant connection networks (P<0.05). The unipolar memristors can only be in two states, and as such the possible network attractor space is significantly more constrained during a trial than that of the bipolar network. As the GA is responsible for setting up useful network activity — attractors that produce pathfinding behaviour — the relationship between topology and in-trial behaviour can be more expediently explored. The plasticity provided by the unipolar network is still useful for behaviour generation, hence the significant speedup over constant connection networks.

Average best fitness and average mean fitness are shown in Figs. 5(a) and (b) respectively. Although bipolar synapses hold a slight fitness advantage, best fitness and average fitness values are comparable between the synapse types (P>0.05). Fig. 5(b) shows that the unipolar population as a whole initially optimises faster than the other network types, but loses its advantage around generation 150 before finishing slightly behind them. As bipolar memristors are capable of more gradual weight (and hence behaviour) changes, the pathfinding function is better approximated compared to the other synapse types, although unipolar memristors generate fitter behaviour than constant-connection networks Fig. 5(a).

In terms of topology (the last two columns of Table 1), the numbers of connected hidden layer nodes (Fig. 5(c)) and connections (Fig. 5(d)) do not vary significantly between the three network types.

Justification for use of self-adaptive parameters was provided as context-sensitivity was shown — some parameters varied significantly between network types, other values varied significantly between parameters for the same network type. In particular, ψ (rate of node addition/removal events) was statistically higher in unipolar networks (avg. 0.102) than either bipolar (avg. 0.087) or constant-connection (avg. 0.074) networks (P<0.05). τ (rate of connection addition/removal) has statistically higher in unipolar networks (avg. 0.049) than in constant-connection networks (avg. 0.024). This indicates that unipolar networks require higher numbers of topology alteration events than the other network types, although the exact reason for this is still an open question.

Table 1. Averages and standard deviations for controller parameters for the three synapse types

	Best fit	Avg fit	Gens. to solve	Nodes	% Connectivity
Unipolar	1602.5 (422)	3115.0 (631)	12.47 (10.7)	17.01 (0.62)	52.98 (3.7)
Bipolar	1368.3 (806)	2679.6 (966)	47.93 (70.8)	17.07 (0.56)	51.7 (5.98)
Constant	1671.6 (656)	2837.1 (1284)	27.73 (38.9)	16.9 (0.69)	52.38 (4.32)

Fig. 6(a) shows the average synaptic weight in the best network of each memristor type during the first 900 robot steps of activation. It is immediately obvious that the networks internally function differently — average weight is much smoother in the bipolar case (avg. weight 0.528), whereas the unipolar synapses are much more distcontinuous (avg. weight 0.629). In contrast, the total number of synaptic weight changes over the same time period (67968 total for unipolar, 75478 total for bipolar) display a smoother profile in the unipolar case. Fewer total switches in the unipolar case indicates that physical unipolar networks will be more long-lasting as the chemical mechanism is less likely to wear down or break (given that a unipolar switch is no more damaging to the device than a bipolar switch).

It was initially thought that binary nature of unipolar resistance switching would lead to "twitchy" controller behaviour. Some of the less fit/early generation unipolar networks showed slight oscillations in path generation, but later, fitter networks were shown to avoid this problem by synchronising switching between two synapses to the same neuron, e.g. where one is in the LRS and the other is in the HRS simulataneously, the receiving neuron receives a constant input of 0.1 + 0.9 /2 = 0.5. By switching at the same time, this constant input can be preserved, and used to stabilise the network making behaviour generation easier.

6.2   Discussion

The focus of this paper was the unipolar memristor synapse, which was evolved for a dynamic-reward robotics task. For both memristor synapse types, evolution was used to set up topologies that could cause useful Hebbian events/enable useful network attractors. Evolution was shown to find solutions statistically faster when the networks used unipolar memristors when compared to the other

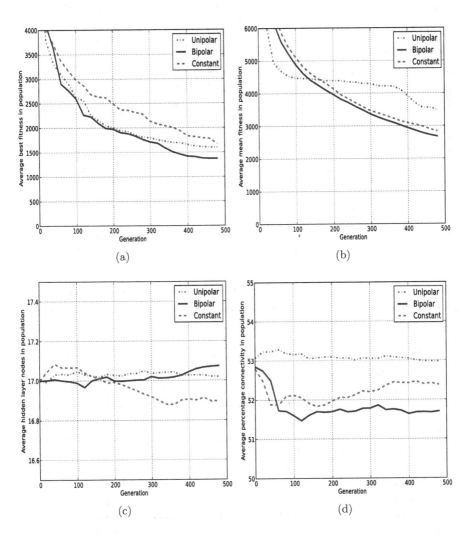

Fig. 5. Comparing mean (a) best fitness (b) avg. fitness (c) hidden layer nodes (d) percentage connectivity for unipolar, bipolar, and constant synapse networks

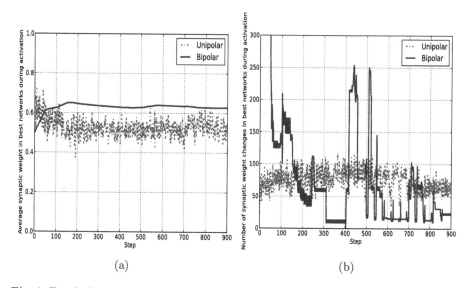

(a)   (b)

Fig. 6. For the best network of each memristor type, (a) average synapse weight during (b) average number of total synaptic weight changes, during network activation

synapse types. More expedient goal-finding behaviour can be attributed to the simpler unipolar attractor space compared to bipolar memristors. It is assumed that the ability to adapt behaviour online gives the unipolar memristor a similar advantage over constant synapses.

As this speedup in useful behaviour generation does not come with a cost in terms of degraded solution fitness, unipolar synapses are here highlighted as a promising alternative to current memristive STDP network implementations. The more coarse-grained attractors and restricted binary plasticity scheme do not overtly impede the unipolar network's ability to generate highly-fit pathfinding behaviour. This result raises interesting questions regarding the direction of neuromorphic engineering, in particular the issue of biological realism vs. computational efficiency. Do we aim for computing like a human brain, or would some hybrid analog/digital approach be more efficient?

The main motivation for testing networks of homogenous unipolar memristors relates to hardware implementations — a homogenous synapse would be easier to manufacture *en masse*. Using a single voltage polarity coupled with binary unipolar plasticity could lead to more robust circuits that can function reliably, and unlike bipolar networks would not rely on potentially complex analog STDP interactions. One lingering question relates to the timescale that unipolar memristor networks could operate on, which is related to the switching frequency — and hence filament creation/breaking speed. The actual relation between S_n and possible switching frequencies is the topic of future research.

References

1. Afifi, A., Ayatollahi, A., Raissi, F.: Stdp implementation using memristive nanodevice in cmos-nano neuromorphic networks. IEICE Electronics Express 6(3), 148–153 (2009)
2. Bi, G.Q., Poo, M.M.: Synaptic modifications in cultured hippocampal neurons: Dependence on spike timing, synaptic strength, and postsynaptic cell type. J. Neurosc. 77(1), 551–555 (1998)
3. Blynel, J., Floreano, D.: Exploring the T-maze: Evolving learning-like robot behaviors using cTRNNs. In: Raidl, G.R., et al. (eds.) EvoIASP 2003, EvoWorkshops 2003, EvoSTIM 2003, EvoROB/EvoRobot 2003, EvoCOP 2003, EvoBIO 2003, and EvoMUSART 2003. LNCS, vol. 2611, pp. 593–604. Springer, Heidelberg (2003)
4. Chua, L.: Memristor-the missing circuit element. IEEE Transactions on Circuit Theory 18(5), 507–519 (1971)
5. Doolittle, W., Calley, W., Henderson, W.: Complementary oxide memristor technology facilitating both inhibitory and excitatory synapses for potential neuromorphic computing applications. In: International Semiconductor Device Research Symposium, ISDRS 2009, pp. 1–2 (2009)
6. Erokhin, V., Fontana, M.P.: Electrochemically controlled polymeric device: a memristor (and more) found two years ago. ArXiv e-prints (Jul 2008)
7. Floreano, D., Dürr, P., Mattiussi, C.: Neuroevolution: from architectures to learning. Evolutionary Intelligence 1, 47–62 (2008)
8. Gerstner, W., Kistler, W.: Spiking Neuron Models - Single Neurons, Populations, Plasticity. Cambridge University Press (2002)
9. Hebb, D.O.: The organisation of behavior. Wiley, New York (1949)
10. Hodgkin, A.L., Huxley, A.F.: A quantitative description of membrane current and its application to conduction and excitation in nerve. The Journal of Physiology 117(4), 500 (1952)
11. Holland, J.H.: Adaptation in natural and artificial systems. The University of Michigan Press, Ann Arbor (1975)
12. Howard, G.D., Gale, E., Bull, L., de Lacy Costello, B., Adamatzky, A.: Evolution of plastic learning in spiking networks via memristive connections. IEEE Transactions on Evolutionary Computing (2012) (in press)
13. Linares-Barranco, B., Serrano-Gotarredona, T.: Memristance can explain spike-time- dependent-plasticity in neural synapses. Available from Nature Preceedings (2009), http://hdl.handle.net/10101/npre.2009.3010.1
14. Mead, C.: Neuromorphic electronic systems. Proceedings of the IEEE 78(10), 1629–1636 (1990)
15. Michel, O.: Webots: Professional mobile robot simulation. International Journal of Advanced Robotic Systems 1(1), 39–42 (2004)
16. Nolfi, S., Floriano, D.: Evolutionary Robotics. MIT Press, Cambridge (2000)
17. Rabaey, J.M.: Digital integrated circuits: a design perspective. Prentice-Hall, Inc., Upper Saddle River (1996)
18. Rechenberg, I.: Evolutionsstrategie: optimierung technischer systeme nach prinzipien der biologischen evolution. Frommann-Holzboog (1973)
19. Rocha, M., Cortez, P.C., Neves, J.: Evolutionary neural network learning. In: Pires, F.M., Abreu, S.P. (eds.) EPIA 2003. LNCS (LNAI), vol. 2902, pp. 24–28. Springer, Heidelberg (2003)
20. Snider, G.: Spike-timing-dependent learning in memristive nanodevices. In: IEEE International Symposium on Nanoscale Architectures, NANOARCH 2008, pp. 85–92 (June 2008)

21. Soltoggio, A.: Neural plasticity and minimal topologies for reward-based learning. In: Proceedings of the 2008 8th International Conference on Hybrid Intelligent Systems, pp. 637–642. IEEE Computer Society, Washington, DC (2008)
22. Soltoggio, A., Bullinaria, J.A., Mattiussi, C., Dürr, P., Floreano, D.: Evolutionary Advantages of Neuromodulated Plasticity in Dynamic, Reward- based Scenarios. In: Bullock, S., Noble, J., Watson, R., Bedau, M.A. (eds.) Proceedings of the 11th International Conference on Artificial Life (Alife XI), pp. 569–576. MIT Press, Cambridge (2008)
23. Strukov, D.B., Snider, G.S., Stewart, D.R., Williams, R.S.: The missing memristor found. Nature 453, 80–83 (2008)
24. Sun, X., Li, G., Ding, L., Yang, N., Zhang, W.: Unipolar memristors enable stateful logic operations via material implication. Applied Physics Letters 99(7), 72101–72101 (2011)
25. Urzelai, J., Floreano, D.: Evolution of adaptive synapses: Robots with fast adaptive behavior in new environments. Evol. Comput. 9, 495–524 (2001), http://dx.doi.org/10.1162/10636560152642887
26. Waser, R., Aono, M.: Nanoionics-based resistive switching memories. Nature Materials 6(11), 833–840 (2007)
27. Xia, G., Tang, Z., Li, Y., Wang, J.: A binary hopfield neural network with hysteresis for large crossbar packet-switches. Neurocomputing 67, 417–425 (2005)

A Genetic Algorithm Solver for Pest Management Control in Island Systems

Jana Brotankova[1], Marcus Randall[2], Andrew Lewis[3], Bob Pressey[1], and Amelia Wenger[1]

[1] ARC Centre of Excellence for Integrated Coral Reef Studies,
James Cook University, Townsville, Australia
`jana.brotankova@jcu.edu.au`
[2] Faculty of Business, Bond University, Gold Coast, Australia
[3] School of Information and Communication Technology, Griffith University,
Brisbane, Australia

Abstract. Island conservation management is a truly multidisciplinary problem that requires considerable knowledge of the characteristics of the ecosystem, species and their interactions. Nevertheless, this can be translated into an optimisation problem. Essentially, within a limited budget, a manager needs to select the conservation actions according to expected payoffs (in terms of protecting or restoring desired species) versus cost (the amount of resources/money) required for the actions. This paper presents the problem in terms of a knapsack formulation and develops optimisation techniques to solve it. From this, decision-support software is being developed, tailored to meet the needs of pest control on islands for conservation managers. The solver uses a Genetic Algorithm and incorporates a simplified model of the problem. The solver derives strategies that reduce the number of threats, allowing the preservation of desired species. However, the problem model needs further refinement to derive truly realistic options for conservation managers.

Keywords: conservation management, genetic algorithms, knapsack problem.

1 Introduction

Systematic conservation planning began to emerge as a discipline just over 30 years ago [11] and is now extensively applied and influential worldwide [12]. As well as guiding the design of new spatial management for conservation, systematic methods can be applied within established reserves to inform zoning [2] or, potentially, the allocation of actions to mitigate threats. Given the number of introduced species that act as threats to native species and ecosystems and limited budgets, prioritising of conservation actions in space and time is necessary to identify the most cost-effective programmes for the eradication of pests.

Existing conservation planning software systems have been used extensively for conservation-related research, but also for real-world applications that have led to gains in conservation. However, these tools are limited in various ways in

S.K. Chalup et al. (Eds.): ACALCI 2015, LNAI 8955, pp. 273–285, 2015.

addressing the full complexity of day-to-day management decisions. Marxan [15], C-Plan [13], and Zonation [7], are mainly targeted to selection of new reserve networks. RobOff [9], [10] does work with conservation actions including pest eradication, but is non-spatial.

Furthermore, most of the research on multiple-action planning (as opposed to planning generic "conservation" applications) has been at a spatial resolution too coarse to be useful for managers on the ground (e.g., [1] and [16]). For our purposes, we need data, and software capable of analysing those data, at a very fine resolution (e.g., typically 1–10 ha) and across hundreds of sites.

Given the limitations of capability of existing software systems and the challenges, in terms of acquisition and analysis of data for fine-resolution applications, a solver system, based around the Genetic Algorithms (GA) optimisation is created to address these limitations. GA was selected as it is a well-established technique that has a track-record of producing good solutions [3], and which is naturally formulated to work with 0-1 problems.

Additionally, the software behind the solver must have an intuitive and attractive visual and spatial interface to facilitate its use by conservation managers. The new software is being designed initially for use by managers of islands in north-western Western Australia (the Pilbara region) and the southern part of the Great Barrier Reef, both regions having biodiversity values of national and global significance.

The remainder of this paper is organised as follows. Section 2 explains the mathematical formulation of the problem, detailing the choice of objective function as well as how it becomes a knapsack polytope. Section 3 describes general the mechanics of a GA as well as setting forth the way in which it is applied to this problem. The computational experiments, results and analyses of these are given in Sections 4 and 5. Finally, along with the conclusions, the direction for developing both the problem definition and solver techniques is outlined in Section 6.

2   Formulation of the Problem

Conservation managers face the following problem when planning pest eradication measures for islands: they need to optimise the selection of actions on the islands in the most cost-effective way considering the evolution of the system in a given time scale. As such, in the first instance, a model needs to be developed that can describe the ecosystem, at least in simple terms, and the changes due to the actions taken.

Several input tables are required to describe the ecosystem. First are the abundances or the extent of features (native species and ecosystems) and threats on the islands. Features are the native animals and plants that need protecting. Threats are the invasive species (animals or weeds) that adversely affect the features. Capturing the interactions amongst the features and threats is a non-linear problem that includes thresholds and depends on the ratios of the predators and prey. In terms of testing the optimisation process, a simplified model was used that considers linear relations among threats and species: each individual of the threats reduces a constant number of each (impacted) feature per year.

Variables are defined as the actions on islands, e.g., shooting goats, trapping or poisoning cats, spraying weeds. One action on one island is one variable. Every action has a defined efficiency (percentage of the targeted threat knocked down), and cost (how much must the managers pay to perform this action on this island).

The ecosystem model gives two knapsack formulations referred as Scenario 1 and Scenario 2:

1. Minimise total cost of actions
   s.t. The number of features is greater than a defined threshold
2. Maximise the number of features
   s.t. The total cost is less than a budget amount

The knapsack problem belongs to a class of problems in combinatorial optimisation, dating to the late 20th century [6]. The task is to find the best combination of items with given parameters, meeting given requirements, to meet some specific objective (e.g. what to pack in a knapsack of given size to maximise the value of the load). The 0-1 formulation of the problem refers to a parameterisation that expresses whether an item is omitted, "0", or included, "1", in the solution.

The whole model must run over a certain time interval, typically 3–5 years, with a time step of one year. The funding in conservation usually works on a year-to-year budget scheme, so this paper will focus on the second knapsack formulation.

To capture the dynamics of the system, a model was developed that predicts abundances of features and threats on each island in each of the given time slices. Each time slice is connected to the previous and the following one via coefficients of birth and mortality. Two basic equations are needed for the model: the time evolution of Threats and of Features.

2.1 Threats

The threats breed on the islands and are killed by the selected actions. In the first simplified approach, we consider only one action for one threat. Thus, the population y_t of Threat t in time c on island i can be written as:

$$y_{c,i,t} = y_{c-1,i,t} + \beta_t \times y_{c-1,i,t} - y_{c-1,i,t} \times z_{c,i,a} \tag{1}$$

where the index $c-1$ depicts the previous year, β_t is the coefficient of breeding (growth rate) of the threat t, and $z_{c,i,a}$ is the action a on island i performed in time c. $z_{c,i,a} = 1$ or 0 if the action is or is not performed, respectively. The growth rate is defined as an increment of the threat population per year in an absence of any predation.

2.2 Features

A similar equation can be written for features, with the only difference being that they are killed by the threats:

$$x_{c,i,f} = x_{c-1,i,f} + \alpha_f \times x_{c-1,i,f} - \sum_{t=1}^{n_{i,f}} \sigma_{f,t} \times y_{c-1,i,t} \qquad (2)$$

Here $x_{c,i,f}$ is the population of feature f at time c on island i; α_f is the growth rate of feature f; $\sigma_{f,t}$ is the coefficient of interaction between feature f and threat t, i.e., how many features f are predated per year by threat t. The last term on the right is summed over $n_{i,f}$ which is the number of all the present threats that reduce feature f on island i. If the sum is greater than the actual abundance of this feature on the island, the whole population is set to 0.

2.3 Method

The variable z represents actions on the islands, as mentioned previously. The solver suggests a combination of a set of these z values for each year and each combination of actions on islands. This will be an input to the model, together with the abundances of threats and features, as well as the coefficients. The model takes into account abundances of threats in year 0 (before any actions are taken) and calculates abundances of threats in year 1. Then it calculates abundances of features in year 1, using the input abundances and information about the threats reducing the features. These two steps are repeated until the last year. The cost of each solution z is calculated from the combination of zeros and ones.

3   Genetic Algorithm Implementation

Genetic algorithms belong to a broader class of evolutionary algorithms. Their origins date back to the 1960s [5] and were inspired by the natural selection of species choosing fitter individuals and allowing them to breed and produce new solutions.

The standard operations of GAs are selection, mutation, and crossover [4]. Each individual (a chromosome) represents one solution to the problem. Chromosomes consist of a combination of genes taking the values of either 0 or 1. All the chromosomes have equal length. The genetic information propagates to the next generations either directly, or by crossover. The point is to find the best solution by improving the genetic information with respect to the desired criterion translated to a fitness function.

The mechanics of a standard GA implementation are as follows. At the beginning, a random set of individuals is generated as the initial population. Their quality is determined by the fitness function and in the case of the test problem, the number of features of concern over all the islands. The individuals are ranked and assigned mating probabilities. The best few individuals ("elite individuals") are transferred directly to the new generation. Crossover is performed on the rest of the individuals. That is, chromosomes are selected randomly using the roulette wheel selection mechanism to "mate". "Mating" means that the two parent chromosomes are split at a random point(s), and exchange parts of themselves with one another. After that, mutation is performed with a small probability. In this, some of the genes will randomly change value. Mutation is vital to avoid search stagnation, which can lead to locally optimum solutions.

The implementation details of the GA for this problem are described in Algorithm 1. One chromosome represents one combination of variables Y. The variables can take values of either 1 or 0 which represent the actions that were or were not performed on a particular island.

Algorithm 1. Genetic algorithm

Generate the initial population of random knapsack solutions
for 1 to the number of iterations **do**
  Assess feasibility: feasible individuals are placed in the mating pool
  Assess the quality of the chromosomes, based on the fitness function
  Transfer the elite individuals into the next generation
  repeat
    Roulette wheel selection: allocate probabilities of selection based on quality of each individual in the mating pool
    Crossover: fill the next generation by two offspring of two randomly selected parents from the mating pool
  until the new generation is filled
  Mutation: randomly change some of the genes with small probability (not for the last run)
  if the best individual in this generation is better than the best one recorded so far **then**
    Make it the best individual
  end if
end for
end
Output the best individual and its objective cost

For Scenario 1, the fitness function is the total cost of actions, subject to the constraint of the given desired final population levels. For Scenario 2, the fitness function is the number of features, subject to the constraint that the collective cost of the selected actions is below a particular budget amount. For each feature, the initial population is taken as 100%; they are summed at the end. Thus, if the population of a feature doubled in abundance during the total time of the model, its contribution was 200%, while if its population halved, its contribution was 50%.

The task for the solver is to select the best combination of actions on islands that still meets the objectives and constraints. For example, for scenario 2 the solver selects the combination with the best fitness function (the maximum of protected features) out of the solutions under the budget level.

Until now, the budget was the only constraint: only individuals with costs smaller or equal to the budget passed into the mating pool. For complex cases, it may be useful to introduce more constraints. For example, apart from the budget, there may be need to focus on a particular island or species. The problem is then while keeping within the budget, achieve at least 150% species a increase, and remove all weeds b from island c. Obviously, this may lead to the situation in which all the constraints cannot be met. Also, the managers may formulate the objectives in a more tentative way: certain things would be good to do, but if it is too hard, they are not performed. To cover this complexity, *hard* and *soft* constraints can be introduced. If a chromosome does not meet a hard constraint (e.g., because of the size of the budget), it will be excluded from breeding. If it does not satisfy the soft constraints, it will be excluded with a certain probability (e.g., 80% if we really want to meet it or 30% if we do not). Refining the handling of these constraints will be examined in more detail in future work.

4   Computational Experiments

The algorithm has been tested on a laptop with an Intel® Core™ i7-4600U CPU @ 2.10 GHz 2.70 GHz processor, with 16 GB RAM and 64-bit operating system under Windows 7. Matlab is used to implement the solver. The trial dataset included only 13 islands, 32 features, and 19 threats, as a simple subset intended to demonstrate the feasibility of the proposed approach. In future work investigations will be extended to use the full set of islands (numbering one hundred and twenty for the Great Barrier Reef, or even more in the Pilbara).

An example of the performance of the solver is given in Figure 1. The top panel shows the convergence of the solution: the average and the best value of the fitness function. The bottom panel shows the percentage of feasible solutions.

Another information about the solver performance needs to be derived from the average and standard deviation. In future work, the solver will be run multiple times by varying the random seed.

An important part of the process is to interpret and visualise the output. A key aspect of visualisation will be a spatial interface in a geographic information system, showing which actions are allocated to which islands, with capability for querying the spatial output by pulling up tables and graphics. The spatial interface is still in development, but some of the background graphics are shown here.

The results need to be shown in the context of the abundance of the features. For this, the model needs to be run again with the final combination of the actions. An example of the temporal trends in abundances of features and threats is shown in Figure 2. The top panels show the trends in threats, the bottom panels trends in features. The left panels are population levels of each single threat/feature on a single island, while the right panels are the sums of each threat/feature across all islands. The reductions in the threats (see in the top left panel) indicate that an action was performed. The indicative budget was set at $200,000.

The solver efficiency needs to be tested. One of the tests is shown in Figure 3. The dashed curve with stars shows the percentage of the budget used, e.g., our budget (on the x-axis) is $250,000, but our solver found a solution of $225,000, so the dashed line shows 90%. The fluctuations in the dashed line can indicate two things: i) that a local minimum was found which may be a bit far from the global one (we do not know where the global maximum is but we assume that it corresponds to 100% of protected features), or ii) there is no action that would be "cheap enough" to be taken within the budget, while being efficient enough to make a difference. To understand this better, the vertical dashed black line shows the maximal cost of the actions, where every possible action is taken on every island. Naturally, after crossing the 100% limit, the dashed line decreases as the maximal cost becomes lower than the budget.

The full line with circles in Figure 3 indicates the cost-effectiveness of the whole conservation process, which is interesting information, highly relevant to the conservational managers. It shows a typical curve in conservation science: the effect of conservation actions rises fast at the beginning, but there are long-established diminishing marginal returns [14]. In this case, the fast rise at the

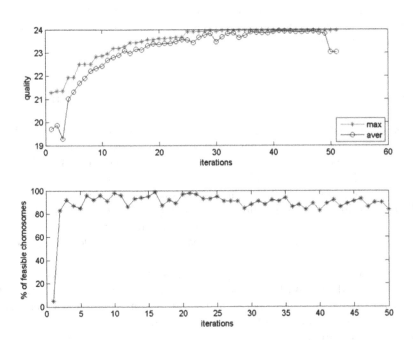

Fig. 1. Example of the convergence of the GA solver: the line with stars shows the quality of the best chromosome, while the one with circles shows the average (top), and the percentage of feasible solutions (bottom).

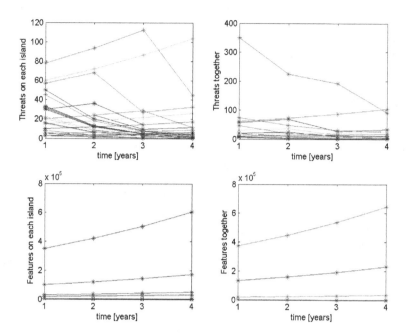

Fig. 2. Temporal trends in abundances of threats and features. Top panels: threats; bottom panels: features. Left panels: each line represents one threat/feature on one island; right panels: one line represents the sum of one threat/feature across all the islands.

beginning is extreme, which is caused by the simplifying assumptions in the model.

A better understanding of the model can be obtained by comparison of the "no actions anywhere" and "all actions everywhere" cases (in other words, the chromosome consists of zeroes only or ones only, respectively). This is given in Figure 4. The top panels again show threats, while the bottom ones show features. The left panels show the time evolutions when nothing was done, the middle is the solution from the solver, and the right when everything was done. The bottom panels are zoomed in. Abundant features (out of the scale; see in Figure 2) practically do not see the impact of threats, while low populated features respond to the actions.

The left two panels show the temporal trends in threats and features when no actions were done anywhere. The right two panels, on the contrary, show when all possible actions were performed on all islands. These data were used for establishing the boundaries (minimum and maximum of possible impact of the actions) in Figure 3.

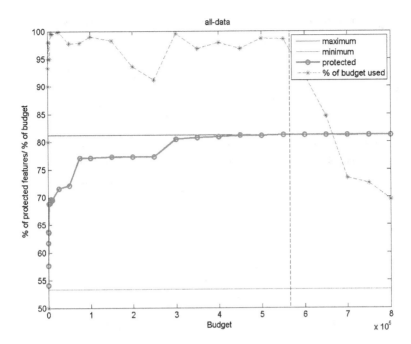

Fig. 3. Efficiency test of the model. The full line (circles) indicates the percentage of protected features achieved, for different budget expenditure. The populations achieved for maximum and minimum impact of actions are depicted by the horizontal full lines. The dashed line (stars) shows the percentage of the budget that was used. The dashed black line shows the maximal cost: when all actions are performed on all islands.

The bottom right panels in each group show how great a difference we can actually make. In this particular case, the initially most populous features show virtually no impact, so the contribution of the actions looks minor. However, the populations of a large number of features with smaller initial populations (that could be considered "more at risk") have survived when actions were taken, instead of being completely obliterated when no action was taken.

5   Discussion

The first model of the conservation problem includes several important simplifications. One reason is that the aim of this paper is to test and implement the solver rather than making a highly realistic model. Furthermore, the precise model requires very specific data which are being currently collected as part of a larger research project[1]. The process of elicitation is very complicated, time-consuming and ongoing, and needs to be considered in the model development.

---

[1] See the Acknowledgements for details of the project.

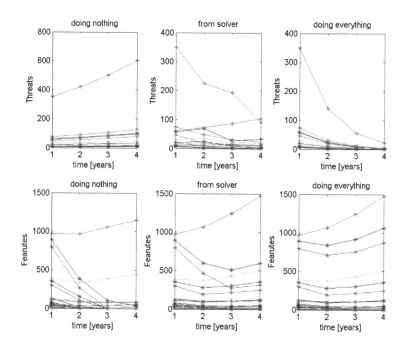

Fig. 4. Temporal trends in abundances of threats and features. Top panels: threats; bottom panels: features (zoomed in). Left panels: nothing was done; middle: solution from solver; right: everything was done.

The advantage of this simplified model is its straight-forwardness, so it is not difficult as a test of the solver. There are some simplifications of the present work that will be overcome by the subsequent development of the model:

- The relation among threats and features is not as simple as a constant. We obviously cannot say, for example, "one cat eats three curlews a day". Predation depends on the abundance of the threat and also of the prey. We also need to distinguish the case when a threat is established on an island, and is in a stable state. This is the case where there have been no actions performed in the past couple of years. In that case, we can consider the abundance of the threats constant with no intervention. The abundance of features may still be declining.
- Recovery functions (recovery of features after the threat is suppressed) are not uniform. Each island has a "capacity" to carry certain populations of native species and growth curves for populations are typically logistic in form.
- The response of the features to the elimination of threats is usually not linear. It has thresholds, e.g., we need to eliminate at least 2/3 of goats to see the native vegetation recover.

- The model considers one action to suppress one threat. In reality, the actions break down into several methods: shooting, baiting, trapping, spraying or pulling weeds etc. Individual methods have different efficacies, which also depend on the repetition: e.g., aerial shooting of goats will only be efficient at the beginning; after one or two fly-overs, the goats will learn to hide.
- The response of threats to actions is not linear [17]. There is a rule of thumb in pest management: eliminating the last 1–10% of a pest may cost the same as reducing the first 90–99% [8]; the most expensive is to remove the last threat (e.g., goat/cat/rat) from the island. This needs to be captured in the model, because it is an important factor for deciding whether eradication or control is chosen.
- The model considers that one action has an impact on one threat only. In reality, one action can influence more threats, and also many features. For example, if we decide to bait rats, cats may also be impacted, but some native birds will eat the baits too, or die from side effects (such as eating a poisoned rat).
- The costs of actions will break down into several items, like fuel for the boat, wages of the staff, and the baits or other material. Fuel costs may be a significant overhead, so once staff are already there, it may be efficient to do other things that would not normally be considered as worth the cost of the overheads. Thus, actions may be clustered.
- We do not consider the reintroduction of threats on some islands (the contra-action may be quarantine) or reintroduction of features by migration (especially birds). This is again an important factor when we decide between eradication or control strategies.
- The budget is not the only constraint we can expect, as mentioned above. Managers in conservation science need to take decisions which are of social-political origin and/or based on their experience which is not captured by the model. The advantage of the constraints model approach is that these special requirements can be implemented by simply adding other constraints. This feature will enable the system to work interactively, which is a vital condition for the new software.

The real-world extent of the problem is 120 islands (for Great Barrier Reef) or roughly 400 islands (for the Pilbara), 40 features, 25 threats, and 30 actions. The heuristic solver can enable managers to explore different options of the system, with different objectives and budgets. The point is not to get the best possible solution, but several near-optimal options to get an idea of the system. To explore several options it needs to be fast (in the order of tens of seconds or minutes) but it may be necessary to compromise on accuracy.

6   Conclusions

The management of invasive species on island systems is an ongoing challenge for conservation managers and decision makers alike. Automated decision making tools have been developed in the past, but have had only limited applicability and success. In this paper, a new model is developed of the problem that is based on optimisation of a form of the well-known knapsack problem in which every potential action on an island is a potential item in the knapsack. Using a genetic algorithm, it was shown that the solver was able to derive strategies that reduced the number of threats in island ecosystems, allowing the preservation of desired plants and animals.

Other combinatorial-oriented techniques, such as Extremal Optimisation or Tabu Search, will be tested in future versions. They will enable i) showing the quality of the solver in the terms of distance of the solution from the overall optimal one, ii) gauging the difficulty of the problem and iii) characterising some of the terrain features (such as the extent of local optima).

This paper presents an initial and simplified version of the problem. The next stage of development will be to refine this model, elaborating it where a number of conditions were imposed for the purposes of developing a simplified, early prototype. Importantly, it will be necessary to account for the real-world interactions that actions have on threats and features to provide a realistic and comprehensive system that can provide conservation managers with reliable, effective and credible decision-making support.

Acknowledgements. The main support for this work has been from the project "Decision support for prioritizing and implementing biosecurity on Western Australia's islands", funded by the Gorgon Barrow Island Net Conservation Benefits Scheme. Key support also came from Project 9.3 "Prioritising management actions for Great Barrier Reef islands", funded by the Tropical Ecosystem Hub of the National Environmental Research Program. We would like to acknowledge our many collaborators on our island projects in the Great Barrier Reef and Western Australia who have shaped the thinking reflected in this paper and are providing data for the analyses. Particular thanks go to Ian Craigie, Lesley Gibson, John Hicks, Cheryl Lohr, Keith Morris, John Olds and Malcolm Turner.

References

1. Carwardine, J., O'Connor, T., Legge, S., Mackey, B., Possingham, H., Martin, T.: Prioritizing threat management for biodiversity conservation. Conservation Letters 5, 196–204 (2012)
2. Fernandes, L., Day, J., Kerrigan, B., Breen, D., De'ath, G., Mapstone, B., Coles, R., Done, T., Marsh, H., Poiner, I.: A process to design a network of marine no-take areas: lessons from the Great Barrier Reef. Ocean and Coastal Management 52, 439–447 (2009)
3. Frévilla, A.: The multidimensional 0-1 knapsack problem: An overview. European Journal of Operational Research 155(1), 1–21 (2004)
4. Goldberg, D.: Genetic algorithms in search, optimization and machine learning. Addison Wesley, Reading (1989)
5. Holland, J.: Outline for a logical theory of adaptive systems. Journal of the ACM 3, 297–314 (1962)

6. Mathews, G.: On the partition of numbers. Proceedings of the London Mathematical Society 28, 486–490 (1897)
7. Moilanen, A.: Landscape zonation, benefit functions and target-based planning: Unifying reserve selection strategies. Biological Conservation 4, 571–579 (2007)
8. Myers, J.: Eradication and pest management. Annual Review of Entomology 43, 471–491 (1998)
9. Pouzols, F., Burgman, M., Moilanen, A.: Methods for allocation of habitat management, maintenance, restoration and offsetting, when conservation actions have uncertain consequences. Biological Conservation 153, 41–50 (2012)
10. Pouzols, F., Moilanen, A.: Roboff: software for analysis of alternative land-use options and conservation actions. Methods in Ecology and Evolution 4, 426–432 (2013)
11. Pressey, R.: The first reserve selection algorithm - a retrospective on jamie kirkpatrick's 1983 paper. Progress in Physical Geography 26, 434–441 (2002)
12. Pressey, R., Bottrill, M.: Approaches to landscape- and seascape-scale conservation planning: convergence, contrasts and challenges. Oryx 43, 464–475 (2009)
13. Pressey, R., Watts, M., Barrett, T., Ridges, M.: The C-Plan conservation planning system: origins, applications, and possible futures. In: Spatial conservation prioritization: Quantitative methods and computational tools, Oxford University Press, Oxford (2009)
14. Rebelo, A., Siegfried, W.: Where should nature reserves be located in the Cape Floristic Region, South Africa? Models for the spatial configuration of a reserve network aimed at maximizing the protection of floral diversity. Conservation Biology 6, 243–252 (1992)
15. Watts, M., Ball, I., Stewart, R., Klein, C., Wilson, K., Steinback, C., Lourival, R., Kircher, L., Possingham, H.: Marxan with zones: Software for optimal conservation based land- and sea-use zoning. Environmental Modelling & Software 24, 1513–1521 (2009)
16. Wilson, K., Underwood, E., Morrison, S., Klausmeyer, K., Murdoch, W., Reyers, B., Wardell-Johnson, G., Marquet, P., Rundel, P., McBride, M.: Conserving biodiversity efficiently: What to do, where, and when. PLoS Biology 5, 1850–1861 (2007)
17. Yokomizo, H., Possingham, H., Thomas, M., Buckley, Y.: Managing the impact of invasive species: The value of knowing the density-impact curve. Ecological Applications 19, 376–386 (2009)

An Evolutionary Algorithm for Deriving Withdrawal Rates in Defined Contribution Schemes

Kerem Senel[1] and Jason West[2]

[1] Istanbul Bilgi University, Turkey
kerem.senel@bilgi.edu.tr
[2] Bond University, Gold Coast, Australia
j.west@bond.edu.au

Abstract. Risk-averse investors typically adopt a fixed spending strategy during retirement to prevent against the premature depletion of their retirement portfolio. But a constant withdrawal rate means that retirees accumulate unspent surpluses when markets outperform and face spending shortfalls when markets underperform. The opportunity cost of unspent surpluses associated with this strategy can be extreme. We employ a genetic algorithm to find optimal asset allocation and withdrawal levels for a retirement portfolio. Using US and international data we compare this approach to existing strategies that use basic investment decision rules. Our results show that allocations to riskier assets early in retirement generates rising incomes later in retirement, without increasing the probability of ruin. A rising income profile remains optimal under different levels of risk aversion. This finding disputes the safe withdrawal rate conventions used in contemporary financial advice models.

Keywords: asset allocation, pension fund, safe withdrawal rate, genetic algorithm.

1 Introduction

Investors face two unknowns when determining the best strategy for funding their retirement using an appropriate withdrawal rate; (1) the future returns of the portfolio, and (2) the duration of their retirement period. If investors had perfect information of future returns and life expectancy, they could easily determine the income that could be generated from the portfolio, eliminating the possibility of a shortfall or surplus, assuming their spending plans are by some measure accurate. Both constant withdrawal rate and fixed horizon planning, which are the most common approaches in retirement withdrawal assessments, ignore important aspects of what is relevant to a real failure or success of the retirement investment and spending decision.

In general, determining the optimal withdrawal strategy is complicated since there are two stochastic variables (life expectancy and portfolio returns) that have a dramatic effect on both the level of potential income available and in income stability. No single comparison metric has emerged to compare the efficacy of different investment and withdrawal strategies due to the complex interaction between spending rates, asset allocation, and mortality. Common rules such as drawing a fixed

S.K. Chalup et al. (Eds.): ACALCI 2015, LNAI 8955, pp. 286–296, 2015.

percentage of the initial savings pool (such as the 4% Rule [1]), drawing a fixed percentage of the current (volatile) account balance or drawing the inverse of the retiree's life expectancy have emerged but none offer a rich appreciation demanded of dynamic retirement portfolios.

When holding withdrawal rates fixed, other research has shown that, predictably, asset allocation significantly affects the sustainability of a retirement portfolio. Portfolios with lower equity allocations over the drawdown phase tend to generate higher probabilities of ruin [2,3]. Forward-looking estimates to determine a sustainable withdrawal rate and highlighted the significant differences in the safety of various static withdrawal rates [4]. Implementing basic decision rules that prioritise the source of retirement funding through dividend and interest returns from the cash account over the stock account significantly dominates a retirement funding schedule without such priorities [5]. Analytical solutions to the multi-period asset allocation problem using dynamic programming have also been developed [6,7]. This research dwelt on asset allocation during the accumulation phase but stopped short of optimising pension withdrawals.

A solution to the multi-period asset allocation problem relied on GARCH effects to derive an asset allocation solution to cater for time-dependent volatility of the underlying assets without recourse to dynamic programming [8]. This shows that an analytical model that fails to incorporate GARCH effects leads to suboptimal portfolio performance. This approach was advanced by comparing two types of multi-period stochastic optimisation models and suggested that the 'efficient frontier' for a fixed-proportion strategy using the hybrid model strictly dominates a scenario tree model using a set of simulated asset return paths [9]. A new approach used an evolutionary algorithm to optimally allocate assets over multiple periods while remaining cognisant of regulatory constraints, investor constrains, increasing risk aversion and other more subjective quality measures [10]. An advanced method used genetic algorithms and stochastic search techniques to model the optimal allocation of assets within the constraint of discontinuities (e.g. short selling restrictions, asset illiquidity) and other empirical nonlinearities (e.g. quadratic terms in portfolio variance for classical portfolio optimisation or nonlinear cost or disutility functions) [11,12]. These results show that genetic algorithms and stochastic search techniques outperform analytical models as well as other accepted heuristic methods such as life cycle allocation and threshold allocation approaches using a range of risk metrics.

Previous scholars have thus used genetic algorithms to examine portfolio asset allocation for the purposes of maximising wealth at a single retirement date. However the more complex problem of defining a withdrawal process in the form of pension income to investors who face stochastic return outcomes from assets across multiple classes coupled with an uncertain investment horizon has not been adequately addressed. The use of a genetic algorithm to apply a range of asset allocation and withdrawal strategies permits a richer analysis of the best performing strategies available to investors. In the presence of volatile markets existing approaches to this problem such as simulation-based optimisation can only reliably obtain asset allocation weights or withdrawal amounts while holding other key parameters fixed. An optimisation approach that can tackle both asset allocation and withdrawal rates in a stochastic asset return setting may be superior to existing methods.

The purpose of this study is to examine the optimal profile of retiree income using a genetic algorithm approach that allows both the allocation of assets of the portfolio and the withdrawal rate to vary interdependently subject to market volatility and mortality considerations. We employ a genetic algorithm approach because it is an efficient method for determining how dynamic withdrawal rates can be prioritised by asset class. Using historical data allows the approach to retain both correlations across asset classes and serial correlation within asset classes. We show that the genetic algorithm approach robustly outperforms comparable methods over a wide array of initial conditions and market parameters.

This paper is organised as follows. In Section 2 we introduce the framework of the defined contribution pension scheme used for the simulations. Section 3 defines the genetic algorithm approach used to optimise the withdrawal rate for a retirement scheme, as well introducing some alternative methods. Section 4 presents the results and Section 5 offers some concluding remarks.

2   Genetic Algorithms and Alternative Solutions

2.1   Genetic Algorithms

In this model we use a floating point chromosome in the algorithm to minimise an expected cost function for the next period in the sequence. We adapt the cost function from [7,8] as follows:

$$C_t = (V_t - v_t)^2 + \alpha(V_t - v_t), \tag{1}$$

where C_t is the 'cost' incurred during period t, V_t is defined as the 'target' level for the retirement portfolio at t, v_t is the actual level of funds at t and α; $\alpha > 0$ is an arbitrary risk aversion parameter.

For the retirement portfolio, funds can be invested in n asset classes. The risk and return characteristics of each asset class are empirically derived using historical data. The withdrawal of income is assumed to be the only decrement from the retirement portfolio and tax implications are ignored (but can be included without loss of generality).

The cost function ensures that negative deviations from some target level are heavily penalised while positive deviations from the target level may either be rewarded or penalised, depending on the size of the deviation. Large positive deviations are penalised to prevent against an excessive exposure to risk (via the $(V_t - v_t)^2$ term) while smaller positive deviations are rewarded (via the $\alpha(V_t - v_t)$ term). Risk aversion decreases with increasing risk aversion parameter (at the limit where $\alpha \to \infty$ large positive deviations are not penalised). The fixed target level V_t is set *a priori* to a level of wealth empirically derived as the value an investor needs to maintain a comfortable annual income with a very low probability of ruin (<5%).

The optimisation problem is stated as

$$\min E[C_{t+1}|I_t], \tag{2}$$

where I_t represents all information available at time t. This formulation is taken from [11].

The actual level of funds at time $t+1$ can be expressed as

$$v_{t+1} = (v_t - y_t)(\theta'W), \tag{3}$$

where y is the withdrawal rate, θ is the vector of portfolio weights and W is the vector of real (gross) asset returns. Note that y and W can explicitly be written as

$$y' = [y_{1t} \quad y_{2t} \quad \cdots \quad y_{nt}] \text{ and}$$
$$W' = [W_{1t} \quad W_{2t} \quad \cdots \quad W_{nt}], \quad W_{it} = e^{X_{it}}, \quad X_{it} \sim N(\mu_i, \sigma_{it}^2), \tag{4}$$

where X_{it} is the return on the ith asset in period t, which is assumed to be constant throughout each period (one year). Asset returns are assumed to be lognormally distributed and the covariance matrix is assumed to be time-variant.

Following the approach in [11] we use a real value encoded genetic algorithm where the solution vector is comprised of $n-1$ elements, corresponding to the portfolio weights of $n-1$ assets. The sum of all portfolio weights must equal 1. With a non-zero probability of obtaining portfolio weights outside the range 0 to 1 (due to the mutation operator), we use a mirroring technique that takes the mirror image of the solution outside the range with respect to the violated boundary until the solution lands in the search space [11].

The cost function in Equation (1) is minimised as a proxy for the fitness function. We assume that there are seven separate underlying asset classes; US stocks, foreign stocks, US bonds, foreign bonds, US cash, listed real estate and unlisted real estate. We use seven bits to represent each portfolio weight to create the population. This corresponds to an interval size of 0.79% (=1/(2^7-1)) between discrete values. For each solution vector the random number generation is repeated until the sum of the $n-1$ portfolio weights remains below 1 and thus the portfolio weight of the nth asset remains positive (and to ensure no short sales). The cost function uses a transformed vector equal to the original vector used by the genetic algorithm divided by the sum of its elements to ensure that the sum of portfolio weights adds to 1.

The parameter settings used for each of the genetic algorithm phases dictate the efficacy of the search process. We introduce such settings for the crossover, election tournament and mutation phases. During the crossover phase, the potential for suboptimal 'offspring' could violate the short selling restriction for the nth asset. For computational efficiency we leave the elimination of such solutions to the election tournament phase of the algorithm. In addition, to maintain the integrity of the search algorithm to wander away from the initial conditions where it is optimal, we employ the shuffle crossover method with an arbitrary 50% probability of shuffle. For the mutation phase we impose an arbitrary restriction on mutation given by

$$\Pr(mutation) = 0.15 + \frac{0.33}{Gen\ No.}, \tag{5}$$

to ensure the probability of mutation decreases with time. This is the same restriction as applied in [11] which offered a relatively robust mutation process relative to other parameter choices. The following arguments were applied to the genetic algorithm:

- *strMin*: Each gene corresponds to the weight of an asset in the portfolio (a vector of 0's).
- *strMax*: Vector of 1's.
- *pSize*: Population size is set equal to 1000.
- *iter*: Number of iterations is 500.
- *mutChance*: Chance of mutation is 1/(chromosome length + 1).
- *elite*: Number of chromosomes carried over to the next generation is 20% of population size.

An initial population is randomly generated using a uniform distribution of values between *strMin* and *strMax*. A fitness score is then derived for each member of the population with the fittest members of the population being carried over to the next generation (via the elitism mechanism). The remaining members of the following generation are derived using a single-point crossover coupled with a non-uniform mutation operator based on a decreasing dampening factor as *t* increases. This mechanism provides flexibility to fine tune the veracity of outcomes and to assist in the process of landing on a global optimum.

2.2   Analytical Model

The cost function in (1) is minimised for the analytical approach. This is largely aligned with the stochastic search techniques devised in [11,12]. The analytical model solves the following objective function:

$$\min E[C_{t+1}|I_t] \text{ s.t. } \mu' y_T = 1, \tag{6}$$

where μ is a vector comprised of all $e^{-\mu_i}$'s. The optimisation problem is solved using the Lagrangian

$$\min E[C_{t+1}|I_t] - \lambda(\mu' y_T - 1). \tag{7}$$

The y_T is derived by transforming the optimal portfolio weights to minimise the cost function at *t+1* by

$$y_T = \frac{(2V_{t+1}+\alpha)(v_t+c)H^{-1}E(W_T|I_t)+\lambda H^{-1}\mu}{2(v_t+c)^2}, \tag{8}$$

where

$$H = E[W_T W_T'|I_t] \text{ and } \lambda = \frac{2(v_t+c)^2-(2V_{t+1}+\alpha)(v_t+c)\mu'H^{-1}E(W_T|I_t)}{\mu'H^{-1}\mu}. \tag{9}$$

Since the analytical model does not explicitly incorporate the restriction on short selling, the portfolio weights are truncated to [0, 1]. This assumption can be relaxed without loss of generality.

2.3   Asset Class Prioritisation Strategy

This strategy applies a decision rule to source pension withdrawals from both bonds and cash before sourcing stocks. The rule states that interest earned on cash and bond assets as well as dividends on stocks are first used to fund pension fund withdrawal, followed by the cash and bond assets themselves in equal portions, followed by withdrawing from stocks. By prioritising assets, this strategy accesses the high return-high risk asset classes later through the retirement cycle. While this approach will naturally increase asset volatility, it offers potentially higher withdrawal rates through retirement than more static approaches. We only employ three asset classes for this approach (stocks, bonds and cash).

3   The Algorithm

3.1   Asset Selection and Data

To calibrate the simulation data were obtained to cover the period January 1976 to January 2014. A range of indexes were used to serve as a proxy for the main asset classes. The S&P500 return series is used to represent US stocks while the MSCI ACWI (All Country World Index - excluding the U.S.) is used to represent foreign stocks. US bonds are represented by the Barclays US Aggregate, the Barclays Global Aggregate is used to represent foreign bond data and the 3-month T-bill yields are used to represent US cash returns. The FTSE NAREIT U.S. Real Estate Series is used as a proxy for listed US real estate investment returns while an NFI-ODCE Equal Weighted Index is used to represent unlisted real estate investment returns. Table 1 outlines the summary statistics for the data.

Table 1. Summary statistics for quarterly gross returns of US stocks, foreign stocks, US bonds, foreign bonds, 3-month T-bills and listed and unlisted real estate, January 1976 - January 2014

	US Stocks	Foreign Stocks	US Bonds	Foreign Bonds	US Cash	Real Estate (listed)	Real Estate (unlist)
Mean	12.52%	8.21%	7.87%	6.64%	5.07%	13.90%	8.38%
St Dev	15.82%	18.90%	6.59%	6.11%	1.79%	17.72%	5.53%
Skew	-0.90	-0.63	0.93	0.25	0.55	-1.76	-3.07
Kurt	1.57	0.89	5.06	-0.69	0.10	9.46	13.47
JB-Stat	34	10	174	3	7	611	1,315
P-value	0.00	0.01	0.00	0.23	0.02	0.00	0.00
n	144	104	144	96	144	144	144
Max	21.35%	27.94%	18.78%	8.93%	3.81%	33.28%	6.44%
Min	-22.53%	-22.29%	-8.71%	-3.83%	0.00%	-38.80%	-13.69%

3.2   Simulations

The portfolio withdrawals for each strategy are summed over the life of the investor and converted into a net drawdown ratio, defined as the proportion of total withdrawals to wealth at retirement. Wealth at retirement is set to US$500,000. We assume the investor retires at the age of 65. For expected mortality, we use the 2009 US Division of Vital Statistics (unisex) mortality table to calculate mortality and hold this horizon fixed for the initial simulation.

The annual target rate of return for calculating interim fund levels is set to expected return of an equally weighted portfolio of all seven assets. In fact a naïve portfolio dominates the Kelly strategy in risk adjusted terms [13]. We set the risk aversion parameter α in the cost function to 0, 20 and 50 for high, medium, and low risk aversion levels, respectively. Using the seven asset classes we consider three cases matched to the different risk aversion parameters used in the simulation. In total, 1000 simulations for each case are conducted to simulate the withdrawal rates, portfolio weights and the interim and final fund levels for the four alternative methods.

To compare the performances of each strategy, it is instructive to use total wealth outcomes along with downside risk metrics to represent the maximisation of wealth and the probability of ruin respectively. The total wealth outcome is measured as the ratio of total withdrawals to wealth at retirement ($500,000); that is, the ratio is equal to $\sum_{t=1}^{T} y_t / v_0$ where T is the retirement horizon. The risk metrics we use include the probability of failure (p-value associated with ruin), 5th percentile value at risk (VaR) and mean shortfall or conditional VaR (CVaR) [14]. We apply this approach to the genetic algorithm, the analytical approach and the asset prioritisation approach.

4   Simulation Results

4.1   Distributional Properties

We investigate a range of retirement withdrawal strategies. In this analysis, we define the optimal withdrawal rate as one that neither depletes a retiree's portfolio of savings nor unnecessarily constrains their desired spending needs. We also consider the opportunity to rebalance a pension portfolio through time as asset returns are revealed, and how this action may contribute to sustainable spending patterns during retirement.

Table 2 summarises the distributional properties of the simulated average withdrawal rates (measured as a net drawdown ratio) for the seven asset portfolio. The results show that the genetic algorithm outperforms both the analytical method and the prioritised withdrawal strategy at high and medium risk aversion levels and is roughly equivalent to both alternative methods for a low risk aversion level. The risk aversion parameter heightens the sensitivity to a greater degree for downside loss relative to high-side gain. The narrow income variability for the medium risk aversion portfolio suggests that it offers the most stable account for the retirement portfolio relative to other risk levels. At either risk aversion extreme greater asset switching occurs, especially early in the retirement period.

Table 2. Distributional properties of withdrawal rates using total wealth outcome (7 asset classes (apart from the prioritised strategy which only uses three); high, medium and low risk aversion; target withdrawal rate = 0.04)

	Mean	Std. Dev.	Min.	Max.
High Risk Aversion				
Analytical	2.670	1.447	0.188	3.981
Genetic algorithm	3.112	1.002	0.266	4.673
Prioritised	2.981	1.671	0.345	4.737
Medium risk aversion				
Analytical	3.091	0.975	2.251	4.308
Genetic algorithm	3.623	0.318	3.194	4.526
Prioritised	3.248	0.898	2.112	4.534
Low risk aversion				
Analytical	3.910	0.778	2.321	6.161
Genetic algorithm	3.975	0.847	2.116	5.746
Prioritised	4.001	0.989	2.210	5.998

The asset allocation time series for the genetic algorithm at various levels of risk aversion and minimum income withdrawal rates are provided in Figure 1. Panel (a) illustrates the asset allocation with income restricted to 4% and Panel (b) illustrates the same profile but for a slightly higher minimum income withdrawal rate. Both profiles represent an investor with a low risk aversion level (high alpha). Each diagram shows that high allocations to risky assets occur until a point where the portfolio can sustain the minimum income level until death. Riskier assets are used more for higher income needs, but no more than necessary.

Panel (c) illustrates the asset allocation profile for a high level of risk aversion (low alpha) with income restricted. The allocation varies in response to market conditions and allocates a considerable (relatively constant) amount to riskier assets through the retirement period. Panel (d) shows the profile for a low level of risk aversion without income restrictions (e.g. a retiree supported by a state-based pension). The allocation to defensive assets takes priority unless the portfolio value falls to an unsustainable level where it reverts to growth (riskier) assets to replenish value.

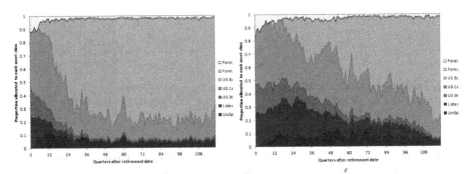

Fig. 1a. Asset allocation for GA with income restricted to 4% and alpha is high (50)

Fig. 1b. Asset allocation for GA with income restricted to 4.6% and alpha is high (50)

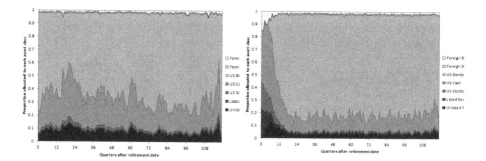

Fig. 1c. Asset allocation for GA with income restricted to 4% and alpha is low (20)

Fig. 1d. Asset allocation for GA with no income restrictions and alpha is high (50)

The portfolio value measured through the retirement period along with the average withdrawal rates for the four risk aversion and minimum income withdrawal rates introduced in Figure 1 are provided in Figure 2. The wealth profile in Panel (a) is slightly humped for low risk aversion levels which reflects the allocation to riskier assets early in retirement. In contrast high risk aversion levels translates into a smooth downward trajectory that achieves zero portfolio value at death. Panel (b) provides the profile for the income levels for each of the four scenarios. All profiles demonstrate an upwards shift in income through retirement as the probability of ruin decreases (due to the shorter time horizon) and they all generally converge to the same level in the second half of retirement despite the withdrawal rate during the first half of retirement. However there does not appear to be a discernible shift in the probability of ruin from one risk aversion level to another.

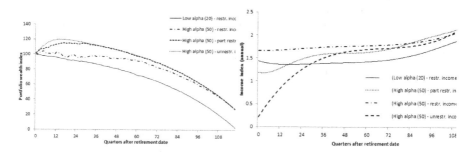

Fig. 2a. Portfolio wealth index level from retirement date for each GA simulation

Fig. 2b. Asset allocation for GA with income restricted to 1.6 and alpha is high (50)

4.2   Risk Measures

Table 3 summarises the risk measures computed for the simulated withdrawal rates for a seven asset class portfolio. The probability of failure shifts slightly higher as the risk aversion level increases. This is due to the higher allocation to defensive assets (because excess wealth is heavily penalised) which allows a limited buffer in the event of market downturns. Low levels of risk aversion allow the portfolio wealth level to recover through a higher allocation to growth assets during market downturns (excess portfolio wealth is only marginally penalised relative to insufficient portfolio wealth).

The probability of failure for both the analytical and prioritised methods exceeds that of the genetic algorithm for each risk aversion level. In addition, the 5th percentile value at risk (VaR) and mean shortfall illustrate that the probability of ruin is extremely sensitive to income level. For instance, while the prioritised approach to investing (withdraw from cash first, then bonds, then stocks) may yield a higher income through retirement, the probability of ruin can also be high, especially late in retirement when all assets are in stocks and the possibility of an adverse market event may deplete portfolio value such that it is unrecoverable. In contrast, the genetic algorithm does not prioritise asset withdrawals but rather relies on a higher allocation to growth assets early in retirement. This strategy outperforms the asset prioritisation approach, not only in terms of the probability of ruin, but also in the reduced variability of potential outcomes.

Table 3. Risk measures for withdrawal rates (7 asset classes; high, medium and low risk aversion; target withdrawal rate = 0.04)

	Prob. Failure	Mean shortfall ($ CVaR)	5th Percentile ($ VaR)
High Risk Aversion			
Analytical	0.060	2.144	2.270
Genetic algorithm	0.042	2.573	2.673
Prioritised	0.069	2.223	2.381
Medium risk aversion			
Analytical	0.062	2.651	2.891
Genetic algorithm	0.051	2.924	3.256
Prioritised	0.091	2.580	2.848
Low risk aversion			
Analytical	0.034	3.551	3.910
Genetic algorithm	0.012	3.442	3.772
Prioritised	0.121	3.706	4.001

The analytical method performs comparatively well for low risk aversion levels but is outperformed by the genetic algorithm at higher risk aversion levels. The optimisation function used in the analytical method, while faster, derived poorer results than the genetic algorithm. The complexity of the problem appears to better suit the genetic algorithm for the scenarios used in this analysis, which represent typical risk aversion and income requirement characteristics observed in retirees.

5   Conclusions

The simulation results show that there is no one model that exhibits superior fitness across all investment strategies. However the genetic algorithm serves as a relatively robust method for the optimisation for all levels of risk aversion. Other than the number of assets, there are numerous potential factors that affect the relative performance of different strategies such as correlation structure, length of withdrawal period and upper and lower limits on portfolio weights. The results highlight that allocation to riskier assets early in retirement generates rising incomes later in retirement, without necessarily increasing the probability of ruin. A rising income profile also remains optimal under different levels of risk aversion. This finding is in direct contrast to the safe withdrawal rate conventions used in contemporary financial advice models.

Our results confirm that there is great potential for the use of genetic algorithms in selecting optimal withdrawal rates along with multi-period asset allocation in defined contribution pension plans. Further studies in this area may extend this analysis and adopt more complex algorithms to better articulate the retirement portfolio withdrawal process using more dynamic feedback mechanisms.

References

1. Bengen, W.P.: Determining Withdrawal Rates Using Historical Data. J. Fin. Plan. 7(4), 171–180 (1994)
2. Cooley, P.L., Hubbard, C.M., Walz, D.T.: Sustainable Withdrawal Rates from Your Retirement Portfolio. Fin. Counsel. Plan. 10(1), 39–47 (1999)
3. Cooley, P.L., Hubbard, C.M., Walz, D.T.: Does International Diversification Increase the Sustainable Withdrawal Rates from Retirement Portfolios? J. Fin. Plan. 16(1), 74–80 (2003)
4. Pfau, W.D.: Can we predict the sustainable withdrawal rate for new retirees? J. Fin. Plan. 24(8), 40–47 (2011)
5. Drew, M.E., Walk, A.N., West, J.M., Cameron, J.: Improving Retirement Adequacy Through Asset Class Prioritization. J. Fin. Serv. Mark. 19(4), 291–303 (2014)
6. Vigna, E., Haberman, S.: Optimal Investment Strategy for Defined Contribution Pension Schemes. Insur. Math. Econ. (28), 233–262 (2001)
7. Haberman, S., Vigna, E.: Optimal Investment Strategies and Risk Measures in Defined Contribution Pension Schemes. Insur. Math. Econ. 31, 35–69 (2002)
8. Tuncer, R., Senel, K.: Optimal Investment Allocation Decision in Defined Contribution Pension Schemes with Time-Varying Risk. In: 8th Int. Congress on Insur. Math. Econ. (2004)
9. Hibiki, N.: Multi-Period Stochastic Optimization Models for Dynamic Asset Allocation. J. Bank. Financ. 30, 365–390 (2006)
10. Baglioni, S., da Costa Pereira, C., Sorbello, D., Tettamanzi, A.G.B.: An Evolutionary Approach to Multiperiod Asset Allocation. In: Poli, R., Banzhaf, W., Langdon, W.B., Miller, J., Nordin, P., Fogarty, T.C. (eds.) EuroGP 2000. LNCS, vol. 1802, pp. 225–236. Springer, Heidelberg (2000)
11. Senel, K., Pamukcu, A.B., Yanik, S.: Using Genetic Algorithms for Optimal Investment Allocation Decision in Defined Contribution Pension Schemes. In: 10th Int. Congress on Insur. Math. Econ. (2006)
12. Senel, K., Pamukcu, A.B., Yanik, S.: An Evolutionary Approach to Asset Allocation in Defined Contribution Pension Schemes. In: Brabazon, A., O'Neill, M. (eds.) Natural Computing in Computational Finance. SCI, vol. 100, pp. 25–51. Springer, Heidelberg (2008)
13. García-Álvarez, L., Luger, R.: Dynamic Correlations, Estimation Risk, and Portfolio Management During the Financial Crisis. Working Paper CEMFI (2011)
14. Jorion, P.: Value At Risk: The New Benchmark for Managing Financial Risk, 3rd edn. McGraw-Hill, New York (2007)

Evolving Point Packings in the Plane

Daniel Ashlock[1], Philip Hingston[2], and Cameron McGuinness[1]

[1] University of Guelph
[2] Edith Cowan University

Abstract. The problem of packing a fixed number of points into a square while maximizing the distance between them is a good test bed for comparing representations for real optimization problems not based on a simple mathematical formula. The problem does permit the applications of forms of gradient search and so allows simple and hybrid algorithms to be compared. In this study we compare a simple representation comprised of an array of points to a more complex generative representation called the walking triangle representation.

Keywords: representation, point packing, operators, generative representations.

1 Introduction

Real parameter optimization problems in test suites are usually posed with a mathematical formula and a set of constraints on permissible parameter values. Applied problems such as circuit component layout, control of biomedical or industrial processes, and even abstract combinatorial problems do not have formulae which can be used in optimization. In this study we examine a class of problems posed in an online forum that are in this latter class of optimization tasks. While the problem is phrased as an abstract combinatorial problem, it is related to the 2D stock cutting problems [5] and other potential applications are outlined in the future work section.

Definition 1. *The* **point packing problem in the square** *or* **PPPS problem** *seeks to place a specified number of points into the unit square, including its boundary, so that the minimum distance between any pair of points is maximized.*

An example solution for $n = 8$ points is shown in Figure 1. We note that a simple affine transformation makes point and circle packing equivalent problems in the square.

If we simply place a circle of the correct radius about each point then we have placed circles with *centers* in the unit square. If a point appears on the boundary of the unit square it extends no more than the circle's radius outside of the square. Scaling the square through the map:

$$x \to (x + r)/(1 + 2r)$$
$$y \to (y + r)/(1 + 2r)$$

places all possible circles within or within and tangent to the unit square. The radii of the circle must be pre-adjusted to deal with the scaling by a factor of $(1 + 2r)$ but this

S.K. Chalup et al. (Eds.): ACALCI 2015, LNAI 8955, pp. 297–309, 2015.

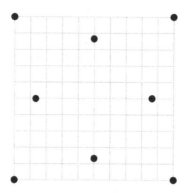

Fig. 1. The unique optimum for the PPPS with $n = 8$ points

map does provide a bijection of point packings with circle packings. If the problem is generalized to more dimensions the map remains shifting each coordinate by r to place all circles in the positive orthant then scaling them to restore containment in the unit hypercube. The problem of packing points (or circles) in the unit square is typically attacked with deterministic algorithms [6]. In this study we compare two representations for solving the problem with evolutionary computation.

A natural question to ask about the PPPS problem is its algorithmic complexity. Typically we would like a problem to belong to a difficult complexity class, e.g. NP-hard, before we go to the trouble of developing an evolutionary computation system to attack instances of it. Unfortunately the PPPS problem is, in general, an unsolved mathematical problem and work on the complexity of finding approximate solutions waits on a more complete development of the mathematical theory. The known optimal solutions, with proofs of optimality, are all special cases. This study compares two representations on a small case of the problem with a known optimal solution. This sets the stage for exploration with more points and in higher dimensions. A number of possible applications for approximate solutions to the PPPS problem are given in Section 5.3.

The remainder of this paper is structured as follows. The representation and algorithm for evolving point packings in the unit square is given in Section 2. The design of experiments is given in Section 3. Results on evolving point packings are given and discussed in Section 4. Section 5 draws conclusions and examines next steps and gives potential applications to both evolutionary computation and Monte-Carlo integration.

2   Representations for Evolving Point Packings

This study compares different representations for the point packing problem. The first is a standard type of representation, a linear array of parameters, albeit with a novel mutation operator that enables more efficient hill climbing for the PPPS problem. The second is a type of generative representation from a class of representations called *walking triangle* representations. These representations are first defined in [1].

The fitness function used is quite simple to specify. Each representation is able to specify a collection of points in the unit square. The fitness of an array of points is simply the minimum distance between any two points, to be maximized. Notice that the overall fitness is determined by exactly two points. That means that most of the points can be moved without affecting the fitness. For the standard representation this means that there are huge neutral networks in the fitness landscape. The second representation, in which each loci in the generative representation can move all the points, was chosen because it is likely to have much smaller neutral networks and hence permit evolution to function more efficiently.

Neutral networks are a critical and possibly underappreciated factor in the design of representations for evolutionary computation.

Definition 2. *A **neutral mutation** is a mutation that does not change the fitness value of the population member being mutated.*

Definition 3. *The **neutral network** of a population member p is the subset of the population that may be reached by applying a sequence of neutral mutations to p.*

We note the joint membership in a neutral network is an equivalence relation on the population. With these definitions in place it is easy to see that any point packing instantiated in the standard representation has many neutral mutations. Any displacement of a point that does not produce a new smallest distance or move one of the two points generating the current smallest distance will be neutral. Since the representation stores machine reals, there are billion of neutral mutants of most potential population members. The walking triangle representation, as we will see, moves all the points in the point packing, meaning packings instantiated using it will have far fewer neutral mutants. This discussion of neutral networks shows, irrespective of other factors, that the fitness landscapes for these two representations are very different.

2.1 Point Array Representation

The first representation used is a simple **point array** (PA) representation for evolving point packings. It takes the form of an array of $2n$ real values of the form

$$(x_1, y_1, x_2, y_2, \ldots, x_n, y_n)$$

that directly specify the coordinates of the points being packed in the unit square. The variation operators used with the point array representation are two point crossover and a complex, domain specific, mutation operator. The mutation operator begins by filling in an array with dimension equal to the problem dimension with numbers in the interval [-1,1] with a probability w that a location is zero and distributed uniformly at random otherwise. The vector is then scaled to have a length of

$$0.01 + \frac{1}{10m}$$

where m is the number of mating events (evolutionary time) so far. The vector is then added, coordinate by coordinate, to the chromosome being mutated. This mutation operator moves all the points with the total size of the motion bounded and decreasing as evolution proceeds.

This mutation operator makes small changes in the position of some of the points in the evolved packing. The parameter w probabilistically controls the number of points that move and so is referred to as the *mutation rate*. Decreasing the total amount of change that is made by mutation over evolutionary time simply acknowledges that, as we approach an optimum, there is less need for exploration and more need for hill-climbing.

An alert reader will have noticed that the mutation operator can produce values outside of the unit square. After application of a mutation operator all negative values are changed to zero and all values exceeding one are changed to one. This is not usually a good choice for real optimization – points will tend to pile up on the boundaries. For the PPPS problem it permits the algorithm to place points on the boundary of the square with positive probability which is a feature of many known global optima. In other words this choice makes the mutation operators specifically friendly to the PPPS problem.

2.2 Walking Triangle Representation

Definition 4. *The **walking triangle** (WT) representation starts with a simplex in $D = 2n$ dimensions with vertices that are the union of the standard basis and the origin. The point packing represented by the simplex is derived from the center of mass of the simplex. Pairs of coordinates from the center of mass are the points in the packing. The representation is generative and so modifies the simplex with three types of moves.*

1. *The first type of move reflects a vertex through the opposite face of the simplex. This move is called a* walk.
2. *The second type of move moves a vertex to the center of mass of the simplex. This move is called* centering.
3. *The third type of move is the inverse of the second; notice that the second move is a linear operation and so invertible. This move is called* decentering.

All three operations have one instance for each vertex of the simplex and so the representation has $6n$ operations. These are treated as an alphabet and the representation is implemented as a string of simplex modifying operations. The point encoded is general in the plane and so, before evaluating fitness, the point encoded is normalized to the range [0,1] by an affine map

$$N(x) = \frac{x - min}{max - min}$$

Diagrams of the three walking triangle moves used are shown in Figure 3. An example of the expression of a walking triangle chromosome is given in Figure 2. The representation as used in evolution freely mixes centering, decentering, and walk moves. The example used a preponderance of walk moves because the other two moves change the size of the simplex on an exponential schedule and so make an illustration unreadable if many of them appear.

Notice that the normalization of the WT representation has the same effect, placing some points on the boundary of the unit square, that the truncation mutation did for the PA representation. Since only four point-coordinates can end up at the boundary of

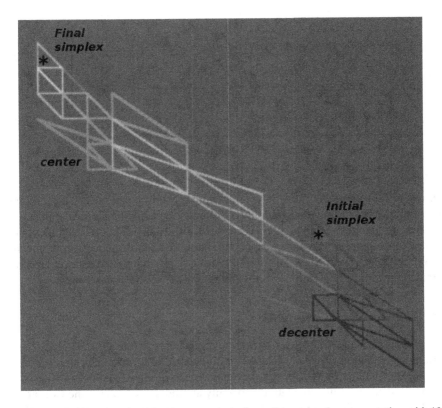

Fig. 2. Shown is the expression of a chromosome in the walking triangle representation with 100 moves in two dimensions. Note that the triangle covers many positions more than once so 100 separate triangles are not visible. All but two of the moves are walk moves. The 33rd move is a decenter, the 66th move is a center. The Star in the final simplex represents the point in the plane represented by the chromosome. If the figure is viewed in color the simplices are shown in order via HSV color from red to yellow.

the square, we modify the expression of this representation by placing points (0,1) and (1,0) in the square and then adding the points specified by the simplex's center of mass to the square.

The variation operators used for the WT representation are two point crossover and k-point mutation with the number of characters changed by the mutation operator selected uniformly at random in the range 1 to MNM. The name MNM is an abbreviation of *maximum number of mutations*. This parameter controls the mutation rate and is the subject of a parameter study.

The normalization of the center of mass before its use has an interesting effect on the search space. The normalization depends on the maximum and minimum x and y values of any coordinate of any point. When a mutation of the sequence of moves changes which point supplies these values, there is potentially a very large change in the arrangement of the post-normalization points. This means that many mutations produce small changes in the relative position of the points in the encoded solution but some provide very large ones.

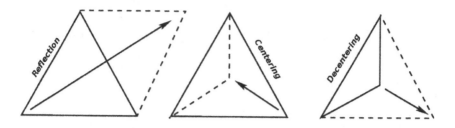

Fig. 3. Schematics of the three types of moves for the WT representation

Representation Length. The WT-representation specifies points as the center of mass of a simplex and operates by modifying the simplex by applying a series of operators. The dimension of the search problem is encoded as the dimension of the simplex and is not tied to the number of operators applied. That means, unlike the PA-representation, the WT-representation has the length of the string of operators used as an independent parameter that must be studied. We call this parameter *representation length*.

2.3   The Evolutionary Algorithm

The evolutionary algorithms used to find point packings are steady state [10]. The algorithm uses single tournament selection with the size of the tournament T studied as an algorithm parameter. This model of evolution performs a population updating by selecting T member of the population uniformly at random and having the two most fit breed and replace the two least fit. Breeding consists of copying the parents, and performing crossover and mutation on the copies. The crossover and mutation operators used are given in the specification of the representations. This very simple evolutionary algorithm design is chosen to permit transparent comparison of the two representations.

3   Experimental Design

Three parameter setting experiments were performed with the evolutionary algorithm for the PA representation. The first changes the mutation rate, which is controlled by the probability a location is zero : set to w =0.5, 0.6, 0.7, 0.8, and 0.9. The second tests population sizes of 10, 32, 100, 320, and 1000. The third tests tournament sizes of T=4, 7, 10, 13, and 16. The eight point packing problem shown in Figure 1 was used for testing because the problem is relatively small and the optimal solution is known (maximal minimum distance $\frac{\sqrt{6}-\sqrt{2}}{2} \cong 0.518$) so that it is possible to assess the behavior of the evolutionary algorithm [7].

For the WT-representation four parameter setting experiments were performed. The first tested the same populations sizes as were tested for the PA-experiment. The second tested the same tournament sizes used for the PA-experiment. The third compares values of 1, 2, 3, 4, and 5 for the MNM parameters. The fourth contrasts representation lengths of 20, 30, 40, 50, and 60.

In each of the studies, the problem is considered solved if a fitness of 0.49 or better is found. Experimentation with a simple stochastic hill-climber showed that solutions with this fitness value rapidly converge to the optimum making it an acceptable finish line for comparing the representations.

The algorithm is permitted up to 1,000,000 mating events to try to find a solution. The times to solution and number of failures are recorded. Times to solution are displayed as inflected box plots which do not include the runs that failed. The times are transformed by the natural log to permit cleaner display and comparison. The number of failures are displayed separately across the bottom of a plot. When a parameter is not being varied we use population size 100, mutation rate $w = 0.8$, and tournament size 7 for the PA-representation and population size 32, maximum number of mutations 2, tournament size 4, and representation length 40 for the WT representation. These default values were chosen during preliminary experimentation. Since a known optimal fitness value is available, comparing time to locate it gives us a good forum for comparing the representations.

4   Results and Discussion

The parameter studies for the PA representation are shown in Figure 4. The immediate result is that the algorithm is remarkably robust to changing parameters. Given the trade off of number of failures against solution time, the population size 100 is the best compromise value. The mutation rate study comes down in favor of $w = 0.6$ and so changing about 40% of the points yields the best performance. The tournament size study suggests tournament size 13, but again the parameter choice is soft. It is important to remember that lower times to solution are better.

For the four parameter studies performed for the WT-representation we also observe substantial robustness to the change of parameters. The best population size, yielding a good completion-time trade off, is 320. The best tournament size, with best mean time and fewest failures, is 4. For the maximum number of mutations there is very little to choose between $MNM = 2$ and $MNM = 3$; 2 has a slight, if not significant, edge. For the representation length the shortest length tested yields absolutely the best results.

Juxtaposing the two representations, it is clear that the WT representation takes fewer fitness evaluation to locate a good point packing than the PA representations. Both representations were optimized for the PPPS problem. The mutation operator used by the PA representation and the placement of two initial points in the WT representation both encode the domain knowledge that it is good to have points on the boundary of the unit square and, in fact, often it is good to have points at the corners. The comparison is not clearly a fair one, given that the algorithms do not even use the same parameters for tuning. From the perspective of finding the better algorithm, the comparison is useful.

The data show that the WT representation is, roughly, 2-3 times faster than the PA representation. To estimate this it is important to remember that the logarithm used in the natural log to that one point difference in the vertical scale represents a factor of 2.71 in time to solution. It is important to note that executing the generative steps in the WT representation is not too expensive, it involves manipulation of an $n \times n + 1$ matrix of coordinates of the vertices of the simplex. The PA representation requires

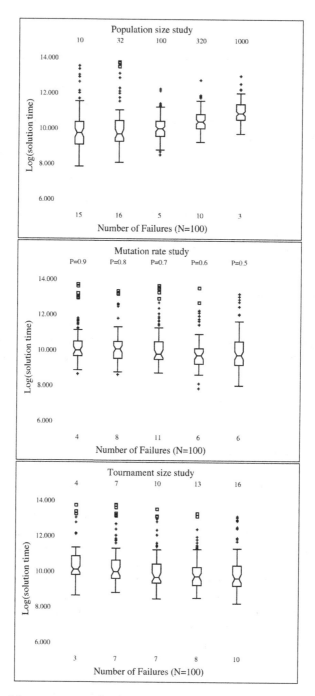

Fig. 4. Results of the parameter studies for placing eight points in the square with the PA representation. The top panel compares population sizes, the middle panel compares mutation rates, and the bottom panel compares tournament sizes.

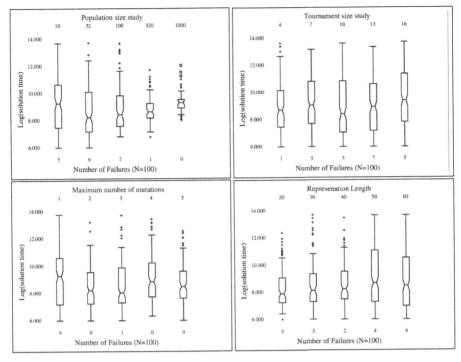

Fig. 5. Results of the parameter studies for placing eight points in the square with the WT representation. In reading order the panels show studies on population size, tournament size, maximum number of mutations, and representation length.

no computations to unpack the set of points in the unit square that it represents. This means that the desirability of the WT representation must be juxtaposed against the cost of expressing the representation. In this study there is a large difference in mean time to solution between the two representations for their tuned best values.

Another factor in favor of the WT representation is that, for the eight point test problem, the shortest and hence least expensive version of the representation yields the best performance. The cost of expressing an instance of the WT representation is linearly proportional to its length. Exploiting this phenomenon is possible and a proposal to do so appears in Section 5.

5   Conclusions and Next Steps

For a test instance of the PPPS problem this study provides proof-of-concept for two different representations for evolving solutions. The WT representation, in spite of its higher overhead costs, was found to yield superior performance. A collection of seven sets of 100 runs of the evolutionary algorithm were performed to tune and compare the representations. Beyond demonstrating the superiority of the WT representation on the test problem, these tests demonstrated that both representations are relatively robust to the parameter settings of the algorithms.

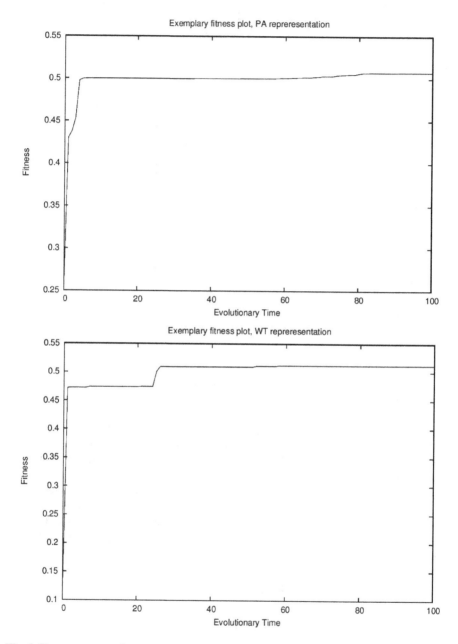

Fig. 6. Shown are exemplary plots of the maximum fitness within and evolving population over evolutionary time for the PA representation (left) and the WT representation (right). These are typical in that the PA representation shows slow smooth progress while the WT representation exhibits large jumps.

The two representations compared yield very different parameter settings on those parameters they have in common and require very different number of fitness evaluations to reproduce the known optimal solution for the test case. This supports the view that the fitness landscapes are very different. As noted previously, the fitness landscape for the PA representation contains enormous neutral networks. Moving points other than the two that are the witness to the minimum intra-point distance, unless it generates a smaller distance and hence a worse fitness, represents a fitness neutral change. Since every operator in the WT representation non-trivially modifies the center of mass, and so moves every point represented, there are constructively far smaller neutral networks. It seems likely that the fitness landscapes are very different with the PA landscape being more friendly to incremental discovery while the WT landscape is more likely to have sudden improvements. Figure 6 shows examples of the way maximum fitness changes during evolution for one run for each of the two representations.

1. The superior time to solution for the WT representation represents less time wandering in neutral networks.
2. The specially designed mutation operator used for the PA representation, intended to reduce the probability of neutral mutation, did not reduce the incidence of neutral mutations sufficiently.

5.1 Possible Improvements

The representation length study in the last panel of Figure 5 shows the shortest representation is best. As we enlarge the number of points being packed into the unit square, it is likely that the best representation lengths will get longer, but it is not at all clear how fast. A simple method of dealing with this is to make the representation length adaptive. In addition to the simplex we encode a real parameter in range $(0, 1)$ that says what initial fraction of the moves encoded by the WT representation are performed. When two fitness values are similar, within a comparison threshold, we would favor the representation that executed the fewest operations. Since the operations used to express the WT representation have a modest but positive cost this is a form of evolvable parsimony pressure for the WT representation.

In the study that introduced the walking triangle representation [1], several operations besides the walk, centering, and decentering were introduced. It is worth checking these additional operations to see how they influence performance. For the PA representation, fitness changes only when the smallest distance changes. This strongly suggests that a mutation operator that moves one of the two points that is part of the witness to a configurations fitness is a good idea.

5.2 Next Steps

This study concentrates on a simple case of the PPPS problem with a known, unique global optimum in order to permit clean parameter setting and comparison of the WT and PA representations. The obvious next step is to explore larger cases of the problem. A dozen exact solutions and thousands of "best known" results are given at:

$$http://hydra.nat.uni-magdeburg.de/packing/csq/csq.html$$

It is likely that well-designed evolutionary search could improve some of these bounds.

Since the PPPS problem is motivated by stock cutting, solutions in 3 or more dimensions have not, so far as we can tell, been studied. Unstudied domains of this sort are typically appropriate domains for evolutionary computation and the generalization to points in more dimensions is not difficult.

5.3   Potential Applications

Convergence to local optima is an undesirable property of evolutionary computation which is combated by techniques as diverse as using very large populations, niche specialization [9], the use of geographically structured algorithms [11,3,8], and even restart based sampling. When using evolutionary computation for real parameter optimization, a well spread out initial population yields many of the same benefits as a large initial population. Higher dimensional version of the PPPS problem provide exactly such initial populations - the need to maximize the minimum distance spreads the population out in a fashion that maximizes the probability of hitting as many basins of attraction in the fitness landscape as possible for a given population size. The points in the unit square or hypercube are simply rescaled to fit the desired search domain.

This idea of using solutions to the generalized (higher dimensional) PPPS as initial populations can be made more powerful by applying hypercuboidal symmetries to the initial points. These symmetries consist of applying the function $f(x) = 1 - x$ to a coordinate of the points and shuffling the coordinates. These two operations are respectively face swaps and coordinate transformation of the hypercube containing the points, before they are rescaled to make an initial population. A library of such sets of points could be saved and the fact there are $n! \cdot 2^n$ hypercuboidal symmetries means that, unless an absurd number of replicates were performed, the initial populations could be distinct in each replicate, further improving the search power.

The application to Monte Carlo integration is very similar to that of generating initial populations. Monte-Carlo integration [4] is used on problems where numerical integration is to be performed but a regular sample grid has a prohibitive number of points. In fifty dimensions, having a grid of points with three members per dimensions yields 7.18×10^{23} sample points, for example. It is possible to bound the integration error of selecting sample points for numerical integration uniformly at random and so get by with a much smaller random sample of points. Point packing designs provide far more even spacing than random points and so might served as *spatial designs* that reduce the number of sample points required or improve the accuracy of Monte Carlo integration techniques.

In [2] *single parent crossover* was introduced. In this model of evolutionary computation, a population of unchanging ancestors is picked and a new variation operator introduced that consists of crossover with an ancestor - a special one sided crossover operator that does not modify the ancestor. The initial application of single parent crossover was in genetic programming where, in addition to maintaining operator diversity in a population it also helped control tree size (bloat) in the evolving population. Solutions to the generalized PPPS problem would be natural ancestor sets for introducing single parent crossover in real optimization when preservation of diversity is valuable. The application to single parent crossover would require much smaller numbers of points than would be needed when using such a solution as an initial population.

References

1. Ashlock, D., Krisk, N., Fogel, G.: Functions for the analysis of exploration and exploitation. In: Proceedings of the 2013 Congress on Evolutionary Computation, pp. 2020–2027. IEEE Press, Piscataway (2013)
2. Ashlock, W., Ashlock, D.: Single parent genetic programming. In: Proceedings of the 2005 Congress on Evolutionary Computation, pp. 1172–1179 (2005)
3. Bryden, K.M., Ashlock, D.A., Corns, S., Willson, S.J.: Graph based evolutionary algorithms. IEEE Transactions on Evolutionary Computation 10, 550–567 (2006)
4. Caflisch, R.E.: Monte carlo and quasi-monte carlo methods. Acta Numerica 7, 1–49 (1998)
5. León, C., Miranda, G., Rodríguez, C., Segura, C.: 2D cutting stock problem: A new parallel algorithm and bounds. In: Kermarrec, A.-M., Bougé, L., Priol, T. (eds.) Euro-Par 2007. LNCS, vol. 4641, pp. 795–804. Springer, Heidelberg (2007)
6. Locatelli, M., Raber, U.: Packing equal circles in a square: A deterministic global optimization approach. Discrete Appl. Math. 122(1-3), 139–166 (2002), doi:10.1016/S0166-218X(01)00359-6
7. Markot, M.C., Csendes, T.: A new verified optimization technique for the 'packing circles in a unit square; problems. SIAM J. Optimization 16(1), 193–219 (2005)
8. McEachern, A., Ashlock, D., Shonfeld, J.: Sequence classification with side effect machines evolved via ring optimization. Biosystems 113(1), 9–27 (2013)
9. Smith, R.E., Forrest, S., Perelson, A.S.: Searching for diverse, cooperative populations with genetic algorithms. Evolutionary Computation 1(2), 127–149 (1993)
10. Syswerda, G.: A study of reproduction in generational and steady state genetic algorithms. In: Foundations of Genetic Algorithms, pp. 94–101. Morgan Kaufmann, San Francisco (1991)
11. Tomassini, M.: Spatially Structured Evolutionary Algorithms. Springer, New York (2005)

The Effect of Reactant and Product Selection Strategies on Cycle Evolution in an Artificial Chemistry

Thomas J. Young and Kourosh Neshatian

University of Canterbury, Christchurch, New Zealand
thomas.young@pg.canterbury.ac.nz

Abstract. The molecules within an Artificial Chemistry form an evolutionary system, capable under certain conditions of displaying interesting emergent behaviours. We investigate experimentally the effect on emergence of the combinations of selected strategies for choosing reactants (Uniform and Kinetic selection) and products (Uniform and Least Energy selection) as measured by three measures of reaction cycle formation. Emergence is maximised by a Kinetic reactant selection strategy; the choice of product selection strategy has minimal effect.

Keywords: artificial chemistry, emergence, open-ended evolution.

1 Introduction

Artificial Chemistries of discrete atoms provide an interesting testbed for investigating various evolutionary phenomena. Fundamentally, they provide a tuneable evolutionary system, capable of highly complex behaviour, built around familiar metaphors (real-world Chemistry, and potentially Biology). A set of interaction rules describing how atoms interact gives rise to emergent forms—molecules. At a higher level, these molecules, under the same interaction rules, also interact in patterns—reactions.

Still higher emergent levels emerge under favourable conditions. Reactions may form cycles, where a sequence eventually returns to an earlier product. Our interest is in identifying the factors that influence the emergence of these higher levels. Cycles in particular are interesting as many biological processes are cyclical. Replication, resulting in an exact copy of an entity, is a macro-example of a cycle; metabolism is another. Building on the apparent correspondence between higher emergent levels in Artificial Chemistry evolution and Biology, we believe like others (e.g., [18]) that cycles, of some form, are a necessary building-block for more complicated structures again in Artificial Chemistries.

Unfortunately, although the emergence of cycles from a solely reaction-based system is certainly possible, and indeed likely under many conditions, more complicated structures are very rare. Perhaps it is simply a matter of probabilities—they may be theoretically possible, but in practice highly unlikely and so most

S.K. Chalup et al. (Eds.): ACALCI 2015, LNAI 8955, pp. 310–322, 2015.

reaction sequences do not do anything interesting: a strongly constructive chemistry can generate an infinite number of reaction types, and it is of course possible for these to combine in sequences that are interesting. But from other work the probability of this happening appears to be very low [3,16].

In an attempt to improve these odds we turn to heuristics, or strategies, inspired by our analogy, the real-world, to tune the Artificial Chemistry. We categorise these strategies into two types—those to do with the selection of reactants for the next reaction, and those to do with the selection of products from the set of all products possible given a particular set of reactants. The combination of the two completely describes a reaction. In this work we explore the following research questions:

RQ1: Is there a quantitative difference between different reactant and product selection strategies?

RQ2: Is there a combination of reactant and product selection strategies that leads to increased emergence as measured by cycles?

RQ3: Is emergence significantly affected by the values of other parameters of an Artificial Chemistry, such as initial kinetic energy or bond energies?

To the best of our knowledge, this is the first time that reaction and product selection strategies in Artificial Chemistries have been experimentally compared. Instead, the general approach of previous work, where there has been a quantitative evaluation, has been to propose a particular strategy, build, and evaluate against the initial goals, rather than against alternatives.

2   Previous Work

Artificial Chemistries are often found employed in three main areas: as models for the study of real-world chemistry; to explore biochemical processes, often in connection with questions regarding the origins or life; and finally purely for the exploration of artificial life.

In the first two areas, the primary requirement is fidelity with real-world chemistry, which requires either a library of empirically derived reaction definitions and rates, or a model capable of accurately simulating quantum-mechanical processes. The latter approach has been taken by a family of Artificial Chemistries, beginning with Benkö et al [1], built on Extended Huckel Theory with parameters taken directly from chemical experiments and later extended (for example in [2]) to a general purpose model with parameters derived from theoretical chemistry. The model was used in [10] for the study of the behaviour and topology of chemical reaction networks, specifically Diels-Alder and Formose reaction networks, and in a series of papers (e.g, [7] and [20]) for the examination of the evolution of metabolic networks in early organisms using a simple model of RNA coding for catalysts.

Real-world chemical processes are also important to modelling scenarios for the origin of life or of other related areas such as the formation of metabolic networks in the earliest protocells. In many cases though the specific focus is less on the bottoms-up model from the most elementary elements, and more on task-based models of processes where the particular starting point is predetermined by the researcher.

For example, in Lattice Artificial Chemistry [17,15], the study of membrane formation and cell division assumes five different types of particles (some hydrophilic and some hydrophobic) that together form an autocatalytic cycle similar to those observed in biological cells. Three types of particle are employed by the Substrate-Catalyst-Link (or SCL) chemistry of [21,19]: the eponymous Substrate, Link and Catalyst. Cells are formed from links around a catalyst, with a single predefined reaction rule $S + S + C \Rightarrow L + C$ and some straightforward constraints on movement of the particles in the matrix (for example, bonded Link particles cannot cross each other.)

Most such work concentrates on the behaviour of individuals; by contrast in [5] the focus is on an ecosystem, based on a set of atoms interacting in pre-specified ways that represent biological photosynthesis, respiration and biosynthesis (or growth). The goal is to explore the interactions in an ecosystem made up of a set of organisms pre-built to perform various defined roles.

Finally, in Artificial Life, Artificial Chemistries have been used in the exploration of open-ended or creative evolution. Squirm3 [11,12,14] adopts fixed molecule types, and pre-defined reactions for replication and gene-sequence transcription, and so although capable of interesting behaviour is not capable of unlimited extension. Stringmol [9] - a bacterial inspired microprogram chemistry - though does demonstrate a rich heredity for open-ended evolution using string-matching to model binding between sequences, and RBN-World [6] shows that a form of Random Boolean Network, with the addition of a bonding mechanisms to allow for composition and decomposition of RBNs, can be used to build a chemistry capable of almost limitless extension out of non-traditional components.

3   The ToyWorld Artificial Chemistry

ToyWorld, our Artificial Chemistry for the exploration of emergent behaviours, was first introduced in [22]. The elements of the model - Atoms, Molecules, Reactions, a Reaction Vessel - are recognisable from real-world chemistry, but in highly simplified forms. Familiarity is important for understanding, but only in so far as the analogy is consistent, and therefore we endeavour to maintain a basic correspondence wherever possible. However, there is no requirement to provide chemically-realistic results - our model cannot be used to investigate real-world chemical behaviours.

The lowest level component in the ToyWorld model is the atom, and atoms can be joined by bonds to form molecules. Reactions between molecules are the only mechanism in the model to modify molecules; a reaction is simply the addition or subtraction of a single bond between any two atoms in two molecules. ToyWorld provides a strongly constructive chemistry ([8]) where completely new forms of molecules may be generated by reactions, and where the new molecules may in turn take part in further reactions: the chemistry emerges from the lower level atomic properties.

All atoms, and therefore molecules and reactions, are contained within a reaction vessel. ToyWorld provides a basic energy model, where molecules have kinetic energy and bond breaking requires energy input and bond formation releases energy. The reaction vessel, which provides the strategies by which reaction reactants (or input molecules) and products (output molecules) are determined, is described in detail in the following section.

4   The Reaction Vessel – Reactant and Product Selection Strategies

Importantly for this work, a reaction may be seen as two stages in sequence: first, the choice of reactants from a population of possible reactant molecules (the Reactant selection strategy, denoted here by S_{Reactant}), and second, the determination of products given that set of reactants (Product selection strategy, denoted S_{Product}).

4.1   Selecting Reactants for a Reaction

Two generic strategies are described in [6] for the selection of reactants—spatial and aspatial—where the primary difference is whether molecular position is a factor in reactant selection. It is possible to further generalise this scheme by considering other differentiating factors. Analogous with real-world chemistry, a cumulative scheme presents itself starting with the pure aspatial, or uniform probability strategy, and then proceeding through the spatial strategy, based on molecular kinetics, to kinetics plus intra-molecular and external forces such as electromagnetism. These strategies can be viewed as being based on increasing derivatives of position or location in the reaction vessel; from no position (uniform selection), through fixed position (uninteresting as we cannot have a sequence of reactions without motion) to the first derivative (velocity or kinetic selection) and finally to the second derivative (acceleration, or force selection.) Accordingly we adopt this more detailed classification for the descriptions below.

Uniform Selection. In a uniform selection strategy ($S_{\text{Reactant}} = $ Uniform), reactants are chosen at random with equal (uniform) probability from the population: no property of a molecule has an effect on the selection. Conceptually we have a well-stirred reaction container with no intra-molecular forces.

Kinetic Selection. By contrast, in a kinetic selection strategy ($S_{\text{Reactant}} = $ Kinetic) molecules have spatial position (and implicitly, velocity) within some assumed reaction vessel, and selection is determined by molecular position—molecules which are spatially co-located (that is, in collision) form a reactant set. Molecules move at constant velocity until they collide with something else (either another molecule or possibly a boundary of an explicit reaction vessel) and then either react, or bounce. Currently in our work we assume that all molecules have a fixed and common size and shape (circular in two-dimensions), irrespective of molecular formula.

Intra-molecular Selection and External Force Selection. More complicated forms, where molecular velocities are not constant, can be generated by the introduction of some combination of intra-molecular forces (such as electromagnetism) or external forces (such as gravity or heat.)

4.2   Determining the Products of a Reaction

For each reaction we can generate a number of alternative product sets [22,2] by enumerating all possible single bond additions, bond subtractions, and changes in bond type between the reactants (more complicated alternatives can be generated by combining these single bond changes).

How should we choose between alternative sets of possible products for the same reactants? Various product strategies appear plausible: the random choice of an alternative; the most complex alternative; least complex; rarest; most common, and so on, but each strategy requires effort to develop and evaluate. We have chosen to focus in this work on a strategy which supports an argument by analogy, where there is a reasonable parallel between the strategy and real-world chemistry: the strategy of Least Energy.

When following a Least Energy strategy ($S_{\text{Product}} = \text{LeastEnergy}$) we select a reaction by choosing with uniform probability from a distribution of reaction alternatives weighted by the total of the energy changes associated with the bond changes. This biases selection towards the Least Energy alternative; the strength of the bias is determined by the degree of the weighting.

As an experimental control, we also evaluate a strategy with minimal bias: a Uniform selection strategy ($S_{\text{Product}} = \text{Uniform}$), where every alternative product set has equal probability of selection.

5   Evaluation

Following on from the research questions, our two primary factors, or independent variables, are S_{Reactant} and S_{Product}. We also introduce two secondary factors, overall reaction vessel energy (E_{Vessel}) and bond energy (E_{Bonds}), to assess the sensitivity of the simulation to other parameters. For simplicity of analysis, all of our factors are two-level, meaning they take one of two possible levels, or values, in each run. The parameter values chosen for each level of E_{Vessel} and E_{Bonds} were chosen as representative from a set of alternatives used in initial exploratory experiments; in each case they allowed the simulation to run for an extended period without running out of possible reactions (from lack of energy for example.)

Table 1. Factors, or independent variables

Factor	+1 value	-1 value	Description
$S_{Reactant}$	Kinetic	Uniform	See Section 4.1
$S_{Product}$	LeastEnergy	Uniform	See Section 4.2
E_{Vessel}	300	100	Initial kinetic energy of each molecule in the reaction vessel
E_{Bonds}	Single=50, Double=100, Triple=200	Simplified real-world chemistry. Average values for Single=77.7, Double=148.2, and Triple=224.3	Energy required to break a bond of the given type

We concentrate on three related response, or dependent, variables—Number of cycles, Length of longest cycle, and Count of most common cycle. All three are derived from a reconstruction of the network of reactions that occur during each experiment run, where every edge represents a specific reaction connecting a particular set of reactants with a particular set of products. Note that the nodes in the constructed network capture specific molecules, rather than molecular types or species that share the same chemical formula (as would be more usual in the construction of a Reaction Network for real-world chemistry.)

We exclude all unique cycles, and all cycles with three or fewer elements (for example, where a molecule loses, then regains, an atom repeatedly). Unique cycles by nature are unlikely to be representative; very short cycles on the other hand are so common as to dominate other more interesting cycles in any analysis.

5.1 Experiment Design

The experiments follow a full factorial design over four factors ($S_{Reactant}$, $S_{Product}$, E_{Vessel} and E_{Bonds}), each at two levels, run in a randomized order, with three (3) replicates of each combination of factors executed in sequence before beginning the next combination. The first replicate of each combination starts with a predefined random seed incremented by one for each successive replicate of the same combination. The factor levels used are given in Table 1.

Each replicate used the same initial population of 800 molecules, made up of 100 molecules each of [H][H], O=O, [O-][N+](=O)[N+]([O-])=O, and N(=O)[O] and 200 molecules each of O and O=C=O (all represented in SMILES [4].) This initial population is somewhat arbitrary, although reasonable; given that Toy-World is a strongly constructive chemistry, we would expect that any differences between initial populations would reduce as the simulation proceeds.

For details of the Artificial Chemistry, see [22]. The chemistry makes use of some low-level components from RDKit [13], open-source software for chem-informatics. RDKit provides a number of useful capabilities, including format conversions to and from SMILES and graphical forms of molecules; standard sanity checks for molecular structure, and molecular manipulations. In Toy-World, atoms are closely based on real-world chemistry atoms, and in fact are implemented as wrappers around the Atom definitions provided by RDKit; we allow any atom type provided by RDKit. Bonds in ToyWorld are represented by RDKit bonds, but the addition or subtraction mechanism makes use of the parameterised ToyWorld energy model.

6   Results

All replicates completed a set of 20,000 reactions; given the initial population size of 800 molecules, and from the summary of results below, we believe that this captures a representative set of reactions. This also simplifies the analysis as we can assume a balanced set of treatments in the statistical sense (that is, the sample sizes for all treatments are equal).

Table 2. Summary of results over 2^4 runs of 3 replicates

Statistic	Number of cycles	Length of longest.cycle	Count of most common cycle
Reactions 4750 to 5000			
Min.	0.00	0.00	0.00
1st Quartile	0.00	0.00	0.00
Median	1.50	3.50	2.50
Mean	219.06	5.04	215.80
3rd Quartile	91.25	7.75	96.00
Max.	5704.00	20.00	2728.00
Reactions 9750 to 10000			
Min.	0.00	0.00	0.00
1st Quartile	0.00	0.00	0.00
Median	6.00	4.00	6.00
Mean	62.10	4.65	169.21
3rd Quartile	68.75	8.25	27.75
Max.	526.00	13.00	6684.00
Reactions 14750 to 15000			
Min.	0.00	0.00	0.00
1st Quartile	1.00	3.00	2.00
Median	5.00	4.50	5.00
Mean	27.17	4.79	42.27
3rd Quartile	34.50	7.00	16.25
Max.	237.00	12.00	862.00
Reactions 19750 to 20000			
Min.	0.00	0.00	0.00
1st Quartile	0.00	0.00	0.00
Median	3.50	4.00	4.00
Mean	20.04	3.90	14.62
3rd Quartile	20.25	6.00	13.25
Max.	199.00	12.00	216.00

A view of the results is given in Table 2: reaction networks built from the full dataset of 20,000 reactions can be too large for easy analysis. Instead, we choose to partition the reaction data into four equally spaced blocks of 250 reactions each and analyse each block independently.

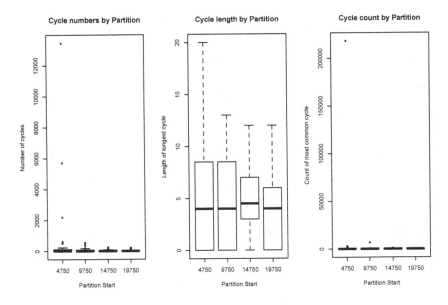

Fig. 1. Cycles by reaction partition (starting reaction number for each partition along x-axis)

7   Analysis and Discussion

Figure 1 suggests that the first partition, representing the vessel a quarter of the way into its lifespan, is quantitatively different from the other three partitions, with a significantly greater range for all three response variables. Intuitively this corresponds with an initial period where the diversity in the reaction vessel rapidly increases from the limited starting set of molecules, as seen in some (e.g, Figure 2) but not necessarily all of the replicates. Diversity here is measured by (average molecular quantity)$^{-1}$. All following sections therefore exclude data from the first partition of reaction numbers from 4750 to 5000.

7.1   RQ1: Is There a Quantitative Difference between the Different Reactant and Product Selection Strategies?

From visual inspection of Figure 3, there appears to be a significant difference between the Uniform and Kinetic reactant selection strategies for number and length of cycles. Kinetic reactant selection seems to result in significantly higher levels of emergent behaviour than Uniform reactant selection. Similarly, from Figure 4, there is very little apparent difference between the two product strategies, Uniform selection and Least Energy selection.

We use ANOVA (Analysis of Variance) to further examine the relationship of S_{Reactant} and S_{Product} to the response variables using a two-factor with two-levels (2x2) model (degrees of freedom=1) with interaction effects. There is a

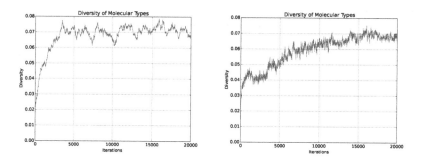

Fig. 2. Diversity for two example replicates (12-0 and 16-1)

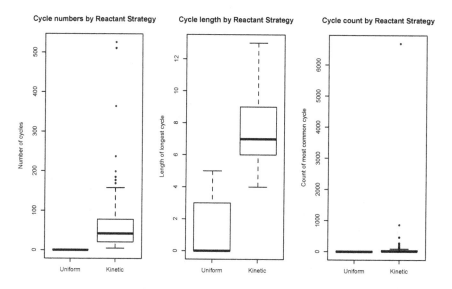

Fig. 3. Response by S_{Reactant}

highly significant difference (p<0.001) between the Uniform and Kinetic reactant selection strategies when comparing the number of cycles (f-value=40.442) and length of cycles (f-value=361.891) (confirming the impression given by Figure 3), although again without difference for the count of the most common cycle. The effect of S_{Product} on cycle number and length is also significant (f-value=4.050 and 5.705 respectively, p<0.05) and there is a first-order interaction between S_{Reactant} and S_{Product} for number of cycles (f-value=4.011, p<0.05).

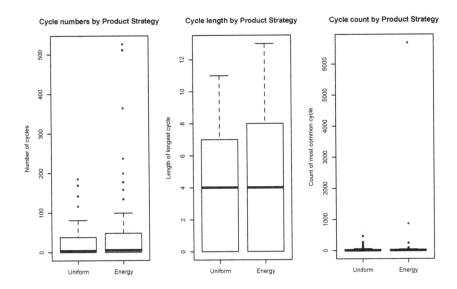

Fig. 4. Response by S_{Product}

7.2   RQ2: Is There a Combination of Reactant and Product Selection Strategies That Leads to Increased Emergence as Measured by Cycles?

From Figure 5c it is clear that there is no significant relationship between strategy and the number of occurrence of the most common cycle. However, from Figures 5a and 5b it seems that such a relationship does exist for the number and length of cycles, with the strongest effect as a result of S_{Reactant}, and a lesser effect from the choice of S_{Product}.

We conclude that the greatest levels of emergence are likely to be seen with the combination of $S_{\text{Reactant}} = \text{Kinetic}$ and $S_{\text{Product}} = \text{LeastEnergy}$.

7.3   RQ3: Is Emergence Significantly Affected by the Values of Other Parameters of an Artificial Chemistry, Such as Initial Kinetic Energy or Bond Energies?

We constructed a two-factor with two-levels (2x2) ANOVA model (degrees of freedom=1) with interaction effects to examine the relationship of the independent variables E_{Vessel} and E_{Bonds} to the response variables, and applied it to our dataset (summarised in Table 2). E_{Bonds} is significant (f-value=4.221, p<0.05) to number of cycles. No other significant relationships exist.

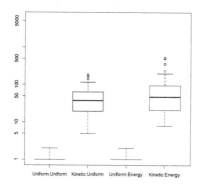
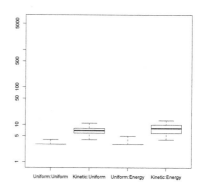

(a) Cycle Count by Strategy Combination (S_{Reactant}:S_{Product})

(b) Cycle Length by Strategy Combination (S_{Reactant}:S_{Product})

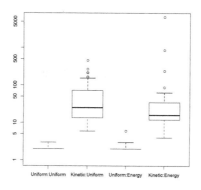

(c) Count of Most Common Cycle by Strategy Combination (S_{Reactant}:S_{Product})

Fig. 5. Effect of the combination of S_{Reactant} and S_{Product} on Response Variables

8   Conclusions

The choice of S_{Reactant} is critical to the behaviour of an emergent Artificial Chemistry; S_{Product} on the other hand appears to have a lesser effect on the emergence of cycles in our experiments. Furthermore, $S_{\text{Reactant}} = $ Kinetic is more effective for cycle emergence than $S_{\text{Reactant}} = $ Uniform.

The most significant limitation of our analysis overall is that the values chosen for the high and low values of E_{Bonds} make it impossible to determine the cause of the difference observed in RQ3. There are two alternative explanations: first, the energy required to make or break bonds is simply different between the two factor levels; second, in the low factor level, based on real-world values, the bond make and break energies for even a single bond vary depending on the atoms involved, while in the high factor level these values are consistent for all bonds of the same degree. To distinguish between the two explanations we would need at least the average levels at each degree to be the same for each factor; this is a suggestion for a future experiment.

In future work we intend to examine the sensitivity of the results to parameter selection, and to extend the ToyWorld Reaction Vessel to include the option of intra-molecular forces such as are seen in real-world chemistry between charged regions on adjacent molecules. These forces give rise to accelerations, which would allow us to continue the Reactant selection strategy series that extends from uniform selection (no physics) through location then velocity and finally to acceleration.

References

1. Benkö, G., Flamm, C., Stadler, P.F.: A graph-based toy model of chemistry. Journal of Chemical Information and Computer Sciences 43(4), 1085–1093 (2003), http://pubs.acs.org/doi/abs/10.1021/ci0200570, PMID: 12870897
2. Benkö, G., Flamm, C., Stadler, P.F.: The toychem package: A computational toolkit implementing a realistic artificial chemistry model (2005), http://www.tbi.univie.ac.at/~xtof/ToyChem/
3. Channon, A.: Unbounded evolutionary dynamics in a system of agents that actively process and transform their environment. Genetic Programming and Evolvable Machines 7(3), 253–281 (2006), doi:10.1007/s10710-006-9009-3
4. Daylight Chemical Information Systems, Inc. Daylight theory manual (2011), http://www.daylight.com/dayhtml/doc/theory/index.html
5. Dorin, A., Korb, K.B.: Building virtual ecosystems from artificial chemistry. In: Almeida e Costa, F., Rocha, L.M., Costa, E., Harvey, I., Coutinho, A. (eds.) ECAL 2007. LNCS (LNAI), vol. 4648, pp. 103–112. Springer, Heidelberg (2007)
6. Faulconbridge, A.: RBN-World: sub-symbolic artificial chemistry for artificial life. Ph.D. thesis, University of York (2011)
7. Flamm, C., Ullrich, A., Ekker, H., Mann, M., Hogerl, D., Rohrschneider, M., Sauer, S., Scheuermann, G., Klemm, K., Hofacker, I., Stadler, P.: Evolution of metabolic networks: a computational frame-work. Journal of Systems Chemistry 1(1), 4 (2010), http://www.jsystchem.com/content/1/1/4
8. Fontana, W., Wagner, G.P., Buss, L.W.: Beyond digital naturalism. Artificial Life 1(2), 211–227 (1994)
9. Hickinbotham, S., Clark, E., Stepney, S., Clarke, T., Nellis, A., Pay, M., Young, P.: Molecular microprograms. In: Kampis, G., Karsai, I., Szathmáry, E. (eds.) ECAL 2009, Part I. LNCS, vol. 5777, pp. 297–304. Springer, Heidelberg (2011), http://dx.doi.org/10.1007/978-3-642-21283-3_37
10. Högerl, D.: Simulation of prebiotic chemistries. Master's thesis, Institute for Theoretical Chemistry, University of Vienna (2010)
11. Hutton, T.J.: Evolvable self-replicating molecules in an artificial chemistry. Artificial Life 8(4), 341–356 (2002), http://www.sq3.org.uk/Evolution/Squirm3/EvSelfReps/
12. Hutton, T.J.: The organic builder: A public experiment in artificial chemistries and self-replication. Artificial Life 15(1), 21–28 (2009), http://dx.doi.org/10.1162/artl.2009.15.1.15102 (October 9, 2012)

13. Landrum, G.: Rdkit: Open-source cheminformatics (2013), `http://www.rdkit.org`
14. Lucht, M.W.: Size selection and adaptive evolution in an artificial chemistry. Artificial Life 18(2), 143–163 (2012)
15. Madina, D., Ono, N., Ikegami, T.: Cellular evolution in a 3D lattice artificial chemistry. In: Banzhaf, W., Ziegler, J., Christaller, T., Dittrich, P., Kim, J.T. (eds.) ECAL 2003. LNCS (LNAI), vol. 2801, pp. 59–68. Springer, Heidelberg (2003)
16. Maley, C.: Four steps toward open-ended evolution. In: GECCO-99: Proceedings of the Genetic and Evolutionary Computation Conference, pp. 1336–1343. Morgan Kaufmann (1999)
17. Ono, N., Ikegami, T.: Self-maintenance and self-reproduction in an abstract cell model. Journal of Theoretical Biology 206(2), 243–253 (2000), `http://www.sciencedirect.com/science/article/pii/S0022519300921210`
18. Steel, M., Hordijk, W., Smith, J.: Minimal autocatalytic networks. Journal of Theoretical Biology 332(0), 96–107 (2013), `http://www.sciencedirect.com/science/article/pii/S0022519313002002`
19. Suzuki, K., Ikegami, T.: Shapes and self-movement in protocell systems. Artificial Life 15(1), 59–70 (2008), `http://dx.doi.org/10.1162/artl.2009.15.1.15104` (October 9, 2012)
20. Ullrich, A., Flamm, C., Rohrschneider, M., Stadler, P.F.: In silico evolution of early metabolism. In: Fellermann, H., Dorr, M., Hanczyc, M., Laursen, L.L., Maurer, S., Merkle, D., Monnard, P.A., Sta, Y.K., Rasmussen, S. (eds.) Proceedings of the Twelfth International Conference on the Synthesis and Simulation of Living Systems (Artificial Life XII), The MIT Press, Cambridge (2010)
21. Varela, F.G., Maturana, H.R., Uribe, R.: Autopoiesis: The organization of living systems, its characterization and a model. Biosystems 5(4), 187–196 (1974)
22. Young, T.J., Neshatian, K.: A constructive artificial chemistry to explore open-ended evolution. In: Cranefield, S., Nayak, A. (eds.) AI 2013. LNCS, vol. 8272, pp. 228–233. Springer, Heidelberg (2013)

Use of a High-Value Social Audience Index for Target Audience Identification on Twitter

Siaw Ling Lo, David Cornforth, and Raymond Chiong

School of Design, Communication and Information Technology
Faculty of Science and Information Technology
The University of Newcastle, Callaghan, NSW 2308, Australia
siawling.lo@uon.edu.au,
{david.cornforth,raymond.chiong}@newcastle.edu.au

Abstract. With the large and growing user base of social media, it is not an easy feat to identify potential customers for business. This is mainly due to the challenge of extracting commercially viable contents from the vast amount of free-form conversations. In this paper, we analyse the Twitter content of an account owner and its list of followers through various text mining methods and segment the list of followers via an index. We have termed this index as the High-Value Social Audience (HVSA) index. This HVSA index enables a company or organisation to devise their marketing and engagement plan according to available resources, so that a high-value social audience can potentially be transformed to customers, and hence improve the return on investment.

Keywords: Twitter, topic modelling, machine learning, audience segmentation.

1 Introduction

Twitter and Facebook are no longer a fad but a gold mine for any business to reach out to potential customers, since both platforms have a huge active user base of over 1.28 billion [1]. More companies are putting emphasis upon, or have started, their social media marketing strategy plan in hopes of standing out from the increasingly crowded social space and attracting prospective customers from the audience. A recent study [2] found that nearly 80% of consumers would more likely be interested in a company due to its brand's presence on social media. It is therefore not surprising that 77% of the Fortune 500 companies have active Twitter accounts and 70% of them maintain an active Facebook account to engage with their potential customers [3].

While a company can rely on incentive referrals to boost its fans' or followers' count, this approach may only provide short-term gain. Furthermore, values from the fans' count and number of retweets are not able to directly provide any actionable insights in customer engagement, although they can be used as one of the measurements in a social media campaign. With the growing "sophistication" of social media users, it can be rewarding for any company if personalised services and quality contents can be offered directly to the fans or followers. Mass marketing can no longer be

S.K. Chalup et al. (Eds.): ACALCI 2015, LNAI 8955, pp. 323–336, 2015.
© Springer International Publishing Switzerland 2015

justified by the effort and amount of money spent. Moreover, there is a thin line between broadcasting a general message and spamming, so instead of attracting a greater audience, there is a high risk of losing current customers. Hence, it makes sense to identify a target audience in order to maximise marketing efficiency and improve the return on investment.

Every profit-oriented business would aim to increase profit, build a long lasting brand name, grow its customer base and further engage its current customers. It is therefore essential to understand the needs and behaviours of customers. This understanding can be achieved through different means and at different levels of detail. Most companies define segmentation of their customers according to their traits or behaviours. All other marketing efforts, such as customer engagement activities, are targeted and measured according to the segmentation.

However, this segmentation is typically restricted to customer relationship management (CRM) or transaction data obtained either through customer surveys or tracking of product purchases, to understand the customer demand. Demographic variables, RFM (recency, frequency, monetary) and LTV (lifetime value) are the most common input variables used in the literature for customer segmentation and clustering [4, 5]. With the rise of social media, there is an emerging model of CRM called "social CRM" [6], which addresses the effect of social media on CRM and its pitfalls. Recent work in this area focuses on a framework of the social CRM model [7], where one of the challenges is violation of customer privacy due to the linking of disparate sources of data. In view of this, it is of interest to analyse alternative approaches (such as using the content shared on social media) in order to determine whether these approaches can be used to complement the traditional CRM in identifying a target or high-value social audience for a company or a product.

There have been efforts in deriving or estimating demographics information [8, 9] from the available social media data, but it may not be feasible to use this set of information directly in targeted marketing, as temporal effects and types of products to be targeted are usually not considered. Besides that, demographic attributes such as age, gender and residence areas on social media platforms may not be updated and hence may result in a misled conclusion. Recently, eBay has expressed that, due to viral campaigns and major social media activities, marketing and advertising strategies are evolving. Targeting specific demographics through segmentation, although still has its value, is being replaced by new strategies. For example, eBay is focusing on "connecting people with the things they need and love, whoever they are" [10]. Other research on predicting purchase behaviour from social media has shown that Facebook categories such as likes, and text analysis methods such as n-grams, significantly outperform demographic features shared on Facebook [11]. Due to the privacy policy of Facebook profiles, our work focuses on Twitter, where most of the contents and activities shared online are open and available.

Considering the vast amount of available social media data, it is not practical to annotate tweets manually to construct a training data for an analysis method. Consequently, the contents from a Twitter account owner are used to extract a list of seed words as the positive training data for the various text mining methods considered in this paper, which include keyword matching through Fuzzy Keyword Match, statistical topic modelling through Latent Dirichlet Allocation (LDA) [12], and machine learning through the Support Vector Machine (SVM) [13]. The scores derived from each of the methods are analysed and combined for the construction of a High-Value Social Audience (HVSA) index, which can subsequently be used in segmenting the list of followers of the account owner for targeted engagement and marketing.

The major contributions of this work can be summarised as follows:

- To the best of our knowledge, our work in this paper is the first attempt to define an index capable of identifying a high-value social audience for segmenting the list of followers of a Twitter account owner.
- From the result observation, the content shared by the account owner can be used for customer segmentation as it contains information that is relevant to identify the target audience.

2   Methods

The focus of this research was to establish an index that can be used to segment the social audience (or the list of followers) of a Twitter account owner using the content shared by the account owner. The architecture of our system is given in Fig. 1.

Tweets from various parties - owners, followers, and owners from other domains - were cleaned and pre-processed before preparing for seed words generation and SVM training and testing datasets. The owner's tweets were used as the positive training data while tweets of owners from other domains were extracted as the negative training data. 10-fold cross validation was applied on both the positive and negative training data for the SVM model before the classification of followers' tweets (or the testing data) was conducted. The seed words generated were used by both Fuzzy Keyword Match and Twitter LDA. A string similarity score derived from Dice coefficient was calculated through a fuzzy comparison with the seed words on the testing data. A list of topics was learned from testing data using Twitter LDA and followers with relevant topic numbers were identified. Details of each component are described in the following sections.

2.1   Data Collection

We have used the Twitter Search API [14] for data collection. As the API is constantly evolving with different rate limiting settings, our data gathering has been done through a scheduled program that requests a set of data for a given query. For this particular research, we selected Samsung Singapore or "samsungsg" (its Twitter username) as the subject or brand. At the time of this work, there were 3,727 samsungsg followers. In order to analyse the contents or tweets of the account owner, the last 200 tweets by samsungsg were extracted. The time of tweets was from 2 Nov 2012 to 3 Apr 2013. For each of the followers, the API was used to extract their tweets, giving a total of 187,746 records.

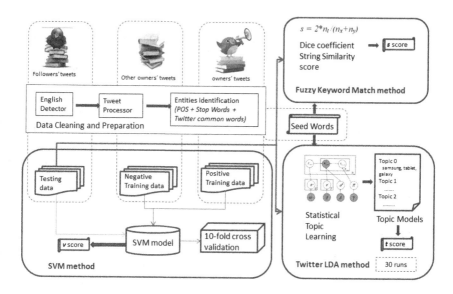

Fig. 1. The system architecture

2.2   Data Cleaning and Preparation

Tweets are known to be noisy and often mixed with linguistic variations. It is hence very important to clean up the tweet content prior to any content extraction:

- Non-English tweets were removed using the Language Detection Library for Java [15];
- URLs, any Twitter's username found in the content (which is in the format of @username) and hashtags (with the # symbol) were removed;
- Each tweet was pre-processed to lower case.

As tweets are usually informal and short (up to 140 characters), abbreviations and misspellings are often part of the content and hence the readily available Named Entity Recognition (NER) package may not be able to extract relevant entities properly. As such, we derived an approach called Entities Identification, which uses Part-of-Speech (POS) [16] tags to differentiate the type of words. In this approach, all the single nouns are identified as possible entities. If the tag of the first fragment detected is 'N' (noun) or 'J' (adjective) and the consecutive word(s) is of the 'N' type, these words will be extracted as phrases. This approach was then complemented by another process using the comprehensive stop words list used by search engines (http://www.webconfs.com/stop-words.php) in addition to a list of English's common words (preposition, conjunction, determiners) as well as Twitter's common words (such as "rt", "retweet" etc.) to identify any possible entity. In short, the original tweet was sliced into various fragments by using POS tags, stop words, common words and punctuations as separators or delimiters. For example, if the content is "Samsung is holding a galaxy contest!", two fragments will be generated for the content as follows: (samsung) | (galaxy contest).

2.3   Seed Words Generation

All the tweets extracted from samsungsg were subjected to data cleaning and preparation mentioned in the previous section. The process enables each tweet to be represented by the identified fragments or words and phrases. This set of data was further processed using term frequency analysis to obtain a list of seed words (which include "samsung", "galaxy s iii", "galaxy camera" etc.). The words in a phrase were joined by '_' so that they could be identified as a single term but the '_' was later filtered in all the matching processes.

These seed words were used to generate results for Fuzzy Keyword Match (see Section 2.4) and identify suitable topic numbers in the Twitter LDA method (see Section 2.5).

2.4   Fuzzy Keyword Match

It is not uncommon for Twitter users to use abbreviations or interjections or a different form of expression to represent similar terms. For example, "galaxy s iii" can be represented by "galaxy s 3", which is understandable by a human but cannot be captured through a direct keyword match method. As such, a Fuzzy Keyword Match method using the seed words derived was implemented in this study.

The comparison here is based on a Dice coefficient string similarity score [17] using the following expression:

$$s = 2*n_t/(n_x+n_y) \qquad (1)$$

where n_t is the number of characters found in both strings, n_x is the number of characters in string x and n_y is the number of characters in string y. For example, consider the calculation of similarity between "process" and "proceed":

x = process	bigrams for x = {pr ro oc ce es ss}
y = proceed	bigrams for y = {pr ro oc ce ee ed}

Both x and y have 6 bigrams each, of which 4 of them are the same. Hence, the Dice coefficient string similarity score is 2*4/(6+6) = 0.67. Each of the tweets of every follower is compared with the seed words and the highest score of any match is maintained as the s score of the follower.

2.5   Twitter LDA

Recently, LDA [12], a renowned generative probabilistic model for topic discovery, has been used in various social media studies [18][19]. LDA uses an iterative process to build and refine a probabilistic model of documents, each containing a mixture of topics. However, standard LDA may not work well with Twitter as tweets are typically very short. If one aggregates all the tweets of a follower to increase the size of the documents, this may diminish the fact that each tweet is usually about a single topic. As such, we have adopted the implementation of Twitter LDA [18] for unsupervised topic discovery among all the followers.

As the volume of the tweets from all the followers in this study was within 200,000, a small number of topics (from 10-30, with an interval of 10) from Twitter LDA were used. We ran these topic models for 100 iterations of Gibbs sampling while keeping the other model parameters or Dirichlet priors constant: $\alpha = 0.5$, $\beta_{word} = 0.01$, $\beta_{background} = 0.01$ and $\gamma = 20$. Suitable topics were chosen automatically via comparison with the list of seed words. The result or the audience list identified by each topic model was a consolidation of 30 runs. The score assigned to each follower can be calculated using the following equation:

$$t = n_m/n_r \tag{2}$$

where n_m is the total number of matches and n_r is the total number of runs. If a particular follower is found in five runs then the t score assigned is $5/30 = 0.17$.

2.6   The SVM

The SVM is a supervised learning approach for two- or multi-class classification, and has been used successfully in text categorisation [13]. It separates a given known set of $\{+1, -1\}$ labelled training data via a hyperplane that is maximally distant from the positive and negative samples respectively. This optimally separating hyperplane in the feature space corresponds to a nonlinear decision boundary in the input space. More details of the SVM can be found in [20].

In this work, the positive training data was generated using processed tweets from samsungsg, the selected account owner. The negative data was randomly generated from account owners of 10 different domains (online shopping deals, food, celebrities, parents, education, music, shopping, politics, Singapore news, traffic), which include ilovedealssg, hungrygowhere, joannepeh, kiasuparents, MOEsg, mtvasia, tiongbahruplaza, tocsg (TheOnlineCitizen), SGnews and sgdrivers respectively. These domains were chosen as they were the main topics discovered using Twitter LDA from the tweets of the followers of samsungsg. The respective account owners were selected as they were the popular Twitter accounts in Singapore according to online Twitter analytic tools such as wefollow.com.

The LibSVM implementation of RapidMiner [21] was used in this study and the sigmoid kernel type was selected as it produces higher precision prediction than other kernels, such as the radial basis function and polynomial.

A v score was assigned for each follower according to individual tweet classification based on the SVM. The v score can be generated using the following equation:

$$v = n_p/n_a \tag{3}$$

where n_p is the total number of tweets that are classified as positive and n_a is the total number of tweets shared by a follower. If a follower has tweeted two related tweets out of a total of 10 tweets, the v score assigned will be 0.2.

2.7   Construction of the HVSA Index

While it is possible to use the s, t and v scores individually as an index for segmenting and identifying a high-value social audience member, each method has its own strengths and limitations. It is therefore of interest to analyse if the combination of the various scores can generalise the identification task and help to improve the classification result.

An average value of scores from five methods, namely Fuzzy Keyword Match, Twitter LDA with 10, 20 and 30 topic models, and the SVM, was used in this study to generate the combined score. As there were three Twitter LDA methods considered, an analysis was done to assess if it would be feasible to use just one of the Twitter LDA methods in developing a representative HVSA index.

The threshold used for the HVSA index was based on the ranking of the scores generated. For example, the HVSA index at top 100 represents the average score value of the top 100 scorers according to the methods of scoring. This top scorer segmentation approach has been adopted as it resembles a real world scenario where a company will more likely be interested in identifying the top n potential customers in an attempt to maximise the use of their marketing resources.

3   Experiments and Results

The results obtained from the various methods were compared with a random annotated sample of the followers of samsungsg. The contents of a total of 300 followers (which were randomly sampled) were annotated manually as either a potential high-value social audience according to the content shared by the account owner or not a target audience. This set of data was used in the evaluation of the various methods and detailed analyses can be found in Sections 3.1, 3.2 and 3.3.

3.1   Results of Various Methods

To compare the various methods, Receiver Operating Characteristic (ROC) curves, as shown in Fig. 2, were plotted for all the results using the various scores derived (Fuzzy Keyword Match uses the s score, Twitter LDA methods use the t score, and the SVM uses the v score). It is observed that Fuzzy Keyword Match has obtained the largest area under the curve (AUC), followed by the Twitter LDA topic modelling methods and the SVM.

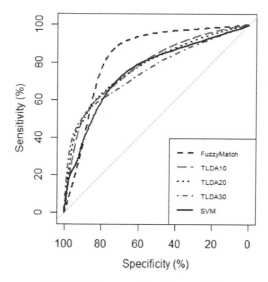

Fig. 2. ROC curves of various methods

The corresponding AUC value can be found in Table 1. It is interesting to note that the Twitter LDA methods have generated similar AUC values irrespective of the number of topics used. It is therefore worth analysing whether it is possible to use just one of the Twitter LDA methods to represent the HVSA index instead of all three methods.

Table 1. AUC for various methods

Methods	AUC
Fuzzy Keyword Match	0.88
Twitter LDA 10 topics	0.81
Twitter LDA 20 topics	0.81
Twitter LDA 30 topics	0.78
SVM	0.80

3.1.1   Results of Twitter LDA

As shown in Fig. 2 and Table 1, the various Twitter LDA methods have achieved similar trends and results. A further analysis was done and the group of audience members identified with topic numbers greater than 30 remained the same. Hence, only the results of topic models from 10, 20 and 30 are included in this paper.

Table 2 presents some sample topic groups and their topical words. The table shows that using seed words derived from the account owner can identify relevant contents from the list of followers.

Table 2. Sample topic groups and their topical words (ID is the topic group id)

Models	IDs	Top topical words
Twitter LDA 10 topics	3	google, android, apps, mobile, galaxy, tablet
	4	samsung, galaxy, mobile, phone, android, tv, camera, smartphone
Twitter LDA 20 topics	8	galaxy, samsung, android, phone, mobile, apps, smartphone
	17	samsung, galaxy, app, tablet
	19	samsung, tv, led, mobile, smart, phone, laptop
Twitter LDA 30 topics	3	samsung, galaxy
	18	samsung, galaxy, android, google, app, phone, mobile, tablet, smartphone
	25	samsung, tv, led, camera, lcd, smart, hd

3.1.2   Results of the SVM

The 10-fold cross validation of the training data yields an accuracy of 88%, with class precision and recall as presented in Table 3. However, when we applied the model on the testing data of the followers' tweets, the denominator (or the normalisation process) used in Eq. (3) plays an important role as further investigation has shown that using an average value of all the tweets only yields an AUC value of 0.66 [22] instead of 0.80 (as shown in Table 1). In this study, the total number of tweets was used to normalise the score instead of an average value of all the tweets due to the fact that the resulted score is more capable in representing the true interest of a follower. For example, if follower1 has tweeted two related tweets out of a total of 10 tweets, the e score assigned will be 0.2. While the e score for follower2 is 0.02 if only two related tweets are classified as positive out of a total of 100 tweets. This is in contrast to using an average value, as both follower1 and follower2 will be assigned the same e score, which may not fully represent the interests of the followers.

Table 3. SVM 10-fold cross validation results

	True samsungsg	True others	Class precision
Predicted samsungsg	165	13	92.7%
Predicted others	35	187	84.2%
Class recall	82.5%	93.5%	

3.2   Analysis of HVSA Index Construction

As mentioned in Section 2.7, the construction of the HVSA index was based on the ranking of average scores generated from various methods. In other words, the segmentation was done such that the top 100 threshold represents the top 100 scorers. The percentage of match with the annotated data together with the s, t and v scores under different segmentations can be found in Table 4. As expected, the s score has a better coverage and hits 92% at the top 1000 threshold. However, it is worthwhile to note that it has not performed as well as the Twitter LDA methods at the top 250 mark.

In general, all three Twitter LDA methods have the similar trend but Twitter LDA with 20 topic models is able to cover all 100% of the annotated dataset at the top 2000 threshold. The SVM (i.e., the v score) does not cover the percentage match as well as the others but as it is a machine learning approach, it has the potential to be better with more training data. Furthermore, it is possible that the SVM is more selective as it is not directly using any keyword matching approach. Besides that, the t scores from the Twitter LDA methods are generally more evenly distributed while the s score of Fuzzy Keyword Match has a higher value and the v score of the SVM has a lower value as shown in Table 4.

Table 4. Comparison of the various scores and their percentage of match with the annotated data (where $t10$ score represents the t score from Twitter LDA 10 topics and $t20$ represents the t score from Twitter LDA 20 topics and so on)

Top	s score	% match	$t10$ score	% match	$t20$ score	% match	$t30$ score	% match	v score	% match
100	1.0	27%	1.0	33%	1.0	29%	0.97	24%	0.38	8%
250	1.0	27%	0.97	40%	0.97	32%	0.87	35%	0.25	22%
500	0.83	84%	0.8	54%	0.6	51%	0.53	52%	0.17	40%
750	0.83	84%	0.5	65%	0.33	67%	0.3	63%	0.13	60%
1000	0.75	92%	0.37	75%	0.2	79%	0.2	70%	0.11	70%
1500	0.6	98%	0.2	92%	0.1	87%	0.1	86%	0.07	87%
2000	0.57	100%	0.03	97%	0.03	100%	0.03	95%	0.01	90%

Table 5. Comparison of various HVSA index constructions

Top	Five-method average score	% match	Three-method average score	% match
100	0.82	16%	0.72	16%
250	0.75	35%	0.65	27%
500	0.56	54%	0.51	59%
750	0.39	67%	0.41	78%
1000	0.31	86%	0.36	86%
1500	0.23	95%	0.29	97%
2000	0.18	100%	0.23	100%

As the Twitter LDA 20 topics model has performed well, as shown in Table 4, it is used as a representative of the Twitter LDA methods for the HVSA index construction. In order to evaluate if it is sufficient to use the score from just one of the topic models (instead of all three), the average score from all the five methods considered in Table 4 and the average score from three of the methods, namely Fuzzy Keyword Match, Twitter LDA with 20 topic models and the SVM, are presented in Table 5. In general, the three-method average has a better coverage as compared to the five-method one even though it has a lower percentage match at the top 250 threshold.

3.3   Percentage of High-Value Social Audience Identified through Analysis of Top Scorers

By using the three-method average score (as shown in Table 5) as the HVSA index, each of the followers has a corresponding HVSA index calculated according to the average of the s, $t20$ and v scores. These indices were compared with the top scorer of the respective segmentations and followers with indices falling within the range will be considered as a match. The percentages of match based on the respective HVSA index for all followers of samsungsg as well as the annotated followers are listed in Table 6. Here, the HVSA index generated for top 100 is the value assigned to the top 100 scorers based on the index construction approach mentioned in Section 3.2. With a HVSA index of 0.36 or at the threshold of top 1000 scorers, 86% of the annotated followers are identified, which covers 28% of all the followers. All the annotated followers or the potential target audience actually have HVSA indices greater than 0.23, while this value covers half of all the followers. In short, by introducing the HVSA index, ranking of the followers and selection of the target audience can be done and potentially be more effective as compared to randomly selecting anyone from all the followers.

Table 6. Top scorers with the corresponding percentage for all the followers and the annotated followers

Top	HVSA Index	% within all the followers	% in the annotated followers
100	0.72	3%	16%
250	0.65	7%	27%
500	0.51	14%	59%
750	0.41	21%	78%
1000	0.36	28%	86%
1500	0.29	42%	97%
2000	0.23	56%	100%

4   Discussion

It is interesting to observe from the results that, the proposed HVSA index is able to identify the high-value social audience from the annotated random users. While the percentage of matches in the annotated data can be used as a guide to assess the potential usefulness of this HVSA index, it is also worthwhile to analyse the detailed contents of some of the followers whose scores from various methods are not in agreement. Some examples are listed in Table 7.

From the table, we can see that `follower1` has consistent high scores for four of the five methods (except the SVM). A closer look at the tweets shows that the follower shares mostly technology and mobile news with tweets like "RT @ZDNet: Samsung announces Galaxy S Wi-Fi 3.6" and "Google Chrome has 70 million Active Users". Having an HVSA index of 0.49 put the follower in the

Top 500 to Top 750 range making them likely to be considered a member of a high-value audience. In contrast, the v score of 0.06 derived from the SVM method alone does not reveal this.

Another scenario of inconsistency is when any two scores, for example, s and v scores (or the scores from Fuzzy Keyword Match and the SVM respectively), are high but the three Twitter LDA methods are not. `follower2` falls under this scenario but the HVSA index indicates that this follower is highly likely to be a target audience member. A detailed study on the contents shared by `follower2` indeed shows a tweet asking samsungsg about the Samsung galaxy S3 workshop.

Although Fuzzy Keyword Match has performed well, the method seems to have consistently higher scores than the other methods. This may lead to the identification of false positives due to the higher value assigned. In Table 7, `follower3` was scored badly by all the other methods except for Fuzzy Keyword Match (the s score has the value of 1.0). A detailed investigation on the user's tweets reveals that 98 tweets extracted were mostly about school studies and daily activities, even though there were also two tweets mentioning about the phone: "`My phone is useless now after updating my phone!!!`" and "`resetting my phone :( `". This follower was in fact a non-target audience member (as per the manual annotation). As such, it is worth combining the various scores in deriving a more suitable score or index for identifying the high-value social audience. The HVSA index for `follower3` is 0.3, which falls within the range of top 1000 to top 1500. In actual fact, as the threshold of top 1500 is 0.29, this follower is likely to be in the upper range and less likely to be identified as a target audience member as compared to having a single s score of perfect 1.0.

As discussed above, there is some benefit in using the HVSA index over individual scores, as each method has strengths and weaknesses. By combining the scores, a more general index could be derived, that would be more practical and useful in real-world applications.

While the above discussion is about the annotated target audience, we have also done some detailed study on the top scorers of the annotated non-target audience. A total of six followers having a HVSA index between 0.5 and 0.6 were identified. A close look at each of the followers shows that three of them are indeed target audience members who had shared similar contents as the account owner, samsungsg. These three followers are mainly technology and mobile news Twitter users while the other three are not directly related. One of the latter had shared mainly contents related to iPhone/iPad, while the other two mentioned Samsung in some of their tweets but the tweets were really about doing business and launching a complaint with Samsung.

Although a human annotator is preferred most of the time, it is a challenge to annotate tens of hundreds of tweets, and mistakes are inevitable. On the other hand, the HVSA index can be handy as a first cut to identify the high-value social audience from a huge list of followers without the need to manually annotate each of them. In order to increase accuracy, verification through a human can be applied on followers with inconsistent scores, which definitely aids in minimising the annotation effort. Engagement done through this approach is definitely better than selecting followers randomly or manually selecting them based on keywords.

Table 7. Interesting followers identified. The higher scores of each user are bolded. The *s* score is generated by Fuzzy Keyword Match, *t10* score is generated by Twitter LDA 10 topics, *t20* score is generated by Twitter LDA 20 topics, *t30* score is generated by Twitter LDA 30 topics and *v* score is generated by the SVM.

Twitter name	*s* score	*t10* score	*t20* score	*t30* score	*v* score	HVSA index
follower1	**0.83**	**0.97**	**1.0**	**0.8**	0.06	0.49
follower2	**1.0**	0.53	0.43	0.53	**0.33**	0.52
follower3	**1.0**	0.37	0.17	0.0	0.03	0.3

5   Conclusion and Future Work

In this study, we have constructed a High-Value Social Audience (or HVSA in short) index from various text mining methods to identify the high-value social audience from a list of followers using the contents of a Twitter account owner, samsungsg. It is assumed that those who have tweeted similar contents are more likely to be interested in the owner's tweets, compared to those who have not been sharing similar contents.

Our results show that the HVSA index is a better indicator than individual scores from the various methods, as the index is an aggregate of those scores and hence it is capable of combining all the findings and providing a more generalised outcome. It is more practical and possibly more useful for a real-world marketing application.

While currently the index is the average value of several methods, other index construction approaches considering the precision or recall values may be incorporated to derive a more robust indicator. It should be noted that the index is developed as a guide for customer segmentation in the application area of targeted marketing. This means any improvement over mass marketing is going to be beneficial for business companies.

We have used samsungsg as a case study in this paper. It has been shown that contents extracted from the account owner can be used to identify the target audience. For future work, we plan to extend it to include other account owners to verify if the observation is consistent across Twitter or if there is any pattern observed for different types of Twitter accounts. For example, a more generic account on parent groups or current affairs may have contents that are more diverse and conceptual and may not work well with keyword-based matching methods like Fuzzy Keyword Match. As such, a more sophisticated feature generation method based on domain-specific and common-sense knowledge may be required to enrich the bag of words with new, more informative features.

References

1. How Many People Use Facebook, Twitter and 415 of the Top Social Media, Apps & Tools (updated March 2014), http://expandedramblings.com/index.php/resource-how-many-people-use-the-top-social-media/#.Uz0f4Vc4t5E
2. Unlocking the Power of Social Media | IAB UK, http://www.iabuk.net/blog/unlocking-the-power-of-social-media
3. 2013 Fortune 500 - UMass Dartmouth, http://www.umassd.edu/cmr/socialmediaresearch/2013fortune500/

4. Mo, J., Kiang, M.Y., Zou, P., Li, Y.: A two-stage clustering approach for multi-region segmentation. Expert Systems with Applications 37, 7120–7131 (2010)
5. Namvar, M., Khakabimamaghani, S., Gholamian, M.R.: An approach to optimised customer segmentation and profiling using RFM, LTV, and demographic features. International Journal of Electronic Customer Relationship Management 5, 220–235 (2011)
6. Greenberg, P.: CRM at the Speed of Light: Social CRM 2.0 Strategies, Tools, and Techniques for Engaging Your Customers. McGraw-Hill Osborne Media (2009)
7. Malthouse, E.C., Haenlein, M., Skiera, B., Wege, E., Zhang, M.: Managing customer relationships in the social media era: introducing the social CRM house. Journal of Interactive Marketing 27, 270–280 (2013)
8. Mislove, A., Viswanath, B., Gummadi, K.P., Druschel, P.: You are who you know: inferring user profiles in online social networks. In: Proceedings of the Third ACM International Conference on Web Search and Data Mining, pp. 251–260. ACM (2010)
9. Kosinski, M., Stillwell, D., Graepel, T.: Private traits and attributes are predictable from digital records of human behavior. Proceedings of the National Academy of Sciences 110, 5802–5805 (2013)
10. How Ebay Uses Twitter, Smartphones and Tablets to Snap Up Shoppers, http://www.ibtimes.co.uk/how-ebay-uses-twitter-smartphones-tablets-snap-shoppers-1443441
11. Zhang, Y., Pennacchiotti, M.: Predicting purchase behaviors from social media. In: Proceedings of the 22nd International Conference on World Wide Web, pp. 1521–1532 (2013)
12. Blei, D.M., Ng, A.Y., Jordan, M.I.: Latent dirichlet allocation. Journal of Machine Learning Research 3, 993–1022 (2003)
13. Joachims, T.: Text Categorization with Support Vector Machines: Learning with Many Relevant Features. Springer (1998)
14. Using the Twitter Search API | Twitter Developers, https://dev.twitter.com/docs/using-search
15. Nakatani, S.: Language-detection - Language Detection Library for Java - Google Project Hosting, http://code.google.com/p/language-detection/
16. Toutanova, K., Manning, C.D.: Enriching the knowledge sources used in a maximum entropy part-of-speech tagger. In: Proceedings of the 2000 Joint SIGDAT Conference on Empirical Methods in Natural Language Processing and Very Large Corpora: held in conjunction with the 38th Annual Meeting of the Association for Computational Linguistics, vol. 13 (2000)
17. Kondrak, G., Marcu, D., Knight, K.: Cognates can improve statistical translation models. In: Proceedings of the 2003 Conference of the North American Chapter of the Association for Computational Linguistics on Human Language Technology: companion volume of the Proceedings of HLT-NAACL 2003–short papers, vol. 2 (2003)
18. Zhao, W.X., Jiang, J., Weng, J., He, J., Lim, E.-P., Yan, H., Li, X.: Comparing twitter and traditional media using topic models. Advances in Information Retrieval, pp. 338–349. Springer (2011)
19. Yang, M.-C., Rim, H.-C.: Identifying interesting Twitter contents using topical analysis. Expert Systems with Applications 41, 4330–4336 (2014)
20. Burges, C.J.: A tutorial on support vector machines for pattern recognition. Data Mining and Knowledge Discovery 2, 121–167 (1998)
21. Predictive Analytics, Data Mining, Self-service, Open source - RapidMiner, http://rapidminer.com/
22. Lo, S.L., Cornforth, D., Chiong, R.: Identifying the high-value social audience from Twitter through text-mining methods. In: Proceedings of the 18th Asia Pacific Symposium on Intelligent and Evolution Systems, vol. 1, pp. 325–339 (2014)

Detecting Anomalies in Controlled Drug Prescription Data Using Probabilistic Models

Xuelei Hu[1], Marcus Gallagher[1], William Loveday[2],
Jason P. Connor[3,4], and Janet Wiles[1]

[1] School of Information Technology and Electrical Engineering
The University of Queensland, Brisbane, Australia
{xuelei.hu,marcusg,j.wiles}@uq.edu.au
[2] Medicines Regulation and Quality Unit, Queensland Health, Brisbane, Australia
bill.loveday@health.qld.gov.au
[3] Discipline of Psychiatry, The University of Queensland, Brisbane, Australia
[4] Centre for Youth Substance Abuse Research
The University of Queensland, Brisbane, Australia
jason.connor@uq.edu.au

Abstract. Opioid analgesic drugs are widely used in pain management and substance dependence treatment. However, these drugs have high potential for misuse and subsequent harm. As a result, their prescribing is monitored and controlled. In Queensland, Australia, the Medicines Regulation and Quality Unit within the state health system maintains a database of prescribing events and uses this data to identify anomalies and provide subsequent support for patients and prescribers. In this study, we consider this task as an unsupervised anomaly detection problem. We use probability density estimation models to describe the distribution of the data over a number of key attributes and use the model to identify anomalies as points with low estimated probability. The results are validated against cases identified by healthcare domain experts. There was strong agreement between cases identified by the models and expert clinical assessment.

Keywords: anomaly detection, probabilistic model, controlled drug, prescription data.

1 Introduction

Opioid analgesic drugs play critical roles in pain management and substance dependence treatment. These drugs also have high potential for misuse and subsequent harm such as drug-related deaths, overdoses, dependence formation and the diversion of these drugs to illicit drug markets. In Australia, pharmaceutical drugs and medicines are regulated under the Therapeutic Goods Act, 1989 [10]. This Act is administered by the Therapeutic Goods Administration (TGA) that lists all medicines and poisons under The Schedule for the Uniform Scheduling of Medicines and Poisons (SUSMP) [11]. The SUSMP includes nine schedules that broadly equate with the abuse potential and therefore degree of accessibility of these substances. Schedule 8 (controlled, S8) includes drugs such as opioid analgesics and psycho-stimulants.

S.K. Chalup et al. (Eds.): ACALCI 2015, LNAI 8955, pp. 337–349, 2015.

In the USA, reports from the last 15-20 years have shown that the increasing prescription volume of Prescription Opioid Analgesic (POA) drugs is related to greater drug-related harm [12,21,23]. This includes growing numbers of persons being admitted for opioid dependence treatment and for overdose at emergency departments where S8 drugs are the principal drugs of concern. S8 drugs have also been more frequently found as significant contributors in cases of drug-related deaths [5,7,6,19,25,29]. In Australia, the licit and illicit use of S8 drugs is also increasing. For example, there has been a substantial increase in the utilisation of morphine based drugs (four-fold since 1991) and oxycodone (ten-fold since 2000) [13,37,3,22]. The use of S8 drugs is recognised as an emerging public health concern, presenting significant challenges to treatment providers and regulators [35,15,14,4,13]. S8 drugs are the front line treatment for many pain and addiction disorders and carry a strong evidence base when prescribed within treatment guideline [24,27]. The increasing prevalence of chronic pain and evidence from north America of growing POA use suggest there will be a growing role for the use of S8 drugs in management of these conditions [1]. Over-prescribing could inadvertently create risks of harm to some sections of the community [14,15]. National [34,36,14] and international [12,21,5,7,25,29,18,8,31,23,19] data supports a dramatic increase in harm caused by misuse of S8 drugs.

The inappropriate use of these drugs outside treatment guidelines is leading to greater costs to the publicly subsidised health system. Medicare Australia in 1996/97 identified more than 10,000 persons as doctor shoppers for any class of drug and nine percent of those drugs dispensed for doctor shoppers were for S8 drugs [20]. Medicare defined "doctor shoppers" as those people who saw 15 or more GPs in a year, had 30 or more Medicare consultations and appeared to obtain more PBS medications than were clinically necessary. This equated to 1,270 "doctor shoppers" for every 1,000 general practitioners [17]. It was estimated that this cost the community over $31 million per year in unwarranted consultations and subsidised prescriptions. Further socio-economic costs of persons developing drug dependence from POA have not been formally quantified but include deterioration of relationships and social networks, occupational roles, poverty and homelessness.

Internationally, both the USA and Canada have experienced some of the highest levels of pharmaceutical opioid prescribing and subsequent health related problems. This has led to both countries making significant advances in implementing jurisdiction based prescription monitoring programs. The Canadian province of British Columbia has the most advanced Prescription Monitoring Programs (PMPs): 'PharmaNet' that extends to prescribing doctors the ability to access full prescription records of patients. Recent evidence suggests this program has led to reduced prescription volumes of pharmaceutical opioids and resultant harms in comparison to other provinces where PMPs were not in use. In the USA, many States now possess some form of PMP. However, there is considerable inconsistency between states in regards to which agencies control these PMPs (law enforcement or health) and variation in how the information in these programs is applied in responding to suspected prescription problems [26]).

Under Queensland legislation [33] community pharmacies are required to submit records of dispensed S8 drugs prescriptions to Queensland Health on a monthly basis. Since 1996, the Medicines Regulation and Quality Unit (MRQ) within Queensland Health has maintained the Monitoring of Drugs of Dependence (MODDS) database to collate and store this information and conduct its regulatory compliance functions. MODDS is used by MRQ staff to try and identify potentially problematic prescribing behavior. A rule-based alert system is regularly applied. For example, when a patient seeks controlled drugs from more than 15 doctors within a 12-month period, the system will generate an alert to indicate possible doctor shopping. However, these rule-based alerts are typically based on single variable thresholds and often miss complex aberrant drug prescribing and consumption behavior. MRQ, together with many researchers recognise that research is needed to improve the use of routinely collected data from monitoring [32].

In this paper we describe collaborative research with the MRQ at Queensland Health, which has one of the most sophisticated procedures for routine data collection of S8 medications based on international standards. More specifically, we apply probability density estimation as a means of anomaly detection to S8 drug prescribing data. Anomaly detection is a problem with enormous practical applications and has been the subject of a large amount of research across machine learning, data mining and statistics (see, e.g. [9,30] for recent reviews). Several different classes of techniques have been developed for anomaly detection, each having their own advantages, disadvantages and underlying assumptions. In this paper, we chose to take a statistical approach, whereby a probability density estimator is fitted to the data and anomalies are then defined as points that have lowest probability under the model. The main advantages of this approach are:

- It is applicable for unsupervised data.
- The model produces a "score" function as its output for a given input, which allows the human domain expert to specify a threshold for deciding whether a point is an anomaly or not. Alternatively, the model can return, e.g. the 10 points in the dataset with the lowest probability.
- The assumptions of the model are relatively clear, particularly if parametric distributions are used.

Data mining and machine learning techniques have been applied to many different problems in the healthcare and biomedical domains. Within this domain, the nature of the data available varies considerably, which has led to the application of many different classification, prediction, clustering and other techniques [28,39]. However, anomaly detection in healthcare has received less attention. A notable exception is recent work on the detection of disease outbreaks [38].

Our approach makes several assumptions (see Section2). The model takes a simple "point" approach to anomaly detection, ignoring issues such as the contextual nature and meaning of an anomaly. We also do not take into consideration the temporal nature of the data (and therefore anomaly detection techniques developed for time-series datasets). Nevertheless, we believe that simplifying the model as much as possible (at least initially) is a sound approach that can yield valuable insight into a problem and is good for domain experts to validate and use.

In Section 2, we describe the properties of the data and the statistical models used. Section 3 presents analysis of the resulting models and their potential usage as a tool for domain experts. Section 4 concludes the paper and discusses possible future work.

2   Methods

2.1   Prescription Data and Preprocessing

The Medicines Regulation and Quality unit records details of all prescriptions of Controlled (Schedule 8) drugs dispensed at community pharmacies in Queensland. The details of each prescriptions held in the MODDS database include patient's information, prescriber's information, dispenser's information, drug's information, date of prescribing, dispensing and receiving, and so on. After indepth discussions with domain experts, in this study, we focus on detecting abnormal behaviors of patients that were dispensed fentanyl patches during a quarter of a year. Fentanyl is a high potency prescription opioid that, in the transdermal patch preparation, was listed for use for chronic pain as a Government funded medication under Australia's Pharmaceutical Benefits scheme in 2006 to allow greater use and access [2]. Fentanyl is manufactured in a transdermal patch with a controlled release matrix to allow for drug release through the skin over a 3 day window. Increased access to fentanyl can lead to increased misuse and diversion and has been associated with a number of overdose deaths since its general release for wider use. Current analysis to identify problematic use of fentanyl is usually based on a 3-month window. Therefore, by combining the knowledge of domain experts, for each patient dispensed fentanyl patches in a specific quarter, we focus on eight variables that are defined as follows:

x_1 (# **patches**) The total number of patches that the patient was dispensed in the quarter. This variable is a positive integer.

x_2 (# **prescriptions**) The total number of prescriptions that the patient was prescribed in the quarter. This variable is a positive integer.

x_3 (# **prescribers**) The number of different prescribers that prescribed the drug to the patient in the quarter. This variable is a positive integer.

x_4 (# **dispensers**) The number of different dispensers that dispensed the drug to the patients in the quarter. This variable is a positive integer.

x_5 (# **days_between**) The average number of days between each pair of the patient's two adjacent dispensing in the quarter. If only one dispensing occurred, the variable is set to 0. This variable is a nonnegative integer.

x_6 (**# days_minmax**) The number of days between the first dispensing and the last dispensing of the patient in the quarter. If only one dispensing occurred, the variable is set to 0. This variable is a nonnegative integer.

x_7 (**age**) The age of the patient at the first dispensing in the quarter. This variable is a positive integer.

x_8 (**gender**) The gender of the patient. This variable is a binary variable (1 means female and 2 means male).

Consequently, for each quarter, we construct a dataset, $\mathbf{D} = \{\mathbf{x}^t\}_{t=1}^N$ where $\mathbf{x}^t = [x_1^t, x_2^t, ..., x_8^t]^T$, from the original data in MODDS. Note that the above feature extraction strategy and the following anomaly detection techniques are general that can be also extended to the analysis of other drugs and the analysis of prescriber's or dispenser's abnormal behaviors.

2.2 Unsupervised Anomaly Detection Procedure

Assume that instances in dataset $\mathbf{D}$ are independently and identically drawn from an unknown probability distribution $P(\mathbf{x})$. According to one common assumption of unsupervised anomaly detection techniques that normal data instances tend to occur in high probability regions of $P(\mathbf{x})$, while anomalies often occur in the low probability regions of $P(\mathbf{x})$, anomalies can be detected by the following steps:

Training. An estimation of the probabilistic model $P(\mathbf{x})$ according to a certain learning principle (e.g., maximum likelihood) based on the dataset $\mathbf{D}$. We will introduce specific estimation methods for different probabilistic models in Section 2.3.

Testing. For each data point $\mathbf{x}^s$, we calculate the log-likelihood value $log(P(\mathbf{x}^s))$ as his/her anomaly score. Then an analyst may choose to either analyse the top few anomalies or use a threshold to select the anomalies.

2.3 Probability Models

In this paper we use three different probabilistic models: independent discrete model, independent smooth model, and dependent discrete model.

Independent Discrete Model (Model: ID). Under the assumption that each variable is independent of others, the joint distribution $P(\mathbf{x}) = \prod_{i=1}^8 P(x_i)$. Therefore, the joint distribution can be estimated by the product of the density function of each variable.

As described in Section 2.1, all features are specified by discrete random variables. Thus for each variable we design a discrete model $P(x) = P_a$ when $x = a$ where $a \in \Omega$ and Ω is a set of all possible values of x. We calculate the frequency of each value to obtain the maximum likelihood estimation of this probabilistic model.

$$\hat{P}_a = \frac{count(x^t = a)}{N} \tag{1}$$

Independent Smooth Model (Model: IS). In this model, we still assume that variables are independent of each other as above. However, with the exception of the binary variable x_8 (gender), the other 7 variables are treated as continuous variables. Since most of these variables are positive and asymmetrically distributed, the Gamma density function defined in Eq. 2 is chosen as the probabilistic model for each variable.

$$p(x) = gamma(x; k, \theta) = \frac{x^{k-1}e^{-\frac{x}{\theta}}}{\theta^k \Gamma(k)} \text{ for } x > 0 \text{ and } k, \theta > 0 \qquad (2)$$

Again, the parameters k and θ in the Gamma distribution are estimated using maximum likelihood estimation as follows.

$$\hat{\theta} = \frac{1}{kN} \sum_{t=1}^{N} x^t. \qquad (3)$$

There is no closed-form solution for k. The function is numerically very well behaved, so if a numerical solution is desired, it can be found using, for example, Newton's method. An initial value of k can be found either using the method of moments, or using a approximation. We use the method of moments to initialize k and Newton's method to obtain the numerical solution of k.

Here we note that for x_5 (# days_between) and x_6 (# days_minmax) we use discrete and continuous mixture model defined in Eq. 4 because they have a special value zero which means only one dispensing occurred.

$$p(x) = \begin{cases} P_0, & \text{for } x = 0; \\ (1 - P_0)gamma(x; k, \theta), & \text{for } x > 0. \end{cases} \qquad (4)$$

Dependent Discrete Model (Model: DD). Since the assumption of independence is often not strictly true in practice, a dependent discrete probabilistic model is employed. In order to avoid estimating too many unknown parameters, discretization of the data into a small number of values is desirable. There are two simple ways that are often used for discretization: quantile discretization and interval discretization. In quantile discretization each bin receives an equal number of data values [16]. The data range of each bin varies according to the data values it contains. Methods based on quantile discretization seem less suitable for frequency-based anomaly detection because we cannot only use frequency as anomaly score since each bin almost has equal frequency. In interval discretization the data range of each bin is equal. The number of data values in each bin varies according to the bin range. In this paper we begin with interval discretization to divide each variable into 4 groups. In addition, since interval discretization is very sensitive to outliers and may produce a strongly skewed range we adjust the range of the last bin to ensure that every bin contains at least one data point. We group the values of each variable as shown in Table 1.

Although there are still a large number of unknown parameters, due to the constraints in the real-world situation (e.g., the number of prescriptions $\geq$ the number of prescribers), the probability values of many bins are equal to 0.

Table 1. The grouped values of each variable for dependent discrete model

values	1	2	3	4
# patches	[1,30]	[31,60]	[61,90]	[91,∞)
# prescriptions	[1,10]	[11,20]	[21,30]	[31,∞)
# prescribers	[1,3]	[4,6]	[7,9]	[10,∞)
# dispensers	[1,3]	[4,6]	[7,9]	[10,∞)
# days_between	0	[1,10]	[11,20]	[21,∞)
# days_minmax	0	[1,30]	[31,60]	[61,∞)
age	[1,20]	[21,40]	[41,60]	[61,∞)
gender	female	male		

3 Results

3.1 Data Description

In this paper, we investigated fentanyl patch prescription data from 2013. We conducted experiments for each quarter of 2013 individually. The total number of fentanyl patch prescriptions in MODDS and the total number of patients after data cleaning, including removing the missing data and merging the redundant data, are shown in Table 2.

Table 2. The total number of fentanyl patch prescriptions and the total number patients used fentanyl patch in each quarter of 2013 in Queensland

	Q1	Q2	Q3	Q4
the total number of prescriptions	36338	37139	38603	39033
the total number of patients	7628	7676	7856	7685

We obtained 4 groups of data by using the features selected (Section2.1) on the four quarters of data. The actual value ranges of the extracted eight variables for the first quarter of 2013 are shown in Table 3.

Table 3. The actual value ranges of the extracted eight variables for the first quarter of 2013

	x_1	x_2	x_3	x_4	x_5	x_6	x_7	x_8
ranges	[1,365]	[1,74]	[1,54]	[1,54]	[0,42]	[0,89]	[10,114]	1,2

We applied the anomaly detection techniques based on different probabilistic models as described above on the four data sets and validate our models with MRQ domain experts. Since it is difficult to obtain a fully established ground truth we submitted top anomalies detected by our methods to domain experts and used their feedback on those cases to evaluate our models.

3.2   Distribution Estimation

We estimated each probabilistic model according to the methods in Section 2 on every quarter's data set (Q1, Q2, Q3, and Q4). Figure 1 shows the estimation of the probability values of each variable for Model ID (independent discrete model) and the estimation of the density function of each variable for model IS (independent smooth model), both on the 2013 Q1 dataset. Model DD (dependent discrete model) is an 8-dimensional joint distribution. We observed that the probability values for many unit bins are equal to zero.

These distribution estimation results as well as their visualization aid to better understand population behaviours and improve clinical treatment. For example, the distribution of gender shows that more female patients than male obtain fentanyl drugs. In addition, from estimated distributions of age over different time windows, there is also an evidence of growing rates of persistent pain in an ageing population.

3.3   Automatic Detection

After obtaining the estimation of a probabilistic model, we calculate the log-likelihood value of each instance and then sort all instances based on their log-likelihood value in ascending order. In general, the smaller the likelihood value, the greater the chance to be a problematic instance. For each dataset and for each model, we asked domain experts to check the top few anomalies. Table 4 shows the number of anomalies recognized as problematic use of drug by experts among the top anomalies detected by our methods.

Table 4. The number of anomalies recognized as problematic use of drug by experts among the top anomalies detected by our methods on each dataset

2013	Q1		Q2		Q3		Q4		Average	
	Top 5	Top 10	Top 5	Top 10	Top 5	Top 10	Top 5	Top 10	Top 5	Top 10
Model: ID	5	8	5	9	5	9	5	9	100%	87.5%
Model: IS	5	8	5	7	5	9	5	8	100%	80%
Model: DD	10/18		8/14		13/22		12/20		58%	

Experimental results show that all top 5 anomalies detected by our methods Model ID and Model IS are consistent with human experts' judgment. Among top 10 anomalies detected by Model ID across the four datasets, (40 anomalies), only 5 cases had been previously identified by MRQ staff as normal cases. Following consultation with MRQ colleagues, the main reasons for these cases are: 1). 2 Elderly patients, usually over 65 years old. Clinically, it is not unusual that elderly patients use larger doses of fentanyl; 2). 1 Cancer patient. Typically cancer patients require more than the usual dose of the drug; 3). Administration reasons. For example, the patient was approved to take special treatment. These reasons are mainly derived from the practical knowledge of experts or

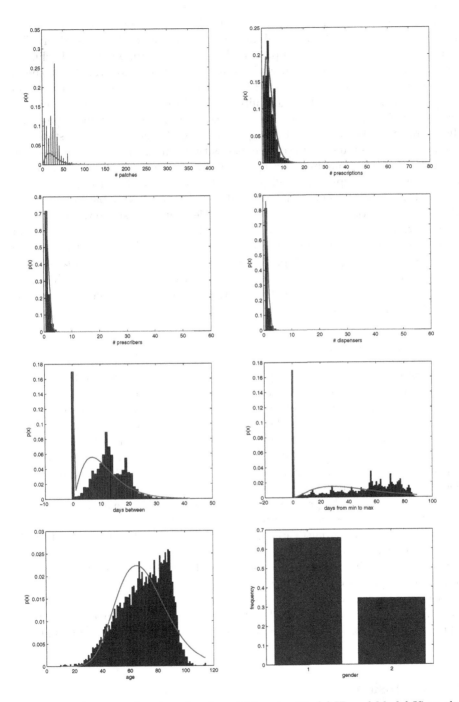

Fig. 1. Distribution estimation of each variable using Model ID and Model IS on the 2013 Q1 dataset. Blue columns show the probability values of Model ID. Red curves show the density functions of Model IS.

extra information beyond the data in MODDS. The average accuracy of top 10 anomalies for Model ID and Model IS are 87.5% and 80% respectively. For Model DD, since more than 10 patients have the same minimum log-likelihood value, Table 4 shows the number of anomalies previously identified by experts among rank first anomalies detected by Model DD. Please note that not all detected anomalies by Model DD are fully checked by experts. The current average accuracy is 58% for Model DD. Meanwhile, it is worth noting that our method discovered two new cases that had previously undetected by MQR staff. For both cases, the number of prescribers is less than three, so they were missed by current query-based monitoring program. After comprehensively analysing these cases, the domain experts identified them as problematic drug users.

We also tried to detect anomalies based on only a single variable and our models based on 8 variables outperformed the model using any single variable. None of the variables including age, gender, # days_between, and # days_minmax can provide sufficient information for abnormal detection. Meanwhile, the variable # patches, # prescriptions, # prescribers, and # dispensers contribute more to abnormal detection. However, since many instances share the same value for a particular variable, it is difficult to effectively distinguish different instances or set a threshold by using only one variable.

3.4   Analysis and Discussion

The results suggest that the proposed automatic detection methods based on probabilistic models can provide effective assistance in practice. First, the experimental results show that most judgments from our proposed techniques are consistent with domain experts. Therefore, it can provide a valuable pre-selection among large volumes of prescription data to reduce human efforts. Second, the results obtained by our methods can be used as an extra verification to make existing monitoring system more reliable. Third, our methods also can help to detect anomalies that may be ignored by current methods.

At the same time, the proposed methods can be easily extended to analysing prescribers and dispensers, as well as other drugs. Combining those analysis results will offer more sophisticated and reliable means of identifying problematic patterns of drug obtaining.

Currently, labelled data (i.e. cases previously identified as problematic prescribing) are quite limited. With the development of our collaborative research project, our models will be further verified and improved as more labelled data is provided. For example, for model DD (dependent discrete model), since not all top anomalies have been fully checked by experts further validation might be needed.

4   Conclusion

In this paper, we apply unsupervised anomaly detection technique based on probability density estimation models on controlled drug prescription data to identify problematic use of controlled drug. Experimental results show that the majority of abnormalities (100% of top 5 anomalies and 87.5% of top 10 anomalies for Model ID) detected by our methods are reliably associated with human expert judgment. Our methods offer efficient and reliable assistance to identifying problematic patterns of drug obtaining and could improve public health outcomes in managing large volumes of prescription information.

This study has demonstrated proof of concept of the capacity for a unsupervised, automated detection system to effectively and reliably identify clinically relevant anomalies in large and complex health databases. Misuse of POA represent a growing and substantial disease burden and fully integrated, real time anomaly monitoring system is the next phase of this body of work. Visualisation techniques will also be developed to allow more effective interface with front-line domain experts.

Recent work on disease outbreak detection also takes a statistical approach to anomaly detection, but applies more complex distribution models (e.g. Bayesian networks) and utilises the temporal nature of the data. In future work we will consider applying these techniques to our prescription data.

Acknowledgement. The authors would like to thank the staff from the Medicines Regulation and Quality, Department of Health for their support and assistance. In particular, the authors would like to thank Abhilash Dev, Shoshana Davies, Rebekah Steele, and Susan Ballantyne for their helpful suggestions and valuable validation of our models. This research was supported by an Australian Research Council Linkage Project Grant (LP120200121). Jason P. Connor is supported by a National Health and Medical Research Council (NHMRC) of Australian Career Development Fellowship (APP1031909).

References

1. Access Economics Pty Ltd. The high price of pain: the economic impact of persistent pain in australia. MBF Foundation in collaboration with University of Sydney Pain Management Research Institute (2007)
2. Australian Government: Fentanyl, transdermal patch, releasing approximately 12, 25, 50, 75 or 100 micrograms per hour, Durogesic 12/25/50/75/100 (March 2006), http://www.pbs.gov.au/info/industry/listing/elements/pbac-meetings/psd/2006-03/fentanyl
3. Bell, J.R.: Australian trends in opioid prescribing for chronic non-cancer pain, 1986-1996. The Medical journal of Australia 167(1), 26–29 (1997)
4. Bruno, R.: Benzodiazepine and pharmaceutical opioid misuse and their relationship to crime, tasmanian report. NDLERF Monograph Series (22) (2007)
5. Centers for Disease Control: Unintentional drug poisoning in the united states (2010), http://www.cdc.gov/HomeandRecreationalSafety/Poisoning/index.html
6. Centers for Disease Control and Prevention: Overdose deaths involving prescription opioids among medicaid enrollees-washington, 2004-2007. MMWR: Morbidity and Mortality Weekly Report 58(42), 1171–1175 (2009)

7. Centers for Disease Control and Prevention: Emergency department visits involving nonmedical use of selected prescription drugs-united states, 2004-2008. MMWR: Morbidity and Mortality Weekly Report 59(23), 705–709 (2010)

8. Centers for Disease Control and Prevention: Drug overdose deaths–florida, 2003-2009. MMWR. Morbidity and mortality weekly report 60(26), 869 (2011)

9. Chandola, V., Banerjee, A., Kumar, V.: Anomaly detection: A survey. ACM Computing Surveys (CSUR) 41(3), 15 (2009)

10. Commonwealth of Australia: Therapeutic goods act 1989 (1989), http://www.comlaw.gov.au/Series/C2004A03952

11. Commonwealth of Australia: Schedule 1-standard for the uniform scheduling of medicines and poisons, therapeutic goods act 1989 (2010), http://www.comlaw.gov.au/Series/C2004A03952

12. Compton, W.M., Volkow, N.D.: Major increases in opioid analgesic abuse in the united states: concerns and strategies. Drug and Alcohol Dependence 81(2), 103–107 (2006)

13. Degenhardt, L., Degenhardt, L., Black, E., Degenhardt, L., Black, E., Breen, C., Degenhardt, L., Black, E., Breen, C., Bruno, R., et al.: Trends in morphine prescriptions, illicit morphine use and associated harms among regular injecting drug users in australia. Drug and Alcohol Review 25(5), 403–412 (2006)

14. Dobbin, M.A.: Misuse of pharmaceutical drugs in australia. Ministerial Council on Drug Strategy, Melbourne (2009)

15. Dobbin, M.A.: Australian evidence on opioids. personal communication (2010)

16. Dougherty, J., Kohavi, R., Sahami, M.: Supervised and unsupervised discretization of continuous features. In: Proceedings of the Twelfth International Conference of Machine Learning, pp. 194–202 (1995)

17. Drugs and Crime Prevention Committee: Final report on inquiry into misuse/abuse of benzodiazepines and other pharmaceutical drugs. Tech. rep., Parliament of Victoria (2007)

18. Fischer, B., Nakamura, N., Rush, B., Rehm, J., Urbanoski, K.: Changes in and characteristics of admissions to treatment related to problematic prescription opioid use in ontario, 2004–2009. Drug and Alcohol Dependence 109(1), 257–260 (2010)

19. Fischer, B., Rehm, J.: Deaths related to the use of prescription opioids. Canadian Medical Association Journal 181(12), 881–882 (2009)

20. Health Insurance Commission: Annual report 1996–1997. Tech. rep., HIC, Canberra (1998)

21. Joranson, D.E., Ryan, K.M., Gilson, A.M., Dahl, J.L.: Trends in medical use and abuse of opioid analgesics. Jama 283(13), 1710–1714 (2000)

22. Leong, M., Murnion, B., Haber, P.: Examination of opioid prescribing in australia from 1992 to 2007. Internal Medicine Journal 39(10), 676–681 (2009)

23. Manchikanti, L., Singh, A.: Therapeutic opioids: a ten-year perspective on the complexities and complications of the escalating use, abuse, and nonmedical use of opioids. Pain Physician 11(2 Suppl.), S63–S88 (2008)

24. Mattick, R.P., Kimber, J., Breen, C., Davoli, M.: Buprenorphine maintenance versus placebo or methadone maintenance for opioid dependence. Cochrane Database of Systematic Reviews 2 (2014)

25. Merrick, M.: Prescription opioids and overdose deaths. JAMA 301(17), 1766–1769 (2009)

26. Nielsen, S., Barratt, M.J.: Prescription drug misuse: is technology friend or foe? Drug and Alcohol Review 28(1), 81–86 (2009)

27. Noble, M., Treadwell, J.R., Tregear, S.J., Coates, V.H., Wiffen, P.J., Akafomo, C., Schoelles, K.M.: Long-term opioid management for chronic noncancer pain. Cochrane Database Syst. Rev. 1(1) (2010)
28. Obenshain, M.K.: Application of data mining techniques to healthcare data. Infection Control and Hospital Epidemiology 25(8), 690–695 (2004)
29. Okie, S.: A flood of opioids, a rising tide of deaths. New England Journal of Medicine 363(21), 1981–1985 (2010)
30. Patcha, A., Park, J.M.: An overview of anomaly detection techniques: Existing solutions and latest technological trends. Computer Networks 51(12), 3448–3470 (2007)
31. Paulozzi, L.J., Budnitz, D.S., Xi, Y.: Increasing deaths from opioid analgesics in the united states. Pharmacoepidemiology and Drug Safety 15(9), 618–627 (2006)
32. Paulozzi, L.J., Kilbourne, E.M., Desai, H.A.: Prescription drug monitoring programs and death rates from drug overdose. Pain Medicine 12(5), 747–754 (2011)
33. Queensland Government: Health (drugs and poisons) regulation 1996 (1996), http://www.legislation.qld.gov.au/LEGISLTN/CURRENT/H/HealDrAPoR96.pdf
34. Rintoul, A.C., Dobbin, M.D., Drummer, O.H., Ozanne-Smith, J.: Increasing deaths involving oxycodone, victoria, australia, 2000–09. Injury Prevention, p. ip–2010 (2010)
35. Rintoul, A., et al.: Coronial deaths involving prescription opioids. victoria, 2000-2009. Presented at the Australian Mortality Data Interest Group, Melbourne (2010)
36. Roxburgh, A., Bruno, R., Larance, B., Burns, L.: Prescription of opioid analgesics and related harms in australia. The Medical Journal of Australia 195(5), 280–284 (2011)
37. The Royal Australasian College of Physicians: Prescription opioid policy: Improving management of chronic non-malignant pain and prevention of problems associated with prescription opioid use (2009), http://www.racp.edu.au/index.cfm?objectid=EA87198D-CA47-AB21-072D9B2F26FD4AA3
38. Wong, W.K., Moore, A., Cooper, G., Wagner, M.: Bayesian network anomaly pattern detection for disease outbreaks. In: ICML, pp. 808–815 (2003)
39. Yoo, I., Alafaireet, P., Marinov, M., Pena-Hernandez, K., Gopidi, R., Chang, J.F., Hua, L.: Data mining in healthcare and biomedicine: a survey of the literature. Journal of Medical Systems 36(4), 2431–2448 (2012)

Multi-Phase Feature Representation Learning for Neurodegenerative Disease Diagnosis

Siqi Liu[1], Sidong Liu[1,2], Weidong Cai[1,2], Sonia Pujol[2], Ron Kikinis[2], and David Dagan Feng[1,3]

[1] BMIT Research Group, School of Information Technologies, University of Sydney, NSW, Australia
[2] Surgical Planning Laboratory, Brigham and Womens Hospital, Harvard Medical School, Boston, MA, USA
[3] Med-X Research Institute, Shanghai Jiaotong University, Shanghai, China

Abstract. Feature learning with high dimensional neuroimaging features has been explored for the applications on neurodegenerative diseases. Low-dimensional biomarkers, such as mental status test scores and cerebrospinal fluid level, are essential in clinical diagnosis of neurological disorders, because they could be simple and effective for the clinicians to assess the disorder's progression and severity. Rather than only using the low-dimensional biomarkers as inputs for decision making systems, we believe that such low-dimensional biomarkers can be used for enhancing the feature learning pipeline. In this study, we proposed a novel feature representation learning framework, Multi-Phase Feature Representation (MPFR), with low-dimensional biomarkers embedded. MPFR learns high-level neuroimaging features by extracting the associations between the low-dimensional biomarkers and the high-dimensional neuroimaging features with a deep neural network. We validated the proposed framework using the Mini-Mental-State-Examination (MMSE) scores as a low-dimensional biomarker and multi-modal neuroimaging data as the high-dimensional neuroimaging features from the ADNI baseline cohort. The proposed approach outperformed the original neural network in both binary and ternary Alzheimer's disease classification tasks.

Keywords: classification, deep learning, neuroimaging.

1 Introduction

To aid the clinical decision making, feature learning methods have been applied on learning the correlations between the high dimensional features extracted from neuroimaging data recently [1,2,3]. Low-dimensional biomarkers, such as the Mini-Mental-State-Examination (MMSE) and the cerebrospinal fluid measurements (CSF), are known as supportive diagnostic tools for clinic diagnosis of brain diseases, accompanied with the high-dimensional neuroimaging biomarkers, such as Magnetic Resonance Image (MRI) and Poistron Emission Tomography (PET). However unlike the application of high-dimensional neuroimaging

S.K. Chalup et al. (Eds.): ACALCI 2015, LNAI 8955, pp. 350–359, 2015.

biomarkers [4,5,6,7,8,9,10,11,12], they have not been sufficiently explored in current machine learning based feature representation methods. There have been studies using the low-dimensional biomarkers, such as CSF, as input features for machine learner [13]. However, low-dimensional biomarkers might not be equally sensitive to the cognitive impairment as high-dimensional biomarkers and can be easily overwhelmed when they are fed into the machine learner together. Whereas, other studies attempted to predict low-dimensional clinic assessments, such as Alzheimer's Disease Assessment Scale-Cognitive Subscale (ADAS-Cog), by building the joint regression models with inputs selected from both high-dimensional and low-dimensional biomarkers [14,15]. However, these methods require the subjects to have paired clinical scores and imaging data, which may lead to shrinkage of training dataset, because of the extra expense on data collection.

In an attempt to solve the above-mentioned problems, we proposed a Multi-Phase Feature Representation (MPFR) framework that have low-dimensional biomarkers embedded in the feature representation learning rather than directly using them as features. MPFR learns the features by assessing the associations between the low-dimensional biomarkers and the high-dimensional biomarkers based on a deep neural network consisting of stacked auto-encoders (SAE), linear regression and softmax regression. The feature representation network is optimised to estimate the low-dimensional biomarkers before it is finally used for classification. The prominent advantage of the proposed framework is the separation of different training phases. Thus, it does not require every training instance to be attached with a diagnostic label nor low-dimensional biomarkers. In addition, the low-dimensional biomarkers will not be overwhelmed by the high-dimensional biomarkers. We validated the proposed framework with the performance of Alzheimer's Disease (AD) diagnosis with 3 groups from the ADNI cohort and selected the MMSE scores as the low-dimensional biomarkers for feature learning. We modelled the AD diagnosis as a classification problem with 3 classes, including Normal Control (NC), Mild Cognitive Impairment (MCI) and AD. These learnt features revealed the associations between MMSE and the neuroimaging patterns and outperformed the features extracted by the state-of-the-art methods as well as conventional deep-learning-based methods without MPFR in both binary and ternary classification tasks.

2   Multi-Phase Feature Representation

There are three phases of MPFR framework, as shown in Fig. 1. Phase A depicts the unsupervised layer-wised pre-training of the feature representation network which learns a manifold to reconstruct the features at the previous layer. The parameters of the auto-encoders learned by Phase A are unfolded and stacked in Phase B. In Phase B, the feature representation network is enhanced by training to output the low-dimensional features. The outputs of Phase B are the low-dimensional biomarkers estimated with the extracted high-level features. In Phase C, after replacing the output layer with softmax regression, the entire

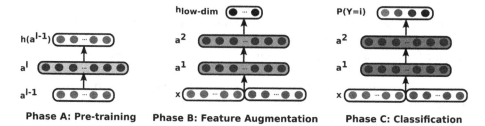

Fig. 1. The illustration of the 3 phases of training the proposed MPFR framework. The grey neurons are the high-dimensional biomarker inputs and the blue neurons are the hidden layer neurons. The neurons with different colors at the bottom layer in Phase B indicate inputs from different neuroimaging modalities, such as MRI and PET, and the black neurons are the estimated low-dimensional biomarker outputs. The darker brown nodes in Phase C indicate more sever stages along the disease progression.

structure is finally fine-tuned for the purpose of classification. The learnt features in Phase C are expected to be more sensitive to the training labels since the hidden layers could learn high-level disorder-specific features.

2.1 Phase A: Pre-training Stacked Auto-encoders (SAE) with Neuroimaging Biomarkers

The biomarkers extracted from brain images, such as MRI and PET, are initially used as the inputs for the feature representation learner. They are fed into a multi-layered neural network with non-linear activation function. Each hidden layer of the neural net is seen as a higher level of representation of the previous layer. To obtain high-level features that can represent the original inputs, we used stacked autoencoders (SAE) to form the hidden layers of the neural network. The feature representations can be computed by feed-forwarding the activation signals with sigmoid function $S(x) = \frac{1}{1+e^{-x}}$. The parameters of each auto-encoder are optimised to reconstruct the previous input a_{l-1}. The optimisation criterion is to minimise the representation loss:

$$L(W, b, x, z) = \min_{W,b} ||h(W, b, x) - x||_2^2 + \lambda ||W||_2^2 \qquad (1)$$

where $h(W, b, x)$ is the reconstruction yielded from the auto-encoder; x is the input vector of the auto-encoder; W and b are the weight and bias parameters to be trained; the second term is the weight decay to control over-fitting. Gradient descent based algorithms, such as L-BFGS algorithm [16], can be applied to train auto-encoders, following the greedy layer-wised training strategy by training each hidden layer at once (Phase A in Fig. 1) [17]. To fully extract the synergy between different image modalities, we zero-masked a small proportion of feature parameters from one single modality randomly when training the first hidden layer [18].

2.2   Phase B: Feature Representation Optimisation with Low-Dimensional Biomarkers

Before using the pre-trained network for the classification, the hidden layers are firstly fine-tuned to estimate continuous low-dimensional biomarkers. The network is also expected to extract the correlations between image biomarkers and the low-dimensional biomarkers. For example, if MMSE is chosen to be estimated, the features provided by the fine-tuned feature representation network can be sensitive to the cognitive status of subjects as well as the risk of being diagnosed as AD. However, by observing (a) and (b) in Fig. 2, it is also obvious that neuroimaging data are expected to be more sensitive to the cognitive impairment.

Linear regression is used to estimate the low-dimensional biomarkers. One output layer with linear activation filter is stacked on the top of the pre-trained SAE (Phase B in Fig. 1). The prediction can be demonstrated as

$$h(W, a^{(l)}) = W a^{(l)} + b \tag{2}$$

where $h(W, a^{(l)})$ is the vector of the estimated low-dimensional biomarkers; $a^{(l)}$ is the l-th layer of high-level features obtained from the pre-trained SAE; W and b are the parameters that can be optimised by jointly propagating the error gradients. Since Phase B is designed for augmenting the feature learning network, early stopping is applied in Phase B training to control the over-fitting on the low-dimensional biomarkers in the training set.

2.3   Phase C: Classification with AD Labels

The trained linear regression layer is replaced with a softmax regression output layer (Phase C in Fig. 1). The softmax layer uses a different activation function, which might introduce non-linearity different from the sigmoid function in SAE:

$$P(Y = i|x) = \frac{e^{W^i a + b^i}}{\sum_j e^{W^i a + b^i}} \tag{3}$$

where a is the feature vector obtained by the fine-tuned SAE. Y is assigned to possible stages of a particular disease, such as NC, MCI and AD of AD progression. The prediction $P(Y = i|x)$ with the highest probability is chosen as the final decision. The network is then fine-tuned by back-propagating the classification loss with the pre-labelled training subjects as a supervised classification neural network.

3   Experiments

3.1   Data Acquisition and Feature Extraction

The dataset used in this study was acquired from the ADNI database [20]. We selected 331 subjects from the ADNI baseline cohort, including 77 NC-, 169 MCI- and

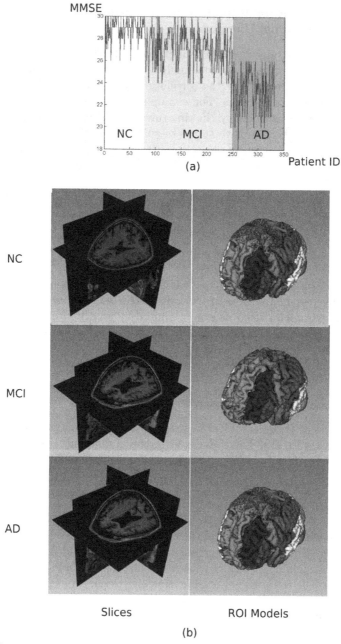

Fig. 2. The comparison between the variations of low-dimensional biomarkers and neuroimaging data. (a) is the plot of MMSE scores. (b) are slices and MAPER whole brain mask models from ADNI baseline cohort, generated using 3D Slicer 4.3.1 [19]. The neuroimaging data contains more information than MMSE. Some sophisticated features, such as ventricle sizes and atrophy, cannot be captured by MMSE, but can be shown in neuroimaging data.

85 AD-subjects. For each subject, an FDG-PET image and a T1-weighted volume acquired on a 1.5 Tesla MR scanner were retrieved. All the 3D MRI and PET data were registered following the ADNI image correction protocols [20,21]. The PET images were align to the corresponding MRI image using FSL FLIRT [22]. The MRI images were then non-linearly registered to the ICBM 152 template [23] with 83 functional regions using the Image Registration Toolkit (IRTK) [24]. The outputted registration coefficients of MRI images were used to aligned PET images into the ICBM 152 template. Finally, all registered MRI and PET image were mapped to brain functional regions using the multi-atlas propagation with MAPER approach [25]. Three types of features were extracted from each of the brain regions, including the grey matter volume [25,26,27], solidity [10,28,29] features from MRI data, and the cerebral metabolic rate of glucose consumption (CMRGlc) from PET data [7,30]. Elastic Net [31,32,33] was applied to choose the most predictive dimensions of features. 85 feature parameters were eventually selected for each subject evaluated in this study.

3.2   Performance Evaluation

The performance on AD diagnosis of the proposed MPFR framework was compared to the state-of-the-art work-flow with multi-kernel SVM (MKSVM) [13] and the conventional deep learning method without embedding MPFR. We chose MMSE scores of patients in the training set to evaluate MPFR in this study, because the variation between the NC/MCI groups and the AD group is obvious (Fig. 2-a). All of the experiments were evaluated with the same features extracted from MRI images and PET images.

MKSVM was implemented using LIBSVM library with the radial basis function (RBF) kernel [34]. We applied the 'one against all' approach to allow MKSVM to perform the trinary classification problem [35]. The proposed deep learning framework was implemented on Matlab 2013b. The approximated random search strategy was applied to choose the hyper-parameters [36].

We used 10-fold cross-validation to evaluate different learning structures. For each fold of cross validation, about 90% subjects were collected for training (including the pre-training, feature optimisation and classification training) and the rest subjects were used for testing. In the experiments of the MPFR framework, the MMSE scores of the testing set were neglected.

3.3   Results

The examination of the high-level features is displayed in Fig 3. Comparing the features learnt with 2 different phases, it is clear that the Phase A only extracted features that represented the neuroimaging data. After Phase B, some dimensions of the learnt features showed variations along the progression of AD.

In Phase B, by comparing the different AD stages, most of high-level features at layer 1 tend to vary according to the severity of AD. Whereas only few dimensions of high-level features at layer 2 showed remarkable variance. It is

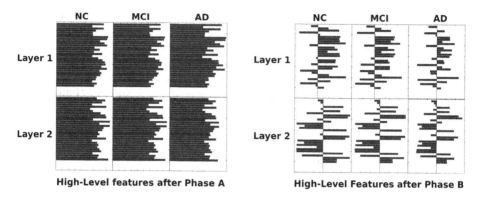

Fig. 3. The examination of the high-level features extracted by Phase A and Phase B (applied MMSE scores) of MPFR. These features were obtained from a network with 2 hidden layers.

reasonable to assume that after the Phase B of MPFR, the higher layers may tend to extract more abstract patterns by flatting the local variations.

Table 1. The performance (%) of the AD binary classification between NC and AD. The first two columns are precisions on each class. The last three columns depict the overall performance (accuracy, sensitivity and specificity).

	NC	AD	ACC	SEN	SPE
MKSVM	89.10 ± 1.26	90.13 ± 1.02	89.60 ± 0.91	89.09 ± 1.39	90.10 ± 1.12
SAE	89.39 ± 10.73	85.67 ± 14.94	88.20 ± 7.68	87.66 ± 9.50	87.50 ± 15.04
Proposed	91.17 ± 8.54	88.35 ± 8.17	90.11 ± 3.06	84.45 ± 10.51	93.89 ± 6.31

The performance of the binary classification between NC and AD is displayed in Table 1. The proposed method outperformed the conventional SAE in both precisions of classifying NC and AD. It also achieved the highest overall accuracy (90.11%) and specificity (93.98%) among the other two methods. The higher sensitivity achieved by MKSVM (89.09%) can be attributed to the limitation on the quantity of the available training data. Parametric models such as SAE and the proposed method tend to have higher standard deviation than non-parametric models like SVM. However, it is notable that the proposed method performed lower standard deviation than SAE. Table 2 shows the performance of trinery classification, including NC, MCI and AD, which was designed for evaluating the effects on the early detection of AD. The proposed method outperformed the conventional SAE and MKSVM in the overall accuracy (59.19%) and the overall sensitivity (50.98%). It is reasonable to convince that the enhancements of classification performance, comparing to the conventional SAE, were primarily benefited from the robust high-level features learnt with MPFR.

Table 2. The performance (%) of the trinary AD classification between NC, MCI and AD. The first three columns are precisions on each class. The last three columns depict the overall performance (accuracy, sensitivity and specificity).

	NC	MCI	AD	ACC	SEN	SPE
MKSVM	47.53 ± 2.59	57.29 ± 0.90	49.74 ± 2.33	53.2 ± 1.27	44.59 ± 2.89	85.00 ± 1.92
SAE	46.97 ± 21.71	61.87 ± 12.26	60.78 ± 15.88	58.57 ± 9.21	49.16 ± 16.60	83.53 ± 6.56
Proposed	49.00 ± 22.42	61.29 ± 12.94	61.52 ± 13.87	59.19 ± 9.20	50.98 ± 16.08	84.36 ± 6.71

4   Conclusions

In this study, we presented a novel framework, the Multi-Phase Feature Representation (MPFR), for the feature representation of neuroimaging data. It differs between the conventional deep learning architecture by learning features to output low-dimensional biomarkers before the deep network is fine-tuned with classification labels. The preliminary results showed that MPFR framework outperformed SAE as well as the state-of-the-art classification method (Multi-Kernel SVM) and had a great potential to embed other low-dimensional biomarkers in feature representation learning without constraining the size of available training data.

Acknowledgements. This work was supported in part by the Australian Research Council (ARC), Alzheimers Australia Dementia Research Foundation (AADRF), NA-MIC (NIH U54EB005149), and NAC (NIH P41EB015902).

References

1. Suk, H.-I., Shen, D.: Deep learning-based feature representation for AD/MCI classification. In: Mori, K., Sakuma, I., Sato, Y., Barillot, C., Navab, N. (eds.) MICCAI 2013, Part II. LNCS, vol. 8150, pp. 583–590. Springer, Heidelberg (2013)
2. Liu, S.Q., Liu, S., Cai, W., Pujol, S., Kikinis, R., Feng, D.: Early Diagnosis of Alzheimer's Disease with Deep Learning. In: 2014 IEEE 11th International Symposium on Biomedical Imaging (ISBI), pp. 1015–1018. IEEE (2014)
3. Liu, S.Q., Liu, S., Cai, W., Che, H., Pujol, S., Kikinis, R., Fulham, M.J., Feng, D.: High-level Feature based PET Image Retrieval with Deep Learning Architecture. Journal of Nuclear Medicine 55(Supple. 1), 2018 (2014)
4. Fischl, B., Dale, A.M.: Measuring the Thickness of the Human Cerebral Cortex from Magnetic Resonance Images. Proceedings of the National Academy of Sciences 97(20), 11050–11055 (2000)
5. Schaer, M., Cuadra, M.B., Tamarit, L., Lazeyras, F., Eliez, S., Thiran, J.P.: A Surface-Based Approach to Quantify Local Cortical Gyrification. IEEE Transactions on Medical Imaging 27(2), 161–170 (2008)
6. Liu, S., Cai, W., Wen, L., Eberl, S., Fulham, M.J., Feng, D.: A Robust Volumetric Feature Extraction Approach for 3D Neuroimaging Retrieval. In: 2010 Annual International Conference of the IEEE Engineering in Medicine and Biology Society (EMBC), pp. 5657–5660. IEEE (2010)
7. Cai, W., Liu, S., Wen, L., Eberl, S., Fulham, M., Feng, D.: 3D Neurological Image Retrieval with Localized Pathology-Centric CMRGlc Patterns. In: 2010 17th IEEE International Conference on Image Processing (ICIP), pp. 3201–3204 (2010)

8. Liu, S., Cai, W., Wen, L., Eberl, S., Fulham, M.J., Feng, D.: Localized Functional Neuroimaging Retrieval using 3D Discrete Curvelet Transform. In: 2011 IEEE International Symposium on Biomedical Imaging: From Nano to Macro (ISBI), pp. 1877–1880. IEEE (2011)

9. Cash, D.M., Melbourne, A., Modat, M., Cardoso, M.J., Clarkson, M.J., Fox, N.C., Ourselin, S.: Cortical folding analysis on patients with alzheimer's disease and mild cognitive impairment. In: Ayache, N., Delingette, H., Golland, P., Mori, K. (eds.) MICCAI 2012, Part III. LNCS, vol. 7512, pp. 289–296. Springer, Heidelberg (2012)

10. Liu, S., Song, Y., Cai, W., Pujol, S., Kikinis, R., Wang, X., Feng, D.: Multifold Bayesian Kernelization in Alzheimer's Diagnosis. In: Mori, K., Sakuma, I., Sato, Y., Barillot, C., Navab, N. (eds.) MICCAI 2013, Part II. LNCS, vol. 8150, pp. 303–310. Springer, Heidelberg (2013)

11. Liu, S., Cai, W., Wen, L., Feng, D.: Neuroimaging Biomarker Based Prediction of Alzheimer'S Disease Severity with Optimized Graph Construction. In: IEEE 10th International Symposium on Biomedical Imaging (ISBI), pp. 1336–1339. IEEE (2013)

12. Cai, W., Liu, S., Song, Y., Pujol, S., Kikinis, R., Feng, D.: A 3D Difference of Gaussian based Lesion Detector for Brain PET. In: 2014 IEEE International Symposium on Biomedical Imaging: From Nano to Macro (ISBI), pp. 677–680. IEEE (2014)

13. Zhang, D., Wang, Y., Zhou, L., Yuan, H., Shen, D.: Multimodal Classification of Alzheimer's Disease and Mild Cognitive Impairment. NeuroImage 55(3), 856 (2011)

14. Wang, Y., Fan, Y., Bhatt, P., Davatzikos, C.: High-Dimensional Pattern Regression Using Machine Learning: From Medical Images to Continuous Clinical Variables. NeuroImage 50(4), 1519 (2010)

15. Zhang, D., Shen, D.: Multi-Modal Multi-Task Learning for Joint Prediction of Multiple Regression and Classification Variables in Alzheimer's Disease. NeuroImage 59(2), 895 (2012)

16. Ngiam, J., Coates, A., Lahiri, A., Prochnow, B., Ng, A., Le, Q.V.: On Optimization Methods for Deep Learning. In: Proceedings of the 28th International Conference on Machine Learning (ICML 2011), pp. 265–272 (2011)

17. Bengio, Y., Lamblin, P., Popovici, D., Larochelle, H., et al.: Greedy Layer-Wise Training of Deep Networks. Advances in Neural Information Processing Systems 19, 153 (2007)

18. Ngiam, J., Khosla, A., Kim, M., Nam, J., Lee, H., Ng, A.: Multimodal Deep Learning. In: Proceedings of the 28th International Conference on Machine Learning (ICML 2011), pp. 689–696 (2011)

19. Fedorov, A., Beichel, R., Kalpathy-Cramer, J., Finet, J., Fillion-Robin, J.C., Pujol, S., et al.: 3D Slicer as an Image Computing Platform for the Quantitative Imaging Network. Magnetic Resonance Imaging 30(9), 1323–1341 (2012)

20. Jack, C.R., Bernstein, M.A., Fox, N.C., Thompson, P., Alexander, G., Harvey, D., Borowski, B., et al.: The Alzheimer's Disease Neuroimaging Initiative (ADNI): MRI Methods. Journal of Magnetic Resonance Imaging 27(4), 685–691 (2008)

21. Jagust, W.J., Bandy, D., Chen, K., Foster, N.L., Landau, S.M., Mathis, C.A., Price, J.C., et al.: The Alzheimer's Disease Neuroimaging Initiative Positron Emission Tomography Core. Alzheimer's & Dementia 6(3), 221–229 (2010)

22. Jenkinson, M., Bannister, P., Brady, M., Smith, S.: Improved Optimization for the Robust and Accurate Linear Registration and Motion Correction of Brain Images. Neuroimage 17(2), 825–841 (2002)

23. Mazziotta, J., Toga, A., Evans, A., Fox, P., Lancaster, J., Zilles, K., Woods, R., et al.: A Probabilistic Atlas and Reference System for the Human Brain: International Consortium for Brain Mapping (ICBM). Philosophical Transactions of the Royal Society of London. Series B: Biological Sciences 356(1412), 1293–1322 (2001)
24. Schnabel, J.A., Rueckert, D., Quist, M., Blackall, J.M., Castellano-Smith, A.D., Hartkens, T., Penney, G.P., Hall, W.A., Liu, H., Truwit, C.L., Gerritsen, F.A., Hill, D.L.G., Hawkes, D.J.: A Generic Framework for Non-rigid Registration Based on Non-uniform Multi-level Free-Form Deformations. In: Niessen, W.J., Viergever, M.A. (eds.) MICCAI 2001. LNCS, vol. 2208, pp. 573–581. Springer, Heidelberg (2001)
25. Heckemann, R.A., Keihaninejad, S., Aljabar, P., Gray, K.R., Nielsen, C., Rueckert, D., Hajnal, J.V., Hammers, A.: Automatic Morphometry in Alzheimer's Disease and Mild Cognitive Impairment. Neuroimage 56(4), 2024–2037 (2011)
26. Liu, S., Cai, W., Song, Y., Pujol, S., Kikinis, R., Wen, L., Feng, D.: Localized Sparse Code Gradient in Alzheimer's Disease Staging. In: 2013 Annual International Conference of the IEEE Engineering in Medicine and Biology Society (EMBC), pp. 5398–5401. IEEE (2013)
27. Che, H., Liu, S., Cai, W., Pujol, S., Kikinis, R., Feng, D.: Co-neighbor Multi-View Spectral Embedding for Medical Content-based Retrieval. In: 2014 IEEE International Symposium on Biomedical Imaging: From Nano to Macro (ISBI), pp. 911–914. IEEE (2014)
28. Batchelor, P.G., Castellano Smith, A.D., Hill, D.L.G., Hawkes, D.J., Cox, T.C.S., Dean, A.: Measures of Folding Applied to the Development of the Human Fetal Brain. IEEE Transactions on Medical Imaging 21(8), 953–965 (2002)
29. Liu, S., Zhang, L., Cai, W., Song, Y., Wang, Z., Wen, L., Feng, D.: A Supervised Multiview Spectral Embedding Method for Neuroimaging Classification. In: 2013 IEEE International Conference on Image Processing (ICIP), pp. 601–605. IEEE (2013)
30. Liu, S., Cai, W., Wen, L., Eberl, S., Fulham, M.J., Feng, D.: Generalized Regional Disorder-Sensitive-Weighting Scheme for 3D Neuroimaging Retrieval. In: 2011 Annual International Conference of the IEEE Engineering in Medicine and Biology Society (EMBC), pp. 7009–7012. IEEE (2011)
31. Zou, H., Hastie, T.: Regularization and Variable Selection via the Elastic Net. Journal of the Royal Statistical Society: Series B (Statistical Methodology) 67(2), 301–320 (2005)
32. Liu, S., Cai, W., Wen, L., Feng, D.: Multi-Channel Brain Atrophy Pattern Analysis in Neuroimaging Retrieval. In: 2013 IEEE International Symposium on Biomedical Imaging: From Nano to Macro (ISBI), pp. 206–209. IEEE (2013)
33. Liu, S., Cai, W., Wen, L., Feng, D.D., Pujol, S., et al.: Multi-Channel Neurodegenerative Pattern Analysis and Its Application in Alzheimer's Disease Characterization. Computerized Medical Imaging and Graphics 38(4), 436–444 (2014)
34. Chang, C.C., Lin, C.J.: LIBSVM: A Library for Support Vector Machines. ACM Trans. Intell. Syst. Technol. 27(3), 1–27 (2011)
35. Liu, Y.F.Y., Zheng, Y.: One-Against-All Multi-Class SVM Classification Using Reliability Measures. In: Neural Networks (IJCNN 2005), IEEE International Joint Conference on. Volume 2. (2005) 849–854
36. Bergstra, J., Bengio, Y.: Random Search for Hyper-Parameter Optimization. The Journal of Machine Learning Research 13, 281–305 (2012)

A Modified Case-Based Reasoning Approach for Triaging Psychiatric Patients Using a Similarity Measure Derived from Orthogonal Vector Projection

Dombawalage Anton Irosh Fernando and Frans Alexander Henskens[*]

The University of Newcastle, Australia
irosh.fernando@uon.edu.au,
frans.henskens@newcastle.edu.au

Abstract. A modified case-based reasoning method is introduced aimed to fulfill the need for a triage tool that differentiates likely psychiatric diagnoses and associated risk level. Clinical cases are represented as a set of clinical features rated on a numerical scale according to level of severity. One standard case is used for each diagnostic category, represented as a vector denoting the expected severity of each clinical feature. A new case represented as another vector denoting the severity of observed clinical features in a patient is assessed against the standard cases. Measurement based on orthogonal vector projection was used as a clinically intuitive measurement of similarity. Using thirty different test cases representing six different diagnostic categories, this measure and alternative similarity measures consisting of cosine similarity and Euclidean distance were evaluated. Results indicated that orthogonal vector projection was superior to the other two methods in differentiating diagnoses and predicting severity.

Keywords: orthogonal vector projection, case-based reasoning.

1 Introduction

Psychiatric conditions are prevalent and disabling [1],[2]. Also, a common psychiatric condition such as major depression is associated with increased suicide risk, and therefore needs to be recognised early [3]. The triage process in health services (e.g. in a hospital emergency department) prioritises and directs patients for treatment based on the nature and severity of their presenting symptoms. General practitioners and junior clinicians, who often have first contact with patients in emergency services, typically perform the triage task. One of the important needs of health services is a triage tool that can be used to screen patients when they present. In the context of this paper, a triage tool would ideally be able to diagnose common psychiatric conditions, severity of symptoms and identify high-risk patients. Such a triage tool would be valuable in prioritising the service delivery and directing the patients for appropriate specialist services. For example, a patient who has severe symptoms with risk of suicide

---

[*] Corresponding author.

S.K. Chalup et al. (Eds.): ACALCI 2015, LNAI 8955, pp. 360–372, 2015.
© Springer International Publishing Switzerland 2015

may require hospital admission whereas someone with less severe symptoms and low risk may attend a psychiatric clinic. Importantly, such a tool can cut down the time of specialist's assessment by collecting part of the required information.

In developing such a triage tool it was important to recognise the specific nature of diagnostic reasoning in psychiatry compared to other medical specialities. Psychiatry differs from other branches of medicine due to lack of diagnostic investigation that gives objective and specific diagnostic measurements. For example, in general medicine, if someone is suspected to have a heart disease, investigations such as electrocardiograms and certain blood tests can provide objective and specific information that is useful in establishing an exact diagnosis. Unfortunately, in psychiatry, no such physical investigations are currently available to confirm even the most common psychiatric conditions such as depression and anxiety disorders. Therefore, diagnostic assessment is largely based on the subjective information gathered during the diagnostic interview(s), which is/are usually more time consuming than in other branches of medicine. Therefore, there is sometimes a level of uncertainty associated with the accuracy of psychiatric diagnosis, and it is not uncommon for different clinicians to have different opinions on diagnosis. Also, sometimes, patients can present with multiple clusters of symptoms that respectively point to different diagnoses, and the clinician is required to establish the primary diagnosis by differentiating the severity of each diagnosis.

This paper describes our strategy for developing a triage tool using a modified case-based reasoning approach that importantly does not require a huge underlying knowledgebase so could, for example, be implemented on a handheld device such as a smartphone or tablet computer. The next section describes: case-based reasoning; the related commonly used techniques that can be used to measure similarity between cases; and the need for a modified approach that suits psychiatry. Commonly used techniques covered in this paper include cosine similarity, Euclidean distance, and neighbour algorithms. We then introduce an approach in which clinical cases are represented as vectors of clinical features. At triage, a patient's case vector is compiled during initial interview, after which it is compared with a set of standard vectors that includes one standard case for each clinical category (i.e. for each different category of diagnosis and patient who is at risk). Comparison involves projecting the patient's case vector on to each of the standard vectors, thus deriving a set of clinically intuitive similarity indices from which the most similar is chosen as indicating the most likely initial case diagnosis. It is important to note that this process is not intended to replace comprehensive clinical investigation of the patient's psychiatric state; rather it provides a means by which less experienced personnel can perform an initial assessment of clinical category and severity.

Finally, the paper uses thirty different test cases representing five clinical categories together with high self-harm risk, to evaluate and compare triage diagnosis using modified case-based reasoning with other relevant diagnostic techniques, and the results are presented.

2   Case-Based Reasoning and Related Approaches

Fernando et al have previously developed algorithms that can be used for comprehensive psychiatric assessments [4],[5],[6]. Implementations of these algorithms are resource intensive, particularly in relation to construction of a large knowledgebase representing individual psychiatric conditions and associated clinical features. However, because of the specific requirement for a screening tool to assist initial evaluation of common psychiatric conditions, these algorithms were not appropriate, and a rather simpler and easy to implement approach was required. This need led to investigation of a case-based reasoning approach.

The generic case based reasoning approach primarily involves maintaining a case base, and retrieving cases to compare their similarity with any given case. As a methodology, case-based reasoning is a cyclical process comprising retrieval, reuse, revision and retaining of cases [7]. However, because psychiatry is different from other branches of medicine as previously described, it is often the circumstance that generic approaches cannot be directly applied. Particularly, in relation to triage screening in psychiatry, the standard case-based reasoning approach is inappropriate because of the highly subjective nature of diagnostic reasoning and lack of specific and objective diagnostic measurements. Also, because there is sometimes a level of diagnostic uncertainty or different opinions on diagnosis, the standard approach requiring maintenance of a case base may lead to gradual accumulation of diagnostic errors.

Therefore, we have adapted the standard case-based reasoning approach to maintain only one standard case for each diagnostic category. Each such standard case is derived from the descriptions of typical cases from the psychiatric literature and standardised diagnostic criteria such as DSM-V [8], and represented as a set of clinical features. The magnitudes of the expected severity of these clinical features are represented as a vector. The same feature set is used to assess new cases, and the observed magnitude of each clinical feature is recorded, resulting in another vector representing the new case. Hence, measuring the similarity between a new case and the standard case involves measuring the similarity of these two vectors. This modified case-based reasoning approach is described in Fig. 1.

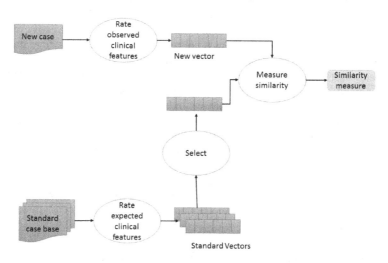

Fig. 1. Modified cased-based reasoning approach

Depending on how cases are structured, there are many available methods for measuring similarity that are broadly categorised as surface similarity and structural similarity methods [9]. Some of the methods used for measuring the surface similarity include k Nearest Neighbour [10], using a binary tree called $K - D$ tree[11], footprint-based retrieval[12], and fish and shrink strategy [13]. Some of the methods used for measuring structural similarity include object-oriented frame based representation[14], spreading activation methods [15], generalised cases [16], graph editing operations [17], and Perspectives [18].

Given that $\vec{A}$ and $\vec{B}$ represent the two vectors that need be compared, the commonly used approach in relation to measuring their similarity includes the following techniques [19]. In *cosine similarity*, the cosine of the angle θ between the two vectors is evaluated using the following formula, in which $\vec{A}.\vec{B}$ represents the dot product and $|A||B|$ represents the product of the lengths of the two vectors.

$$\cos(\theta) = \frac{\vec{A}.\vec{B}}{|A||B|}$$

Euclidean Distance is given by the following formula in which A_i and B_i represent the ith feature of each vector where $i = 1,2,...,n$.

$$d(A,B) = \sqrt{\sum_i^n (A_i - B_i)^2}$$

Using weight w_i for the ith clinical feature and $\Phi(A_i, B_i)$ as a similarity function that compares A_i with B_i , the *Nearest Neighbour Algorithm*, which is commonly used in case-based reasoning, uses the following formula for measuring the similarity [20].

$$\frac{\sum_{i=1}^n w_i \times \Phi(A_i, B_i))}{\sum_{i=1}^n w_i}$$

It is also worthwhile to mention that similarly to the task of matching cases in case-based reasoning, pattern recognition in image processing often involves matching an image with a set of images using similarity measures. For example, Moghaddam and Pentland have introduced a technique known as Probabilistic Visual Learning, which is based on probability density estimation in high-dimensional feature spaces using an eigenspace decomposition [21]. Also, the techniques known as canonical correlation analysis and extended canonical correlation analysis involves measuring the degree of agreement between variations observed in two sets [22]. These techniques are desirable when the patterns of features are represented as different sets of vectors, and an adequately large sample of such feature sets are available so that relevant statistical techniques can be applied (e.g. estimating unimodal and multimodal probability distributions in a given set of features as in Probabilistic Visual Learning). These techniques were deemed unsuitable for the problem that we have addressed in this paper for two reasons. Firstly, the case-based reasoning that we have introduced in this paper involves *suggesting most likely similarity* rather than categorical identification. Accordingly the reasoning involves matching only two vectors rather than two sets of vectors, and rather than using a sample of standard cases it uses only a single standard case for each of a small number of comparisons. Therefore, it is difficult to apply the stated techniques meaningfully to this much simpler problem or use the associated probability measures. Secondly, the meaning of similarity needs to be interpreted in relation to the problem domain, and for example, the meaning of establishing similarity between the facial features in two images is vastly different to suggesting similarity between two clinical cases. The proposed approach involves approximating the *initial* diagnostic reasoning of an expert clinician using a clinically intuitive and meaningful model as described in the following section.

3   Orthogonal Vector Projection Measure

Let $\vec{S}$ be the standard vector representing the expected severity of clinical features in a particular diagnostic category, and $\vec{X}$ be the corresponding vector representing the observed severity of these clinical features in a patient. The orthogonal projection of $\vec{X}$ onto $\vec{S}$ is $\overrightarrow{X_P}$ as shown in Fig. 2.

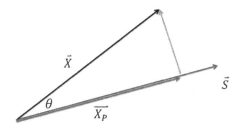

Fig. 2. Orthogonal vector projection

We claim that the ratio, $\frac{|\overrightarrow{X_P}|}{|\vec{S}|}$ serves as a clinically more intuitive measurement of the similarity of $\vec{X}$ to $\vec{S}$. This ratio can be derived as follows.

$$|\overrightarrow{X_P}| = |\vec{X}|cos\theta$$

$$cos\theta = \frac{\vec{X}.\vec{S}}{|\vec{X}||\vec{S}|}$$

$$|\overrightarrow{X_P}| = |\vec{X}|\frac{\vec{X}.\vec{S}}{|\vec{X}||\vec{S}|} = \frac{\vec{X}.\vec{S}}{|\vec{S}|}$$

$$\frac{|\overrightarrow{X_P}|}{|\vec{S}|} = \frac{\vec{X}.\vec{S}}{|\vec{S}|^2}$$

This proposed similarity measure attempts to approximate the expert clinical reasoning based on pattern recognition, which involves comparing: 1) the overall similarity between the individual symptoms of a given case and those of a small number of standard cases; and 2) the severity of the clinical case (i.e. 'how unwell the patient is') based on the overall severity of all the symptoms compared with the each of the standard cases which represent a severe example of the case. When this problem is conceptualised as cases representing vectors: a) the severity of a case is translated to vector length (i.e. the longer the vector the more severe the illness); and b) the direction of a case vector (representing the new case) towards the standard case vector (for each standard case) is translated as the overall similarity of the new case to that standard case. This provides a means to quantify the level of similarity of a given case to each of a given set of standard diagnoses respectively representing a severe example of that diagnosis. The proposed ratio derived from vector projection captures these two aspects best compared to the other two measures (cosine angle is invariant to vector length; Euclidean distance is unable to measure the direction of one vector towards the other). Therefore, the proposed ratio is considered clinically more intuitive.

4   Deriving Standard Cases

Based on their level of prevalence and clinical importance, five diagnostic categories consisting of: depression; anxiety; mania; psychosis; and delirium were chosen for an initial evaluation. A sixth category representing high-risk level (i.e. risk of suicide, aggression, or other form of harm) was also included because of its importance in an initial assessment. Psychiatric assessment involves eliciting clinical features in patients' histories and also features in mental state; accordingly a total of 63 clinical features representing both history and mental state items were carefully selected, using clinical expertise, for this initial evaluation. Selection involved subjective clinical judgement, based on one of the author's domain expertise (author Fernando is a registered practicing clinical psychiatrist), that these 63 features were the minimum number of items required for an adequate representation of a clinical case for the purpose of triaging. Of these 63 clinical features, the first 28 features were rated according to what can be expected in the patient's history, and the remaining 35 items were rated according to what can be expected in the findings of mental state examination. These ratings were based on a typical presentation of the most severe form of the respective illnesses, using the rating scale shown in Fig. 3. The relationships between each selected clinical feature and the six standard diagnostic categories, with ratings on a scale from 0 to 9, are shown in Fig. 4. It is important to emphasise that each standard case represents a typical severe form of the illness for its respective category. For example, in relation to the diagnostic category of depression, the first item 'depressed mood' in Fig. 4 was given a rating of nine, which is interpreted as 'extremely severe'

Score	Description
0	Absent
1	Very mild
2	Mild
3	Mild plus
4	Moderate
5	Moderate plus
6	Severe
7	Severe plus
8	Very severe
9	Extremely severe

Fig. 3. The scale used to score clinical features items

	Cinical Item	Depression	Anxiety	Psychosis	Mania	Delirium	Risk Level
1	Depressed mood	9	4	0	0	0	9
2	Anhedonia	9	0	0	0	0	0
3	Decreased appetite	9	0	0	0	0	0
4	Loss of weight	9	0	0	0	2	0
5	Decreased energy	9	8	0	0	0	0
6	Insomnia	9	8	3	9	3	9
7	Poor concentration	9	8	3	9	5	0
8	Self-harm behaviour	9	0	0	0	0	9
9	Past history of depression	9	0	0	8	0	0
10	Past history of psychosis	5	0	9	0	0	0
11	Past history of mania	0	0	0	9	0	0
12	Past suicidal attempts	9	0	0	5	0	9
13	Past history of agression	5	0	0	3	0	9
14	Increased goal directed behaviour	0	0	0	9	0	0
15	Increased pleasure seeeking behaviour	0	0	0	9	0	0
16	Lack of need for sleep	0	0	0	9	0	0
17	Aggressive behaviour	5	0	0	4	0	9
18	Avoiding certain situations because of anxiety	0	9	0	0	0	0
19	Panic attacks	0	9	0	0	0	0
20	Exposure to trauma	5	8	4	3	0	0
21	Family history of depression	7	0	0	0	0	0
22	Family history of schizophrenia	0	0	9	0	0	0
23	Family history of anxiety	0	9	0	0	0	0
24	Family history of bipolar	0	0	0	9	0	0
25	Excessive use of alcohol	5	5	0	2	3	8
26	Excessive use THC	0	0	8	2	0	0
27	Symptoms of a physical illness	0	0	0	0	9	0
28	Confusion and altered level of consciousness	0	0	0	0	9	0
29	Poor self-care	9	3	6	3	5	0
30	Poor eye contacts	8	0	0	0	3	0
31	Over familiarity	0	0	0	9	0	0
32	Slowing of mortor activity	9	0	0	0	5	0
33	Distractibility	2	7	7	9	7	0
34	Agitation	5	8	5	9	7	9
35	Irritability	5	2	4	8	3	8
36	Lack of reactivity of affect	9	2	9	0	5	0
37	lability of affect	4	0	0	9	0	0
38	Level of anxiety	5	9	0	0	5	7
39	Level of depression	9	4	0	0	4	9
40	Lack of prosody in speech	9	2	0	0	0	0
41	Reduced volume in speech	9	0	0	0	3	0
42	Reduced flow of speech	9	0	0	0	3	0
43	Increased flow of speech	0	6	0	9	0	0
44	Tangential thought form	0	0	6	9	5	0
45	Lack of coherence in speech	0	5	9	7	8	0
46	Grandiosity	0	0	0	9	0	0
47	Guilt and self-blame	9	4	0	0	0	9
48	Low self-esteem and confidence	9	4	0	0	0	0
49	Increased self-esteem	0	0	0	9	0	0
50	Worrying thougths	5	9	4	0	4	8
51	Pessimistic thoughts	9	4	0	0	0	9
52	Self-harm thoughts	8	0	0	0	0	9
53	Persecutory thoughts/delusions	4	0	9	0	7	0
54	Bizarre duelsions	0	0	9	0	5	0
55	Non-bizarre delusions	3	0	7	0	5	0
56	Auditory hallucinations	3	0	9	0	5	5
57	Mood congrency of psychotic symptoms	9	0	0	9	7	9
58	Visual hallucinations	0	0	0	0	9	0
59	Lack of insight	1	0	8	9	8	0
60	Impaired concentration	3	9	4	5	9	0
61	Impaired registration	3	9	2	3	9	0
62	Impaired recall	3	9	2	3	9	0
63	Disorientation	0	0	0	0	9	0

Fig. 4. Standard cases

using the rating scale shown in Fig. 3. This was because, in a typical and most severe case of depression, the depressed mood is expected to be extremely severe. On the other hand, in a typically most severe case of mania, the depressed mood was rated as zero (absent) as is appropriate for that diagnostic category. The resulting vectors of 63 clinical items are approximate representations of the expert domain knowledge achieved using subjective clinical judgement.

5   Evaluation of Similarity Measures Using Test Cases, and the Results

In order to test our claim that the similarity measure derived from orthogonal vector projection was better, and to choose the most appropriate similarity measure for this application, we carefully derived 30 different test cases using clinical expertise. These include five different test cases representing an increasing gradient of the severity of the clinical features for each diagnostic category (i.e. for each category, case $i + 1$ is more severe than case i, where $i = 1,2,3,4$). These thirty test cases are shown in Fig. 5a and Fig. 5b.

Each of the test cases was compared to each of the standard cases, and similarity measures were obtained using cosine angle, Euclidean distance, and the orthogonal vector projection. The aims of the evaluation were: 1) to identify which similarity measure was able to differentiate test cases in relation to both diagnostic category and severity; and 2) to test our claim that orthogonal vector projection was a better measure to achieve the above based on clinical intuition.

The method of evaluation using 30 test cases should not to be interpreted as an attempt to test our technique statistically. Test cases were chosen carefully, and do not represent a random sample. The testing presented here is similar to testing a computer algorithm using test data, in which a programmer would choose carefully depending on those different parts of the algorithm that need to be tested. Given that the severity and similarity of symptoms are rated on 0-10 scale, five cases were considered to be adequate to reasonably represent different gradients within this range. Five cases for each diagnostic category were chosen in such a way that this 0-10 range was evenly covered. In terms of the accuracy of the measure there is fuzziness because of the highly subjective nature of the domain knowledge. Therefore, the evaluation was about determining which comparison technique was able to best differentiate both the diagnosis and severity of test cases, and not about comparing the results with any "gold standard".

Fig. 6, and Fig. 7 show the results of similarity measures obtained using cosine angle and Euclidean distance methods respectively. The Nearest Neighbourhood method could not be directly compared with these other methods used in evaluation since our approach did not use weights, however, we have mentioned it earlier for the sake of completeness. The results of similarity measure obtained by using orthogonal vector projection are shown in Fig. 8. The row-column intersection gives the similarity score of the test case given in the column, which corresponds to the diagnostic category given in the row.

Cinical Item	Depression Cases					Anxiety Cases					Psychosis Cases				
	1	2	3	4	5	1	2	3	4	5	1	2	3	4	5
1 Depressed mood	5	6	7	8	9	0	0	0	3	5	0	0	4	5	6
2 Anhedonia	5	6	6	7	8	0	0	0	0	0	0	0	0	0	0
3 Decreased appetite	4	5	6	8	8	0	0	0	0	0	0	0	0	0	0
4 Loss of weight	5	5	6	7	8	0	0	0	0	0	0	0	0	0	0
5 Decreased energy	5	7	7	8	9	0	0	5	6	6	0	0	0	0	0
6 Insomnia	6	6	7	7	8	0	5	6	7	8	0	0	5	6	8
7 Poor concentration	4	5	6	7	7	0	4	5	6	7	3	4	5	5	7
8 Self-harm behaviour	2	5	7	8	9	0	0	0	0	0	0	0	0	0	0
9 Past history of depression	0	5	9	0	5	0	0	0	0	0	0	0	0	0	0
10 Past history of psychosis	0	0	0	0	0	0	0	0	0	0	0	0	5	5	9
11 Past history of mania	0	0	0	0	0	0	0	0	0	0	0	0	0	0	0
12 Past suicidal attempts	0	0	5	0	9	0	0	0	0	0	0	0	0	0	0
13 Past history of agression	0	0	6	0	0	0	0	0	0	0	0	0	0	0	5
14 Increased goal directed behaviour	0	0	0	0	0	0	0	0	0	0	0	0	0	0	0
15 Increased pleasure seeking behaviour	0	0	0	0	0	0	0	0	0	0	0	0	0	0	0
16 Lack of need for sleep	0	0	0	0	0	0	0	0	0	0	0	0	0	0	0
17 Aggressive behaviour	0	4	5	0	0	0	0	0	0	0	0	0	0	0	5
18 Avoiding certain situations because of anxiety	0	0	0	0	0	5	6	7	8	9	0	0	0	0	0
19 Panic attacks	0	0	0	0	0	0	5	6	7	8	0	0	0	0	0
20 Exposure to trauma	5	5	0	5	5	0	0	5	7	9	0	0	0	0	0
21 Family history of depression	5	0	7	9	9	0	0	0	0	0	0	0	0	0	0
22 Family history of schizophrenia	0	0	0	0	0	0	0	0	0	0	0	5	5	9	9
23 Family history of anxiety	0	0	5	9	9	0	5	5	9	9	0	0	0	0	0
24 Family history of bipolar	0	0	0	0	0	0	0	0	0	0	0	0	0	0	0
25 Excessive use of alcohol	5	6	7	4	0	0	0	5	5	9	0	0	5	5	5
26 Excessive use THC	0	0	0	0	0	0	0	0	0	0	5	5	0	5	9
27 Symptoms of a physical illness	0	0	0	0	0	0	0	0	0	0	0	0	0	0	0
28 Confusion and altered level of consciousness	0	0	0	0	0	0	0	0	0	0	0	0	0	0	0
29 Poor self-care	5	6	7	8	9	0	0	0	0	4	0	0	5	5	7
30 Poor eye contacts	6	7	7	7	8	0	0	0	0	0	0	0	0	0	6
31 Over familiarity	0	0	0	0	0	0	0	0	0	0	0	0	0	0	0
32 Slowing of mortor activity	4	5	6	7	8	0	0	0	0	0	0	0	0	0	0
33 Distractibility	0	0	0	0	0	0	3	3	5	3	0	4	6	6	7
34 Agitation	2	3	5	6	6	0	3	4	4	5	4	0	4	6	7
35 Irritability	3	4	5	5	5	0	0	0	0	0	0	4	4	0	3
36 Lack of reactivity of affect	5	6	7	7	8	3	0	4	6	6	5	5	7	7	8
37 lability of affect	0	0	4	5	6	0	0	0	0	0	0	0	0	0	0
38 Level of anxiety	0	3	5	6	6	5	6	7	8	9	0	4	0	6	5
39 Level of depression	7	8	8	9	9	0	0	3	3	4	0	0	0	0	5
40 Lack of prosody in speech	3	5	6	7	8	0	0	0	4	4	0	0	0	5	0
41 Reduced volume in speech	3	5	6	7	8	0	0	0	0	0	0	0	0	0	0
42 Reduced flow of speech	3	5	6	7	8	0	0	0	0	0	0	0	0	0	0
43 Increased flow of speech	0	0	0	0	0	0	0	3	3	4	0	0	0	0	0
44 Tangential thought form	0	0	0	0	0	0	0	0	0	0	0	0	6	6	0
45 Lack of coherence in speech	0	0	0	0	0	0	0	0	0	0	0	0	0	5	0
46 Grandiosity	0	0	0	0	0	0	0	0	0	0	0	0	0	0	0
47 Guilt and self-blame	6	6	7	8	9	0	0	0	0	0	0	0	0	0	0
48 Low self-esteem and confidence	6	6	7	8	9	0	0	0	0	5	0	0	0	0	0
49 Increased self-esteem	0	0	0	0	9	0	0	0	0	0	0	0	0	0	0
50 Worrying thoughts	5	6	7	7	8	5	6	7	8	9	0	0	0	4	4
51 Pessimistic thoughts	6	6	7	8	9	0	0	0	0	7	0	0	0	0	0
52 Self-harm thoughts	6	6	7	8	9	0	0	0	0	0	0	0	0	5	0
53 Persecutory thoughts/delusions	0	0	0	5	9	0	0	0	0	0	6	0	6	7	9
54 Bizarre duelsions	0	0	0	0	0	0	0	0	0	0	0	7	8	7	7
55 Non-bizarre delusions	0	0	0	0	0	0	0	0	0	0	6	0	0	5	8
56 Auditory hallucinations	0	0	0	0	9	0	0	0	0	0	6	7	8	8	8
57 Mood congrency of psychotic symptoms	0	0	0	0	9	0	0	0	0	0	0	3	0	0	6
58 Visual hallucinations	0	0	0	0	0	0	0	0	0	0	0	0	0	0	0
59 Lack of insight	0	0	0	0	7	0	0	0	0	0	6	7	8	7	8
60 Impaired concentration	0	0	5	6	8	3	4	5	5	5	0	4	5	6	6
61 Impaired registration	0	0	0	0	0	0	0	0	0	0	0	0	0	4	4
62 Impaired recall	0	0	0	5	6	0	0	0	4	4	0	4	4	6	6
63 Disorientation	0	0	0	0	0	0	0	0	0	0	0	0	0	0	0

Fig. 5a. Test cases for the diagnostic categories of depression, anxiety and psychosis

Clinical Item	Mania Cases					Delirium Cases					Risk Cases				
	1	2	3	4	5	1	2	3	4	5	1	2	3	4	5
1 Depressed mood	0	0	0	0	0	0	0	0	5	5	5	7	6	8	9
2 Anhedonia	0	0	0	0	0	0	0	0	0	0	6	5	7	7	8
3 Decreased appetite	0	0	0	0	0	0	0	0	0	0	0	0	5	6	7
4 Loss of weight	0	0	0	0	0	0	0	5	5	7	0	0	0	0	5
5 Decreased energy	0	0	0	0	0	0	0	6	5	7	0	5	5	0	0
6 Insomnia	6	7	8	8	9	0	0	6	8	8	6	7	7	8	9
7 Poor concentration	5	6	7	8	9	0	0	5	5	0	0	5	5	0	5
8 Self-harm behaviour	0	0	0	0	0	0	0	0	0	0	5	7	5	7	9
9 Past history of depression	0	0	5	5	0	0	0	0	0	0	0	0	0	5	9
10 Past history of psychosis	0	0	0	0	0	0	0	0	0	0	0	0	0	0	0
11 Past history of mania	0	0	9	9	9	0	0	0	0	0	0	0	0	0	0
12 Past suicidal attempts	0	0	0	0	0	0	0	0	0	0	5	5	9	5	9
13 Past history of agression	0	0	5	5	0	0	0	0	0	0	0	5	6	8	0
14 Increased goal directed behaviour	5	7	7	8	9	0	0	0	0	0	0	0	0	0	0
15 Increased pleasure seeeking behaviour	5	6	6	7	9	0	0	0	0	0	0	0	0	0	5
16 Lack of need for sleep	6	7	7	8	9	0	0	0	0	0	0	0	0	0	0
17 Aggressive behaviour	0	0	5	5	7	0	0	0	0	0	5	6	8	8	9
18 Avoiding certain situations because of anxiety	0	0	0	0	0	0	0	0	0	0	0	0	0	0	0
19 Panic attacks	0	0	0	0	0	0	0	0	0	0	0	0	0	0	0
20 Exposure to trauma	0	0	0	0	0	0	0	0	0	0	0	0	0	0	0
21 Family history of depression	0	0	0	0	0	0	0	0	0	0	0	0	0	0	0
22 Family history of schizophrenia	0	0	0	0	0	0	0	0	0	0	0	0	0	0	0
23 Family history of anxiety	0	0	0	0	0	0	0	0	0	0	0	0	0	0	0
24 Family history of bipolar	5	5	9	9	9	0	0	0	0	0	0	0	0	0	0
25 Excessive use of alcohol	0	0	0	5	5	0	0	0	0	7	0	0	5	5	9
26 Excessive use THC	0	5	5	0	7	0	0	0	0	0	0	0	5	0	8
27 Symptoms of a physical illness	0	0	0	0	0	5	5	6	7	9	0	0	0	0	0
28 Confusion and altered level of consciousness	0	0	0	0	0	6	8	8	9	9	0	0	0	0	0
29 Poor self-care	0	0	0	0	5	4	6	7	6	8	0	0	0	5	5
30 Poor eye contacts	0	0	0	0	0	0	0	2	4	5	0	0	0	0	0
31 Over familiarity	5	6	6	8	5	0	0	0	0	0	0	0	0	0	0
32 Slowing of mortor activity	0	0	0	0	0	0	0	5	4	6	0	0	0	0	0
33 Distractibility	5	5	7	7	8	4	5	5	6	8	0	0	0	0	0
34 Agitation	4	6	4	7	6	4	5	5	7	5	6	7	7	8	9
35 Irritability	0	5	5	4	6	0	0	3	5	0	0	6	8	5	7
36 Lack of reactivity of affect	0	0	0	0	0	0	0	4	4	5	0	0	0	0	0
37 lability of affect	0	5	3	7	8	0	0	0	0	0	0	0	0	0	0
38 Level of anxiety	0	0	0	0	5	3	4	5	5	6	5	0	0	5	7
39 Level of depression	0	0	0	0	0	0	0	2	0	4	5	5	0	6	6
40 Lack of prosody in speech	0	0	0	0	0	0	0	0	4	4	0	0	0	0	0
41 Reduced volume in speech	0	0	0	0	0	0	0	2	2	4	0	0	0	0	0
42 Reduced flow of speech	0	0	0	0	0	0	0	2	4	5	0	0	0	0	0
43 Increased flow of speech	5	6	7	6	8	0	0	0	4	0	0	0	0	0	0
44 Tangential thought form	5	6	6	7	8	0	4	2	6	8	0	0	0	0	0
45 Lack of coherence in speech	0	0	0	4	6	4	5	6	5	6	0	0	0	0	0
46 Grandiosity	4	5	5	7	6	0	0	0	0	0	0	0	0	0	0
47 Guilt and self-blame	0	0	0	0	0	0	0	0	0	0	0	5	0	7	8
48 Low self-esteem and confidence	0	0	0	0	0	0	0	0	0	0	0	0	0	0	0
49 Increased self-esteem	5	7	6	7	9	0	0	0	0	0	0	0	0	0	0
50 Worrying thougths	0	0	0	0	0	0	4	0	6	8	0	0	0	6	7
51 Pessimistic thoughts	0	0	0	0	0	0	0	0	0	0	5	5	0	6	8
52 Self-harm thoughts	0	0	0	0	0	0	0	0	0	0	6	6	7	8	8
53 Persecutory thoughts/delusions	0	0	0	5	8	5	4	5	6	8	0	0	0	0	0
54 Bizarre duelsions	0	0	0	0	0	0	0	0	0	0	0	0	0	0	0
55 Non-bizarre delusions	0	0	0	6	8	0	4	5	6	8	0	0	0	0	9
56 Auditory hallucinations	0	0	0	0	0	0	4	5	6	8	0	0	0	0	0
57 Mood congrency of psychotic symptoms	0	0	0	8	8	0	0	0	0	0	0	0	0	5	9
58 Visual hallucinations	0	0	0	0	0	0	2	4	6	8	0	0	0	0	0
59 Lack of insight	4	5	6	7	8	5	4	6	8	9	0	0	0	0	0
60 Impaired concentration	0	3	4	6	6	6	6	6	7	8	0	0	0	0	0
61 Impaired registration	0	0	0	0	2	4	5	6	8	9	0	0	0	0	0
62 Impaired recall	0	2	4	6	6	6	6	8	9	9	0	0	0	0	0
63 Disorientation	0	0	0	0	0	6	5	8	8	9	0	0	0	0	0

Fig. 5b. Test cases for the diagnostic categories of mania and delirium, and high-risk category

According to the results all three methods are reasonably capable of differentiating the test cases in relation to primary diagnostic category, except test case 1 of anxiety test cases. The smallest Euclidian distance measured for this test case was 31 for both anxiety and psychosis, and the maximum value of the orthogonal vector projection method was 0.1 for anxiety, psychosis, delirium and risk categories. However, this test case represents the lowest form of severity because of the overlap of symptoms across diagnostic categories, so failure to discriminate this test case in relation to the primary diagnostic category was not clinically very significant.

On the other hand, both the cosine angle method and the Euclidean distance method were unable to accurately differentiate the severity gradient. For example, using the cosine angle method, it was not possible to differentiate the severity of anxiety for test cases 3, 4, and 5 since all three scored 0.9. In addition, some Euclidian distance measures failed to identify the test cases in relation to the severity gradient. For example, test cases 4 and 5 under mania in Fig. 6 scored 15 and 19 respectively, and this was incorrect since test case 5 is more severe than test case 4 (i.e. the resulting Euclidean distance for case 5 should be less than that for the case 4). In contrast, the measure derived from orthogonal vector projection was able to accurately differentiate severity in all test cases.

	Depression Cases					Anxiety Cases					Psychosis Cases				
	1	2	3	4	5	1	2	3	4	5	1	2	3	4	5
1 Depression	0.86	0.9	0.93	0.9	0.9	0.2	0.2	0.4	0.4	0.5	0.2	0.25	0.4	0.4	0.5
2 Anxiety	0.47	0.5	0.5	0.6	0.5	0.5	0.8	0.9	0.9	0.9	0.1	0.3	0.4	0.5	0.5
3 Psychosis	0.22	0.2	0.21	0.3	0.4	0.2	0.2	0.3	0.3	0.3	0.7	0.69	0.8	0.9	0.8
4 Mania	0.17	0.2	0.29	0.2	0.3	0	0.2	0.3	0.3	0.3	0.2	0.32	0.4	0.4	0.4
5 Delirium	0.28	0.3	0.33	0.4	0.5	0.3	0.3	0.3	0.4	0.3	0.4	0.52	0.6	0.6	0.6
6 Risk	0.49	0.5	0.57	0.5	0.5	0.2	0.2	0.3	0.3	0.4	0.3	0.3	0.4	0.5	0.6

	Mania Cases					Delirium Cases					Risk Cases				
	1	2	3	4	5	1	2	3	4	5	1	2	3	4	5
1 Depression	0.15	0.2	0.24	0.3	0.3	0.2	0.2	0.5	0.5	0.5	0.6	0.64	0.6	0.7	0.7
2 Anxiety	0.29	0.3	0.32	0.4	0.4	0.4	0.5	0.5	0.6	0.5	0.3	0.37	0.3	0.4	0.4
3 Psychosis	0.26	0.3	0.31	0.4	0.5	0.4	0.5	0.5	0.6	0.5	0.1	0.14	0.2	0.2	0.3
4 Mania	0.82	0.9	0.9	0.9	0.9	0.3	0.3	0.4	0.4	0.3	0.2	0.31	0.3	0.3	0.4
5 Delirium	0.25	0.3	0.3	0.4	0.5	0.8	0.9	0.9	0.9	0.9	0.2	0.17	0.2	0.2	0.3
6 Risk	0.17	0.2	0.27	0.3	0.4	0.3	0.4	0.4	0.4	0.5	0.6	0.66	0.6	0.8	0.8

Fig. 6. Results using Cosine angle

	Depression Cases					Anxiety Cases					Psychosis Cases				
	1	2	3	4	5	1	2	3	4	5	1	2	3	4	5
1 Depression	28.6	24	18.8	22	22	46	45	43	43	41	46	45.8	44	43	42
2 Anxiety	31.7	33	35.8	35	43	31	25	20	17	16	36	34	34	32	36
3 Psychosis	35.4	38	43	44	48	31	32	32	34	38	24	22.9	18	16	21
4 Mania	44	45	46.4	51	52	42	40	40	42	44	40	39.1	38	40	42
5 Delirium	36.5	38	41.4	42	45	34	33	34	35	38	31	29.7	28	27	30
6 Risk	37.7	37	37.3	42	44	42	42	42	43	42	41	41.3	41	39	36

	Mania Cases					Delirium Cases					Risk Cases				
	1	2	3	4	5	1	2	3	4	5	1	2	3	4	5
1 Depression	47.6	48	48.8	49	51	47	47	42	42	44	40	36.7	38	33	33
2 Anxiety	34.3	35	37.6	40	41	31	31	31	31	36	33	33.5	36	36	41
3 Psychosis	32	33	35.7	38	37	29	26	28	30	34	35	36	36	39	43
4 Mania	27.9	23	19.1	15	19	39	39	40	41	47	41	40.1	40	42	44
5 Delirium	35	36	38.2	37	38	23	20	16	16	18	36	38	40	40	43
6 Risk	43.9	44	45	45	45	41	40	41	41	43	35	32.8	34	27	26

Fig. 7. Results using Euclidean distance

		Depression Cases					Anxiety Cases					Psychosis Cases				
		1	2	3	4	5	1	2	3	4	5	1	2	3	4	5
1	Depression	0.45	0.6	0.73	0.8	0.9	0	0.1	0.2	0.2	0.3	0.1	0.1	0.2	0.3	0.4
2	Anxiety	0.33	0.4	0.53	0.7	0.7	0.1	0.3	0.5	0.7	0.8	0.1	0.15	0.3	0.4	0.5
3	Psychosis	0.17	0.2	0.24	0.3	0.5	0.1	0.1	0.2	0.2	0.3	0.3	0.4	0.6	0.8	0.9
4	Mania	0.1	0.2	0.26	0.2	0.4	0	0.1	0.1	0.2	0.2	0.1	0.14	0.2	0.3	0.3
5	Delirium	0.2	0.3	0.35	0.4	0.6	0.1	0.1	0.2	0.3	0.3	0.2	0.27	0.4	0.6	0.6
6	Risk	0.37	0.5	0.67	0.6	0.8	0.1	0.1	0.2	0.3	0.4	0.1	0.1	0.2	0.3	0.4

		Mania Cases					Delirium Cases					Risk Cases				
		1	2	3	4	5	1	2	3	4	5	1	2	3	4	5
1	Depression	0.06	0.1	0.15	0.2	0.3	0.1	0.1	0.3	0.4	0.4	0.2	0.31	0.3	0.4	0.6
2	Anxiety	0.15	0.2	0.27	0.4	0.5	0.2	0.3	0.4	0.6	0.6	0.2	0.24	0.2	0.3	0.4
3	Psychosis	0.15	0.3	0.29	0.4	0.6	0.2	0.4	0.5	0.6	0.7	0	0.1	0.1	0.1	0.3
4	Mania	0.37	0.5	0.65	0.8	0.9	0.1	0.2	0.3	0.3	0.3	0.1	0.17	0.2	0.2	0.4
5	Delirium	0.14	0.2	0.25	0.4	0.6	0.4	0.5	0.7	0.9	1	0.1	0.11	0.1	0.2	0.3
6	Risk	0.07	0.1	0.19	0.3	0.4	0.1	0.2	0.3	0.3	0.4	0.3	0.35	0.4	0.5	0.7

Fig. 8. Results using orthogonal vector projection

6   Conclusion

This paper described a case-based reasoning approach that was adopted according to the nature of domain knowledge (i.e. specific nature of diagnosis in psychiatry compared to other branches of medicine) and the requirements of its application as a triage tool in initial psychiatric assessment. A more clinically intuitive method derived from orthogonal vector projection, which similarity measure better suits the required clinical reasoning of the application, was used. Evaluation of the orthogonal vector projection similarity measure was applied to test cases and shown to be superior compared to two commonly used alternative similarity measures, cosine angle and Euclidean distance.

The development of generic clinical reasoning applications that cover different medical specialities is challenging due to their complexity and the large knowledge-base required. This paper demonstrates the feasibility of developing clinical reasoning applications for preliminary diagnosis by adopting generic methods according to the specific nature of a chosen subdomain (e.g. a particular medical subspecialty) and application requirements. As the next stage of development, we intend to evaluate this approach by applying it as the triage tool for real patients. Also, further tuning and adjustments to both the set of chosen clinical features and the vector representation of the standard cases will be undertaken in order to further improve the differentiation of diagnoses and severity of cases.

References

1. Eaton, W.W., Martins, S.S., Nestadt, G., Bienvenu, O.J., Clarke, D., Alexandre, P.: The Burden of Mental Disorders. Epidemiologic Reviews 30, 1–14 (2008)
2. Paykel, E.S., Brugha, T., Fryers, T.: Size and burden of depressive disorders in Europe. European neuropsychopharmacology: The Journal of the European College of Neuropsychopharmacology 15, 411–423 (2005)
3. May, A.M., Klonsky, E.D., Klein, D.N.: Predicting future suicide attempts among depressed suicide ideators: a 10-year longitudinal study. J Psychiatr Res 46, 946–952 (2012)
4. Fernando, I., Henskens, F., Cohen, M.: An approximate reasoning model for medical diagnosis. In: Lee, R. (ed.) SNPD 2013. Studies in Computational Intelligence, vol. 492, pp. 11–24. Springer, Heidelberg (2013)

5. Fernando, I., Henskens, F.: ST Algorithm for Diagnostic Reasoning in Psychiatry. Polibits 48, 23–29 (2013)
6. [6] Fernando, I., Henskens, F.: Drill-Locate-Drill Algorithm for Diagnostic Reasoning in Psychiatry. International Journal of Machine Learning and Computing 3, 449–452 (2013)
7. Aamodt, A., Plaza, E.: Case-based reasoning: foundational issues, methodological variations, and system approaches. AI Commun. 7, 39–59 (1994)
8. Association, A.P.: Diagnostic and Statistical Manual of Mental Disorders: Dsm-5. Amer Psychiatric Pub Incorporated (2013)
9. Lopez de Mantaras, R., McSherry, D., Bridge, D., Leake, D., Smyth, B., Craw, S., et al.: Retrieval, reuse, revision and retention in case-based reasoning. The Knowledge Engineering Review 20, 215–240 (2005)
10. Cover, T., Hart, P.: Nearest neighbor pattern classification. IEEE Trans. Inf. Theor. 13, 21–27 (2006)
11. Wess, S., Althoff, K.-D., Derwand, G.: Using k-d trees to improve the retrieval step in case-based reasoning. In: Wess, S., Richter, M., Althoff, K.-D. (eds.) EWCBR 1993. LNCS, vol. 837, pp. 167–181. Springer, Heidelberg (1994)
12. Smyth, B., McKenna, E.: Competence guided incremental footprint-based retrieval. Knowledge-Based Systems 14, 155–161 (2001)
13. Schaaf, J.: Fish and Shrink. A next step towards efficient case retrieval in large scaled case bases. In: Smith, I., Faltings, B.V. (eds.) EWCBR 1996. LNCS, vol. 1168, pp. 362–376. Springer, Heidelberg (1996)
14. Aamodt, A.: Knowledge-intensive case-based reasoning in CREEK. In: Funk, P., González Calero, P.A. (eds.) ECCBR 2004. LNCS (LNAI), vol. 3155, pp. 1–15. Springer, Heidelberg (2004)
15. Brown, M.: An underlying memory model to support case retrieval. In: Wess, S., Richter, M., Althoff, K.-D. (eds.) EWCBR 1993. LNCS, vol. 837, pp. 132–143. Springer, Heidelberg (1994)
16. Mougouie, B., Bergmann, R.: Similarity assessment for generalizied cases by optimization methods. In: Craw, S., Preece, A.D. (eds.) ECCBR 2002. LNCS (LNAI), vol. 2416, pp. 249–263. Springer, Heidelberg (2002)
17. Bunke, H., Messmer, B.T.: Similarity measures for structured representations. In: Wess, S., Richter, M., Althoff, K.-D. (eds.) EWCBR 1993. LNCS, vol. 837, pp. 106–118. Springer, Heidelberg (1994)
18. Arcos, J., de Mántaras, R.: Perspectives: A declarative bias mechanism for case retrieval. In: Leake, D.B., Plaza, E. (eds.) ICCBR 1997. LNCS, vol. 1266, pp. 279–290. Springer, Heidelberg (1997)
19. Qian, G., Sural, S., Gu, Y., Pramanik, S.: Similarity between Euclidean and cosine angle distance for nearest neighbor queries. presented at the Proceedings of the 2004 ACM symposium on Applied Computing, Nicosia, Cyprus (2004)
20. Watson, I., Marir, F.: Case-based reasoning: A review. The Knowledge Engineering Review 9, 327–354 (1994)
21. Moghaddam, B., Pentland, A.: Probabilistic visual learning for object detection. In: Proceedings Fifth International Conference on Computer Vision, pp. 786–793 (1995)
22. Arandjelović, O.: Discriminative extended canonical correlation analysis for pattern set matching. Machine Learning 94, 353–370 (2014)

The MST-kNN with Paracliques

Ahmed Shamsul Arefin, Carlos Riveros, Regina Berretta, and Pablo Moscato

The Priority Research Centre for Bioinformatics Biomarker Discovery and
Information-based Medicine
Information-based Medicine Program, Hunter Medical Research Institute,
School of Electrical Engineering and Computer Science,
The University of Newcastle, Australia
{ahmed.arefin,carlos.riveros,regina.berretta,
pablo.moscato}@newcastle.edu.au

Abstract. In this work, we incorporate new edges from a paraclique-identification approach to the output of the MST-kNN graph partitioning method. We present a statistical analysis of the results on a dataset originated from a computational linguistic study of 84 Indo-European languages. We also present results from a computational stylistic study of 168 plays of the Shakespearean era. For the latter, results of the Kruskal-Wallis test 1 (observed vs. all permutations) showed a p-value of a 1.62E-11 and a Wilcoxon test a p-value of 8.1E-12. Overall, our results clearly show in both cases that the modified approach provides statistically more significant results than the use of the MST-kNN alone, thus providing a highly-scalable alternative and statistically sound approach for data clustering.

Keywords: data clustering, graph partitioning, MST-kNN, paracliques.

1 Introduction

Data clustering is perhaps the most common and widely used approach in data analytics. Over the years, a large number of methods have been developed for clustering. Among those, the graph-based approaches are well-known for their advantages in partitioning both real-world and artificial data [22]. Graph based methods generally take a distance matrix computed from the input and build a proximity graph $(G(V, E))$, where each vertex represents a data element, each edge represents the presence of a proximity relationship and the weight of the edge represents, in some way, the degree of proximity of the pair of vertices [31,1]. This is followed by the computation of some subgraphs [7], the Minimum Spaning Tree (MST), the k-Nearest Neighbour Graph (k-NNG), the Relative Neighbourhood Graph (RNG) and so forth.

Among the various known graph clustering methods, the MST-kNN [19] (see also [15]) is of interest for our work as it does not require any ad hoc user-defined parameter. Further, in terms of homogeneity and separation index [30], it has been shown that it performs better than the classical clustering algorithms such as K-Means and SOMs [21]. The MST-kNN's scalability and performance have

S.K. Chalup et al. (Eds.): ACALCI 2015, LNAI 8955, pp. 373–386, 2015.

been demonstrated in its external-memory [2] as well as in data-parallel variants [6,4]. Furthermore, it has been employed in the analysis of large-scale real-world data of various kinds, such as stock market data [19], yeast [20], prostate cancer [9], breast cancer [2] and Alzheimer's disease [3].

In this work, we extend the MST-kNN method by integrating kNN based paraclique structures. A clique is a set of vertices in which every vertex has an edge to every other vertex in the set. A maximal clique is a clique that cannot be extended by adding another vertex. The maximum clique of a graph is a maximal clique that has the largest number of vertices and is arguably the most "natural" cluster in a proximity graph [27]. The computation of vertex-disjoint sets of maximum cliques in a graph seems an interesting approach, however, the problem of finding the maximum clique is a well-known $\mathcal{NP}$-hard problem. We do not expect to have polynomial-time algorithms for this problem for the general case– as the decision version is $\mathcal{NP}$-complete [14].

In contrast, the identification of *paracliques* provides a viable alternative [10]. Given some experimental settings, in which the "proximity" relation may behave some false positives, the identification of maximum cliques in the proximity graph brings some assurance in "filtering out" many of these false positives. However, both the intractability of the problem and the fact that "false negatives" may conspire to find highly dense subgraphs which do not reach "clique status", synergise to point at the identification of paracliques as a good research direction. In this contribution, we identify paracliques via the identification of the maximal cliques of size 3 or higher present in the kNN graphs, reconstructed from the MST-kNN components. In other words, we collect the neighborhood networks as paracliques that are present within the MST-kNN components, but lack only a few edges to become cliques of a larger size. The results provide more insightful networks among the core vertices in each MST-kNN partition than the ones portrayed by the MST alone.

The rest of the paper is organised as follows. Section 2 describes the original MST-kNN algorithm and its proposed extension. It also explains the graph randomisation procedure we utilise to evaluate the methods. Section 3 explains the experimental data for the method evaluation. Section 4 depicts the clustering outcomes and statistical results obtained through using the methods and Section 5 gives our future plans and concluding remarks.

2   Methods

2.1   The MST-kNN Algorithm

The MST-kNN algorithm, as presented in [19], receives as input an undirected complete weighted graph, $G(V,E,W)$, and first computes two proximity graphs: a minimum spanning tree (G_{MST}) and a k-nearest neighbour graph (G_{kNN}), where the value of k is determined by Eq. 1:

$$k = \mathbf{min}\{\lfloor \ln(n) \rfloor \, ; \mathbf{min} \; k \; / \; G_{kNN} \, \mathbf{is \; connected}\} \tag{1}$$

Subsequently, the algorithm inspects all edges in the G_{MST}. If for a given edge (u,v) in this graph, neither u is one of the k nearest neighbors of v, nor v is one of the k nearest neighbors of u, the edge is eliminated from the G_{MST}. This results in a new graph $= G_{MST} - \{(u,v)\}$. Since the G_{MST} is a tree, after the deletion of first edge, it becomes a forest. The algorithm continues to apply the same procedure recursively to each subtree in with a value of k re-adjusted by Eq. 1, where n is now the number of nodes in each subtree, until no further partition is possible. The final partition of the nodes of induced by the forest is the result of the clustering algorithm. Here the computation of the MST, for example using the Prims algorithm requires $O(|E|log|V|)$ operations and the kNN requires $O(k|V|^2)$ operations.

2.2   The MST-kNN with Paracliques

The modified algorithm, termed as the MST-kNN WITH PARACLIQUES is presented in Algorithm 1 . It adopts the working procedure of the MST-kNN, but using an iterative approach (steps 7-11). It follows the concept that "a partitioned subtree is also an exact MST of the relevant component in the complete graph" [2]. Therefore, it computes the MST only once, at the beginning at step 2, instead of, at each iterative step. Where an additional method (the kNN PARACLIQUES) computes the paracliques (step 8) of the MST-kNN components obtained at step 4. A merge graph method (the MERGE GRAPHS) merges the paracliques with those components (step 9) and at the end, all of the graph components are aggregated to build the final MST-kNN with paracliques at step 10.

Algorithm 1. MST-kNN WITH PARACLIQUES (D: Distance matrix)

---

1 Compute G (D);
2 Compute G_{MST} (G);
3 Compute G_{kNN} according to Eq. 1;
4 $G_{cluster} \leftarrow \{V_{cluster} = V, E_{cluster} = E_{MST} \cap E_{kNN}\}$;
5 $G_{connectedComponents} \leftarrow$ connected components $(G_{cluster})$;
6 $G_{cluster} \leftarrow \emptyset$;
7 **for** *each connected component* C *in* $G_{connectedComponents}$ **do**
8 | $C_{pCliques} \leftarrow k$NN PARACLIQUES(d_submatrix(C));
9 | $C \leftarrow$ MERGE GRAPHS$(C, C_{pCliques})$;
10 |_ $G_{cluster} \leftarrow G_{cluster} + C$;
11 Return $G_{cluster}$;

The kNN Paracliques method (Algorithm 2) has as input the distance submatrix D' between the objects represented by the vertices of each of the MST-kNN components and it computes the kNN graph G_{kNN} $(G(D'))$, where the value of k is re-defined by Eq. 1. Next, for each kNN graph component, it finds all the cliques of size greater than 3 (step 6) and extracts the top k maximal cliques. Cliques are then aggregated (collectively forming the aforementioned paracliques at step 7) and returned (step 9) to the modified MST-kNN, for merging with the relevant MST-kNN component.

Algorithm 2. kNN PARACLIQUES (D': Distance matrix)

---

1 Compute G (D');
2 Compute G_{kNN} according to Eq. 1;
3 $G_{pCliques} \leftarrow \emptyset$;
4 $G_{connectedComponents} \leftarrow$ connected components (G_{kNN});
5 **for** *each connected component* C *in* $G_{connectedComponents}$ **do**
6   *Find all cliques in* C *with size greater than 3*;
7      $G_{pCliques} \leftarrow G_{pCliques} +$ *top k maximal cliques*;
8 Return $G_{pCliques}$;

The procedure for merging graphs (the MERGE GRAPHS) is given in Algorithm 3. It first finds the symmetric difference between the graph inputs, i.e., it identifies the vertices and edges that are in one graph but not in the other, respectively (step 1). Then it finds the vertices and edges that are at the intersection (step 2). Finally, it then aggregates all of these graph components to form the merged graph (step 3), which is subsequently returned (step 4) to the MST-kNN with Paracliques method (step 9, Algorithm 1) for further processing.

Algorithm 3. MERGE GRAPHS ($G1$ and $G1$: Graphs)

---

1 $G1' \leftarrow G1 - G2$ **and** $G2' \leftarrow G2 - G1$;
2 $G_{intersect} \leftarrow G1'$ intersect $G2'$;
3 $G_{merged} \leftarrow G_{intersect} + G1' + G2'$;
4 Return G_{merged};

2.3 Method Implementation

We implement the MST-kNN and its proposed variant in R using the *igraph* package [12]. For computing the MST and kNN we use minimum.spanning.tree (Prim's) and graph.adjacency functions, respectively. For finding the maximal cliques we use decompose.graph, maximal.cliques and induced.subgraph functions and for retrieving the k maximal cliques we use an order function. For aggregating the maximal cliques we use graph.edgelist and simplify functions. For merging the graphs, we compute the symmetric graph differences by using graph.difference.by.name and graph intersections by using graph.intersection.by.name functions and finally we aggregate the graph components by using function called internal.add.edges.

2.4   Statistical Analysis via a Permutation Test Approach

We assess the proposed method's strength particularly in identifying further associations among the input elements, using a random permutation test [17]. The test utilises class labels (types) of the nodes, which we embed apriori in the node names. For instance, a node with name "NodeA.TypeA" is considered as NodeA (node label) with class TypeA (class label). The underlying idea is, in a perfectly clustered graph, the nodes with same class labels are expected appear together, but this is unlikely to happen in the same graph when labels are randomised. We investigate the affinity of the node class types in the graph partitions against n random placement of the nodes labels.

Algorithm 4. RANODMISE GRAPHS (G : Graph, N: Randomisations)

---

1 *same* ← 0;
2 *different* ← 0 ;
3 *nodeLabels* ← Node labels (G) // NodeA.TypeA ;
4 *classLabels* ← Class labels (*nodeLabels*) // TypeA;
5 **for** *each test t in N* **do**
6 | Randomise (*nodeLabels*);
7 | **for each edge** *e* **in** *G* **do**
8 | | **if** *classLabel (source(e)) = classLabel(target(e))* **then**
9 | | | *same* ← *same* + 1;
10 | | **else**
11 | | | *different* ← *different* + 1 ;

12 Return the *same* and *different* scores for each *classLabel*;

Given the class labels, the RANDOMISE GRAPHS procedure (Algorithm 4) randomises and measures the number of connections towards the 'same' and 'different' classed nodes, in the outcomes of the MST-*k*NN and its paracliques variant (observed graphs) as well as in the randomised graphs.

We randomise the graph node names using **random_shuffle** from the STL library in C++. This function re-arranges the node names using a uniform random generator [23]. We then assign two scores (*same* and *different*) to each class labels. For each graph edge, if the class label of the source node matches with the targets class label, we increase the *same*, else the *different* score (steps 6-11).

Furthermore, when a node contains more than one class (for instance, a node with name NodeA.TypeA.TypeB), we consider both of the class labels (TypeA and TypeB) and halve the scores while computing the same and different scores. A scoring rule example is shown in Table 1. It illustrates a graph with two nodes containing up to four class labels. The label matching at step 7 utilises the STLs **set_union**, **set_intersection** and **set_symmetric_difference** functions. The scores are then stored in a matrix for further statistical tests as described in the Section 4.3.

Table 1. The scoring rule for four class labels (A–D) in two nodes (Node 1 and 2)

Labels Node 1		Node 2		A same	diff	B same	diff	C same	diff	D same	diff
A	-	A	-	1	0	0	0	-	-	-	-
A	-	B	-	0	1	0	1	-	-	-	-
A	B	A	-	0.5	0.5	0	0.5	-	-	-	-
A	B	C	-	0	0.5	0	0.5	0	1	-	-
A	B	C	D	0	0.5	0	0.5	0	0.5	0	0.5

3   Experimental Data

In this work, we utilised two publicly available datasets. The first one is contributed by Dyen et al. [13] and is digitally provided as a (84 × 84) distance matrix, where the distances were computed by calculating mean percent difference of cognacy in 200 *Swadesh* words. We term this as the **84 Indo-European languages** dataset.

Table 2. List of the Indo-European languages organized by the language family

Classes	Elements
Celtic	IrishA, IrishB, WelshN, WelshC, BretonList, BretonSE, BretonST
Romance	RumanianList, Vlach, Italian, Ladin, Provencal, French, Walloon, FrenchCreoleC, FrenchCreoleD, SardinianN, SardinianL, SardinianC, Spanish, PortugueseST, Brazilian, Catalan
Germanic	GermanST, Penn.Dutch, DutchList, Afrikaans, Flemish, Frisian, SwedishUp, SwedishVL, SwedishList, Danish, Riksmal, IcelandicST, Faroese, EnglishST, Takitaki
Baltic	LithuanianO, LithuanianST, Latvian
Slavic	Slovenian, LusatianL, LusatianU, Czech, Slovak, CzechE, Ukrainian, Byelorussian, Polish, Russian, Macedonian, Bulgarian, Serbocroatian
Indo-Iranian	GypsyGk, Singhalese, Kashmiri, Marathi, Gujarati, PanjabiST, Lahnda, Hindi, Bengali, NepaliList, Khaskura, Ossetic, Afghan, Waziri, Persian- List, Tadzik, Baluchi, Wakhi
Greek	GreekML, GreekMD, GreekMod, GreekD, GreekK
Armenian	ArmenianMod, ArmenianList
Albanian	AlbanianT, AlbanianTop, AlbanianG, AlbanianK, AlbanianC

There exist a number of studies that report classifications of this data by utilising different partitioning approaches (e.g., see [8,24,18]). Among those, the clustering presented by Bryant et al. [8] by building a *phylogenetic* network of languages demonstrates a total of nine classes in these languages (see Table 2). In this work, we adopt these classes as the languages class labels and utilise them to evaluate the performance of our method outcomes.

The second data set, termed as the **168 Shakespearean era plays** dataset has been constructed using a text corpus containing texts of unambiguous authorship of a total of 39 authors (see Table 3) from the 16th and 17th centuries.

It has been produced using a software called *Intelligent Archive* by Craig and Whipp [11]. This software generates counts of word-forms according to a parameterised user input, taking into account the variations in spelling commonly found in those century plays. It also facilitates disambiguation of words by both context and frequency. For each play, the frequency of a total of 55,116 words was calculated and the results were stored in the form of a (55,116 × 168) matrix, which is publicly available as described in [25]. We use the authors of each work as class labels to evaluate the performance of our method.

Table 3. List of authors and their contributions in the 168 Shakespearean era plays dataset

Authors	Plays	Authors	Plays	Authors	Plays
Shakespeare	28	Webster	3	Davenant	1
Middleton	18	Wilson	3	Day	1
Jonson	17	Haughton	2	Edwards Richard	1
Fletcher	15	Kyd	2	Goffe	1
Chapman	13	Marston	2	Greville Fulke	1
Lyly	8	Massinger	2	Lodge	1
Ford	7	Rowley	2	Marmion	1
Dekker	5	Beaumont	1	Nashe	1
Heywood	5	Brandon Samuel	1	Porter Henry	1
Marlowe	5	Brome	1	Sidney Mary	1
Peele	5	Carey	1	Suckling	1
Greene	4	Chettle	1	Tourneur	1
Shirley	3	Daniel	1	Wilmot	1

4 Results

The computational tests were performed on a developer workstation with Intel Xeon processors (2 E5640 @ 2.67 GHz), 1.5 terabytes of HDD and 24 gigabytes of RAM and a 64 bit Linux OS (kernel version 3.13). The MST-kNN [19] and its proposed paraclique-based extension were implemented in R version 3.0.2. The randomisation procedure was written in C++ with STL and Boost library (version 1.56.0) and compiled in g++ version 4.8.2.

4.1 Results from the 84 Indo-European Languages Dataset

We first applied the MST-kNN method on the 84 Indo-European languages data. It produced a total of nine clusters (Fig. 1). The clustering outcome mostly captured the groupings found by Byrant et al. [8] (see Table 2).

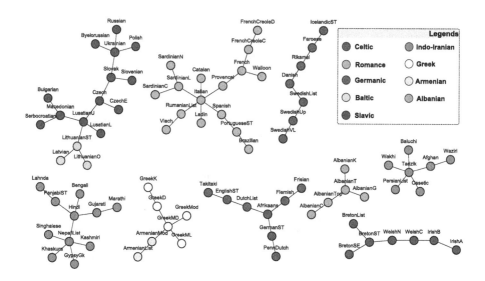

Fig. 1. The MST-kNN on the 84 Indo-European Languages

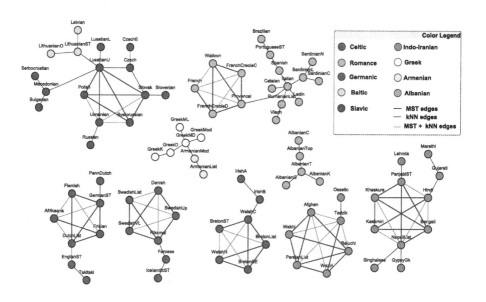

Fig. 2. The MST-kNN with Paracliques on the 84 Indo-European languages

For instance, the *Romance, Celtic* and *Albanian* were completely confined into three separate clusters. Two others *Germanic* and *Indo-European* were placed into four clusters; that is the MST-kNN detected further partitions in these cases.

The rest of the groups: *Baltic* and *Slavic*, and *Greek* and *Armenian* were merged into two separate clusters, respectively. The rationales for these mergings as well as separations have been discussed in [18]. These language groups appeared as either 'close' or 'far' pairs in the phylogenetic network constructed by Bryant et al. [8].

Next, we applied the proposed extension of the MST-kNN with paracliques (Fig. 2). A total of seven paracliques were formed in seven clusters, which essentially indicate the further interactions among the relatively closer elements within those clusters. For instance, the clique structure formed by the *French*, *FrenchCreoleD*, *FrenchCreoleC*, *Provencal* and *Wallon* indicates a higher level of affinity among these languages, which separates them from the others (*Italian*-origin languages) in that cluster. The same argument is valid for the clique formed by the Celtic languages, which separates them from the Irish. Therefore, even though the overall classification of the languages largely remained the same as the MST-kNN, the extended outcome resulted in further insights in relation to closer associations among the languages.

4.2 Results from the 168 Shakespearean Era Dataset

For the 168 Shakespearean era plays dataset, same as with the previous dataset, we first applied the MST-kNN method [19] by creating a (168 × 168) distance matrix from this data. We used the Jensen-Shannon Divergence (JSD) [26] as a metric for the computation of distance. The advantages of using the JSD on this data have been demonstrated in [5,28]. As an outcome, the MST-kNN produced only two clusters out of the 168 plays (Fig. 3).

We then applied the proposed method which resulted in the same two clusters but now with additional 10 paracliques (Fig. 4). Amongst which, six were cliques with size 4 to 6. In order to further investigate these structures, we highlighted the seven most contributing authors from Table 3. This provided us further insights within each cluster. For instance, in the larger cluster (cluster 1), a total nine paracliques were formed where most of the works by *Shakespeare*, *Chapman*, *Middleton*, *Lyly* and *Jonson* grouped together. The other cluster (cluster 2) was mainly formed by the works of *Fletcher* including a paraclique. Essentially, these additional structures further enhanced the final outcome. For instance, in the MST-kNN's outcome, the plays by Shakespeare correlated with many others works, while their internal associations/ inter-relations were not clearly evident. In contrast, the outcome with paracliques clearly highlights the inter-associations amongst Shakespear's works. The same is valid for the other major authors.

Therefore, it is evident from this result that if a data set contains a set of similar (same class or category) elements, the proposed method would result in paracliques formed by those elements. This affinity cannot be obtained by random grouping or placement of the elements or their labels, which we prove next.

4.3 Statistical Significance

To assess the significance of the clustering results, following the graph randomisation procedure in Section 2.4, we randomised the outcomes of the MST-kNN

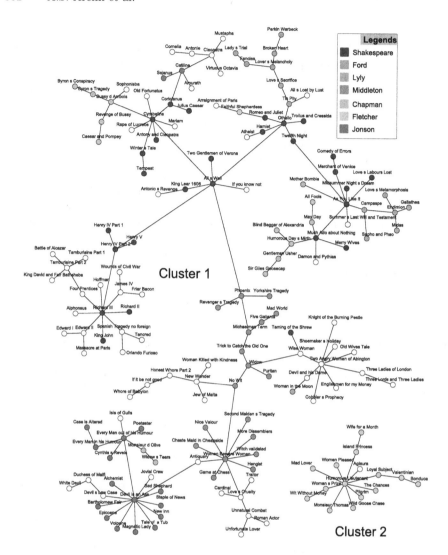

Fig. 3. The MST-kNN partitioning of the 168 Shakespearean era plays

and its proposed paraclique-based variant. The aforementioned *same* and *different* scores were computed considering two different forms of tokens, the nine groups of languages (Table 2) and the 39 Shakespearean era authors (Table 3).

We then used two different configurations for computing the observed outcomes significance over the randomised outcomes. First, we used the *Wilcoxon signed-rank test* [16], where we compared the mean rank of differences between the number of edges connecting works of same and different tokens in our observed data and random labelling. In the second configuration we performed the same but using the *Kruskal-Wallis test* [16]. Finally, in our third configuration, we considered each of the differences from the permutations as an independent

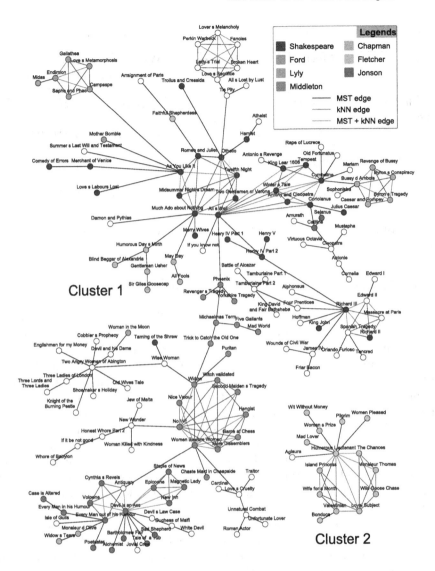

Fig. 4. The MST-kNN with paracliques on the 168 Shakespearean era plays dataset

sample and performed the Kruskal-Wallis test on 1,001 samples (one observed data labelling and 1000 permutations of the labelling of the nodes in the outcome graph). The outcomes of our random permutation test are presented in Table 4. It is clearly evident from this table that the MST-kNN with paracliques produces better p-values (i.e., higher inter-relations amongst elements within same class) than the MST-kNN alone. As the number of input elements and their classes grow high, the outcomes become even more significant.

Table 4. Significance of clusterings by the MST-kNN and its paraclique variant

Data	Method	Scoring Class	Wilcoxon test p-Value	Kruskal-Wallis test p-Value
84 Indo-European languages data set	MST-kNN	9 language groups	1.04E-07	2.09E-07
	MST-kNN with Paracliques		**1.02E-07**	**2.04E-07**
168 Shakespearean era plays data set	MST-kNN	39 authors of the plays	1.13E-10	2.26E-10
	MST-kNN with Paracliques		**8.10E-12**	**1.62E-11**

*The Kruskal-Wallis test 2, on the original vs. the individual 1000 random permutations resulted in p-values close to 0.

5   Conclusion and Future Research Directions

In this work, we have enhanced the existing MST-kNN method by adding insightful paracliques to its outcome. The paracliques are formed by the maximal cliques found in the kNN components of the relevant MST-kNN partitions. The modified approach provides statistically better results than the original MST-kNN, especially when we examined the edge connections against a thousand of randomised node labellings. We have described the proposed method from its implementation perspective. We aim to publish it as a package for R in the near future. At the moment, on smaller data sets, our method's time performance is similar to the MST-kNN, however at a large scale, e.g., with a data set having more than 10,000 elements, it performs at least 10 times slower, which is mainly due to its maximal clique finding component. We aim to re-implement this part using a data-parallel approach (e.g., as shown in [29]), which we expect to give a better speedup gain.

In relation to method comparisons, so far we only compared our outcomes against the MST-kNN. This is because, we initially aimed at enhancing the MST-kNN performance only, where the original method has already been shown to perform better against the traditional clustering methods, such as CLICK and SOMs [19]. In order to draw a more robust comparison, we now aim to compare our outcomes against the other data partitioning methods, such as DBSCAN for graphs, affinity propagation, spectral clustering, etc. This would also help us to identify the data types, for which the proposed method is more appropriate.

Finally, in this work, we presented an interesting variant of the MST-kNN method, termed as the MST-kNN WITH PARACLIQUES, which provides more insights of the inter-relations among the partitioned elements. We envision that the modified method will be a useful data clustering approach for the analysis of data sets in several areas, including– bioinformatics, artificial intelligence, image and video analysis, creative arts, and finance.

Acknowledgments. The authors would like to thank Ms. Natalie Jane de Vries for proof-reading the final version of this manuscript. This work has been supported in part by the Australian Research Council (ARC) Discovery Project Grants DP120102576 and DP140104183. Professor Pablo Moscato is funded by the ARC Future Fellowship FT120100060.

References

1. Anders, K.-H.: A hierarchical graph-clustering approach to find groups of objects. In: Proceedings 5th Workshop on Progress in Automated Map Generalization, pp. 1–8 (2003)
2. Arefin, A.S., Inostroza-Ponta, M., Mathieson, L., Berretta, R., Moscato, P.: Clustering nodes in large-scale biological networks using external memory algorithms. In: Xiang, Y., Cuzzocrea, A., Hobbs, M., Zhou, W. (eds.) ICA3PP 2011, Part II. LNCS, vol. 7017, pp. 375–386. Springer, Heidelberg (2011)
3. Arefin, A.S., Mathieson, L., Johnstone, D., Berretta, R., Moscato, P.: Unveiling clusters of RNA transcript pairs associated with markers of Alzheimers disease progression. PloS One 7(9), e45535 (2012)
4. Arefin, A.S., Riveros, C., Berretta, R., Moscato, P.: kNN-MST-Agglomerative: A fast and scalable graph-based data clustering approach on GPU. In: 2012 7th International Conference on Computer Science & Education (ICCSE), pp. 585–590. IEEE (2012)
5. Arefin, A.S., Vimieiro, R., Riveros, C., Craig, H., Moscato, P.: An Information Theoretic clustering approach for unveiling authorship affinities in Shakespearean era plays and poems. PLoS ONE 9(10), e111445 (2014)
6. Arefin, A.S., Riveros, C., Berretta, R., Moscato, P.: kNN-borůvka-GPU: A fast and scalable MST construction from kNN graphs on GPU. In: Murgante, B., Gervasi, O., Misra, S., Nedjah, N., Rocha, A.M.A.C., Taniar, D., Apduhan, B.O. (eds.) ICCSA 2012, Part I. LNCS, vol. 7333, pp. 71–86. Springer, Heidelberg (2012)
7. Berkhin, P.: A survey of clustering data mining techniques. In: Grouping multidimensional data, pp. 25–71. Springer (2006)
8. Bryant, D., Filimon, F., Gray, R.D.: Untangling our past: languages, trees, splits and networks. In: The Evolution of Cultural Diversity: Pylogenetic Approaches, pp. 67–84 (2005)
9. Capp, A., Inostroza-Ponta, M., Bill, D., Moscato, P., Lai, C., Christie, D., Lamb, D., Turner, S., Joseph, D., Matthews, J.: Is there more than one proctitis syndrome? a revisitation using data from the TROG 96.01 trial. Radiotherapy and Oncology 90(3), 400–407 (2009)
10. Chesler, E., Langston, M.: Combinatorial genetic regulatory network analysis tools for high throughput transcriptomic data. In: Eskin, E., Ideker, T., Raphael, B., Workman, C. (eds.) RECOMB 2005. LNCS (LNBI), vol. 4023, pp. 150–165. Springer, Heidelberg (2007)
11. Craig, H., Whipp, R.: Old spellings, new methods: automated procedures for indeterminate linguistic data. Literary and Linguistic Computing 25(1), 37–52 (2010)
12. Csardi, G., Nepusz, T.: The igraph software package for complex network research. Inter Journal, Complex Systems 1695(5) (2006)
13. Dyen, I., Kruskal, J.B., Black, P.: An Indoeuropean classification: a lexicostatistical experiment. Transactions of the American Philosophical Society, iii–132 (1992)

14. Feige, U., Goldwasser, S., Lovsz, L., Safra, S., Szegedy, M.: Approximating clique is almost NP-complete. In: 2013 IEEE 54th Annual Symposium on Foundations of Computer Science, pp. 2–12. IEEE Comput. Soc. Press (1991)

15. Gonzlez-Barrios, J.M., Quiroz, A.J.: A clustering procedure based on the comparison between the k nearest neighbors graph and the minimal spanning tree. Statistics & Probability Letters 62(1), 23–34 (2003)

16. Hollander, M., Wolfe, D.A., Chicken, E.: Nonparametric statistical methods, vol. 751. John Wiley & Sons (2013)

17. Huh, M.H., Jhun, M.: Random permutation testing in multiple linear regression. Communications in Statistics-Theory and Methods 30(10), 2023–2032 (2001)

18. Inostroza-Ponta, M.: An integrated and scalable approach based on combinatorial optimization techniques for the analysis of microarray data. NOVA — The University of Newcastle's Digital Repository (2008)

19. Inostroza-Ponta, M., Berretta, R., Mendes, A., Moscato, P.: An automatic graph layout procedure to visualize correlated data. In: Bramer, M. (ed.) Artificial Intelligence in Theory and Practice. IFIP, vol. 217, pp. 179–188. Springer, Heidelberg (2006)

20. Inostroza-Ponta, M., Berretta, R., Moscato, P.: QAPgrid: A two level QAP-based approach for large-scale data analysis and visualization. PloS One 6(1), e14468 (2011)

21. Inostroza-Ponta, M., Mendes, A., Berretta, R., Moscato, P.: An integrated QAP-based approach to visualize patterns of gene expression similarity. In: Randall, M., Abbass, H.A., Wiles, J. (eds.) ACAL 2007. LNCS (LNAI), vol. 4828, pp. 156–167. Springer, Heidelberg (2007)

22. Jain, A.K., Murty, M.N., Flynn, P.J.: Data clustering: a review. ACM Computing Surveys (CSUR) 31(3), 264–323 (1999)

23. Knuth, D.E.: The Art of Computer Programming. Seminumerical algorithms, vol. 2, pp. 229–279. Addison-Wesley, Reading (1969)

24. Mahata, P., Costa, W., Cotta, C., Moscato, P.: Hierarchical clustering, languages and cancer. In: Rothlauf, F. (ed.) EvoWorkshops 2006. LNCS, vol. 3907, pp. 67–78. Springer, Heidelberg (2006)

25. Marsden, J., Budden, D., Craig, H., Moscato, P.: Language individuation and marker words: Shakespeare and his Maxwell's demon. PloS One 8(6), e66813 (2013)

26. Menndez, M., Pardo, J., Pardo, L., Pardo, M.: The Jensen-Shannon divergence. Journal of the Franklin Institute 334(2), 307–318 (1997)

27. Ngomo, A.-C.N.: Clique-based clustering. Evaluation 1, 10 (2006)

28. Rosso, O.A., Craig, H., Moscato, P.: Shakespeare and other english renaissance authors as characterized by information theory complexity quantifiers. Physica A: Statistical Mechanics and its Applications 388(6), 916–926 (2009)

29. Schmidt, M.C., Samatova, N.F., Thomas, K., Park, B.-H.: A scalable, parallel algorithm for maximal clique enumeration. J. Parallel Distrib. Comput. 69(4), 417–428 (2009)

30. Sharan, R., Maron-Katz, A., Shamir, R.: CLICK and EXPANDER: A system for clustering and visualizing gene expression data. Bioinformatics 19(14), 1787–1799 (2003)

31. Zemel, R.S., Carreira-Perpin, M.A.: Proximity graphs for clustering and manifold learning, pp. 225–232. MIT Press (2005)

Mechanical Generation of Networks with Surplus Complexity

Russell K. Standish

Mathematics and Statistics
University of New South Wales
hpcoder@hpcoders.com.au

Abstract. In previous work I examined an information based complexity measure of networks with weighted links. The measure was compared with that obtained from by randomly shuffling the original network, forming an Erdös-Rényi random network preserving the original link weight distribution. It was found that real world networks almost invariably had higher complexity than their shuffled counterparts, whereas networks mechanically generated via preferential attachment did not.

In this paper, I report on a mechanical network generation system that does produce this complexity surplus. The heart of the idea is to construct the network of state transitions of a chaotic dynamical system, such as the Lorenz equation. This indicates that complexity surplus is a more fundamental trait than that of being an evolutionary system.

Keywords: information based complexity, chaos, graphs, dynamical systems, networks.

1 Introduction

This work situates itself firmly within the *complexity is information content* paradigm, a topic that dates back to the 1960s with the work of Kolmogorov, Chaitin and Solomonoff. Indeed, the seminal work of Mowshowitz in 1968 [6–9] describes an information-based network complexity measure called *graph entropy*, that is essentially a generalisation of the measure presented here, work that has by and large been forgotten by the complex systems community, only to be reinvented in recent times [1].

The idea is fairly simple. In most cases, there is an obvious *prefix-free* representation language within which descriptions of the objects of interest can be encoded. There is also a classifier of descriptions that can determine if two descriptions correspond to the same object. This classifier is commonly called the *observer*, denoted $O(x)$.

To compute the complexity of some object x, count the number of equivalent descriptions $\omega(\ell, x)$ of length ℓ that map to the same object x under the agreed classifier. Then the complexity of x is given in the limit as $\ell \to \infty$:

$$\mathcal{C}(x) = -\log P(x) = \lim_{\ell \to \infty} (\ell \log N - \log \omega(\ell, x)) \tag{1}$$

S.K. Chalup et al. (Eds.): ACALCI 2015, LNAI 8955, pp. 387–394, 2015.

where N is the size of the alphabet used for the representation language. Loosely speaking, $P(x)$ here is the probability that a description chosen uniformly at random will describe the object x. This probability measure is essentially Solomonoff and Levin's *universal prior*, which is a kind of formalised Occam's razor that gives higher weight to simpler (in the KCS sense) computable theories for generating priors in Bayesian reasoning, in the situation where descriptions are programs of some universal Turing machine, and $\omega(\ell, x)$ is the number of such programs of length less than ℓ that output x and halt.

The relationship of this algorithmic complexity measure to more familiar measures such as Kolmogorov (KCS) complexity, is given by the coding theorem [3, Thm 4.3.3]. The difference between this version of $\mathcal{C}$ and KCS complexity is bounded by a constant independent of the complexity of x, so these measures become equivalent in the limit as message size goes to infinity.

To fix the representation language of graph using a binary alphabet (N=2), we start with a prefix of $\lceil \log_2 n \rceil$ 1s followed by a '0' stop bit. This indicates the number of bits needed to store n, the number of nodes. Next we encode the number of links l, which for a directed graph requires $\lceil \log_2 n + \log_2(n-1) \rceil$ bits. Finally, we encode the linklist, as a *rank index* within the

$$\Omega = \binom{L}{l}$$

possible linklists with l links, where $L = n(n-1)$. So each description of an n-node, l-link graph is precisely $\ell_{n,l} = 1 + 2\lceil \log_2 n \rceil + \lceil \log_2 n + \log_2(n-1) \rceil + \lceil \log_2 \Omega \rceil$ bits long. Descriptions longer than that represent the same graph as the initial leading sequence just described, with the trailing bits irrelevant, thus $\omega(\ell, x) = \omega(\ell_{n,l}, x) 2^{\ell - \ell_{n,l}}$. Substituting into equation (1) gives (in bits):

$$\mathcal{C}(x) = \ell_{n,l} - \log_2 \omega(\ell_{n,l}, x). \tag{2}$$

In setting the classifier function, we assume that only the graph's topology counts — positions, and labels of nodes and links are not considered important. Links may be directed or undirected and can have a positive real number weight attached to them.

If all links have the same weight, then the counting problem of determining $\omega(\ell_{n,l}, x)$ for networks turns out to be equivalent to the automorphism group problem of determining if two graphs are automorphic. Whilst this problem is suspected of being combinatorially hard [4], several practical algorithms are available for computing the size of the automorphism group for reasonable sized networks of thousands of nodes.

To handle weighted links, the idea is to interpolate between the graph with the link, and without the link, according to the link's weight. For instance if a network X has the same network structure as the unweighted graph A, with b links of weight 1 describing the graph B and the remaining $a - b$ links of weight w, then we would like the network complexity of X to vary smoothly between that of A and B as w varies from 1 to 0.

The most obvious way of defining this continuous complexity measure is to start with normalised weights $\sum_i w_i = 1$. Then arrange the links in weight order, and compute the complexity of networks with just those links of weights less than w. The final complexity value is obtained by integrating:

$$C(X = N \times L) = \int_0^1 C(N \times \{i \in L : w_i < w\})dw, \tag{3}$$

where in this formula, N refers to the set of node labels, and $L \subset N \times N$ is the set of links making up the graph X. Obviously, since the integrand is a stepped function, this is computed in practice by a sum of complexities of partial networks.

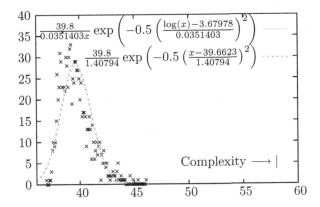

Fig. 1. The distribution of complexities of the shuffled Narragansett Bay food web[5]. Both a normal and a log-normal distribution have been fitted to the data — the log-normal is a slightly better fit than the normal distribution. In the bottom right hand corner is marked the complexity value computed for the actual Narragansett food web (58.2 bits). Reproduced from [12].

In [12], this measure is applied to a number of well-known naturally occurring networks, mostly published food webs. The measure is also compared with an ensemble of networks obtained by shuffling the link structure, with a positive complexity difference (*complexity surplus*) usually found, indicating it is measuring something structurally important about the network. The same technique was applied to Edös-Rényi generated networks, which unsurprisingly had no complexity surplus, and to networks generated via preferential attachment, which also generates no significant complexity surplus.

In [11], I made the observation that artificial evolutionary processes, such as EcoLab and Tierra also did not lead to a complexity surplus, making this property of natural networks a mysterious one. However, this later turned out to be due to a bug in the analysis [12], and when corrected, led to significant complexity surpluses being generated for EcoLab and Tierra, though not for WebWorld, another evolutionary ecology model similar to EcoLab.

In this paper I report on another (non-evolutionary) mechanical technique for generating networks that does generate significant amounts of complexity surplus.

2 Generating Networks from Timeseries Tata

Michael Small has been analysing timeseries data by generating networks that represent the dynamics behind the timeseries, and then applying network analysis techniques to tease out features of the data. His most recent version of the technique [10], which I shall describe below, can be applied to any timeseries, continuous or discrete, and of any dimension. Of particular interest are timeseries derived from chaotic dynamics, which generate particularly beautiful filigree networks, that are prime candidates for high structural complexity.

Consider first a discrete timeseries $(x_1, x_2, \ldots, x_n)$ where $x_i \in X \subset \mathbb{Z}$. Each element of X labels a node of the target network, and links of the network are weighted by the number of transitions (x_i, x_{i+1}) in the timeseries between the labels of source and target nodes of the network link. Concretely, consider a simple timeseries 1,2,3,1,2,1. The generated network is shown in figure 2, where the link $1 \to 2$ has double the weight of the other links.

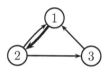

Fig. 2. Example network generated from the timeseries 1,2,3,1,2,1

If the timeseries data is continuous rather than discrete, then a means to convert real-valued data into integer labels is required. In this paper, I use a simple coarse graining, where the number of cells in each dimension of the timeseries is chosen to give a target network size. For example, with three dimensional data, one can choose 10 cells along each dimension to give a target network size of 1000 nodes.

It should be pointed out that Small gives a more sophisticated approach aimed at extracting the maximum dynamic information from the timeseries, which involves choosing a window size w, and ranking the values within the window to give a well defined sequence of integers. For example, the sequence (0.5, 0.2, 0.35, 0.4, 0.3) will for $w = 3$ give the sequence of ranks: (3,1,2), (1,2,3), (2,3,1). The generated networks will have $m(w) \leq w!$ nodes. Finally, the parameter w is not arbitrary, but chosen to maximise the amount of information captured. The curve

Table 1. Node and link count, network complexity, average shuffled complexity, surplus and the number of standard deviations of the shuffled distribution that the surplus represents. Listed here are the well-known *C. elegans* neural network, the Narrangansett bay food web, which also features in Figure 1, preferential attachment with outdegree 1 (from [12]), networks generated from the Lorenz and Hénon-Heiles systems, and the well-known rules 30 (a chaotic cellular automata) and 110 (Wolfram class 4 CA proven to be capable of universal computation). The other CA rules shown here are chaotic rules that produced the most complex networks.

Dataset	nodes	links	$\mathcal{C}$	$e^{\langle \ln \mathcal{C}_{ER}\rangle}$	$\mathcal{C} - e^{\langle \ln \mathcal{C}_{ER}\rangle}$	$\frac{\ln \mathcal{C} - \langle \ln \mathcal{C}_{ER}\rangle}{\sigma_{ER}}$
celegansneural	297	2345	442.7	251.6	191.1	29
Narragansett	35	219	58.2	39.6	18.6	11.0
PA1	100	99	98.9	85.4	13.5	2.5
Lorenz	8000	62	560.2	56.0	504.2	58.3
Hénon-Heiles	10000	31	342.0	57.3	284.7	55.6
Rule 30	1024	15	130.7	44.4	86.3	27.4
Rule 110	1024	25	204.3	46.8	157.5	28.9
Rule 45	1024	430	943.2	276.3	666.9	13.2
Rule 75	1024	430	943.2	272.9	670.3	15.2
Rule 89	1024	430	943.2	269.9	673.3	14.2
Rule 101	1024	430	943.2	274.3	668.9	15.1

$m(w)$ is roughly sigmoidal in shape, and the optimum value w_{opt} occurs at the point of inflection, where $\Delta m(w_{opt})$ is maximised.

3   Results

The first study looked at applying Small's network generation technique to the dynamics of two well-known chaotic dynamical systems — the Lorenz system, given by equation (4) and the Hénon-Heiles system, given by equation (5).

$$\dot{x} = \sigma(y - x)$$
$$\dot{y} = x(\rho - z) - y \qquad (4)$$
$$\dot{z} = xy - \beta z$$
$$\sigma = 10, \rho = 28, \beta = 8/3$$

$$\ddot{x} = -x - 2xy$$
$$\ddot{y} = -y - (x^2 - y^2) \qquad (5)$$

The networks were generated according to the scheme described in §2. Shown in table 1 are the node and link counts of the generated network, the complexity value $\mathcal{C}$ computed according to eq (1), the average complexity value of shuffled networks, the difference between the complexity and the average shuffled complexity (ie surplus) and finally the number of standard deviations of the shuffled distribution that the surplus corresponds to. It is reported this way, as the p value is far too ridiculously small to be comprehensible. For more detailed discussion of the analysis, please refer to [12]. Also shown, for comparison, are a couple of results from that paper.

The next experiment performs the same analysis on timeseries generated by 1D binary cellular automata with a neighbourhood of 3. The number of cells chosen was 10, so the generated network will have 1024 nodes (2^{10} possible states). The CAs were initialised to a random state, and the first 1000 steps discarded to eliminate transient effects. Figure 3 shows the complexity, and average shuffled complexity plotted as a function of Langton's λ [2], for all 256 neighbourhood 3 binary CAs. Figure 4 shows the complexity surplus for these same networks. What is clear is that there a large spike in the complexity values (and in the surplus) around $\lambda = 0.5$, corresponding to chaotic rules.

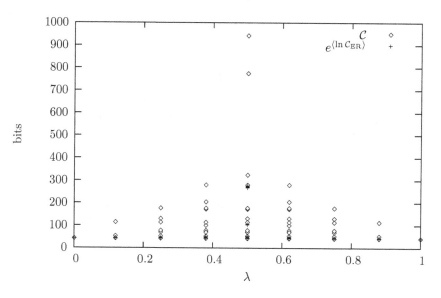

Fig. 3. Plot of $\mathcal{C}$ and averaged shuffled $\mathcal{C}$ for networks generated from all 256 1D CAs with a 3 cell neighbourhood, plotted as a function of Langton's λ

Source code used for these experiments can be found as part of $Ec\varrho ab$ version 5.D19, available from http://ecolab.sourceforge.net.

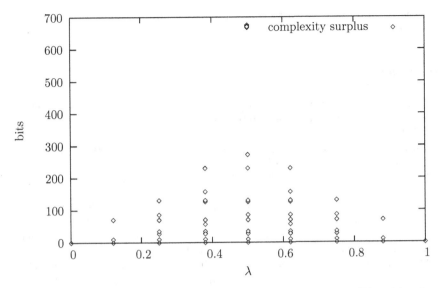

Fig. 4. Complexity surplus for networks generated from all 256 1D CAs with a 3 cell neighbourhood, plotted as a function of Langton's λ

4 Discussion

Generating networks from chaotic dynamical systems proves to be a good means of generating networks with complexity surplus. It raises the very pertinent question of what, exactly, is this complexity surplus measuring. On the one hand, we know that it is a structural complexity that is destroyed by rearranging a network's link randomly. We also know that it appears in networks generated as a result of an evolutionary process, which tends to result in an integrated network, where dynamical activity in one part of the network will influence distantly related parts of the network in a scale free manner. But standard preferential attachment does not produce the necessary complexity. In this study, we discovered that networks derived from chaotic dynamics also exhibit large amounts of complexity surplus, presumably also due to long-range influences between different parts of phase space.

We can now begin to study systems that can be tuned across a range of behaviour from ordered to chaotic. A preliminary experiment showed that chaotic behaviour is associated with the presence of large amounts of network complexity. One might suspect that the complexity surplus is associated with complex dynamics, or with Wolfram class 4 cellular automata. The preliminary experiment reported here did not specifically support that, as the peak occurred for chaotic (class 3) cellular automata, however the class 4 regime tends to be a very small part of the λ spectrum, so enumerating all 1D 3-neighbourhood CA can resolve the issue. Instead, transition to chaos experiments, such as Langton's original study with a 4-state, 5-neighbourhood CA [2] will probably be more suitable.

Acknowledgments. I wish to thank Michael Small for helpful discussions on this topic.

References

1. Dehmer, M., Mowshowitz, A.: A case study of cracks in the scientific enterprise: Reinvention of information-theoretic measures for graphs. Complexity (2014), doi:10.1002/cplx.21540
2. Langton, C.G.: Computation at the edge of chaos: Phase transitions and emergent computation. Physica D 42, 12–37 (1990)
3. Li, M., Vitányi, P.: An Introduction to Kolmogorov Complexity and its Applications, 2nd edn. Springer (1997)
4. Lubiw, A.: Some NP-complete problems similar to graph isomorphism. SIAM Journal on Computing 10(1), 11–21 (1981), http://link.aip.org/link/?SMJ/10/11/1
5. Monaco, M., Ulanowicz, R.: Comparative ecosystem trophic structure of three U.S. Mid-Atlantic estuaries. Mar. Ecol. Prog. Ser. 161, 239–254 (1997)
6. Mowshowitz, A.: Entropy and the complexity of graphs: I. an index of the relative complexity of a graph. Bulletin of Mathematical Biology 30(1), 175–204 (1968)
7. Mowshowitz, A.: Entropy and the complexity of graphs: II. the information content of digraphs and infinite graphs. Bulletin of Mathematical Biology 30(2), 225–240 (1968)
8. Mowshowitz, A.: Entropy and the complexity of graphs: III. graphs with prescribed information content. Bulletin of Mathematical Biology 30(3), 387–414 (1968)
9. Mowshowitz, A.: Entropy and the complexity of graphs: IV. entropy measures and graphical structure. Bulletin of Mathematical Biology 30(4), 533–546 (1968)
10. Small, M.: Complex networks from time series: Capturing dynamics. In: IEEE International Symposium on Circuits and Systems Proceedings, pp. 2509–2512 (2013)
11. Standish, R.K.: Network complexity of foodwebs. In: Fellerman, H., et al. (eds.) Proceedings of Artificial Life XII, pp. 337–343. MIT Press, Cambridge (2010)
12. Standish, R.K.: Complexity of networks (reprise). Complexity 17, 50–61, arXiv: 0911.3482 (2012)

Efficient Sensitivity Analysis of Reliability in Embedded Software

Indika Meedeniya[1], Aldeida Aleti[2], and Irene Moser[1]

[1] School of Software and Electrical Engineering,
Swinburne University of Technology, Melbourne, Australia
[2] Faculty of Information Technology, Monash University, Melbourne, Australia

Abstract. The reliability of software architectures is an important quality attribute in safety-critical systems. Researchers have developed a number of models that can estimate the reliability of software systems at design time. These models use matrix operations of considerable complexity. During the design process of an embedded system as used by the automotive industry, the reliability of a system has to be evaluated after each change. Safety-critical systems are often subjected to sensitivity analysis, where a single parameter is changed numerous times, with a subsequent re-evaluation of the system's reliability. In this paper, we introduce an efficient sensitivity analysis, which computes the change in reliability of the part of the system architecture which was affected by a change. Results from experiments based on a real case-study from the automotive industry indicate a significant improvement in time of the proposed approach compared to traditional sensitivity analysis methods.

Keywords: sensitivity analysis, reliability, delta evaluation.

1 Introduction

In software reliability prediction, Discrete Time Markov Chain (DTMC) based models are a common formalisation technique [10,15]. Since its first introduction by Cheung [2], this probabilistic model has been used as the basis of hierarchical reliability evaluations [11]. Goševa-Popstojonava et al. [15] illustrated the applicability of the model in various scenarios by analysing the state-of-the-art in reliability evaluation. The authors also discussed the usefulness of the model in uncertainty analysis when the 'method of moments' [14] and Monte Carlo simulation [13] are applied.

The design phase of embedded software systems generally comprises a sensitivity analysis, bottleneck identification, exploration of design options and uncertainty analysis. State-of-the-art techniques re-evaluate reliability models in their entirety regardless of the size of the change.

Probabilistic model evaluation is a computation- and memory-intensive process. Extensive re-evaluations of practically sized problems are often impossible due to complex matrix operations. Matrix inversions in DTMC based evaluations have a complexity of $\mathcal{O}(n^3)$. Having to re-evaluate the entire model with every change of the architecture is particularly time-consuming in sensitivity analysis.

S.K. Chalup et al. (Eds.): ACALCI 2015, LNAI 8955, pp. 395–408, 2015.

Sensitivity analysis constructs graphs to analyse the response characteristics of a quality attribute of interest with respect to possible variations of one or more parameters. Cheung [2] presented a method to obtain the sensitivity of DTMC-based reliability evaluation model to component reliabilities. This method is purely analytical, and consists of 2nd and 3rd order partial derivatives of system reliabilities which are hard to estimate in real cases. Goševa-Popstajanova et al. [14] proposed using the method of moments to calculate the sensitivity of the system reliability to component reliabilities and transition probabilities. In this approach, variances and covariances of model parameters are employed. A similar approach is proposed by Cortellessa et al. [5], who analyse the sensitivity of system reliability on failure propagation.

Goševa-Popstojanova et al. [12] have shown that analytical methods of uncertainty analysis do not scale well. To address this issue, they proposed a Monte Carlo simulation-based method, demonstrating that it scales better than the previous approaches [12]. In the safety evaluation domain, Förster et al. [8] have introduced a similar approach to obtain the sensitivity of hazard probabilities to the probability uncertainties of low level failure events, which also applies Monte Carlo simulations to obtain a probability distribution of the output hazard probability.

Monte Carlo simulation-based methods are more scalable compared to analytical methods [12] while still requiring the re-evaluation of the quality attributes for every sampled parameter value. In this paper, we introduce a novel architecture-based sensitivity analysis method for reliability. Rather than re-evaluating the entire system, Δ Evaluation [20] uses previous evaluation results to compute the changed reliability by estimating the impact of the architectural change on the overall system reliability. Only the changed part of the system Δ has to be re-evaluated and incorporated into the whole system reliability.

In previous work [19,20], Δ Evaluation was introduced to render the re-evaluation of software models after change more efficient. Following the recommendations for future work made earlier [20], in this paper, we use Δ Evaluation for the sensitivity analysis of software systems with the aim of predicting the overall reliability of the system and the propensity of failure of individual components, investigating the efficiency and applicability of the approach.

2   State-of-the-Art in Reliability Evaluation

Many of the probabilistic models used in software architecture evaluation are mathematical abstractions of certain aspects of the system which are relevant to an attribute of interest. Probabilistic model checking [16,6] is one way of verifying probabilistic properties from the system model. In cases where the quality attributes are given as algebraic functions of architectural parameters, the attributes can be computed by analytical methods.

The majority of reliability evaluation methods are based on Cheung's model [2]. These studies focus mainly on component-based systems where the architecture is modelled using architecture description languages.

Cortellessa et al. [5] used Cheung's model to consider the effects of error propagation among components, whereas Wang et al. [22] presented the use of Cheung's model for reliability evaluation in different architectural styles. Gokhale et al. [11] have used the model as the basis for their extension to hierarchical reliability evaluation. Goševa-Popstojonava et al. [15] illustrated extensive use of the model in their reliability evaluation survey.

These reliability evaluation methods provide only an indication of how the system reliability would change for a small change in component reliability from its original prediction. It does not produce the range of system reliability, which is a common practical requirement. To address this problem, Goševa-Popstojanova et al. [14] introduced the use of the method of moments. The approach calculates the sensitivity of a system's reliability to component reliabilities and transition probabilities. This sensitivity analysis method can help identify the most critical system components.

Coit et al. [23,3] used the means and variances of the reliability estimates of software components to derive the mean and variance of the reliability of a redundancy allocation analytically. With the assumption of normally distributed input parameters, Finodella et al. [7] derived the distribution of system reliability from a multinomial distribution. Coit et al. [4] presented an analytical approach to obtain the lower bound of the reliability values in series-parallel systems.

The methods described above use an analytical approach to quantifying the sensitivity. All approaches discussed assume the parameter distributions to be normal and variations to be characterised by the mean and variance alone. To address this issue, Gošva-Popstojanova et al. [12] investigated the use of a combined analytical and simulation-based method for uncertainty analysis, and confirmed that Monte-Carlo-simulation-based methods scale better than the analysis using the method of moments. One major drawback of the Monte Carlo simulation based uncertainty analysis is that it requires the creation of a large number of sample variations of an architecture from the probability distributions of parameters, which can be very computationally expensive [1,12,17]. The reliability models have to be re-evaluated for each variant.

3   DTMC-Based Reliability Prediction

A Discrete Time Markov Chain (DTMC) is a tuple (S, P) where S is a finite set of states, and $P : S \times S \to [0,1]$ is the transition probability matrix. A DTMC is *absorbing* when at least one of its states has no outgoing transition.

The program flow graph of a terminating application has a single entry and a single exit node. This model can easily be extended to support multiple initial nodes and multiple final states by introducing *super-initial, super-final* states. The transfer of control among modules can be described by an absorbing DTMC with transition probability matrix $P = [p_{ij}]$, where p_{ij} denotes the probability of jth module being called after executing the ith module.

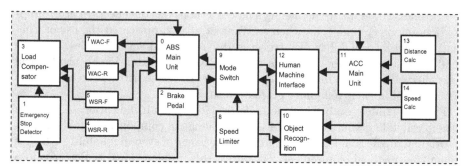

WAC : Wheel Actuator Controllers (Front and Rear)
WSR : Wheel Sensor Readers (Front and Rear)

Fig. 1. Automotive composite system

An assumption of Cheung's model is that the components fail independently. According to this model, the reliability of component i is characterized by the probability R_i that the component produces the correct output and transfers control to the next component without a failure.

Two absorbing states C and F are added, representing the correct output and failure respectively. The transition probability matrix P is modified to $\hat{P}$, which incorporates these two states. The original transition probability p_{ij} between the components i and j is modified to $R_i p_{ij}$, which represents the probability that the module i produces the correct result and the control is transferred to component j. From the final (exit) state n, a directed edge to state C is added with transition probability R_n to represent the correct execution.

The failures of a component i are considered by creating a directed edge to failure state F with transition probability $(1 - R_i)$. This process integrates the failure behaviour of the components into the functional behaviour described in the original control flow. Figure 2 illustrates a control flow graph of a software system and the corresponding DTMC when the two states C and F are added. The reliability of the system is the probability of reaching the absorbing state C of the DTMC.

Let Q be the matrix obtained from $\hat{P}$ by deleting rows and columns corresponding to the absorbing states C and F. $Q_{(1,n)}^k$ represents the probability of reaching state n from 1 through k transitions. From initial state 1 to final state n, the number of transitions k may vary from 0 to infinity. It can be proved that the infinite summation converges as follows [2]:

$$S = I + Q + Q^2 + Q^3 + \dots = \sum_{k=0}^{\infty} Q^k = (I - Q)^{-1} \qquad (1)$$

The matrix S is called the *fundamental matrix* of the DTMC, and $S_{(i,j)}$ represents the expected number of visits to the state j starting from state i before

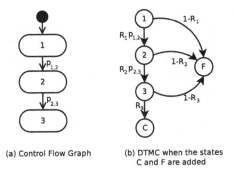

(a) Control Flow Graph   (b) DTMC when the states
C and F are added

Fig. 2. Control flow graph and corresponding DTMC for Cheung's model

it is absorbed. Cheung [2] introduced an architecture based reliability prediction method in which the reliability of the overall system can be computed from S as follows:

$$R_s = S_{(1,n)} R_n \qquad (2)$$

4   Automotive Case Study

In the automotive domain, reliability is an important quality characteristic, because specific functions (e.g. brake assistance) are safety critical. The case study represents a subsystem which implements an *Anti-lock Brake System (ABS)* and *Adaptive Cruise Control (ACC)* functionality [9]. The components in the system refer to Electronic Control Units (ECU)s, which are microprocessors with built-in software. The component failure rates and the estimated execution times per visit, have been chosen as closely to a real system as possible given the exact information is not in the public domain.

Anti-lock Brake System (ABS): ABS is currently used in the majority of modern cars to minimise hazards associated with skidding and loss of control due to locked wheels during braking. Proper rotation during brake operations allows better manoeuvrability and decreases the speed more effectively.

Adaptive Cruise Control (ACC): Apart from the usual automatic cruise control functionality, the main aim of the ACC is to avoid crashes by reducing speed once a slower vehicle is detected ahead.

The *ABS Main Unit* is the major decision-making component regarding the braking levels of individual wheels, while the *Load Compensator* unit assists with computing adjustment factors from the wheel load sensor inputs. Components 4 and 5 represent the components that communicate with wheel sensors, whereas components 7 and 8 represent the electronic control units that control the brake actuators. *Brake Pedal* is the component that reads from the pedal sensor and sends the data to the *Emergency Stop Detection* unit.

Execution initialisation is possible at the components that communicate with the sensors and user inputs. In this case study the *Wheel Sensors, Speed Limiter, Object Recognition, Mode Switch* and *Brake Pedal* components contribute to the triggering of the service. The data from the sensors is processed by a number of components in the system and triggers are generated for the actuators like *Brake Actuators* and *Human Machine Interface*. The software components are characterised by three externally observable parameters:

(a) Failure Rate (λ_c), the failure intensity of the exponential distribution of failure behaviour of a component [21]. Component failures in the model are assumed independent.

(b) Estimated Time per Visit (t_c), the estimated time taken by component execution within a single visit of the component measured in milliseconds (ms).

(c) Execution Initiation Probability (q_0), the probability of the program execution starting at this component.

The interaction between two components C_i and C_j have the following observable characteristics:

(a) Failure Rate (λ_l), the failure intensity of the exponential distribution of failure behaviour of a communication link between two components, assumed independent for different links and given per time unit.

(b) Transfer time for a link per visit (t_l), the communication time between two components measured in a model with no redundancy, given in time units (ms).

(c) Next-step probability (p), the probability that a service calls component C_j after component C_i.

5   Efficient Reliability Analysis

In order to obtain quantitative metrics on the reliability of a software-intensive system, an appropriate reliability model has to be constructed. Several aspects of the system such as execution model, usage behaviour and failure characteristics have to be captured to assess the degree of reliability.

5.1   Reliability Model Construction

In this work, we assume a DTMC-based reliability model which has been widely-accepted in the field. We consider two types of possible failures in the reliability evaluation.

Execution Failures: Components are considered as self-contained micro-computers with the software to fulfil a specific functionality. Failures may occur during the execution of a process in a software component. This type of failure is expressed in the *failure rate* values.

Communication Failures: A failure of a data communication bus at a time when a software component communicates with another over the bus leads to a failure of the service that depends on this communication.

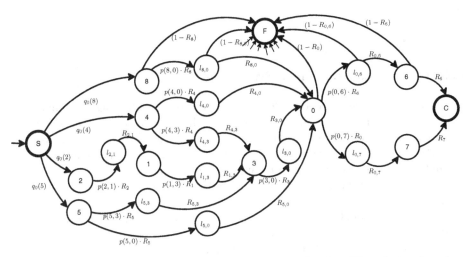

Fig. 3. Annotated DTMC [18] for service reliability evaluation. Note that only a few of the possible failure transitions are included in the diagram as an illustration. Similar arcs exist from each transient state to the final state F.

Figure 3 [18] shows the DTMC for the case study described in Section 4. The digits in the node labels point to the corresponding nodes in Figure 1. Single digit nodes represent execution of a software component, and nodes labelled $l_{i,j}$ denote the communications between software components. A super-initial node has been added to represent the start of the software execution, and arcs originating at the node have been annotated with relevant execution initialization probabilities(q_0). Two new absorbing states C and F have been added, representing the *correct output* and *failure* states respectively.

Failures during execution are mapped to arcs from each execution node c_i to F state with a probability $(1 - R_i)$ and communication failures are mapped to arcs from each communication node l_{ij} to F with a probability $(1 - R_{ij})$, where R_i, R_{ij} represent component reliability and execution link reliability respectively. Note that only a few of these failure transitions have been added for the clarity of the figure.

The failure probabilities during the execution of a software component (c_i) can be obtained from it's estimated failure rate parameter and the execution time as follows:

$$R_i = e^{-\lambda_{c_i} \times t_{c_i}} \tag{3}$$

A similar computation can be employed to establish the reliability of the communication elements, which, in our model, is characterised by the failure rates of the link, and the time taken for inter-component communication. Therefore, the reliability of the communication between component c_i and c_j is defined according to Equation 4.

$$R_{l_{ij}} = e^{-\lambda_{l_{ij}} \times t_{l_{ij}}} \tag{4}$$

5.2 Incremental Reliability Evaluation

Many of the analyses needed at design-time require re-evaluating the reliability model. For instance, *Sensitivity Analysis*, which is widely used as a technique to determine the impact of parameters on the behaviour of the composite system. Parameter sweeps are most commonly applied for this purpose and quality evaluations are necessary at each change of parameter.

The relationship between architecture and probabilistic quality model maps architectural elements (e.g. software components, interactions) to the elements of probabilistic model (e.g. nodes, transition probabilities). When a change is made to the architecture, the change is identified and propagated without a complete reconstruction of the quality evaluation model.

The model evaluation process can be enhanced by propagating the change through the model using Δ Evaluation [19,20]. With the annotations in Figure 4 and using $\Rightarrow$ to represent derivation, the approach can be formally defined as $(A, \Delta A, M) \Rightarrow \Delta M \Rightarrow M'$ and $(M, \Delta M, R) \Rightarrow R'$.

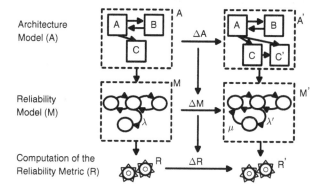

Fig. 4. Outline of the proposed approach

5.3 Δ Evaluation for Sensitivity Analysis

Δ Evaluation [19,20] can be applied in the architecture-based reliability evaluation by using it for the calculation of the probability of reaching the correct execution completion state C in the DTMC-based model. Suppose the transitions of the system have been changed and the change is expressed by ΔQ such that the new matrix Q' is $Q' = Q + \Delta Q$. The new system reliability is $R'_s = S'_{1,n} R_n$, where $S' = (I - Q')^{-1}$.

The change matrix ΔQ can be expressed as a row vector r and a column vector c such that $\Delta Q = cr$.

With the notation of $A = (I - Q)$ and B to denote the matrix obtained by deleting the nth row and the 1st column from A, $A' = A + \Delta A = A + c'r'$ where $c'r' = I - cr$

Similarly, $B' = B + c''r''$ where c'', r'' are obtained by removing the nth row and the 1st column from $c'r'$.

Meedeniya et al.[19] have shown that,

$$S'_{1,n} = \frac{(-1)^{n+1}|B'|}{|A'|} = \frac{(-1)^{n+1}|B|(1 + r''B^{-1}c'')}{|A|(1 + r'A^{-1}c')} \tag{5}$$

$$= S_{1,n}\frac{1 + r''B^{-1}c''}{1 + r'A^{-1}c'} \tag{6}$$

The results obtained in above derivation can be generalized to any single element modification (δ_{ij}) in the transition matrix Q,

$$S'_{(1,n)} = S_{(1,n)}\frac{1 - \delta_{ij} \times B^{-1}_{(j-1,i)}}{1 - \delta_{ij} \times A^{-1}_{(j,i)}} \tag{7}$$

In summary, if only one element of the transition matrix is changed, the updated reliability can be obtained simply by computing Equation 7. If more than one element in one row or column in the matrix is changed, Equation 6 is applicable which requires significantly less computation power than the computation of $(I - Q)^{-1}$. The next section further illustrates the significance of the computational gain in various analysis activities.

6   Validation

In order to validate the computational advantage of the Δ Evaluation in reliability analysis, we have conducted a series of analyses to compare the results obtained using:

- Full evaluation of the reliability model by Cheung [2] after each change,
- Δ Evaluation, and
- PRISM tool for reachability formulae evaluation.

6.1   Objectives of Reliability Analysis

The most relevant aspects to analyse during the design stage of automotive software are:

- What is the predicted reliability of the automotive software system for the given configuration?
- Which are the most sensitive software components that affect the system's reliability?
- How sensitive is the system reliability to behavioural model estimation?

In this work, we show how the proposed method can help in answering these questions quicker and with less computational effort.

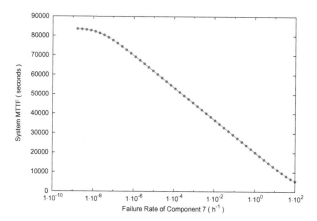

Fig. 5. Sensitivity of MTTF with respect to failure rate of component 7

6.2   Scenario 1: Sensitivity Analysis with Respect to the Failure Rate

Estimating susceptibility to failure is difficult in embedded systems where environment conditions affect the system's reliability. For example, the operating temperature of a hardware host directly affects its failure rate. Therefore, it is important to analyse how the system reliability would vary if the component failure rate changed. The experiment analyses the sensitivity of the mean time to failure (MTTF) when the failure rate of the brake actuator is changed.

For the purpose of these experiments, the values for execution initiation probability q_0 were chosen uniformly randomly in the range 0 - 1.17, the failure rate λ_c in the range $4x10^{-6}$, while the time per visit t_c takes uniform random values between 10 and 33. The failure rate λ_l is assumed to have values in the range $4x10^{-5}$ and the transfer time t_l is assigned values of 10, 20, 30 and 40 uniformly randomly, while the probability of a communication failure between two components is set in the range 0.2 - 1.

Figure 5 is a sensitivity graph, which depicts the variation of system MTTF against a parameter sweep of the failure rate for the range $[10^{-9} - 10^2]$, i.e. sensitivity of the the system MTTF to failure rate of component 7. For the purpose of this experiment, only one parameter (failure rate of component 7) was changed in 50 homogeneous steps across the range $[10^{-9}-10^2]$ while all other parameters were fixed. This change affects the changes in two probabilities in the reliability model given in Figure 3: transitions $7 \rightarrow SF$, and $7 \rightarrow F$. Since the rows and columns corresponding to state F are removed to obtain the modified matrix Q, only one value is changed.

The sensitivity analysis uses the simplified formulae in Equation 6 instead of the complete model evaluation. It can be observed that the system MTTF is very sensitive to the failure rate of component 7. The impact on MTTF is not significant when component 7's failure rate is below $10^{-7}h^{-1}$ where as the MTTF drops rapidly with increasing failure rate from about $10^{-7}h^{-1}$.

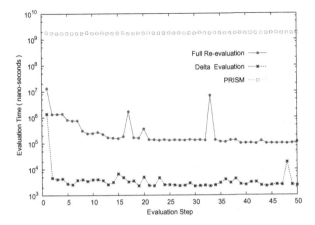

Fig. 6. The computation time for each evaluation step in the analysis

Figure 6 illustrates the computation time for each evaluation step in the sensitivity analysis experiment. It can be observed that Δ Evaluation usually takes less than 10^4 nanoseconds, whereas the complete model evaluation requires more than 10^5 nanoseconds. The extremely high evaluation time arising from the PRISM evaluation compared to the Cheung [2] model evaluation is largely explained by calls to third party applications.

6.3 Scenario 2: Sensitivity Analysis with Respect to Behaviour of Model Parameters

One key advantage of Markov Chain-based reliability models is their ability to combine many aspects of the system, including systems execution behaviour, usage profile and failure characteristics. At the design phase of an embedded system, it is important to analyse how the system's reliability would vary according to various user profiles. Considering this analysis requirement, we conducted a sensitivity analysis experiment with respect to a set of user behaviour parameters.

For illustration, we will consider the estimated call probabilities of brake pedal sensor component. Figure 7 presents the values of system reliability (MTTF) for different parameter values.

For the purpose of this experiment, only two transition probabilities were changed in the reliability model: $2 \rightarrow 1$ and $2 \rightarrow 9$. The new Δ Evaluation formula described in Equation 7 was applied and compared to the process of re-evaluating the whole model for each parameter value.

Similar to the other two scenarios, Figure 8 presents considerably lower computation time for each change in comparison to conventional model evaluation. Table 1 summarises the results. Similar to the previous scenario, the computational time of the Δ Evaluation technique is high for the first evaluation of the system reliability, hence the high maximum value, and very low for the subsequent re-evaluations of the system.

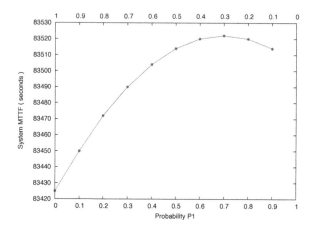

Fig. 7. System reliability (MTTF) change for different parameter values

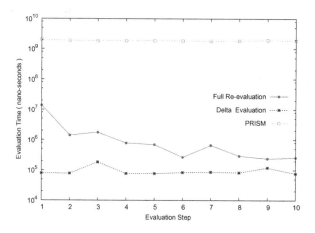

Fig. 8. The computation time for each evaluation step in the analysis

Table 1. The time in milliseconds taken by the three sensitivity analysis schemes

Time	Minimum	Average	Median	Maximum	Std Dev
Complete	2.02	0.67	13.84	0.24	4.18
Δ Eval.	0.07	0.09	0.08	0.18	0.03
PRISM	1854.00	1909.00	1889.00	2062.00	63.00

7 Conclusion and Future Work

Models for reliability evaluation are computationally expensive due to the complex matrix operations involved. The time-consuming aspect of model calculations is especially crucial in sensitivity analysis. The reliability of the system has to be re-evaluated for every change made. The approach introduced in this paper helps reduce the computational complexity of sensitivity analysis by using Δ Evaluation, which builds on previous evaluation results by evaluating a change in the architecture to estimate its reliability rather than re-evaluating the architecture in its entirety. Experiments on a practical example demonstrate significant economies in computation time compared to state-of-the-art sensitivity analysis methods without incurring any loss of accuracy.

References

1. Beyer, H.-G., Sendhoff, B.: Robust optimization - a comprehensive survey. Computer Methods in Applied Mechanics and Eng. 196(33-34), 3190–3218 (2007)
2. Cheung, R.C.: A user-oriented software reliability model. IEEE Transactions on Software Engineering 6(2), 118–125 (1980)
3. Coit, D.W., Jin, T., Wattanapongsakorn, N.: System optimization with component reliability estimation uncertainty: a multi-criteria approach. IEEE Transactions on Reliability 53(3), 369–380 (2004)
4. Coit, D.W., Smith, A.E.: Genetic algorithm to maximize a lower-bound for system time-to-failure with uncertain component weibull parameters. Computers & Industrial Engineering 41(4), 423–440 (2002)
5. Cortellessa, V., Grassi, V.: A modeling approach to analyze the impact of error propagation on reliability of component-based systems. In: Schmidt, H.W., Crnković, I., Heineman, G.T., Stafford, J.A. (eds.) CBSE 2007. LNCS, vol. 4608, pp. 140–156. Springer, Heidelberg (2007)
6. Filieri, A., Ghezzi, C., Tamburrelli, G.: Run-time efficient probabilistic model checking. In: Proceedings of the 33rd International Conference on Software Engineering, ICSE 2011, May 21-28, pp. 341–350. ACM, Waikiki (2011)
7. Fiondella, L., Gokhale, S.S.: Software reliability with architectural uncertainties. In: IEEE International Symposium on Parallel and Distributed Processing, pp. 1–5. IEEE Computer Society (2008)
8. Förster, M., Trapp, M.: Fault tree analysis of software-controlled component systems based on second-order probabilities. In: IEEE International Symposium on Software Reliability Engineering (ISSRE 2009), pp. 146–154. IEEE Computer Society (2009)
9. Fredriksson, J., Nolte, T., Nolin, M., Schmidt, H.: Contract-based reusable worst-case execution time estimate. In: The International Conference on Embedded and Real-Time Computing Systems and Applications (RTCSA), pp. 39–46 (2007)
10. Gokhale, S.S.: Architecture-based software reliability analysis: Overview and limitations. IEEE Transactions Dependable and Secure Computing 4(1), 32–40 (2007)
11. Gokhale, S.S., Trivedi, K.S.: Reliability prediction and sensitivity analysis based on software architecture. In: International Symposium of Software Reliability Engineering (ISSRE 2002), pp. 64–78. IEEE Computer Society (2002)
12. Goševa-Popstojanova, K., Hamill, M., Wang, X.: Adequacy, accuracy, scalability, and uncertainty of architecture-based software reliability: Lessons learned from large empirical case studies. In: International Symposium of Software Reliability Engineering (ISSRE 2006), pp. 197–203. IEEE Computer Society (2006)
13. Goševa-Popstojanova, K., Kamavaram Assessing, S.: uncertainty in reliability of component-based software systems. In: IEEE International Symposium on Software Reliability Engineering (ISSRE 2003), pp. 307–320. IEEE Computer Society (2003)

14. Goševa-Popstojanova, K., Kamavaram, S.: Software reliability estimation under uncertainty: Generalization of the method of moments. In: High-Assurance Systems Engineering (HASE 2004), pp. 209–218. IEEE Computer Society (2004)
15. Goševa-Popstojanova, K., Trivedi Architecture-based, K.S.: approach to reliability assessment of software systems. Performance Evaluation 45(2-3), 179–204 (2001)
16. Kwiatkowska, M.Z., Norman, G., Parker, D.: Probabilistic model checking in practice: case studies with prism. SIGMETRICS Performance Evaluation Review 32(4), 16–21 (2005)
17. Marseguerra, M., Zio, E., Podofillini, L.: Multiobjective spare part allocation by means of genetic algorithms and monte carlo simulation. Reliability Engineering & System Safety 87(3), 325–335 (2005)
18. Meedeniya, I., Aleti, A., Avazpour, I., Amin, A.: Robust archeopterix: Architecture optimization of embedded systems under uncertainty. In: 2012 2nd International Workshop on Software Engineering for Embedded Systems (SEES), pp. 23–29 (June 2012)
19. Meedeniya, I.: An incremental methodology for quantitative software architecture evaluation with probabilistic models. In: Proceedings of the 32nd ACM/IEEE International Conference on Software Engineering, ICSE 2010, May 1-8, vol. 2, pp. 339–340. ACM, Cape Town (2010)
20. Meedeniya, I., Grunske, L.: An Efficient Method for Architecture-Based Reliability Evaluation for Evolving Systems with Changing Parameters. In: IEEE International Symposium on Software Reliability Engineering (ISSRE 2010), pp. 229–238. IEEE (2010)
21. Shatz, S.M., Wang, J.-P., Goto, M.: Task allocation for maximizing reliability of distributed computer systems. IEEE Trans. Computers 41(9), 1156–1168 (1992)
22. Wang, W.-L., Pan, D., Chen, M.-H.: Architecture-based software reliability modeling. Journal of Systems and Software 79(1), 132–146 (2006)
23. Wattanapongskorn, N., Coit, D.W.: Fault-tolerant embedded system design and optimization considering reliability estimation uncertainty. Reliability Engineering & System Safety 92(4), 395–407 (2007)

Identifying Verb-Preposition Multi-Category Words in Chinese-English Patent Machine Translation

Hongzheng Li[1,2], Yun Zhu[1,2], and Yaohong Jin[1,2]

[1] Institute of Chinese Information Processing, Beijing Normal University, Beijing, China
[2] CPIC-BNU Joint Laboratory of Machine Translation, Beijing Normal University, China
lihongzheng@mail.bnu.edu.cn, {zhuyun,jinyaohong}@bnu.edu.cn

Abstract. Multi-category words are widely distributed in Chinese patent documents, and identification of them has been one of the difficulties in machine translation (MT). This paper proposes a rule-based method for identifying verb and preposition multi-category words in Chinese-English patent machine translation. Based on principles of boundary perception and according to syntactic and semantic information of multi-category words as well as context information, some reliable disambiguation rules are designed to help the MT system analyze proper categories of words, then proposes adverbial and predicate identification rules to determine and identify the words further. Related experiments and BLEU evaluations show that the method is efficient to recognize verbs and prepositions better, and is also helpful to improve final translation quality.

Keywords: multi-category words, verb identification, preposition identification, machine translation.

1 Introduction

Patent documents play a positive and important role in technology progress and economic development all over the world [1]. In recent years, patent machine translation (MT) has become one of major application fields of MT, and gains more and more attention from various organizations and research communities [2,3].

Chinese patent documents usually feature longer sentences with more complex grammatical structures, more tedious and rigorous expressions, resulting in more difficulties in Chinese-English patent MT, one of which is verb and preposition multi-category words (V-P words in short). Such words not only can serve as components of prepositional phases (PP), but also as predicate verb or non-predicate verbs under some conditions, V-P words can influence syntactical analysis and final translation results in MT system.

Following are two examples in Chinese patent texts.

E.g.1 本发明可以为该装置提供技术支持。(This invention can provide technical support *for the instrument*.)

E.g.2 化合物A的盐可以为药理学可接受的盐。(The salt of compound A can *be* pharmacologically acceptable salt.)

S.K. Chalup et al. (Eds.): ACALCI 2015, LNAI 8955, pp. 409–421, 2015.

In example 1, the Chinese word "WEI" is a preposition (prep.), while in example 2 it is a verb, thus it can be regarded as multi-category word. PP often serves as an adverbial (adv.) in a sentence, contrary to the position of adv. in Chinese, adv. is usually located behind the VP in English, consequently, when translated from Chinese to English, as shown in Fig.1, positions of PP and VP in example 1 should be reordered to be more consistent with expression habits in English. On the other hand, example 2 does not need to reorder the positions of words and chunks.

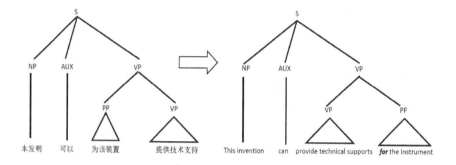

Fig. 1. Syntax tree of example 1

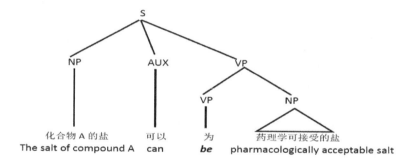

Fig. 2. Syntax tree of example 2

The two examples indicate that multi-category words not only have important impacts on part of speech (POS) tagging and word sense disambiguation (WSD), but also on syntactic analysis and reordering of words while translating Chinese into English. In a word, correct identification of multi-category words is of great significance.

As Chinese lacks inflectional changes between words, there always exist some difficulties in recognizing multi-category words. Based on the principle of boundary perception, this paper will propose a rule-based method of identifying V-P words for Chinese-English patent MT. According to the syntactic and semantic information of V-P words, some reliable disambiguation rules are designed to help the MT system analyze properties of words, then proposes adverbial chunks and predicate identification rules to further determine and recognize whether the words can be verbs or prepositions.

This paper is organized as follows: Section 2 discusses some related work. Section 3 briefly discusses our patent MT system. Section 4 introduces V-P multi-category words in Chinese patent texts. Section 5 will propose the identification method and rules. Experiments and analysis will be conducted in Section 6. And the last section will present some conclusions and future work.

2   Related Work

Multi-category words research, which is closely related to POS and WSD, has been one of the hot issues in the field of Natural Language Processing (NLP). The standard classification of WSD systems (Agirre and Edmonds, 2006) used the term "knowledge-based" for systems that use man-made lexical resources and splits corpus-based approaches into two types: "supervised" and "unsupervised" systems [4,5].

There usually exist two methods of identifying multi-category words: rule-based and statistical-based approaches. While rule-based methods depend on linguistic rules to describe the information appearing in the context, statistical-based methods employ statistical models such as Maximum Entropy (ME) model, Conditional Random Field (CRF) and N-gram model to recognize the words [6]. The two methods have both advantages and weaknesses. Some research (Zhang, 2002) also uses a hybrid method by combining the rule-based method with statistical method to identify multi-category words [7].

If the V-P words are identified as preposition, identifying PPs should be next step. Researches on identifying PPs in Chinese usually focuses on determining the boundaries of PP and identify them as whole chunks [8], since the left boundary is preposition itself, the key issue is to determine the right boundary. Some researchers proposed an identification method based on Support Vector Machine (SVM) [9], and some others also tried to combine rule methods with statistical method [10].

Generally, basic approaches to MT include statistical-based MT (SMT), rule-based MT (RBMT) and hybrid method MT. While SMT has been considered as the mainstream of translation, RBMT has tended to be more effective for limited subject domains than SMT [11]. Take patent MT for instance, patent text usually has fixed expression structures, rules can describe the features more precisely. SMT, on the other hand, finds it more difficult to deal with the word reordering in the translation between distant language pairs such as Japanese and English [12].

Considering research on identification of multi-category words in patent MT field is limited, on the basis of previous studies, we will apply rule-based method to the research, hoping to propose some efficient ideas and concise formal rules to identify V-P words.

3   Chinese-English Patent MT System

Our C-E patent MT system, designed and developed by C++ program, is rule-based. Knowledge base and rules are essential components of the system, only after integrating them into the system, can it parse source language sentences and generate final translation.

As shown in Fig.3, the system mainly contains four modules: word segmentation, semantic analysis, transitional transformation and target words generation. And identification of V-P words belongs to semantic analysis module.

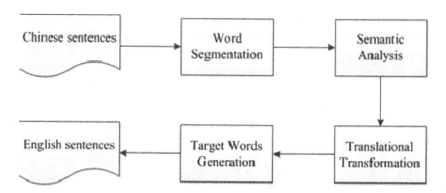

Fig. 3. Processing modules of patent MT system

4   Verb-Preposition Words in Patent Texts

We analyzed 500 sentences randomly extracted from different patent documents, the result showed that 226 sentences contained V-P words, accounting for 45.2% of the sample, while words in 154 sentences were prepositional, accounting for 68.1% of the 226 sentences. These data clearly indicated V-P words are widely distributed in Chinese patent documents, and most V-P words served as preposition has strong relations with the inherent organizational forms and expression features of patent texts.

4.1   V-P Words as Verbs

Assuming V-P words have been identified as verbs, if they need to be identified as predicate verbs further, they should meet the condition that no other verbs or no VPs serve as predicates in the sentences.

E.g.1:本发明的实施例可以**使用**一个弹性的接口40。(Embodiments of the present invention can ***employ*** a flexible interface 40.)

E.g.2: 权利要求1中的电缆能够**通过**具有调节装置的加热器。(Cables in claim 1 can ***pass through*** the heater that has adjusting devices.)

In example 1, the V-P word "使用" is the only verb in the sentence, so it should be selected as predicate; Except for the V-P word "通过", although other verbs and VP also appear in example 2, as VP is actually a clause in the NP behind the word "通过", thus, the V-P word is still predicate.

On the other hand, if the V-P words serve as parts of NPs, they should be identified as common non-predicate verbs, just as shown in the following example, predicate verb is "具有(have)" instead of "通过(pass through)".

E.g.3: **通过**加热器的电缆具有特殊的生产工艺。(The cables ***passing through*** the heater ***have*** special production progress.)

4.2   V-P Words as Prepositions

Expressions of Adverbials
Most V-P words serve as prepositions in patent texts. One common syntactic function of prepositional phases is acting as adverbial chunks. After analyzing large scale corpus, we concluded several common forms of adverbials in patent texts as follows.

(Subject) + Adv. + Predicate. The adverbial located between subject and predicate, and subject sometimes can be omitted. This is the most common form.
　　E.g. 本发明的清洗过程不需要【通过清洗热处理】来去除残留有机物。(The cleaning process of the present invention does not require to remove residual organics *by washing heat treatment*.)

Adv. + ", " + (Subject) + Predicate. In order to highlight the adverbial, sometimes adverbial is split by comma, standing in front of subject and predicate structure.
　　E.g. 【在一个实施方式中】，清洗剂组合物也包含至少一种碱性盐和缓冲剂。(*In one embodiment*, the cleaning composition also comprises at least one kind of alkaline salts and buffers.)

(Subject) + Adv.1 + Adv.2 +......+Predicate. In this form, several parallel adverbials can appear in the same sentence.
　　E.g. 罐子【在此温度下】【采用含镁的合金】【通过深冲工艺】制成。The jar is made *at this temperature using magnesium alloy by deep drawing process*.)

Adverbial chunks in Chinese patent texts usually have complex syntactic structures and compositions, forming long distance structures. But they still have obvious boundaries, one of which is preposition itself. The boundary words are very useful in identifying adverbials.

In some adverbials, words of right boundaries are collocations of certain prepositions, such as "在......中/时/内". In this paper, prepositions are marked as "L1", and collocation words like "中/时/内" are marked as "L1H", adverbials with L1 and L1H are called as *double boundaries adverbial*; Adverbials which only have L1 are *single boundary adverbial*.

Table 1 shows some common Chinese V-P words in patent corpus.

Table 1. Common V-P words in patent corpus[1]

monosyllabic words	two-syllable words
在(ZAI, in), 为(WEI, for), 经(JING, through),用 (YONG, using)......	采用(CAIYONG, using), 使用(SHIYONG, using), 利用(LIYONG,), 参考(CANKAO, refer to),参照 (CANZHAO, according to), 经过(JINGGUO, through),通过(TONGGUO, by), 作为(ZUOWEI, as), 基于 (JIYU, based on) ......

---

[1] The capital letters in each bracket represent *Pinyin* of the Chinese words.

Levels of Adverbials

Hierarchy is the basic property of syntactic structure. Adverbials located in different syntactic positions in a sentence usually have different syntax levels. In order to distinguish and parse various adverbials, this paper divides them into two levels named "LEVEL 1" and "LEVEL 2".

LEVEL 1: Adverbials that are immediate constituents of sentences belong to this level, and they must locate in the first levels in a tree diagram. Adverbials in the above examples are all LEVEL 1.

LEVEL 2: Adverbials serving as components of chunks instead of immediate constituents of sentences usually belong to LEVEL 2. Some adverbials of LEVEL 1 often contain adverbials of LEVEL 2. Such adverbials, as showed in the following example, are usually called as *nested adverbials*.

E.g. 该真空工具【通过 [在控制器中]/LEVEL2连接这些网络环片段】/LEVEL1能够控制至少一个低温泵。(The vacuum tool can control at least one cry pump *by connecting the network rings in the controller*.)

In the example, the prepositional phrase (PP) "in the controller" is part of the PP beginning with the word "by", so the syntactic level of the phrase "in the controller" is LEVEL 2.

Level information is important to determine syntactic levels in the progress of syntactic analysis, which will also have further impacts on transformation and generation processing.

5   Identification Method

In this section, methods of identifying V-P words will be proposed. It is necessary to first introduce some information about the rules related to the methods.

5.1   Rule Description

All the rules in the system are manually written in *Backus-Naur Form* (BNF), which is a kind of simple, clear grammar rules to describe languages [13]. The general form of rules is conditions => actions, while the left parts determine the necessary conditions for the application of the rules, the right parts describe the actions taken by applying the rules. Following is an example rule.

(0){LC_CC[L1]&CHN[通 过 , 利 用 , 用]&BEGIN%%}+(f){(1)LC_CC[LA]}=> LC_TREE(ABK,0,1][2]

It can be seen that the rule contains much information including POS (LC_CC), logic information (&), word location information (Arabic numbers) in a sentence and so on. Such formal expression is easy to read and understand for both human beings and computer systems.

Based on the principles of boundary perception [14], the rules make full use of syntactic and semantic information of words and context information to determine the boundaries of different chunks in the sentence. Once the boundaries are determined,

---

[2] (0, 1] in the right part of the rule is similar to interval in mathematics, it means the word in location 0 is within the range of adverbial chunk, while the word in location 1 is not.

words and components inside the chunk will not interfere with processing of other chunks, which is particularly beneficial to long distance collocation chunks.

For example, suppose in the sentence $S=W_1, W_2, W_3 \ldots\ldots W_n$, if string $W_i, W_{i+1} \ldots\ldots W_j$ ($i<j\le$ n) is recognized as a specific chunk, such as PP, all the words in the chunk will not be analyzed as immediate constituents of the sentence.

Another obvious advantage is, the rules just need to pay attention to local linguistic phenomena instead of overall situation in the sentence, which increases the efficiency of rule matching, and greatly reduces the difficulties in designing and writing the rules.

5.2   Identification Modules

Following are basic steps of identifying V-P words:

Step1: Pre-processing of source language sentences, including word segmentation and segment sentences into several chunks according to the punctuations such as commas and periods.

Step2: Disambiguating the multi-category words first. If the preposition POS of V-P words is excluded in this process, then go to step4; if not, go to step 3.

Step3: Identifying adverbial chunks. If the V-P words can match the adverbial identification rules successfully, the words will be recognized as prepositions, and adverbial chunks will be also identified; if not, go to step 4.

Step4: Identifying predicate and non-predicate verbs. If the V-P words can match the rules in this module successfully, the words will be identified as core predicate verbs; if not, they will be identified as non-predicate verbs.

The last three steps involve about 600 different rules of three processing modules, since the adverbial chunks are usually located before predicate, adverbial identification is also designed to be prior to predicate identification in the MT system. Considering the limit of this paper, while introducing each module in the following, we will only take at most 2 rules for each instance.

Multi-category Disambiguation
As the first stage of syntactic analysis in the translation system, the purpose of this module lies in disambiguating some multi-category words with obvious syntactic features to reduce interference on subsequent processing caused by multi-category words. Since each word should have exactly single POS in specific contexts and sentences, only if the POS of multi-category words is determined, can guarantee proper analysis in subsequent processing. By examining the properties of verbs and prepositions in corpus, as well as the context information, some reliable rules are designed. Just take two rules for example:

Rule 1:
(0)CHN[通过,利用]+(f){(1)CHN[来,而]}=>!LC_SELECT(0,LC_CC,V)

The rule means, in a sentence, if the Chinese words "来" or "而" can be found behind "通过"or "利用", then the POS of "通过"or "利用"should not be identified as verb. Because in patent sentence pattern *"(NP)* + 通过/利用 +......+ *VP"*, VP is usually identified as predicate chunks, and when translated into English, string between "通过/利用" and VP will be reordered to the end of the sentence as adverbial chunks.

E.g. 然后该制剂可以**通过**启动与容器连接的计量阀而被喷散。(The formulation may then be dispersed *by activating a dose-metering valve affixed to the container*.)

Rule 2:

(0){LC_CC[L1]&LC_GCC[V]&END%}=>!LC_SELECT(0,LC_CC,L1)

This rule means that if the V-P word is located at the end of a sentence, the word should not selected be preposition.

E.g. 本产品不会改变权利要求中的材料**使用**。(The product will not change the *use* of the materials in the claim.)

Note that, natural languages are so complex that the disambiguation rules definitely cannot cover all the contexts that V-P words may appear. What the rules can do is to exclude more multi-category words as much as possible.

Adverbial Chunk Identification

If POS of V-P words hasn't been determined temporarily at previous stage, the words will enter current stage to be further judged through serial rules. As prepositions are necessary to adverbials, the V-P words will be identified as preposition if matching the adverbial rules successfully.

The key issue in identifying adverbial chunks is to determine the right boundaries. In our method, we first assume that all the words with the marks "L1"and "L1H" can be identified as boundary words, then find the adverbial chunk in the string that begins with the preposition. Information of preposition is necessary in each rule.

Adverbials with Single Boundary

For adverbials with single boundaries, it is necessary to determine the right boundary words according to some specific words next to the right boundary, such as some conjunctions.

Suppose string $W_i, W_{i+1}......W_j$ is in the sentence $S=W_1, W_2, W_3......W_n (i,j< n)$, if W_i is the preposition, W_j is a conjunction between phases, and W_{j+1} is predicate, considering the expression features in patent texts, the string $W_i, W_{i+1}......W_{j-1}$ is determined as adverbial chunk. The formal rule is described below.

(0)LC_CC[L1]+(f){(1)LC_CC[LA]}=>LC_TREE(ABK,0,1]

E.g. 本发明【**通过**/L1权利要求中的产品说明】/ABK 而/LA提高汽车的生产效率。(The invention improves the production efficiency of cars *through the product description in the claim.*   )

Adverbials with Double Boundaries

For adverbials with double boundaries, if W_i is preposition(L1)in the string $W_i, W_{i+1}......W_j$, and W_j is L1H, the two words are first identified, then $W_i, W_{i+1}......W_j$ will be identified as adverbial chunk.

(0)LC_CHK[L1] +(f){(1)LC_CC[L1H] }=>LC_TREE(ABK,0,1)

E.g. 组通信业务【在/L1通信系统内/L1H】/ABK 变得越来越普遍。(Group communication service is becoming more and more popular **in communications systems**.)

Parallel Adverbials

For such adverbials, it is necessary to recognize prepositions of each adverbial and determine their levels according to the context. In the sentence $S=W_1, W_2 \cdots W_i, W_{i+1}, \cdots W_j, W_{j+1}, \cdots W_k, W_{k+1} \cdots W_n$, suppose W_i and W_j are both L1 of LEVEL 1, then the strings $W_i, W_{i+1}, \cdots W_{j-1}$ and $W_j, W_{j+1}, \cdots W_{k-1}$ are usually parallel adverbials.

E.g. 该实验装置【在/L1, LEVEL1此温度下/L1H, LEVEL1】【采用/ L1, LEVEL1含镁的合金】【通过/L1, LEVEL1深冲工艺】制成。(The experiment instrument is made *at this temperature using magnesium alloy by deep drawing process*.)

Nested Adverbials

For those adverbials of LEVEL 1 containing double boundaries adverbials of LEVEL 2, as several boundaries of different levels appear in the same chunk, the system should guarantee the L1H words of LEVEL 2 inside cannot be identified as the right boundary of L1 in adverbials of LEVEL 1. That is, boundary words with different syntactic levels cannot form adverbial chunk.

(0)LC_CHK[L1]&LEVEL1+(f){(1)LC_CC[L1]&LEVEL2}+(f){(2) LC_CC[L1 H]&LEVEL2} =>LC_TREE(ABK,1,2)&PUT(ABK, LEVEL2)

E.g. 本发明需要【根据/ L1, LEVEL1 在/L1, LEVEL2 样本数据中/L1H, LE VEL2 得到的结果】来提高私人汽车的产量。(This invention needs to improve production of private automobiles *according to the results in the sample data*.)

Predicate Verb Identification

As the processing steps show, words that have excluded the preposition POS in step 2 or haven't matched the adverbial rules successfully will enter predicate identification stage.

Chinese lacks morphological changes between words, what's more, patent sentences often have more than one verb. Consequently, it's hard for translation system to determine proper predicate from several verbs. Aiming at the problem, we present a method by giving weights to different verbs [14]. Several kinds of weights are designed for verbs to represent the possibilities serving as predicate verb. Different weights are shown in the right parts of rules related to verb identification, the system first gives weights to each verb including V-P words according to context conditions and the rules it matches, then compares levels of the weights, and finally selects the verb with the highest weights as core predicate.

The V-P words which two POS are not excluded will also have a weight in lower level, but it doesn't mean they cannot be selected as predicate at all. Because during the progress of syntactic analysis, the words may be given different weights when matching various rules. Except the V-P words, if no other verbs exist in the same sentence, or, the system is unable to find verbs whose weights are higher than V-P word's, then the V-P word will be identified as the final predicate; otherwise, the V-P word will be chose as non-predicate verb.

E.g.1 当移动节点208离开覆盖区域时,节点208可使用其全部资源能力。 (When the mobile node 208 moves from the coverage area, node 208 can *use* all resources capacity.)

E.g.2 在厨房里使用这种燃料的容器需要被涂覆。(The container *using* the fuel in the kitchen needed to be coated.)

In example1, there exists no other verbs except the V-P word "使用", as a result, it will be identified as predicate, although it has a low weight. While in example2, as the same word "使用" is part of the attributive, it is definitely not predicate verb, and it will be translated into English in the form of a clause.

After the three processing modules, POS of V-P words will be finally determined and identified, and generate related information on the parsing tree.

6   Experiments and Analysis

In this part, we first conducted experiments to examine identification effects of V-P words with our Chinese-English patent MT system after integrating all the rules, then evaluated the performance of the system with BLEU score by comparing it with baseline. Both the identification tests and BLEU evaluations included closed tests and open tests. We randomly selected 3000 patent sentences from bilingual patent paralleled corpora provided by *State Intellectual Property Office of China* (SIPO) as closed test set, and chose test set of patent machine translation subtask [3] in the NTCIR-9 workshop meeting as open test set, which contained 2000 bilingual (Chinese-English) patent sentence pairs.

6.1   Identification Tests

In the tests, we aimed to examine the identification effects of multi-category words. We would observe identification of verbs and prepositions respectively.

Following were the experimental procedures:

1. Manually extracting all sentences containing V-P words from the test sets.
2. Counting respectively the total number of V-P words that should be identified as verbs or prepositions. If the same word appeared more than once, or different multi-category words existed in a sentence, we would double count the times they appeared.
3. Testing the extracted sentences with current MT system and manually checked ultimate results, then calculating related data according to the following equations.

$$\text{Precision (P)} = \frac{\text{Number of Correctly identified multi-category words}}{\text{Number of identified multi-category words}} \times 100\% \quad (1)$$

$$\text{Recall(R)} = \frac{\text{Number of Correctly identified multi-category words}}{\text{Total Number of multi-category words in test sets}} \times 100\% \quad (2)$$

---

[3] http://research.nii.ac.jp/ntcir/ntcir-9/data.html

$$\text{F-measure (F1)} = \frac{2 \times P \times R}{P+R} \times 100\% \tag{3}$$

Table 2. Identification results of closed test

	Total Number	Totally Identified	Correctly Identified	P (%)	R (%)	F1 (%)
V-P as Verb	372	336	301	89.58	80.91	85.02
V-P as Preposition	908	843	797	94.54	87.78	91.03

Table 3. Identification results of open test

	Total Number	Totally Identified	Correctly Identified	P (%)	R (%)	F1 (%)
V-P as Verb	261	248	212	85.48	81.22	83.29
V-P as Preposition	784	738	665	90.11	84.82	87.39

6.2 BLEU Evaluation

BLEU score evaluation [15], proposed by IBM in 2002, has been considered as one of the most commonly used methods for automatic evaluation in MT field [16]. In order to evaluate the translation effects after adding V-P words identification rules to the current system, we used the Interactive BLEU Tool [17] (ibleu-2.6.2.zip [4]) to get BLEU-4 scores, and compared them with baseline. Note that baseline was BLEU scores of the system without adding any multi-category disambiguation rules.

Table 4 showed the scores.

Table 4. Comparison of BLEU-4 scores

	Baseline (%)	RB System (%)
Closed tests	26.16	37.58
Open tests	21.44	30.37

6.3 Experimental Analysis

In the identification tests, precision and recall rates reached over 80%, indicating that methods proposed in this paper had better effects in identifying V-P words. However, after analyzing the results, we also found some factors that may result in error identification, these factors included: some rules were too strict to cover all the contexts where the V-P words appeared; some bugs in the translation system also resulted in improper syntactic analysis for some sentences. We should also recognize that, recall rates were lower than precision rates because of some too strict rules.

---

[4] http://code.google.com/p/ibleu/

In the BLEU evaluation, both scores of two tests were higher than the baseline. The score of closed tests improved 11 percent and open test score improved about 9 percent. These also verified that the rules were helpful to improve the system's translation results. The reason why BLEU scores improved mainly lay in the fact that, identification of multiple-category words have impacts on syntactic analysis of source language sentences, after correct identification, the system will choose proper English words according to the POS of multiple-category words when transforming Chinese into English.

On the other hand, the scores of open tests were lower than those of closed tests. The main reason was, all the words included in the knowledgebase and translation dictionary of the system are derived from large scale corpus provided by SIPO, but many words and terms in open test set are out of vocabulary (OOV), as a result, they had no corresponding English words, and had to appear in final translation in the form of Chinese characters, which largely decreased the scores in return.

7   Conclusion and Future Work

In this paper, we first studied syntactic and semantic features of common V-P multi-category words in Chinese patent documents, and then presented a rule-based method of identifying such words in Chinese-English patent MT. Related experiments and BLEU evaluations showed that our method and rules were efficient to identify the multi-category words and helpful to improve whole translation quality of the system, although there still existed some error identification.

In the future, we will modify the improper values of words in the knowledge base, take more factors and conditions into account to present more precise and detailed rules, and select more patent passages as test sets to verify the rules.

Acknowledgements. This work was supported by the National Hi-Tech Research and Development Program of China (2012AA011104).

References

1. Jiang, H., Jiang, T., Zhang, K., et al.: Some Key Issues in Chinese-to-English Patent Machine Translation. In: Proceedings of the 9th China Workshop on Machine Translation, CWMT 2013 (2013)
2. Wang, D.: Chinese to English automatic patent machine translation at SIPO. J. World Patent Information. 31(2), 137–139 (2009)
3. Goto, I., Lu, B., Chow, K.P., Sumita, E., Tsou, B.K.: Overview of the patent machine translation task at the ntcir-9 workshop. In: Proceedings of 9th NTCIR Workshop Meeting, pp. 559–578 (2011)
4. Eneko, A., Edmonds, P.: Word sense disambiguation, algorithms and applications. Springer, Heidelberg (2006)
5. McCarthy, D.: Word Sense Disambiguation: An Overview. J. Language and Linguistics Compass (3/2), 537–558 (2009)

6. Xia, J.: Automatic Recognition Research on Syntactic Category of Common Words (2012) (in Chinese)
7. Zhang, L.: Multi-category words processing mechanism combined rule with statistical methods (2002) (in Chinese)
8. Gan, J., Huang, D.: Automatic Identification of Chinese Prepositional Phrase. J. Journal of Chinese Information Processing 19(4), 17–23 (2005) (in Chinese)
9. Wen, M., Wu, Y.: Feature-rich Prepositional Phrase Boundary Identification based on SVM. J. Journal of Chinese Information Processing. 23(5), 19–24 (2009) (in Chinese)
10. Zan, H., Zhang, T., Zhang, K.: Automatic recognition research on preposition's usage based on combinations of rules and statistics. J. Computer Engineering and Design 34(6), 2153–2157 (2013) (in Chinese)
11. List, J.: Review of machine translation in patents–Implications for search. J. World Patent Information 34, 193–195 (2012)
12. Isozaki, H., Hirao, T., Duh, K., et al.: Automatic Evaluation of Translation Quality for Distant Language Pairs. In: Proceedings of the 2010 Conference on Empirical Methods in Natural Language Processing, pp. 944–952. MIT, Massachusetts (2010)
13. Wei, X., Zhang, Q.: Study on the computer-proceeding rules of V+V in Chinese. J. Application Research of Computers. 1, 43–46 (2006) (in Chinese)
14. Zhu, Y., Jin, Y.: A Chinese-English patent machine translation system based on the theory of hierarchical network of concepts. J. The Journal of China Universities of Posts and Telecommunications 19(Suppl. 2), 140–146 (2012)
15. Papineni, K., Roukos, S., Ward, T., et al.: BLEU: a Method for Automatic Evaluation of Machine Translation. In: Proceedings of the 40th Annual Meeting on Association for Computational Linguistics, pp. 311–318 (2002)
16. Liu, Q., Qian, Y.: Summary on Chinese Information Processing Technology Evaluation. J. Communications of China Computer Federation 02, 11–18 (2008) (in Chinese)
17. Madnani, N.: iBLEU: Interactively Debugging & Scoring Statistical Machine Translation Systems. In: Proceedings of the Fifth IEEE International Conference on Semantic Computing, pp. 213–214. IEEE Press, USA (2011)

Wavelet Based Artificial Intelligence Approaches for Prediction of Hydrological Time Series

Vahid Nourani[*] and Gholamreza Andalib

Department of Water Resources Engineering, Faculty of Civil Engineering,
University of Tabriz, Iran, P.B. 51666
vnourani@yahoo.com,
gholamreza.andalib@gmail.com

Abstract. In this paper, the efficiency of a Wavelet-based Least Square Support Vector Machine (WLSSVM) model was examined for prediction of monthly Suspended Sediment Load (SSL) of the Aji-Chay River. First the SSL was predicted via ad hoc Least Square Support Vector Machine (LSSVM) and Artificial Neural Network (ANN) models. Thereafter in hybrid models, streamflow and SSL time series were decomposed into sub-signals via a wavelet transform and the decomposed subseries were fed into LSSVMs and ANNs to simulate a discharge-SSL relationship. The results showed that ANNs led to better outcomes with Determination Coefficient (DC)=0.62 than ad hoc LSSVMs with DC=0.59. On the other hand, WLSSVMs performed better than wavelet-based ANN (WANN) models in monthly SSL prediction and wavelet data preprocessing could lead to more accurate results.

Keywords: suspended sediment load, least square support vector machine, wavelet, artificial neural network, Aji-Chay river.

1   Introduction

Suspended sediment load is a serious pollutant in streams and estuaries. In addition, sedimentation is an ongoing maintenance problem for reservoirs, limiting reservoir storage capacity and navigation. Sediment transport in a river can cause significant damage to the nature, agriculture, water quality and water installations. Considering the significance of sediment phenomenon and its environmental impacts, the prediction of the carried sediment volume by a river is an important and interesting issue for river engineers. Therefore, several models have been presented for simulation of sediment phenomenon [1,2]. Due to the complexity of sediment transport in a river, the black box (lumped) modeling may have some avails over the modeling by the theoretical ruling equations [3]. Recently, Artificial Intelligence (AI) approaches as a new generation of robust tools have been developed for time series forecasting purpose. As such forecasting tools, Artificial Neural Network (ANN) [4], Least Square Support Vector Machine (LSSVM) [5], Genetic Programming [6], Extreme Learning Machine

---

[*] Corresponding author.

S.K. Chalup et al. (Eds.): ACALCI 2015, LNAI 8955, pp. 422–435, 2015.
© Springer International Publishing Switzerland 2015

[7], Relevance Vector Machine [8] etc. have been extensively employed at different engineering fields. Among such AI models, the capability of commonly used ANN models to approximate nonlinear mappings between inputs and outputs makes it a useful tool for modeling hydrological phenomena [9,10,11].

However, ANN-based modeling may include some shortcomings, such as overfitting, convergence to local minima and slow training, which make it difficult to achieve adequate efficiency when dealing with complex hydrological processes [12]. Support Vector Machine (SVM), proposed in [13], is one of the most persuasive forecasting tools as an alternative method to ANN. SVM is based on the structural risk minimization principle and Vapnik–Chervonenkis theory, and involves solving a quadratic programming problem, thus can theoretically get the global best consequence of the primal problem [13]. In recent decades, SVMs have been implemented in several hydrological fields [14,15,16]. As well, in suspended sediment estimation, SVM was used with Gaussian radial basis function as kernel in order to estimate SSL for two rivers located in the USA [17]. SVM was also applied for simulation of runoff and sediment yield [18,19].

On the other hand, wavelet analysis gains considerable insight into the physical forms of the data by presenting information in both time and frequency domains of the time series. It has been found that a proper data pre-processing which uses wavelet analysis can enable the models to adequately describe the real characteristics of the basic system. The neuro-wavelet model is created by conjunction of ANN and wavelet transform. Wavelet-ANN (WANN) models are usually efficient in modeling nonlinear and non-stationary time series due to integrated capability of both wavelet analysis and ANN framework. Wavelet transform can decompose a non-stationary signal into a certain number of stationary sub-signals. Then, ANN is combined with wavelet transform to improve precision of the prediction [20]. Hybrid WANN model has been successfully applied in recent years to forecast hydrological and hydrogeological processes [21,22]. In the content of SSL modeling, neuro-wavelet technique was used for forecasting river daily SSL [23,24]. ANN was conjugated with threshold based wavelet denoising approach to predict SSL [25]. Results revealed that mother wavelet, resolution level and selected threshold value of noise directly affect the prediction results. The aforementioned studies confirm that the ANNs calibrated using the pre-processed data may result in better efficiency with regard to the ANNs calibrated using un-decomposed, noisy and raw time series. Although the hybrid Wavelet-SVM (WSVM) model has been used in several engineering fields [26,27], a few studies have pointed out the ability of WSVM in hydrological modeling [28,29,30]. The comparison of the methods revealed that the ANN and SVM models linked to wavelet transform are able to supply more accurate forecasting results than the ad hoc ANN and SVM models. Furthermore, it was found that SVM model coupled with wavelet transform provides a bit better forecasting results than WANN.

In this paper, the conjunction of LSSVM, as a developed version of SVM [31] and the wavelet-based data pre-processing is examined by proposed WLSSVM for modeling discharge-sediment relationship. Whereas, ad hoc models as LSSVM and ANN can't cover non-stationary time series, wavelet presents seasonalities in the process by decomposing non-stationary signal into the stationary sub-signals. To catch this aim, monthly streamflow and SSL time series of the Aji-Chay River are decomposed into sub-signals at various resolution levels. Then, the obtained sub-signals are imposed to the LSSVM and ANN models to reconstruct the original predicted time series of SSL to appraise the modeling ability. The proposed models are also compared with single LSSVM and ANN models.

2   Materials and Methods

2.1   Least Square Support Vector Machine

LSSVM has been originated from SVM as a powerful methodology for solving problems in non-linear classification, function estimation and density estimation [31,32]. Via LSSVM, a non-linear function can be shown as [31]:

$$f(x) = w^T \phi(x) + u \tag{1}$$

where f indicates the relationship between the streamflow and SSL, w is the m-dimensional weight vector, ϕ is the mapping function that maps x into the m-dimensional feature vector and u is the bias term [33]. Considering the complexity of function and fitting error, the regression problem can be given according to the structural minimization principle as [31]:

$$\min J(w,e) = \frac{1}{2} w^T w + \frac{\gamma}{2} \sum_{i=1}^{m} e_i^2 \tag{2}$$

with the following constraints for $i=1,2,\ldots,m$:

$$Y_i = w^T \phi(X_i) + u + e_i \tag{3}$$

where γ is the margin parameter and e_i is the slack variable for X_i. To solve the optimization problem given by equation (2), the objective function can be obtained using the Lagrange multipliers of α_i and the optimal condition can be obtained by taking the partial derivatives from objective function of unconstraint problem with respect to the parameters which yields the linear regression of [31]:

$$\begin{bmatrix} 0 & -Y^T \\ Y & ZZ^T + \dfrac{I}{\gamma} \end{bmatrix} \begin{bmatrix} u \\ \alpha \end{bmatrix} = \begin{bmatrix} 0 \\ 1 \end{bmatrix} \tag{4}$$

where $Y = Y_1,\ldots,Y_{ym}, Z = \phi(X_1)^T Y_i,\ldots,\phi(X_m)^T Y_m, I = [1,\ldots,1], \alpha = [\alpha_1,\ldots,\alpha_i]$.

By defining a non-linear kernel function, $K(X,X_i) = \phi(X)^T \phi(X_i)$, the LSSVM non-linear regression becomes [31]:

$$f(x) = \sum_{i=1}^{m} \alpha_i K(X, X_i) + u \tag{5}$$

The radial basis function (RBF) is a commonly used kernel function in regression problems. The RBF kernel represents the normal probability distribution form and since most stochastic hydrological processes like SSL obey the normal distribution probability or have capabilities of changing to such normal distribution, the RBF kernel is used as the LSSVM main kernel function in this study as [31]:

$$K(X, X_i) = \exp(-\frac{\|X - X_i\|^2}{2\sigma^2}) \tag{6}$$

where, σ is the kernel width parameter.

2.2   Proposed Hybrid Wavelet–LSSVM and Wavelet–ANN Models

The proposed WLSSVM and WANN models contain a two-stage framework, wavelet-based pre-processing stage and one-time step-ahead prediction stage. The schematic of developed modeling strategy is shown in Fig. 1. In the first stage using wavelet transform, the streamflow ($Q(t)$) and SSL ($SSL(t)$) time series are decomposed into sub-signals at different scales, i.e., a large-scale sub-signal and several small-scale sub-signals in order to extract the temporal characteristics of the input signals. Dyadic discrete wavelet transformation of a signal at level L yields $L+1$ sub-signals, one approximation (at level L) which denotes to the general trend of time series and L detailed sub-signals each representing a specific periodicity and seasonality of the process, e.g., 2^1-mode, 2^2-mode, ... and 2^L-mode. This helps the ANN and LSSVM models in the second stage to identify the dominant and important sub-signals and features of the process via the training phase. Therefore, the prediction model applies higher weights (W_i) on the dominant sub-signals. For an objected signal, the signal corresponding to $a(t)$ (i.e., $SSL_a(t)$ or $Q_a(t)$) is approximation sub-signal (large scale) of the original signal and ith or jth detailed sub-signal (small scale) is recognized by i or j (i.e., $SSL_i(t)$ or $Q_j(t)$) where i and j are decomposition levels of the SSL ($SSL(t)$) and runoff ($Q(t)$) time series, respectively. Annual or seasonal features are decomposed into large scale approximation sub-signal and on the other hand, daily, monthly and weekly fluctuations in the small periods are decomposed into detailed sub-signals. The details of multi-layer feed-forward network used in the WANN model of this study can be found in [20]. For the LSSVM modeling, both γ and σ parameters should be determined for each input data set. For this purpose in this study, γ and σ were determined through a grid search trial-error process. The grid search algorithm performs a direct search through the parameter space of a learning algorithm to solve the problem of model selection (i.e., finding the optimal parameters for a dataset) [34].

2.3   Study Area and Data

The data used in this study are from Akhula hydrometric station on the Aji-Chay River which is the closest station to the river Delta connected to Urmieh Lake, the second saltiest lake in the world. The Aji-Chay River (Fig. 2) contains high level of sediment

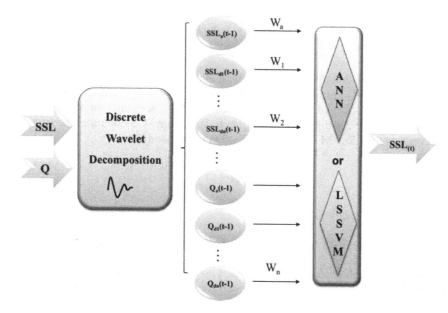

Fig. 1. Schematic of proposed hybrid WLSSVM and WANN models

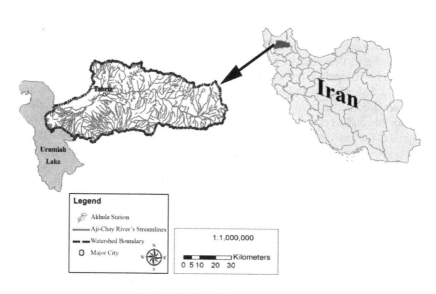

Fig. 2. Aji-Chay River watershed

and salinity concentrations and its watershed is located in northwest Iran at Azarbay-jan province and east of Urmieh Lake (between 37°24' and 38°37' North latitude and 45°30'and 47°45' East longitude). The length of river reaching Urmieh Lake's Delta is about 276 km and the watershed's area is about 13853 km². The monthly stream-flow and SSL data for 31 years (from 1981 to 2013, 372 months) were utilized in this study (Table 1). Due to the training and verification goals, data set was divided into two parts. The first part as 75% of the total data used for the training and the rest 25% data were used for the verification purpose. As it can be seen in Table 1, X_{max} and standard deviation (S_d) values of calibration data set are higher than those for the veri-fication data set which denote to the heterogeneity of the calibration data set with regard to the verification data. This is a crucial issue in data division step since ANN and LSSVM as interpolators can perform reliable predictions for unseen data if they are trained using a wide range of data.

Table 1. Statistics of time series for calibration, verification and all data

Statistical Parameters	All Data		Training Data		Verifying Data	
	$Q(m^3/s)$	SSL (tons/day)	$Q(m^3/s)$	SSL (tons/day)	$Q(m^3/s)$	SSL (tons/day)
X_{mean}	8.5	1164.8	9.6	1169.4	5.4	1151
X_{max}	107.3	16030	107.3	16030	41.3	7597
X_{min}	0	0	0	0	0	0
S_d	14.4	1625.7	15.6	1662.2	7.7	1519.5

2.4   Efficiency Criteria

Several conventional performance evaluations such as correlation coefficient, coeffi-cient of determination, root mean square error (*RMSE*) and sum of square error (*SSE*) were reviewed by [35] and it was concluded that the correlation coefficient is not a suitable measure for evaluation of a prediction model. They indicated that a perfect evaluation of model performance should include at least one 'goodness-of-fit' (e.g., Determination Coefficient (*DC*)) or relative error measure and at least one absolute error measure (e.g., *RMSE* or mean absolute error (*MAE*)). The model that yields the best result in terms of *DC* as equation (7) and *RMSE* as equation (8) in the training and verifying steps can be determined through a trial and error process [20].

$$DC = 1 - \frac{\sum_{i=1}^{N} (O_{obs_i} - O_{com_i})^2}{\sum_{i=1}^{N} (O_{obs_i} - \bar{O}_{obs})^2} \tag{7}$$

$$RMSE = \sqrt{\frac{\sum_{i=1}^{N} (O_{obs_i} - O_{com_i})^2}{N}} \tag{8}$$

where N, O_{obs_i}, O_{com_i} and $\bar{O}_{obs}$ are number of observations, observed data, com-puted values and mean of observed data, respectively.

The *RMSE* is utilized to measure prediction accuracy which gives a positive value by squaring the errors. The *RMSE* decreases from large positive values for poor performance to zero for perfect forecasts. Clearly, small value for *RMSE* and high value for *DC* (up to one) show higher efficiency of the model.

The utilized data were normalized due to the fact that the model training process could be speeded up by normalizing the input and target data before training [36]. In this study, the input and target data were normalized between 0 and 1 as:

$$s_i = \frac{x_i - x_{min}}{x_{max} - x_{min}} \tag{9}$$

in equation (9), x_i is the desired variable, x_{min} and x_{max} are the minimum and maximum values, respectively. s_i is the normalized variable.

3   Results and Discussion

3.1   Results of Ad Hoc LSSVM and ANN Models

At first, LSSVM model via RBF-kernel was employed to predict one-step-ahead SSL using raw runoff and SSL data. This kind of LSSVM is more desirable than other versions of SVM due to: first, unlike the linear kernel, the RBF kernel can handle the case when the relation between class labels and attributes is non-linear. Second, the RBF kernel tends to give better performance under general smoothness assumptions. Third, it has fewer tuning parameters than the polynomial and the sigmoid kernels [15]. As well as LSSVM, a multi-layer perceptron feed-forward ANN model without any data pre-processing was also used to model the runoff–SSL process of the river. This kind of ANN model accompanied by back propagation training algorithm has been widely used in hydrological modeling [15]. The architectures of LSSVM and ANN models were arranged according to the antecedents of streamflow and SSL values. Streamflow and SSL time series usually behave as Markovian process, so that the parameter values at the current time step are related to the conditions at the previous time steps. Therefore, 4 combinations of streamflow and SSL antecedent values were used as inputs of models at the input layer of ANN and LSSVM to predict monthly SSL. As well, the Comb. 4 was employed whereas the volume of current month SSL may have a satisfactory correlation with the SSL value at the same month in the previous year due to the seasonality of the process.

Input combinations for SSL prediction were consumed as:

Comb. 1: SSL_{t-1}
Comb. 2: Q_{t-1}
Comb. 3: SSL_{t-1}, Q_{t-1}
Comb. 4: $SSL_{t-1}, SSL_{t-12}, Q_{t-1}, Q_{t-12}$

in all cases, t demonstrates the current time step. The output layer comprised only one variable, i.e., SSL at current time step (SSL_t). In order to get appropriate predictions of SSL, the input layer should be arranged in a way that could access all pertinent information on the target data. Based on sensitivity analysis, the input layer was optimized with only the most important time memories.

Table 2. Grid search result of LSSVM for input Comb. 1

γ	σ	RMSE (Normalized)		DC	
		Calibration	Verification	Calibration	Verification
1	1	0.088	0.083	0.28	0.23
	2	0.089	0.083	0.27	0.23
	8	0.091	0.086	0.24	0.16
	20	0.093	0.091	0.19	0.08
	40	0.095	0.092	0.17	0.05
	50	0.095	0.092	0.16	0.04
2	1	0.088	0.083	0.28	0.23
	2	0.088	0.082	0.27	0.24
	8	0.090	0.085	0.25	0.18
	20	0.092	0.090	0.21	0.10
	40	0.094	0.092	0.18	0.05
	50	0.094	0.092	0.17	0.04
50	1	0.087	0.083	0.29	0.23
	2	0.088	0.083	0.28	0.23
	8	0.089	0.083	0.27	0.23
	20	0.089	0.084	0.26	0.20
	40	0.090	0.087	0.24	0.16
	50	0.091	0.088	0.23	0.13
100	1	0.087	0.083	0.29	0.23
	2	0.087	0.082	0.29	0.23
	8	0.089	0.083	0.27	0.23
	20	0.089	0.084	0.26	0.21
	40	0.090	0.085	0.25	0.18
	50	0.090	0.086	0.24	0.16
150	1	0.087	0.083	0.29	0.22
	2	0.088	0.083	0.28	0.23
	8	0.089	0.083	0.27	0.23
	20	0.089	0.083	0.26	0.22
	40	0.090	0.085	0.25	0.19
	50	0.090	0.086	0.25	0.17

For each input combination, the RBF-kernel parameters in LSSVMs were adapted to achieve highest performance. For this purpose, various pairs of (γ, σ) values were tried with a grid search procedure and the pair with the best accuracy was chosen. For example, the grid search result for input Comb. 1 has been presented in Table 2 for a few pairs of parameters. Then, the trained LSSVM was just applied to verify the model in SSL prediction. The arrangement of the ANN model was a three-layered ANN including input, hidden, and output layers. In the hidden layer, the number of neurons was varied up to 10 neurons to choose the appropriate hidden neuron number. After determination of proper ANN architecture in terms of performance criteria, training was terminated and the weights were saved in order to be used in the verification step. Monthly SSL prediction results are presented in Table 3. It is inferred from results of Combs.1 and 2 that SSL in forward time step has more dependency to SSL values at previous time steps with regard to streamflow's antecedents. As it is observed in Table 3, input Comb. 4 for

LSSVM and ANN models led to better performance with regard to other input combinations. Implication of input Comb. 4 which considers involved seasonality of the process (with period of one year) in addition to the autoregressive characteristic of the data, could yield better results than other input combinations which only take the Markovian property (autoregression property) into account.

3.2   Results of Hybrid Models

As the second step of modeling, proposed hybrid models were applied to predict the SSL values and in this way, we tried to investigate the effects of the used mother wavelet (*MW*) as well as Decomposition Level (*DL*) on the efficiency of WLSSVM and WANN models. The selection of an appropriate *MW* is a challenge in hybrid WANN and WLSSVM modeling, since the type of utilized *MW* can affect the modeling results.

Table 3. Results of ANNs and LSSVMs for different input variables in monthly SSL predictions

Input	Structure	Model	*RMSE* (Normalized)		*DC*	
			Calibration	Verification	Calibration	Verification
Comb. 1	$(2,2)^a$	LSSVM	0.088	0.082	0.27	0.24
	$(170,9)^b$	ANN	0.085	0.081	0.34	0.26
Comb. 2	(20,2)	LSSVM	0.095	0.09	0.17	0.1
	(10,8)	ANN	0.097	0.088	0.13	0.13
Comb. 3	(25,2)	LSSVM	0.087	0.082	0.29	0.24
	(40,10)	ANN	0.081	0.079	0.39	0.32
Comb.4	(2,2)	LSSVM	0.064	0.06	0.62	0.59
	(20,6)	ANN	0.05	0.058	0.76	0.62

^{a} (γ, σ)
^{b} (Epoch No., Number of hidden neurons)

The essence of wavelet transform is to discover the similarity between the analyzed time series and utilized wavelet prototype. In this way, Daubechies family of wavelets (*Haar*, *db2*, *db3*, [25]) were examined as the used *MW*s. The Daubechies wavelets have associated minimum-phase scaling filters, are both orthogonal and bi-orthogonal, and do not have an explicit analytic expression except for the *db1* (or *Haar*) form. It has been already deduced that in monthly time scale, an optimum *DL* could be chosen based on the signal length as [24]:

$$DL = \text{int}[Log\,(N\,)] \tag{10}$$

in which N is monthly time series length, so, for the current study *N=372* yielded *DL=2*. Other dominant seasonalities with longer periods may also be involved in the process. Therefore, *DL*= 3 and 4 were also examined to obtain optimum *DL*.

Table 4 shows the best structures of hybrid models for SSL predictions using both WLSSVM and WANN models. The same *MW* and *DL* (*db1*, *DL=4*) indicated better performance with $DC_{WLSSVM}=0.79$ and $DC_{WANN}=0.7$. It could be deduced that *db1* may originate from the form of wavelet, which is in coincidence to the streamflow and SSL signal forms. In Table 4, it should be noted that by alteration of *MW* and *DL*, the efficiency of both WLSSVM and WANN models is changed significantly.

3.3   Comparison of Models

The comparison of applied models has been summarized in Table 5. It can be pointed out that in one-step-ahead SSL prediction, ANN performs slightly better than LSSVM. In monthly modelling, poor Markovian property of the process prevents the LSSVM to model runoff-SSL in a single iteration; but ANN could conduct the monthly SSL predictions a bit better than LSSVM with more iteration and minimizing error using only a few data points.

Table 4. Results of WLSSVMs and WANNs for investigation of *MW* and *DL* impacts in monthly SSL predictions

Model	MW	DL	Structure	RMSE (Normalized)		DC	
				Calibration	Verification	Calibration	Verification
WLSSVM	db1	2	(8,4)	0.05	0.047	0.77	0.75
		3	(8,8)	0.044	0.046	0.82	0.76
		4	(8,7)	0.046	0.044	0.8	0.79
	db2	2	(8,15)	0.054	0.052	0.73	0.69
		3	(8,15)	0.054	0.056	0.72	0.64
		4	(8,22)	0.05	0.062	0.87	0.56
	db3	2	(5,10)	0.047	0.079	0.79	0.3
		3	(5,40)	0.053	0.077	0.73	0.34
		4	(1,20)	0.031	0.069	0.91	0.47
WANN	db1	2	(20,4)	0.066	0.061	0.6	0.58
		3	(150,4)	0.059	0.054	0.68	0.68
		4	(30,4)	0.055	0.051	0.72	0.7
	db2	2	(120,3)	0.059	0.069	0.66	0.47
		3	(10,8)	0.055	0.067	0.72	0.5
		4	(30,6)	0.056	0.069	0.71	0.47
	db3	2	(80,4)	0.053	0.081	0.73	0.25
		3	(80,4)	0.064	0.084	0.62	0.19
		4	(90,6)	0.067	0.085	0.57	0.19

By imposing the wavelet analysis to the LSSVM and ANN models, the seasonal characteristics of SSL process were exposed and therefore, instead of imposing the values of inputs at previous months, the decomposed sub-details of time series were applied to the models. Consequently, WLSSVM and WANN models absorbed the wavelet transform ability to predict SSL more robustly. Fig.3 shows the observed and computed time series using single and hybrid models for prediction of SSL values.

Table 5. Comparison of models

Model	DC		RMSE (Normalized)	
	Calibration	Verification	Calibration	Verification
LSSVM	0.62	0.59	0.064	0.06
ANN	0.76	0.62	0.05	0.058
WLSSVM	0.8	0.79	0.046	0.044
WANN	0.72	0.7	0.055	0.051

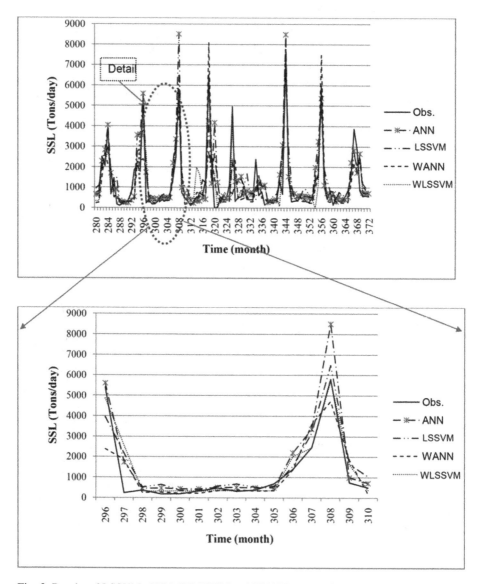

Fig. 3. Results of LSSVM, ANN, WLSSVM and WANN models for monthly SSL predictions in validation step

4   Conclusions

SSL is one of the most important water quality parameter which directly influences the water transparency, turbidity and water color etc, as well as affecting the design and management of water resources systems and structures. According to the SSL importance as a complex phenomenon, employment of intelligent black box models like LSSVM could lead to accurate estimation of SSL. The LSSVM model was used to predict 1-month-ahead Aji-Chay River SSL values. Also, LSSVM's ability was assayed in comparison to the ANN, and finally the efficacy of wavelet transform was investigated as proposed hybrid wavelet-LSSVM model.

The optimized inputs were determined via sensitivity analysis for LSSVM and ANN models based on Markovian property of monthly data. The results indicated that in monthly time series, ANN performs slightly better than LSSVM. In order to upgrade model efficiency and figure out seasonality effects, the wavelet transform, which can capture the multi-scale features of a time series, was used to decompose the runoff and SSL time series into different sub-signals. Then, the sub-signals were used as inputs to the LSSVM and ANN models to predict the monthly SSL. The hybrid WLSSVM and WANN models led to improved outcomes of runoff–SSL modelling compared to the ad hoc LSSVM and ANN models. It should be noted that mother wavelet and *DL* are effective factors in both WLSSVM and WANN models.

Due to the large size of the study watershed, it is suggested to apply the presented method via a multi-station framework and combine WLSSVM with other models like Adaptive Neuro Fuzzy Inference System-LSSVM. Whereas sediment process depends not only on the streamflow but also on the other parameters like rainfall intensity and evaporation, it is suggested to consider these hydro-climatological parameters as inputs of the model as well as the streamflow.

Acknowledgements. This study was supported by the East Azerbaijan water company under grant No. 40201244.

References

1. Verstraeten, G., Poesen, J.: Actors controlling sediment yield from small intensively cultivated catchments in a temperate humid climate. Geomorphology 40, 123–144 (2001)
2. Ward, P., Balen, R.T., Verstraeten, G., Renssen, H., Vandenberghe, J.: The impact of land useand climate change on late Holocene and future suspended sediment yield of the Meuse catchment. Geomorphology 103, 389–400 (2009)
3. Nourani, V., Mano, A.: Semi-distributed flood runoff model at the sub continental scale for southwestern Iran. Hydrol. Process. 21, 3173–3180 (2007)
4. ASCE Task Committee on the application of ANNs in hydrology.: Artificial neural networks in hydrology, II: Hydrologic applications. J. Hydrol. Eng. 5(2), 124–137 (2000)
5. Kisi, O.: Modeling discharge-suspended sediment relationship using least square support vector machine. J. Hydrol. 456, 110–120 (2012)
6. Nourani, V., Komasi, M., Alami, M.T.: Hybrid wavelet–genetic programming approach to optimize ANN modeling of rainfall–runoff process. J. Hydrol. Eng. 17, 724–741 (2012)

7. Shang, Z., He, J.: Confidence-weighted extreme learning machine for regression problems. Neurocomputing 148, 544–550 (2015)
8. Nicolaou, M., Gunes, H., Pantic, M.: Output-associative RVM regression for dimensional and continuous emotion prediction. Image Vision Comput 30, 186–196 (2012)
9. Wu, C.L., Chau, K.W., Li, Y.S.: Predicting monthly streamflow using data-driven models coupled with data-preprocessing techniques. Water Resour 45, W8432 (2009), doi:10.1029/2007WR006737
10. Abrahart, J.R., Anctil, F., Coulibaly, P., Dawson, C.H., Mount, N., See, L., Shamseldin, A., Solomatine, D., Toth, E., Wilby, L.R.: Two decades of anarchy? Emerging themes and outstanding challenges for neural network river forecasting. Prog. Phys. Geog. 36(4), 480–513 (2012)
11. Nourani, V., Kalantari, O., Baghanam, A.H.: Two semi-distributed ANN-based models for estimation of suspended sediment load. J. Hydrol. Eng 17(12), 1368–1380 (2012)
12. Guo, J., Zhou, J., Qin, H., Zou, Q., Li, Q.: Monthly streamflow forecasting based on improved support vector machine model. Expert Syst. Appl. 38, 13073–13081 (2011)
13. Vapnik, V., Cortes, C.: Support Vector Networks. Machine Learning 20, 1–25 (1995)
14. Chen, S.T., Yu, P.S., Tang, Y.H.: Statistical downscaling of daily precipitation using support vector machines and multivariate analysis. J. Hydrol. 385, 13–22 (2010)
15. Noori, R., Karbassi, A.R., Moghaddamnia, A., Han, D., Zokaei-Ashtiani, M.H., Farokhnia, A., Ghafari Gousheh, M.: Assessment of input variables determination on the SVM model performance using PCA, Gamma test and forward selection techniques for monthly stream flow prediction. J. Hydrol. 401, 177–189 (2011)
16. Ch, S., Anand, N., Panigrahi, B.K., Mathur, S.: Streamflow forecasting by SVM with quantum behaved particleswarm optimization. Neurocomputing 101, 18–23 (2013)
17. Cimen, M.: Estimation of daily suspended sediments using support vector machines. Hydrolog. Sci. J. 53, 656–666 (2008)
18. Misra, D., Oommen, T., Agrawal, A., Mishra, A.K.: Application and analysis of support vector machine based simulation for runoff and sediment yield. Biosyst. Eng. 3, 527–535 (2009)
19. Kakaei, E., Moghddamnia, A., Ahmadi, A.: Daily suspended sediment load prediction using artificial neural networks and support vector machines. J. Hydrol. 478, 50–62 (2013)
20. Nourani, V., Komasi, M., Mano, A.A.: multivariate ANN-wavelet approach for rainfall–runoff modeling. Water Resour. Manag. 23, 2877–2894 (2009)
21. Nourani, V., Alami, M.T., Aminfar, M.H.: A combined neural-wavelet model for prediction of Ligvanchai watershed precipitation. Eng. Appl. Artif. Intel 22, 466–472 (2009)
22. Nourani, V., Kisi, O., Komasi, M.: Two hybrid Artificial Intelligence approaches for modeling rainfall–runoff process. J. Hydrol. 402, 41–59 (2011)
23. Partal, T., Cigizoglu, H.K.: Estimation and forecasting of daily suspended sediment data using wavelet-neural networks. J. Hydrol. 358, 317–331 (2008)
24. Rajaee, T., Nourani, V., Zounemat Kermani, M., Kisi, O.: River suspended sediment load prediction: Application of ANN and wavelet conjunction model. J. Hydrol. Eng. 16(8), 613–627 (2011)
25. Nourani, V., Baghanam, A.H., Yahyavi Rahimi, A., Nejad, F.H.: Evaluation of wavelet-based de-noising approach in hydrological models linked to artificial neural networks. In: Computational Intelligence Techniques in Earth and Environmental Sciences, pp. 209–241. Springer, Heidelberg (2014)
26. Dogantekin, E., Dogantekin, A., Avci, D.: An expert system based on Generalized Discriminant Analysis and Wavelet Support Vector Machine for diagnosis of thyroid diseases. Expert Syst. Appl. 38, 146–150 (2011)

27. Chen, F., Tang, B., Chen, R.: A novel fault diagnosis model for gearbox based on wavelet support vector machine with immune genetic algorithm. Measurement 46, 220–232 (2013)
28. Kisi, O., Cimen, M.: A wavelet-support vector machine conjunction model for monthly streamflow forecasting. J. Hydrol. 399, 132–140 (2011)
29. Kisi, O., Cimen, M.: Precipitation forecasting by using wavelet-support vector machine conjunction model. Eng. Appl. Artif. Intel. 25, 783–792 (2012)
30. Kalteh, A.M.: Monthly river flow forecasting using artificial neural network and support vector regression models coupled with wavelet transform. Comput. Geosci. 54, 1–8 (2013)
31. Suykens, J.A.K., Vandewalle, J.: Least square support vector machine classifiers. Neural Process. Lett. 9(3), 293–300 (1999)
32. Kumar, M., Kar, I.N.: Non-linear HVAC computations using least square support vector machines. Energy Convers. Manage. 50, 1411–1418 (2002)
33. Shu-gang, C., Yan-bao, L., Yan-ping, W.: A forecasting and forewarning model for methane hazard in working face of coal mine based on LSSVM. J. China U. Mining Tech 18, 172–176 (2008)
34. Lee, C.Y., Chern, S.G.: Application of a support vector machine for liquefaction assessment. J. Sci. Tech. 21, 318–324 (2013)
35. Legates, D.R., McCabe, J.R.: Evaluating the use of goodness-of-fit measures in hydrologic and hydroclimatic model validation. Water Resour. Res. 35(1), 233–241 (1999)
36. Rogers, R.: Neural Networks: A Systematic Introduction. Springer, Berlin (1996)

Ranking-Based Vocabulary Pruning
in Bag-of-Features for Image Retrieval

Fan Zhang[1], Yang Song[1], Weidong Cai[1], Alexander G. Hauptmann[2],
Sidong Liu[1], Siqi Liu[1], David Dagan Feng[1,3], and Mei Chen[4]

[1] Biomedical and Multimedia Information Technology (BMIT) Research Group,
School of Information Technologies, University of Sydney, Australia
[2] School of Computer Science, Carnegie Mellon University, United States
[3] Med-X Research Institute, Shanghai Jiaotong University, China
[4] Intel Science and Technology Center on Embedded Computing,
Carnegie Mellon University, United States

Abstract. Content-based image retrieval (CBIR) has been applied to
a variety of medical applications, e.g., pathology research and clinical
decision support, and bag-of-features (BOF) model is one of the most
widely used techniques. In this study, we address the problem of vocabulary pruning to reduce the influence from the redundant and noisy
visual words. The conditional probability of each word upon the hidden
topics extracted using probabilistic Latent Semantic Analysis (pLSA) is
firstly calculated. A ranking method is then proposed to compute the
significance of the words based on the relationship between the words
and topics. Experiments on the publicly available Early Lung Cancer
Action Program (ELCAP) database show that the method can reduce
the number of words required while improving the retrieval performance.
The proposed method is applicable to general image retrieval since it is
independent of the problem domain.

Keywords: image retrieval, bag-of-features model, vocabulary pruning.

1 Introduction

Content-based image retrieval (CBIR), i.e., searching for images similar to the
query under certain similarity metric, has been an active research field [1–3]. It
can be a powerful tool for diagnosis assistance and decision support [4–17]. Most
of the state-of-the-art approaches build upon the bag-of-features (BOF) model
[18–21], which represents one image as a frequency histogram of visual words
based on a vocabulary obtained by quantizing the local features of all images in
the database.

In general, the main steps involved in BOF-based CBIR include feature extraction, vocabulary construction, BOF generation, and similarity calculation
[22]. Firstly, feature extraction is conducted by computing local descriptors for
the regions of interest (ROIs). Then, a codebook is built offline within the feature space. The obtained codebook is usually referred to as a visual vocabulary,

S.K. Chalup et al. (Eds.): ACALCI 2015, LNAI 8955, pp. 436–445, 2015.

and the cluster centers are visual words. The BOF representation of an image is obtained by assigning a visual word to each of the feature descriptors, resulting in a frequency histogram of the visual words to calculate the similarity [23–25].

Current work on BOF model mostly tackles the feature design and neighbor identification problems [26–31]. In this study, we focus on the vocabulary construction step, particularly on vocabulary pruning. Visual vocabulary is usually redundant, over-complete and noisy, which leads to a high-dimensional feature space [32]. It reduces the retrieval accuracy due to the sparse data problem, and increases the computational cost. Therefore, it is preferable to obtain a more meaningful and compact vocabulary. The supervised method [33] is considered as an option by giving the prior knowledge, e.g., the prefixed vocabulary size. It has limited adaptability since the words used are different under various imaging conditions. An unsupervised approach was proposed in [32] by extracting the latent associations between image set and vocabulary with probabilistic Latent Semantic Analysis (pLSA). The visual words were ranked according to the conditional probability upon the extracted hidden topics, and a significance threshold was selected to eliminate the unimportant words. However, this method does not achieve an observable retrieval accuracy improvement; and we hypothesize that it is due to the pruning based on the conditional probabilities only without considering the relative significance among the words.

We present an unsupervised ranking algorithm to prune the vocabulary to improve the BOF-based image retrieval. We suggest that the hidden topics should normally not be of equal importance, and the words should not be equally linked to each topic. We thus propose to model the mutually reinforced relationship between the visual words and hidden topics to calculate their significance values. The proposed method was evaluated on the publicly available Early Lung Cancer Action Program (ELCAP) [34] database as a case study. The experimental results showed that it can improve image retrieval accuracy.

2   Method

2.1   Dataset

In this study, ELCAP database, which contains 50 sets of low dose computed tomography (CT) images, was used for evaluation. A total of 379 slices are provided with the centroids of lung nodules annotated, which are divided into four different types based on their relative locations to the surrounding anatomical structures (e.g., pleural surfaces, vessels, etc. [35]): well-circumscribed (W-15%), vascularized (V-16%), juxta-pleural(J-30%) and pleural-tail (P-39%). Example images of the four type nodules are shown in Figure 1(a), with the nodules displayed in the center.

2.2   Method Outline

The overall BOF-based retrieval with the proposed vocabulary pruning method is illustrated in Figure 1. The Scale Invariant Feature Transform (SIFT) descriptor is firstly extracted with each pixel in the area around the nodule centroid as the keypoint, so that both the nodule and surrounding anatomical structures are included. Next, we use k-means clustering to construct the vocabulary, and obtain the frequency histogram of the visual words for each image. The Term Frequency Inverse Document Frequency (TF-IDF) weighting scheme is then applied followed by the L2 normalization on the frequency histogram matrix, i.e., a $N \times M$ matrix where N is the number of images and M is the size of vocabulary that is the number of clusters obtained by k-means clustering, and k-nearest neighbor (k-NN) method is used to perform the retrieval. In our proposed method, instead of using the entire vocabulary generated by k-means, we would like to prune the vocabulary by keeping the most useful words. In particular, as show in Figure 1(e), we use pLSA to extract a total of K hidden topics and design a ranking method to compute the significance of each word. The words with higher significance values sv are reserved as the pruned vocabulary.

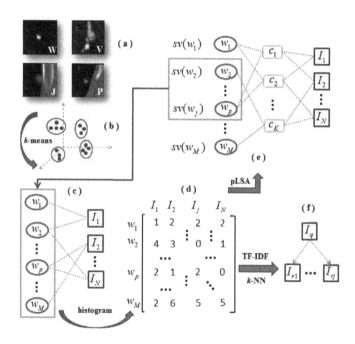

Fig. 1. Outline of BOF-based retrieval with the proposed vocabulary pruning method: (a) sample nodule images from ELCAP database; (b) vocabulary construction with k-means clustering; (c) feature assignment to visual words; (d) frequency histogram matrix; (e) hidden topic discovery and visual works ranking; (f) retrieval results

2.3   Vocabulary Pruning with pLSA

pLSA, which was originally used in linguistic studies, can be used to extract the hidden topics to bridge the semantic gap between documents (images) and words (visual words) [36–38]. It is a general model assuming that documents (images) can be interpreted by a set of hidden variables c, i.e., the hidden topics, each of which is the probability distribution upon the words (visual words). Given the document-word co-occurrence matrix, i.e., the frequency histogram matrix, the conditional probability of the words upon each hidden topic, $p(w|c)$, can be learned (see [39] for details).

The hidden topics are object categories [40] describing the common characteristics of different ROIs, e.g., nodules, pleural surfaces, and vessels in lung nodule images, so that the words would be more meaningfully linked to the ROIs than the individual images. Therefore, the conditional probability can be used to measure the significance / meaningfulness of the visual words. For a given hidden topic c, we consider the word w meaningless if its conditional probability $p(w|c)$ is below a certain significance threshold [32]. A word is removed for vocabulary pruning if it is meaningless to all topics.

2.4   Vocabulary Pruning with the Proposed Ranking Method

While the conditional probability $p(w|c)$ provides an effective criterion to evaluate the significance of visual words, it is insufficient to perform vocabulary pruning with the above scheme. Firstly, the extracted topics are not equally important, and the words linked to the more important topics should have higher significance values. Secondly, the words should be evaluated based on the overall relationship with all topics rather than individual ones, which means a word might be removed even if it is meaningful for some topics especially if these topics are not important. Based on these motivations, we propose a ranking method to calculate the significance value sv of the hidden topics and visual words by analyzing the overall mutual interactions between them. This is the main difference from [6], which uses $p(w|c)$ directly as the significance value.

Our method is based on the underlying algorithm that the significance values of topics and words are calculated conditioned on each other. This means that, a topic c with higher significance value $sv(c)$ tends to connect with words of higher significance, and a word w with higher significance value $sv(w)$ tends to connect with topics of higher significance. This mutual relationship can be formulated as:

$$sv(c_q) = \sum_{w_p \in L(c_q)} sv(w_p) \tag{1}$$

$$sv(w_p) = \sum_{c_q : w_p \in L(c_q)} sv(c_q) \tag{2}$$

where $L(c)$ is the list of words that are meaningful for topic c, which is obtained according to the conditional probability as described in Section 3.

Next, the significance values are updated iteratively based on Eqs. (1) and (2), as shown in Figure 2. During each iteration, the significance values of all words and topics are calculated based on each other from the overall perspective. This helps to determine the significance of a word based on all topics collectively, and the significances of various topics can be differentiated based on the related words. Across the iterations, the significance of a certain word, e.g., $sv(w_p)$, is diffused to the topics at the current iteration and gathered at the next iteration for updating the other words. This helps to encode the mutual relationship into the significance values in an iterative manner. Based on the experiments, we observe that the significance values tend to converge with more iterations. 20 iterations were chosen to balance between efficiency and performance.

Inputs:

L for each topic, number of iteration T

Outputs:

sv of each word and each topic

Steps:

Initialize $sv_0(w) = 1$ and $sv_0(c) = 1$.

for $t = 1 : T$

    for $q = 1 : K$

        Compute $sv_t(c_q)$ based on $sv_{t-1}(w)$ using Eq.(1);

    for $p = 1 : M$

        Compute $sv_t(w_p)$ based on $sv_{t-1}(c)$ using Eq.(2);

        Normalize $sv_t(c)$ and $sv_t(w)$;

Return:

$sv_T(w)$ and $sv_T(c)$

Fig. 2. The pseudo code of significance value computation for words and topics. Bold w and c represent the sets of words and topics, respectively.

Finally, all words are ranked according to their significance values obtained at the final iteration, and vocabulary pruning is performed by removing the words below a significance threshold $th \in (0, 100)$, i.e., the top $th\%$ words are reserved.

3   Experiments

In the experiments, we conduct leave-one-case-out cross-validation and compute the average retrieval accuracy (recall) of all queries to evaluate the performance. To obtain a fair comparison, we selected the first 100 descriptors near the centroid for each image producing the same number of descriptors per image, and extracted vocabularies with different sizes from 500 to 2000 with an interval of 100. The list of meaningful words for each topic consisted of the top 10% with higher conditional probabilities, which generated the best performance in general.

We first discuss the effect of the pruned vocabulary. Figure 3 shows the average accuracy of the first four retrieved items over different percentages of words reserved. The statistics generated by extracting different numbers of topics at

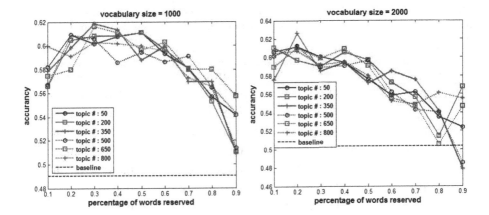

Fig. 3. Evaluation of the pruned vocabularies obtained by reserving different percentages of high significance value words in the original vocabularies. The curves show the accuracy distribution over various topic numbers, and the result from baseline (standard BOF model) is also given.

two different original vocabulary sizes (1000 and 2000) are displayed. The standard BOF approach on the original vocabulary is regarded as the baseline. It can be observed that considerable improvements were obtained by pruning the vocabulary. Typically, the best performance was achieved when 60% to 80% of the words were pruned from the overall perspective.

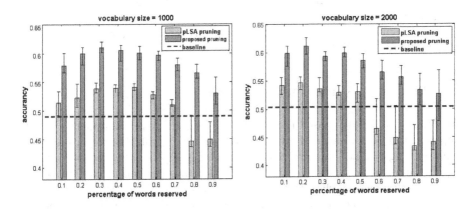

Fig. 4. Comparison with pLSA pruning approach. The bars indicate the average accuracy, and the error bars show the lowest and highest.

Figure 4 shows the comparisons with vocabulary pruning using pLSA only. For each pruned vocabulary, the average, minimum and maximum of retrieval accuracy are displayed. The words in the pLSA approach were reserved according to the conditional probability upon the topics. The average accuracies across

Table 1. Average retrieval results (varying original vocabulary sizes and hidden topic numbers) regarding various numbers of outputs from the baseline, pLSA pruning and proposed approaches

Output number	Baseline	pLSA pruning	Proposed pruning
1	0.630 ± 0.129	0.675 ± 0.076	**0.731 ± 0.066**
2	0.687 ± 0.034	0.680 ± 0.043	**0.720 ± 0.017**
3	0.566 ± 0.031	0.579 ± 0.045	**0.639 ± 0.025**
5	0.454 ± 0.027	0.488 ± 0.052	**0.546 ± 0.037**
8	0.392 ± 0.025	0.427 ± 0.057	**0.481 ± 0.046**
10	0.370 ± 0.019	0.403 ± 0.058	**0.456 ± 0.050**
15	0.342 ± 0.022	0.366 ± 0.056	**0.417 ± 0.051**
20	0.328 ± 0.023	0.346 ± 0.052	**0.395 ± 0.050**

all pruned vocabularies of pLSA pruning are 0.5094 and 0.4969, which are similar to that of the baseline, which are 0.4901 and 0.5033 respectively. This is in accordance with the finding in [6] that pLSA can be used to reduce the vocabulary but with no obvious effect on the retrieval accuracy. Using our approach, the retrieval performances were 0.5843 and 0.5738 on average with about 8% improvement over the baseline, which suggests the advantage of the proposed ranking-based significance value computation method.

The overall performance of the proposed method regarding various numbers of retrieval output is given in Table 1. The average accuracy and standard deviation across all dictionaries (from 500 to 2000), and topics (from 50 to 800) are listed. Overall, the proposed pruning method outperforms the standard BOF and pLSA pruning by about 8% and 10%, respectively.

4   Conclusions and Future Work

We propose an unsupervised ranking-based vocabulary pruning method, which improves the performance of BOF-based image retrieval. The experimental results on lung nodule image retrieval show that the proposed method can identify the most meaningful visual words to describe the image content so that the retrieval quality is significantly enhanced even the vocabulary is pruned significantly. The reduction of the vocabulary leads to a low-dimensional feature representation, which reduces the computational cost and is more applicable to large scale data analysis.

The method is currently used on medical image analysis, and we would expect a better performance if a customized BOF model is used, e.g., more sophisticated feature design and better regions of interest detection. In addition, we are currently extending the proposed method to general image analysis due to the domain independent characteristic.

Acknowledgments. This work was supported in part by ARC grants.

References

1. Smeulders, A.W.M., Worring, M., Santini, S., Gupta, A., Jain, R.: Content-based image retrieval at the end of the early years. IEEE Transactions on Pattern Analysis and Machine Intelligence 22(12), 1349–1380 (2000)
2. Torres, R., Falcao, A.: Content-based image retrieval: Theory and applications. Revista de Informtica Terica e Aplicada 13(2), 161–185 (2006)
3. Zhang, S., Yang, M., Cour, T., Yu, K., Metaxas, D.: Query Specific Rank Fusion for Image Retrieval. IEEE Transactions on Pattern Analysis and Machine Intelligence (2014), doi:10.1109/TPAMI.2014.2346201
4. Mller, H., Michoux, N., Bandon, D., Geissbuhler, A.: A Review of Content-based Image Retrieval Systems in Medical Applications Clinical Benefits and Future Directions. International Journal of Medical Informatics 73(1), 1–23 (2004)
5. Cai, W., Kim, J., Feng, D.: Content-based Medical Image Retrieval. Biomedical Information Technology, Chapter 4, 83–113 (2008)
6. Kumar, A., Kim, J., Cai, W., Fulham, M.J., Feng, D.: Content-Based Medical Image Retrieval: A Survey of Applications to Multidimensional and Multimodality Data. Journal of Digital Imaging 26(6), 1025–1039 (2013)
7. Song, Y., Cai, W., Eberl, S., Fulham, M.J., Feng, D.: Discriminative pathological context detection in thoracic images based on multi-level inference. In: Fichtinger, G., Martel, A., Peters, T. (eds.) MICCAI 2011, Part III. LNCS, vol. 6893, pp. 191–198. Springer, Heidelberg (2011)
8. Liu, S., Cai, W., Wen, L., Feng, D.: Multi-channel Brain Atrophy Pattern Analysis in Neuroimaging Retrieval. IEEE International Symposium on Biomedical Imaging (ISBI), 206-209 (2013)
9. Akgl, C.B., Rubin, D.L., Napel, S., Beaulieu, C.F., Greenspan, H., Acar, B.: Content-based image retrieval in radiology: current status and future directions. Journal of Digital Imaging 24, 208–222 (2011)
10. Song, Y., Cai, W., Huang, H., Wang, Y., Feng, D.: Object Localization in Medical Images based on Graphical Model with Contrast and Interest-Region Terms. In: The 25th IEEE Conference on Computer Vision and Pattern Recognition (CVPR) Workshop on Medical Computer Vision, pp. 1–7 (2012)
11. Liu, S., Liu, S.Q., Pujol, S., Kikinis, R., Feng, D., Cai, W.: Propagation graph fusion for multi-modal medical content-based retrieval. To be presented at the 13th International Conference on Control, Automation, Robotics and Vision (ICARCV), Singapore (2014)
12. Song, Y., Cai, W., Eberl, S., Fulham, M.J., Feng, D.: Thoracic Image Case Retrieval with Spatial and Contextual Information. In: IEEE International Symposium on Biomedical Imaging (ISBI), pp. 1885–1888 (2011)
13. Zhang, X., Liu, W., Dundar, M., Sunil, B., Zhang, S.: Towards Large-Scale Histopathological Image Analysis: Hashing-Based Image Retrieval. IEEE Transactions on Medical Imaging (2014), doi:10.1109/TMI.2014.2361481
14. Cai, W., Feng, D., Fulton, R.: Content-Based Retrieval of Dynamic PET Functional Images. IEEE Transactions on Information Technology in Biomedicine 4(2), 152–158 (2000)
15. Che, H., Liu, S., Cai, W., Pujol, S., Kikinis, R., Feng, D.: Co-neighbor Multi-view Spectral Embedding for Medical content-based Retrieval. In: IEEE International Symposium on Biomedical Imaging (ISBI), pp. 911–914 (2014)

16. Song, Y., Cai, W., Zhou, Y., Fulham, M.J., Feng, D.: Volume-of-interest retrieval for PET-CT images with a conditional random field alignment. The Journal of Nuclear Medicine 55(Suppl.1), 20–65 (2014)

17. Liu, S., Cai, W., Wen, L., Feng, D., Pujol, S., Kikinis, R., Fulham, M.J., Eberl, S.: Multi-channel neurodegenerative pattern analysis and its application in Alzheimer's disease characterization. Computerized Medical Imaging and Graphics 38(4), 436–444 (2014)

18. Song, Y., Cai, W., Eberl, S., Fulham, M.J., Feng, D.: A Content-based Image Retrieval Framework for Multi-Modality Lung Images. In: IEEE International Symposium on Computer-Based Medical System (CBMS), pp. 285–290 (2010)

19. Haas, S., Donner, R., Burner, A., Holzer, M., Langs, G.: Superpixel-based Interest Points for Effective Bags of Visual Words Medical Image Retrieval. In: Second MICCAI International Workshop on Medical Content-Based Retrieval for Clinical Decision Support (MCBR-CDS), pp. 58–68 (2012)

20. Song, Y., Cai, W., Zhou, Y., Wen, L., Feng, D.: Pathology-centric Medical Image Retrieval with Hierarchical Contextual Spatial Descriptor. In: IEEE International Symposium on Biomedical Imaging (ISBI), pp. 202–205 (2013)

21. Song, Y., Cai, W., Eberl, S., Fulham, M.J., Feng, D.: Structure-Adaptive Feature Extraction and Representation for Multi-Modality Lung Images Retrieval. In: The International Conference on Digital Image Computing: Techniques and Applications (DICTA), pp. 152–157 (2010)

22. Yang, J., Jiang, Y.G., Hauptmann, A.G., Ngo, C.W.: Evaluating Bag-of-visual-words Representations in Scene Classification. In: Proceedings of the International Workshop on Multimedia Information Retrieval, pp. 197–206 (2007)

23. Song, Y., Cai, W., Feng, D.: Hierarchical Spatial Matching for Medical Image Retrieval. In: The Annual ACM International Conference on Multimedia Workshop on Medical Multimedia Analysis and Retrieval (ACM MMAR), pp. 1–6 (2011)

24. Liu, S., Cai, W., Song, Y., Pujol, S., Kikinis, R., Feng, D.: A Bag of Semantic Words Model for Medical Content-based Retrieval. Presented at the 16th International Conference on MICCAI Workshop on Medical Content-Based Retrieval for Clinical Decision Support, Japan (2013)

25. Song, Y., Cai, W., Eberl, S., Fulham, M.J., Feng, D.: Thoracic Image Matching with Appearance and Spatial Distribution. In: The 33rd Annual International Conference of the IEEE Engineering in Medicine and Biology Society (EMBC), pp. 4469–4472 (2011)

26. Arandjelovic, R., Zisserman, A.: All about VLAD. In: IEEE Conference on Computer Vision and Pattern Recognition (CVPR), pp. 1578–1585 (2013)

27. Qin, D., Gammeter, S., Bossard, L., Quack, T., Van Gool, L.: Hello Neighbor: Accurate Object Retrieval with K-reciprocal Nearest Neighbors. In: IEEE Conference on Computer Vision and Pattern Recognition (CVPR), pp. 777–784 (2011)

28. Cai, W., Zhang, F., Song, Y., Liu, S., Wen, L., Eberl, S., Fulham, M.J., Feng, D.: Automated Feedback Extraction for Medical Imaging Retrieval. In: IEEE International Symposium on Biomedical Imaging (ISBI), pp. 907–910 (2014)

29. Sivic, J., Zisserman, A.: Video Google: A Text Retrieval Approach to Object Matching in Videos. In: IEEE International Conference on Computer Vision (ICCV), pp. 1470–1477 (2003)

30. Liu, S., Cai, W., Wen, L., Eberl, S., Fulham, M.J., Feng, D.: A robust volumetric feature extraction approach for 3D neuroimaging retrieval. In: IEEE Annual International Conference of the Engineering in Medicine and Biology Society (EMBS), pp. 5657–5660 (2010)

31. Cai, W., Liu, S., Song, Y., Pjuol, S., Kikinis, R., Feng, D.: A 3D Difference-of-Gaussian based lesion detector for brain PET. In: IEEE International Symposium on Biomedical Imaging (ISBI), pp. 677–680 (2014)

32. Foncubierta-Rodríguez, A., Herrera, A.G.S.D., Müller, H.: Medical Image Retrieval using Bag of Meaningful Visual Words: Unsupervised Visual Vocabulary Pruning with pLSA. In: Proceedings of the 1st ACM International Workshop on Multimedia Indexing and Information Retrieval for Healthcare, pp. 75–82 (2013)

33. Bilenko, M., Basu, S., Mooney, R.J.: Integrating Constraints and Metric Learning in Semi-supervised Clustering. In: Proceedings of the Twenty-first International Conference on Machine Learning (ICML), pp. 11–18 (2004)

34. ELCAP Public Lung Image Database, http://www.via.cornell.edu/databases/lungdb.html

35. Diciotti, S., Picozzi, G., Falchini, M., Mascalchi, M., Villari, N., Valli, G.: 3-D Segmentation Algorithm of Small Lung Nodules in Spiral CT Images. IEEE Transactions on Information Technology in Biomedicine 12(1), 7–19 (2008)

36. Castellani, U., Perina, A., Murino, V., Bellani, M., Rambaldelli, G., Tansella, M., Brambilla, P.: Brain morphometry by probabilistic latent semantic analysis. In: Jiang, T., Navab, N., Pluim, J.P.W., Viergever, M.A. (eds.) MICCAI 2010, Part II. LNCS, vol. 6362, pp. 177–184. Springer, Heidelberg (2010)

37. Cruz-Roa, A., González, F., Galaro, J., Judkins, A.R., Ellison, D., Baccon, J., Madabhushi, A., Romero, E.: A visual latent semantic approach for automatic analysis and interpretation of anaplastic medulloblastoma virtual slides. In: Ayache, N., Delingette, H., Golland, P., Mori, K. (eds.) MICCAI 2012, Part I. LNCS, vol. 7510, pp. 157–164. Springer, Heidelberg (2012)

38. Zhang, F., Song, Y., Cai, W., Lee, M.-Z., Zhou, Y., Huang, H., Shan, S., Fulham, M.J., Feng, D.: Lung Nodule Classification With Multi-level Patch-based Context Analysis. IEEE Transactions on Biomedical Engineering 61(4), 1155–1166 (2014)

39. Hofmann, T.: Probabilistic Latent Semantic Indexing. In: Proceedings of the 22nd Annual International ACM SIGIR Conference on Research and Development in Information Retrieval, pp. 50–57 (1999)

40. Bosch, A., Zisserman, A., Muñoz, X.: Scene classification via pLSA. In: Leonardis, A., Bischof, H., Pinz, A. (eds.) ECCV 2006. LNCS, vol. 3954, pp. 517–530. Springer, Heidelberg (2006)

Author Index